Sixties Ireland

This is a provocative new history of Ireland during the long 1960s which exposes the myths of Ireland's modernisation. Mary Daly questions traditional interpretations which see these years as a time of prosperity when Irish society – led by a handful of key modernisers – abandoned many of its traditional values in its search of economic growth. Setting developments in Ireland in a wider European context, she shows instead that claims for the economic transformation of Ireland are hugely questionable: Ireland remained one of the poorest countries in Western Europe until the end of the twentieth century. Contentious debates in later years over contraception, divorce and national identity demonstrated continuities with the past that long survived the 1960s. Ranging from Ireland's economic rebirth in the 1950s to its entry into the European Economic Community (EEC) in 1973, this is a comprehensive reinterpretation of a critical period in Irish history with clear parallels for Ireland today.

MARY E. DALY is Professor Emeritus in Modern Irish History at University College Dublin. In 2014, she was elected as the first woman President of the Royal Irish Academy in its 229-year history.

Sixties Ireland

Reshaping the Economy, State and Society,
1957–1973

Mary E. Daly
University College Dublin

CAMBRIDGE
UNIVERSITY PRESS

CAMBRIDGE
UNIVERSITY PRESS

University Printing House, Cambridge CB2 8BS, United Kingdom

One Liberty Plaza, 20th Floor, New York, NY 10006, USA

477 Williamstown Road, Port Melbourne, VIC 3207, Australia

4843/24, 2nd Floor, Ansari Road, Daryaganj, Delhi - 110002, India

79 Anson Road, #06-04/06, Singapore 079906

Cambridge University Press is part of the University of Cambridge.

It furthers the University's mission by disseminating knowledge in the pursuit of education, learning and research at the highest international levels of excellence.

www.cambridge.org
Information on this title: www.cambridge.org/9781316509319

First published 2016

A catalogue record for this publication is available from the British Library

Library of Congress Cataloging in Publication data
Daly, Mary E., author.
Sixties Ireland : reshaping the economy, state and society,
1957–1973 / Mary E. Daly.
Cambridge, United Kingdom : Cambridge University Press, 2016. | Includes bibliographical references and index.
LCCN 2015042971 | ISBN 9781107145924 (hardback)
LCSH: Ireland – History – 1922– | Ireland – Economic conditions –
1949– | Ireland – Social conditions – 1922–1973. | Ireland – Politics and government – 1949– | Economic development – Ireland – History –
20th century. | Social change – Ireland – History – 20th century.
| Political culture – Ireland – History – 20th century.
LCC DA963 .D35 2016 | DDC 941.7082/3–dc23
LC record available at http://lccn.loc.gov/2015042971

ISBN 978-1-107-14592-4 Hardback
ISBN 978-1-316-50931-9 Paperback

For Conor, John, Aidan, Peter and Kilian

Contents

Acknowledgements

I have been working on this book for over a decade – the inordinate delays were due to my commitments as Principal of the UCD College of Arts and Celtic Studies, a job that allowed little time for research and writing. However that decade also saw the publication of an extraordinary number of monographs and articles on Ireland in the 'long 1960s', which made it less necessary for me to carry out primary research on a number of topics, so I would like to begin by acknowledging the work of every author who is cited in the footnotes and bibliography. This book benefited enormously from a two-month stay at the European University Institute (EUI) in 2012 – which gave me time for research and reflection. My thanks go to the archivists and librarians who made this book possible: the National Archives in Ireland and Kew; the Historical Archives of the EU in Florence; Dublin Diocesan Archives, and most especially the UCD Archives (UCDA), which holds the most important collection of private papers relating to independent Ireland; the Library at the EUI – especially Dr Tom Burke; the UCD library, which facilitated innumerable requests, and the Library of the Royal Irish Academy, which proved invaluable as I completed the final stages of this work.

This book has drawn on my experience as a lecturer and supervisor over many years, and on the generosity of many friends and colleagues. Patrick Honohan supplied copies of some World Bank archives relating to *Economic Development*; John Horgan generously gave me copies of his interview notes for his biography of Seán Lemass; and Frank Barry shared his unpublished work on the ownership of Irish industry in the early 1960s. My thanks also to Sarah Campbell, Catherine Cox, Tom Feeney, Carole Holohan, John McCafferty, Dermot McDonald, Declan Meagher, Brian Murphy, William Murphy, Margaret O'Callaghan, Brendan O'Donoghue and Conor Ward. My special thanks to Lindsey Earner-Byrne and Paul Rouse, who read and commented on an earlier draft of this work, and to Mark Duncan, who helped me find the cover image. John Bergin compiled a meticulous index. Michael Watson at Cambridge University Press encouraged me to complete this book, and

I really appreciate his support; my thanks also to Rosalyn Scott and to an anonymous reader. My greatest debt is to the expanding Daly family: to Paul, Dee, Conor, John and Peter; to Elizabeth, Dominik, Aidan and Kilian to Nicholas and Steph, Alice and John, and most especially to my beloved PJ.

Abbreviations

AFT	An Foras Talúntais
AIFTAA	Anglo-Irish Free Trade Area Agreement
AOH	Ancient Order of Hibernians
B&F	*Business and Finance*
CAP	Common Agricultural Policy
CFP	Common Fisheries Policy
CIO	Committee on Industrial Organisation
CSJ	Campaign for Social Justice
DD	Dáil Debates
DEA	Department of External Affairs
DFA	Department of Foreign Affairs
DHAC	Dublin Housing Action Committee
DIB	*Dictionary of Irish Biography*
DO	Dominions Office
DOE	Department of Education
EEC	European Economic Community
EFTA	European Free Trade Area
ESB	Electricity Supply Board
ESR	*Economic and Social Review*
ESRI	Economic and Social Research Institute
FCO	Foreign and Commonwealth Office
FII	Federation of Irish Industry
FO	Foreign Office
GAA	Gaelic Athletic Association
GATT	General Agreement on Tariffs and Trade
GMS	General Medical Service
GNP	Gross National Product
HAEU	Historical Archives of the European Union
ICA	Irish Countrywomen's Association
ICD	Irish Catholic Directory
ICMSA	Irish Creamery Milk Suppliers' Association

ICTU	Irish Congress of Trade Unions
IDA	Industrial Development Authority
IER	*Irish Ecclesiastical Record*
IES	*Irish Educational Studies*
IESH	*Irish Economic and Social History*
IFJ	*Irish Farmers' Journal*
IFPA	Irish Family Planning Association
IHA	Irish Housewives' Association
IHS	*Irish Historical Studies*
II	*Irish Independent*
IMF	International Monetary Fund
IMI	Irish Management Institute
IMT	*Irish Medical Times*
IP	*Irish Press*
IPS	*Irish Political Studies*
ISIA	*Irish Studies in International Affairs*
ISPCC	Irish Society for the Prevention of Cruelty to Children
IT	*Irish Times*
ITGWU	Irish Transport and General Workers Union
JSSISI	*Journal of the Statistical and Social Inquiry Society of Ireland*
NAI	National Archives of Ireland
NATO	North Atlantic Treaty Organisation
NESC	National Economic and Social Council
NFA	National Farmers' Association
NICRA	Northern Ireland Civil Rights Association
NIEC	National Industrial and Economic Council
NLI	National Library of Ireland
NUI	National University of Ireland
OECD	Organisation for Economic Co-Operation and Development
OEEC	Organisation for European Economic Co-Operation
PAYE	Pay As You Earn
PR	Proportional Representation
RTC	Regional Technical College
RTÉ	Radio Teilifís Éireann
SD	Seanad Debates
SFADCO	Shannon Free Airport Development Company
SI	*Sunday Independent*
SDLP	Social Democratic and Labour Party
TCD	Trinity College Dublin
TD	Teachta Dála (parliamentary deputy)
TNA	The National Archives (Kew)

UCC	University College Cork
UCD	University College Dublin
UCDA	University College Dublin Archives
UCG	University College Galway
VHI	Voluntary Health Insurance

Introduction

> Ireland is not the place it used to be. The sweet, slow, sorrowful land
> of cheerful indolence and doleful memory is being overtaken by some-
> thing called progress. Ireland is changing. It is changing today more
> profoundly than at any time since the Great Hunger of more than a
> century ago.[1]

This is a book about change and continuity in the years 1957–1973: the
tensions and interaction between the two as Ireland embarked on a
programme of economic development and a campaign to join the EEC.
The independent Irish state which came into existence in 1922 was the
hybrid product of revolution and democratic elections. Despite its turbulent birth, it settled down to become a stable, conservative democracy.
The main preoccupations of the new state were asserting its independence and preserving/creating (we could debate which) a rural, Gaelic
society, whose values were closely aligned with those of Catholicism, the
religion of the overwhelming majority of the population. The social and
cultural values were, at least in theory, the obverse of those embraced by a
modern industrial, anglicised world. Government policies privileged the
family farm and rural life, Gaelic culture and Catholic teaching. There
was an obvious contradiction at the heart of the new state between the
aspiration to achieve a united Ireland and the failure to take account of the
differing religion and culture of Northern Ireland's Protestant/Unionist
majority. The ideology of the newly independent Ireland fostered a pre-
disposition towards introversion and separation, which might be intelli-
gible in a new country trying to come to grips with its independence and
the fallout from the struggle for independence and subsequent civil war.[2]
  Ireland was neutral in the Second World War and did not join the
North Atlantic Treaty Organisation (NATO) despite sharing its opposition to communism. Strict censorship of film and print media insulated

---

[1] Donald Connery, *The Irish* (London: Eyre & Spottiswoode, 1969), p. 11.
[2] Karl Deutsch, *Nationalism and social communication. An inquiry into the foundation of
nationality* (Cambridge, MA: MIT Press, 1966), p. 83.

1

society from what was seen as the decadence and sexual permissiveness of modern life. This isolation should not be over-stated. With emigration increasingly directed towards England, there was a constant traffic between the two islands. Returning emigrants brought home stories of life in England – which probably played down the hardships and often-squalid living conditions, while exaggerating the high pay and more exciting aspects of their lives. The British Broadcasting Corporation (BBC) and other foreign stations gave households with a radio some exposure to a wider world. British newspapers and magazines circulated freely, provided that they did not carry advertisements for contraceptives. Up to 400,000 English Sunday newspapers were imported every week in the 1950s.[3] Delaney points out that Irish people had quite a sustained engagement with modernity during the 1940s and 1950s 'in the sense of experiencing aspects of life or value systems that were widely acknowledged to be new and very different', and he identifies the cinema, British newspapers and emigration as some of the sources for these experiences.[4] Yet while emigration provided a window into a wider world and was a potential agent of modernity, it also reinforced social stability: providing jobs for those who could not find a livelihood in Ireland, reducing the proportion of young adults in the population, removing potential malcontents and social misfits. Social stability was especially evident in Ireland's marriage and fertility, where the patterns that emerged in the decades after the famine survived into the 1950s. Almost one-quarter of adults never married, and those who did, married at a late age, but families were large – averaging four to five children in marriages that lasted for twenty to twenty-four years. Family size was almost unchanged from the 1920s until the late 1950s.[5] The decade or so after the end of the Second World War was the period when Ireland became most out of step with Western Europe. Successive governments embarked on programmes to expand the health services, and tackle shortfalls in housing, but this activity was not matched by a corresponding expansion in agriculture or manufacturing industry. At a time when other countries were enjoying full employment, a rapid rise in living standards, a post-war marriage boom and an expanding urban population, Ireland only experienced these forces vicariously, through the net emigration of over 500,000 young men and women to Britain.

---

[3] Enda Delaney, 'Modernity, the past and politics in post-war Ireland', in Thomas E. Hachey (ed.), *Turning-points in twentieth-century Irish history* (Dublin: Irish Academic Press, 2012), p. 109.

[4] Delaney, 'Modernity', p. 111.

[5] Mary E. Daly, *The slow failure. Population decline and independent Ireland, 1920–1973* (Madison, WI: University of Wisconsin Press, 2006), p. 130.

The conventional wisdom is that all this changed in the late 1950s – a decade 'of crisis leading to a transition from protection to free trade'.[6] Ireland's economic policy changed course. The economy began to grow. Rising living standards resulted in a marriage boom and some liberalisation of society, which was marked by the coming of television, and a weakening of the authority exercised by the Catholic Church. In 1959, Eamon de Valera, the dominant politician in the early decades of the new state, was elected President of Ireland, a largely symbolic role. His departure from active politics is seen as marking the transition to a younger generation, and the dilution or abandonment of their political and cultural values – such as a united Ireland and the revival of the Irish language. Seán Lemass' announcement in August 1961 that Ireland would apply for membership of the EEC signalled a commitment to abandon economic protection in favour of joining a European economic union. The historic 1965 meeting between Lemass and Northern Ireland Prime Minister Terence O'Neill, the first such meeting of the two heads of government since 1922, is viewed as evidence that the Irish government had abandoned its traditional dogmatic line on partition. As Garvin commented in *Preventing the Future*, '(I)t took what was seen as the economic disaster of the mid-1950s and the ageing of the Boys of the Old Brigade to force real change' – changes that nullified the special interests of older business, ecclesiastical, cultural and labour elites.[7] A 'political New Departure' coincided with major shifts in the economy and 'ecclesiastical upheaval'.

The patriots had come reluctantly or otherwise to the conclusion that economic and cultural protectionism would have to be abandoned in favour of free trade, and that multinational capital would have to be used to supplement local capital. It was also concluded that cultural protectionism in the form of book and film-censorship was stultifying and that, in particular, education designed to produce pious patriots and nationalist priests would have to be replaced by education and training for economic growth. ... Essentially this is what duly happened, and happened very rapidly.[8]

Garvin's account suggests that Ireland had embarked on the inexorable path towards modernisation, where economic development was accompanied by the emergence of a more liberal and secular society. Terence Brown – in one of the earliest accounts of this period – suggested that in the late 1950s economic growth became 'the new national imperative',

[6] Brian Girvin, *Between two worlds. Politics and economy in independent Ireland* (Dublin: Gill & Macmillan, 1989), p. 196.
[7] Tom Garvin, *Preventing the future. Why was Ireland so poor for so long* (Dublin: Gill & Macmillan, 2004), p. 27.
[8] Garvin, *Preventing the future*, p. 144.

and Ireland made 'this major cultural and ideological shift without undue strain', partly because the scale and pace of urbanisation was moderate.[9] He writes of a country under the influence of 'the modernizing virus'.[10]

Girvin provides a more cautionary account:

> During his short period as Taoiseach, Lemass shifted the balance of power within Irish society. His administration initiated the most comprehensive attempt at modernisation which had occurred in Ireland. In a broad sense Ireland acquired 'modernity' during this decade, becoming increasingly industrialised, secularised, urbanised and bureaucratised. In retrospect the achievements of the 1960s were partial: more traditional norms quickly reasserted themselves; yet the achievements were real.[11]

In 1968, US journalist Donald Connery identified five recent events that 'converged to revitalize Ireland': the new demands and new confidence resulting from economic growth; a shift towards more outward-looking national policies; 'the sweeping in of all manner of foreign influences'; the arrival of television; and a more liberal Catholicism inspired by Pope John XXIII.[12] While all of the above is correct, I would argue that the degree of change is overstated. More importantly, it suggests that Ireland decided, of its own volition, to abandon protection, whereas I would argue that there was no alternative if the nation was to survive in a world where international trade and economic integration were seen as pre-requisites for economic growth. With net emigration in the 1950s running at levels last seen in the depressed 1880s, it was evident that Irish citizens would not accept living standards that were significantly inferior to other Western nations. Once we start from the position that Ireland had no alternative, other than to abandon protection and work to become a member of the EEC, the focus shifts somewhat, and it implicitly requires greater analysis of the pressures and the difficulties involved in this process of change. There has been a tendency to understate the difficulties involved in this major change of direction; a failure to acknowledge that while many were more than willing to embrace the benefits, they were not necessarily prepared to accept the costs, above all a tendency to hype the achievements.

The focus on Seán Lemass, or 'the Lemass era',[13] has tended to concentrate attention on the early/mid-1960s, with the later 1960s and the early 1970s being treated in a more cursory manner. In 1969, Lemass,

---

[9] Terence Brown, *Ireland. A social and cultural history 1922–1979* (London: Fontana, 1981), pp. 202–3.

[10] Brown, *Ireland*, p. 245. [11] Girvin, *Between two worlds*, p. 200.

[12] Connery, *The Irish*, p. 37.

[13] Brian Girvin and Gary Murphy (eds), *The Lemass era. Politics and society in the era of Seán Lemass* (Dublin: UCD Press, 2005).

now retired from politics, told a journalist that 'Progress once it is properly started must accelerate all the time you see: this is the law of life.'[14] Yet by 1969 the momentum for economic growth had slackened; the numbers at work were static or contracting; politicians were failing to confront thorny problems such as a regional development strategy and a sustainable local taxation base. Elections were increasingly transformed into bidding wars, with parties promising tax concessions or higher spending. EEC membership in 1973 was a major achievement that could not have been taken for granted in the early 1960s. But the gap between Ireland's growth rate and living standards and those of other Western European countries actually widened between 1960 and 1973; the only gap closed was between Northern Ireland and Britain. The numbers at work in 1971 were almost identical to 1961 and significantly below the 1951 figure, at a time when developed economies of Western Europe enjoyed full employment.

The argument that Ireland experienced modernisation, that it was transformed during the 1960s, comes into question when we look at the 1970s and 1980s, and here the analysis of social scientists is unequivocal. Breen et al., writing about the post-1973 period, noted that 'despite the depth of the transformation Ireland experienced since 1958, in some crucial respects stability rather than change proved to be the chief outcome.... The "rising tide" had not sufficed to erase some of the continuities of Irish society.'[15] Higher economic growth between 1958 and 1973, though disappointing by European standards, was not sustained. In the early 1990s, Ireland remained one of the poorest countries in Western Europe, and the gap between Ireland and the EU average was almost identical to 1960.[16] Ó Gráda and O'Rourke describe Ireland as 'clearly a bad underachiever from the standpoint of GNP/capita growth'.[17]

Continuity with earlier times was not confined to the economy. Fahey noted that for Irish Catholicism the 1960s gave 'the appearance of a watershed', but he concludes that 'change has not been so dramatic'.[18]

---

[14] Quoted in Garvin, *Preventing the future*, p. 164.

[15] Richard Breen, Damien Hannan, David Rottman, and Christopher T Whelan, *Understanding contemporary Ireland: state, class, and development in the republic of Ireland* (Dublin: Gill & Macmillan, 1990), pp. 16–17.

[16] Kieran A. Kennedy, 'The context of economic development', in John H. Goldthorpe and Christopher T. Whelan (eds), *The development of industrial society in Ireland* (Oxford: Oxford University Press, 1992), pp. 7–12.

[17] Cormac Ó Gráda and Kevin O'Rourke, 'Irish economic growth 1945–88', in Nicholas Crafts and Gianni Toniolo (eds), *Economic growth in Europe since 1945* (Cambridge: Cambridge University Press, 1996), p. 395.

[18] Tony Fahey, 'Catholicism and industrial society in Ireland', in Goldthorpe et al., p. 255.

Small agricultural holdings survived – often owned by the same family – despite all the doomsayers, though many landholders were now part-time farmers, whose main income came from a job in a factory, or construction – and they continued to exert a strong influence over politics and society.[19] When Liam Ryan compared social values in Ireland with those in other Western European countries in the early 1980s, he concluded that 'It is scarcely surprising to learn that what marks Ireland off from the rest of Europe is largely a matter of conservatism – conservative in religion, in morality, in politics, in views on work and marriage and the family.'[20] The 1980s referendums on the right to life of the unborn and divorce left 'Ireland in a quite exceptional position in developed countries on these issues'.[21] In 1990, Coleman described Ireland's demographic transition (to a low rate of natural increase) as 'still incomplete', going on to note that 'Ireland's demography challenges demographic theory. It cannot adequately account for Irish exceptionalism.'[22] Whether Irish politics is exceptional remains a topic for debate, though Peter Mair does suggest that during the period covered by this book, it is possible to detect the emergence of an ideological distinction between Fianna Fáil and Labour/Fine Gael.[23]

Once we accept the importance of 'continuities', the question is how to explain them? I would argue that far from embracing economic growth in an uncritical fashion, and abandoning the political and cultural priorities of earlier decades, in the 1960s the process of economic and social development was carefully controlled – insofar as this was possible – to preserve strong elements of continuity with the past. So while Ireland had no alternative other than to modernise its economy, dismantle economic protection, apply for EEC membership and recruit foreign-owned firms, there was a determined effort to ensure that the impact was contained. While the 1960s is seen as the decade when Ireland moved from being an agricultural economy, the key policy changes of the period – the 1965 Anglo-Irish Free Trade Area Agreement (AIFTAA) and EEC membership – were designed to preserve the rural, farming community, and the major costs of both developments were carried by industrial firms established under the protectionist regime of the 1930s and their workforce.

---

[19] Damien Hannan and Patrick Commins, 'The significance of small-scale landholders in Ireland's socio-economic transformation', in Goldthorpe et al., p. 102.

[20] Michael Fogarty, Joseph Lee and Liam Ryan, *Irish values and attitudes: the Irish report of the European value systems study* (Dublin: Dominican Publications, 1984), p. 97.

[21] Fahey, 'Catholicism and industrial society in Ireland', p. 258.

[22] D. A. Coleman, 'The demographic transition in Ireland in international context', in Goldthorpe et al., p. 52.

[23] Peter Mair, *The changing Irish party system: organisation, ideology and electoral competition* (London: Pinter, 1987).

While many of the factories that disappeared or shed jobs were based in Dublin and the larger cities, the new foreign-owned successors tended to locate in small towns whose hinterland and culture was dominated by agriculture and rural life. So, while superficially Ireland ceased to be a predominantly agrarian economy, continuities with traditional life styles and values remained strong, though there were obviously some disconti- nuities. Despite doomsday predictions that thousands of smaller farms would vanish, they survived – bolstered by a favourable welfare system and by a refusal to implement any measures that would interfere with farm ownership. In 1981, 44 per cent of the population lived in rural areas, and many of those living in small towns (classified as urban) remained closely associated with rural life. Indeed, we can argue that Ireland never really became an industrial economy – it moved from an agrarian economy in 1961 to become a modern service economy at the end of the twentieth century, with an uncertain hybrid existence in the intervening period.[24]

The 1960s brought new wealth to certain groups in Irish society, but the weakness of the industrial sector meant that the expanding native business elite was concentrated in property development and the service economy – a concentration that can be seen as a continuation of the value system associated with the family farm. The failure to become a fully industrialised economy might in hindsight have been auspicious since Ireland was not left with massive numbers of redundant workers from heavy industries such as steel or shipbuilding – an IDA advertisement in the 1990s boasted that Ireland had avoided the Industrial Revolution. But industrial policies that were designed to shore up provincial/rural Ireland and to limit the emergence of large urban, industrial complexes undoubt- edly weakened the post-1970 industrial structure. The consequences were fewer jobs, greater poverty and more emigrants. Emigration did not end in the 1960s. For much of the 1970s it was simply replaced by rising unemployment; it revived again in the 1980s as economies else- where boomed; Ireland did not succeed in closing the gap in living standards with other Western economies until the 1990s.

Ferriter criticises the failure in the 1960s to address social ills and social inequalities, 'squalor and neglect in the midst of a new-found opulence: the degree to which promises of a more egalitarian Ireland had been continually reneged on over 40 years of Irish independence'.[25] Yet these comments are made with the benefit of the hindsight afforded by the

---

[24] Hartmut Kaeble, *A social history of Europe 1945–2000. Recovery and transformation after two world wars* (New York and Oxford: Oxford University Press, 2013), p. 57.

[25] Diarmaid Ferriter, *The transformation of Ireland 1900–2000* (London: Profile, 2004), p. 537.

explosion in professional research on social and economic inequality, and he too readily accepts the official rhetoric of 1960s economic success. Ireland remained significantly poorer than other Western European countries; the 'new-found opulence' was limited. The multi-factoral causes of social inequality and their deep roots were not adequately understood by social scientists at this time, either in Ireland, where social science research was in its infancy, or internationally, and many ambitious programmes launched during these years have produced at best mixed results.[26] Delaney is more perceptive when he suggests that 'the challenges to cultural orthodoxies through the media, especially television, and the attempts to reduce social inequality by allowing greater access to the secondary and university system may be paradoxically seen as merely the political establishment following on what were widely perceived by the state's citizenry to be the basic features of a developed equitable and "modern" society'. He suggests that there are 'tantalising questions about how subaltern groups drove on social and cultural change in post-war Ireland'.[27] While the expansion of educational opportunities is generally and rightly lauded as one of the major achievements of the 1960s, most of the additional school places were created in existing academic schools, the majority of them under church control. Ownership and control tended to remain in the hands of the church; the syllabus was much as before. It may not be coincidental that Ireland's economic boom – the so-called Celtic Tiger – was delayed until the 1990s, a time when an expansion in service employment – more suited to the educational values of academic secondary schools and related third-level courses, and the wishes of Irish parents – became a major driver of economic growth.

Improvements in health and social welfare can also be described as modifying rather than transforming the previous arrangements. They preserved the principle of a health service that differentiated between people on the basis of need, rather than uniform, universal access as a right – as in Britain's National Health Service. Health and welfare continued, like education, to be a partnership between the state and voluntary agencies – and once again this partnership was renegotiated to take account of changing circumstances, but it did not disappear, and there was a general assumption that the Catholic Church should retain a significant role in Ireland's voluntary health and welfare sector.

Demography is a more complex story. On the one hand, rising living standards resulted in a wave of earlier marriages, and a rising marriage

---

[26] For an evaluation of Lyndon Johnson's War on Poverty, Martha J. Bailey and Sheldon Danziger (eds), *Legacies of the war on poverty* (New York: Russell Sage Foundation, 2013).

[27] Delaney, 'Modernity', p. 118.

rate, which enabled Ireland to belatedly join the international post-war marriage and baby boom, which ended elsewhere in the mid-1960s. The total number of births continued to rise until 1980, and Irish fertility remained significantly out of line with other Western countries. This distinct population profile is partly a reflection of the continuing strength of Irish Catholicism and traditional family values, including the valorisation of large families which was particularly pronounced in farming and rural communities, where fertility remained above the national average. However, it also reflects the frustrations of earlier decades when lack of economic opportunities prevented many men and women from marrying and having children. Girvin and Murphy concede that in the early 1970s, 'the moral community reflected in the 1937 Constitution and the influence of the Church on policy and society remains largely intact'.[28] This is confirmed by statistics of religious practice; most Irish people continued to attend church at least weekly well into the 1980s, and while for some this may have been a matter of conformity, their attendance gave the Catholic clergy an opportunity to exercise their influence with respect to critical issues, especially sexuality and reproduction. While the numbers of newly ordained priests, nuns and religious brothers fell from the mid-1960s, the decline from a post-famine peak in numbers did not cause an immediate crisis. The immediate fall-out from the 1968 Papal Encyclical *Humanae Vitae* among religious and laity was much less evident than in the United States or Europe. Admittedly the late 1960s/early 1970s brought contraception to Ireland, with the contraceptive pill, and the opening of the first family planning clinics, and there is evidence of a more liberal attitude towards sexual relations on the part of young people. However, the strength of more traditional values is evident in the protracted political campaigns relating to divorce, contraception and the 'pro-life' campaign.

Politics is one of the greatest examples of continuity. Expectations that the retirement of the founding fathers of the state, coupled with a growing economy, would bring a realignment of political parties on a clearer ideological, left/right basis were not fulfilled. The existing party system survived, though all parties took opportunistic advantage of more buoyant tax revenue to make commitments for increased public spending, and elections came to be dominated by competing promises of additional benefits or tax relief. The 'parish pump' – local constituency needs – remained paramount; indeed, with a more dynamic economy and higher government spending it offered additional scope for political patronage.

---

[28] Girvin and Murphy, 'Whose Ireland? The Lemass era', in Girvin and Murphy (eds), *The Lemass era*, p. 10.

As for Northern Ireland, Lemass' emphasis on economic growth, his over-tures to Northern Ireland businessmen and the Northern Ireland govern-ment can be seen as a new approach to securing a united Ireland – an argument built on economic interests in place of traditional nationalist rhetoric; it should not be seen as an abandonment of the traditional aspiration. The outbreak of violence in 1969 showed that ethnic and religious identities and historic grievances continued to be potent forces in both parts of Ireland, and the rhetoric of militant republicanism and a united Ireland still resonated with some voters.

So this is the story of how Ireland accepted a need to make some critical changes, and then ensured that the impact of these changes was moder-ated in such a manner that many of the core institutions and core values survived and even thrived. It would probably be unwise to assume that the political and administrative leadership made a conscious decision that 'we must change in order to stay the same'.[29] It is more probable that those in authority – whether political, social or economic – lacked the capacity or the commitment to transform the state and the economy, and they con-sciously or unconsciously adopted measures that would modify such a strategy in order to protect their own interests and placate farmers, con-stituents, the Catholic Church and other interest groups. The practice of circumscribing economic goals with social criteria, which was the keynote of Fianna Fáil policy in the 1930s, continued in the 1960s; all the key goals of the 1930s, such as decentralising industry, and promoting jobs for men rather than women survived, with one notable exception – the aspiration to economic self-sufficiency. Lemass' commitment to eco-nomic and political change is not in question; what is more doubtful however is the extent to which this was supported by other leading politicians. Lee commented that 'Nor was there much evidence that the younger generation had more fire in their bellies than the young, or even the old Lemass'.[30] His successor, Jack Lynch, may have deployed similar rhetoric in many speeches; however, Lynch's first period as Taoiseach (1966–1973) was marked by a loss of momentum and a greater tendency to placate groups such as farmers or opponents of a selective regional development policy. It is no coincidence that Fianna Fáil's electoral support became stronger in rural areas under Lynch's leadership. By the late 1960s, EEC membership was increasingly seen not only as the major economic objective – which indeed it was – but as a means of resolving demanding socio-economic aspirations: protecting markets and living

---

[29] Giuseppe de Lampedusa, *The Leopard*, (London: Collins, 1960), p.40.

[30] J. Lee, *Ireland 1912–1985. Politics and society* (Cambridge: Cambridge University Press, 1989), p. 390.

standards for farmers; enabling the government to improve welfare benefits, because they no longer had to subsidise agriculture; making Ireland more attractive to foreign industries; and perhaps offering a potential pathway towards a united Ireland.

Ireland's EEC membership can be seen as symptomatic of a more general approach to thorny political and social issues. Questions about whether it was compatible with neutrality and the implications of membership for Irish sovereignty were largely ignored; the focus remained on economic and financial benefits. Similarly, while there was a warm, if vague, welcome for government efforts to create closer links with Northern Ireland, the changes that might be required in Ireland's laws and constitution were not seriously contemplated. Lemass was willing to review the 1937 Constitution with a view to making it more acceptable to minority and unionist interests, but this point of view was not shared by his successor Jack Lynch, nor was it widely known or accepted by the electorate. The removal of Article 44 in the Constitution, which referred to the 'special position' of the Catholic church was not accompanied by a reflective debate on what that 'special position' meant, or the degree to which the Constitution and laws should continue to reflect Catholic teaching on issues such as divorce or contraception. Garret FitzGerald's 'constitutional crusade' in the 1980s, a later venture along similar lines, met a similar fate. What this suggests is that much of the process of change and modernisation did not happen until the 1980s, or perhaps the 1990s, and that as in other aspects of its history, Ireland pursued a *sonderweg*.

This book is a contribution to the examination of Irish modernity, and Ireland's interaction with socio-economic change in the mid-twentieth century. This emphasis on tradition and continuity chimes with Joe Lee's argument about the dominance of 'possession' rather than 'performance' in post-independence Ireland up to and including the 1950s, when Seán Lemass attempted to 'shift the balance', determined 'to elevate the performer principle at the expense of the possessor principle'.[31] Lee noted that judgement on Lemass must wait until the archives had been opened; this book has the advantage of both my personal research in those archives and the remarkable output of monographs and articles written by others about this period, plus the work of social scientists.[32] The years covered in this book, 1958–1973, are generally recognised as the key period, when Ireland began to experience economic growth and social change, so by focusing in detail on this period, I hope to identify some of the factors that explain the

[31] Lee, *Ireland 1912–1985*, pp. 392–404; quotations pp. 396, 400.
[32] For a reflective series of essays embodying current research see *IHS*, xxxviii, no. 154, May 2013. Special issue, 'The origins of contemporary Ireland: new perspectives on the recent past', Guest editor, Brian Girvin.

survival and modification of traditional forces. The period has a political unity; the general election of 1957 saw a coalition government of Fine Gael and Labour succeeded by Fianna Fáil, who held office through four successive general elections, until 1973, when they give way to a Fine Gael/Labour coalition government. The year 1973 also marks Ireland's entry to the EEC – an entity that first begins to take shape in 1957; 1973 is also accepted as the end date for the post-war economic 'golden age'. The time period broadly coincides with Arthur Marwick's 'long sixties', which begin in 1958 and end in 1973–1974. Marwick argues that this was a 'self-contained period ... of outstanding historical significance in that what happened during this period transformed social and cultural development for the rest of the century', and his sparkling account of the cultural revolution during these years in Britain, France, Italy and the United States has prompted many contributions that critique or confirm his.[33]

All histories of this period give the economy a central role, so the opening section – one of three – concentrates on the economy, beginning with an overview of Ireland's economic growth and how it compared with other Organisation for Economic Co-Operation and Development (OECD) countries. This is followed by a chapter that looks at the process of economic planning and commitment and capacity of key groups, including the civil service to lead a process of economic development. The remaining chapters in this section examine how industry, rural Ireland and the processes for physical and regional planning coped with the changing economy. The second section, headed 'Society' looks at changing life styles, changes in marriage and demography, reforms in state provision for those in need, including children in institutional care. Several chapters in this section look at women: changes in work pattern, provision for widows, single mothers, the impact of the emerging second-wave feminist movement, contraception and fertility decline. This section also looks at health and education and the Catholic Church. The final section looks at political parties, elections and candidates, arguing that while there is evident change in the passing of the revolutionary generation, and the adoption of more radical social policies by at least two major parties, continuity in terms of the preoccupation with local clientelist issues, and also the two and a half party configuration, is evident. This is followed by a chapter on foreign policy – examining the predominance of the EEC as an issue, despite the rhetoric of Ireland's independent foreign policy. A chapter on Northern Ireland unites both foreign and domestic policy, and it also brings us back to the economy and its significance.

---

[33] Arthur Marwick, *The Sixties* (Oxford: Oxford University Press, 1998).

Part I

The economy

1 'Bringing up the rear of the pack'[1] in Europe's golden age of economic growth

On 12 July 1963, the *Time* magazine cover story featured the Taoiseach Seán Lemass with the headline: 'New spirit in the ould sod'. Lemass was pictured against a garish green curtain, covered with shamrock motifs, which opened to reveal an electricity generating station and modern high-rise buildings. The story juxtaposed traditional images such as the Lakes of Killarney, horse-racing and GAA football with a factory assembling Volkswagen Beetles, a traffic jam on Dublin's O'Connell St and a vegetable processing plant. Economic success was, and remains, the central image of 1960s Ireland.[2]

This chapter casts a critical eye on that representation. My underlying argument is that the economic turnaround over the period 1958–1973, though dramatic when compared with the previous performance, is much less impressive when Ireland is compared with other European countries: not just Germany, France, Italy and the Benelux, but less developed and more peripheral economies, such as Spain, Portugal and Greece. During the 1960s, the economies of OECD countries grew by more than 50 per cent. Ireland (with Britain) was among the minority who failed to achieve this target. Furthermore, while the story is generally presented as one where an Irish government decides to abandon long-established protectionist policies and introduce a programme for economic development, Ireland had no alternative other than to do this, in the light of the creation of two Western European trading blocs and increasing competition in the British market from Commonwealth countries and Britain's European Free Trade Area (EFTA) partners. The popular story of Ireland's economic success fails to acknowledge how difficult it was to transform an economy that had been slumbering complacently for many decades and how partial that transformation proved to be. Despite achieving significantly higher growth than in previous decades, the gap in GNP and living

---

[1] Barry Eichengreen, *The European economy since 1945: coordinated capitalism and beyond* (Princeton: Princeton University Press, 2007), p. 119.
[2] The article was written by Donald Connery.

15

standards between Ireland and the rest of the OECD actually widened during these years. The 1960s are also celebrated as the decade when the population of independent Ireland began to rise after more than a century of decline – the decade when it appeared that emigration had ended. Yet while the 1971 Census recorded a population of 2,978,248, which was 6,256 higher than 1926, the numbers in employment were 40,000 fewer than in 1951 and only 2,300 above the historically low 1961 figure. Emigration had fallen significantly, but this may owe more to young people remaining longer in school and Britain's economic difficulties than to Ireland's economic progress, and unemployment was high when compared with other countries.

Rather than seeing the 1960s as 'The best of decades',[3] I would like to emphasise the challenges and the shortcomings in Ireland's economic record. This should not be read simply as a condemnation of Ireland's economic performance and the key actors – politicians, civil servants, businessmen, farmers and trade union leaders. That would be to under-estimate the inherent difficulties in transforming an economy in a modern democracy, especially in a country where the process of change had been slow, and the reforms threatened to undermine Ireland's self-image as a rural, agrarian society. Yet Irish people aspired to living standards that were comparable to those in Britain – comparisons that were inevitable given the high rates of emigration. But there was a lack of realism about the external economic environment, and Ireland's lack of capacity to control this. The prospects of achieving economic prosperity and higher living standards within a short period were undoubtedly inflated, espe-cially by politicians. Above all, there was a failure to acknowledge the trade-offs that were necessary. The real losers were those condemned to either emigrate or survive on long-term benefits, not just in the years covered by this book, but in decades to come.

On 20 July 1959, the Irish Council of the European Movement held a conference in Dublin, which was addressed by Walter Hallstein, President of the EEC Commission; John Cahan, Deputy Secretary-General of the Organisation for European Economic Co-Operation (OEEC); Maurice Faure, a former French Foreign Minister; and Alfred Robens, President of the UK Council of the European Movement.[4] The timing is significant,

---

[3] Fergal Toibín, *The best of decades: Ireland in the 1960s* (Dublin: Gill & Macmillan, 1996).

[4] Historical Archives of the European Union, Florence, hereafter HAEU, Hallstein papers. N1266/1769. Visit to Dublin. The Irish Council of the European Movement was estab-lished in 1954 to assist those connected with the economic life of the country to keep in touch with developments in Europe and to promote an understanding in other European countries of Irish problems and attitudes. Hallstein described the Movement as 'recently reconstituted'.

less than a month after Seán Lemass became Taoiseach on 23 June in succession to Eamon de Valera. On the same day, the 'outer seven' – seven European nations who were not EEC members – were meeting in Stockholm to establish the EFTA. Hallstein noted that this 'gave the meeting a special note – because Ireland was not involved in the Stockholm event'. Although EFTA was confined to trade in manufactures, Denmark, which like Ireland was very dependent on agricultural exports, had managed – as part of the negotiations on membership – to secure a highly favourable agreement with Britain, which removed the tariff on bacon imports and gave Denmark concessions on processed foods.[5] Danish bacon now had access to the UK market on similar terms to Ireland. This concession was rightly seen as eroding the value of the 1948 Anglo-Irish trade agreement – which had given Ireland preferential access to the UK market for agriculture produce. News of the agreement with Denmark prompted a hastily arranged meeting between Lemass and the Irish Ministers for Agriculture and Industry and Commerce and the UK President of the Board of Trade. Although Irish government sources described the meeting as a continuation of earlier talks relating to a European free trade area, this was putting a positive spin on events. The only outcome was a commitment to explore ways of improving trade between the two countries. It is clear that all the pressure for talks and proposals for a new trade agreement originated in Dublin.[6]

The Anglo-Danish agreement, and the establishment of a seven-member EFTA, which is generally seen as a reaction to the formation of the six-member EEC in 1958, highlighted Ireland's parlous position. At a time when the impetus within the Western world was towards trade liberalisation, multi-national agreements and closer integration of national economies, Ireland remained isolated. Despite being an independent state for almost forty years, Irish links to the international economy were almost entirely via Britain. Ireland's privileged access to the British market was being eroded by the rapid expansion of British agriculture, which was boosted by generous government supports. Irish produce was also facing growing competition from Commonwealth and EFTA producers, who had secured concessions in the British market, at a time when Britain and Germany offered the only significant export markets for livestock, pork and dairy produce. In European circles, the formation of EFTA and the Anglo-Danish agreement were read as evidence that Ireland's privileged bilateral trading relationship with Britain was

---

[5] *IT*, 14 July 1959 The Anglo-Danish pact. By a special correspondent.
[6] *IP*, 14 July 1959 Taoiseach in London talks.

coming to an end.[7] John Cahan told the Dublin audience that 'you badly need a jolt ... some of you were getting a bit complacent'. He warned that Ireland was going to lose 'probably forever, your privileged position in the United Kingdom agricultural market' and would face greater competition from Denmark and the Netherlands. The creation of the 'little free trade area' – EFTA – would 'hit you also on the industrial side'. Cahan outlined two options for Ireland: raising protection on industry 'to astronomical heights, or to get rid of protection and make your industries fully efficient. You have no terribly bright picture in front of you.' He claimed that Ireland would have a 'hard road to the end of the century'![8] Hallstein was more positive. He praised the 1958 Programme for Economic Expansion and suggested that European manufacturers might establish plants in Ireland. But in his private notes he suggested that the government was caught between the current agricultural crisis and pressure from the opposition for failing to anticipate this new threat to agricultural exports to Britain. He claimed that Lemass was aware that the Irish relationship with Britain was that of the beggar (*als Bettler vor Grossbritannien*), despite Ireland being Britain's second-best market in Europe. He also highlighted the government's recent defeat in a referendum and by-election losses.[9] While Hallstein overstated the political difficulties, his concerns about the economy were realistic.

The 1950s

By the late 1950s, Ireland's economic policy had changed little over the past twenty years. When Fianna Fáil came into government in 1932, it embarked on a programme of self-sufficiency for agriculture and industry, but by the end of the decade ideological zeal had given way to a more pragmatic arrangement, which was symbolised by the 1938 Anglo-Irish trade agreement. This gave Irish agricultural produce privileged access to the British market in return for a commitment to review the high rate of protection for Irish manufactures, which had no practical impact, perhaps because of the outbreak of war in 1939. Although an Irish Central Bank was established in 1943, the Irish currency was pegged to sterling and fully backed by sterling reserves. Exchange and interest rates were determined in Whitehall and the Bank of England, not in Dublin. Ireland did not join the World Bank and the International

---

[7] European Nachrichten 136/1959 Frankfurt, 14 Juli 1959. III/2. Irland um seinen Agrarmarkt besorgt – zwischen EWG und kleiner Freihandlszone.

[8] *IT*, 21 July 1959. All press clippings cited are in Hallstein's papers.

[9] N1266/1769. Visit to Dublin.

Monetary Fund (IMF) until 1957; until then all access to international currency was via Britain.[10]

The combination of highly protected industries and an agricultural sector, part of it geared to exporting livestock to Britain and part based around a complex array of protectionist measures, survived largely unchanged until the 1960s. Throughout most of Western Europe, the 1950s was a decade of economic transformation with unprecedented growth, near-full employment, modest price increases and steadily rising living standards. In Ireland, it was marked by economic stagnation and the highest level of emigration since the 1880s. When Eichengreen reviewed the performance of Europe's economies after 1945, he described Britain, Belgium and Ireland as 'laggards ... bringing up the rear of the pack'; Ireland was 'the most dramatic outlier'. In the 1950s, Ireland's growth was one-third of the Western European average, as was the return on capital investment.[11] In 1957, the IMF (which Ireland had just joined) noted 'how different the Irish position is from that of most members of the Fund. Almost without exception, the problem with which members of the Fund are faced are those of over-expansion, of rapid growth which taxed the resources of member countries in productive capacity, foreign exchange, and in many cases of labour ... In Ireland, by contrast, we are dealing with an economy which – with few interruptions – has been contracting for more than a hundred years'. Despite a sharp fall in population, unemployment was 'very much higher than usually found in Western countries'.[12]

Ireland's poor performance was due to a combination of factors, not least its dependence on the sluggish British economy. In 1950, 92.7 per cent of exports went to Britain. Danish economist Lars Mjoset has described Ireland as 'a free rider on Britain's decline'.[13] The dominance of agriculture was both a weakness and an opportunity. In France and Italy, post-war growth was fuelled by rising agricultural productivity and a flexible labour supply, as workers moved to better-paying, more productive industrial jobs – but not in Ireland. The 1950s were also marked by a new agricultural revolution: crop yields soared, thanks to the intensive use of fertiliser and chemical spraying against disease; intensive farming of pigs and poultry brought cheap, year-round supplies of eggs, and cheaper

---

[10] For background to Ireland's belated membership of the IMF, see Ronan Fanning, *The Irish department of finance, 1922–58* (Dublin: Institute of Public Administration, 1978), pp. 386–91.

[11] Eichengreen, *The European economy since 1945*, pp. 118–19.

[12] NAI, DFA E 6, International Monetary Fund Statement by Louis Rasminsky, Irish Consultations, 14 May 1958.

[13] Lars Mjoset, *The Irish economy in a comparative institutional perspective* (Dublin: NESC, 1992), p. 9.

bacon. Chicken became an everyday food, no longer a luxury. The eradication of livestock disease and selective breeding, using artificial insemination, resulted in bigger and better cattle. In post-war Europe, where many people had previously gone hungry, cheap and plentiful food constituted an economic miracle. But Ireland was in the last place yet again when it came to agricultural productivity. Soil fertility remained low; farmers used less fertiliser than elsewhere because high tariffs were levied on fertilisers in order to protect local manufacturers. Milk and butter production remained highly seasonal – with lots of milk in the summer and a winter shortage, which meant that Ireland occasionally had to import butter during the winter. Bovine tuberculosis was rife; farmers opposed eradication programmes and the government was reluctant to challenge this powerful interest group. Only the threat that Irish cattle would be excluded from the British market spurred the government to undertake a full-scale eradication programme in the late 1950s. Pig and poultry farming was uncompetitive, especially in comparison with Northern Ireland, because animal feed had to contain a specified proportion of expensive home-grown grain – part of the government's commitment to promoting self-sufficiency and viable small farms.[14]

Rising agricultural productivity brought an over-supply of produce and greater competition in international markets. By the late 1950s, Britain and West Germany were the only countries in Western Europe that imported significant quantities of agricultural produce. Young live cattle (store cattle) were the only item that Ireland could export to Britain without a subsidy. Yet, despite low productivity and the indifferent quality of Irish produce, the economy remained dependent on agricultural exports. Eighty per cent of Irish exports consisted of live animals, food and beverages, which included Guinness stout (a beer).[15] Employment in agriculture declined, though at a slower rate than elsewhere; workers moved to English construction sites and factories – not to jobs in Ireland.

The continuing reliance on agriculture for export earnings and significant employment reflected the appalling state of the manufacturing industry.[16] The self-sufficiency programme of the 1930s had resulted in the establishment of numerous small firms, which were protected by high tariffs and draconian quotas. Under the Control of Manufactures Acts, foreign-owned or foreign-controlled industries could only operate under licence, producing goods that did not compete with domestic firms, and

---

[14] Mary E. Daly, *The First Department. A history of the department of agriculture* (Dublin: Institute of Public Administration, 2002).

[15] Kieran A. Kennedy, Thomas Giblin and Deirdre McHugh, *The economic development of Ireland in the twentieth century* (London: Routledge, 1988), Table 9.2, pp. 184–5.

[16] Girvin *Between two worlds*, pp. 196–9, presents a more positive account of Irish industry.

this legislation remained in place despite a new drive to attract foreign industries, launched in 1949.[17] When US economic consultants IBEC[18] were asked in 1952 to identify the industries that had the best prospects of securing export markets in the United States, they reported that they had failed to find any.[19] The few foreign industrialists who set up plants in Ireland, often German family businesses fearful of a communist takeover, were directed to small towns in the rural west and south-west, in keeping with a socio-economic philosophy that privileged rural living and deplored the growth of major cities.

The overall level of investment was low when compared with other European economies, and too low a proportion of this sum was invested in economically productive projects. There was little innovation, whether in agriculture or industry, and an introspective, defensive suspicion of economic change. Politicians complained that most of Ireland's Marshall Aid came in the form of loans rather than grants, but the money was badly spent; many dollars were used to buy tobacco – a valuable source of revenue for the exchequer but useless in terms of generating economic growth or higher productivity.[20] A post-war investment drive concentrated on housing and hospitals, which were undoubtedly socially desirable but produced no long-term economic dividend. The Land Project, which reclaimed wasteland for agricultural use, absorbed large sums of money. The sole benefit came in the wages paid to workers – as the marginal land was being reclaimed, large tracts of better land lay neglected by emigrants or elderly farmers.[21] Other European countries made better use of the opportunities and resources offered. A study of the European Productivity Agency, which provided trans-Atlantic assistance to raise European productivity – describes Ireland as one of the four 'ghosts' – countries that rarely took part in the agency's activities and never commented on its work.[22]

Although Ireland was a founding member of the OEEC, she did not join the World Bank or the IMF until 1957. Despite a strong current of anti-British sentiment, and a nationalist version of economic history that

---

[17] Mary E. Daly, ' "An Irish-Ireland for Industry"? The Control of Manufactures Acts, 1932 and 1934', *IHS*, vol. 24, no. 94, November 1984, pp. 246–72.

[18] Not to be confused with the Irish business organisation which has the same initials.

[19] IBEC Technical Services Corporation, *An appraisal of Ireland's industrial potential*, 1952 Department of Industry and Commerce I. 98.

[20] Bernadette Whelan, *Ireland and the Marshall Plan, 1947–1957* (Dublin: Four Courts, 2000).

[21] Daly, *First Department*, pp. 282–6.

[22] Bent Boel, *The European productivity agency and transatlantic relations 1953–1961* (Copenhagen: Museum Tusculanum Press, 2003), p. 245. The others were Portugal, Luxembourg and Iceland.

represented Ireland as a victim of British policies, when it came to international economic relations, Ireland remained dependent on Britain, and
even trusted Britain as its intermediary. The decision not to join the
World Bank or the IMF in the late 1940s was made on the assumption
that Britain would provide Ireland with sufficient access to foreign
reserves (but it didn't). Anglo-centrism meant that Ireland failed to notice
that Britain was a declining power, which was being overtaken by other
European nations. Ireland was slow in grasping the significance of the
OEEC, moves towards a European free trade area or the political significance of agencies such as the European Coal and Steel Community or
the EEC. Proposals for a European free trade area were seen as threatening Ireland's privileged access to the British market – a euro-sceptic
response that mirrored Britain's. At the OEEC, Ireland branded itself
as a developing country on a par with Greece and Turkey, demanding
that any reduction in tariff protection should be spread over twenty years,
with only a 10 per cent reduction in tariffs over the first ten years.[23]

In many respects the cards were stacked against Ireland. The OEEC
saw trade liberalisation and rising manufacturing output as the key to
economic growth. This message was not welcome in a country with a
small, inefficient and highly protected manufacturing sector, which
regarded agriculture and rural living as fundamental bedrocks of society.
Furthermore, while the OEEC was committed to liberalising trade for
both agriculture and industry, the main pressure was on reducing tariffs
on manufactures. Industrial countries such as Germany and Britain
continued to cosset their farmers with subsidies and encouraged them
to increase output. In contrast agricultural countries such as Ireland and
Denmark were under pressure to open their markets for manufactured
goods to outside competition. Joining EFTA, a free trade area that
applied only to manufactures, would have exposed Ireland's protected
industrial sector to the full blast of competition, without any corresponding gains in agricultural markets. The EEC, which was an economic
union, not a free trade area, offered much better prospects for farmers.
But Irish membership would only be practicable if Britain also joined.

While the OEEC's John Cahan believed that Ireland needed a jolt, and
senior officials in the World Bank were equally adamant that Ireland had
to face up to the need for economic change, the options were limited and
appeared to be contracting. *Economic Development*, the 1958 white paper
by Ken Whitaker, the young secretary of the Department of Finance, was

[23] UCDA P 175/2 Whitaker Papers, J. C. B. Mc Carthy (Industry and Commerce) to
Murray, 14 October 1959 rejoining the outer Seven (EFTA); Maurice Fitzgerald,
Protectionism to liberalisation. Ireland and the EEC, 1957 to 1966 (Aldershot: Ashgate,
2000), p. 57.

written as a 'wake-up call'. It set out the 'problems and opportunities' that Ireland faced in achieving economic development, including the need 'sooner or later' to abandon self-sufficiency and face the challenge of free trade.[24] Among its key recommendations were encouraging foreign investment and policies designed to increase livestock output, rather than tillage. Both proposals involved the repudiation of traditional Fianna Fáil ideology. *Economic Development* recommended that public capital investment should be redirected from social projects such as housing, hospitals or telephones to productive purposes. (Eichengreen cites this hostility to investing in telephones and roads, and the fact that by 1960 Ireland had a mere 50 telephones per 1,000, compared with 150 in the United Kingdom and 400 in the United States as evidence of Ireland's 'outlier' status.)[25] Whitaker urged that policy should concentrate on one objective: the growth rate – ignoring goals to create jobs, promote regional development or preserve small farms, which had been central to government policy since the 1930s. He recommended reducing taxes on incomes and removing subsidies – traditional recommendations from the Department of Finance. Given this relentless rejection of existing policies, it is not surprising that one backbencher described this document as 'more in the line of economic destruction'.[26] He set a target of doubling the annual growth rate from 1 to 2 per cent – a derisory figure, at a time when Italy was recording 7 per cent growth. He identified agriculture as offering the best growth prospects. This was at variance with what was happening elsewhere in Europe, where industrial development was the main dynamic, but Whitaker obviously regarded Irish industry as a hopeless cause, and in seeing Ireland as an agrarian economy he was firmly in the traditions of the Department of Finance.

Whitaker's report and the government's *Programme for Economic Expansion* – a watered-down version of *Economic Development* that expunged or diluted many of the tougher, politically unpalatable recommendations – were both drafted in 1958 against the background of a serious recession. Although the international uncertainty resulting from the 1956 Suez crisis was a contributory factor, the primary responsibility for this recession rested with the government. In the autumn of 1955, Gerard Sweetman, Minister for Finance in the Second Inter-Party government,[27] decided not to raise interest rates in line with a rise in UK rates. Irish banks reacted to this break with established practice by moving capital to London, resulting in a sharp fall in external assets and a

[24] *Economic Development*, F/58 (Dublin, 1958), Foreword.
[25] Eichengreen, *The European economy since 1945*, p. 119.
[26] Wycherley, DD, vol. 171, col. 1567, 3 December 1958.
[27] A Fine Gael, Labour, Clann na Talmhan coalition supported by Clann na Poblachta.

soaring balance of payments deficit. Sweetman tried to redress this deficit (which was primarily a capital outflow) with a grim menu of import levies, consumer credit restrictions, increased taxes and cuts in the public capital programmes, driving the economy into a deep recession lasting several years. The construction sector did not regain pre-depression levels until 1961/62; employment in manufacturing did not overtake the 1955 figure until 1962; fixed investment (by volume) did not recover to the 1955 level until 1961 and only surpassed it in 1963; the 1955 share of fixed investment in GNP was not reached again until 1962. Agriculture did not regain its 1957 output until 1961.[28] The impact of this severe depression on living standards, on the thousands forced to emigrate and the crisis in national morale cannot be exaggerated. Fine Gael lost office in the 1957 general election and did not return to government until 1973. Memories of the economic debacle of 1956 permanently damaged the political career of Gerard Sweetman, 'the Iron Chancellor'.[29]

Economic growth in the 1960s: rhetoric and reality

Between 1958 and 1963, the years of the first *Programme for Economic Expansion*, the economy grew at an average annual rate of 3.4 per cent, which was regarded as a major triumph. However, a cold look at the statistics indicates that much of this growth can be attributed to the economy rebounding after a deep recession. The 1961 census showed that total employment and industrial employment were lower than in 1951, and the population was the lowest recorded. A chilling headline in the *Belfast Newsletter* – 'Fleeing Irish and East Germans', written shortly after the construction of the Berlin Wall and the publication of the census returns – noted that Ireland and East Germany were the only countries in Europe with declining populations; it described both as failed entities. But Lemass, anticipating the census figures several weeks before they were published, suggested that employment in all sectors, including agriculture, had stabilised since the middle of 1959 (when Lemass became Taoiseach) 'following upon a long period of continuous decline'. A leading article in the *Irish Press*, which was owned by the de Valera family, claimed that Ireland had reached 'the half-way mark' in the process of developing the economy[30] – an assertion that would not withstand scrutiny.

[28] Kieran Kennedy and Brendan Dowling, *Economic growth in Ireland: the experience since 1947* (Dublin: ESRI, 1975), pp. 6–8, 33.
[29] *Hibernia*, 9–22 May 1969. Profile Gerard Sweetman.
[30] Daly, *The slow failure*, pp. 211–19.

Lemass' optimism was designed to pave the way for Ireland's application for EEC membership. This option emerged for two reasons – an absence of alternatives and the fact that British Prime Minister Harold Macmillan was preparing to apply for membership and Ireland's fate was tied to Britain's. The determination to apply for EEC membership marked a change in policy in both Britain and Ireland. Negotiations on the establishment of a European free trade area, led by the OEEC, coincided with Ireland's 1957 general election, which meant that Ireland was only represented by civil servants. Throughout the campaign, all the political parties adopted a cautious attitude to the proposed European free trade area. Britain remained Ireland's primary concern. In July 1959, a committee of senior civil servants determined that it was essential to establish closer economic relations with Britain in order to protect the market for agricultural produce 'and avoid being squeezed between the emergent trading blocs in Europe'. Their goal was to have British support prices – the higher prices paid to UK farmers – extended to Irish farmers. *The Economist* summarised Ireland's goals as 'the economic equivalent of rejoining the United Kingdom, combined with the emotional satisfaction of remaining politically independent'.[31] Ireland also wanted Britain to encourage UK firms to open factories in Ireland. Something would have to be offered in return – and the only concession of value for Britain was to grant UK manufacturers duty-free entry to the Irish market, which Ireland was not (yet) prepared to offer. The President of the Board of Trade, Reginald Maudling, told Lemass that no concessions that Ireland could offer would induce him to grant what Ireland was seeking.[32] A bilateral trade agreement signed in April 1960 brought minimal benefits for Irish farmers, and no change in existing arrangements for manufactures; most Irish manufactures already enjoyed duty-free access to the British market.[33]

By 1960, it appeared that the option of a closer trading relationship with Britain had been closed off, or would only be secured through joint EEC membership. When Lemass outlined Ireland's policy on Europe in Dáil Éireann in July 1960, he noted that the first objective would be to protect the trade relationship with Britain – 'the keystone of our external trade structure'.[34] Forewarned of Britain's intention to apply for EEC membership, Ireland wrote a letter of application on 31 July 1961. Denmark, forewarned, also applied. Although the EEC opened negotiations with Britain and Denmark, Ireland's application was left to one side,

[31] *The Economist*, 26 September 1959.
[32] D. J Maher, *The tortuous path: the course of Ireland's entry into the EEC 1948–1973* (Dublin: Institute of Public Administration, 1986), p. 104.
[33] Daly, *First Department*, pp. 358–60.   [34] Daly, *First Department*, p. 364.

allegedly because the economy was regarded as underdeveloped, but more probably because the EEC was unwilling to admit to full membership a country which was not a member of NATO. Despite these unpromising signals, and the possibility that Britain and perhaps Denmark might become members, while Ireland was excluded, the underlying economic strategy of the early 1960s was geared to preparing industry for EEC membership in the not too distant future. In January 1963, Ireland introduced a unilateral tariff cut – an indication of intent to move towards free trade. In addition to domestic speeches, where he 'talked up the economy', Lemass gave many interviews to foreign journalists, all designed to highlight the transformation that was underway.[35] He made a determined effort to represent the country as a modern developed economy, in marked contrast to the strategy in 1957 when Ireland had bracketed itself with Greece and Turkey as a developing economy needing a long transitional period before it could cope with free trade. The many interviews given to foreign journalists formed part of a strategy to advance the case for EEC membership and attract foreign investment.[36]

Although Britain's application was suspended early in 1963, the *Second Programme for Economic Expansion*, launched several months after French President Charles de Gaulle had vetoed British membership, assumed that Ireland would have joined the EEC by 1970, and the growth targets and projections were apparently based on this assumption. The Programme was a conscious attempt to link Ireland with the growth and trade liberalisation targets set by the OECD – the successor to the OEEC. Ireland belatedly signed up to the OECD target of a 50 per cent rise in GNP over the decade 1960–1970, which the Council of Ministers had adopted in December 1961 at the first meeting of the new, expanded organisation. The target was literally plucked out of the air; the OECD never made any projections to see whether it was attainable.[37] The target reflected a hubris about the capacity to achieve growth and full employment that seems remarkable today, a hubris which Ireland fully embraced. The target would only have been feasible if Ireland had joined the EEC in the mid- to late 1960s; yet when the Programme was launched, this was highly unlikely.

Nevertheless the *Second Programme* began well; growth was on target in 1963 and 1964. The year 1964 was a boom year. A 'National Wage Recommendation' awarded most wage and salary earners a 12 per cent

[35] NAI DT, S16699 D/61 – F/95.
[36] NAI DT Private Office files, 97/9/1511/1512/1546/1946 give Lemass' interviews 1959–62.
[37] HAEU, OECD 41. First meeting OECD Executive Committee – 19 October 1961 OECD/CE/M (61) 1.

pay increase over thirty months. Farmers fared even better: incomes rose by 20 per cent per capita; net agricultural output by 15 per cent; agricultural prices by 11 per cent. A Europe-wide beef shortage resulted in record cattle prices. The 1964 'farmers' budget' announced higher guaranteed prices for most produce and additional relief on rates – the tax levied on agricultural land.[38] But the boom and euphoria were short-lived. During the 1950s, economic growth in Western Europe was promoted by industrial peace and steady but controlled growth in wages. Wage increases lagged behind rising profits, leaving businesses and government with sufficient funds for increased investment, which in turn ensured further growth. However, by the 1960s, workers had higher expectations of better pay and improved working conditions. Their bargaining power was strengthened by acute labour shortages in countries such as Germany and the Netherlands. Rising inflation stoked labour militancy. Although Ireland was far from enjoying full employment, prices were rising faster than in the past, aggravated by the introduction of a general sales tax (turnover tax) in 1963. Regular speeches by politicians about Ireland's prospering economy ramped up pay demands. Powerful groups of workers regarded the 12 per cent national pay increase as the starting point in pay negotiations and set out to exceed it. Dublin building workers downed tools in August 1964 demanding a reduction in working hours from 42.5 to 40 hours; by October, the strike threatened to become nationwide. When Industry and Commerce Minister Jack Lynch conceded their demands, Agriculture Minister Patrick Smith resigned in protest, calling on the government to fight the plague of trade union militancy.[39] Smith's description appears justified: more than 500,000 days were lost to strikes in 1964 – a figure reached on only four occasions from 1923 to 1961; it was little consolation that the Irish trend was almost identical to Britain.[40]

One of the underlying premises behind economic programming was that medium or long-run strategies should not be derailed by short-term difficulties. This principle went out the window in 1965. The economy was in crisis with a soaring balance of payments deficit, which was a direct consequence of the 1964 incomes boom. The Central Bank introduced credit restrictions in an attempt to reduce imports. Livestock and beef exports fell by almost 18 per cent, forcing the government to introduce a livestock export subsidy for the first time since the 1930s. Exports of

[38] John Horgan, Seán Lemass: the enigmatic patriot (Dublin: Gill & Macmillan, 1997), p. 235.
[39] Daly, First Department, p. 458.
[40] Charles McCarthy, The decade of upheaval. Irish trade unions in the nineteen sixties (Dublin: Institute of Public Administration, 1973), pp. 20–1.

manufactured goods fell when Britain imposed a 15 per cent import surcharge in an effort to protect its balance of payments. The 1966 Budget, brought forward to March (the normal date was April/May), ostensibly so that it would not clash with the 1916 Golden Jubilee celebrations, but probably to ease pressures on the exchequer, continued the deflationary process with higher taxes and further reductions in capital spending. A mini-budget in June raised taxes on petrol and tobacco and introduced a new wholesale tax of 5 per cent, resulting in further price increases. Cattle exports almost ceased from May to July because of a UK shipping strike, but its ending brought little relief. The EEC had imposed stringent import duties on produce from outside its member countries – a foretaste of things to come. The government introduced a subsidy on fat cattle exported to Britain, which gave farmers prices equal to the guaranteed price paid to British farmers.[41] Attempts to borrow money on the international market – for the first time since 1927 – were badly timed; they ended up with a loan in Deutschmarks at record-high interest rates. Whitaker ruefully reflected that 'we arrived just at the wrong time … if you want to borrow then borrow when you don't need to borrow'.[42] Deteriorating trade conditions, credit restrictions and spending controls combined to reduce the growth rate to 2.25 per cent in 1965 and 1.75 per cent in 1966. Yet despite an end to the boom, the number of days lost through strikes increased in 1965 and 1966 and strikers became more militant: a telephonist strike resulted in protest marches and hunger strikes. In the autumn of 1966, the National Farmers' Association (NFA) took to the roads to protest at low incomes and the government's failure to involve them in economic discussions. The 1965 downturn was felt throughout Western Europe. By 1966 however, most countries had returned to rapid growth – albeit with higher inflation and greater labour unrest. Ireland remained in the doldrums – Europe's worst-performing economy in 1965, 1966 and 1967. Although historians have generally applauded Lemass' economic record as Taoiseach, the shortcomings in economic strategy were becoming evident by the time that he retired.

The 1965 Anglo-Irish Free Trade Area Agreement

The Anglo-Irish Free Trade Area Agreement, signed in December 1965, was Lemass' last significant achievement on the economic front. It opened the Irish market to UK manufacturers in return for assurances that Irish farmers would have better access to the British market – an option that Ireland had refused to contemplate in 1960. The Agreement

---

[41] Daly, *First Department*, p. 475.   [42] OECD EPC Minutes 16 March 1966.

appeared to grant significant benefits to Irish farmers, while forcing manufacturers to face greater competition. Lemass spoke of a 'two-country common market concept'[43] and Ireland represented the Agreement as an interim step on the road to EEC membership. Negotiations were long drawn-out: Britain held most of the cards. Commonwealth countries like New Zealand and Australia were targeting the British market, as was Denmark, whose farmers were being excluded from their traditional market in Germany, and as part of their campaign they attacked the concessions granted to Irish farm produce. It was probably no coincidence that Britain opened bilateral talks with Denmark in March 1963, five days before scheduled talks with Ireland. Multilateral talks on meat and livestock exports also took place between Ireland, Britain, Australia, New Zealand, Argentina and Uruguay, with Australia demanding an investigation of Ireland's store cattle trade with Britain. By December 1964, Britain indicated agreement in principle on an Anglo-Irish free trade area but wished to keep concessions to Irish agriculture to a minimum. The priorities of Irish and British farmers were radically different. Britain wished to ensure a continuing and indeed an increasing supply of store cattle – younger animals which would be fattened and slaughtered in Britain, whereas Ireland wanted to increase exports of beef and fat cattle (ready for slaughter), which would give a higher return. Ireland was insistent on retaining duty-free entry for agricultural produce and securing a better deal for textiles.[44]

The final agreement was negotiated by a team of civil servants, led by Whitaker, who were given plenipotentiary powers.[45] It was signed in December 1965 – almost three years after talks opened. Britain agreed to remove all protective duties on imports of Irish-manufactured goods from 1 July 1966. In return, Ireland would progressively remove all protective tariffs on British goods over a nine-year period. Irish fat cattle would qualify for British support prices after two months in Britain – instead of the existing three. Britain agreed to pay UK support prices on 25,000 tons of Irish beef and 5,000 tons of carcase lamb. Ireland gave an undertaking that store cattle exports to Britain would not fall below a specified level and was given firm guarantees that no restrictions would be placed on store cattle exports – which accounted for 40 per cent of Irish agricultural exports to the United Kingdom. Ireland's butter quota was increased, but imports of butter, bacon, poultry eggs and grain continued to be governed by Britain's multinational agreements, which were

---

[43] NAI DT S16674K/95 Trade relations with Britain.
[44] NAI DT, S16674Y; Cabinet minutes 10 December 1965.
[45] Anne Chambers, *T.K. Whitaker. Portrait of a patriot* (London: Doubleday, 2014), p. 171.

proving increasingly restrictive as other countries fought for a share of the British market.

The Agreement failed to reduce the rising cost to the Irish Exchequer of agricultural price supports, and the promised market security proved ephemeral. Although livestock exports and prices rose significantly in 1967 and 1968, and in 1967 for the first time Ireland became the no. 1 exporter of carcase beef to Britain, the Irish taxpayer was now paying a subsidy on all beef exports not covered by the UK support price agreement. A promising export market for cheese, which was carefully fostered by Bord Bainne – the Irish dairy board – was threatened in 1968 when Britain introduced 'voluntary' import restrictions, which was contrary to the Agreement. Import quotas for Irish butter continued to fall. After another round of trade talks in February 1969, Minister for Agriculture Neil Blaney remarked that if the restrictions on cheese exports were extended to other produce, the Agreement would become worthless for Ireland. Towards the end of that year senior civil servants noted that 'our agricultural gains under the Agreement had been limited, contrary to expectations'. They expressed concern at British threats to impose further restrictions on Irish agricultural exports, and to renegotiate the subsidies agreed for Irish beef. Britain planned to increase domestic agricultural output, primarily to reduce its import bill. Despite claims that this would not conflict with commitments given in the Agreement,[46] market opportunities for all Irish farm produce, other than store cattle, were contracting. In the light of these difficult market conditions, perhaps it is not surprising that Irish agricultural output stagnated.

The 1965 Agreement was a trade-off between the interests of agriculture and industry, and by restoring the free-trading relationship between Britain and Ireland that existed pre-1932, it can be seen as the ultimate triumph of the Department of Finance. Most Irish manufactures had duty-free access to the British market since 1948. The only firms to benefit from the Agreement were those producing or using man-made fibres. As manufacturing imports from EFTA members would have duty-free access to the UK market by January 1967,[47] Irish firms faced growing competition in Britain. Garret FitzGerald predicted that AIFTAA would have a much more severe impact than EEC membership, because most firms would gain nothing to compensate for sales lost at home, whereas EEC membership would open up new markets.[48] When the Federation of Irish Industry (FII) consulted members before the Agreement was signed,

[46] Daly, *First Department*, pp. 492–5; *Third Programme*, p. 23.
[47] *Third Programme. Economic and Social Development, 1969–72* (Dublin, 1969), p. 23.
[48] *B&F*, 13 August 1965.

they reported that 'Some started off optimistic and ended up gloomy. Others, a minority, finally decided that their worst fears would not be realised.' Only synthetic fibres manufacturers 'viewed with pleasure the prospect of a trade agreement'. The FII concluded that the Agreement would result in slower industrial growth after 1970 – the half-way point in the tariff reduction time-table. Most firms anticipated greater competition under the Agreement than they would face when they joined the EEC, because membership would diversify Britain's export drive, as opposed to concentrating it on Ireland. Firms who manufactured British brands under licence for the domestic market, Irish subsidiaries of British firms and firms threatened with competition from well-known British brands, which had hitherto been excluded from the Irish market, felt especially vulnerable, as did assemblers of electrical goods such as televisions and fridges, because there was over-capacity in the UK market.[49]

In the mid-1960s Irish manufacturing industry had a significantly better growth record than agriculture. Output and exports of textiles and hosiery was growing well ahead of the targets in the *Second Programme*.[50] New foreign-owned firms (see Chapter 3) were making a significant contribution to export earnings. By 1971, nominal tariff rates had halved, though effective tariff rates were still more than double the UK and EEC average.[51] Ireland's trade deficit with Britain doubled between 1965 and 1970. British imports increased by 79 per cent and Ireland moved from being Britain's ninth-best market to third-best. By 1973, New Industries– the majority of them foreign-owned – accounted for 30 per cent of manufacturing output, 29 per cent of employment and 62 per cent of manufacturing exports.[52] While this might be seen as evidence of success in attracting foreign direct investment, it also reflects the inability of formerly protected manufacturing industries to adapt to changing circumstances. Mining was another major source of jobs and export earnings, with the large silver and lead and zinc deposits at Tynagh, county Galway, which were exploited by Irish emigrant Pat Hughes. By 1965, Tynagh was the largest industry in the west of Ireland.[53]

---

[49] *B&F*, 1 October 1965, 8 October, 1965.   [50] *B&F*, 5 February, 1965.

[51] Dermot McAleese, *Effective tariffs and the structure of industrial protection in Ireland* (Dublin 1971: ESRI paper 62), p. 38.

[52] Dermot McAleese, *A profile of grant-aided industry in Ireland* (Dublin: IDA, 1977), pp. 16–17. McAleese, p. 9 defines New Industry as 'Enterprises which received new industry grants from the IDA (or its predecessor organisation) and which were one full year in operation by 1974'. Firms grant-aided by Shannon Free Airport Development Company SFADCO were excluded.

[53] *B&F*, 17 September 1965.

International stories about Ireland's economic miracle – the parallel with Germany's *Wirtschaftswunder* is obvious – petered out around 1965/66. An *Economist* story in 1965 was headed 'Ireland's bumpy flight'. A *New Society* article, 'Ireland's economy under fire', opened with positive comments about the growing economy, 'the industrial complex around Shannon airport ... huge power stations towering over miles of bog', before noting that 'the kind of hyperbolical description of economic progress that one used to hear only a year ago is now hard to find. The economy is suffering from the identical ills that are besetting the British economy and a few others thrown in for extra measure.'[54] The cover featured an Aer Lingus plane under attack from rockets labelled 'rising prices; balance of payments; British levy; rising wages; gold reserves down'. In May 1967 the Irish delegate to the OECD's Economic Policy Committee confessed that 'we have at home laid most of the blame on our own mistakes ... [for] ... the serious interruption of growth' in 1965 and 1966. 'Excessive increase in money incomes, credit and public expenditure' triggered a large balance of payments deficit and the need for corrective measures which depressed growth. Ireland's growth rate consistently fell below target – so much for economic planning. In June 1966, officials predicted that the annual growth of 3.7 per cent would rise to 5 per cent in 1967; by September projections had been reduced to 2.1 per cent for 1966 and 4 per cent for 1967, which, though far below other OECD countries, proved too optimistic.[55]

The most severe shortfalls related to agriculture; output increased by only 2 per cent in the years 1964–1967 – the target was 16 per cent. Industrial output increased by 25.5 per cent, against a target of 31 per cent. Although 1967 saw a return to 4 per cent growth, this was short-lived. After 1968, GNP grew at a lower rate than in the early 1960s, with the exception of 1969, when it was fuelled by another round of very generous pay increases following a lengthy strike by maintenance workers. The generous settlement[56] probably helped Fianna Fáil to victory in a June general election, at the cost of higher inflation and further balance of payments difficulties.

By 1968, net agricultural output was only 12 per cent higher than in 1957; it actually fell in 1969–1970. Nevertheless, major changes were underway in Irish farming. By 1970, cattle numbers had increased to almost 6 million, from 4.7 million in 1960; the number of cows had increased from 1.20 million to 1.66 million. Beef exports rose; milk

[54] Jeremy Bugler, 'Ireland's economy under fire', *New Society*, 2 September 1965.
[55] HAEU, OECD 164(2) short-term economic forecasting 30 June 1966.
[56] McCarthy, *Decade of upheaval*, p. 27.

output soared from 480 million gallons in 1960 to 775 million; dairy herds grew larger. Many farmers switched to dairying, because it offered the best prospect of a decent family income. Incomes of dairy farmers were heavily subsidised by taxpayers; in 1968/1969 the exchequer subsidy on milk accounted for 40 per cent of the price paid to farmers, the unsubsidised market price was lower than in 1960. Much of the additional milk was processed as cheese or powdered milk, rather than the traditional butter. But world markets were awash in all dairy produce, so taxpayers also had to subsidise sales of butter, cheese and milk powder on global markets.[57]

Assessing Ireland's economic performance

The late 1960s marked the beginning of the end of the post-war economic miracle. The oil crisis following the 1967 Arab-Israeli War, the inflationary spiral in the United States because of the Vietnam War and Johnson's Great Society Programme resulted in large volumes of dollars awash on the international markets and rampant inflation. The post-war monetary system introduced at Bretton Woods was unravelling; the Deutsch mark was too strong, sterling lurched from crisis to crisis and the French franc remained vulnerable. Monetary instability added to inflation.[58] No European country managed to hold the line against escalating wage and prices. The mass strikes and protests of 1968 reverberated throughout the Western world, bringing industrial unrest and higher inflation. The 1968 'évenements' shattered the post-war consensus on growth and rising prosperity. Unemployment, which had disappeared from much of Western Europe began to rise, though this failed to dampen wage demands.[59] By the end of the decade, governments were more concerned with controlling inflation and the consequences of unstable currencies than with promoting economic growth and full employment. Yet by 1970, the OECD had exceeded its target of a 50 per cent growth in gross national product (GNP). Ireland experienced most of the downside of the late 1960s – long and disruptive strikes, rising inflation and currency uncertainties – but failed to achieve the OECD target. Growth in 1971 and 1972 was below 3 per cent; employment fell between 1968 and 1972, wiping out the gains achieved earlier in the decade.

---

[57] Daly, *First Department*, pp. 484–503.
[58] Eichengreen, *The European economy since 1945*, p. 220.
[59] Robert J. Flanagan, David W. Soskice and Lloyd Ulman, *Unionism, economic stabilization and incomes policies. European experience* (Washington: Brookings Institution, 1983), p. 5; Eichengreen, *The European economy since 1945*, pp. 216–19.

One welcome change, however, was the reversal of more than a century of population decline. In 1966, the population was 2,884,000 – substantially above the 1961 figure of 2,818,000 – which was an all-time low, though still below the 1956 figure. The 1971 Census, with a population of 2,978,000, was the highest figure recorded since independence. In 1961, Dublin was the only region with a population greater than in 1951. In 1966, fourteen counties – mainly in the west and the midlands – recorded a decline; by 1971, population loss was confined to all Connacht counties except Galway, plus Cavan, Longford, Donegal and Kerry (which had thirteen fewer inhabitants than in 1966).

Better terms of trade (the relative prices of exports and imports, including falling oil prices) meant that in 1973 Ireland could buy 39 per cent more imports than in 1957 for a similar quantity of exports.[60] Nevertheless, while the economy performed better than in the past, it lagged behind the rest of the OECD, on almost every indicator. In 1960, Irish Gross Domestic Product (GDP) per capita was 60.8 per cent of the average for fifteen Western European countries;[61] by 1973, it was 58.9 per cent. Per capita private consumption (what the average person had to spend) fell from 77 to 65 per cent of the OECD average.[62] Although Irish people were more prosperous than in 1960, in relative terms they were poorer. Growth in exports and imports and the rate of capital investment remained below the OECD average; more worryingly, the return on investment fell significantly in later years. Why then were/are the 1960s regarded as a successful decade for Ireland? One explanation rests with Lemass' consistent practice of talking up Ireland's economic achievements, a story that was widely covered in the media both in Ireland and internationally. A second explanation is that the economy *was* growing; people were more prosperous; and furthermore Ireland was growing faster than Britain and Northern Ireland. But Ó Gráda and O'Rourke argue convincingly that doing better than Britain was no cause for celebration, because as a poorer country Ireland would have been expected to grow faster than the European average. Indeed, they go as far as to state that 'UK growth was more or less what would have been expected given its initial level of GDP per capita. Ireland should have been growing faster than the UK but was not; it is Ireland which appears to be the sick man of Europe, not the UK.'[63] Ireland's rate of investment, though higher than

---

[60] Kennedy and Dowling, *Economic growth in Ireland*, p. 47.
[61] The fifteen countries that were members of the EEC in 1995.
[62] John Bradley, 'The Irish economy in comparative perspective', in Brian Nolan, Philip J. O'Connell and Christopher T. Whelan (eds), *Bust to Boom? The Irish experience of growth and inequality* (Dublin: ESRI, 2000), pp. 12–16.
[63] Gráda and O'Rourke, 'Irish economic growth 1945–88', p. 395.

Britain's, was below the European average, and although unemployment was lower than in the 1950s, or after 1973, it was above the average.[64] The most significant comparisons are between Ireland and less developed European economies. In Spain, GNP per capita grew from 56.9 per cent in 1960 to 74.8 per cent of the EU-15 average in 1973; Portugal went from 43.2 to 61.1; Greece from 42.5 to 62.4; they all overtook Ireland.[65]

Ó Gráda and O'Rourke suggest that no single factor explains Ireland's poor performance. They identify 'the small size of the economy, the importance of agriculture, low-quality investment decisions, and rent seeking in industrial relations' – though they believe that this is not the whole story.[66] Ireland's economic profile was not an advantage. As already noted, by the 1960s European agriculture was facing a crisis of over-production and low prices. The British market was becoming more competitive, and the AIFTAA failed to protect Ireland's position. EEC entry would have given farmers higher prices and secure markets, but this was not secured until 1973, leaving the Irish taxpayer carrying an increasing burden of price supports and other subsidies. Yet the postponement may have been providential, because it is not clear that Ireland would have been given full membership in the early 1960s, at a time when the EEC had aspirations to become a significant political union, and would not have welcomed a non-NATO member. The fact that Ireland was regarded as an underdeveloped economy was another potential barrier against full membership; by the end of the decade however, Ireland had managed to shake off that label.

The Irish economy remained heavily dependent on Britain – the slowest-growing major economy in Western Europe. An overvalued sterling and the loss of competitiveness of British industry meant that the 1960s was marked by a series of balance of payments crises and measures to counteract this: import deposit schemes and 'voluntary' restrictions on imports – not to mention restrictions on personal spending. The belated devaluation of sterling in November 1967 failed to solve Britain's difficulties; it was followed by further measures to curb demand and restrict imports, which had a significant impact on Ireland. Britain remained the major destination for agricultural and manufactured exports – because there was no alternative, and British attitudes towards Ireland reflected

---

[64] Nicholas Crafts and Gianni Toniolo, 'Postwar growth: an overview', in Crafts and Toniolo (eds), *Economic growth in Europe*, pp. 1–32; Ó Gráda and O'Rourke, 'Irish economic growth', pp. 391–5.

[65] Bradley, 'The Irish economy in comparative perspective', p. 12; Frank Barry, 'Economic integration and convergence. Processes in the EU cohesion countries', *Journal of Common Market Studies*, vol. 41, no. 5, 2003, p. 899.

[66] Ó Gráda and O'Rourke, 'Irish economic growth', pp. 419–21.

this reality. While Britain gave advance notice of the 1967 devaluation to a number of key trading partners, in order to limit the adverse reaction, 'There was a presumption that Ireland's economy was so interwoven with Britain's that it would continue inside the Sterling area indefinitely, no matter what happened.'[67] In March 1968, the British embassy in Dublin reported considerable criticism that Ireland had to devalue in line with Britain. Ireland was seriously considering reducing its sterling holdings – not surprising, given that other countries in the sterling area had already done so, and sterling was once again coming under pressure in international currency markets. By May, the proportion of Irish reserves in sterling had fallen to 77 per cent, and the British authorities were increasingly concerned at this trend; Ireland was the second-largest international holder of sterling. When he met senior British officials to discuss this, Whitaker raised the question of the 'voluntary' restrictions imposed on British firms investing in Ireland, in a manner that suggests that if Britain made some concessions on that front, Ireland might delay its plans to reduce sterling balances, but Britain rejected this proposal; indeed, officials began to contemplate unspecified retaliation if Ireland continued to reduce its sterling holdings.[68]

The falling value of sterling was only one potential cause of friction between Britain and Ireland. Ireland appears to have negotiated the 1965 Agreement on the assumption that both countries would be members of the EEC before tariff cuts would begin to bite. With the date of EEC membership drifting into an uncertain future, Irish industrialists complained that the AIFTAA was having a severe impact on their domestic market, as British industries targeted the Irish market. In Ireland, EEC membership was increasingly seen as the Promised Land and the delay in arriving there was often blamed on Britain. In February 1968, Andrew Gilchrist, the British ambassador, told a senior Foreign Office official that 'This business about Britain being a dog-in-the-manger over the Common Market is coming up more and more in the newspapers and also in the Dáil' – he was keen to use a speaking engagement to 'put in a counter-word'.[69] Whether the reduction in tariff barriers under the AIFTAA – almost a decade before it would have happened following EEC entry – was good for Irish industry is questionable; manufacturing jobs were lost that could otherwise have survived for some years.

Barry suggests that inability to control wage inflation was probably the critical factor in Ireland's disappointing growth performance. Having

[67] Anthony Craig, *Crisis of confidence. Anglo-Irish relations in the early troubles* (Dublin: Irish Academic Press, 2010), p. 24.

[68] TNA Kew, FCO 48/26 Finance Sterling Irish Republic diversification of.

[69] FCO 62/91 Gilchrist to Ken Gallagher 23 February 1968.

compared Ireland, Spain, Portugal and Greece, he concluded that 'only in Ireland however was there a coincidence of strong wage growth, high unemployment and high emigration'. In Spain, Portugal and Greece, 'state corporatist' regimes controlled wage increases (though real wages rose by 81 per cent in Spain and 60 per cent in Portugal), making it possible to have higher investment and higher economic growth. Irish real wages increased by 90 per cent between 1960 and 1973, compared with 56 per cent in Britain, making many Irish firms uncompetitive in both home and export markets. Only FDI 'propped up the manufacturing sector'.[70] Rising inflation afflicted all Western economies, but Ireland was the worst affected. Between 1969 and 1973, consumer prices rose at an annual rate of 9.3 per cent, double the rate of 1961–1969 (4.6 per cent); the highest rate of inflation in Western Europe – higher even than Britain.[71] Irish pay increases consistently outstripped other countries; in the years 1968 and 1969, they were rising at an annual rate of 15.4 per cent, the highest in Europe.[72] In 1969, Whitaker told the OECD's Economic Policy Committee that 'what we have seen in Ireland – a kind of social psychological change; a tendency for workers not to look across the social structure and think of comparability with other workers in the same sphere but to look up the social structure and want to make a significant and quick improvement in their real standards as against the higher income brackets'.[73] Repeated references to a growing economy, and a greater awareness of international comparators, had encouraged workers to demand living standards comparable to their wealthier neighbours.

Lower growth, lower investment and higher inflation meant fewer jobs. Additional jobs in industry and services just compensated for those disappearing in agriculture. Between 1968 and 1972, the numbers in employment fell; the 1972 figure was the lowest recorded.[74] Unemployment was above the European average, and would have been higher, if a growing number of young people hadn't remained in school to take advantage of the expansion in secondary- and third-level education.[75] In 1967, the National Industrial and Economic Council (NIEC) *Report on Full Employment* set

---

[70] Barry, 'Economic integration and convergence', pp. 902–3.

[71] Christopher Alsopp, 'Inflation', in Andrea Boltho (ed.), *The European economy. Growth and crisis* (Oxford: OUP, 1982), p. 79.

[72] Kennedy and Dowling, *Economic growth in Ireland*, pp. 267–8; Eichengreen, *The European economy since 1945*, p. 217; Alsopp, 'Inflation', p. 85.

[73] HAEU EPC OECD 205 EPC 23rd meeting; 30 June–1 July 1969.

[74] Kennedy and Dowling, *Economic Growth in Ireland*, p. 257; James F. O' Brien, *A study of national wage agreements in Ireland* (Dublin, 1981) ESRI paper no. 104, p. 7.

[75] Denis Conniffe and Kieran A. Kennedy (eds), *Employment and unemployment policy for Ireland* (Dublin: ESRI, 1984), p. 5.

out what would be needed to ensure that everybody actively seeking work in Ireland could find a job. While this seems a rather ambitious goal given Ireland's history, full employment or near full employment was the norm in most Western countries at this time. The report conceded that full employment was unlikely 'in the foreseeable future'. Achieving full employment by 1981, assuming that money incomes rose in line with Britain, would require an additional 7,000–12,800 jobs annually, an average growth rate of 5.5 per cent, and an investment of 27–30 per cent of GNP. All of these targets were significantly higher than the achievements of the 1960s. If this did not happen, the NIEC predicted that the 1970s would bring either rising unemployment or a resumption of emigration – a prediction that sadly proved to be correct. If one of the key challenges facing Ireland was to bring a deeply engrained practice of mass emigration to an end, then the period 1958–1973 must be deemed a failure. Although the rate of emigration fell sharply, and indeed during the early 1970s many emigrants returned home from Britain, that proved to be a short-term trend. Later decades brought a return to high levels of emigration. The change appears to be from long-term emigration to more cyclical patterns, with low rates of emigration often coinciding, as in the 1970s, with soaring unemployment.[76]

[76] NIEC, *Report on Full Employment*, 1967, F66/19 Return emigration in the early 1970s was partly driven by a belief that the Irish economy had turned a corner, partly I suspect by rising anti-Irish sentiment in Britain, following the onset of violence in Northern Ireland, and partly by a slowing economy in Britain.

2 Transforming the economy
Whose plan?

> Some years ago in the County Mayo
> This story all began,
> Before emigration was finally cured
> By the first economical plan.[1]

Economic plans do not commonly feature in ballads, but the 1958 *Programme for Economic Expansion* was known in rural Ireland, and it was credited with transforming the economy and ending emigration. Economic planning was very much in vogue in the 1950s and 1960s. This was prompted by both Marshall Aid, which required recipient countries to devise a plan, and the development of national income statistics and a literature on economic growth.[2] By the 1960s, France, the Netherlands, Italy and Britain had all engaged in some form of planning. Ireland appears to have been heavily influenced by the success of Italy's Vanoni Plan and by France, which transformed itself into a dynamic prospering economy, apparently because of the Commissariat du Plan. Yet the most successful economy at the time, West Germany, was averse to such exercises, and many scholars have questioned whether planning had any significant effect on economic growth during these years.[3] Nevertheless, by adopting an economic programme Ireland was following the European fashion. Contrary to what is often stated, this was not Ireland's first effort at economic planning. While the self-sufficiency programme introduced by Fianna Fáil after 1932 did not set targets for GNP (the concept had not been developed), it did set out ambitious and

---

[1] TO MY SON IN AMERICAY. By the Author of THE GROCER'S OPINIONS to the air of THE ROCKS OF KNOCKANURE, as quoted in Hugh Shields, 'Printed aids to folk singing 1700–1900', in Mary E. Daly and David Dickson (eds), *The origins of popular literacy in Ireland: Language change and educational development 1700–1920* (Dublin: TCD & UCD, 1990), p. 146.

[2] Robert W. Fogel, Enid Fogel, Mark Guglielmo and Nathaniel Grotte, *Political arithmetic. Simon Kuznets and the empirical tradition in economics* (Chicago: Chicago University Press, 2013).

[3] Alec Cairncross, *The British economy since 1945. Economic policy and performance, 1945–1990* (Oxford: Oxford University Press, 1992), pp. 142–3.

often unrealisable targets for the share of the domestic market to be supplied by industry and agriculture. Wartime neutrality also demanded considerable planning to ensure sufficient fuel, grain and other products – again not always successfully. Ireland also had to devise a plan to qualify for Marshall Aid, though Whitaker suggested that this was regarded as 'an exercise that had to be undertaken to persuade the Americans to give us Marshall Aid'.[4]

While many words have been written about the significance of the publication in November 1958 of the government's *Programme for Economic Expansion* and Whitaker's *Economic Development,* the events passed largely unnoticed at the time. John McCarthy claims that all members of the Oireachtas (Parliament) received copies of the *Programme for Economic Expansion* on 11 November, and 'Eamon de Valera invited Whitaker to attend the parliamentary session and personally congratulated him', but the Dáil was not sitting on that date, and there is no record in the Oireachtas Debates of the publication, or of Whitaker being congratulated. McCarthy is correct in noting that TDs (Teachtaí Dála) were given no opportunity to debate the Programme.[5] Were it not for Garret FitzGerald, then writing in the *Irish Times,* under the pseudonym 'Analyst', it is probable that neither document would have been noticed by the press. On the one hand, the lack of publicity is remarkable given the modern hype of press releases/photo opportunities, but governments operated in a different manner at this time. On the other hand, lack of publicity might also indicate a less-than-wholehearted commitment to the programme.

Economic Development proposed a neo-liberal approach to the economy, reducing taxes and subsidies and exercising tight control over public expenditure. The published version removed some of the more contentious recommendations, and the *Programme for Economic Expansion* further diluted this message. Furthermore, while a near-final draft of *Economic Development* was available before work began on the *Programme for Economic Expansion,* the *Programme* appeared first.[6] These details may appear pernickety and overly academic, but they are significant. While in many respects *Economic Development* was a classic Department of Finance (Treasury) document, advocating cutting taxes and subsidies and favouring a free market – for example, abolishing rent

---

[4] Quoted in Fanning, *Finance,* p. 406.
[5] John F. McCarthy, 'Ireland's turnaround: Whitaker and the 1958 Plan for Economic Development', in McCarthy (ed.), *Planning Ireland's future. The legacy of T.K. Whitaker* (Dublin: Glendale, 1990), p. 57.
[6] The *Programme for Economic Expansion* was published on 12 November 1958; *Economic Development* on 22 November.

control – the *Programme for Economic Expansion* toned down that message significantly. Whitaker's recommendations to remove regional incentives for industries and reduce agricultural rates relief and use the savings to subsidise fertiliser were ignored (rates relief continued and a fertiliser subsidy was introduced). Whitaker wanted to submit proposals to construct a government-owned nitrogen fertiliser plant and make a major investment in the state-owned Irish Steel Co. to the World Bank for their scrutiny, but the Departments of Industry and Commerce and Agriculture successfully opposed this.[7] But the government's wish to develop nitrogen and steel industries reflected a continuing commitment to old-style protectionism, indicating that some sections of government were not yet convinced of the merits of free trade.

A second issue concerns the control/oversight of the planning process. In the first draft of *Economic Development*, which was titled 'Has Ireland a Future?' Whitaker wrote:

The senior Civil Servant's principal function must always be that of advising Ministers – of presenting to them a rounded view of the facts and considerations which should guide public policy, of making recommendations, but once policy has been decided, of carrying it out faithfully and effectively. But something more is needed in an economy like ours. It is, of course, essential that Civil Servants should keep out of party politics and a great responsibility must always rest on them to be discreet in their behaviour and utterances ... In a small country like this where not information only but talent as well is locked up in the Civil Service, it is desirable that there should be free communication between the service and the public. Even the Border has its 'approved roads'![8]

This can be read as advocating that civil servants should have a greater role in determining policy and should be permitted to act as an intermediary between the state and the public in shaping this policy; the corollary would be a reduced role for politicians. Whitaker also suggested that the *Programme for Economic Expansion* should be subject to regular review by a team of external economists. He sent an advance copy to the World Bank, which was rather critical; one official described it as 'a retrograde step from the Whitaker Report' and complained that 'there is still jam for everyone'.[9] Lemass ruled out any external evaluation. 'The Government must be in full control of policy and I think that it might tend to undermine this position – or at least create the danger of misunderstanding about it – if modifications or extensions of the Government's

---

[7] NAI 2001/3/16 Economic Development.

[8] Has Ireland a Future? Copy on NAI DT, S16660A. Approved roads were cross-border roads, not policed by customs' posts, which locals were permitted to use.

[9] IBRD King to Zafariou, Ireland – Economic Development Program, 27 January 1959. My thanks to Patrick Honohan for supplying me with material from the World Bank Archives.

published programme could be discussed by our officers on their own initiative with persons outside the civil service.'[10]

Government control (i.e., political control) is evident in the diluting of the *Economic Development*'s focus on the free market and indeed in the roll-out of the *Programme*, though this did not extend to scheduling a debate in Dáil Éireann.[11] Bew and Patterson claim that the high rate of trade union membership among non-agricultural workers ensured that the hard-nosed free market approach of Whitaker to the reconstruction of the Irish economy was not followed.[12] But Fianna Fáil had never accepted a hard-nosed free-market approach, and this was especially so with Lemass. When Lemass became Taoiseach, he began to exercise a subtle shift in the message associated with the *Programme for Economic Expansion*. The concept of switching public investment from non-productive to productive activities gave way to a more positive attitude towards public investment. Within weeks of succeeding de Valera, Lemass in a letter to the Lord Mayor of Dublin emphasised the 'Government's stated policy that the state should in future participate to an even greater extent than heretofore in developmental activities, *which while not commercial* [my emphasis], contribute to overall expansion of the economy and help in the achievement of economic production'. Similar messages to all local authorities prompted funding requests for swimming pools, car parks, swamp drainage and similar schemes – whose connection with the Programme was tenuous to say the least; these were often a rehashing of failed applications under various job creation programmes in previous years.[13] The government also received numerous applications for funding from private individuals, including proposals to produce heather honey, a potato crisp factory in Longford, organic vegetables (ahead of its time!), caravan parks and retirement homes for American citizens, not to mention some recycled hardy perennials, such as the manufacture of carrageen moss and seaweed meal. In all, over seven hundred proposals were received.[14]

John Horgan, Lemass' biographer, noted that traditionally the Department of the Taoiseach 'was only tangentially concerned with

---

[10] NAI, DT, S16474 Lemass to Ryan 2 December, 1958.

[11] Lee, *Ireland 1912–1985*, comments that 'The de-politicisation of "planning" was too useful an asset to be wantonly surrendered to the capricious vagaries of Dáil debate', p. 352.

[12] Paul Bew and Henry Patterson, *Seán Lemass and the making of modern Ireland* (Dublin: Gill & Macmillan, 1982), p. 189.

[13] Mary E. Daly, *The buffer state. The historical roots of the Department of the Environment* (Dublin: Institute of Public Administration, 1997), pp. 440–1.

[14] For a list of topics, see index of files Department of Finance Development Division 1960 files; Chambers, *Whitaker*, p. 153.

policy'.[15] This was not the case under Lemass. During his years as Taoiseach, he relied heavily on a committee of secretaries of the Departments of Finance, Agriculture, Industry and Commerce and External Affairs to formulate policy on issues that crossed departmental lines, such as EEC membership, foreign trade or north–south relations.[16] Lemass applied the language of enterprise and economic development to the public service; he spoke of 'making every Department of the Government into a development corporation'.[17] Ten days after he became Taoiseach, he wrote to the presidents of the NFA, the Federation of Irish Industries (FII) the Irish Congress of Trade Unions (ICTU) and the Association of Chambers of Commerce of Ireland, inviting them to meet him to discuss what could be done to increase economic growth.[18] Lemass' concept of planning included quasi-corporate committees, councils, and endless papers and discussions between civil servants, businessmen (they were all men) and trade union leaders; the Department of Industry and Commerce complained that there were too many meetings.[19] If Lemass' concept of planning was rather different from what Whitaker had envisaged, the consummate civil servant adapted to the new model.

The newly created Economic Development Branch in Finance – later known as 'Development Division' – became the flagship troubleshooting group that drove economic planning and related activities. It was headed by Charlie Murray, with TCD economist Louden Ryan (who had examined Whitaker's London university PhD thesis) as a part-time technical director. Ryan was seconded to Development Division full-time from 1964 to 1966 – so Whitaker's wish to have an external economist involved was partly achieved. Development Division took on a daunting array of activities: producing regular updates on the *Programme for Economic Expansion* and quarterly data on national income; drafting the Second and Third Programmes; reviewing state aid for agriculture and industry, industrial research and design and management education; and ensuring that these activities supported the government's development strategy. Many of these projects trespassed into the domain of other departments; so it is not surprising that according to Louden Ryan, the unit was seen as 'a bit of an upstart'. Garret FitzGerald noted that their activities 'met with resistance from a number of quarters, as other departments reacted against initiatives, which they felt to be within their own areas of

---

[15] Horgan, *Seán Lemass*, pp. 191–2. [16] Daly, *First Department*, p. 342.
[17] Seán Lemass, 'The organisation behind the Economic Programme', *Administration*, vol. 9, no. 1, 1961, pp. 3–10.
[18] Daly, *First Department*, p. 343.
[19] NIEC *Report on Economic Planning*, 1965, paras 32 and 33.

responsibility'.[20] Development Division had the thankless task of assessing all applications for funding and ideas for new investments. No aspect of economic policy escaped their scrutiny. Indeed, the long list of files in the National Archives prompts the suspicion that they may have cast their net too indiscriminately. Nevertheless, the overriding impression is of a country buzzing with ideas. In that respect the energy and range of proposals – some good, others downright crazy – are reminiscent of the 1930s when Fianna Fáil embarked on quite a different programme for economic development – one based on self-sufficiency.

Schonfield's classic study of 1960s capitalism and planning noted that Britain concentrated on two aspects of planning– 'the propaganda aspect, and the plan as a forum for the establishment of a new consensus among the main economic interest groups'.[21] While the 1958 *Programme* was drafted by civil servants, the *Second Programme* drew heavily on consultative meetings with employers and trade union leaders, in keeping with the processes followed by other Western European planning agencies. When French planning supremo Pierre Massé addressed the Institute of Public Administration (IPA) in 1962, he emphasised that the key concept behind the plan was 'the harmonisation of all the economic and social resources of the nation'.[22] The underlying assumption was that if key interest groups were involved in discussing issues that directly affected them, a consensus would emerge that would transcend the traditional divisions between employer and worker or farmer and industrialist. The early 1960s saw the creation of a network of committees and consultation groups, drawn from industry and employers, trade unions, senior civil servants and leading figures in state companies – all engaged in exercises designed to transform the economy, though we would be naïve not to acknowledge that for some the primary objective was to defend their sectoral interests.

Once the government had announced its determination to join the EEC, the state of Irish industry emerged as the major challenge. When Lemass and Whitaker met a deputation from ICTU in July 1961, Lemass told them that the main adjustment problems following EEC membership would fall on industry.[23] Although Lemass had been converted to the merits, or more

[20] Ivor Kenny, *In good company. Conversations with Irish leaders* (Dublin: G&M, 1987), p. 145. Garret FitzGerald, *Planning in Ireland. A PEP study* (Dublin and London: Institute of Public Administration/PEP, 1968), p. 68.

[21] Andrew Schonfield, *Modern Capitalism. The changing balance of public and private power* (Oxford: Oxford University Press, 1970 edition), p. 151.

[22] Pierre Massé, 'French planning', in Patrick Lynch and Basil Chubb (eds), *Economic development and planning* (Dublin: IPA, 1969), pp. 219–32.

[23] Committee on Industrial Organisation (CIO), Main File NAI, DT, 2001/3/201, 11 July 1961.

probably the inevitability of free trade, Industry and Commerce, the department where he had spent almost his entire career as minister retained a strong attachment to protection, as did many firms that had developed a close – perhaps too close – relationship with that department. Industry and Commerce had given Whitaker minimal assistance when he was writing *Economic Development*; indeed their attitude could be described as bordering on hostility, and this persisted. During 1959/1960, Whitaker and Murray battled to convince J. C. B. McCarthy, Secretary of Industry and Commerce, that industry should be exposed to 'the tough discipline of external competition', as soon as possible. They argued that protection created a vicious circle; every effort must be made to persuade industrialists to adapt and change, and while government subsidies could help to achieve this, they were of the opinion that industry lacked the will to change unless forced to do so. Data on manufacturing exports would confirm Whitaker and Murray's views: since 1948 almost 80 per cent of Irish manufactures had access to the UK market free of duties, but in 1956 agricultural produce, food, drink and tobacco accounted for 79 per cent of Irish exports to Britain. Whitaker painted a grim scenario of Ireland 'being left stranded on a high and narrow protectionist plateau on which acceptable living standards could be provided only temporarily and for a diminishing number of our people'. Industry and Commerce countered that free trade threatened the survival of up to 100,000 manufacturing jobs, and they were determined to postpone the evil day. In January 1960, Whitaker and McCarthy agreed that there was little point in continuing this exchange.[24] Industry and Commerce continued to place obstacles in the way of the Development Division, denying them access to data about Irish industry. They introduced new tariffs and quotas in annual budgets, and despite strong advice to repeal the Control of Manufactures Act, which required all foreign-owned firms to operate under restrictive licences, this did not happen until 1964. The continuing imposition of new tariffs – some as high as 75 per cent – did not escape notice in Brussels; a report by the European Council in October 1961 queried whether Ireland was fully committed to membership.[25] Industry and Commerce were insistent that Development Division should not initiate contact with industrialists; all communications should be via them.[26] When Development Division

---

[24] UCDA, P 175/2.
[25] Jérôme aan de Wiel, 'The commission, the council and the Irish application for the EEC, 1961–73', in Mervyn O'Driscoll, Dermot Keogh and Jérôme aan de Wiel (eds), *Ireland through European eyes. Western Europe, the EEC and Ireland, 1945–1973* (Cork: Cork University Press, 2013), pp. 329–30.
[26] NAI Industrial Surveys. DIC. Extract from record of discussions between JCD and C Murray on 19/8/60 D1/12/59.

proposed establishing a committee to examine the composition of Irish industry as the first step in a process of restructuring, Louden Ryan recalled more than twenty years later that 'Charlie Murray and I prepared a memorandum. It went to the relevant Assistant Secretary in Industry and Commerce who sat on it for long enough to give every reason for supposing he had considered it carefully. Then he said no.'[27] Such inaction was in the time-honoured traditions of the Irish civil service, but this tactic proved less effective than in the past. Ryan bypassed this road block by setting out the case for rationalizing industry in the *Irish Banking Review*. The paper comes across now as rather bland and benign: it plays down the prospect of redundancies, suggesting that firms would see obvious advantages in cooperating on marketing, research and other activities; it was obviously written as part of a public relations campaign.[28]

Lemass presented similar arguments in a speech to the annual conference of the Irish Management Institute (IMI): encouraging 'the right kind' of structural change might become 'an important part of national industrial development'. Some industries offered scope for enhancing efficiency; this would enable them to withstand increased competition. The government would find it much easier to contemplate joining the EEC if they were aware that Irish manufacturers were actively preparing for membership. He warned that some industries were not exporting 'as much as they could'; there were some 'lame ducks' in 'our industrial brood'.[29] Within weeks the Federation of Irish Industry (FII) and senior civil servants had agreed to establish a Committee on Industrial Organisation (CIO) to determine the measures needed to adapt Irish industry to withstand greater competition in domestic and foreign markets.[30]

Initial plans were that the CIO should consist of representatives of industry, civil servants plus externally recruited economists and technical experts, but ICTU pressed to be included and Lemass conceded to their demands.[31] No technical experts were appointed, because the industries refused to accept them, despite repeated pressure from government to do so. The twenty-six CIO surveys covered industries employing 58 per cent of the manufacturing workforce. The Department of Agriculture, which was not represented on the CIO, demanded that food processing industries be omitted. As a compromise these industries were examined by Agriculture with the assistance of Finance – yet another instance where a

---

[27] Kenny, *In good company*, p. 145.
[28] Kenny, *In good company*, p. 145; W. J. L. Ryan, 'The need for structural change in Irish industry', *Irish Banking Review*, March 1961, pp. 9–15.
[29] CIO Main File now NAI 2001/3/201 formerly D3/8/61.
[30] FitzGerald, *Planning in Ireland*, pp. 55–6.   [31] NAI DT 2001/3/201.

department protected its patch irrespective of the wider national interest. An additional twenty-four industries consisting of a small number of firms were subjected to less comprehensive surveys conducted by Industry and Commerce. All reports had to be approved by the CIO before publication. A preliminary review of findings by civil servants in October 1962 (before the information was given to the CIO) indicates some omissions from the published reports. This review highlighted restrictive labour practices, inadequate training, the need for a better-educated labour force and problems posed by the multiplicity of trade unions. None of these featured in the published reports, which went so far as to suggest that labour relations were not a problem, and there were few restrictive practices! However, the published reports criticised the management for failing to make adequate use of techniques such as production planning and budgetary and stock controls, failing to take workers into confidence, and more generic difficulties associated with small family-owned businesses.[32]

The profile of Irish industry presented by the CIO reports reflected the legacy of three decades of economic protection and the policies of discouraging domestic competition and scattering firms throughout provincial Ireland. Firms were predominantly small in size; many did little more than assemble imported components. Few attempted to specialise, most produced a wide range of lines; consequently production runs were short. Productivity was below the European average because of the small size of firms, less capital-intensive production methods and poor training.[33] In short, the picture strikes me as very similar to the late 1930s, except that the firms were older and more set in their ways. The most politically sensitive issue identified was location: the additional transport and other costs resulting from the decentralised nature of Irish industry. It suggested that creating industrial estates would help to surmount some of these difficulties. The surveys also highlighted shortcomings in marketing, industrial design and packaging and the lack of industrial research. Managers were not facing up to the challenge of free trade and the need to modernise with sufficient urgency. Only seven of the twenty-two major industrial sectors exported over 20 per cent of output; half exported less than 10 per cent. If measures were not taken to prepare for free trade, the CIO report anticipated that almost one-quarter of the 150,000 manufacturing jobs would disappear. Job losses of the order of 10,000 were anticipated even if firms took steps to make their operations more efficient in anticipation of competition.[34]

[32] FitzGerald, *Planning in Ireland*, pp. 57–63.   [33] FitzGerald, *Planning in Ireland*, p. 61.
[34] FitzGerald, *Planning in Ireland*, p. 61.

In April 1962, while the surveys were still underway, the CIO published an interim report on state aid to industry. It recommended additional grants to assist with marketing, technical improvements or switching product lines and additional tax concessions and interest free loans to finance new capital equipment or to encourage joint industrial enterprises. Many of these measures were introduced in the 1962 Finance Act, with the government adding a further sweetener – industrialists could get either grants or tax relief for new equipment. Further grants were introduced for training, consultancy services and overseas trips.[35] These carrots were accompanied by the announcement of a unilateral tariff reduction of 10 per cent from January 1963, in the hope that 'that this will reduce the tendency, in some quarters to hold up measures of reorganization and adaptation'.[36]

The years 1962/3 marked the beginning of a new relationship between industry and the state involving frequent tripartite meetings between industrialists, civil servants and trade unions. The emergence of the CIO was followed in October 1963 by the establishment of the National Industrial and Economic Council (NIEC) – yet another tripartite organisation with members drawn from employers, trade unions and the state. J. C. B. McCarthy claimed that the 'real justification' for establishing some form of economic council was to gain a commitment from employers and unions to restrain income increases, 'ensuring that relatively "unpopular" measures will receive the approval of both sides of industry in advance [and] ensure their ready acceptance by public opinion'.[37] When Lemass and other ministers trumpeted the news of record economic growth, workers responded with demands for a five-day week and generous pay increases. In 1961, Lemass had suggested that the determination of pay should not be left to market forces and the power of trade unions: regard must be had to the good of the community. He cited *Mater et Magistra*, a recent encyclical by Pope John XXIII, to support his case.[38] A consultative Employer/Labour Conference was established in 1962 to review working practices and industrial relations with a view to raising productivity, but it was a weakling. Lemass 'continued to woo the trade unions'[39] and to talk to employers in the hope of establishing a more

---

[35] FitzGerald, *Planning in Ireland*, p. 62, NAI DT S13776d/63 Taxation on industry: general. Peter Murray, *Facilitating the future. US Aid. European integration and Irish industrial viability, 1948–73* (Dublin: UCD Press, 2009), p. 72.

[36] Lemass speech to Cork Chamber of Commerce 15 November 1962. On NAI 2001/ 3/201.

[37] NAI DT S17419D Proposals to establish the NIEC.

[38] NAI 2001/3/201, 14 September 1961. One of the key messages in *Mater et Magistra* was the need to subordinate sectional interests to the common good.

[39] McCarthy, *Decade of discontent*, p. 55.

formal consultative employer/labour organisation.[40] A government White Paper, *Closing the Gap*, issued early in 1963 called for wage increases to be linked to higher productivity and suggested that a mechanism for negotiating an incomes policy should be devised, but the trade unions objected to any restrictions being placed on the process of free collective bargaining,[41] an attitude that reflects their close affinity with British trade unions, and one that contrasts with trade unions in some other European countries.

FitzGerald claimed that 'it was intended that it [NIEC] should concern itself solely with incomes policy', but Louden Ryan, interviewed in the 1980s, claimed that this goal was not explicit, and 'if it had been made explicit, I don't think he [Lemass] would have got the willing involvement of the trade unions'.[42] Tadhg Ó Cearbhaill, then a senior official in the Department of the Taoiseach, cautioned that employers wanted a mechanism for resisting demands for further pay increases whereas the unions believed that they had achieved the long-held dream of a National Economic Council. Given this ambiguity, it is not surprising that the terms of reference for the NIEC were somewhat opaque: they began by setting out the principles that should apply to economic development, including 'the realisation and maintenance of full employment at adequate wages with reasonable price stability' and reasonable equilibrium in the balance of payments. The reference to incomes was relegated to the second sentence, and the definition was extended to include profits and rents.[43] The composition of the NIEC was broadly similar to the CIO, though the remit was wider, encompassing economic development, full employment and wages policy.[44] ICTU's opposition to an incomes policy meant that the NIEC devoted its time to reviewing the *Second Programme* and writing worthy reports on the economy, industrial estates, the Anglo-Irish Trade Agreement and other topics.[45] In short, they engaged with practically every topic, except pay increases!

Irish economic planning: rhetoric and reality

This burst of corporate activity peaked c.1963/1964 with the drafting of the *Second Programme for Economic Expansion*. The *Second Programme* marks the apogee of Ireland's love affair with planning. The fact that the economy grew between 1958 and 1963 at almost double the target set

---

[40] NAI DT S17419E Tadhg Ó Cearbhaill, 31 July 1963.   [41] NAI DT S17419B.
[42] Kenny, *In good company*; Louden Ryan, p. 147.
[43] Terms of reference and composition DD vol. 205, cols. 22–23, 23 October 1963.
[44] NAI DT S17419D/63 National Industrial and Economic Council.
[45] FitzGerald, *Planning*, p. 157.

in the first *Programme* gave rise to a belief that planning was the magic key to economic growth. Yet the success of the 1958 *Programme* demonstrated its fallibility. In 1958, agriculture was seen as the sector that would produce a higher growth rate, yet by 1963 agricultural output was only 1 per cent higher than in 1958, despite the fact that public investment in agriculture was double the figure set out in the *Programme*. By comparison, industry, which Garret FitzGerald described as the 'the Cinderella of Irish economists – if not, indeed the ugly duckling of the Irish economy',[46] grew by 47 per cent. Yet while FitzGerald acknowledged the serious shortcomings of the first *Programme* and the gap between targets and outcomes, he, and many others, argued that the primary benefit was psychological; 'it is not too much to say that it saw a transformation of the economy of the Republic and, most important of all perhaps a transformation of the outlook of the Irish people'.[47] While sentiment is an important factor driving economic activity, both positively and negatively, this emphasis on national psychology was not without risks. There appears to have been an assumption that setting even more ambitious and detailed targets in the *Second Programme* would encourage a national effort to achieve, even exceed them. This strategy reflects Lemass' personality; his economic plans in the 1930s were also characterised by very ambitious targets, though many were not realised. However, the entire process has a strong element of snake-oil medicine.

The OECD's 50 per cent growth target was treated as sacrosanct (which was not the OECD's intention).[48] In the *Second Programme* this translated into an annual growth rate of 4.2 per cent for 1963–1970. Although agricultural output had been stagnant under the previous *Programme*, and there was clear evidence that agriculture was in crisis throughout the developed world, the *Second Programme* assumed that agriculture would expand at an annual rate of 2.8 per cent (later raised to 2.9 per cent); cattle numbers would increase by an annual average of 83,000 – more than five times the increase over the previous decade. These ambitious targets, set by the Department of Agriculture, would only have been feasible if Ireland joined the EEC several years before 1970. Yet although Whitaker queried 'the repeated and unqualified assumptions about membership of the EEC',[49] these targets were

[46] FitzGerald, *Planning*, p. 49.   [47] FitzGerald, *Planning*, p. 41.

[48] J. C. B. McCarthy (DIC) claimed that that an examination of the plan carried out by the NIEC convinced him that the projections were 'based on as comprehensive a survey as one could reasonably expect'. Quoted in Bew and Patterson, *Seán Lemass*, pp. 156–7. HAEU OECD Council of Ministers 16–17 November 1961, draft communique; Minutes of 14th meeting 132 Feb. 1962.

[49] Quoted in Daly, *First Department*, p. 444.

included. Industry was given an annual growth target of 7 per cent, calculated not on the basis of any considered estimate of the capacity for industrial expansion but because this was the figure necessary if the 50 per cent overall growth target was to be achieved.[50] Worse still was the statement that if agriculture failed to meet its targets 'industry will have to step up its contribution' – that is, achieve a higher growth rate.[51]

The *Second Programme* devised a complex input–output model for the economy, which included detailed projections for the main agricultural and industrial sectors, export targets for fifty-two industries and detailed investment targets across the economy. Planners ran numerous statistical models of the economy up to 1970 – with repeated cross-checks to ensure that estimates for expenditure, investment, employment and other data were mutually consistent, though no check appears to have been carried out to see if the overall target was feasible. CIO committees provided advice and information for sectoral targets. Reading the *Second Programme* and the huge swathe of accompanying material, published and unpublished, evokes conflicting emotions: admiration for the extraordinary statistical detail and complex calculations – done without the aid of modern computers – coupled with a sense that the medium had become the message, and the message had become so complicated that it would be unintelligible to the majority of industrialists, workers and politicians.

The *Programme* was set out within the framework of detailed national accounts – treating Ireland as one would treat a private business, farm or household. Whitaker claimed that 'a national programme or plan is merely an attempt to apply to the nation's economic affairs the same foresight, organisation and determination as a competent and prudent person applies to the management of his own household or business'.[52] A cynic might suggest that few businesses or households operated on this basis, and it was soon evident that neither did the government. Nevertheless, if we strip away the detail, the core message was extremely relevant. The developed world was moving ever more rapidly towards freer trade. There was 'an urgent need to adapt, re-equip, extend and reorganise all sectors of the economy to ensure the greater strength and efficiency needed to prosper in a more acutely competitive world'.[53]

---

[50] FitzGerald, *Planning*, pp. 68–80; W. J. L. Ryan, 'The methodology of the second programme of economic expansion', *JSSISI*, vol. xxi, no. ii, 1963–4, pp. 120–4.

[51] *Second Programme*, chapter 6, quoted FitzGerald, *Planning*, p. 95.

[52] T. K. Whitaker, 'Merits and problems of planning', in Basil Chubb and Patrick Lynch (eds), *Economic Development and Planning*, vol. 1 (Dublin: Institute of Public Administration, 1969), p. 266.

[53] *Second Programme* (Chapter 1, para 4)

A shorter, less technical document concentrating on projections of the numbers of men and women seeking work, a short list of measures designed to improve the skills of workers, farmers and managers, and a clear strategy to communicate the message that moderate pay increases would bring significantly higher living standards in the future might have proved more effective.

Setting ambitious growth targets was seen as a means of driving change and promoting consensus. But this was a high-risk strategy. Repeated statements that the economy could grow by 50 per cent over the decade generated unrealistic expectations for higher incomes, and there was a strong temptation to massage the figures for political purposes. Maurice Moynihan, Governor of the Central Bank, expressed concerns about 'dangerously optimistic assumptions and targets'; he feared that the *Second Programme* might 'do irreparable harm' unless there were some 'unpredictable developments in our favour' – presumably EEC membership.[54] Finance Minister James Ryan queried the overall growth target and in a memo to Lemass suggested that the Cabinet Committee overseeing the draft *Programme* should decide whether, 'on political and psychological grounds, this target should be adhered to or a less ambitious one substituted'.[55] Louden Ryan, one of its authors, claimed that the trade unions saw it as an election document; he worked hard to persuade them that it was much more than this.[56]

The *Second Programme* was quietly shelved after 2–3 years, because the targets were not being achieved. FitzGerald noted that annual reports produced by the Department of Finance in 1966 and 1967 made 'very little reference to *Second Programme* targets ... there was certainly no attempt to measure performance against a comprehensive list of targets'.[57] Taxes, spending and credit controls were determined by short-term factors with scant regard to the *Programme*. The NIEC's culture of consensus and compromise meant that they failed to confront the thornier issues – such as the reality that many Irish industries would not survive under free trade, unless they were radically transformed. In 1966, the NIEC Council noted a widespread agreement that the industrial reviews were not having any deep impact on management or unions.[58] It was probably unrealistic to have expected Irish employers and unions to engage in frank discussions on difficult topics, as happened in the Netherlands. Irish trade unions shared the British culture of distrust in such exercises, and trade unionists seen to be co-operating with employers and government risked losing support to

---

[54] NAI DT S17437B *Second Programme*, 15 July 1963, Moynihan to Whitaker.
[55] S17537B Ryan to Lemass, 17 July 1963.   [56] Kenny, *In good company*, p. 147.
[57] FitzGerald, *Planning*, p. 184.   [58] FitzGerald, *Planning*, pp. 149–52.

more radical voices. Lemass hoped that engaging the union leadership in discussions about economic policy would embolden them to persuade rank-and-file members to adopt a less militant attitude towards industrial relations. But while union leaders attended regular meetings with government ministers, business leaders and senior civil servants, the rank-and-file members engaged in lengthy strikes that were often not sanctioned by union leadership. Lemass' strategy failed, not least because unions that adopted a moderate position were in danger of being superseded by more militant groups.

Lemass' retirement in the autumn of 1966 probably sealed the fate of economic planning. While he showed a strong personal commitment to modernising the economy, it is uncertain how far his Cabinet supported these goals. Whereas de Valera presided over lengthy Cabinet meetings, giving time for ministers to express their views at such length that consensus was eventually achieved by exhaustion, Lemass' cabinets often lasted for under one hour – indicating that they were largely perfunctory and did not engage in lengthy discussions on key issues. James Ryan, the Minister for Finance, was undoubtedly sympathetic to economic planning: as Fanning notes, de Valera's decision to appoint Ryan, rather than Seán MacEntee to Finance, was crucial;[59] it is almost unthinkable that *Economic Development* or a *Programme for Economic Expansion* would have emerged under MacEntee. The commitment of Minister for Agriculture Paddy Smith is questionable: he remained strongly committed to supporting Ireland's small farmers and their way of life. Charles Haughey, who succeeded Smith in 1964, was obviously more in tune with Lemass' wishes.

Jack Lynch's contribution as Minister for Industry and Commerce remains something of a mystery. Keogh's chapter on Lynch's time in this key department (1959–1965) lists a bewildering array of legislation on hire purchase, mines and quarries, restrictive trade practices and so forth, and he provides details of Lynch's efforts to bring new industries to Cork, which is simply traditional parish-pump politics, but there is little sense of any drive to promote exports, increased productivity or attract foreign industries.[60] There is no evidence to suggest that Lynch, who became Taoiseach in November 1966, shared Lemass' commitment to transforming the economy. Lynch emerged as a compromise candidate, which meant that he had less control over the Cabinet than Lemass. Desmond O'Malley, an undoubled admirer, who became Chief Whip in 1969 and Minister for Justice the following year, noted that 'His style

[59] Fanning, *Department of Finance*, p. 508.
[60] Dermot Keogh, *Jack Lynch. A biography* (Dublin: Gill & Macmillan, 2008), pp. 69–88.

was to remain relatively detached; ministers and parliamentary secretaries were allowed to get on with their jobs with little interference'.[61] In July 1967, Lynch announced that while a review of progress under the *Second Programme* would be carried out, the Programme was effectively being abandoned. 'A programme of policy and action' would be drawn up when Ireland's position with respect to EEC membership became clearer.[62] Instead of trying to meet or revise targets, or reflect on why they were not achieved, Ireland abandoned the *Second Programme* and wrote another one. Did anybody notice? By that stage the commitment to economic planning was largely perfunctory. The failure to engage seriously with the difficulties exposed by economic plans was similar to what happened in Britain. FitzGerald quoted Sam Brittan's comment, 'One of the worst features of the contemporary [British] approach to planning is the attempt to paper over the conflict between economic growth and other objects of policy by frequently changing the time horizon. On each occasion we are told ... that growth will be slow at first, but we will catch up later. By the time "later" has arrived, the old plan has been replaced by a new one stretching further ahead. Thus we are always in the early stages, and promise is never checked against fulfilment.'[63] Tom Barrington noted with regret that over time the link between the planning system, the annual budget and the public capital programme became weaker.[64]

The *Third Programme, Economic and Social Development 1969–72*, launched in March 1969, attracted much less interest than its predecessor. Economic planning was losing favour not just in Ireland. The reference to social development reflected the criticism in Fine Gael's 1965 strategy document 'A Just Society', which highlighted the neglect of social development.[65] The *Programme* also anticipated a changing focus in the OECD, from economic to social development – in response to the unrest in 1968 and greater awareness of the social and environmental costs associated with economic growth. The *Programme* described itself as 'a step on the road' to the goal of achieving full employment. It set a growth target of 17 per cent for the years 1969–1972 (an annual growth rate similar to the discarded *Second Programme*), a modest 16,000 rise in total employment and a reduction in net emigration to 12–13,000 annually, which would bring the population to over 3 million by 1972. It

[61] Desmond O'Malley, *Conduct unbecoming. A memoir* (Dublin: Gill&Macmillan, 2014), p. 44.
[62] FitzGerald, *Planning*, pp. 185–6.
[63] Samuel Brittain, *Inquest on planning in Britain*, PEP pamphlets, no. 499, Jan. 1967, p. 23.
[64] Tom Barrington, 'Whatever happened to Irish government', in Frank Litton (ed.), *Unequal achievement: The Irish experience, 1957–1982* (Dublin: Institute of Public Administration, 1982), p. 92.
[65] Fine Gael, *Towards a Just Society* (Dublin: Fine Gael policy, 1965).

emphasised that economic growth was essential to provide sufficient jobs for Irish men and women 'to develop themselves as individuals to the limits of their ability without being compelled to do so in an alien environment' and to help the state in meeting 'the special needs of the underprivileged and the collective needs of the community'.[66] The Department of Finance had suggested 1 per cent per annum as a realistic growth target for agriculture; predictably, the Department of Agriculture insisted on a higher figure. By the end of the decade, economic programmes and their targets had effectively been superseded by a single target – EEC membership – and the resources of Development Division and other senior officials increasingly concentrated on that goal.

'Sitting by Nelly': the Irish civil service

While ministers and senior civil servants were not slow to tell farmers and industrialists that they had to change their attitudes and working practices if Ireland was to be ready for EEC membership, there is no evidence that the civil service was subjected to similar pressure. A government commission on the civil service – commonly known as the 'Devlin Commission' – was not appointed until 1966 and did not report until 1969. Implementation of its recommendations was delayed for another two to three years. The Commission gathered evidence of civil service practice in Britain, France, Germany and the Netherlands. The report was strongly influenced by the 'Fulton Report on the British Civil Service'[67] – yet another example of Ireland's dependence on its former governing power. Devlin revealed that the vogue for planning had not extended into the civil service; there was no assessment of future staffing requirements, no succession planning – 'a failure to come to terms with developments in managerial skills and methods'. It identified a number of major structural weaknesses, including the ill-defined roles and responsibilities of various units.[68] Management accounting was gradually introduced from the late 1960s and was operational throughout the service by 1975.[69] Some government departments – including the key economic Departments of Agriculture and Industry and Commerce – remained wedded to the policies and practices that they had been following for decades. While there was undoubtedly a civil service culture, there was

---

[66] Third Programme; Economic and social development, 1969–72 (Prl 431, Paras 11, 8.
[67] The Civil Service/Chairman: Lord Fulton. Vol. I Report of the Committee 1966–68, HMSP 1968.
[68] Report of public service organisation review group, 1966–69 (Dublin: Dept. Finance, 1969, F.81), 8.3.30; 10.10.2; 11.3.1–11.4.4 (hereafter cited as Devlin).
[69] DIB online – Charles Murray.

also perhaps a more powerful culture associated with individual departments. The civil service consisted of a series of silos; officials who happened to be appointed to one department, regardless of interests,
education or expertise, generally remained there – working their way up
the ranks and absorbing the departmental culture.[70] Many senior officials
failed 'to see outside their own Departmental structures'; they tended 'to
see things from the comparatively narrow perspective of their own
Departments rather than that of government as a whole'.[71]

Consequently, disproportionate responsibility for economic development and other miscellaneous programmes fell on the twenty-eight
administrative staff in the Development Division of the Department of
Finance – one-third of the Department of Finance compliement.
Whitaker's biographer suggests that concentrating key decision-making
in a small section of Finance was a means of 'bypassing interdepartmental
bureaucracy and rivalry',[72] but apart from the heavy workload, this
centralised responsibility raised questions about the commitment to
implementing change across the wider public service. Garret FitzGerald
described Industry and Commerce as 'acting largely as observers', as
Finance and industrialists agreed targets for manufacturing industry
under the *Second Programme*.[73] The Department of Agriculture likewise
adopted a rather semi-detached approach to economic planning –
insisting on producing their own Second Programme – 'the brown
book', with utterly unrealistic estimates for increased agricultural output;
however, they conveniently ignored these targets – and the massive
shortfalls in their 1967 review of agriculture, probably with good reason.
This suggests that two of the three key economic departments were less
than wholly committed to the programmes for economic growth.

One possible explanation for this attachment to past policies and
departmental agendas may lie in the low level of education. In contrast
to Britain or France, the Irish civil service lacked an elite cohort. A survey
carried out in the mid-1950s showed that 75 per cent of the 163 civil
servants surveyed (from assistant secretaries down to clerical officers) had
received their secondary education from the Irish Christian Brothers –
which would, according to the author, have exposed them to 'strongly
nationalist tendency, both linguistic and political'. Of this sample, 84 per
cent had entered the civil service as clerical officers, executive officers or

---

[70] O'Malley, *Conduct unbecoming*, p. 64, re the Department of Justice. In the 1960s there
were still tensions within the Department of Local Government between those who have
formerly served in the Irish Local Government Board (pre 1922) and those recruited after
independence.
[71] *Devlin*, p. 127.   [72] Chambers, *Whitaker*, pp. 134–5.
[73] FitzGerald, *Planning*, p. 203.

customs and excise officers – low- or middle-grade positions, where work would have been largely routine.[74] Although an administrative grade was introduced in the 1920s to recruit university graduates, with the expectation that they would be fast-tracked into senior positions, by the mid-1950s two-thirds of recently appointed administrative officers had been promoted from the executive grade. Tom Barrington, a relentless critic of the system, despite or perhaps because he had been a senior civil servant, commented that 'we seek to train for the highest posts the man or woman whose mind has been enlarged by a glimpse of the universe of knowledge; but in fact fill them by men whose formative years have been cabined by consideration of the narrowest issues'.[75]

This apparent hostility to graduate recruitment may well be a legacy of Ireland's civil service under the Union. The British administration in Ireland, including the Royal Irish Constabulary, effectively ran a dual-career structure, with senior officials, appointed mainly by patronage from Anglo-Irish gentry, military or clergyman families, and a rank and file recruited from a more nationalist and plebeian background – many of them past pupils of the Irish Christian Brothers.[76] After independence the Christian Brothers pupils had their revenge. The Irish civil service was predominantly Catholic; Protestant workers were much less likely to be employed in the civil service, the gardaí or the army[77] – occupations where recruitment was on the basis of competitive examinations (and other criteria such as height). In 1961, only sixty-five of the almost 2,000 senior officials in the civil service and local authorities were members of the Church of Ireland or Presbyterian congregations. Michael Viney speculated that the requirement to meet a certain standard of Irish might be a factor in the low Protestant representation; alternatively, it may reflect a certain detachment from the state, plus the fact that Protestant school-leavers may have found it easier to get white-collar jobs in private industry. Most civil servants were practising Catholics, and often actively committed to their religion; many were members of the St Vincent de Paul Society in Westland Row.[78] This undoubtedly coloured their attitudes towards social policy and the role of the church with respect to education, health and welfare.

---

[74] S Ó Mathúna, 'The Christian Brothers and the Civil Service', *Administration*, vol. 3, 1955, pp. 69–74.

[75] Tom Barrington, 'Elaborate contrivance', *Administration*, vol. 3, 1955, p. 104.

[76] Fergus Campbell, *The Irish establishment, 1879–1914* (Oxford: Oxford University Press, 2009).

[77] Michael Viney, *The five per cent. A survey of Protestants in the Republic* (Dublin: Irish Times, 1965), pp. 10–12.

[78] Personal information from a retired senior civil servant.

In 1955, Barrington claimed that 'the system has broken down, both from its inner contradictions and because the recruits are substantially different from those for which it was devised'.[79] Lee however detected a more positive attitude towards change among younger civil servants, with the Institute of Public Administration, founded in 1957, with Barrington as director, providing 'a forum for sustained self-appraisal'.[80] Yet statistics from the mid- to late 1960s suggest that the educational standards of civil servants were falling – at a time when the numbers with secondary or university education had risen. Many recruits in earlier decades were among the brightest school-leavers, who often rejected university scholarships – which were few in number – in favour of a civil service job, perhaps because they were expected to contribute to family income, or because the economic climate set a high premium on job security. Promotion was 'almost automatic', even for the lazy and the mediocre.[81] By the late 1960s, however, the improved economic climate, and perhaps more secure family incomes, meant that the brightest school-leavers were opting for university, and by 1968 the civil service was finding it difficult to recruit qualified candidates as executive officers. An increasing number of positions were filled by promoting clerical officers. An agreement with the civil service unions provided that half of executive positions were reserved for internal candidates; in reality, a majority were being filled on that basis. This meant that the educational standard of new executive appointees was lower than in the past. This was equally so in more senior grades: of ninety-nine appointments as assistant principal in 1967 and 1968 only five were university graduates when they joined the civil service. Three-quarters had entered as clerical officers or lower grades, indicating a low standard in secondary-school examinations. Some had graduated from evening degree programmes, mainly in UCD (approximately 40 per cent of senior civil servants had studied for a degree part-time), but graduates from full-time degree programmes were conspicuous by their absence, except in the Departments of External Affairs and Finance. Some departments had a 'deliberate policy ... to restrict or even to exclude all Administrative Officer [i.e. graduate] recruitment'. The majority in professional grades were graduates – scientists, meteorologists, engineers, and so on; however, they were precluded from becoming secretaries or assistant-secretaries of government departments. *Devlin* concluded that the system of recruitment and promotion fostered 'a tendency towards mediocrity in the whole organisation'.[82] Training consisted of ' "sitting by Nellie": i.e. a quasi-apprenticeship-system, for a period of about six

[79] Barrington, 'Elaborate contrivance', p. 97.   [80] Lee, *Ireland 1912–1985*, pp. 341–2.
[81] Barrington, 'Elaborate contrivance', p. 103.   [82] *Devlin*, pp. 87, 95, 98.

weeks – the last recruited EO [Executive Officer] in the section trained the new recruit'.[83] Modern equipment such as comptometers (machines capable of complex calculations) could only be used by specialist staff. When the Irish civil service held competitions for secretarial positions in the EEC Commission in Brussels in 1973/74, they did not have sufficient electric typewriters to carry out the tests and had to lease machines.[84]

There were some exceptional civil servants, some of whom had been recruited as graduate administrative officers. Three of the first seven graduate administrative officers – Leon Ó Broin, John Garvin and Maurice Moynihan – rose to head government departments.[85] Ken Whitaker, educated by the Christian Brothers in Drogheda, entered as a clerical officer. His father was about to retire on a small pension, so the family could not afford to send him to university to study medicine, and a civil service place seemed a safer option than hoping that he could secure a university scholarship.[86] Whitaker went on to attain a bachelor's degree and a PhD as an external student in London University. Charlie Murray, Whitaker's successor as Secretary of the Department of Finance, and his key collaborator on *Economic Development*, abandoned his studies as a medical student to take a civil service position because of family pressures; he too studied for a London University degree. Denis Maher, another key official in the Development Division, abandoned a scholarship to study at UCD to take an executive officer position in the Department of Lands.[87] But these and other exceptional officials (graduate recruits to the Department of External Affairs included many talented writers and scholars) do not detract from the overall mediocrity. *Devlin* noted a tendency to allocate more work 'to the more capable, the more expert, the more willing'; practices that made it possible for 'substandard officers [to] get by at the expense of their more efficient colleagues'.[88]

Devlin's main recommendation was to create separate sections dealing with policy and its execution in every government department. A small 'core' unit – the Aireacht 'grouped around the Minister' – would concentrate on determining policy; 'satellite bodies' would be responsible for executing policies. A new Department of Public Service would coordinate the activities of all government departments.[89] Whether this distinction between policy and execution was realistic, given the immediate pressures that land on a minister's desk, does not concern us. It is

[83] Áine Hyland, 'The investment in education report 1965 – recollections and reminiscences', *Irish Educational Studies*, vol. 33, no. 2, June 2014, p. 125.
[84] Hyland 'The investment in education report', p. 133 and personal knowledge.
[85] Fanning, *Finance*, pp. 76–7.   [86] Chambers, *Whitaker*, pp. 23–4.
[87] *DIB* online – Charles Murray, Denis Maher.   [88] *Devlin Report*, pp. 125–6.
[89] *Devlin Report*, p. 430.

more important to note that the reform of the civil service only begins in the 1970s and it is unclear whether the creation of a Department of Public Service resulted in any serious change in the culture of the Irish civil service – the Department was abolished in 1987.

State companies offered a more flexible and more responsive agency for implementing public policy, and Lemass was the minister who had been responsible for establishing the largest number of such companies. State-owned enterprises featured prominently in the mixed economies of post-war Europe, where many governments believed that they could play an active role in specific economic niches. Irish state enterprises were loosely divided between 'commercial' companies – such as those responsible for generating electricity, processing peat fuel or sugar-beet – and running the railways and buses, and those responsible for promoting tourism, exports, regional development or attracting foreign investment. The 'commercial' companies had much greater freedom than the others, which were reliant on an annual budget allocated by their parent department. Lemass claimed that state enterprises 'set standards of performance which can inspire private enterprise to greater achievements and will help to build up confidence in the country's future'. He was keen that they be given some 'freedom of action'.[90] This new lease of life for state enterprise in the 1960s reflected a fusion of ideologies, fashion and pragmatism. Todd Andrews, who headed three state enterprises, argued that without state companies, 'the country would be little better than a cattle ranch, managed by what someone once described as the finest herdsmen in the world'. Andrews claimed that 'the companies have given to the administrators and technologists in Ireland opportunities for advancement which would never be available to them in an economy where the family-owned firm was dominant and the crown prince blocked promotion to the top posts'.[91] Many state enterprises were headed by former civil servants, and it could be argued that they stripped the civil service of dynamic potential leaders. Some heads of state companies took full advantage of the 'freedom of action', to which Lemass referred. In contrast to senior civil servants, who generally remained anonymous (Whitaker was the major exception), their names were known to the public; they were profiled in the newspapers, and this strong profile may have given them the freedom and the courage to question instructions given by government ministers, something that was unlikely to happen within the civil service. Kevin McCourt – whose career straddled the public and private sectors – became

[90] Lemass, 'The role of state-sponsored bodies'; reprinted in Chubb and Lynch (eds), *Economic development and planning* (Dublin: Institute of Public Administration, 1969), p. 194.
[91] C. S. Andrews, comments on Lemass, 'The role of state-sponsored bodies', in Chubb and Lynch (eds), *Economic development and planning*, p. 198.

director-general of Teilifís Éireann, the state television service, in November 1962. During his term at Teilfís Éireann, he rebutted several attempts by Lemass and Charles Haughey – Minister for Justice and later Minister for Agriculture – to ensure that the broadcaster reflected the government line on political issues. He adopted a similar approach towards the Archbishop of Dublin John Charles McQuaid.[92] One member of the management of Shannon Free Airport Development Company (SFADCO) described Brendan O'Regan, the chief executive, as a 'one-man state company'. O'Regan initially headed a company to handle catering and sales at Shannon Airport, and in 1957, through his personal relationship with Lemass, was given responsibility, and considerable freedom, to develop tourism, freight traffic and industries and housing at Shannon.[93] In 1959, Michael Joseph Costello, chief executive of Comhlucht Siúicre Éireann Teo (CSÉT), the Irish Sugar Company, who was passionately committed to helping small farmers in the west of Ireland, established a subsidiary company, Erin Foods, to process vegetables, which he planned to sell in Britain and the domestic market. Costello joined forces with Fr James McDyer, parish priest of Glencolumbkille, who was another crusader for small western farms.[94] But CSÉT were monopoly producers of sugar in a protected market, whose products were packed in a style that would have been worthy of any Communist regime; they had little marketing experience. Their decision to produce freeze-dried vegetables may have met Irish consumer needs in 1959, but in Britain and indeed in Ireland, most families aspired to owning a fridge, and frozen vegetables, which tasted better, were capturing an increasing share of the market. While Costello's aspiration to save small western farms by promoting vegetable growing may have been admirable, it failed to take account of climate, land quality or market trends. The enterprise proved a costly failure. A consultant's report, initiated by his successor Tony O'Reilly, showed that it lost £1 for every £1 of turnover. Erin Foods was finally taken over by the Heinz Corporation.[95]

By the mid-1960s state companies were increasingly being run by a younger generation. Tony O'Reilly, who had headed up the state-owned dairy marketing board, An Bord Bainne, and succeeded Costello as head of CSÉT by the age of thirty, was described to journalist Donald Connery as

---

[92] Eugene McCague, *My dear Mr McCourt* (Dublin: Gill & Macmillan, 2009), pp. 74–5, 82–7, 104–5.

[93] Brian Callanan, *Ireland's Shannon Story. Leaders, visions and networks. A case study of local and regional development* (Dublin: Irish Academic Press, 2000), pp. 45–55, 171–3.

[94] Vincent Tucker, 'Images of development and underdevelopment in Glencolumbkille, County Donegal, 1830–1970', in John Davis (ed.), *Rural change in Ireland* (Belfast: Queen's University, Institute of Irish Studies, 1999), pp. 111–2. *DIB* online – Michael Joseph Costello.

[95] *B&F*, 21 October 1966; 1 December 1967; *Hibernia*, 11–25 April 1969.

'the prototype of the first really free Irishmen'. Connery saw O'Reilly and 'others of his breed' as 'unencumbered by the old baggage of unrealistic national dreams ... an arch-pragmatist; proud to be an Irishman but well aware that the nation cannot prosper in splendid isolation'.[96] By 1960, sales of Irish butter to the UK market were strongly outstripped by Danish and New Zealand butter, which were packaged and marketed to suit the needs of new supermarket chains and British consumers. The Kerrygold export brand launched in 1962 was the first serious attempt to market Irish agricultural produce to consumers. It capitalised on Irish images and stereotypes, to the extent of giving away 'Larry the leprechaun dolls' as promotional gifts. O'Reilly claimed correctly that 'had it been replicated in the bacon and beef industries, it would have added a substantial notch to the prosperity of the people of Ireland, and in particular to the agriculture sector'.[97] O'Reilly left the Irish Sugar Company in 1969 to join Heinz Corporation, where he later became chief executive. Michael Killeen, a former civil servant, who joined the state export promotion company Córas Tráchtála in the early 1950s and became its head, before becoming chief executive of the reformed Industrial Development Authority in 1970, was another example of dynamic leadership in a state company.[98] But some of the state enterprises of the time were ill-conceived, such as NET – the Nitrogen factory established at Arklow; it increased the cost of fertiliser for Irish farmers, while failing to give a return on the public investment. While short-term profitability cannot be the sole criterion, the scrutiny exercised over 'commercial' state companies was limited – and many of their investments were ill-advised. Economist John Bristow remarked on the lack of a coherent policy for state enterprise: 'a wide range of activities has been brought into the public sector, the only common feature being the extremely vague notion that each of these activities contribute to economic development in some way'.[99] 'Some way' was poorly defined, and thus capable of manipulation and distortion.

Economic planning was a new venture for the Irish government sector, one that some resisted and others embraced with enthusiasm. Yet the capacity of many of those who were engaged in the exercise to transform the economy must be questioned, likewise the commitment of some officials and ministers. The remaining chapters in this section examine the responses of industry and agriculture to the challenges of economic development and impact of a developing economy on regional and physical planning.

[96] Connery, *The Irish*, p. 103.   [97] Kenny, *In good company*, p. 168.

[98] *DIB* online – Michael Killeen.

[99] John Bristow, 'Public enterprise', in J. A. Bristow and A. A. Tait (eds), *Economic policy in Ireland* (Dublin: Institute of Public Administration, 1968), pp. 193–5.

3   Coping with change 1
Industry and trade unions

The story of Irish industry is one of birth and death. Existing industries, established under the protectionist regime from the 1930s to the early 1960s, struggled to survive or sold out, while new foreign-owned firms were being attracted to Ireland by tax incentives and grant assistance. In 1959, UCD economist Paddy Lynch noted that 'one of the major tasks in Ireland is to raise the efficiency of uncompetitive private firms to the level of those that do compete'.[1] The introversion and intellectual mediocrity identified in the civil service applied with equal and perhaps greater force in business. Many firms were family-owned, with succession determined by birth, family networks and the old school tie rather than education and ability. Banks gave preference in recruitment to the children of bank employees – though this practice ended when the Irish banks merged in the 1960s. Many domestic firms enjoyed a near monopoly of the Irish market, which guaranteed them a comfortable livelihood and an easy life. A 1964 survey by the IMI revealed that over 78 per cent of companies had never carried out a formal study of the market for their products.[2] Why bother when consumers had no alternative, or – as also happened, firms had reached an informal agreement to share the market? The percentage of managers with no professional qualifications ranged from 80 per cent for firms with 20–99 employees to 57 per cent in those employing more than 500.[3] The CIO reports of the early 1960s revealed what one writer has described as 'the detritus of three decades of protection: small-scale units, little specialisation, short production runs, plant under-utilisation, poor design, scarcely any R&D and negligible marketing'.[4] Michael Smurfit claims that most of the machinery in his father's packaging

---

[1] Patrick Lynch, 'The economics of Independence: Some unsettled questions of Irish economics', *Administration*, vol. 7, no. 2, 1959, p. 93.
[2] Breffni Tomlin, *The management of Irish industry. A research report by the Irish Management Institute* (Dublin: IMI, 1966), pp. 176–8.
[3] Tomlin, *The management of Irish industry*, pp. xxix, 42.
[4] Tom Cox, *The making of managers. A history of the Irish Management Institute 1952–2002* (Cork: Oak Tree, 2002), p. 86.

plant was home-made; 'sometimes it worked, sometimes it didn't'. It was only when he worked in a large US firm that he realised that this was not inevitable.[5] Changing cultures was not easy – given the low level of education and widespread complacency. J. C. B. McCarthy reported that 'All the industries surveyed [by the CIO] were urged seriously to consider engaging the services of experienced consultants and were told the Government was prepared to pay half the costs involved. None of the industries have acted on that suggestion.'[6] This might suggest that the frenzied activity of CIO committees was a mirage – but that would probably be an overstatement; some businessmen responded to the challenges and opportunities, many didn't. But change wasn't easy. When a young Michael Smurfit returned from the United States in the early 1960s, brimming with ideas about modernising the family firm, his father, who had arranged for him to learn the most modern techniques in Continental Can, would not permit him to apply them. So the son went to England and set up his own firm. When he returned in 1965 at his father's invitation, his business was worth more than the long-established family firm.[7] Clashes between two generations or between an established family firm and a professional manager recruited from outside must have been common. When Kevin McCourt was appointed as the first managing director of United Distillers of Ireland, a company formed by merging three long-established family firms, he discovered that there was a serious dearth of people with management skills, and no personnel department, because the firms had been run on a traditional paternalist basis.[8]

Government assistance for business was generous and extensive, offering a growing array of grants and tax concessions to support capital investment, export marketing, design and training. The state export company Córas Tráchtála chivvied industrialists to participate in trade missions and industry fairs. The IMI,[9] Irish National Productivity Committee, Institute of Industrial Research and Standards and Kilkenny Design all offered assistance. In October 1964, the IMI reported that its business had doubled; more than 1,200 executives from Irish commercial companies attended courses, which were government-subsidised, during that year.[10] Between 1963 and 1968 existing

---

[5] Michael Smurfit, *A life worth living* (Cork: Oak Tree, 2014), pp. 41–47.
[6] Quoted in Cox, *The making of managers*, pp. 87–8.
[7] Smurfit, *A life worth living*, pp. 47–65.
[8] McCague, *My dear Mr. McCourt*, pp. 127–9.
[9] The Irish Management Institute was founded in 1952 with the objective of raising the standard of management in Ireland. Tomlin, *The management of Irish industry*, p. xvii.
[10] *B&F*, 9 October 1964.

firms received approximately £15 million in grants towards the cost of new machinery or premises,[11] half of which went to food, textiles and clothing companies.[12] A separate programme for small industries, employing less than fifty, was launched in 1967 in response to political pressures. Re-equipment grants were introduced in 1969, ostensibly to help firms withstand increased competition as tariff barriers fell, but grants were also paid to bakeries, brick and block works and provincial newspapers – industries that could not credibly be described as threatened by imports, except perhaps in border counties. A case of 'jam for everybody'!

Some domestic firms responded well to the challenges and support available. In 1965, *Business and Finance* reported that many textile firms established in the 1930s were 'rationalising at break-neck speed', with mergers underway between Cork-based Sunbeam Wolsey, Salts (Tulllamore) and Gentex (Athlone).[13] Sunbeam Wolsey had developed strong export sales to the United Kingdom, cashing in on the growing market for man-made fibres. Arklow Pottery, another 1930s company, had developed new markets mainly in the United Kingdom; Carrigaline Pottery announced a four-year development plan.[14] Print and paper output was ahead of *Second Programme* targets.[15] Ford and Dunlop – two iconic long-established international firms – announced major expansions.[16] Carpet producers in Navan and Youghal were particularly successful – as homeowners in Britain and Ireland covered every inch of floor space with fitted carpets.[17] Economic recovery at home and a booming UK market saw profits rise for shoe firms. Dundalk manufacturer John Halliday – the most successful firm – had developed new brands of children's and women's shoes. Firms that had traditionally made heavy boots fared less well,[18] evidence of changing lifestyles and spending patterns. This buoyant market was reflected in the Irish stock exchange. A 1965 flotation by Edenderry Shoes was over-subscribed ten times; shares in Cork textiles firm Martin Mahony had doubled in value since their flotation in 1962.[19] But for many firms the boom was short-lived. By the end of the decade sales to Britain were proving more difficult as Britain opened its market to EFTA countries; at the same time, British

---

[11] National Economic and Social Council, *Industrial policy and development: a survey of literature from the early 1960s* (NESC, no. 56, December 1980), p. 8.

[12] McAleese, *A profile of grant-aided industry in Ireland* (Dublin: IDA, 1977), p. 13.

[13] *B&F*, 21 May 1965.   [14] *B&F*, 13 November 1964; 16 October 1964.

[15] *B&F*, 26 March 1965.   [16] *B&F*, 19 November 1965.

[17] *B&F*, 17 May 1968; 30 August 1968.

[18] Jon Press, *The footwear industry and Ireland, 1922–1973* (Dublin: Irish Academic Press, 1989), pp. 132–6.

[19] *B&F*, 4 June 1965; 11 June 1965.

firms were taking a rising share of the Irish market. When import quotas for shoes ended in 1968, Dundalk manufacturers Rawson and Munster Shoes went into liquidation.[20] Shoe imports trebled within three years, reaching almost one-quarter of domestic sales, at a time when Irish footwear exports to Britain were hit by the British import deposit scheme (yet another British device to reduce imports and protect the value of sterling) and competition from low-cost imports from third countries. Although the footwear industry had made considerable progress over the past decade, a 1971 report concluded that it was not competitive in a free market; some manufacturers were more interested in lobbying for government assistance than in raising productivity.[21] Sixty per cent of Irish consumer goods exported to the United Kingdom were marketed under distributors' brand names, which left manufacturers vulnerable to being undercut by competitors,[22] at a time when Irish cost inflation was significantly above the European average. In 1969, Britain imposed 'voluntary' restrictions on imports of man-made fibres because of overcapacity in British firms. The Cork town of Youghal, one of the boom towns of the decade, with Youghal Carpets and textile firm Sunbeam Wolsey flourishing in both the domestic and British markets, was seriously affected by this measure. By 1969, the outlook for Sunbeam Wolsey was described as 'problematic'; another textile firm Glenabbey closed its jersey division. The closure of Seafield Gentex Athlone plant in 1970, with the loss of 320 jobs, was also blamed on Britain's 'voluntary' restrictions, though the refusal of the unions to co-operate with planned rationalisation was also a factor.[23] The Youghal textile factory Blackwater Cotton closed in 1971.[24]

Grants and tax concessions helped to offset some of the impact of the AIFTAA, keeping jobs alive, though perhaps only for a few years. Ireland was not the only country where long-established firms were disappearing, because of mergers, greater competition and labour-saving technologies. Investment in technologically advanced plants and equipment, often subsidised by governments, wiped out thousands of manual jobs across Europe. A major re-equipment by Guinness's brewery, which received generous grants, reduced the workforce from 4,000 to 1,400. Most established industries were only accustomed to supplying the small domestic market, so the prospect of free trade forced them to operate on a completely different scale. Michael Smurfit realised that once the

---

[20] *B&F*, 2 June 1967; 5 April 1968; 11 April 1968.
[21] *B&F*, 19 June 1970. Press, *Irish footwear industry*, pp. 160–8. The Committee on Industrial Progress, *Report on the Irish Footwear Industry* (1971).
[22] *B&F*, 16 June 1967.   [23] *Hibernia*, 28 August 1969; 12–25 June 1970.
[24] *B&F*, 23 September 1971.

AIFTAA tariff reductions came into effect, his family's firm would be too small to withstand competition from larger British firms, so he embarked on an aggressive programme of taking over other Irish firms, including several that were significantly larger than Smurfits. By the early 1970s they were the second-largest company in Ireland.[25] While many firms failed to withstand the competition from UK and European firms, the mergers and rationalisations, plus the recruitment of managers with professional education, and perhaps some international education or experience, enabled others to survive. Nevertheless, despite repeated urging by politicians and business leaders, and the support of a state export board, many firms continued to focus on the home market, because the level of protection remained extremely high despite a phased reduction in tariffs from 1963. McAleese claimed that Ireland's tariff protection created a bias against exports, which was not offset by grants or tax reliefs.[26] The continuing legacy of protection counteracted the government drive to increase manufacturing exports.

Rather than change their ways, some companies sold out to a foreign owner, or entered partnerships with foreign companies.[27] This might reflect a realisation that they lacked the necessary technical and marketing expertise, or simply a wish to take the easy way out. By the early 1960s, almost 40 per cent of jobs in firms dating from the protectionist era were in foreign ownership or producing under licence to foreign firms,[28] and a growing number of established firms were being taken over by foreign concerns. Urney, the chocolate manufacturer, was bought in 1963 by US firm W. R. Grace; Beatrice Foods, another major US company, became part owner of Tayto Crisps; Lemon, a long-established Dublin sweet manufacturer, passed into British ownership.[29] Bew and Patterson highlighted the business interests of J. L. Fitzpatrick, president of the FII, 1957–1959, and a key supporter of government efforts to modernise Irish industry, as evidence of the close links between some sections of Irish industry and foreign capital.[30] In September 1965, *Business and Finance* reported that a substantial volume of Irish equities was now in British hands.[31] Many Irish industries followed the British model of merging to create large conglomerates, in the belief that this offered the best prospects of survival. In 1966, the long-established whiskey firms Cork

[25] Smurfit, *A life worth living*, pp. 65–82.

[26] Dermot McAleese, *Effective tariffs and the structure of industrial protection in Ireland* (Dublin: ESRI, general research series no. 62, 1971), pp. 27,45.

[27] *Hibernia*, June 1962.

[28] Frank Barry, Linda Barry, Aisling Menton, 'Foreign ownership and external licensing of Irish business under protectionism', Research Paper, Aug. 2012.

[29] *B&F*, 23 October 1964; 18 June 1965; 13 August 1965.

[30] Bew and Patterson, *Seán Lemass*, pp. 133–4.   [31] *B&F*, 17 September 1965, p. 14.

Distillers, John Jameson and John Power merged to form Irish Distillers, with the goal of creating a company with the capacity to withstand free trade and compete on export markets. Irish whiskey lost its protected domestic market in 1971; from that date Scotch could be sold on equal terms. Although Irish whiskey sales in the United States were rising, they remained insignificant compared with Scotch (15 million cases of Scotch in 1969 against 110,000 cases of Irish). In 1970, plans were announced for a merger between United Distillers, tobacco company P. J. Carroll, the Irish Glass Bottle and Waterford Glass to create a strong Irish industrial company with the potential to market its products internationally. The press release referred to the opportunities and challenges facing industry because of the Anglo-Irish Agreement and EEC membership and noted that 'Such a group would be better placed to meet competition that is already operating on a multi-national basis than would the individual companies acting alone.' In the event, this merger never happened. Shortly after talks broke down, United Distillers – now renamed Irish Distillers – entered into an arrangement with the Canadian distilling company Seagrams in order to gain technical expertise and better marketing opportunities in the United States.[32] In hindsight, serious questions have been asked about the British merger-mania of these years – questions that apply equally to Ireland, but hindsight is always easy. Mergers and foreign takeovers were common throughout Europe at this time, and Ireland was no exception.

Irish industry underwent more change in the 1960s than at any time since the 1930s, and the process was not without casualties. Conditions worsened after 1973 with EEC membership and the onset of an economic recession, and the next decade or so saw the closure of many firms established under the former protectionist regime. There were some dramatic success stories among established industries – notably Waterford Glass, described as 'the kind of product that the country should be putting into the export market', a strong brand name, exporting 90 per cent of output, either directly or through sales to tourists. But Waterford Glass, originally founded by Czech businessman Charles Bacik in 1946, could be regarded as an early, unorthodox example of foreign investment. In 1950, the firm was taken over by Irish businessman Joe McGrath. From the beginning it targeted export markets.[33] Waterford had modern plants and a highly skilled, well-paid workforce. By the early 1970s, Tipperary, Cavan, Dublin, Fermoy, Kilkenny,

[32] McCague, *My dear Mr. McCourt*, pp. 126–37; 141–5.
[33] *DIB* online – Charles Bacik.

Galway and Cork were hoping to emulate Waterford by setting up Irish crystal glass factories.[34]

Attracting new foreign direct investment

Employment in manufacturing industry rose by 34,197 between 1961 and 1971. Over the same period, firms supported by the Industrial Development Authority's New Industries Programme created 33,736 jobs. Thus, New Industries (overwhelmingly foreign-owned) accounted for the entire increase in employment and for almost one-third (30 and 29 per cent) of manufacturing output and employment and 62 per cent of manufacturing exports. These industries were dispersed more widely than established firms, accounting for 60 per cent of manufacturing jobs in the north-west and over 40 per cent in the west and south-west. The Dublin area, with almost half of manufacturing employment, had less than one-quarter of jobs in new industries.[35]

The drive to attract foreign industry began, however, half-heartedly in 1949 with the formation of the Industrial Development Authority (IDA), which was responsible for promoting Ireland as a location for foreign-owned industries. In 1952, it was supplemented by another state organisation An Foras Tionscal, which awarded grants for new industrial development (native or foreign-owned). But there were few applicants. Grants were only available in undeveloped areas, and foreign companies had to comply with the provisions of the Control of Manufactures Act. In 1956, New Industry (grant-aided) accounted for only 1.2 per cent of fixed manufacturing investment.[36] In 1958, Lemass, the architect of the Control of Manufactures Act, amended the legislation to permit any company manufacturing purely for export, or a foreign company that manufactured 'primarily for export' and made a bona fide offer of 50 per cent of its voting shares to Irish citizens, to operate without a licence.[37] The requirement that new grant-aided industries must locate in development areas in the west of Ireland was eased. In 1959, grants – at a lower rate – were extended to firms locating outside development areas, provided that they could present a strong case for doing so, or the project was of exceptional national importance: a large industry or one with strong export potential. This marked a compromise between Whitaker's recommendation to remove

---

[34] *B&F*, 8 June, 1972.
[35] McAleese, *Profile of grant-aided industry*, pp. 16–17, 23; P. N. O'Farrell, *Regional industrial development trends in Ireland, 1960–1973* (Dublin: Institute of Public Administration, 1975), table 1, and pp. 52–5.
[36] McAleese, *Profile of grant-aided industry*, table 7.1, p. 67.
[37] *Economic Development*; app. 2, p. 232.

all regional incentives[38] and the determination of the Department of Industry and Commerce to maintain them. In 1963, the conditions determining eligibility for grants outside the undeveloped areas were further eased.[39] Grants were discretionary, not calculated on a formulaic basis as in Britain and Northern Ireland, where grants of up to one-third of the cost of plant and equipment were available. This left the Irish process open to charges that it favoured foreign rather than domestic firms.

While these changes were important, indeed essential, most foreign investors were attracted to Ireland by Export Profits Tax Relief, which was first introduced in 1956 as a temporary incentive to encourage Irish firms to increase exports and help relieve a balance of payments crisis. This concession was proposed in a submission by the Irish Exporters Association to the Committee on the Taxation of Industry. It first appeared in the 1953 report by the consultancy firm IBEC.[40] But in the face of strong objections from the Revenue Commissioners, who regarded this as 'a dangerous precedent', the Committee did not include it among their recommendations. Lemass, then in opposition, opposed the measure, claiming that it discriminated against existing firms.[41] Nevertheless, in 1961 the tax concession was extended to 100 per cent of profits on exports, with full relief granted for a ten-year period (25 years in the Shannon Free Airport zone), followed by five years of tapering relief. Initially, only firms that were in operation by April 1964 were eligible for ten years' relief, but this deadline was extended under the *Second Programme*.[42] Tax concessions remain the bedrock of Ireland's strategy for attracting foreign direct investment to the present day, though they have been modified on a number of occasions to conform to EU regulations. Given that the combined rate of corporation tax and income tax in Ireland in the early 1960s was 41.7 per cent, and only four OECD countries had lower rates,[43] the concession was a significant benefit for any profitable industry.

Foreign industries were widely seen as symbolising a changing Ireland. In July 1959, *Daily American* ran a story, 'Emerald Isles opens doors to foreign capital'. The story continued: 'Pastoral Ireland has embarked on

---

[38] *Economic Development*, pp. 159–60.

[39] *Survey of Grant-Aided Industry*, October 1967, Prl. 117, p. 14; Loraine Donaldson, *Development Planning in Ireland* (London: Praeger, 1966), pp. 64–5.

[40] My thanks to Professor Frank Barry for identifying this.

[41] Peter Clarke, 'The introduction of exports sales relief – a fifty year review', *Accountancy Ireland*, vol. 38, no. 1. February 2006, pp. 85–6.

[42] Donaldson, *Development planning in Ireland*, p. 63.

[43] Donaldson, *Development planning in Ireland*, p. 124. No country charged less than 30 per cent *Business International* report – referenced below.

an all-out effort to industrialize the Emerald Isle.' It noted Ireland's position 'on the doorstep of Europe' and government efforts to create the 'proper investment climate' so that 'foreign capital will want to invest in the whimsical island of shamrocks, leprechauns and Guinness stout'.[44] The *Wall Street Journal*, the United States' premier business newspaper covered this story in November 1960 under the heading 'Why Irish Eyes are Smiling'. 'A couple of years ago, Ireland scrapped its restrictive investment policies and flung open the country to foreigners with heavy pockets and big plans. Lured by remission of rates, subsidies, tariff advantages with British Commonwealth nations and almost every other incentive wit could desire, Germany, English, American and Japanese businessmen have started some 90 new factories – nothing to be sneered at in a small country.'[45] In February 1963, the London *Evening Standard* reported that 'An industrial revolution is gathering pace only 60 miles from the shores of Britain'.[46] Between 1960 and 1973, a total of 418 firms were established with grant assistance totalling £92 million – the overwhelming majority were foreign-owned; 352 were still in business in June 1973, employing almost 45,000 workers. The peak year for new industries was 1969, with 59 new firms and over 7,000 jobs; although the pace of investment subsequently slowed, it remained well above the early 1960s, with roughly 3,500 additional jobs annually.[47]

While these achievements were laudable they should be set in an international context. Between 1950 and 1970, US foreign direct investment grew at an annual rate of 10 per cent.[48] In 1959, new direct US private investment in Western Europe totalled $439 million: US investments in the United Kingdom were valued at $2.6 billion and $1.9 billion in EEC countries. Total investment in New Industries in Ireland that year was under £1.4 million (less than $4 million). Ireland was competing with countries offering access to large domestic markets or a European free trade area.[49] By the 1960s, firms were shopping around to see which country offered the best grants and taxes, market access and other variables.[50] Until the late 1960s, Northern Ireland was much more

[44] *Daily American*, 20 July 1959, clipping on NAI DT S2850 F/94, Control of Manufactures Act.

[45] *Wall Street Journal*, 1 November 1960, Clipping on NAI DT S2850G/94.

[46] *Evening Standard*, 8 February 1963, clipping on NAI DT S17437.

[47] McAleese, *Profile of grant-aided industry*, p. 23; O'Farrell, *Regional industrial development trends*, table 1, and pp. 52–5.

[48] David Kurt Jacobsen, *Chasing progress in the Irish Republic. Ideology, democracy and dependent development* (Cambridge: Cambridge University Press, 1994), p. 31.

[49] Attracting US investments. A study made for Shannon Free Airport Development Co. Ltd. April 1960 by *Business International* on NAI DT S 2850G/94.

[50] McAleese, *Profile of grant-aided industries*, pp. 26–7.

successful than the Republic in attracting overseas investment; it was earlier in the field with its marketing campaign, and it offered very generous capital concessions and modern factories for lease. The outbreak of violence wrecked Northern Ireland's investment programme.

Some German and Dutch firms opened factories in Ireland because of labour shortages at home. A 1961 report by *Business International* suggested that 'Although it is a matter of some delicacy', the promotional campaign should highlight Ireland's privileged access to the United Kingdom and Commonwealth markets. They also suggested that given its history, Ireland would be a good manufacturing base for products targeted at newly independent African states.[51] However, until the late 1960s, efforts to attract overseas industries were handicapped by amateurish marketing and too many agencies. The IDA was responsible for promotion. Grants for would-be investors were negotiated with An Foras Tionscal, though the Department of Industry and Commerce liked to be involved – not least because this gave the minister some influence over location. Gaeltarra Éireann assisted firms in Irish-speaking areas. The Shannon Free Airport Development Corporation (SFADCO), which was established to help Shannon diversify its activities at a time when transatlantic flights were increasingly by-passing Shannon airport, ran its own promotion campaign, apparently independent of other agencies.[52] This plethora of competing organisations confused outsiders, but a recommendation that responsibility for promoting and negotiating with new industries (excluding Shannon) should be handled by one agency was excised from *Economic Development* before publication.[53]

In 1960, a hard-hitting report by *Business International* commissioned by SFADCO recommended that an 'An aggressive Irish promotion Office in the US' should market Ireland; a separate promotion campaign for Shannon would confuse US businessmen and be 'a wasteful duplication of efforts'; the special attractions of Shannon could be sold within the overall Irish message. Remaining restrictions under the Control of Manufactures Act should be repealed. *Business International* described them as 'difficult to understand in light of Ireland's drive for US investments and US managerial and technical skills ... a serious psychological block for foreign managers interested in Ireland ... most detrimental' to efforts to attract foreign investment.[54] Restrictions preventing new

[51] Attracting US investments, p. 43.
[52] Bernard Share, *Shannon Departures, A study in regional initiatives* (Dublin: Gill & Macmillan, 1992), pp. 58–62.
[53] D/F, memo for Govt. F96/10/57 Economic Development, 4 July 1958, The unpublished version of Economic Development is available on NAI D/F 2001/3/5.
[54] Attracting US investments, pp. 4, 38, 49.

overseas firms from selling in the Irish market represented a form of continuing protection for domestic industry, limiting the spill-over benefits from foreign companies, such as better training of executives and craftsmen and the potential for foreign industry to promote greater productivity within Irish–owned industries. Although Lemass described this report as 'a very valuable document' whose recommendations should be considered in full, he handed responsibility for implementation to Industry and Commerce, which was tantamount to ensuring that they would be ignored. They implied that the report contained nothing of value.[55] The Control of Manufactures Act was eventually repealed in 1964, but restrictions persisted on new industries selling in the Irish market.

Throughout most of the 1960s the IDA focused on family-owned businesses in Germany and the Netherlands. In 1960, the IDA office in New York was staffed only by a secretary, who mailed brochures to interested companies. The Dutch firm Wavin Pipes, located in Swords – north of Dublin airport, was the first major foreign firm established outside the development areas, but it was exceptional. Few major foreign firms located in Dublin before the 1980s. Donaldson suggests that German firms invested in Ireland in order to gain access to the UK market, because they were 'not as welcome in Britain as in Ireland', and they wished to be as far as possible from 'the conflicts of the continent'. This latter argument is supported by the fact that a number of Germans were buying land in Ireland at this time, often in the teeth of strong local opposition. In 1960, the Irish Embassy in Bonn sought to have an article published in the German press indicating that while German industrialists were welcome, this did not extend to the buying of land by Germans.[56] The IDA's concentration on Germany is evident in the composition of the Industrial Promotion Panel – a panel of Irish-based industrialists who would assist the IDA in attracting new industries: seven of the fourteen-man panel represented German companies; there were no US representatives.[57] The Survey of Grant-Aided Industry in 1966/67 suggested that labour availability was a major attraction for German firms – this is understandable given that West Germany had a severe labour shortage and had signed several bilateral agreements to recruit workers from southern Europe and Turkey.[58] In hindsight, it is perhaps surprising that more German firms did not set up branches in Ireland.

[55] D/F Inducements to industrialists NAI 2001/3/121.
[56] Donaldson, *Development planning in Ireland*, p. 91. NAI DT S2850 F/94.
[57] DD, vol. 224, col. 429, 29 September 1966.
[58] *Survey of Grant-Aided Industries*, p. 57.

The early US companies investing in Ireland were not blue-chip entities. They included a plant to manufacture ladies housedresses, a small
cosmetics and hair products plant, two manufacturers of coin-operated
amusement tables, bowling alley equipment and Leaf chewing-gum plant
in Kilcock.[59] There is a strong impression that the government wished to
concentrate US investment in Shannon – though this was never explicitly
stated. The first significant investment at Shannon was a branch of the US
company SPS (Standard Pressed Steel), which opened in 1960. Another
household name, the South African diamond firm, De Beers arrived in
1961, closely followed by EI – the American giant General Electric. In
1961, the Shannon Free Zone employed 463 workers; by 1968 this had
risen to almost 4,000 workers.[60]

In 1966, Minister for Industry and Commerce Patrick Hillery told the
Dáil that there was need 'for a thorough re-appraisal in all its aspects of the
programme for the attraction of industry from abroad'. The 1965 Anglo-
Irish Agreement would result in free trade with Britain within ten years.
Ireland's Export Profits Tax Relief was due to expire at the same time. The
incentives offered to new industries by competitors, especially Northern
Ireland and Britain, had significantly improved in recent years.[61] In 1966,
the IDA was given responsibility for evaluating proposals for new developments by Irish firms, and a new division was established to assist small
industries. An Foras Tionscal took responsibility for adaptation and expansion grants to existing firms, and for the industrial estates recently established at Waterford and Galway.[62] The IDA commissioned US consultants
Arthur D. Little to review its structures. Their report was forthright: 'Unless
the Government is willing to commit the Irish people to a standard of living
lower than that enjoyed by their neighbours, industrialization must be
accelerated'; 'to be even marginally successful ... the I.D.A. will, in our
view, require considerably greater resources than are now provided. Ireland
has not yet made the critical minimum effort needed to attract new industry.' They recommended an expanded role for IDA and a significantly
increased budget, citing Northern Ireland's success in attracting new
industry;[63] if Lemass, now a backbench TD, read this report, he would
probably wince, given his speeches in the early 1960s contrasting the
economic successes of the Republic with failure in Northern Ireland.

---

[59] NAI 2001/3/122.
[60] Brian Callanan, *Ireland's Shannon story: leaders, visions and networks – a case study of local and regional development* (Dublin: Irish Academic Press, 2000), p. 89.
[61] DD, vol. 222, col. 1081, 3 May 1966.
[62] DD, vol. 230, cols. 1758–9, 26 October 1967.
[63] Arthur D. Little, *Review of the structure of the Industrial Development Authority* (May, 1967), pp. 3, 5, 6.

Arthur D. Little recommended that the IDA take over the functions of An Foras Tionscal, create a new research unit and expand the number of staff involved in overseas promotion and support new firms when they located in Ireland. They were insistent that the IDA should no longer be part of the civil service; they must have greater freedom to recruit key staff and make decisions. They also emphasised that 'the United States deserves greater attention than the I.D.A has been able to devote to it'. There were more 'truly international companies' in the United States than elsewhere. Because US industry had a technological lead, they were being courted by representatives of many other countries, 'each bringing his package of incentives and conveying a strong interest on the part of his Government to attract the company to build a factory'.[64] Over the past decade the Netherlands had attracted 120 US firms and 30 joint US/ Dutch ventures with a total investment of $140 million.

The reorganised IDA began its operations in 1969. The former executive chair was summarily removed, a decision described as 'quite a shock to the Dublin business community'; he was succeeded by Michael Killeen, the young managing director of the Irish Export Board, Córas Tráchtála.[65] The reformed structures and greater focus on the United States, which accounted for more than half of global FDI, proved successful. In 1973, Ireland accounted for 1.9 per cent of existing FDI within the nine members of the EEC; by 1981 this had risen to 5 per cent,[66] but one could argue that Ireland had missed the boat, because the volume of FDI fell during the post-1973 recession.

Foreign industries attracted considerable media attention. Lemass opened many new factories, often using the occasion to promote a message about the economy. Good news about foreign industries attracted publicity; bad news attracted even greater attention – whether this related to a lengthy industrial relations dispute at the EI factory in Shannon or the failure of the French-owned Potez aerospace plant, south of Dublin. With projected investment of £3 million and annual projected sales of £12 million, Potez would have marked a quantum leap in Ireland's bid to attract new industries, because it was a capital-intensive, hi-tech company.[67] A receiver was appointed to the firm less than three years after the initial announcement.[68] Fine Gael used a picture of the factory with the slogan 'Why is the factory empty?' in its 1969 general election campaign.[69] A plant opened in Dundalk by the UK firm GEC closed within eight months of receiving a large grant,

[64] Little, *Review of the structure of the Industrial Development Authority*, pp. 3, 5, 6.
[65] *B&F*, 5 December 1969.
[66] UK Department of Trade and Industry, *Multi-national investment strategies in the British Isles*, HMSO 1983, By Neil Hood and Stephen Young, p. 16.
[67] *B&F*, 2 October 1964.   [68] *B&F*, 19 April 1967.   [69] *Hibernia*, 6–26 June 1969.

though in this case one-third of the jobs transferred to a nearby plant in Dunleer, which became the nucleus of a successful Irish company Glen Dimplex.[70] But a spectacular failure such as Potez was atypical: most new firms were much smaller. The 1967 Survey claimed that fewer than 10 per cent of assisted firms failed. Allowing for those which were subsequently taken over and reopened, the net failure rate was 7 per cent. The firms in question had received approximately £1 million. in grant assistance from a total of £35 million.[71] By 1973, the failure rate had risen to 15.8 per cent; following the onset of economic recession later that year it increased to 20 per cent by 1975, accounting for 6.9 per cent (mid-1973) and 12.6 per cent (end 1975) of grant payments. A disproportionate number of the 1970s failures were firms established in the 1950s. Most failing firms were in sectors where domestic firms were also under pressure: one-third of grant-aided textiles and footwear firms closed during these years.[72]

Tax incentives encouraged foreign firms to concentrate on export markets. There was little linkage between new and existing firms. Foreign companies bought relatively little raw materials or intermediate products locally, and they sold little of what they produced in the Irish market. This lack of contact between the two industrial sectors was the outcome of government policy – which continued to favour the dispersal of foreign-owned firms, and prevented them from selling on the local market in order to protect established firms. These restrictions limited the interaction between the two groups and limited the opportunities for existing firms to learn from the newcomers. The dispersal of foreign firms in regions with little or no manufacturing tradition was another inhibiting factor.[73] In time this changed, but closer interaction between domestic and foreign firms – however threatening to existing firms – would have ultimately been more beneficial. So the story is mixed: significant losses among long-established industries which were compensated by the arrival of new foreign-owned firms, but those who lost their jobs were not necessarily employed by the incoming firms, which often located in different places and required different skills.

Trade unions: resentment and rising expectations

The changes in the economy were good for trade unions. Although the numbers at work in 1971 were almost identical to that a decade earlier,

---

[70] *B&F*, 14 May 1965.   [71] *Survey of Grant-Aided Industry*, pp. 28, 37–8.

[72] McAleese, *Profile of grant-aided industries*, pp. 77–81.

[73] John Bradley, 'The history of economic development in Ireland, north and south', in Anthony F. Heath, Richard Breen and Christopher T. Whelan (eds), *Ireland: north and south. Perspectives from the social sciences* (Oxford: Oxford University Press, 1999), p. 61.

there was a major shift from self-employment and working within the family economy, to waged and salaried jobs, so the number of potential union members rose significantly. In 1959, the trade union movement, which had been split into two rival groups for over a decade, reunited to form the Irish Congress of Trade Unions. The timing was fortuitous; a reunited movement strengthened the unions' hand in negotiating with government and helped to secure their place in the CIO and the NIEC. Lemass had a history of friendly relations with the trade unions, and shortly after he became Taoiseach he invited ICTU to meet him to discuss economic development.[74] The membership affiliated to ICTU rose from 432,000 in 1960 to 510,000 by 1970 and 570,000 by 1974. While ICTU had members in Northern Ireland, most of the expansion was in the Republic, where membership rose from 328,000 in 1961 to 499,000 by 1979. Membership of the Irish Transport and General Workers Union (ITGWU) – the country's largest union – increased from 91,300 in 1960 to 117, 000 by 1971 and 141,100 by 1976.[75] In 1961, just over half of employees (51 per cent) were members of a trade union; by 1967 this had risen to 56 per cent, a substantially higher proportion than in Britain or most western European countries. By 1979 almost two-thirds of employees belonged to a trade union. The biggest relative increases were in white-collar unions.[76]

But despite an expanding membership and closer connections with government, the trade unions faced many challenges. The heady combination of rising inflation, a belief that long-term economic growth was now assured, and the significant rise in trade union membership, especially among younger workers, resulted in numerous strikes, official and unofficial, some lasting for months. By 1970, Ireland had overtaken Britain in the number of days lost in industrial disputes and was second only to Italy. In 1971, Ireland had the unenviable record of topping that league; on both occasions the days lost per worker were double the UK rate and many multiples of the figures for Germany or the Netherlands.[77] Charlie McCarthy, a leading trade unionist, wrote that 'In the early nineteen sixties, for the first time, we experienced economic growth, but

---

[74] Brian Girvin, 'Trade unions and economic development', in Donal Nevin (ed.), *Trade Union Century* (Cork: Mercier, 1994), p.125.

[75] Nevin (ed.), *Trade Union Century*, Appendices: Congress Membership, 1894–1994, pp. 433–4.

[76] McCarthy, *Decade of upheaval*, pp. 38–9. David Rottman and Philip O'Connell, 'The changing social structure', in Litton (ed.), *Unequal Achievement*, p. 75.

[77] In 1970 and 1971, days lost in strikes were 146,555 and 138,337 days per 100,000 non-agricultural wage earners; the UK figures were 51,994 and 64,209 days; the Netherlands, 7,172 and 2,608. Peter Flora, *State, economy and society in Western Europe, 1815–1974: a data handbook*(London: Macmillan, 1987), vol. II, chapter 10.

we seemed unable to absorb it into the economy.'[78] *Business and Finance* claimed that 'affluent society propaganda has rebounded and created the very dissatisfaction that now stirs within the trade union movement'.[79]

As union leaders became more involved in national committees, they had less time to devote to local disputes and the everyday matters that rankled with rank–and–file members; this was particularly significant for the large general unions.[80] A vacuum emerged at grass-roots level and there would appear to have been a lack of attention to local issues. This proved a major factor in the proliferation of unofficial strikes, which was one of the least welcome features of the decade.[81] Given the lack of expertise in civil service and business, it would be surprising if similar shortcomings did not apply to trade union staff. Some disputes were triggered by insecurity and fear of change and threats of containerisation in the docks or an end to bus conductors. Strikes by Dublin busmen over plans to introduce one-man buses were a regular feature of the decade; these were prompted by fears of job losses. In this instance the problem was compounded because the busmen had abandoned their traditional large general union to form a breakaway group, because they believed that the established unions did not reflect their views.[82]

Lee has suggested that in the difficult circumstances of 1950s Ireland wage relativities became extremely rigid; craftsmen sought to maintain these differentials and their relative status vis-à-vis unskilled workers.[83] The wage inflation of the 1960s, the more dynamic labour market and national wage rounds destabilised long-term wage differentials and labour practices, as did the emergence of new cohorts of wage and salaried workers in provincial Ireland. Trade union membership spread into industries and to places where it was formerly unknown – such as the Shannon area and the midland bogs. Bord na Móna – the state-owned turf production company – had been a major employer throughout the midlands from the late 1940s, but there was no tradition of union membership among the general workers until 1965 when Bord na Móna and the group of trade unions negotiated an agreement making membership a condition of employment. Wages for unskilled and semi-skilled turf workers were traditionally related to agricultural wages; craft workers were paid on a par with craft workers elsewhere. The gap between unskilled

---

[78] McCarthy, *Decade of upheaval*, p. 95.   [79] *B&F*, 16 July 1965 Cover Story.

[80] McCarthy, *Decade of upheaval*, pp. 67, 70.

[81] Martin Maguire, *Servants to the public. A history of the local government and public services union* (Dublin: Institute of Public Administration, 1998), p. 180.

[82] McCarthy, *Decade of upheaval*, pp. 62–65.

[83] Joe Lee, 'Workers and society in modern Ireland', in Donal Nevin (ed.), *Trade unions and change in Irish society* (Cork: Mercier, 1980), p. 13.

and skilled wages was one of the largest in the state, and the unions demanded parity with Electricity Supply Board (ESB) workers. This demand was not altogether surprising given that the ESB employed many workers in the midlands at their peat-fired power stations, and unlike Bord na Móna their wages were linked to Dublin workers.[84]

A disproportionate number of strikes were initiated by workers in relatively well-paid secure jobs, including skilled craft workers, or white-collar workers in the public service and banking. Between 1937 and 1960, the state-owned ESB experienced seven official (sanctioned by unions) and unofficial strikes by manual workers and one strike by non-manual workers; between 1961 and 1968, manual workers engaged in two official strikes and twenty-four unofficial strikes, and non-manual workers were involved in nine official strikes and three unofficial strikes.[85] The ESB Officers Association was the most militant group of white-collar workers. Threats and realities of power cuts became a regular part of Irish life. Legislation introduced in 1966 outlawing strikes where electricity supplies were threatened did little to improve matters; indeed, the government's reputation for controlling industrial disputes was further damaged in 1968 when ESB workers on unofficial strike were jailed, only to be released. Their fines were paid by the ESB, who then opened talks with the former strikers.[86] One cause of unrest was the different status and treatment of manual and white-collar workers: the latter had a separate canteen, better sick leave and pensions. Skilled electricians resented seeing clerks free to leave work to attend mass on a church holiday, or go to the shops in the middle of the working day, whereas they had to clock in and clock out.[87] ESB clerks were recruited on the basis of their results in the Leaving Certificate examination and competition was keen. They were relatively well paid, yet the work was often routine, so in a growing economy they felt increasingly frustrated,[88] and appear to have sought compensation for their frustration by pay demands. As the ESB was a capital-intensive company without a direct competitor, pay increases were not a significant additional cost and were often conceded without dispute. However, increases for ESB clerks triggered demands for comparable increases in other parts of the public sector. The government tried to establish a common scale across the public sector in order to stop the escalating cycle of wage and salary increases. In 1966, the Quinn Tribunal

[84] *Report of inquiry into strikes in Bord na Móna in November 1967 and February/March 1968 conducted by Charles Mulvey* (Dept. of Labour, 1968, V5).
[85] *Final Report of the Committee on Industrial Relations in the ESB* (Dept. of Labour, 1969, V2/1).
[86] Maguire, *Servants to the public*, p. 186.   [87] McCarthy, *Decade of upheaval*, pp. 101–4.
[88] McCarthy, *Decade of upheaval*, pp. 134–5.

recommended one salary grade across the public service[89] – a recommendation that challenged history and tradition.

The arrival of foreign-owned industries could give rise to problems in industrial relations. Many located in areas lacking an industrial tradition and some rural workers found difficulty in adjusting to factory discipline. The German crane manufacturer Liebherr, one of the first of the new wave of foreign-owned industries, complained that it was difficult to hire and retain workers in its Killarney plant. One official described the Irish worker as 'a bird of passage', who would take a job for a while and then move on. Liebherr found it difficult to deal with a population where 'the mentality of the industrial worker did not exist'; there was an absence of the kind of vocational training that would be common in Germany, so they had a very high proportion of trainees. Liebherr were surprised to discover that workers from neighbouring counties and districts would not settle in Killarney. However, they conceded that when trained, Irish workers 'learned well and were adapting themselves to desired routines, such as punching the clock and changing out of overalls before going to the restaurant'.[90] The Irish structure of trade unions and labour relations was very different to Germany or Holland. Liebherr, who was reputed to have faced fifteen strikes in the first five years of operations, complained of having to conduct separate negotiations with eighteen labour unions; in Germany, negotiations were conducted with a single works council. Many disputes in new foreign industries related to requirements that workers meet quality and productivity targets. A long-established leather goods factory in the Midlands was taken over by a German owner, who threatened to close if output did not increase; he also threatened to send a report on his experiences to 'all competent German authorities in order to warn all German Factories of what they have to expect in Ireland'. Production was low, quality unsatisfactory, workers were not trying to increase their incomes by achieving the promised productivity bonus and the productivity of some Irish workers who had been trained in Germany had fallen since their return to Ireland. This factory also faced a series of wage demands as rival trade unions sought to recruit workers by escalating pay claims.[91] The IDA was unwilling to become involved in this dispute, referring the matter to Industry and Commerce, who were equally determined to sit on the fence.[92]

In the Shannon industrial estate, however, SFADCO attempted to anticipate labour relations difficulties by recruiting a Dutch expert (Vermullen) to advise on industrial relations. They held regular meetings

[89] McCarthy, *Decade of upheaval*, p. 110.
[90] NAI DT S2850 H/61; F-G/94 Control of Manufactures Act Proposed amendment: encouragement of Foreign Capital.
[91] *IT*, 24 January 1962.   [92] NAI DT S2850 F-G/91.

with trade union representatives; SFADCO recognised the ITGWU as the primary trade union negotiator/recruiter on the estate. SFADCO also tried to resolve industrial disputes through local negotiations before the matter went to the Labour Court. These arrangements presupposed that new firms locating at Shannon were willing to recognise trade unions. Given Shannon's concentration on US companies, this was rather improbable, and in 1967 a very bitter dispute erupted over trade union recognition between the ITGWU and EI – a subsidiary of the giant US firm General Electric, which was a flagship company on the industrial estate. The ITGWU, which had recruited approximately 300 of the 1,000 workers, made a claim for improved working conditions on behalf of their members. EI refused to negotiate (the company had a no union policy), arguing that trade union members were in a minority. During the ensuing strike buses transporting workers to the plant were burned and there were many allegations of intimidation. EI brought a case to the High Court, arguing that no dispute existed, because only a minority of workers were union members. In April 1968, the Supreme Court determined that a trade dispute did exist and the strike ended shortly afterwards with the company recognising the union.[93] While the EI dispute has come to be seen as a landmark industrial dispute – and it set an important precedent for the recognition of trade union rights in foreign-owned industries – in other respects it was atypical. The striking workers were mainly young women working in unskilled/semi-skilled jobs on assembly lines, not the typical figure who was involved in major strike-action during that decade.

Public sector workers such as teachers and guards were among the most militant, fearing a loss of relative income vis-à-vis the private sector. In the 1950s, they were viewed as privileged workers (as were bank clerks), holding secure pensionable posts in a country where such jobs were hotly contested. The more dynamic economy however saw relative affluence spread more widely and this resulted in a loss of status among these previously privileged groups. Bank officials recruited in the 1920s were guaranteed to reach an income level three to four times the average male industrial wage, even if they failed to become managers; those recruited in the mid-1930s could aspire to earn three times the average industrial wage; by the early 1970s the gross maximum pay of a senior bank official – the male career grant – was roughly twice the industrial wage, and this differential was further eroded by income tax.[94] The prestige of a career in

---

[93] Callanan, *Ireland's Shannon story*, pp. 88–91.
[94] *Report on dispute of 1970 between the Associated Banks and the Irish Bank Officials' Association and recommendations as to what action might be taken to avoid the risk of closures through industrial action in the future*, by Michael P. Fogarty at the request of Joseph Brennan (Dublin, 1971, R112), p. 183.

banking was falling, even in rural Ireland, where it had traditionally ranked high. A background note on a Department of Taoiseach file concerning the national employer/labour conference noted that 'banks and ESB and other white collar workers have helped to create fears that if unskilled workers get an increase others will press for preservation of differentials'.[95]

Industrial relations difficulties in the banks were also a response to changing structures and work practices. During the 1960s, the main Irish banks (other than the Belfast-based Ulster and Northern Banks) merged into two groups: Allied Irish Banks and the Bank of Ireland Group. Before the merger two of the smaller banks, the Royal Bank and the Hibernian Bank, each employed approximately 500 workers, which made them more akin to a large family firm. Management was informal and paternalistic. Amalgamations severed established institutional loyalties, but existing management styles and practices continued unchanged. Staff who had subscribed to the traditional gentlemanly business culture were uncomfortable at being asked to sell a range of financial products to account holders, including hire purchase and life insurance. Michael Fogarty reported particular hostility to the 'Little Red Book' – not Chairman Mao, but a Bank of Ireland manual for staff, titled 'Banking for the Personal Customer', which set targets for product sales. Fogarty suggested that some of the hostility stemmed 'from dislike of the marketing approach to business in an occupation which in the past has been oriented to a professional rather than a commercial outlook'.[96] The banks had recruited large numbers of young staff shortly after the end of the 1914–1918 war, which meant that the banks had 'a severe promotions block' until the early 1960s, with clerks commonly taking up to twenty years to secure a counter job. Promotion to branch manager commonly came only five–six years before retirement. By the mid-1960s, the promotion blockage had lifted, and the expansion in banking brought 'a flood of new recruits'.[97] More formal and professional recruitment processes ended the practice of favouring children of bankers.[98] By the early 1970s, two-thirds of bank staff had less than eleven years of service; the overwhelming majority of these were under thirty years of age; 60 per cent of female staff was under twenty-five years of age – because of the marriage bar.[99]

The garda síochána was established in the 1920s. Most recruits were young – commonly veterans of the War of Independence; few

[95] NAI DT S17419 from S 15453F.   [96] Fogarty, *Report on bank dispute*, p. 116.
[97] Fogarty, *Report on bank dispute*, pp. 7–8.
[98] D. J. Cogan, *The Irish services sector. A study of productive efficiency* (Dublin: Govt. Stationary Office, 1978), pp. 147–9.
[99] Fogarty, *Report on bank dispute*, p. 7.

former members of the Royal Irish Constabulary joined the new force. By the late 1950s, with the first generation retiring there was a brief period of accelerated promotion, with the average length of service of newly promoted sergeants falling from seventeen years in 1952 to eight by 1961. Once the flood of retirements eased, promotions dried up, and in 1963 the average length of service of new sergeants was fourteen years.[100] A tougher entrance examination meant that new recruits were better educated than their predecessors (commonly with some secondary schooling, whereas their predecessors rarely went beyond primary school), indeed better educated than their boss.[101] New garda recruits like new bank officials were less willing to accept restrictive working conditions than their predecessors, such as the requirements that unmarried members live in official accommodation or pay for this accommodation (a bed in the garda barracks) if they did not use it. Gardaí were subject to regular moves, and married guards resented the disruption to family life, not to mention the difficulty in finding houses in provincial towns. Frustration over working conditions and promotion opportunities resulted in gardaí taking unofficial action – which was contrary to regulations.

A report by the NIEC in November 1965 set out broad principles for an incomes policy linking pay increases to increased output; increases above that norm for some workers should be balanced by below-the-norm increases for others.[102] But most workers believed that they were entitled to above-the-norm increases. In 1968 maintenance workers closed down many firms for six weeks, putting up to 30,000 workers out of their jobs and winning a generous pay award, which others sought to replicate.[103] Industrial relations expert Michael Fogarty described it as producing 'a great monstrosity of a settlement', which 'As regard fair shares to the lower-paid workers (it) put the clock back by a generation'.[104] Two long-running bank strikes in 1966 and in 1970 – when banks closed for over six months – prompted the comment that 'Ireland once again showed itself to have all the marks of a banana republic except the bananas'.[105]

---

[100] *Commission on the Garda Síochána: Report on remuneration and conditions of service Presented to Min Justice Jan 1970.* Prl. 933. Judge Conroy Chairman:hereafter, Conroy Commission, 1970. R119, para 884.

[101] Forty-Five per cent of those recruited between 1962 and 1967 had intermediate certificates, and 31 per cent had matriculated or held a Leaving Certificate (Conroy Commission).

[102] NIEC, *Report on the economic situation,* no. 11, Nov. 1965.

[103] McCarthy, *Decade of upheaval,* pp. 161–9. Their award was £3.50 a week

[104] Fogarty, *Report on bank dispute,* pp. 54–7.

[105] Fogarty, *Report on bank dispute,* p. 38.

Incomes policies were much discussed during the 1960s and in some European countries they formed an integral part of the planning nexus. Many Irish workers, especially those in craft unions or white-collar unions, were members of British unions, and their insistence on protecting the principle of free collective bargaining was at odds with government efforts to promote a more European-style consensus among interest groups that would include an incomes policy. ICTU was a new entity, and if the larger Irish-based general unions had contemplated this course (there is no reason to suggest that they did), it would probably have triggered a new split in the trade union movement. Roche notes that in Ireland 'the unions were initially enticed into consultative bodies and into a gradual re-definition of their role during the 1960s ... because of their stake in the possibilities inherent in national economic development ... They were to be further integrated into the process of public policy, and persuaded to fudge their traditional commitment to free collective bargaining.'[106] Roche also remarked that 'The rise in strike participation and days lost during the 1960s and 1970s occurred in spite of the rising incidence of procedures for conflict avoidance and the growing resort to the conciliation and investigation services of the Labour Court ... the system of wage-fixing had become almost entirely unresponsive to market signals and conditions.'[107] Some workers were awarded pay rises, as their employers faced acute and often fatal competition from imports.

In 1969, Minister for Labour Patrick Hillery claimed that 'the priority is in settling strikes at all costs'; Taoiseach Jack Lynch blamed employers for being too willing to buy industrial peace, but the government as an employer was equally guilty.[108] Hardiman summarises Ireland's industrial relations in the 1960s as follows: 'neither exhortation to match wage increases to the growth in national productivity ... nor direct intervention .... was found to be satisfactory, and deflationary fiscal policy was thought to be a poor substitute for voluntary employer-labour restraint as a means of curbing inflationary wage pressures'.[109] In 1969, the *Third Programme* recommended the establishment of 'a central

---

[106] William K. Roche, 'State strategies and the politics of industrial relations in Ireland since 1945', in T. Murphy (ed.), *Industrial relations in Ireland. Contemporary trends and developments* (Dublin: UCD, 1987), pp. 94–8.

[107] William K. Roche, 'The liberal theory of industrialism and the development of industrial relations in Ireland', in Goldthorpe and Whelan (eds), *The development of industrial society*, p. 317.

[108] DD, 238, col. 2356, 5 March 1969 as cited in James F. O'Brien, *A study of national wage agreements in Ireland* (Dublin, 1981) ESRI paper no. 104, pp. 14, 18.

[109] Niamh Hardiman, *Pay, politics, and economic performance in Ireland 1970–1987* (Oxford: Oxford University Press, 1988), p. 48.

body, advisory in character, and representative of employers unions and Government' to keep price and income trends under review and 'advise on desirable criteria for dealing with prices and incomes in the light of economic and social targets' – an entity that sounds remarkably like the NIEC.[110] Progress was slow. Workers in Cement Ltd., which had a near monopoly on cement output, went on strike for more than a hundred days in 1970 – during the middle of a construction boom; the settlement awarded wage increases of up to 24.5 per cent; cement prices rose by over 10 per cent.[111] A National Pay Agreement was finally agreed late in 1970, following a threat to introduce statutory wage controls. The agreement and its successor in 1972 resulted in a significant fall in the number of days lost through strikes,[112] but pay increases remained well above the European average.

Although a number of studies of incomes policy concluded that they were ineffective, bringing at best a temporary reduction in pay demands,[113] Barry's comparison with Spain, Portugal and Greece suggests that governments could play a role in controlling pay increases. However, none of the three countries mentioned were functioning democracies throughout this period. Incomes policy was widely seen as a key ingredient in sustaining economic growth. Although Irish employers were keen on national wage agreements, trade unions were hostile to centralised bargaining unless the economy was depressed.[114] The sorry state of Irish industrial relations reflected the incapacity of government, union leaders and management to cope with the key challenges presented by a modern industrial economy. A report on industrial relations in the ESB reflected as follows:

In Ireland as in other countries the social and economic conditions underlying industrial relations have happily been changing as a result of economic growth. Aspirations are rising as new standards of living come into reach. There is a better choice of jobs and less risk of unemployment than a generation ago, and education, improved communications, and the regular movement of workers in both directions across the Irish Sea make people more aware than in the past of what is going on in industrial relations elsewhere and how it might be relevant to their own case. All these are reasons why employees today are less ready than in the past to accept managers' or union leaders' decisions without question and are readier to strike out for their own interests.

---

[110] *Third Programme*, chapter 12, pp. 142–6.   [111] *B&F*, 3 July 1970.

[112] Hardiman, *Pay, politics, and economic performance*, p. 93.

[113] Niamh Hardiman, 'The state and economic interests', in Goldthorpe and Whelan (eds), *Development of industrial society*, p. 330; Flanagan, Soskice and Ulman, *Unionism, economic stabilization and incomes policies*, p. 3

[114] O'Brien, *A study of national wage agreements in Ireland*, p. 14.

They went on to note 'dangerous complacency' on the part of management and workers, lack of awareness by senior echelons in the ESB that they had lost the confidence of their managers, and a similar complacency on the part of unions who had failed to gain the confidence of their members.[115]

---

[115] *Final Report, Committee on Industrial Relations in the ESB.*

4   Coping with change 2
Agriculture and rural Ireland

It is time to turn our attention to agriculture, the dominant occupation and way of life in Ireland until this period. The most bizarre feature of the complex network of committees and consultative fora that emerged during the 1960s is the absence of farming representation or the failure to create a parallel set of committees focusing on agriculture. The NIEC, a tripartite forum of employers, trade unions and government officials, was the National Industrial and Economic Council. There was no parallel National Agricultural Council. Lemass justified agriculture's exclusion from the NIEC with the claim that 'agricultural policy is determined to a large extent by external conditions, which we cannot hope to alter by discussions taken here'.[1] This was a false distinction: industrial prices and exports were strongly influenced by external conditions, especially by what was happening in Britain, and from the mid-1960s onwards farm incomes were increasingly determined by the guaranteed prices set by government.

In May 1958, the Taoiseach (de Valera) and Minister for Agriculture Patrick Smith met the NFA (established in 1955) to discuss the current position of agriculture. Such meetings became an annual event, with the NFA presenting the government with a list of priority concerns and demands. In the autumn of 1961, the government met farming organisations and the county committees of agriculture (the local committees that oversaw the agricultural advisory service) to discuss Ireland's application for EEC membership.[2] Given this history of regular meetings, agriculture's exclusion from a national economic council is rather surprising and it left Lemass' government open to the charge of neglecting agriculture, at a time when increases in agricultural incomes lagged behind waged and salaried workers. Agriculture's absence from the NIEC resulted in a rather lop sided process of engagement – with formal structures in place

---

[1] Quoted Daly, *First Department*, p. 446.
[2] Louis Smith and Sean Healy, *Farm organisations in Ireland. A century of progress* (Dublin: Four Courts, 1996), p. 167; Daly, *First Department*, p. 367.

for communicating with employers and unions and more informal ad hoc arrangements for agriculture. One complicating factor was the NFA's demand to be treated as the sole representative of farmers, given the existence of the Irish Creamery Milk Suppliers Association (ICMSA) plus the smaller, more specialist Irish Beet-growers' Association. The NFA was popularly described as 'Fine Gael on tractors', which might have left the government reluctant to accord them sole negotiating rights.[3] The composition of farming representation was obviously a complex question, but it could arguably have been resolved if the government had made serious efforts to do so.[4] Irrespective of the reasons, excluding agriculture from the wider consultative process was a mistake. Agriculture was a significant economic and political force, with the capacity to assist or hamper growth and stability. A broader economic council might have promoted better understanding between agriculture and industry at a time when the respective balance between the two sectors was changing. Exclusion left agricultural interests free to play the victim; they claimed that the government's attitude was 'one of instinctive hostility'.[5]

The story of agriculture is paradoxical: on the one hand, it lost its position as the dominant sector in the economy; on the other hand, the low rate of growth in agricultural output was a drag on the economy, and agriculture's omission from the NIEC might suggest that it had lost its previously dominant position. Yet the share of current expenditure devoted to agriculture rose significantly over the decade, and in 1970 agriculture was the largest single item in the annual spending estimates.

In the 1958 *Programme for Economic Expansion*, agriculture was seen as the sector that could raise Ireland's derisory annual growth rate, but by the end of the five-year period it had manifestly failed that test. The 1958 *Programme* identified a number of key objectives – increased output and productivity, eradicating bovine tuberculosis; improvements in agricultural education and the marketing of agricultural produce and redeploying exchequer funds to reduce the cost of inputs as opposed to subsidising agricultural prices. Rouse notes that the only objective in this list that was achieved was the (partial) eradication of bovine tuberculosis. This was costly and was probably only achieved because of the imminent threat that Irish cattle would otherwise be excluded from the British market.[6]

All the criticism rehearsed earlier about Irish industry: the low standards of management and productivity, the lack of education, lack of

---

[3] FitzGerald, *Planning*, p. 164.   [4] Daly, *First Department*, pp. 443–52.
[5] Daly, *First Department*, p. 449.
[6] Paul Rouse, *Ireland's own soil. Government and agriculture in Ireland 1945–1965* (Dublin: Irish Farmers' Journal, 2000), pp. 200–3.

interest in market research and innovation applied probably with even greater force to agriculture. Farms were the family business par excellence; they passed from father (or mother) to son. Given Ireland's large families, the heir was commonly the son who showed least interest in education. There was no systematic programme to educate future farmers, in part because the Departments of Agriculture and Education fought over who should be in control. The majority of students who attended courses in agricultural colleges, commonly with local authority scholarships, opted for careers away from the farm – often in public service jobs related to agriculture, and only 30 per cent of male students who attended a vocational school returned to farming. A survey of farmers in West Cork in the mid-1960s revealed that only 4 per cent had received any fulltime post-primary schooling.[7] Many farmers preferred their inheriting son to have not received any education in farming, because ignorance maximised parental control and presumably reduced inter-generational strife. The Limerick Rural Survey concluded:

Agricultural education is not held in high esteem by the farmer. He considers that traditional methods are better than those learned at an agricultural college, or from the local instructor. The agricultural colleges and the instructors are accused of being too theoretical, or working under ideal conditions, of not making due allowance for local conditions of soil and climate and of not appreciating the practical and economic difficulties which the farmer must overcome.[8]

A report by a US expert on the provision of agricultural credit in the early 1960s noted that 'while progress is being made the majority of the farmers were satisfied to plod along much as their fathers did before them'.[9] Farmers who plodded along were less likely to have their soil tested, though this would provide guidance on the most effective use of fertiliser; they were more likely to cling to established breeds of cattle, such as the dairy-shorthorn, Ireland's beloved 'dual-purpose cow' – an animal that claimed to be suited for both beef and dairying and was second- or third-best in both categories.

The attitudes of the Department of Agriculture mirrored those of farmers: both were conservative and determined to retain control. The sectoral targets for industry in the *Second Programme* were drawn in conjunction with the NIEC. There was no comparable process for agriculture, so the NFA wrote their own programme, setting very ambitious targets requiring a substantial increase in government subsidies. Officials

[7] Daly, *First Department*, pp. 408–10.
[8] Jeremiah Newman (ed.), *Limerick Rural Survey, 1958–64* (Tipperary: Muintir na Tíre, 1964), pp. 213–4.
[9] Fred Gilmore, *Survey of Agricultural Credit in Ireland* (Dublin: Dept. of Agriculture, 1959).

dismissed the NFA targets as a blatant attempt to secure higher government spending.[10] Yet, in an attempt to placate farming interests the Department of Agriculture insisted on raising the growth targets to figures that the Department of Finance planners regarded as unrealistic. Consciously or unconsciously the NFA and the Department were both playing the same game.

The Department jealously guarded its patch against all intruders; they fought hard to control An Foras Talúntais, (AFT) the Agricultural Research Institute (which was funded by the Department), insisting that it submit detailed annual research plans for scrutiny. The Department insisted on retaining its own research laboratories and trial farms, despite the fact that they might duplicate research carried out by AFT – many of whose staff had post-graduate qualifications from leading US universities. In 1962, John Nagle,[11] secretary of the Department of Agriculture, claimed that there was a danger of 'having, in effect, two Departments of Agriculture in the country'. Minister for Agriculture Patrick Smith expressed the view that 'the Institute is developing at too fast a pace'; he believed that many items on their research programme were 'at best, relatively unimportant'.[12] The long-running dispute over control of agricultural research, which is paralleled by battles over agricultural education, weakened the Department's capacity to persuade sceptical farmers of the benefits of research and education.

The rationalisation of creameries – many of which had been established in the early part of the century when the horse and cart or donkey and cart was the common means of transporting milk (it remained so in many areas into the 1960s) – was yet another instance where rival agencies fought for control. This dispute was between the state-owned Dairy Disposal Company, which owned a number of creameries in the south-west, and the Irish Agricultural Organisation Society (IAOS), the umbrella group for the co-operative movement. A report by US agricultural expert Joseph Knapp recommended liquidating the Dairy Disposal Company and strengthening the IAOS, but the Department, again reluctant to cede control, queried Knapp's recommendations, although they had been approved by Lemass. Attitudes changed when Charles Haughey (Lemass' son-in-law) became Minister for Agriculture in 1964, and the process of rationalising creameries commenced. But changing technology meant that the ideal size of creameries continued to rise – larger

---

[10] Daly, *First Department*, pp. 453–8.
[11] Nagle was among the best-educated civil servants, a graduate of University College Cork in commerce and economics and a post-graduate student in Cambridge. He joined the Irish civil service as an administrative officer in 1933. *DIB* online.
[12] Daly, *First Department*, pp. 395–402; Rouse, *Ireland's own soil*, p. 164.

creameries had lower costs and higher quality. Closing a local creamery, which had been a focal point for the community (and a source of jobs), proved contentious, often requiring long and patient negotiations – brokered by the IAOS.[13]

The marketing of agricultural produce also gave rise to demarcation disputes. In 1957, Seán Moylan, who was Minister for Agriculture for a mere six months, established a committee to review the marketing of agricultural produce – the first such investigation since the 1920s. Irish farmers and producers took little account of consumer wishes with respect to beef, bacon or other produce; they had a monopoly of the domestic market, and farmers believed that anti-Irish prejudice accounted for their inability to secure better prices in Britain.[14] Moylan decided that the Department should not be represented on the committee, though it would provide secretarial support. The report criticised the lack of market research, noting that 'Even though market conditions and requirements may be altering fundamentally, most Irish exporting interests appear to trade in what has been the traditional market for the products which they export.'[15] It recommended establishing powerful export agencies to market eggs, poultry, dairy produce and pigs and bacon, in place of the existing multiplicity of exporters.[16] This proposal mirrored practice in Denmark, which had successfully established a strong national brand for agricultural produce. An Bord Bainne (discussed earlier) was established as a result of this report, but that was the extent of its achievements. The thirty firms exporting Irish bacon to Britain mounted an effective opposition campaign against a similar organisation, and they won the day. The outcome was a half-hearted strengthening of the existing Pigs and Bacon Commission.[17] Another omission/ evasion concerns beef and livestock; the committee determined that a centralised marketing agency for meat would be ineffective and they recommended no changes. A livestock and meat marketing board (Córas Beostoic agus Feola) was established in 1969, but its role was purely promotional – running trade stands at food fairs and similar venues; it did not actively engage in marketing or sales.[18] Vested interests may not have been the sole factor in the reluctance to market agricultural produce. Rouse suggests that 'the Department of Agriculture perceived that Irish produce was uncompetitive in foreign markets and, consequently, attempts to develop a presence in such markets were largely

---

[13] Daly, *First Department*, pp. 487–9.   [14] Rouse, *Ireland's own soil*, p. 188.
[15] *Report on general aspects of the Irish export trade in agricultural produce* (1959, A.47), p. 10.
[16] *Advisory Committee on the Marketing of Agricultural produce* (Dublin: Dept. of Agriculture, Seven reports 1958–59, A42–47).
[17] Rouse, *Ireland's own soil*, pp. 192–5.   [18] Daly, *First Department*, p. 495.

perfunctory'.[19] Marketing boards would also involve greater participation by farmers and other agricultural/food organisations in decision-making. In 1964, when the NFA drew up its alternative version of a *Second Programme for Agriculture*, it included ambitious plans for marketing boards covering all major commodities, with at least half the places filled by farmers, and the remainder by marketing and processing interests, with a sole government representative. They proposed that these boards would constitute a mini-Common Agricultural Policy, with intervention schemes to buy produce at agreed minimum prices. It is no surprise that the government recoiled from proposals that threatened to leave them with large tax bills and little control. However, the spiralling cost of agricultural subsidies from the mid-1960s, suggests that they ended up in a broadly similar position.

Some progress was made though it proved expensive. Cattle breeds diversified to include Friesians and Charolais; by 1964, a majority of cows were inseminated by cattle breeding stations, whose progeny were selected on the basis of milk yields and other quality indicators. The number of cows rose from 1.2 million in the late 1950s – almost identical to the number on the eve of the First World War – to 1.7 million by 1970. Between 1957 and 1963 fertiliser usage increased by two-thirds, perhaps because prices fell by one-third between 1957 and 1960 and remained stable until 1965 (thanks to a government subsidy). However, farmers cut back on fertiliser after 1965 when prices were increased to cover the additional cost of production in the new state-owned nitrogen plant in Arklow,[20] yet another instance where the legacy of self-sufficiency continued to handicap current policy. More fertiliser meant more grass and more livestock; some farmers began to switch from hay, which was dependent on good weather, to silage. The number of tractors almost doubled from just under 44,000 in 1960 to 84,000 by 1970. By 1970, roughly two-thirds of farms of over thirty acres owned a tractor. Cattle were increasingly sold in purpose-built livestock markets, instead of the traditional Irish fair, removing a major health hazard, and an exotic sight for tourists. There were more agricultural advisors working with farmers, especially in western counties, where historically they had been fewer in number because the lower local tax base made local authorities reluctant to appoint them. Creameries began to collect milk in bulk tankers, bringing to an end the daily trip to the creamery by horse or donkey and cart; this probably reduced the amount of local gossip, but farmers had more time for other farm tasks. By the early 1970s there were fewer, larger and more efficient creameries.

[19] Rouse, *Ireland's own soil*, p. 182.   [20] Daly, *First Department*, pp. 343–8.

The rise in agricultural output was costly to taxpayers. The increase in cattle numbers was achieved by offering farmers a subsidy to keep more breeding heifers. By 1967, the Department of Finance was complaining that they could no longer afford 'To pay a farmer £15 for buying or retaining a calved heifer, £30 annually in milk subsidies for milk produced by the heifer and sold to a creamery, a further £50 for an as yet unspecified increase in production whether in terms of milk or cattle or otherwise, and finally a beef subsidy of £15 to £20 at recent rates for each animal slaughtered and exported.' They could have thrown in the cost of export subsidies for the dried milk or cheese produced by the additional cows or the cost of subsiding fat cattle exported to Britain.[21] Although the Department of Finance tried to call halt, the costs continued to rise. An increasing proportion of beef and fat cattle exports were being subsidised and successive budgets had to confront the cost of subsidising the 'rising tide of milk'.[22] Dairying was increasingly seen as giving farmers with middling-sized farms the best prospect of an adequate income. The number of dairy farmers rose steadily and dairying spread into new regions, especially the west of Ireland. Milk prices – set by the government – offered farmers a degree of security, and the monthly cheque from the creamery provided a regular income. But every additional gallon had to be exported at a loss, and the price of milk became a contentious lobbying/bargaining issue on a par with regular wage rounds. In 1968, the government introduced an additional payment on the first 7,000 gallons – a subsidy to smaller producers – despite recommendations to the contrary from an expert advisory group. By 1970, when agriculture was the largest vote in the annual budget, dairy subsidies cost £30.5 million, compared with £4.7 million in 1960.[23]

The sharp increase in subsidies on agricultural produce was the agricultural equivalent of the generous pay awards. Both were political responses to demands for higher incomes, but as with industry, concessions did not buy peace. By 1966, relations between the government and farming organisations had deteriorated to the point that the ICMSA picketed government buildings and Leinster House in May. In the autumn, the NFA embarked on a protest march to Dublin, followed by a lengthy sit-in outside the Department of Agriculture, road blocks and a refusal to pay rates. The tactics were obviously modelled on French farmers' protests. The perception of a growing gap between urban and rural lifestyles, which was undoubtedly a reality in the early1960s, fuelled

---

[21] NAI D/T 99/1/405 D/A Memo to government 21 December 1967 – as cited in Rouse, *Ireland's own soil*, p. 225.

[22] The phrase was used by Minister for Agriculture Charles Haughey, DD 29 April 1965, col. 429.

[23] Daly, *First Department*, pp. 486–91, 498.

rural resentment. In 1966, Minister for Agriculture Charles Haughey commented that 'there is probably a great deal more dissatisfaction and agitation [in the farming community] than there was in the 1930s when things were a great deal worse'.[24] In January 1967, his successor, Neil Blaney announced the establishment of a National Agricultural Council (NAC) with a broadly similar remit to the NIEC, but the NFA boycotted the NAC, which was quietly abolished within two years.[25] It would have been difficult, perhaps impossible, for any Irish government to have a harmonious relationship with the farming community at a time when agriculture's role in the economy was declining, but the breakdown in relations did not promote the modernisation of Irish farming. When the *Third Programme for Economic and Social Development* was being drafted, the Department of Agriculture, yet again, pressed for an annual growth target of 2.5 per cent – a fantasy figure; the compromise agreed was 1.75 per cent – which predictably was not achieved. By then, the Promised Land – EEC membership appeared to be in sight, yet there were growing concerns that it might disrupt rural landownership and 'our way of life'.

'Our very way of life is threatened'

Like the rest of the world we want improved living standards, a better social order. But we also want our Way of Life. Our national history has been a struggle to win the right to achieve a reasonable living for our people, but also to preserve our Way of Life. There were times when the immediate, though not necessarily the long-term, choice appeared to be between material gain or the preservation of our Way of Life. Our forefathers, by a majority, always chose the latter when such a choice had to be made. Now that we are to a great extent independent, we are not faced with the problem of making such a choice. We are faced with a fight to preserve our economy, and it depends on us whether with it we continue the fight to preserve our Way of Life.[26]

The *Irish Catholic* saw 'OUR WAY OF LIFE' as synonymous with the family farm. In 1960, just under half of farms were under thirty acres, and almost one-quarter had less than fifteen acres. Small farms were concentrated in western and northern areas – where land was less fertile. Average farm incomes were only 60 per cent of those in southern counties.[27] The preservation of traditional agriculture and achieving a due balance

---

[24] Martin Mansergh (ed.), *The spirit of the nation: speeches and statements of Charles J. Haughey (1957–86)* (Cork: Mercier, 1986), p. 67. Speech to European Society for Rural Sociology, 22 Aug. 1966.

[25] Daly, *First Department*, pp. 478–81.

[26] *Irish Catholic*, February, 1963; copy on S 17419B.

[27] CSO, *National Farm Survey* (1962), I.110 table 5.

between agriculture and industry were core concepts in Pope John XXIII's encyclical *Mater et Magistra*. Lemass advised all his ministers to keep a copy on their desks.[28] It was presumably reading this encyclical that prompted Lemass in 1961 to identify the problem of 'small (mainly western) farms' as 'the main, if not the only question arising in national economic policy to which we have not yet found a satisfactory answer' – a remarkable statement given the many other problems that existed. An inter-departmental committee was asked to come up with solutions. Their list of recommendations included consolidating farms; better marketing of produce; encouraging dairy farming; education and training programmes for farmers, farm wives and their offspring; and measures to support off-farm employment.[29] Most controversially they recommended that farms owned either by emigrants or elderly farmers without a direct heir should be leased or sold to younger farmers, leaving the owner with his house and a small plot of land. While these proposals could potentially improve the living standards of younger farmers struggling to survive on smallholdings, they aroused passionate resistance and emotional recollections of the land wars and evictions of the late nineteenth century. Land redistribution had been a popular form of political patronage since the foundation of the state. In 1957, the Department of Land reported that a sample survey of cases showed that one-third of the land was allocated to individuals who had made no representation to TDs – which suggests that two-thirds went to those who had.[30] Political interests and social preferences ensured that land was divided among the maximum number of claimants, though a more selective approach would have created larger and more economically viable farms. Minister for Agriculture Patrick Smith (1957–1964) was insistent that the Land Commission divide vacant land among all qualified applicants, whereas they wanted to concentrate on creating holdings of 40–45 acres. He told Dáil Éireann that he had spent his life in a community of small farmers and 'they maintain a social pattern far superior to that obtaining in countries where there are large blocks of land run by advanced methods of mechanisation which eliminate the human element practically entirely'.[31]

Irish Times journalist John Healy, who was the unofficial spokesman for the 'Charlestown Group', a lobby group that campaigned to 'save the West', claimed that 'Official Establishment Dublin and unorganised rural Ireland, despite their Siamese dependence, one upon the other, talk two

---

[28] Horgan, *Seán Lemass*, p. 322.   [29] Daly, *First Department*, p. 422.
[30] Terence Dooley, *The land for the people. The land question in independent Ireland* (Dublin: UCD Press, 2004), pp. 216–9.
[31] Daly, *First Department*, p. 426.

different languages, have different senses of values and priorities and apparently fail to recognise a mutual dependency if there is to be a future'.[32] Healy excoriated proposals to take land from people who were not farming it – commonly emigrants or elderly farmers without dependants – refusing to acknowledge that leasing land to young resident farmers or farmers' sons might enable them to marry and raise a family as opposed to emigrating. While early drafts of the 1965 Land Act included measures for compulsory transfer of land that was not being worked, these were removed. The Act introduced a pension scheme for farmers who sold their land to the Land Commission while keeping their home and a small adjoining area. By 1972, only thirty-five farmers had opted for this scheme.[33] This is not surprising because in 1966 all smallholders in eleven 'western' counties and in West Cork and West Limerick became eligible to collect unemployment assistance, 'farmers' dole', irrespective of income earned on their farms. This measure perpetuated many small-holdings; owners also became eligible for a non-contributory old age pension without giving up their farm.[34] In the Fanad peninsula in Donegal in 1970, 356 of the 820 men aged 20–69 (43 per cent) were claiming unemployment benefit (72) or unemployment assistance (284) – which was paid to uninsured workers; in Fanad West, 74 per cent of adult males received unemployment benefit or more probably assistance. Half of the recipients were landowners. Allowing for dependents, almost one-quarter of the population relied on unemployment benefit or assistance.[35] Rural decline was a Europe-wide problem, for which there was no simple solution; nostalgia for rural life co-existed with a mass exodus of younger people. Ireland was not the only country where propo-sals to transfer land from absent or neglectful owners proved politically unacceptable.[36] Respecting the ownership rights of smallholders, enabling to hold on to their farms while collecting benefit, contributed to social harmony and may have ensured the re-election of TDs and local council-lors, but it crippled the prospects for younger farmers who were trying to create modern economically successful farms.

At issue was a conflict between social objectives and economic reality. The 'Charlestown Group' (named after the Mayo town where Healy was born) wanted to preserve a way of life that they valued. However, the most striking feature of the Group is the absence of any farmer in its

[32] John Healy, *The death of an Irish town* (Cork: Mercier, 1968), p. 76.
[33] Dooley, *The land for the people*, p. 181.   [34] DD, vol. 217, cols. 157–60, 29 July 1965.
[35] James Deeny, *The end of an epidemic. Essays in Irish public health, 1935–65* (Dublin: A&A Farmar, 1995), pp. 165–7
[36] Anna-Christina Lauring Knudsen, 'Romanticising Europe? Rural images in European Union policies', *Kontur*, vol. 12, 2005, pp. 49–58.

ranks: it consisted of four priests, a veterinary surgeon, a baker and veteran left-wing republican Peadar O'Donnell. The leader was Fr James McDyer, who had organised a co-operative vegetable processing plant in the remote Donegal parish of Glencolumbkille. They demanded the identification of pilot areas in other western communities that would replicate the Glencolumbkille vegetable processing scheme; other pilot areas should concentrate on pig or dairy production. A public meeting in Charlestown was followed by other mass meetings; Fr McDyer addressed an estimated 500 farmers in Castlerea in November 1963. Lemass met the group and agreed to establish pilot programmes. When Charles Haughey became Minister for Agriculture in 1964, succeeding Patrick Smith, who had been singularly unsympathetic, he created a special unit to address the needs of western agriculture. Additional advisors were appointed and pilot schemes to improve agricultural output or create non-farm employment were developed. (The programme was reminiscent of the activities of the Congested Districts Board in the years 1891–1923.) Nevertheless, the relationship between what was renamed 'the Committee for the Defence of the West' and the government became increasingly acrimonious. There were disputes as to who should control the new government-funded programmes: the self-appointed committee, which had strong support from the Catholic Hierarchy, or the local authorities, including county development committees, and county committees of agriculture, with a democratic mandate. In response to these demands, Haughey established a consultative council for the west, which he chaired. Ultimately the disagreement between the Committee for the Defence of the West and the government was philosophical: should the action programme concentrate on developing the economy in order to provide the population with a satisfactory standard of living, or should its goal be to preserve a way of life? The Committee was determined to select the most remote areas with poorest soil as pilot development areas – which almost guaranteed that they would fail the development test, whereas officials wanted to select less disadvantaged communities with a prospect of economic regeneration. The division is summarised in a letter written by the western bishops to Lemass:

The people of the small western farms are in a special way representative of the nation inasmuch as they have clung longer than people in other parts of the country to the traditions which are characteristic of the Irish way of life and of Irish culture including the native language. Even if this can be attributed in large part to an accident of history, it is nevertheless a fact. Moreover, their homes have always been nurseries of religious vocations, thus contributing to the building up of Ireland's spiritual empire. We believe that it would be an irreparable loss to the nation and to the Church if they were left to thin themselves out under the merciless operation of economic laws.[37]

By the late 1960s, most Western European countries had created an 'agricultural welfare state', where taxpayers supported family farms through price or income subsidies and Ireland was no exception. By 1973, only 32.8 per cent of household income on farms of less than thirty acres came from farming (including price subsidies); the balance came from non-farm incomes, and state transfers – notably the farmers' dole. On farms of 30–50 acres, farm income only accounted for 57 per cent of household income.[38] In Ireland, as elsewhere, the benefits of this 'agricultural welfare state' were not distributed on the basis of individual need. The CAP can be described as an EEC-wide pooling of national supports for agriculture, with the bill now met by the Community rather than national governments; it constituted a transfer of income from workers in industry/services to farming.[39] The family farm was seen as a privileged entity, worth of protection and support, in a way that the small country shop, local craftsman or local industry was not. Given the centrality of farming to Ireland's economy and self-image, it was probably not surprising that farmers succeeded in securing significant support from the taxpayer. Yet while EEC membership offered a lifeline to Irish agriculture, it was increasingly seen as posing a threat to smaller western farms. The Mansholt Plan, published in 1968, anticipated that 5 million people throughout the EEC would leave farming during the 1970s. It identified three types of farm – those that were commercially viable; development farms with the potential to become viable which would be given substantial assistance to do so; and 'others', whose days were numbered. The majority of Irish farms and the overwhelming majority of western farms fell into the last category. Between 1974 and 1982, only 23 per cent of participating farms were classified as 'development farms', and only 4 per cent as commercial farms; more than 70 per cent were classified as 'others', a description that included farms on low income with little or no capacity to raise them.[40] Given this scenario, it is no surprise that when Mansholt, the EEC Commissioner for Agriculture, visited Ireland,

---

[37] NAI DT S170321/95 Small western farms.

[38] Damian Hannan and Patrick Commins, 'The significance of small-scale landholders in Ireland's socio-economic transformation', in John Goldthorpe and Christopher Whelan (eds), *The development of industrial society in Ireland* (Oxford: Oxford University Press, 1992), p. 89.

[39] Ann-Christina Knudsen, *Farmers on welfare. The making of Europe's common agricultural policy* (Ithaca: Cornell University Press, 2009); Adam Sheingate, *The rise of the agricultural welfare state. Institutions and interest group power in the United States, France and Japan* (Princeton: Princeton University Press, 2001).

[40] Daly, *First Department*, p. 516.

protesting farmers held up signs saying 'Go Home Cromwell' or that the western seaboard recorded a higher no vote in the 1972 referendum on EEC membership.[41] In the event, the more punitive aspects of the Mansholt Plan were never implemented. Few Irish farms, even those without an apparent direct heir, came on the market; most remained in family ownership. Hannan and Commins summarised the position as follows: 'Having battled so long for their land, the Irish smallholders have been very loath to give it up.'[42]

---

[41] Sinn Féin were responsible for the Cromwell/Mansholt analogy, aan de Wiel, 'The Commission, the Council and the Irish application for the EEC, pp. 374–5.

[42] Hannan and Commins, 'The significance of small-scale landholders in Ireland's socio-economic transformation', p. 90.

5   Coping with change 3
Regional and physical planning

Ireland showed little interest in regional or physical planning before the 1960s. The satirical columnist Myles na Gopaleen commented that 'the whole country lacks the population that would sustain even the fraction of "planning" that is proper to the temperament and economy of this country . . . The problem to be addressed here is simply that of the falling birth-rate'.[1] Economic development changed the picture, creating new pressures on housing and infrastructure in areas with a growing population and industrial investment, and, paradoxically, even greater pressures from areas where the population was still declining. Ireland, accustomed to population decline and economic stagnation, was ill-equipped to cope with a rising population, industrial development and shortages of houses, office blocks and other trappings of modern life.

Despite efforts to devise measures that would enable small farms to survive, the 1960s brought a growing recognition that manufacturing industry offered a more reliable lifeline to rural Ireland. The spread of industry into small towns, where factories were unknown, changed the culture of communities that were previously dominated by farming. New industries were welcome because they provided much-wanted jobs and their arrival helped to modify some of the traditional prejudices of rural families against factory work. Farmers hoped that children who did not inherit the farm would find work in secure occupations such as the gardaí, nursing, teaching and public service.[2] A 1960 study of rural families in the neighbourhood of the Shannon industrial estate found that they aspired to see their children in white-collar, public service jobs,[3] despite the fact that nearby factories were hiring workers. By the end of the decade, attitudes were changing; Damien Hannan, who surveyed adolescents in

[1] Daly, *Buffer state*, p. 459.
[2] The majority of lower-grade civil servants were Dubliners; the low numbers from rural backgrounds reflect difficulties in accessing secondary schooling. By comparison, the gardaí, where secondary school certificates were not mandatory, recruited large numbers from farming backgrounds.
[3] Callanan, *Ireland's Shannon story*, p. 97.

Cavan – a predominantly rural county – in 1965 and again three years later, reported a more positive attitude towards factory work in 1968 among farmers' sons, though not daughters: 'factory girls' were believed to have less promising marriage prospects; in some instances, local boys were reported as refusing to dance with them.[4] This attitude was not unique to Ireland; French farmers also kept their daughters at school longer than sons and hoped that they would leave the land.[5]

A study of Scariff and Tubbercurry – two small towns in Clare and Sligo – suggested that industrial development offered the best prospect for stabilising the rural population. By 1966, Tubbercurry was home to three factories, established by a returned emigrant, employing 183 workers, making locks, gauges and other metal goods which were exported, or fitted in new Irish houses. The chipboard factory in the village of Scariff (home of the novelist Edna O'Brien) employed approximately 200 workers making veneer for fitted kitchens – a major status symbol of the time.[6] Forty per cent of Tubbercurry workers and 20 per cent of those in Scariff had previously worked in England. Three-quarters of the Tubbercurry workers and half of those in Scariff would have emigrated if these factories had not existed. When farmers took factory jobs, their wives took on more farm tasks.[7] Workers from farming families invested their earnings in farm equipment and fertiliser, and 'generally [that] their farms are better managed'; household spending and living standards rose; most of the money was spent locally, and the population rose.[8]

Irish industrial policy had traditionally favoured the dispersal of industries: one would-be investor in the 1930s was told, 'the farther he decided to go from the city, the greater attraction he would lend to his proposal'.[9] Small factories founded in the 1930s were dotted throughout the midlands and the south, though few had located west of the Shannon. The industrial policy of the 1960s was a modification, but not a reversal of previous practice. Higher regional grants, pressure from the Department of Industry and Commerce and the IDA, ensured that most foreign-owned industries were kept away from Dublin and Cork. By 1973, new grant-aided firms accounted for 60 per cent of manufacturing jobs in the

[4] Damien Hannan, *Rural exodus. A study of the forces influencing large-scale migration of Irish rural youth* (London: Chapman, 1970), p. 253.
[5] Henri Mendras, *The vanishing peasant. Innovation and change in French agriculture* (Cambridge MA, London: MIT Press, 1970), pp. 173–4.
[6] Denis I. F. Lucey and Donald R. Kaldor, *Rural industrialization. The impact of industrialization on two rural communities in western Ireland* (London: Chapman, 1969), pp. 30–40.
[7] Lucy and Kaldor, *Rural industrialization*, pp. 112, 195, 169.
[8] Michael Fogarty, 'Introduction' to Lucy and Kaldor, *Rural industrialization*, pp. 9–11.
[9] Quoted in Mary E. Daly, *Industrial development and Irish national identity, 1922–1939* (Syracuse: Syracuse University Press, 1992), p. 108.

north-west, and over 40 per cent in the west and south-west. The Dublin area, with almost half of manufacturing employment, had less than one-quarter of jobs in new industries.[10] Modern industry needed high-tension electricity, adequate supplies of water, good roads, telephones and housing for managers and specialist workers moving into the locality. A CIO report in December 1962 recommended that a small number of regional development centres should be given priority for investment in essential infrastructure. In 1965 (note the time lag), two pilot industrial estates were announced for Waterford and Galway, with advance factories available for rent, at subsidised rates (Northern Ireland had been offering advance factories for some years). Additional centres would be identified when regional studies carried out on behalf of the Minister for Local Government were complete.[11] The NIEC urged a selective approach to identifying further development centres, but conscious of the political dividends – positive and negative – the government rejected their opinion that development centres were unlikely to be effective in Ulster or Connacht, with the exception of Galway.[12]

When it became evident that regional growth centres and industrial estates were being contemplated, parish-pump politics swung into action with a vengeance. Noel Griffin, managing director of Waterford Glass, wrote a sycophantic letter to Lemass expressing his delight at Waterford's selection. Tralee, Longford and Sligo and Thurles lobbied to be included in the next phase of industrial estates, as did Cork, which was seen as having the necessary infrastructure to attract industries, and therefore not needing an industrial estate. Donegal TD and Minister for Local Government, Neil Blaney reminded the committee charged with identifying future locations that the government did not accept the NIEC's view that industrial estates would be ineffective in the north-west – that is, Donegal.[13] Limerick TD and Minister for Education Donogh O'Malley protested at Limerick–Shannon–Ennis being described as an established centre. He claimed that all development was concentrated at the airport and expressed concern that industries that might have located in Limerick would be diverted to Galway and Waterford. He wanted to see industries in Limerick city of the kind *given* (my emphasis) to Galway and Waterford. The fact that Ireland's

[10] McAleese, *A profile of grant-aided industry*, p. 23. O'Farrell, *Regional industrial development trends*, table 1, pp. 52–5.

[11] CIO, *Interim Report on state aid* (Dublin: Dept. of Industry and Commerce, 1962, I. 109), pp. 9–12; CIO, *Report of Committee on development centres and industrial estates* (Dublin: 1965, Dept. of Industry and Commerce, I. 110); NIEC, *Comments on report of committee on development centres and industrial estates* (Dublin: Dept. of Finance,1965, F.66/8).

[12] NAI 97/6/639A; 97/6/90 Development centres designation.   [13] NAI 97/6/90.

largest industrial estate was at Shannon, a short drive from Limerick appears to have fuelled Limerick's sense of grievance. When Limerick Junior Chamber of Commerce invited Minister for Labour and Clare TD Paddy Hillery to address them in 1967, as part of their campaign for designation as a development centre (distinct from Shannon and Ennis), he responded in a rather high-handed manner: 'I am sure that the people in Ennis and other towns in County Clare, who have gone out and succeeded by their hard work in bringing industry to Clare, will be willing to advise and help their less active brothers. I do not think, however, that Clare people want to tie our County to the less successful people of Limerick and their various gyrations.' Hillery forwarded a copy of this letter to Taoiseach Jack Lynch, emphasising that he was writing on Dáil Éireann, not ministerial notepaper, 'to distinguish the Clare TD from the member of the government'.[14]

The histrionics of Hillery and O'Malley – not to mention Blaney's intervention – reflect intense competition for designation as a growth centre. Growth centres would secure priority investment in advance factories, water, sewerage, telephones, roads and housing; thus the potential benefits were considerable. British planning consultants, Colin Buchanan and Partners was commissioned by the United Nations, in association with An Foras Forbartha – the national planning authority – to draft a report on regional centres, drawing on existing regional plans for Dublin and Limerick. Their report would be reviewed by a ministerial committee, who would report to Cabinet.[15] Buchanan presented several options. The most extreme would concentrate all development in Dublin. He recommended a three-tier strategy, with Cork and Limerick-Shannon as the main development centres outside Dublin. Growth in Dublin would be neither discouraged nor encouraged. Waterford, Dundalk, Drogheda, Sligo, Galway and Athlone were designated as regional growth centres. To placate areas at a distance from these towns, Letterkenny and Tralee were identified as local centres, with the promise that two further local centres would be identified in counties Mayo and Monaghan/Cavan/Longford.

If this strategy was adopted, Buchanan anticipated that every region except the north-west would record a higher population in 1988. He presented the government with a choice: it could opt for dispersion which would mean a lower rate of growth and higher emigration, or for higher growth, less emigration and less dispersion. A continuation of current policies would mean a lower population loss in the north-west, at the cost of a lower national population and

---

[14] NAI 98/6/695.   [15] NAI DT 98/6/887; Regional Development General.

higher emigration.[16] The determination of Hillery, O'Malley and Blaney to maximise constituency interests at the expense of the national interest suggests that Buchanan's recommendations were doomed before they were drafted. The report was submitted to government in September 1968, and there it languished; the succession of pink slips noting that the Cabinet had postponed discussion indicates that the government was seriously divided. Opposition was led by Blaney, now Minister for Agriculture, and Mayo TD and Minister for Lands, Michael Moran. Both complained that Buchanan had neglected the West. Moran invoked a campaign by Achill islanders for 'human rights' and their demand that Achill and Mayo be declared 'disaster areas' to bolster his demand for immediate action on a government pledge to move the Department of Lands (his Department) to Castlebar, Mayo.[17] The Buchanan Report was eventually published in May 1969 (shortly before a general election), without a government endorsement – which was the kiss of death. The accompanying press release merely noted that the recommendations would be referred for further consideration 'in the context of proposals for regional development generally'. Lack of government support negated the endorsement given to Buchanan by the NIEC. They emphasised that 'it is important the Buchanan strategy is seen in its proper perspective. It must not be viewed as a strategy for apportioning the economic growth that will in any case occur, and the benefits that will follow from it, in a particular way along the different parts of the country. It is rather a strategy which will accelerate growth to the rate which will make full employment a realisable objective.'[18] Nobody listened.

The report was welcomed by the small number of selected towns; the remainder were vociferous in expressing outrage, and the losers far outnumbered the winners. What Padraic White describes as 'the west of Ireland triumvirate' – journalists John Healy, Jim Maguire and Ted Nealon 'generated immense firepower in favour of the west through skilful use of the media'. White, one of the authors of the IDA Regional Industrial Plans, 1972–1977, was a native of Leitrim and therefore in sympathy with the 'triumvirate'. The IDA set targets for manufacturing jobs for 172 towns and villages, excluding the Gaeltacht and Mid-West (Limerick region), which was the SFADCO's responsibility.[19] In contrast

[16] Colin Buchanan and partners, *Regional studies in Ireland* (Dublin: An Foras Forbartha, 1969), paras 351–6.

[17] NAI DT 2000/6/338, 10 January 1969.

[18] NIEC, *Report on physical planning*, 1969, paras 13–17.

[19] NESC, *Regional policy in Ireland a review* (Dublin, 1974), p. 48.

to Buchanan, the IDA appeared to offer 'jam for everyone' – or almost everyone, though at a significant cost for the national economy. Retrospective analysis has vindicated Buchanan's plan as offering both national and regional benefits. In 2001, when the Minister for the Environment and Local Government, Noel Dempsey, launched the National Spatial Strategy in Charlestown, he mentioned that he had specifically chosen the location because of the town's links with *Irish Times* journalist John Healy and the campaign for the future of the West. He went on to describe Buchanan Report as 'an opportunity wasted':

Buchanan foretold how Ireland would develop in the decades ahead unless the future was carefully planned. He warned how Dublin would develop at the expense of the rest of the country. He offered an alternative blueprint to ensure balanced regional development. He advocated the establishment of some large centres throughout the country as a counterbalance to the tilt towards the capital city .... There was a groundswell against Buchanan's proposals. Local interests were put first ... by a range of people ... politicians, the local media, the public ... with disastrous consequences for the country as a whole and for the west and midlands in particular. The report was 'shelved' – because people were so parochial in their outlook that they couldn't bear what they saw as neighbouring towns benefiting at the expense of their own localities.[20]

Yet, the IDA's commitment to scattering industries throughout 172 towns and villages was not supported by essential investment in modern infrastructure. In contrast to other Western European countries, Ireland made no attempt to develop a network of motorways. Road spending continued to focus on local rather than national priorities. The main concern was providing jobs for unemployed/under-employed labour, by doling out money annually for labourers to fill potholes. These jobs were a form of political patronage. Tentative efforts to develop modern dual-carriageways were roundly condemned in the media. Suggestions that towns such as Naas – a major bottleneck on all road journeys from Dublin to the south and south-west – should have a bypass aroused vocal opposition from local traders, who feared the loss of business from the passing trade, so industries in remote areas had to contend with roads that were not suited to heavy goods traffic, resulting in additional costs, and record death rates on Irish roads. Although responsibility for national roads was transferred from local authorities to the Department of Local Government in 1970, this did not result in a major investment programme.[21] A similar reluctance to invest in telecommunications

20 Speech at launch of public consultation paper on the national spatial strategy 'Indications for the Way Ahead', Charlestown Co. Mayo, 5 September 2001.
21 Daly, *The buffer state*, pp. 492–3.

meant that it often proved difficult to secure a phone line for a new factory (not to mention the manager's home). In extremis, the IDA had to identify a private phone subscriber who might be willing to relinquish their phone line in return for a financial payment. Although the lack of phones and the quality of service – in many provincial towns it was dependent on a manual exchange – prompted many complaints by industrialists, this was not remedied until the 1980s.[22] An adequate system of motorways was not completed until the twenty-first century.

The focus on 'the west' as *the* underprivileged area is not supported by statistics. The key differentiation was between urban and rural Ireland. By 1966, all 97 towns with 1,500 residents or more (excluding the four county boroughs and Dun Laoghaire), regardless of region, recorded a population increase, and the rate of growth accelerated between 1966 and 1971. 'All provinces share[d] nearly equally.'[23] An ESRI study concluded that 'possibly for the first time in Ireland as regards small and middle-sized towns, many have a great future growth potential'; there was no evidence that '*any* town is doomed to stagnation'.[24] Estimates of county incomes questioned 'the received wisdom' – that the three Ulster counties plus Connacht, Kerry and West Cork were poor, while eastern and southern counties were 'relatively rich'. By 1966, the east-rich, west-poor division no longer applied. Income per head of the workforce and income per capita was higher in Kerry and Clare than in Laois, Offaly or Wexford. As for farm incomes, Westmeath and Offaly fared worse than Clare and Kerry.[25] In 1969, the poorest counties were Leitrim, Donegal, Roscommon, Mayo, Longford, Laois and Cavan; incomes were rising most rapidly in Clare, Monaghan, Mayo and Louth: the greatest relative deterioration was in Meath, Offaly and Laois.[26] The expansion of dairy farming boosted farm incomes in Munster and Monaghan; the impact of the Shannon industrial zone on Clare was also evident. The 1973 Survey of New Industry showed that the west, north and south-west had attracted a higher share of new jobs, relative to population. The big losers were Sligo-Leitrim and midland counties such as Offaly, Laois and Longford. Baker and Ross suggested that instead of the traditional east/west division, it would be 'much more practical to think now in terms of a

[22] Personal knowledge.

[23] D. Curtin, R.C. Geary, T. A. Grimes, B. Mention, *Population growth and other statistics of middle-sized Irish towns* (Dublin: ESRI paper 85, April 1976), table 1.1, p. 14. The percentage increase in Ulster and Leinster was 7.8; Munster 7.5 and Connacht 6.8.

[24] M. Ross, *Further data on county incomes in the sixties* (Dublin: ESRI paper 64, May 1972), table B, pp. 83–4.

[25] T. J. Baker and M. Ross, 'The changing regional pattern in Ireland', *ESR*, vol. 1, no.1, 1969, pp. 155–61.

[26] Ross, *Further data on county incomes in the sixties*, table B.

continuous spectrum of counties, ranging from the very poor and little developed, such as Leitrim, Mayo and Longford, through the majority of counties a little on either side of the average, to the undoubtedly well-developed and relative rich counties such as Louth and Waterford'.[27] But no lobby group campaigned on behalf of the less-romantic and less clearly identifiable midlands, and lobbyists failed to acknowledge the regional impact of non-farming incomes or welfare payments.

Dublin: development and destruction

The obverse to the privileged place assigned to rural life in Ireland's political and cultural discourse was an ingrained hostility to Dublin and the belief that cities were incompatible with Irish nationalist identity. 'Is Dublin too big' was a regular topic for debate, especially in the 1950s when the national population was falling steadily.[28] But despite repeated complaints that Dublin was sucking population from rural Ireland, the rate of internal migration was 'exceptionally low by international standards'.[29] Throughout the first half of the twentieth century, life expectancy in Dublin was lower than in rural Ireland; infant mortality was above the national average. Although the gap had narrowed by the early 1960s, age-specific mortality in urban areas remained above the national average.[30] Dublin was both a winner and a loser as the economy developed. Growing employment in modern services such as banking, insurance and the public sector created many opportunities for young men and women with secondary schooling. The numbers living within the centre city fell as tenements were demolished to make way for modern offices. Until the 1960s, it was possible to walk from the most northerly points of the built-up city in Finglas to the southern extremities in Rathfarnham/Crumlin. By the 1970s, Dubliners were living much farther afield. But after a century of population decline, politicians, officials and the construction sector were ill-prepared to respond to rising demand for housing, modern offices and higher car ownership. While the problems

---

[27] Baker and Ross, 'The changing regional pattern in Ireland', p. 164. Their analysis excluded Dublin.

[28] Symposium, 'Is Dublin too big', *Administration*, vol. 2, 1954 (the fact that this symposium was organised by public servants is especially noteworthy). See *also Commission on Emigration and other Population Problems, 1948–54* (Dublin, 1955 R.63).

[29] David Rottman, 'The changing social structure', in Litton (ed.), *Unequal Achievement*, p. 81.

[30] Mary E. Daly, 'Death and disease in independent Ireland c.1920–c.1970: a research agenda', in Catherine Cox and Maria Luddy (eds), *Cultures of care in Irish medical history, 1750–1970* (Basingstoke: Palgrave Macmillan, 2010), p. 236.

that resulted from ill-thought-out developments were most evident in Dublin, they were also evident in provincial cities.

The 1960s marked the peak of belief in modernism and a relentless urge to discard the urban fabric of the past to make way for large constructions in glass, steel and concrete and car-friendly cities. This was true almost everywhere, not just in Dublin. The dozy state of the economy and neutrality in the Second World War meant that Dublin had experienced very little destruction and rebuilding since the 1920s. Many commercial and government offices were located in Georgian townhouses but legislation introduced in 1958 set minimum standards for offices employing more than five people, which proved difficult to meet in older buildings.[31]

By 1962, plans were well advanced for several large office blocks in central Dublin, including a twelve-storey development on the site of the Carlisle Building, a landmark late Georgian building that framed the southern vista from O'Connell Bridge. Developments were underway along both banks of the Grand Canal with a headquarters for Bord Fáilte (the state tourist board) on Baggot St, which was part of Dublin's core Georgian streetscape, and modern offices for Carroll's Tobacco Company and the state-owned Irish Life Insurance Company.[32] In 1965, the seventeen-floor Liberty Hall, headquarters of the ITGWU, opened – Ireland's tallest building until it was overtaken by Cork County Hall. The opening of the US embassy in Ballsbridge in 1964[33] kicked off a scramble for office and hotel developments in that area, many of them high rise (by Dublin standards), and out of keeping with the high-quality Victorian streetscape. But Victorian architecture was held in low esteem at this time, not just in Dublin.

In 1959, in an effort to revive the depressed construction sector, ministers and officials met British investors to discuss possible commercial developments in central Dublin. Whitaker told representatives of the Norwich Union Assurance Company that Dublin had a shortage of modern offices. They blamed this shortage on laws, protecting tenants against repossession and rent increase.[34] 'So long as this type of legislation existed, the redevelopment of the central areas ... cannot be expected to progress in a manner comparable with that of other capital cities in the world today.' Norwich Union claimed that there was an urgent need for legislation that would give a landlord 'reasonable rights to regain possession of property he wishes to rebuild'. In 1962, another British firm Lang Development approached the government with plans for a major

---

[31] Frank McDonald, *The destruction of Dublin* (Dublin: Gill & Macmillan, 1985), p. 13.
[32] *Hibernia*, Dublin diary, Alex Newman, September 1962; November 1963.
[33] *Hibernia*, June 1964.   [34] Daly, *Buffer state*, p. 460.

redevelopment of central Dublin, which would require legislation to 'facilitate redevelopment' and enable Irish cities and towns to adapt to the motor age. There were plans for an inner ring road to facilitate traffic flows around the city; proposals to fill in the Grand Canal in order to widen the adjoining roadway and to partly cover sections of the River Liffey along the quays to provide parking space for cars – a proposal endorsed by Erskine Childers, Minister for Transport and Power. Although neither of these extreme ideas was implemented, other developments wrought irrevocable damage to the city's architectural heritage.

The 1963 Planning Act was almost a carbon copy of the 1962 Town and Country Planning Act of England and Wales. The primary purpose was to facilitate industrial and commercial development, including the redevelopment of built-up areas regarded as run-down. Much of central Dublin was owned by a large number of small property-owners, and the legislation gave local authorities power to acquire these properties which could then be leased or sold to a developer, as recommended by Norwich Union.[35] The Act created eighty-seven planning authorities, who were required to draw up development plans, zoning land for future use, setting out proposals for current and future traffic needs and future amenities such as parks. Most planning authorities were too small to do this job effectively, so the government designated nine planning regions, and went on to commission consultants' reports on the Dublin and Limerick regions. A 1969 statement emphasised that 'planning authorities will, in future, be more active in using their powers to assist and encourage suitable enterprises in their areas'.[36] In 1972, the Department of Local Government reiterated that local authorities should follow a policy of 'doing all they can to facilitate desirable developments, including housing developments, and not to frustrate these developments by the unduly rigid application of controls'.[37]

Once the 1963 Act was in place, Dublin Corporation commissioned British planner Nathaniel Lichfield to devise plans for the north-city area west of O'Connell St. He proposed a complete reconfiguration of the existing streetscape to create a large shopping precinct. A delegation from Dublin Corporation travelled to British and European cities to view other examples of city-centre planning.[38] The 1960s zeitgeist favoured the

---

[35] Daly, *Buffer state*, pp. 458–68.
[36] NAI Government Information Bureau, 19 May 1969.
[37] NAI 2008/79/724 408/137/2 Pt IX. Monograph prepared by Department of Local Government in response to a UN questionnaire circulated by the UN Economic Commission for Europe, 23 June 1972. Quoted in Elaine A. Byrne, *Political corruption in Ireland 1922–2010. A crooked harp?* (Manchester: Manchester UP, 2012), p. 78.
[38] Erika Hanna, *Modern Dublin. Urban change and the Irish past 1957–1973* (Oxford: Oxford University Press, 2013), pp. 37–8.

relentless remodelling of urban space – Dublin was keen to join this movement, perhaps because this was seen as evidence that Ireland had come of age as a modern economy.

In 1961, the ESB announced a major architectural competition to rebuild its offices in sixteen Georgian houses on Fitzwilliam St. While this was not the first demolition of Georgian buildings, it threatened Dublin's longest surviving Georgian streetscape. A public meeting to protest at this decision attracted 900 people; a further 200 were unable to gain entry.[39] Dublin Corporation rejected the winning design by Dublin architects Sam Stephenson and Arthur Gibney but they were overruled. While Minister for Local Government Neil Blaney has generally been blamed for this decision, Hanna presents convincing evidence that Lemass, not Blaney, was responsible.[40] The demolition of Fitzwilliam St heralded the way for an assault on St Stephen's Green. By 1966, Stephenson was involved in three separate projects on the Green. When Desmond Guinness of the Irish Georgian Society urged him to concentrate on developing the large areas of the city with less architecturally significant properties, Stephenson replied that developers were not interested in these areas, 'They want a building where they want it, not where they are told to have it.' When Guinness protested that St Stephen's Green should be preserved, Stephenson countered that 'this sort of preservation is more than Dublin can afford'.[41] In 1966, An Taisce (Ireland's National Trust) sent Dublin Corporation a document setting out which parts of Dublin should be protected; the area in question accounted for barely one-twentieth of the central city.[42] But given that no planning permission was required for demolition, the odds were stacked against conservation.

The battle over Georgian Dublin saw rival sides invoking the rhetoric of development and preservation, nationalism and the legacy of Anglo-Irish colonialism. Frank McDonald quotes an *Irish Times* article published on New Year's Eve 1959: 'It is well-known that, as far as the central city is concerned, the days of Dublin's Georgian heritage are numbered and that when these decayed and obsolete monuments of a past age come to be demolished, many of their sites will be redeveloped with buildings much larger in bulk and greater in height than the present ones.'[43] John Healy, *Irish Times* journalist and lobbyist for the west of Ireland, claimed that 'over the last five years the preservation of what is, basically, a couple of hundred acres of Dublin, has exercised the public and national mind

[39] Frank McDonald, *The destruction of Dublin* (Dublin: Gill & Macmillan, 1985), pp. 19–22.
[40] Hanna, *Modern Dublin*, pp. 90–3.   [41] *Hibernia*, September 1966.
[42] *Hibernia*, January 1967.   [43] McDonald, *The destruction of Dublin*, p. 7.

more than the rural decay of a people, a land and a way of life'.[44] Healy's comment epitomises the politics of envy that characterised the decade; any comparison of the volume of files in National Archives or newspaper on the two topics (with the possible exception of the *Irish Times* letters page) would refute his argument. Populist nationalist rhetoric joined forces with property developers to campaign for the demolition of Georgian property. When the Green Property company became embroiled in controversy over its plan to demolish houses in Hume St, *Business and Finance* came to their support arguing that 'Dublin badly needs to be torn down and rebuilt. There are too many people in damp, ill-lit poorly-equipped offices.'[45] Developers and architects linked nationalism and modernism, defining Irish modernism in opposition to Georgian architecture. Insofar as they looked to the past, their references came from pre-Norman Ireland.[46]

Disputes over conservation became more heated in 1969 when students squatted in vacant houses in Hume St – adjoining St Stephen's Green – to prevent their demolition. The sit-in ended when security workers broke into the building in the early morning and forcibly removed the squatters. The face-saving compromise agreed was a development with pastiche Georgian buildings. Minister for Local Government Kevin Boland claimed that 'the physical needs of the people must get priority over the aesthetic needs of Lord and Lady Guinness'.[47] 'If I have to choose between preserving the entity of Hume Street and Ely Place for those who have time to enjoy its beauty *and* providing the housing that will eventually eliminate the eyesores on the Naas Road [people living in caravans], I will choose the latter and accept the vilification'[48] though it is unclear how demolishing houses in Hume St would relieve the housing problem.

Tenements and tower-blocks: solving the housing crisis

Boland and the squatting students had one thing in common. Both linked the redevelopment of central Dublin with an acute housing shortage. In the decade after the ending of the Second World War, successive governments had invested heavily in housing – both local authority schemes and assisting owner-occupiers. Investment in housing was significantly reduced during the crisis of 1956–1958. *Economic Development*

---

[44] Healy, *The death of an Irish town*, p. 75.   [45] *B&F*, 15 December 1967.
[46] Hanna, *Modern Dublin*, chapter 2, and especially pp. 59–60
[47] Quoted McDonald, *Destruction of Dublin*, p. 95.
[48] Boland to An Taoiseach, Jack Lynch 21July 1969, NAI 2000/6/650 Planning Appeals General, as quoted in Byrne, *Political corruption in Ireland*, p. 78.

recommended that public investment should be diverted to more productive purposes, because the post-war housing programme was
deemed to be complete. In 1959, shortly after he became Taoiseach,
Lemass told local authorities that he was keen to increase employment
in construction – but in projects other than housing. Between 1958 and
1964, the Departments of Finance and Local Government rejected
applications by local authorities for capital funding for housing or sanitary services so severely that spending fell short of the modest targets set
in the *Programme for Economic Expansion*. Housing only accounted for
one-sixth of the public capital programme, compared with one-third in
the years 1949–1958. The 1957/1958 Report of the Department of
Local Government claimed that many local authority houses and flats
in Dublin were vacant because the tenants had emigrated.[49] But the
reduction in housing investment was too severe and was not reversed in
time.

A survey completed by local authorities in 1963 showed that 60,000
occupied houses were unfit for habitation; 32,000 of these were beyond
repair. The overwhelming majority, 27,000, were in rural areas. In addition, some 1950s emigrants had returned home, and the number of
marriages was rising. The 1964 White Paper on Housing acknowledged
a significant, unmet need at all levels of society. It set an annual target of
12,000–13,000 additional houses, almost double the 7,500 completed in
1964. While the eradication of 'rural slums' was a serious issue, the most
immediate pressures were felt in Dublin, Galway and towns where new
industries had located. Most provincial towns could not cope with an
influx of even ten or twenty families. There were few private houses for
rent. Local authority housing was allocated on the basis of waiting lists,
which gave preference to families long resident in the area. Liebherr had
to build houses for key workers, because there were no houses available
for rent or purchase in Killarney, only to find that they could not get a
mains water connection. They had to draw water from the Killarney
lakes.[50] A government agency, the National Building Agency, was created
to construct housing in such cases.

Dublin had a long history of poor-quality housing, and Dublin
Corporation had an equally long record of lurching from one housing
crisis to another. In June 1963, three tenement houses collapsed in central
Dublin with the loss of four lives. When the dangerous buildings section
of Dublin Corporation surveyed other tenements after these tragedies,
they ordered the evacuation of 367 buildings, which were home to 1,189
families. The displaced families were rehoused in caravans, chalets and

---

[49] Daly, *Buffer state*, pp. 439–40.   [50] NAI DT, S2850 F/94.

the former Richmond Barracks, which was also home to families who had returned from England. Dublin's housing crisis prompted the construction of a new community in Ballymun on the city outskirts: Ireland's first experiment with tower-blocks. The project, carried out by the National Building Agency on behalf of Dublin Corporation, was utopian in its conception – a new community, incorporating modern materials and a modernist style of living. The original blueprint for such schemes came from the Swiss architect Le Corbusier whose first Unité d'Habitation – housing tower blocks – were erected in Marseilles in the late 1940s. By the 1960s, many British cities had followed this model, with tower-blocks, centrally heated, with elevators, erected in large open spaces with communal playgrounds. Ballymun was designed to make maximum use of prefabrication. This was believed to offer the prospect of cheaper housing, which could be erected speedily, at a time when the Irish construction industry was extremely stretched. Before embarking on the Ballymun project, Minister for Local Government Neil Blaney and senior officials travelled to California to view system-built apartment complexes in the Los Angeles area. It was this vision – not yet shattered by race riots or reports of crime and vandalism – that guided the project. Blaney told Dáil Éireann that Ballymun would represent 'a high standard of planning, including play spaces, car parking and landscaping, so as to achieve the optimum integration of this new residential area with the existing city ... shops, schools and other amenities provided *pari passu* with the establishment of the new community ... space for small business and offices, a community hall and meeting rooms, health clinic, swimming pool, sites for churches and 36 acres of open space ... parks and gardens, playgrounds'.[51] Every home would be within easy walking distance of a park, and the entire project would be landscaped.

The first occupants moved to Ballymun in 1966; the seven blocks were named after the signatories of the 1916 Proclamation – a tribute to the Golden Jubilee. It is difficult to know how Ballymun would have fared if the original plan had been followed; such projects are now generally regarded as social and architectural disasters. When it opened, a social worker claimed that 'Most of those rehoused there are delighted with the luxurious accommodation, others have found skyscraper living conditions difficult to adapt to'.[52] One of the first occupants recalled a three-bedroom flat, a tiled bathroom, a gas cooker, central heating and 'all the hot water we could think of ... heaven'.[53] The delay in providing

[51] Daly, *Buffer state*, p. 476.   [52] *Clinical Report, Rotunda Hospital*, 1967, p. 63.
[53] Quoted in Rob Somerville-Woodward, *Ballymun. A history, c.1600–1997.* Synopsis 2 volumes (Dublin: Ballymun Regeneration, 2002), vol. 2, p. 86.

amenities fatally damaged Ballymun's prospects. By 1970, 3,265 dwellings were completed, but work had yet to start on the town centre, shops and cultural and social amenities. Ballymun was already identified with 'faulty lifts and communal psychoses'.[54]

Dublin Corporation provided a record 5,500 houses over a twelve-month period 1967/1968; yet, by 1969 there were 8,302 applications for Corporation housing – more than double the 1963 figure of 3,000 young married couples with two or three children were told that they could not qualify because they had too few children![55] Because of financial pressures, most new developments lacked community services. Eleanor Holmes, the social worker in the Rotunda Maternity Hospital, described the expanding Dublin suburb of Finglas as 'rife with problem families, need[ing] more educational and cultural facilities for all age groups especially the young'.[56]

Housing problems were not confined to Dublin, or to high-rise blocks. Sociologist Rev Liam Ryan described Parkland (a fictional name for a new Limerick local authority estate), where families from overcrowded city-centre properties were relocated, as 'a sprawling low-class residential suburb with its "roads", "avenues", "squares" and "crescents" of monotonous unimaginative houses broken only by a church and a shopping centre'. Houses had three bedrooms, bathroom, sitting room and kitchen with a small garden front and rear. The estate was 'divided by a very wide main road running into the city ... the town-planners made ample provision for the movement of traffic, but unfortunately none at all for the movement of children ... no playgrounds or playing-fields... despite the fact that over half the population of the area is under fifteen years of age. Pushed out of overcrowded homes by distracted mothers, and children with no form of amusement automatically turn to mischief'. The plan involved scattering 'the better families around in the hope that they would set the standard for the locality'. Ryan feared that standards were being determined by the 'lowest common denominator', though he also noted that 'good families' 'where the husband has a steady job, where the wife keeps a reasonably clean house where the children are well dressed and kept under some control ... are in the majority in Parkland and their influence is very slowly helping to transform the whole community'. He concluded by noting that fifteen years earlier 'Parkland was the solution to inadequate housing and city slums. Today it is itself the target for solution'.[57]

---

[54] *B&F*, 18 July 1969.   [55] *Hibernia*, 31 January–11 February 1969.
[56] *Clinical Report, Rotunda Hospital*, 1966, p. 69.
[57] Liam Ryan, *Social dynamite. A study of early school-leavers* (UCC: Sociology Dept., no date but c.1970), pp. 11–13, 18–19, 43.

Girls were reluctant to give a Parkland address when looking for jobs; likewise, girls living in Dublin's Fatima Mansions, a large 1950s flat complex in Dublin, were reluctant to give their home address to boys whom they met at a dance.[58] In a 1971 article titled 'Fatima Mansions: another Unity Flats', *Hibernia* compared Fatima Mansions in Dublin's south inner-city – a large 1950s housing development – with the Unity Flats complex in Belfast which attracted widespread notoriety when violence engulfed that city in the summer of 1969. The comparison was prompted by reports that up to fifty youths had rampaged through Fatima Mansions for several days; yet, the writer claimed that it was 'not a slum; no better and no worse than many other flats'. But the details were grim: 'a financial world ruled by Trading Cheque companies; a visual world from which the colour green has been tidied away by concrete; a world where the dominant smell is the one Brendan Behan described as endemic to all prisons – a smell of excrement and soap'.[59] But inadequate urban housing was not confined to cities: in 1971, only 46 per cent of houses in small Clare town of Kilrush had baths.[60]

Ballymun was an emergency response to Dublin's housing crisis. The Dublin Regional Plan, developed by Myles Wright, recommended that the city's main growth should be westward, where sleepy villages such as Tallaght (population 1956 – 710; 1971 – 6,174), Clondalkin (3,105– 7,009) and Lucan (1,594–4,245) saw their populations soar. But the new houses were not accompanied by investment in schools, shops, leisure facilities or bus routes. The *Second Programme* assumed that the majority of new homes would be owner-occupied and built by private developers, with the state limited to providing serviced sites, and subsidies. Property developers offered buyers thirty-year mortgages, pre-arranged with a building society or insurance company. The close relationship between developers and building societies pushed young couples into outer suburbia; it was almost impossible to get a mortgage on older properties in mature areas, where large tracts of Victorian houses had turned into bedsits. By the end of the decade, building society assets were rising at an annual rate of 17 per cent,[61] and the societies were increasingly calling the shots in the housing market. The Department of Local Government urged them to give preference to first-time buyers and smaller houses, instead of the luxury houses that were beginning to appear, but it is

[58] *Social dynamite*, p. 32, *Hibernia*, 27 August–9 September 1971.
[59] *Hibernia*, 27 August–9 September 1971.
[60] Curtin, Geary, Grimes, and Menton, *Population growth and other statistics of middle-sized Irish towns*, p. 22.
[61] *Statistical Abstract 1972*, Particulars of building societies incorporated under the Building Societies Acts 1874–1942.

probable that the Department's grants to first-time buyers served to further inflate house prices.[62]

Property development and construction were boom industries of the 1960s, and while there was significant investment by British companies, Irish developers – many of them returned emigrants – were also prominent. The decade was marked by a new relationship between politicians and property developers. Office blocks, new houses, factory sites were regarded as essential components of Ireland's developing economy. Politicians were more than happy to facilitate these ventures in the knowledge that this could be justified as supporting the national development agenda. Many state companies and government departments were anchor tenants in new office blocks. Rumours abounded of connections between various ministers and property developers; in 1966, *Business and Finance* reported on stories that 'the Department of X have taken space in the new building on Y Street. The Minister is connected with the crowd who built it.'[63]

The 1963 Planning Act required local authorities to draw up plans and make zoning decisions that would determine future development. If this legislation had been introduced in the mid-1950s when the economy was stagnant, it might have proved relatively uncontroversial. In the heated economic atmosphere of the mid-1960s, however, planning decisions became highly politicised. Councillors commonly overturned zoning decisions made by professional planners under powers given them by Section 4 of the 1955 County Management Act.[64] If councillors failed to approve a proposal, developers could appeal to the Minister for Local Government, who could overrule the council. Denying planning permission might leave a local authority liable to pay compensation. Development land was not subject to a betterment levy – a tax on the increase in value resulting from being zoned for housing or commercial development, or provided with water and sewerage. For property owners, securing development zoning was akin to winning the sweepstake, and they had a strong incentive to lobby for a change of use. An editorial in May 1965 in *Business and Finance*, which cannot be regarded as anti-developer, commented that 'Property speculators and developers in the Dublin area must be greatly encouraged by the first report from Prof.

---

[62] Daly, *Buffer state*, p. 477.   [63] *B&F*, 22 April 1966.

[64] This legislation, introduced to placate councillors who were angered by the power exercised by the salaried county (or city) manager, gave councillors power to override managerial decisions by calling a special meeting if necessary. Any decision, except in relation to personnel or individual health cases, could be overturned by an absolute majority of all councillors, or by more than two-thirds of councillors present. Daly, *Buffer state*, pp. 318–9.

Myles Wright on the pattern of development over the next twenty years. To judge by what he says, land values are certain to rise ... best prospects west of Dublin from Tallaght and Clondalkin to Swords and Malahide.'[65] Bruce Arnold, writing in the same magazine in 1968, noted that 'the whole question of the development of land ... has been the excuse for charges of corruption, of bribery, of unfair speculation, of enormous profits of muddled and in some cases ruinous planning decisions and mistakes, and of unwillingness or inability on the Government's part to straighten things out'. He believed that most of the faults were probably the result of laziness and stupidity rather than 'seamy and corrupt activities', but there was cause for concern, in cases where developers had advance notice of drainage facilities that would enable land to be developed, and used this fore-knowledge to buy sites at low agricultural prices.[66] The 1965 Finance Bill initially provided for a new tax liability on profits realised from property development, but this was removed.[67] Keogh, the biographer of Jack Lynch, who was Minister for Finance in 1965, claimed that the clause was dropped, because of a Supreme Court ruling.[68]

While Dublin offered the greatest potential for speculation, by the end of the decade, Galway was Ireland's fastest growing city. *Hibernia* reported how 'meeting after meeting Fianna Fáil councillors hammered away at rezoning hundreds of acres of farmland on the city outskirts, despite the fact that the city manager had pointed out the "enormous consequences" of their actions'. They rezoned sufficient land to accommodate a town the size of Ballina (population 6,000), cutting across the city's plan to build a new suburb on a 10,000 acre site at Ballybrit.[69] The political scientist Mart Bax, whose research was carried out in the late 1960s, claimed that 'around one-quarter of the MCCs (members of County Councils) of one county council have improved their positions through land speculation, and the farmers among them have increased their own acreage. Of that same council almost all politicians have been able to obtain personal priority for various sorts of local government services: water and sewerage connections, building grants, agricultural grants, the tarring of the road to their houses, to mention but a few personal benefits they have derived from their office.'[70] In 1971, following widespread claims that inflated land prices were pushing up house prices, Minister for Local Government Bobby Molloy established an enquiry into the cost of building land, with a brief to recommend measures to

[65] *B&F*, 21 May 1965.   [66] *B&F*, 21 June 1968.
[67] *B&F*, 22 April 1966; 6 May 1966.   [68] Keogh, *Jack Lynch*, pp. 110–13.
[69] *Hibernia*, 17 November 1972.
[70] Mart Bax, *Harpstrings and confessions. Machine-style politics in the Irish Republic* (Assen and Amsterdam: Van Gorcum, 1976), pp. 63–4.

control prices and to ensure that 'all or a substantial part' of the increased land value 'should be secured for the benefit of the community'.

The Kenny Inquiry found that the price of serviced land in county Dublin had increased by 530 per cent between 1963 and 1971 (consumer prices rose by 64 per cent). They documented many examples of significant windfall profits over a short period: a profit of over 140 per cent in a matter of months; a profit of over 400 per cent within two years which was not liable to tax, thanks to complex manoeuvres with respect to companies. These were not isolated examples. They cited cases of compulsory purchase by the local authority, where owners of agricultural land contested the price offered and were awarded significantly higher sums in court by the Official Valuer because of the potential development value. In all cases, the increased value was dependent on actual or expected local authority investment in water or sewerage. Where a local authority revoked outline planning permission because the land lacked basic services, they were liable to pay compensation. The increase in land values was partly due to a shortage of serviced land, and failure to anticipate the increased demand for housing, but providing more serviced land would not resolve the problem. By the early 1970s, most potential development land in the vicinity of Dublin was owned by a small number of construction firms.

While the diagnosis was comprehensive, the Kenny Inquiry proved less successful at recommending solutions. It proposed that local authorities should designate areas likely to be developed over the next ten years, where land could be compulsorily acquired at existing use value plus a 25 per cent premium; all planning decisions in a designated area should be reserved to the county manager. The Planning Act should be amended to reduce the right to compensation if permission was refused.[71] But their recommendations were seriously weakened by the fact that only four of the six members signed the majority report, and one of these only with an addendum. The Inquiry failed to examine allegations of corruption or potential conflicts of interest in local or national politics relating to planning decisions. The rezoning windfall continued for decades to come; it was the main subject of the Mahon Inquiry published in 2012.[72] Close links between politicians and developers were not confined to local authorities. Although Seán MacEntee, a former Minister for Local Government, argued for the inclusion of an independent planning appeals process in 1963 Act, because when he had to adjudicate on

---

[71] *Committee on the Price of Building Land. Report to the Minister for Local Government*, 1973 K.119

[72] *The Tribunal of Inquiry into certain matters & payments. The final report*, March 2012 (www.planningtribunal.ie).

planning appeals 'I found that I had to withstand pressure from various interests',[73] his advice was ignored. Ministers for Local Government continued to exercise patronage with respect to planning appeals until 1976, when an independent planning appeals board was established.

Housing ranks among the major failures of the 1960s and a major indictment of government planning. The share of public expenditure devoted to housing fell from 6.5 per cent in 1963 to 5.8 per cent in 1968.[74] The 1964 target of 12,000–13,000 new houses annually was not achieved; neither was a revised target set in 1969. The shortfall was serious, because neither target had assumed an increase in population. House prices far outstripped the consumer price index. By 1969, house prices were double the 1953 figure; over the next two years, they increased by a further 35 per cent. The cost of housing was a major factor in the shortfall – investment was higher than projected but fewer houses were built. Much of the blame for rising costs was due to the lack of planning controls, especially over land prices. The 1960s also saw a major shift in housing provision, with private developers and building societies taking on the major role of providing housing in urban areas. By 1981, there were over 360,000 mortgages outstanding on private houses, compared with only 6,449 in 1946.[75]

Local and regional government

Many of the pressures associated with the developing economy fell on a local administration, which was often ill-equipped to cope with them. The county and county borough had been the key local administrative unit since the 1920s. The main changes introduced since independence involved the abolition of rural district councils and the transfer of some key decisions from elected councillors to professional city and county managers. Irish local government was subject to considerable central oversight: when the Maud Committee on the Management of Local Government in England and Wales reviewed structures in various countries, they decided that Ireland had the most stringent central controls over local government.[76] This was partly a legacy of British rule, partly the response of the new state to a legacy of corruption in local government that long predated independence.[77]

---

[73] Daly, *Buffer state*, p. 464.   [74] Kennedy and Dowling, *Economic growth*, p. 294.
[75] Daly, *Buffer state*, p. 534.
[76] Maud Committee on the Management of Local Government, HMSO 1967, vol. 1, p. 13.
[77] K. Theo Hoppen, *Elections, politics and society in Ireland 1832–1885* (Oxford: Clarendon, 1984) Daly, *Buffer state*, chapters 1–3.

The maze of new committees and consultative bodies that characterised Ireland's 1960s development drive was particularly prevalent at
regional level. County development teams were established in the twelve
western counties to promote development, co-ordinate the activities of all
public bodies involved with economic development and encourage local
development proposals. The *Third Programme* exhorted local authorities
to play an active role in development – everything from liaising with
industrialists as to their needs for water and sewerage to improving the
appearance of towns and the countryside and liaising with the IDA's small
industries programme.[78] Whether local authority staff had the skills to
handle these matters is a moot point; many councillors or local authority
staff might have found it difficult to distinguish between responding to
government requests and actively assisting developers. Although some
government initiatives placed additional responsibilities on county authorities, many duties were taken over by regional or national authorities.
The creation of the National Building Agency in 1960, to build houses for
key workers attached to a new industry or tackle an emergency such as
Ballymun, suggests that local authorities were not seen as sufficiently
responsive to changing needs. The 1963 Planning Act created nine planning regions. By the early 1970s, the IDA had developed a regional plan
for industrial development; there were regional tourist programmes,
plans for regional technical colleges and regional health boards – all
threatening to move the centre of power away from the county. Yet,
there was no agreement as to the appropriate regional boundaries.
County Roscommon was in three different regions for health, tourism
and physical planning, and the county was divided into two catchment
areas for technical colleges.[79] Yet, despite this new emphasis on regions, a
1971 White Paper reinforced the county as the key administrative unit. It
recommended transferring authority from smaller urban areas to the
county – because the distinction between town and country was no longer
clear-cut. It also repeated the recommendation in the Devlin
Commission (which did not examine local government) that regional
bodies should be non-executive; their primary role should be securing
co-operation between the various local authorities. The White Paper
favoured granting greater autonomy to local authorities; however, it
emphasised that this was contingent on their capacity to generate revenue
from local sources.[80]

[78] *Third programme*, pp. 162–3; *Devlin report*, pp. 47–8.
[79] Tom Barrington, *From big government to local government. The road to decentralisation*
(Dublin: IPA, 1975), p. 69.
[80] Daly, *Buffer state*, pp. 512–13.

The main source of local authority revenue was rates – a tax levied on property and on land, which was introduced in the mid-nineteenth century. By the early 1960s, it was generally accepted that local taxation was in need of major reform. But the question was how to do this. When Lemass opened the Economic Research Institute (later the ESRI) in 1961, he mentioned that one of their first projects would be a study of local taxation and local finance.[81] Researchers duly produced a series of papers on local incomes, and the incidence of rates, which while worthy and scholarly need not concern us, as they had no impact. Throughout the decade, protests mounted against rates, mainly but not exclusively from farmers. Throughout the 1960s, the Exchequer assumed a growing share of the cost of local services, especially health. But the government never seriously contemplated either reforming the rating system or devising an alternative form of local taxation. This failure to find an effective local tax was not unique to Ireland. In Britain, officials also wrestled with this problem throughout the 1960s and 1970s – eventually opting for the politically disastrous poll tax. Daunton noted reluctance on the part of civil servants to abandon an existing system of taxation and a tendency to identify all the problems associated with a new form of taxation. The default position was to move the costs from local to central taxation – a politically easier solution but one that weakened local democracy and enhanced central control.[82] This centralising solution proved very attractive to Irish politicians.

Physical and regional planning and the structures of local government are probably the issues where economic development confronted Irish political culture in the most direct fashion, and the outcome was not a happy one. Ireland's last serious attempts at urban planning were in the late eighteenth century but that magnificent achievement was dismissed as representative of an alien political ascendancy. In the 1960s, the combination of anti-urban sentiment and modernism proved a dangerous mixture. Local, regional or national planning demanded tough political decisions that could undoubtedly prove unpopular; it also offered temptations in the form of political and financial dividends, though not all the shortcomings should be blamed on politicians – many of the solutions put forward by experts at the time have since been widely criticised.

---

[81] Daly, *Buffer state*, pp. 503–6.
[82] Martin Daunton, *Just taxes. The politics of taxation in Britain, 1914–1979* (Cambridge: Cambridge University Press, 2002), chapter 11.

Part II

Society

6   The optimism of a rising tide

In the late 1950s, Ireland was a country where most people knew their place; a country where stories of rags to riches were uncommon – and most of these related to a returning emigrant who had made his fortune abroad, or to a winning ticket in the Irish Hospitals Sweepstake, less commonly to a successful business venture in Ireland.[1] Birth and family connections determined education, career choice (if we can speak of a choice); whether a man or woman could marry; their marriage partner; who would emigrate, their destination and possibly their job. Emigrants with family connections would have a temporary place to stay and perhaps a job, others had to fend for themselves. The family farm and family business were dominant social forces in rural Ireland, provincial towns and larger cities. Sons of bank managers had an inside track on jobs in the bank, as did the sons of key customers. Entry standards for university or professional courses were low, which meant that it was rarely a barrier to family succession. Many solicitors and general practitioners were succeeded by a son, and the consultant lists in Dublin hospitals showed a recurrence of the same family names. Dr Conor Ward, a consultant paediatrician in Crumlin Children's Hospital, had a serious falling out with his father, when he declined to join his father's medical practice in Monaghan.[2] Most solicitor and accountancy businesses were family firms; if they recruited outsiders, these came from the extended family, close friends and business contacts, or past pupils from a particular school. These informal recruitment networks help to explain why in 1961 non-Catholics accounted for one-third of directors, managers and company secretaries, but only 4.5 per cent of senior officials in the civil

---

[1] Examples of returning emigrants who had prospered include Pat Hughes, who emigrated to Canada and prospered in mining before returning to Ireland where he developed Tynagh mines, or Matt Gallagher, who developed a successful construction business in England, then returned to Ireland where he opened factories in Tubbercurry and became a major player in Dublin's construction boom.
[2] As reported by Dr Conor Ward.

service and local authorities (where appointments were on merit). This changed, though only gradually. In 1973, Protestants constituted 24 per cent of senior business executives.[3] Michael Smurfit claimed that there were many companies where Catholics could never join the management team, 'no matter how good they were at their job or how considerable the contribution that they could make to the success of the business', and it was difficult for a Catholic firm such as Smurfit to make sales to Protestant companies.[4] While the existence of Protestant or Catholic firms was generally acknowledged, people were less comfortable about acknowledging the importance of class. Bertram Hutchinson, a sociologist who moved to Ireland in the 1960s as a research professor at the ESRI, was told on several occasions that social classes 'have totally withered away since Independence'; his research showed that, at least in Dublin, this was not the case.[5]

Church, family and social class combined to determine many aspects of individual lives. The 1960s marked the peak of Ireland's 'devotional revolution' – the remarkable expansion of Catholic religious devotions and observance, and the founding of Catholic institutions that began more than a century earlier. Many families had close relatives who were priests, nuns or lay brothers. Schools were segregated by denomination, and by gender. In Dublin and the larger towns, there was also significant segregation by class; middle-class children generally attended private fee-paying elementary schools. Second-level schooling was determined by social class. Many children from poorer households only attended primary school; vocational schools that taught practical skills plus continuation subjects were dominated by the working class and children of small farmers. Hutchinson's study of intergenerational social mobility in Dublin noted that while there was evidence of upward and downward mobility, the line between manual and non-manual social classes appeared almost impenetrable.[6]

Social life was demarcated by religion and class. Golf and tennis clubs were middle-class preserves, whose members might also exercise a degree of religious segregation; rugby was overwhelmingly middle class, and soccer tended to attract the working class. The GAA attracted support across all classes, but the fact that games were played on a Sunday ruled

[3] Daithí Ó Corráin, *Rendering to God and to Caesar: the Irish churches and the two states in Ireland, 1949–73* (Manchester: Manchester University Press, 2008), p. 88.

[4] Smurfit, *A life worth living*, pp. 79–80.

[5] Bertram Hutchinson, *Social status and inter-generational social mobility in Ireland* (ESRI, 1969), p. 31. Bertam Hutchinson, *Social status in Dublin: marriage mobility and first employment* (ESRI paper 67, Dublin, 1973).

[6] Hutchinson, *Social status and inter-generational social mobility*, p. 32.

out Protestant support; likewise the ban on GAA members playing or attending 'foreign games', such as soccer, rugby, hockey and cricket. Dances in local halls were commonly supervised by a priest; similar chaperoning/scrutiny applied in Protestant church halls in order to ensure that young people would marry co-religionists. But the key determinant of marriage or non-marriage was probably the family. Marriages might be delayed or prevented because a son or daughter was expected to support younger siblings or widowed, elderly or impoverished parent(s), or because succession to the family farm or business had not been determined. Match-making, which played a key role in Irish marriage after the famine, was on the wane, but had not yet disappeared. Robert Cresswell claims that in rural county Galway in the late 1950s, families met to discuss a dowry and a match, after a couple had met and formed an emotional attachment; if these details could be negotiated, they duly married, otherwise they might marry and emigrate.[7] But in 1969, the magazine *Woman's Choice* published several letters from women whose parents objected to their marrying their boyfriend, asking how to deal with this problem, which suggests that parents continued to exercise some influence over a child's marriage.[8]

The state was important, not least as a major provider of income and housing, although the payments were parsimonious, and many welfare recipients relied on charitable organisations such as the St Vincent de Paul Society, or kindly neighbours and friends in order to survive. National and local authorities provided housing for a significant proportion of the population – either directly through local authority housing schemes or indirectly via loans or housing grants. Grants made it possible for rural households to replace thatch with galvanise or slate; add extra bedrooms or a larger kitchen. The state also provided free primary schools, accessible to all, though the local community had to raise part of the capital and running cost. It also guaranteed free access to a doctor for the poorest citizens and free or almost-free hospital care for the majority of the citizens. But health services often divided on the basis of social class. Middle-class women gave birth in private nursing homes, not in large maternity hospitals; they visited specialists in consulting rooms in Dublin's Georgian squares and were treated in private nursing homes, not in large hospital wards. The local national school was almost certainly owned and controlled by a local clergyman, and many of the largest hospitals were also under voluntary, often church, control.

---

[7] Robert Cresswell, *Une communauté rurale d'Irlande* (Paris: Institut d'ethnologies, 1969), p. 484.
[8] *Woman's Choice*, 15 April 1969, p. 4, 17 June 1969, p. 6.

By the mid-1950s, church and state were broadly in agreement as to their respective spheres of influence. The state had expanded its remit with respect to health services during the 1950s, following a public spat with the Catholic Church and the powerful medical profession, but a compromise was reached with the 1953 Health Act. The role of the church in education had not been challenged over the previous twenty-five years. This was equally true of the church's role in running industrial schools and residential institutions for mentally handicapped children and adults, which were funded by the state but under church control. Constitutional and legal restrictions on divorce and contraception, and the censorship of film and publications reflected the teachings of the Catholic Church, and the overwhelming majority of the population appear to have accepted these limitations on their personal freedom. Those who were anti-clerical, non-churchgoing, or atheists, tended to keep their opinions to themselves; however, they were probably few in number.

Economic and social change destabilised this equilibrium between church and state, and the traditional authority of parents over children was undermined. This instability was inherent in the process of economic development. The need for a more educated workforce required an expansion in educational provision, involving a re-negotiation of the church–state relationship in that sphere. In time, it was probable that this more educated workforce might question church teaching with respect to personal morality. The fall in emigration meant that the population now included a higher proportion of young adults, who were more likely to challenge the status quo with respect to sexual morality. In 1971, there were over 80,000 more people aged 20–35 in Ireland than in 1961. Economic development made it possible for more couples to marry and at an earlier age, resulting in a shortage of women workers and a gradual easing of the ban on married women in paid employment. The requirement to bring labour and welfare legislation into line with EEC countries and pressure to abolish Victorian-style dispensaries, where poor patients were treated apart from other patients, prompted reforms in health and welfare services. By the early 1970s, the crisis in Northern Ireland had reopened a debate about a united Ireland, prompting comparisons between welfare services in the two parts of Ireland. Other pressures came from changes in private lives. The falling age of marriage eroded 'family-planning Irish style', where the late age of marriage restricted family size. It became more necessary to confront the medical and social consequences of very large families, prompting the first moves to provide some form of family planning. Widows, deserted wives and single mothers emerged from the shadows to demand that the state provide for their needs.

The government was a rather passive player in this process of social change, reacting to changing attitudes or growing pressures. Another traditional pillar of society, the Catholic Church proved more adroit in navigating its way through the changes. The papal encyclicals of Pope John XXIII and the emergence of a small cohort of reforming, even radical clergy ensured that the Catholic Church was to the fore in debates about poverty and welfare, and successfully protected its key influence in education despite a significant expansion in that sector, though the limits of Irish Catholic reformist tendencies were becoming evident by the end of the decade. Investigative journalists in print and television and an emerging second-wave feminist movement (at the end of our period) were also forces for change. The process was gradual, not revolutionary; nevertheless over a range of issues – poverty and welfare, access to education, healthcare, working women and equal pay – there was a broad acceptance across Irish society of a need for change. The outcomes were generally a compromise: removing the legal ban on married women in state employment, but making little effort to facilitate them or their childcare needs; a lack of follow-up research to ensure that the introduction of free secondary schooling and grants for students in higher education was percolating through to the most disadvantaged areas. Marriage and sexual morality were major exceptions to this process of reform: in 1973, neither the church, nor the state, nor the majority of the electorate were willing to concede a right to access reliable contraception (even for married couples), or a right to divorce. These issues would divide Irish society for decades to come.

In 1961, Ireland was very much a pre-industrial society with 426 out of every 1000 men at work engaged in farming. Almost 44 per cent of those in work were employers, self-employed or assisting relatives. Farming was still the largest source of employment by a considerable margin in 1971, accounting for almost one in three jobs, but the number of employers, self-employed and assisting relatives had fallen to just over one-third of male workers. The decline was most striking in the case of agriculture, where the number of male relatives assisting, who were mainly farmers' sons (most farmers' daughters had already left agriculture), more than halved (95,000–47,000); the numbers of self-employed and assisting relatives in non-agricultural occupations also fell. In 1971, fewer than one-sixth of men aged 20–24 relied on family employment; in 1951, the figure was one-third.[9] The servile dependent relationship of a son

[9] David Rottman, 'The changing social structure of Ireland', in Frank Litton (ed.), *Unequal achievement. The Irish experience, 1957–1982* (Dublin: Institute of Public Administration, 1982), p. 72.

working for his father is poignantly captured by Brian Friel in his play 'Philadelphia here I come' where the young man emigrates in order to gain his freedom. Many young men made a similar choice; however, by the 1960s it was easier to gain freedom without having to emigrate. By 1971, almost two-thirds of workers received a weekly or monthly wage or salary. This was significant. Young wage-earning men and women had much greater independence than those working in a family business. By 1963/1964, waged and salaried workers enjoyed a five-day week and guaranteed holidays with pay, yet another contrast with those in the family economy. The numbers in professional, white-collar and skilled manual jobs increased, as did their share of the total workforce. More workers held better-paid jobs, which presumably offered them greater satisfaction. This change was most notable for women: in 1961, personal service employed the greatest number of women at work; ten years later, this had been superseded by professional employment – mainly teaching and nursing. The demands of a growing economy forced many traditional businesses to merge or transform their working arrangements (the big exception was the family farm), opening up the recruitment process. Yet, a study of social mobility in Dublin in 1968 showed that the proportion of non-Catholics in the top four social categories was four times their share of the population. However, the author concluded that this was a historic legacy; he suggested that 'the erstwhile social dominance enjoyed by non-Catholics is drawing to a close'.[10] Journalist Michael Viney declared that the days of the identifiable Protestant or Catholic employer was passing as family firms disappeared or were taken over, and firms increasingly gave priority to ability and qualifications over family and other connections.[11]

By 1965, average industrial earnings were over 90 per cent higher than that in 1953 – far outstripping the 40 per cent rise in consumer prices. Despite annual price inflation of over 10 per cent by the early 1970s, industrial earnings remained comfortably ahead – almost four times the 1953 figure, whereas prices had doubled.[12] Changes in farm incomes are more difficult to estimate; but with falling number of relatives assisting/ farm labourers, and a growing number of dairy farmers, which gave a high return per acre, many farm households enjoyed better incomes and higher living standards. Between 1960 and 1968, family farm incomes rose by 52 per cent, and as the number of relatives assisting fell by 17 per cent, the average income per head rose by 82 per cent, or 33 per cent in real

---

[10] Hutchinson, *Social status and inter-generational social mobility*, pp. 6–7.
[11] Viney, *The five per cent*, p. 10.
[12] Figures relate to an index of earnings in transportable goods industries, and consumer price index.

incomes.[13] There is considerable evidence of a growing consumer economy in both urban and rural Ireland – the outcome of higher incomes, television and the motor car. Rural electrification and rural water schemes removed a major distinction between urban and rural living.

Television was a major force in promoting a consumer society. In 1960, roughly 30 per cent of households – mainly those living along the east coast or near the border – could receive British television programmes.[14] When Teilifís Éireann – the national station – opened on New Year's Eve 1961, television viewing began to spread more widely. By April 1966, in time for celebrations marking the Golden Jubilee of the 1916 Rising, 98 per cent of the population could receive the Teilifís Éireann signal, though only 55 per cent of homes had a TV set.[15] More than three-quarters of urban households had a television, double the proportion in rural areas.[16] In the early years therefore, watching TV on special occasions – such as an all-Ireland football final – might be a communal occasion, with friends and neighbours gathering around a set, as happened in the early radio years. By the end of the decade, this became less common. Television helped to erode social and geographical distinctions – everybody with a TV could enjoy the same entertainments, and at a time when most households only had access to a single TV channel, there was probably a greater element of shared leisure experience across all ages, occupations and social classes than at any time before or since. The station was funded by a combination of licence fee and advertising. Many households probably welcomed the advertisements, which introduced new products and new aspirations: alcohol, tobacco, clothing, electrical goods and motor cars.

In 1962, an advertisement placed by Teilifís Éireann in the *World's Press News* and *Television Mail and Advertisers' Weekly* – a journal directed at major advertisers –featured a picture of a Ford Cortina under the heading 'An Irish Jaunting Car 1962'. The message was, 'Yes things have changed in Ireland'; the number of cars registered had increased by 30 per cent between 1958 and 1961, and the station was touting for business from motor manufacturers.[17] By 1966, the Ford Cortina had become the best-selling car in Irish motoring history.[18] Car ownership more than doubled between 1957 and 1967; by then, an estimated 30 per cent of urban households and up to 38 per cent of rural households owned

[13] Daly, *First Department*, p. 502.
[14] Martin McLoone and John MacMahon (eds), *Television and Irish Society: 21 Years of Irish Television* (Dublin: RTÉ, 1984), p. 7.
[15] Kevin C. McCourt, 'Broadcasting–A community service', *Administration*, vol. 15, no. 3, Autumn 1967, p. 174; Alacoque Kealy, *Irish Radio Data: 1926–80* (Dublin: RTÉ, 1981), pp. 15–16.
[16] Radio Éireann: *Annual Report 1966*.   [17] NAI, DT S14496 F/62 television general file.
[18] *B&F*, 4 November 1966.

a car, but there was plenty of unsatisfied demand.[19] Demand for larger cars was running at such a rate that Fiat lacked the capacity to assemble smaller cars and decided to import them despite paying an import duty of 75 per cent.[20] Motor cycle numbers grew steadily from the early 1950s until 1964 and then began to fall – presumably because some owners could now afford a car.[21]

Most drivers were male, though I have failed to find any statistics on the gender of license holders. But a 1964 advertisement titled 'A car of her own' told the story of Pat and Jim, who lived in a new suburban house. At first they were very happy there despite the fact that schools and shops were some distance away. Pat could drive, but most days Jim had to take car into town because although there was a bus it did not always get him to work on time. The advertisement showed Pat collecting her eldest child from school (walking) and both getting very wet. Then they bought another car, financed by a finance-house second car plan.[22] When factory workers in Scariff and Tubbercurry were asked how they spent the additional earnings, cars ranked third after savings, and clothing.[23] A thirty mile per hour speed limit in urban areas was introduced in 1961, but until 1964 motorists could get a full driving licence without having to pass a test.[24] Although motorists were charged with drink-driving, enforcement was lax and breathalysers were not introduced until 1969. It is little surprise therefore that fatal road accidents rose sharply; in 1972, 601 people were killed on Irish roads – double the 1959 figure, and significantly higher than the 241 deaths in 2010, when there were more than four times the number of licensed motor vehicles. Yet, road traffic deaths did not attract anything like the concern aroused by the much lower fatalities of the early twenty-first century.

Rising car ownership played a crucial role in transforming shopping, leisure and communities. Until the 1960s most shoppers, whether they lived in towns, cities or the countryside, made their regular purchases within walking, cycling distance or a short bus ride from home, and the choice of shop owed more to custom, family networks or religious and political allegiance than to price comparisons.[25] When Martin Raftery

[19] John Blackwell, *Transport in the developing economy of Ireland* (ESRI paper no. 47, August 1969), p. 15.

[20] *B&F*, 3 February 1967.   [21] Blackwell, *Transport in the developing economy*, p. 23.

[22] *Hibernia*, July–August 1964.

[23] Lucey and Kaldor, *Rural industrialisation*, pp. 154–5; 30.7 per cent in Tubbercurry and 25.2 per cent in Scariff spent money on cars.

[24] Daly, *The buffer state*, p. 430.

[25] As a small child living in a border town where it would have been possibly to buy all your needs on shops owned by Presbyterian or Church or Ireland families, I recall one nun advising the class that we should patronise X, which was a Catholic pharmacy.

took charge of the family pub in Glenamaddy, county Galway, in 1958, it was 'a classical country pub. We were also into provisions, things like pollard, bran flour, and we used to buy wool and we were undertakers – up in the loft there was always half-a-dozen coffins. We did not rise to a hearse, that was subcontracted.'[26] Brody's description of a shop in the fictional village of Inishkillane is typical of many rural shops.

one area of shelving is for tins of vegetables, soups, fruits; another for washing powder and kitchen equipment; fresh vegetables are kept close to the counters; cured meats near the slicing machine; Wellington boots and other footwear are at the bottom of the shelves on the floor; fishing tackle to the right of the till; shirts in their cellophane covers are high on the shelves of one side; children's toys at another; frozen foods are in a large freezer behind the counter; ice creams are in another by the door; soft drinks are kept in their crates on one side of the floor, opposite the boots; in the outhouses are ropes, timber, buoys, nails, canisters of Calor gas; smaller items of fishing tackle are inside the shop; fresh meat is brought to individual order from a butcher relative in a nearby market town; bread least likely to desiccate with storing is stacked in boxes by the counter, white and sweet brown in watertight wrappings; some soda farls are for sale quite fresh two or three times a week; flour, sugar, currants, soda – all the requirements for home baking – are for sale in both small bags and huge sacks; baking mixes, jelly powders and sponge-cake mix in boxes offer the alternatives to home produce, as do the rows of mixed fruit and jams and narrow bottles of ketchup and brown sauces; a few pots and pans are balanced in odd corners. Any and every demand is anticipated by the shops, and most of the parishioners make most of their purchases here ... the wealth of supplies in Michael's reflects an insight into the multitudinous needs and the potential demands for every kind of purchase which have emerged in rural communities like Inishkillane.[27]

Most transactions in Michael's, and probably in the Raftery shop, were on account. Bills were cleared or reduced once or twice a year – coinciding with the sale of livestock or getting emigrant remittances. Although Michael's was a traditional general store in a rural village, the owner was a modern, focused businessman, who ran a large guesthouse, a taxi and minibus service, an expanding farm and two lobster boats; a county councillor who stood out from the community because he did not drink in the local bar.[28] Traditionally, the only serious competition to these local shops came from larger department stores in Dublin Cork and other provincial centres where special purchases were made by mail order, or on a special shopping trip. Increased ownership of cars, vans, motor bikes

[26] Ivor Kenny, *Out on their own. Conversations with Irish entrepreneurs*, (Dublin: Gill& Macmillan, 1991), p. 290.
[27] Hugh Brody, *Inishkillane: change and decline in the west of Ireland* (London: Jill Norman & Hobhouse, 1982), pp. 188–9.
[28] Brody, *Inishkillane*, pp. 184–210.

and tractors resulted in 'far more closures or bypassing of local schools, shops, churches, local halls etc.' and the weakening of local communities. Hannan noted that 'Neighbours no longer share in the same services – schools, churches, shops, fairs and markets, etc. – to the same extent as they did previously, so that they are that less integrated amongst themselves', but greater mobility gave people additional space and opportunities. Hannan noted that part of the opposition to the closing of the local school reflected parental loss of social control: the fact that they could no longer see what their children were doing, or who they were socialising with.[29] Communities may offer support to some; they can also be stifling.

Ireland's first self-service grocery store or supermarket H.Williams opened in the Dublin suburb of Terenure in late 1957; the Quinn family opened the first provincial self-service store in Dundalk in 1960.[30] In 1963, Power Supermarkets, a subsidiary of the Associated British Foods, arrived in Ireland – the advance party of a new wave of British retailers. Yet, in 1964 *Business and Finance* concluded that there was limited potential for supermarkets and shopping centres; most housewives shopped every day or every second-day because they did not have a fridge.[31] Lack of cars to carry home a week's family shopping delayed the growth of supermarkets. With rising car ownership, shoppers increasingly bypassed the local shops. When Power Supermarkets opened in Galway in 1965, the rapid expansion of supermarkets in provincial Ireland was underway.[32] By 1969, they were the dominant force in the Irish grocery trade, with the takeover of Findlaters, the long-established grocery chain that supplied affluent Dublin suburban households for generations.[33]

Shopping had always entailed a degree of social stratification – with more affluent Dubliners shopping in Grafton Street (where the larger department stores still closed on Saturday afternoons in the mid-1960s), and families with more modest incomes favouring Camden Street or George's Street, but the 1960s brought the beginnings of generational segregation with the first shops or sections of shops geared to young people, a trend that coincided with some erosion of social stratification. When Dublin retailer Arnotts opened a new branch in Grafton St, which was targeted at a younger market, they flew in the British model Jean Shrimpton to open the store – there were near riots among the throng of on-lookers; Shrimpton who was paid a reported appearance fee of £1,000

---

[29] Hannan, 'Kinship, neighbourhood and social change in Irish rural communities', *ESR*, vol. 3 (1972), pp. 172, 178–9.

[30] Kenny, *Out on their own*, pp. 276–7.   [31] *B& F*, 19 September 1964.

[32] *B&F*, 11 June 1965.   [33] *B&F*, 3 January 1969.

proved a disappointment to reporters; *Hibernia* reported that she held no strong views on anything.[34]

In 1969, Dorine Rohan claimed that 'Country folk' on shopping trips to a larger town could be identified by how they dressed: 'the poorer ones with a rough mackintosh and a headscarf, or a skirt, almost ankle-length, with the jacket of an old suit, whose skirt has been turned into dusters. Their more well-to-do neighbours in suits, and the inevitable hat. It is not only their attire which distinguishes them – they have an air of determination, a set gait, as they stride along the street, balanced by bulging string bags on either side, or Roche's Stores plastic bags which they have saved from their last visit.'[35] This was changing with the spread of chain stores such as Roche's Stores and Dunne's Stores (both originating in Cork), throughout Ireland, bringing cheaper, more fashionable clothing to a mass market. The reduction of Ireland's prohibitive tariffs under the AIFTAA undoubtedly forced factories to close, but rising imports increased consumer choice and reduced the cost of fashionable clothing and footwear. Children were less likely to wear hand-me-down footwear or clothing than in the past, and Rohan's poor country woman finally had some prospect of dressing in smarter, new clothes. The year 1966 saw the opening by Ben Dunne at Cornelscourt of a 'super discount store',[36] several months ahead of a planned shopping centre nearby in Stillorgan, 'an exceptionally prosperous area'[37] from which Dunne – an established Irish retailer – had been excluded.[38] When the (Dublin) Northside shopping centre opened in 1970, all 56 retail units were already let.[39] Chain stores and supermarkets changed the relationship between the shopper and shopkeeper into a more impersonal transaction, often determined by price or range of goods, whereas in the past family networks and access to credit were often the key factors. Free trade brought cheaper goods into Irish shops, though prices for electrical goods or motor cars remained considerably higher than in Britain or Northern Ireland, partly because of continuing protection. Ireland had traditionally imposed punitive sales taxes on 'luxury' items such as refrigerators and other electrical goods,[40] but the AIFTAA and greater retail competition meant that these items became more affordable. By the end of the decade, the shopping centres and the main streets of larger towns invariably included stores selling electrical goods – televisions, stereo record players, fridges, washing

---

[34] *Hibernia*, June 1966.
[35] Dorine Rohan, *Marriage Irish style* (Cork: Mercier, 1969), p. 30.
[36] *B&F*, 7 October 1966.   [37] *B&F*, 19 September 1964.   [38] *B&F*, 2 December 1966.
[39] *B&F*, 3 October 1970.
[40] In 1959, Whitaker described refrigerators, cameras and motor cars as 'eminently suitable for taxing'. Chambers, *T. K Whitaker*, p. 160.

machines, electric food mixers, electric blankets and other household items, with Hire Purchase available for more expensive items. It would not be an overstatement to see the 1960s as marking the beginnings of an Irish consumer society – for good or ill.

There are two sides to the housing story. In an earlier section, I outlined the failures in national planning that resulted in a housing shortage and a sharp rise in rents and house prices. But the 1960s saw remarkable improvements in standards – many modern homes with running water, bathrooms, fitted kitchens, fridges, even central heating. By 1956, an estimated 200,000 of the 280,000 homes targeted under the ESB's rural electrification programme had been connected; this programme was completed in 1965, but amazingly the target, set in the late 1940s, planned to connect only 69 per cent of rural homes, which suggests that electricity was regarded as an optional, not an essential service. But households who had declined an electricity connection in the past were demanding a connection, as were families living in very remote areas. By 1971, 90 per cent of rural homes had mains electricity; the last outstanding areas, the Black Valley in Kerry and Ballycroy in Mayo were connected by the end of that decade.[41]

In 1961, only 12 per cent of rural homes had indoor water on tap.[42] The campaign for rural water received strong support from the Department of Local Government and the Irish Countrywomen's Association (ICA), but it was opposed by the NFA, and Minister for Agriculture – Patrick Smith. Farmers objected to the cost of rural water schemes being part-funded through rates, despite the fact that improved hygiene was essential to produce quality milk and curtail the spread of bovine tuberculosis. The outcome was a compromise. Rural water was gradually extended, mainly through community schemes, which were grant-assisted by central government; the drive to sign up households for these schemes was often led by women. Yet, a survey of west of Ireland farms in 1970 showed that only half had piped water. Water was the key to many other improvements – such as a bathroom and washing machine. Families with piped water generally had a bathroom, television and a gas or electric cooker; households who owned a washing machine generally had a separate sitting room.[43]

---

[41] Michael Shiel, *The quiet revolution. The electrification of rural Ireland* (Dublin: O'Brien Press, 1984), pp. 154–5.

[42] Caitriona Clear, *Women of the house: women's household work in Ireland, 1926–1961: discourses, experiences, memories* (Dublin: Irish Academic Press, 2000), p. 202.

[43] Damien F. Hannan and Louise A. Katsaiouni, *Traditional families? From culturally prescribed to negotiated roles in farm families* (Dublin: ESRI, 1977), p. 63.

In the 1940s, Eamon de Valera suggested that the low marriage rate among farm families might be improved if a second 'dower-house' was erected on family farms. A report by a committee of politicians rejected that option – in part because of the cost of constructing and equipping a second home.[44] By the 1970s, however, greater affluence meant that young farm couples were more likely to start married life in a home of their own, as opposed to co-habiting with the man's parents. The modernising tendency that resulted in the demolition of Georgian Dublin was not confined to the city. In the countryside, new houses, generally one-storey bungalows, sprang up, and traditional cottages and even larger farm houses were abandoned. The year 1972 saw the first edition of *Bungalow Bliss*, by Jack Fitzsimons, a much-derided best-seller that has gone through multiple editions; it supplied basic plans which enabled small builders, and even amateurs to construct a basic one-storey home. Examples can be found throughout rural Ireland and the outskirts of provincial towns.[45] A site could be readily obtained on family-owned land, with much of the labouring work done by the family, and the cost of materials being met from the local authority housing grant. Fitzsimons' books often carried an introduction by the Minister for Local Government, an indication of the link between his housing plans and the government's rural housing programme. Many existing houses were extended by adding a new kitchen, a bathroom, plus an additional bedroom or two.

There was a major contrast between the generations with respect to housing amenities. Damien Hannan described two farmers, one an old man in his seventies, formerly 'the biggest and most respected man in the area', who continued to live in 'the old two-storey slated house that was built around 1880. His wife still goes to the well for water. The house is very clean, the floors polished, the parlour elegant in a style that was fashionable around the 1920s.' The second, a younger man who inherited a small farm 'wet and poorly stocked' and who had 'coored' with the older farmer in the past. 'Today' the younger farmer 'is married with two sons in the local secondary school. He has a modern three bedroom bungalow with partial central heating, from a modern oil-fired stove. The kitchen, sitting-room, and bedrooms are all furnished in a middle class suburban style. He has a tractor and a range of machinery, and he changed his car two years ago; he has bought two farms in the locality and rents a further 20 acres.'[46]

---

[44] Daly, *First Department*, pp. 108–16.
[45] Jack Fitzsimons, *Bungalow Bashing* (Kells: Kells Publishing Co., 1990).
[46] Damien Hannan, *Displacement and development: class, kinship and social change in Irish rural communities* (Dublin: ESRI, 1979), pp. 185–6.

Contrasting housing standards were not confined to the countryside, though virtually all city homes had running water and electricity. While newspapers and magazines advertised modern three- and four-bedroom houses, with fitted wardrobes, central heating and garages, the suburban dream remained largely confined to middle-class households. Single women and men lived in squalid bedsits in Dublin's inner suburbs. The rent charged in the few purpose-built flats available was beyond the means of the average clerical worker. In 1966, Mary Maher described four 'girls' who shared two rooms and a kitchenette in Rathmines. There was one bathroom and toilet in the house for eleven residents. Maher claimed that sharing a bath and toilet with five or more people was the norm in flatland. Furniture was old and cheap: 'Dark green walls and lavender printed draperies, flowered wallpaper and patterned, stained carpets. Coffin shaped wardrobes, springless beds, glaring neon blue or orange plastic and lino in the cheaply modernised offerings.' There were few regulations governing the Dublin flat market.[47] For many young people, life in a bedsit was often a short-time experience pending marriage and a move to the suburbs, but many working-class couples were living and raising families in conditions not noticeably different to those reported in 1914 or the 1940s. Ruairí Quinn, then an architecture student, has described canvassing tenements in the vicinity of Mountjoy Square during the 1965 general election: 'large families all in one room, where frayed curtains acted as dividers between the sleeping space and the living area. There was no kitchen as such. Food was prepared with water obtained from a tap downstairs and cooked, if lucky, on a gas cooker or else in a frying pan over an open fire ... The tall elegant Georgian rooms were impossible to heat and the one toilet, located down the stairs in the backyard, was used by as many as ten families. The smell of poverty was everywhere, making me want to throw up.'[48] Eleanor Holmes, a social worker in the Rotunda maternity hospital, described couples who feared eviction by a private landlord when he discovered that they were expecting a baby. Some couples rented or bought caravans as their home, unaware that because there was no government grant for rehousing caravan dwellers, they were reducing their chances of getting a local authority home.[49] The social work department in the Coombe maternity hospital reported cases where couples living in 'expensive flats find when the baby is due they are either given notice to quit by the landlord or they

[47] Mary Maher, 'The working girls 2. Economics of flat-dwelling', *IT*, 25 October 1966, p. 10.

[48] Ruairi Quinn, *Straight left. A journey in politics* (Dublin: Hodder Headline Ireland, 2005), pp. 46–7.

[49] *Rotunda Hospital Clinical Report*, 1966, pp. 67–8.

have to move back to their parents' home because they cannot afford the heavy rents with their increasing commitments. This results in over-crowding and friction.'[50] The construction of the Ballymun flats brought some relief; many couples were delighted with the spacious, centrally heated flats, but others found it difficult to adapt to high-rise living. Yet, in 1971, Holmes reported that the housing programme 'has been unable to keep pace with the marriage rate, and unless young couples had managed to save, they had scant hope of a home of their own pending the arrival of two children'.[51] Housing standards were rising, but for many families so too was the gap between their aspirations and current living conditions.

[50] *Coombe Hospital Clinical Report*, 1966, p. 127.
[51] *Rotunda Hospital Clinical Report*, 1971, p. 69.

7 Farewell to 'the vanishing Irish'

In 1954, Notre Dame Professor, Rev John O'Brien, published a book called *The Vanishing Irish*, which purported to explain why Irish men were so reluctant to marry. Although he did not know it, O'Brien and his contributors were writing about a phenomenon that was about to disappear. Between 1963 and 1967, the number of marriages increased by 2 per cent annually; this trend accelerated in 1967, with the numbers marrying rising at an annual rate of 7.5 per cent. The peak in the marriage rate was in 1973 (birth numbers peaked in 1980). Between 1961 and 1971, the proportion of men aged twenty-five to thirty-four who were married increased from 42 to 58 per cent; the comparable figures for women were 63 and 74 per cent. Ireland belatedly experienced the postwar marriage boom, which was common throughout the Western world in the 1950s, but well past its peak by the early 1970s. Although sociologists continued to write about large numbers of permanently celibate Irishmen and women, these were an ageing cohort increasingly confined to small western farms; indeed, we might suggest that they were becoming more conspicuous because they no longer conformed to a norm.[1] Greater prosperity, falling emigration and more jobs outside farming meant that couples could afford to marry and no longer had to wait until they could be sure of inheriting a farm. The fact that Ireland's belated marriage boom started in 1963, at the end of the *First Programme for Economic Expansion*, suggests that contrary to Rev O'Brien and his fellow contributors, Ireland's low marriage rate owed more to socio-economic circumstances than to psychology. Most brides now dressed in white, with bridesmaids in equally elaborate dresses – in marked contrast to the 1950s when many brides opted for a sensible suit or dress that could be worn on later occasions – further evidence of rising living standards, or simply greater optimism about the future.

---

[1] John C. Messenger, *Inis Beag: Isle of Ireland* (London and New York: Holt, Rinehart & Winston, 1969); Brody, *Inishkillane*; Nancy Scheper-Hughes, *Saints scholars and schizophrenics. Mental illness in rural Ireland* (Berkeley, London: University of California Press, 1981).

140

The marriage boom was a major factor in Dublin's housing crisis. Stories of couples setting up home in caravans or in their parents' home indicate a more optimistic, less cautious approach to embarking on married life than in the past, which may also reflect a psychological response to an improving economy, or the local impact of a growing youth culture and sexual revolution that is often seen as characteristic of the 1960s. Social lives of young people became less restrictive. It is more difficult to exercise control over a son or daughter who is earning a regular wage or salary and perhaps living away from home. The commercial dance halls that opened in provincial towns, generally on the outskirts with a large car park, gave young people the opportunity to meet away from the prying eyes of the local priest, who traditionally supervised dances in parish halls. Albert Reynolds, a future Taoiseach, built a prosperous career from a chain of dancehalls, whose names – Cloudland, Roseland, Fairyland and so on – evoke a mood of romantic escapism.[2] The dancehalls were filled on several week nights and on Sundays with showbands who played throughout Ireland, and to Irish audiences in England. There were limits to the dance hall revolution: no dances on Saturday nights because of fears that young people might miss Sunday mass, and no dances during the penitential season of Lent, when bands toured England. Dance halls did not have an alcohol licence. But the young men, who played their own versions of popular hits, attracted a large following of fans in their teens and twenties, who often followed their favourite band to halls up to a hundred miles from home. The Limerick Rural Survey noted that many younger men travelled very long distances to dances – partly to follow a favourite showband, but also because this enabled them to socialise away from the gossip and prying eyes of neighbours, who would probably report back to their parents.[3]

The traditional Irish pub was a male preserve, with women, on their rare visits, confining themselves to the 'snug', a small enclosed area.[4] That began to change in the 1960s. Licensing laws had been liberalised to allow for Sunday opening, and many pubs opened a new lounge bar, designed to attract women, with carpets and soft furnishings. Between 1948 and 1970, per capita consumption of alcohol increased from 3.2 to 5.1 litres; between 1965 and 1970, it increased by one litre per capita.[5] Summer festivals of various types were permitted longer drinking hours.

[2] Albert Reynolds, *My autobiography* (London: Transworld Ireland, 2009), pp. 28–34.
[3] Patrick McNabb, 'Social structure', in Jeremiah Newman (ed.), *Limerick rural survey, 1958–64* (Tipperary: Muintir na Tíre, 1964), pp. 228–9.
[4] Clear, *Women of the house*, p. 208.
[5] Diarmaid Ferriter, *A nation of extremes. The Pioneers in twentieth-century Ireland* (Dublin: Irish Academic Press, 2000), p. 203.

Fleadhanna ceoil – traditional music festivals held in a provincial town – attracted large numbers of young people for a weekend of music, bohemian lifestyle and often sex, much to the outrage of local and national media. John Montague's poem, 'The Siege of Mullingar, 1963', describes the two sounds of the Fleadh Cheoil as

> the breaking
> Of glass and the background pulse
> Of music. Young girls roamed
> The streets with eager faces,
> Shoving for men. Bottles in
> Hand they rowed out a song.
> *Puritan Ireland's dead and gone,*
> *A myth of O'Connor and O'Faolain.*

With more women drinking alcohol, and pubs offering ballad sessions, as a popular alternative to the showbands, dance halls were losing some of their popular appeal by the early 1970s. Women begin to feature in ads for alcohol – such as a Jameson's whiskey Christmas 1965 advertisement, where one bottle carried a gift tag for 'aunty', or an advertisement for Cork Dry Gin featuring a woman, glass in hand, with friends on a boat.[6] Aggressive marketing of vodka or Bacardi rum targeted women.[7] In 1971, Smirnoff vodka ran an ad in Ireland's best-selling Sunday newspaper featuring a Marilyn Monroe look-alike – declaring that 'Smirnoff leaves me breathless',[8] which would have been unimaginable ten years earlier. But such changes were largely confined to younger women. Many older women in rural Ireland rarely left home except to shop in a nearby town, or a day trip to Knock Shrine or Dublin. They never had a holiday (neither did their husband), though they often hoped to travel to Lourdes when the children 'had good jobs'.[9]

The fact that more young women were going to pubs, dancehalls, working outside a domestic environment, living in bedsits, meeting men who were not from their parish or neighbourhood may account for the explosion in advice columns in women's magazines, newspapers and in specialist publications such as the *Irish Farmers' Journal*. Young women and men were often uncertain how to behave on a date, and many were extremely ignorant about sexuality and basic reproductive biology. An experienced nurse in one maternity hospital told Dorine Rohan that many men and some women 'did not know how or where a baby is born when they first became parents'. Michael Smurfit claimed that watching a cow giving birth on television, when he was twenty years old was 'the first time

---

[6] *SI*, 19 December 1965; 27 July 1969.   [7] *SI*, 21 December 1969; 12 July 1970.
[8] *SI*, 18 July 1971.
[9] Dorine Rohan, *Marriage Irish style* (Cork: Mercier, 1969), pp. 30, 35, 38.

I knew anything about sex'.[10] In 'Woman's Page', a lunch-time radio programme, sponsored by Jacob's biscuit manufacturers, Frankie Byrne read letters from readers seeking advice about personal relationships, using them as a vehicle for satirical commentary.[11] 'Mary Dillon' (presumably a pseudonym) in *New Spotlight*, which was primarily a showband magazine, dealt with topics such as teenage pregnancy, homosexuality and masturbation, though she did not write about contraception.[12] Ireland's best-known agony aunt, Angela McNamara, began her column in Ireland's best-selling Sunday newspaper, the *Sunday Press*, in 1963, advising readers about wearing bikinis.[13] Her talks in convent secondary schools dealt with topics such as 'going steady, kissing and petting'.[14] *Hibernia* described her column as

> written against a background of moral indecision and changing moral standards; the new morality is more than the old immorality condoned ... Angela deals in the main with the problems of Mary O'Flaherty and her pursuers (how to distinguish between the friendly kiss, the modest and the immodest touch) ... : 'It is easy to make fun of her column; the girl who inquires if French kissing can make her pregnant; the boy who thinks he may have contracted v. d.; the man who indulges in shameful practise, the middle-aged spinster who is contemplating a moment of ecstasy before it is too late; the mother of twelve who does not want to become a mother of thirteen ... Angela McNamara's achievement is that she tries to offer a positive morality to young people.

The article ended by arguing that 'advice on family planning consistent with religious beliefs of the individual should be available at all health centres. A marriage counselling service should be organised in every parish. Angela MacNamara has shown that a real need exists.'[15]

Advice columns record changes in sexual behaviour and a greater willingness to discuss sexual matters. The prospect of earlier marriages reduced the pressure on couples to control their sexuality; alternatively, it may be that a less puritanical attitude resulted in earlier marriages. In the 1960s, if couples wanted a regular sex life, society required them to be married, and that applied not just in Ireland. Fr Anthony Gaughan, who assisted at approximately a hundred marriages in the working-class parish of Cabra West in the early 1960s, claimed that 'nearly all were marriages of teenagers and quite a few were ARPs – the sign we put after marriages

---

[10] Rohan, *Marriage Irish style*, p. 78; Smurfit, *A life worth living*, p. 38.
[11] Paul Ryan, *Asking Angela Macnamara, an intimate history of Irish lives* (Dublin: Irish Academic Press, 2012), p. 23.
[12] Carole Holohan, 'Every generation has its task: attitudes to Irish youth in the 'sixties' (PhD, 2009), pp. 135–9.
[13] Ryan, *Asking Angela Macnamara*, p. 3.   [14] *Hibernia*, January 1963.
[15] *Hibernia*, 28 February–13 March 1969.

where the young lady was already pregnant'.[16] However, the most remarkable aspect of Ireland's marriage boom is that it was not matched by a proportionate rise in births.

In the 1950s, Ireland's birth rate was close to the Western European average; however, this was achieved through the unique combination of a low marriage rate, and very high marital fertility (children born per married woman). In 1961, the number of legitimate births per married women (ten to forty-nine years) in Ireland was 195.5 per thousand, almost double the figure in England and Wales (108.3), Belgium or Denmark; the closest comparable figure was New Zealand at 154.6.[17] Delaying marriage, or not marrying, reduced Irish fertility: in 1961, women who had married in their early thirties and were married for over thirty years had 327 children per 1,000 compared with 555 for those marrying in their early twenties.[18] More than 10 per cent of women giving birth in the Coombe Hospital in 1963 gave birth to their tenth child; one woman gave birth to her twentieth child. After 1963, despite a rise in the number of births, fertility (per married woman) fell – coinciding with the increasing marriages. There was a further decline in marital fertility after 1966, coinciding yet another rise in marriages. Between 1966 and 1968, the number of births fell by 1,650 or almost 3 per cent; if marital fertility had remained constant, there should have been 2,800 additional births. This amounted to a 7 per cent fall in fertility within two years. In the year ending March 1969, there were 4,400 fewer births than in the year ending March 1965. In 1969, Garret FitzGerald titled an article 'The Baby Boom that Never Was'.[19] Although falling fertility was first evident in Dublin, provincial Ireland was not far behind. By 1970, almost half of births (48.6 per cent) were first or second babies compared with 39.4 per cent in 1958; the percentage of fifth or higher order births fell from 22 to 15 per cent. Brendan Walsh has suggested that while the marriage boom of 1963–1965 could be explained by the upturn in the economy, the further rise in marriages in 1967–1969 may have been a response to declining marital fertility.[20] He suggested that couples were more willing to marry and at an earlier age, because marriage did not inevitably mean a large family. But it is important not to exaggerate the transformation; in 1967 almost one-quarter (23 per cent) of women

[16] Anthony Gaughan, *At the coalface. Recollections of a city and country priest, 1950–2000* (Dublin: Columba Press, 2000), p. 56.

[17] Robert Kennedy, *The Irish. Emigration, marriage and fertility* (Berkeley: University of California Press, 1973), p. 75, table 58.

[18] Kennedy, *The Irish*, p. 176, table 60.

[19] 'The Baby Boom that Never Was', *IT*, 5 November 1969.

[20] Brendan M. Walsh, 'Ireland's demographic transition, 1958–70', *ESR*, vol. III, no. 2, 1972, pp. 260–3.

giving birth in Dublin's National Maternity Hospital gave birth to their fifth child, and the number of births peaked in 1980. Marital fertility in Ireland was still seriously out of line with any other country in the Western world, and remained so because fertility elsewhere was falling sharply.

Nevertheless, younger, middle-class, educated couples were consciously trying to limit their families. Research into falling fertility suggests that changing attitudes are the first crucial factor. Couples take the decision to control fertility and then find the means of doing so; most of the fall in fertility over the past two centuries was achieved using methods that would not be regarded as reliable today: coitus interruption, abstinence and perhaps abortion. Fisher's research on fertility control in Britain prior to the 1960s shows that the key decisions were taken by men, and that most British couples relied on methods of fertility limitation that were available in Ireland: coitus interruptus and abstinence.[21] If we apply Fisher's argument to Ireland, it suggests that the continuing high fertility in Irish marriages reflected a failure/unwillingness by men to control sexual activity and perhaps an unwillingness to consider the needs and wishes of their wives. The teaching of the Catholic Church, especially in confession, may have been critical. The 1935 Criminal Law Amendment Act prohibited the sale and importation of contraceptives and the 1929 Censorship of Publications Act made it a crime to print, publish or distribute works providing information about contraception or advocating contraception. Literature on the safe period, which was tolerated, and indeed approved by Pope Pius XII in 1951, was not banned in Ireland, but it was not readily available. By the 1950s, the Catholic Hierarchies in Britain, the United States and the Netherlands (to take only a small sample of countries) were instructing couples on how to limit family size in a manner that was compatible with Catholic teaching, but the Irish Catholic Hierarchy made no efforts to inform Irish couples. It was only in the late 1960s that branches of a Catholic Marriage Advisory Council, which provided pre-marriage courses and advice on the safe period, opened in Ireland, and these services were poorly advertised. Rohan noted that most of the people that she had spoken to were unaware of their existence.[22] I failed to find any advertisements or information about them in the *Catholic Standard* – Ireland's leading Catholic newspaper until the late 1970s. Although some couples obtained manuals outlining the 'safe period', access was probably limited to middle-class couples, who could get individual advice from a sympathetic doctor; the

---

[21] Kate Fisher, *Birth control, sex & marriage in Britain 1918–1960* (Oxford: Oxford University Press, 2006).
[22] Rohan, *Marriage Irish style*, p. 112.

advice columns in *Woman's Choice* in the late 1960s indicate that many couples were keen to learn about the safe period, but lacked even basic information on the subject.

What was prompting more Irish couples than in the past to limit the number of children? It is possible that the reduction in the age gap between husband and wife, which had been one of the highest in Europe, may have resulted in more companionate marriages and more equal discussion between husband and wife; likewise, the disappearance of dowries, match-making and other more instrumental determinants of marriage partners, or the shift from working within the family to reliance on wages or a salary. Increasing affluence – the nightmare of many Catholic clergy – may well have been a factor – as couples strove to buy a house or car and equip their home with the trappings of modern living. The increasing emphasis on education as the route to economic success and security may also have concentrated parental minds on how many children they could provide for. Changing attitudes were fostered by the beginnings of an open debate on family planning and the difficulties presented by large families. These topics were being discussed even by the Catholic Church in the context of the population explosion in developing countries (a major topic at the time), and the more immediate pressures on married couples.

The contraceptive pill, which was first approved by the US Food and Drugs Administration as safe for use in 1960,[23] played a crucial role in opening a debate on contraception; indeed, the pill was probably more readily available in 1960s Ireland than information about the safe period! Medical practitioners could prescribe the pill to regulate menstrual cycle and therefore bypass the 1935 Criminal Law Amendment Act. It was a contraceptive that was initiated and controlled by women – overcoming the need to rely on men to control fertility. The pill made it easier for women to discuss contraception with a doctor or a friend, because it did not entail an intrusive medical procedure, a discussion of sexual anatomy, menstrual cycles or other potentially embarrassing topics. The liberal window in the early and mid-1960s, when the Catholic Church appeared on the point of approving the pill as an acceptable means of contraception, facilitated this discussion. In 1964, the Irish Jesuit periodical, *Studies* published an article by a leading Belgian theologian in which he stated that 'birth regulation is one of the most urgent questions facing the Church today'; he argued that 'there must be boldness to preach a planned parenthood'.[24] *Studies* was not read by the average men and

---

[23] Marwick, *The sixties*, p. 250.
[24] Joseph Fuchs, 'The Pill', *Studies*, winter 1964, p. 352.

women, but it did reach many Catholic clergy, and the article could be seen as a straw in the wind. More to the point, a new Irish women's magazine *Woman's Way* began to publish occasional articles about contraception.[25] For the first time, family planning became an acceptable topic for discussion. Pope John XXIII's decision to appoint a Special Commission on Family Problems, with a majority of lay members, including five women, created expectations that a major change in Catholic teaching was imminent. In 1966, the Irish-born journalist Peter Lennon noted that 'In a very short time – a matter of less than four years – the ordinary Irish Catholic without apparent difficulty or distress, has come to accept the fact that contraception – a practice which he had always been led to believe was criminal – is, if not yet officially acceptable, at least a possible solution to a human dilemma.'[26] In June 1966, the commission submitted an 800-page report to Pope Paul VI.

It is against that background that the October 1966 Teilifís Éireann Programme, 'Too many children', should be seen. The presenter, Michael Viney played taped responses of Irish mothers to a series of questions: 'When is a family too big? What are the human realities of family planning?' as the prologue to a studio discussion with a panel consisting of a priest, a psychiatrist, a gynaecologist and a social worker. The social worker Noreen Kearney noted that in order to qualify for Dublin Corporation housing, a family had to have at least three children, and this put pressure on couples to have children as rapidly as possible. The gynaecologist, Declan Meagher of the National Maternity Hospital, expressed the view that the safe period was only effective for a minority of couples; coitus interruptus was 'not only emotionally and physically damaging, but it also left a sense of guilt'. One women, heard on the programme, reported that a priest had refused her absolution in confession because she was using contraception, and she did not go to confession for a long time after that; another informed Viney that 'you cannot talk to those priests: they make you feel so low'.[27] Fuller notes that 'Viney expressed the mood of the moment, when he referred to the expectation that "any day now a pronouncement from the Pope may well take this whole issue a big step further" '.[28] Viney claimed that most reactions to the programme had been 'completely approving'; the most common question was why the taped interviews were dominated by Dublin working-class mothers. His response was that the urban working class was 'where the most urgent problems are – the kind of problems, as I said in the programme, which give

[25] Michael Solomons, *Pro Life? The Irish question* (Dublin: Lilliput, 1992), p. 19.
[26] Peter Lennon, 'Sex and the Irish', *IT*, 31 October 1966.   [27] *IT*, 14 October 1966.
[28] Louise Fuller, *Irish Catholicism since 1950. The undoing of a culture* (Dublin: Gill&Macmillan, 2002), p. 197.

family planning its point'. He commented on 'the essential difference between managing a big family on a farm and attempting the same in the concrete desert of a Dublin council estate',[29] but one might argue that this reflects a rather romantic view of life on a farm.

Some gynaecologists had been providing family planning advice for private patients for some years. By the early 1960s, Michael Solomons was providing family planning advice to public patients at his gynaecological clinic in Mercer's Hospital (a general hospital).[30] In 1963, the largest maternity hospital, the National Maternity Hospital (Holles St) which operated under the patronage of the Archbishop of Dublin, established a clinic to provide family planning advice 'in conformity with Catholic moral teaching'. For the first time, family planning (presumably the safe period) became an integral part of the training programmes for midwives, doctors and medical students; 'the clinic was instituted with the full knowledge and at least tacit support of the Archbishop John Charles McQuaid'.[31] By 1965, all three Dublin maternity hospitals were operating 'Marriage Guidance Clinics'. The 1965 annual report of the Coombe noted that 'many patients either for medical or social reasons are anxious to avail of it'.[32] In the same year, 4,000 women who had recently given birth in Holles St attended lectures on family planning. Although the Holles St clinic only provided advice on the safe period, it was so overcrowded that access was restricted to mothers whose babies were delivered in the hospital. Individual consultations were only provided for women with serious medical conditions or 'highly-fertile patients and those with distressing socio-economic conditions' – the majority were under thirty years and had given birth to five or more children. Yet only 33 per cent turned up for consultations.[33] By 1967, Holles Street was prescribing the pill to 'couples who felt in conscience able to take it' – roughly half of those offered it.[34] Lack of resources meant that the family planning clinic in the Rotunda Hospital could only see 'extreme cases'; the 301 women seen in 1968 included tubercular mothers, mothers whose children had TB, women with an alcoholic or unemployed husband, women whose husband deserted them during pregnancy. 'All of these women had ten or more children.'[35]

---

[29] Michael Viney, 'The pill and the programme', *IT*, 26 October 1966.
[30] Solomons, *Pro-Life*, p. 17.
[31] Tony Farmar, *Holles street 1894–1994, the national maternity hospital – a centenary history* (Dublin: A&A Farmar, 1994), p. 152.
[32] *Rotunda Hospital Clinical Report 1964*, p. 59; *Coombe Lying-In Hospital Clinical Report*, 1965.
[33] *National Maternity Hospital, Clinical Report 1966*, p. 95.
[34] Farmar, *Holles street*, p. 153; *National Maternity Hospital, Clinical Report* 1967, p. 95.
[35] Solomons, *Pro-Life?* p. 21.

Hospital clinics were established to assist women with large families and/or serious medical and social conditions; however, the early adopters of family planning were younger, more middle-class couples. By 1967, an estimated 12,000 Irish women were using the pill.[36] The publication on 18 July 1968, of the papal encyclical *Humanae Vitae*, which ruled that the contraceptive pill was contrary to Catholic Church teaching was a major shock. Holles Street ceased prescribing the pill in its clinic.[37] But the contraceptive genie was out of the bottle, and despite the papal pronouncement, it could not be put back. An opinion poll of doctors quoted in the *Irish Medical Times* showed that of 538 who took part, 65 per cent disagreed with the papal ruling; 91 per cent said that it would not lead to major changes in the advice that they gave.[38] There were claims that some Irish women stopped taking the pill as a result of *Humanae Vitae*, and the birth-rate rose as a consequence. In November 1969, Garret FitzGerald expressed the view that the current increase in births might be due to the encyclical. However, Brendan Walsh argued convincingly that the rising number of births was due to the soaring marriage rate, not to the papal ruling.[39] The number of Irish women using the pill is estimated to have fallen from 17,000 to over 15,000, following the papal encyclical, but it soon rose to 19,000.[40] By 1974, it was claimed that more than 38,000 women were using the pill;[41] approximately one-third of married women aged twenty to thirty-four.[42]

Other forms of contraception continued to be prohibited by the 1935 Criminal Law Amendment Act, and this became a critical matter, as evidence emerged of the health risks associated with the pill. In 1969, what Linda Connolly describes as 'the discreetly named Fertility Guidance Clinic' opened in Dublin; it soon changed its name to the Irish Family Planning Association (IFPA) Clinic.[43] Most of the eight men and women who founded the clinic were medical practitioners who had worked outside Ireland at some stage in their career. The clinic received financial support from the International Planned Parenthood

[36] Micheline McCormack, 'Irish women and the Pill Ban', *IP*, 29 July 1968.

[37] Farmar, *Holles street*, p. 154.

[38] 'Doctors give views on birth control ruling', *II*, 21 August 1968, citing a poll reported in the *Irish Medical Times*, August 1968.

[39] Walsh, 'Ireland's demographic transition', p. 261.

[40] Ian Dalrymple, quoted in *Catholic Standard*, April 1973.

[41] SD, vol. 77, col. 208, 20 February 1974.

[42] In 1971, there were 106,776 married women aged 20–34.

[43] Linda Connolly, *The Irish women's movement. From revolution to devolution* (Basingstoke: Palgrave Macmillan, 2003), p. 95.

Federation and the Ford Foundation; most of the early clients were middle class.[44] By the early 1970s, they had opened a second clinic in Mountjoy Square, a more working-class area; both clinics provided access and guidance on all methods of family planning.[45] Yet, despite efforts to attract working-class clients, the clinics tended to be patronised by the middle class; most clients were women, and a growing number were single. The existence of these clinics, reports that an increasing number of couples were importing contraceptives from Britain or Northern Ireland, either in their personal luggage, or by mail order, and the growing instances of contraceptives being seized by customs authorities[46] represented a direct challenge to the 1935 Criminal Law Amendment Act. While there appears to be evidence of an increase in pre-marital sex, and an open acknowledgement of contraception that would have been unthinkable ten to fifteen years earlier, we should not overstate the extent of the sexual revolution. In 1971, 63 per cent of those surveyed opposed the sale of contraceptives; only 29 per cent of women were in favour.[47]

---

[44] Solomons, *Pro-Life?* pp. 23–30; Barry Desmond, *Finally and in conclusion* (Dublin: New Island, 2000), p. 226.

[45] *Commission on the Status of Women*, Report to Minister for Finance, Dec., 1972, para 568.

[46] *IT*, 9 April 1970, David Goldberg, 'Contraception and the Law'. Customs and excise staff were seizing spermicides which had to be used in conjunction with diaphragms which were being fitted by a number of family planning clinics.

[47] *IP*, 15 April 1974. Public opinion was volatile; support had almost doubled by April 1974, only to fall back later.

8   Women, children and families

Women and work

The 1960s afforded women greater opportunities to work as secretaries, clerks and teachers – provided that they had the necessary level of schooling – and much better marriage prospects than in the past, with a hope of settling down in a house with modern amenities. Post-war domestic bliss reached Ireland, just as it was being challenged by an emerging second-wave feminism. There is good reason to believe that many women were content to become full-time wives and mothers, not least because so many of their predecessors had been denied this lifestyle. For most women, paid employment was a transient phase between school and marriage. In the past a significant proportion found themselves in long-term careers, not necessarily by choice (though there exceptions), but because they failed to marry. But women's career options were limited, even when no formal barriers existed. Family and societal expectations and the limitations of the curriculum in girls' schools were only marginally less effective obstacles than legal restrictions. While more girls than boys attended secondary school, girls were more likely to leave after sitting their intermediate certificate (age fifteen–sixteen) and less likely to attend university. Secretarial courses, nursing or primary school teaching were the standard career aspiration among parents and school principals alike. Although a draft manuscript for a book on careers for girls produced in the early 1960s included sections on veterinary medicine and a 'lady barrister', the overall tone favoured jobs that were gendered and conventional. The section on 'Lady Barrister' concluded 'As to whether the lady Barrister is going to be a great success at the Bar, or even to make a living out of it, that is another matter!', whereas air hostess was 'an attractive career for girls', and the chapter on nursing emphasised 'that a nurse needs to be trustworthy and reliable. She must be sympathetic and patient and keep her good humour despite fearful odds. Some of her patients are frightened and nervous with reason, others are merely foolishly afraid and concerned – but a sick person's fears are very real to himself and he looks to the nurse as a rock in the storm.' No mention of medical expertise![1]

In 1966, over one-quarter of women worked in jobs where at least 90 per cent of fellow-workers were women; more than three-quarters were in jobs with a majority female workforce.[2] The 1966 Census recorded only five women engineers (2,878 men), thirty-two architects and surveyors (1,720 men) and 654 women directors, managers and company secretaries (11,195 men), the majority probably in family businesses.[3] Nevertheless, women were more visible in the workforce than in the past when domestic and other forms of service (i.e., waitressing) were the major source of employment. A growing number of women now worked in organisations employing large numbers of men, which made them aware of their lower pay and limited promotion prospects.

Women in public service jobs were required to resign on marriage. This was the norm throughout Europe and North America in the 1930s, but the laws were relaxed during the Second World War, though not in neutral Ireland. Some private sector firms operated a formal marriage bar; in others it was the convention. The marriage bar reduced the number of women with sufficient experience to apply for senior positions, and the assumption that women were 'birds of passage' dissuaded employers from grooming them for promotion. Synthetic turnover made it easy to concentrate women in repetitive, undemanding roles. In 1972, there were only two women in the Irish civil service at Principal Officer grade, and none in a more senior position; no woman was among the seventy-five senior staff in local authorities.[4] Thekla Beere, appointed as Secretary of the new Department of Transport and Power in 1959, the first woman to serve at that grade, retired in 1966.[5] In 1964, the post of Chief Medical Officer in the Department of Health was advertised as open only to men.[6] Gendered pay, promotion and employment structures were equally common in the private sector.[7] The commercial banks recruited a growing number of women, but in the early 1970s, 60 per cent of women in banking were under twenty-five years, because of the marriage bar. Women bank officials were not permitted to work on the bank

---

[1] NAI, Tweedy Papers, 98/17/2/2/13 Careers for Girls.
[2] Brendan M. Walsh, 'Aspects of labour supply and demand with special reference to the employment of women in Ireland', *JSSISI*, xxxii, part iii, p. 96.
[3] *Commission on the status of women*, para 41, p. 25.
[4] *Commission on the status of women*, para 233, pp. 101–2.
[5] Anna Bryson, *No coward soul. A biography of Thekla Beere* (Dublin: Institute of Public Administration, 2009).
[6] NAI DT 96/6/170 Equal Pay for men and women in the civil service Lemass to Ryan 1 December 1964.
[7] Cogan, *The Irish services sector*, pp. 147–9.

counters; a separate career structure kept them on a lower pay scale and offered fewer and more poorly paid promotional prospects than men.[8]

As most Irish women had traditionally worked in family businesses or in jobs that were gender-segregated, the issue of equal pay was somewhat academic. In the public service, where men and women carried out identical work, there were two grades: one for single men and all women, and a higher rate for married men. The more centralised pay bargaining of the 1960s – specifically the 1964 pay round which guaranteed a minimum increase of £1 a week for *men* with lower pro rata increases for women and juveniles – highlighted women's inferior position. The relative pay of men and women remained broadly unchanged throughout the decade: women earned 53 per cent of the average male wage in 1960 and 54 per cent in 1969. In the 1969 pay round, however, women secured a higher percentage increase than men (though a smaller monetary sum); in the next two pay rounds women in the public sector were given equal increases with men and a number of state companies introduced equal pay for clerical workers. By 1971, women were earning 59 per cent of male rates.[9]

Improvements in women's working conditions were initially driven by labour shortages and by international forces; the first stirrings of a proto-feminist movement can also be detected. Politicians, trade unions and employers responded slowly and often reluctantly to pressures for change, and there was no major groundswell in Ireland in favour of increased working opportunities for women during the 1960s. By the end of the decade, however, some employers were complaining of shortages of women workers. As more women married and at an earlier age a growing number of married women were re-employed on temporary contracts in both the private and public sectors.[10] The marriage bar was gradually giving way to a maternity bar, with married women in short-term temporary employment. Although women in insured employment could claim maternity benefit for twelve weeks – six weeks before and six weeks after the expected date of delivery – they had no right to return to their former job. The Commission on the Status of Women noted that none of the firms surveyed had any provision for maternity leave or for women to return to their jobs after giving birth.[11]

---

[8] Fogarty, *Report of banks inquiry*. Paul Rouse and Mark Duncan, *Handling change. A history of the Irish bank officials association* (Cork: The Collins Press, 2012), pp. 154–5.

[9] Mary E. Daly, 'Women work and trade unionism', in Margaret MacCurtain and Donncha Ó Corráin (eds), *Women in Irish society. The historical dimension* (Dublin: Arlen House, 1978), p. 78.

[10] Walsh, 'Aspects of labour supply', pp. 97–9; NAI 96/6/184 *Proposed* commission on the status of women. Memo. Dept. of Labour to Sec. Department Taoiseach, 21 November 1968.

[11] *Commission on the status of women*, p. 98.

Ireland lagged behind Western Europe in its treatment of working women. Article 119 of the Treaty of Rome required member states to ensure equal pay for equal work,[12] though it seems unlikely that this commitment was honoured by all member nations. The 1961 European Social Charter, drawn up by the Council of Europe, set out a range of rights relating to work, health and social protection, including the right of men and women to equal pay for work of equal value, paid maternity leave, protection against dismissal because of pregnancy and time off for breastfeeding mothers.[13] The European Social Charter and UN resolutions were an important source of external pressure, given Ireland's determination to become a member of the EEC and a more general wish to be regarded as a member in good standing in international organisations. Seán MacEntee, Tanaiste and Minister for Health – generally regarded as a conservative voice – warned that ratifying the European Social Charter would mean that 'our policies' would be open to scrutiny by the Council of Europe; 'Adherence to the proposed Charter would represent an immense surrender of national sovereignty in the domestic sphere.' Although the government ratified the European Social Charter, it did not sign up to the equal pay clause, claiming that the maternity benefits available through social insurance meant that Ireland met that requirement.[14] When the Labour Court approved the 1964 wage round giving women a lower minimum pay increase than men, the Association of Women Citizens of Ireland told Lemass that this was 'a particularly retrograde step in view of your own frequently – made statements that this country should prepare itself to enter the EEC'. A letter from Lemass to the Minister for Finance (Ryan) in December 1964 stated that the government had accepted the principle of equal pay, and there is further evidence that several ministers were keen to adopt equal pay (albeit in a restricted form), though the Department of Finance – which was responsible for pay and recruitment throughout the public service – remained resolutely opposed.[15]

In 1968, Ireland signed a UN resolution on the elimination of discrimination against women, which required signatories to take steps to ensure equal rights with men for all women, married or unmarried, including the right to equal pay and equal treatment in respect of work

---

[12] *Commission on the status of women*, p. 18.

[13] *European Social Charter. Collected texts*, 6th edition 30 June 2008, pp. 13–16. The Charter covered a wide range of social rights that extended well beyond women.

[14] UCDA MacEntee Papers P67/319 European social charter, 7 September 1961 memo by the Tanaiste; Dept. External Affairs memo 16 September 1964; Dept. Industry and Commerce 20 April 1964.

[15] NAI 96/6/170 Equal Pay.

of equal value; however, Ireland reserved its position with regard to women in the public service and equal pay and declared that it did not regard the failure to summon women for jury service – a practice dating from the 1920s – or the exclusion of women from certain jobs 'for which by objective standards they are not suitable' as discriminatory.[16] In 1967, the UN Commission on the Status of Women asked women's organisations to put pressure on national governments to establish a Commission on the Status of Women in their country. A broad alliance of women's organisations, brought together by the Irish Housewives Association and the Association of Business and Professional Women, lobbied the government on this matter.[17] In December 1969, more than a year after first being contacted, the Taoiseach Jack Lynch announced that a Commission on the Status of Women would be appointed.

The Commission, appointed in March 1970, was chaired by Thekla Beere, former Secretary of the Department of Transport and Power The terms of reference were almost identical to the memo submitted by the ad hoc committee of women's organisations.[18] It reported to the Minister for Finance, indicating that equal pay, the marriage bar and pensions were regarded as the crucial issues. Shortly after its appointment, members were asked to fast-track a report on equal pay. More than half of the final report was concerned with pay, employment, social welfare, pensions and taxation. The recommendations were designed to remove discrimination against women, married, widowed or single, with respect to employment, pensions, welfare and taxation.[19] By the time that the interim report on equal pay appeared in October 1971, the government was moving gradually to remove gender-based discrimination in the public service – giving equal pay awards and removing male-only job designations. In July 1972, the Employer Labour Conference signed a National Wage Agreement which accepted the principle of equal pay and set out a process for its phased implementation.[20] The public service marriage bar was removed in 1973; an anti-discrimination pay act was enacted the following year.

UN resolutions and Ireland's application for EEC membership were crucial in promoting employment equality. In 1976, the EEC rejected a request by the Irish government for a derogation on the introduction of equal pay. While women's organisations joined forces to campaign for equal employment rights, this was not a universally popular cause. The trade union movement was at best ambivalent: they failed to demand

---

[16] NAI 98/6/184 memo Dept. of External Affairs 23 April 1968; 22 October 1968.
[17] Hillery, Minister for Labour pressed Lynch to take action on several occasions.
[18] NAI 98/6/184; Bryson, *No coward soul*, pp. 166–80.
[19] *Commission on the status of women: summary of recommendations*, pp. 227–37.
[20] *Commission on the status of women*, App. B, pp. 256–8.

equal pay during negotiations on annual wage rounds. The Civil Service Clerical Association, which represented a significant number of women, was formally opposed to removing the marriage bar and other unions may have shared this opinion.[21] Some public officials and ministers tried to claim that different pay scales for married men and women/single men did not breach the EEC commitment to equal pay.[22] In a 1968 survey of male employees carried out by the Economic and Social Research Institute (ESRI), 79 per cent were of the opinion that a single man should have a higher basic wage than a single woman; only fifty-four respondents (5.4 per cent) considered that workers should be paid a common wage, irrespective of gender or marital status.[23] Interviews carried out with management on behalf of the Commission on the Status of Women, revealed extensive gender stereotyping – assumptions that men were more suited to intellectually demanding jobs; that 'jobs with promotional potential' should be assigned to men; that women had a low level of motivation and were not interested in promotion, even 'lacking ability'.[24] This survey also indicated a broad consensus that mothers of young children should not be in paid employment. Insofar as attitudes towards married women in the workforce were evolving, they appeared to favour women returning to work when their children were older. Although 74 per cent of women interviewed by the ESRI approved of married women in paid employment, 'a very substantial proportion ... felt that certain conditions should exist before a woman re-entered employment' – most commonly no young children.[25]

Members of the Commission on the Status of Women were 'unanimous in the opinion that very young children, at least up to three years of age, should if at all possible, be cared for by the mother at home'.[26] They favoured moderate reform, not revolution, which was in line with Irish majority opinion. There were 10,000 fewer women at work in 1971 than in 1961. Nevertheless, the Commission's recommendations, the removal of the marriage bar and the EEC's insistence on Ireland introducing equal pay were major milestones in advancing women's employment. Yet for most women the change was not revolutionary. The number of married women in paid employment did rise, but prohibitive marginal income tax rates on two-income households, social attitudes and lack of childcare meant only a minority continued in the long term. It was only in the 1980s that significant

[21] *Commission on the status of women*, para 252–3 pp. 108–9.
[22] NAI 96/6/170 Equal Pay; 98/6/184.   [23] *Commission on the status of women*, p. 38.
[24] *Commission on the status of women*, pp. 86–8, 93.
[25] *Commission on the status of women*, p. 124.
[26] *Commission on the status of women*, p. 130.

numbers of married women began remaining in employment after childbirth.[27]

Marginalised women and children

The biographer of Thekla Beere, the chair of the Commission on the Status of Women, noted that 'Beere herself was more concerned with what the Commission might achieve for marginalised women in Irish society – widows, unmarried mothers, prisoners' wives and deserted wives – rather than the advancement of career women'.[28] In 1966, there were 732,000 women and 188,843 men over fourteen who were described as 'not gainfully occupied'. The 40,665 widowers were greatly outnumbered by 125,888 widows, 45,000 of them under sixty-four years – many with dependent children. Article 41 of the 1937 Constitution recognised that 'by her life in the home, the woman gives to the State a support without which the common good cannot be achieved. The State shall therefore endeavour to ensure that mothers will not be obliged by economic necessity to engage in labour to the neglect of her duties in the home.' Yet Irish law was seriously in need of reform with respect to women's rights within the family, and social services provided minimal support for widows and other women who were not in paid employment. Welfare payments operated on the principle of the male breadwinner, with payments for unemployment benefit or assistance or disability benefits all going to the male. The only payment to acknowledge that a woman might have dependents was the means-tested widows' pension, first introduced in 1935.

In Britain, the decade following the securing of female suffrage saw the enactment of laws relating to marriage and guardianship of infants; it was not until the late 1950s and 1960s that moves were made to update these laws in Ireland.[29] Pressure for reform came from a network of women's organisations, including the Irish Housewife's Association and the Women Graduates Associations of both Irish universities, Dublin University and the National University of Ireland. Linda Connolly suggests that there was a direct link between the small and low-key feminist

---

[27] Brendan Walsh, 'Labour force participation and the growth of women's employment, Ireland 1971–1991', *ESR*, vol. 24 no. 4, 1993, pp. 369–400.

[28] Bryson, *No coward soul*, p. 144.

[29] Lindsey Earner-Byrne, ' "Aphrodite rising form the waves", Women's voluntary activism and the women's movement in twentieth-century Ireland', in Ester Breitenbach and Pat Thane (eds), *Women and citizenship in Britain and Ireland in the twentieth century. What difference did the vote make?* (London: Continuum, 2010), p. 98.

network that existed in the mid-twentieth century and the strong second-wave feminist movement of the 1970s.[30]

The 1957 Married Women's Status Act, a largely forgotten milestone for Irish women, provided that husband and wife were to be treated as two separate persons for all purposes of acquisition of property, and it permitted a wife to sue a husband for damages in cases such as a car accident, changes that predated similar reforms in Britain.[31] But Ireland was one of the very few countries and, according to the Department of Justice, probably the only one in Western Europe to give absolute freedom of testamentary disposition. A husband could make a will, leaving nothing to his wife or children. The Department of Justice argued that the special position accorded to the family in the Constitution demanded that a man's obligation to maintain his wife and children during his lifetime (which does not appear to have been enforced) should extend to after his death.[32] A 1962 Programme of Law Reform, which recommended recognising women's rights with regard to wills, inheritance and guardianship of infants, was given a warm welcome by the Irish Housewives Association, who noted that it would raise women's civil and economic status and remove legal discrimination.[33] Yet the protracted history of the 1965 Succession Act suggests that a significant section of Irish society – most especially the farming community – was reluctant to give statutory recognition to women as equal partners within the family.

In 1963, Justice Minister Charles Haughey brought proposals to Cabinet to give a widow and all children under the age of twenty-one statutory rights to a share of a husband's estate. These proposals were strongly opposed by the Ministers for Agriculture and Lands who claimed that this would be against the best interests of Irish agriculture and prevent earlier rural marriages. The Minister for Lands wanted the entire farm to pass smoothly to one individual without financial encumbrances; the Minister for Agriculture was concerned that the provisions might result in the division of the estate, or the heir being saddled with debts. He also wished to deny an unfaithful spouse any statutory right of inheritance. When a draft bill, broadly in line with Haughey's proposal, came before Cabinet in 1964, Minister for Lands Michael Moran used the absence of divorce as an argument against giving widows a statutory right to inherit. He referred to marriages 'in which the contracting

[30] Connolly, *The Irish Women's Movement*, p. 89.
[31] James Casey, 'Law and the legal system, 1957–82', in Litton (ed.), *Unequal achievement*, p. 276.
[32] NAI DT S17439A Memo to Govt. 27 February 1963. Reform was first proposed by the Commission on Emigration.
[33] NAI DT S14071b 62 Law Reform.

parties have been separated for years but have no satisfactory legal remedy'; 'a number of "shot-gun" marriages in rural Ireland after which the parties have never cohabited, in respect of which one of the parties quite often emigrates to England or America and is never heard from again until he or she turns up to contest the will of the deceased spouse'.[34]

Married women, who had separated from their husbands, were probably at greatest risk of disinheritance. Fine Gael deputy Riche Ryan (who practised as a solicitor) highlighted a case known to him where a couple, apparently in comfortable circumstances, separated; an agreement was drawn up providing for the man to contribute to the support of his separated wife. However, he made a will leaving her nothing, and when he died she had to apply for public assistance. Ryan emphasised that the absence of statutory inheritance rights for widows and children meant that 'society is now maintaining widows and children of people who, if they had lived, would have been under a moral and statutory obligation to maintain those people'.[35] Childless farming widows were especially vulnerable, since there was a strong tradition (documented in Arensberg and Kimball) of keeping land within the family,[36] and a farm might be willed to a brother or a nephew. An anonymous letter to Seán Lemass in December 1963, written on poor-quality paper, gives an insight to their position.

I am writing to you to ask a request. Will you as Taoiseach see to widows. Will you please protect them It is God's will if they have no children and sure in the eyes of Our Blessed Lord they are entitled to their husband's assets and, even if he makes a will and gives her nothing the Law should be there to protect her and give her what she is entitled to in the eyes of God. The woman with a family has them to help her but the poor unfortunate woman with no family is destitute and has nobody to help her.

I feel you as Taoiseach in whom we all have great trust will protect us.

God bless you for ever.

From a childless person.[37]

When Haughey announced that he would introduce a bill giving statutory rights to widows and dependent children, an editorial in the *Irish Times* commented that 'the principal feature . . . is the improvement in the rights of women'.[38] But a motion tabled at a meeting of the Fianna Fáil National Executive, shortly after this announcement, requested 'the Government to re-consider the provisions of the Succession Bill relating

[34] NAI DT S17439A.   [35] DD vol. 205, cols. 1031–3, 6 November 1963.
[36] Conrad Arensberg and Solon T. Kimball, *Family and community in Ireland* (Cambridge MA: Harvard University Press, second edition 1968), pp. 131–4.
[37] NAI DT S17439A.   [38] *IT*, 11 July 1964.

to compulsory distribution of property having regard to their legal social and political implications particularly in rural Ireland'.[39] Although the Catholic Church was supportive, the measure was opposed by the legal profession and by many leading figures in Fine Gael, including reforming politicians Declan Costello and Garret FitzGerald.[40] The bill, first introduced in October 1964, did not become law until 1965, an indication of the uphill struggle to have it enacted. The NFA issued a press release in October 1964, which noted that 'the Council was convinced that the stability of Irish agriculture depends on the right of a farmer to dispose of his own property, by will or otherwise, within the family circle in the light of his special knowledge of the particular circumstances and requirements of his own family and farm'.[41] County executives of the NFA lobbied local TDs assiduously. The Wicklow County Executive noted that a deputation that met local TDs 'found that all of them seem to agree with the official N.F.A. attitude to the Bill'.[42] The NFA secured some changes, including limiting inheritance rights to a widow and *dependent* children, and some technical and financial clauses, but the core elements survived. A survey of the archives of the Irish Countrywomen's Association suggests that they evaded the issue, though they were happy to express their opinion on topics such as deserted wives and the pension and welfare treatment of single women; this apparent silence indicates that the legislation was highly contentious.[43] The measure was widely discussed in rural Ireland – where Dáil proceedings were not routinely followed.

The Act gave widows a statutory right to a share of the estate. It prevented a husband from disinheriting his wife, by rendering ineffective any disposition of property or assets made within three years of his death, unless she had given her written consent. If a man died intestate, a childless widow would inherit the estate; if there were children she would get two-thirds, with the balance divided among the children. If a husband made a will effectively disinheriting his wife, she could insist on her statutory right to one-half of the estate if there were no children or one-third if there were children. While the Succession Act protected the rights of widows, it left farmers' wives and women who played an active role in their husband's business without statutory entitlement during his life; one writer has described it as 'ironic – not until after his death is a husband

---

[39] UCDA P 176/348 FF National Executive.
[40] Finola Kennedy, *Cottage to crèche. Family change in Ireland* (Dublin: Institute of Public Administration, 2001), pp. 224–8.
[41] *IFJ*, 3 October 1964.   [42] *IFJ*, 31 October 1964.
[43] NLI, Records of Irish Countrywomen's Association MSS 39,284/1–39,890.

required by law to share his property with his wife, regardless of her input to the family enterprise'.[44] Yet, despite this qualification the Succession Act is a significant landmark in protecting the interests of widows and dependent children.

The Act forms part of a wider focus on widows as a deserving group that needed the protection and assistance of the state. Ireland's late age of marriage, especially for men (average age of 33 in 1946), meant that women were often left widowed with dependent children, and without adequate means of support, though a means-tested widows' pension, introduced in 1935, provided some minimal assistance. Few widows qualified for pensions through their husbands' occupational pensions – widows of public servants and primary school teachers, for example, only received one year's salary. Widows of TDs commonly stood for election when their husbands died, because they often had no alternative means of support. Pensions for TDs' widows were introduced in 1968. In 1966, the Royal Medical Benevolent Society of Ireland made a special appeal to its members on behalf of doctors' widows, especially those with children still in education; they distributed £3,905 to ninety-two cases in the previous year.[45]

There were few jobs open to older women wishing to return to work, although the civil service had provision for re-employing widows and deserted wives who were former civil servants, and a number of organisations such as the *Irish Press* group appear to have set aside certain jobs for widows, such as processing the crossword and fashion competitions. The National Association of Widows was established in 1967 by Eileen Proctor, who was widowed in 1962 when she was in her forties, to lobby for pensions and other supports; her letter in the *Irish Press* prompted a major response.[46] Minister for Finance Charles Haughey, whose mother was widowed with young children, was sympathetic. A new pension scheme for widows of civil servants was introduced in 1968; in 1969, special provision was made for existing civil service widows who would not be covered by the new scheme; between 1967 and 1969, pensions for widows was increased by 42 per cent compared with a 16 per cent rise in the cost of living.[47]

Improved pensions for widows were universally welcomed, and it might have been expected that raising the legal age of marriage would likewise have been non-contentious. Irish women's organisations had

[44] Patricia O'Hara, *Partners in production? Women, farm and family in Ireland* (New York/ Oxford: Berghahn, 1998), p. 114.
[45] *IT*, 31 March 1966.   [46] Eileen Proctor, *II* obituary, 9 December 2007.
[47] NAI 96/6/184 Speech on Women in Irish Society June 1969.

been lobbying for such legislation since 1957.[48] In Ireland, the minimum legal age for marriage established by common law was twelve for a girl and fourteen for a boy – ages set by Canon Law in the distant past (in 1917 Canon Law amended them to fourteen and sixteen, respectively). In 1962, the Department of Health proposed legislating to set a minimum age of sixteen, in line with Britain and Northern Ireland; they noted that 'the proposed reform is generally desired by those who can be taken as expressing the feminine view'. While few Irish marriages involved girls in their early teens, there were instances of British men coming to Ireland accompanied by women aged less than sixteen years in order to marry. These cases 'occasionally attract a great deal of unsavoury or sensational publicity particularly in the English Sunday newspapers, and the fact that such marriages may take place in this country cannot enhance its reputation abroad'.[49] In 1961, an Englishman who had 'carnal knowledge' of a twelve-year-old girl travelled to Ireland and married her to avoid prosecution for a sexual offence.[50] The proposed legislation would bring Ireland into line with Western Europe and a proposed UN convention; however, the Department of Health memo noted that a professor of Canon Law, who had been consulted, wanted the bill to provide for exemptions, 'if it was considered in the best interests of that person', 'such as the case of a girl under 16 years who became pregnant, and who wished to marry the man responsible for her condition'. The canon lawyer wanted authority to grant exemptions (to the civil law) to be vested in bishops of the Catholic Church and the Church of Ireland or in the District Court in the case of religions with no recognised head. This 'Reverend Professor' was of the opinion that the age of puberty would decline as living standards increased 'and he felt that it would be unwise in these circumstances to have any age limit below which an exemption could not be given'.[51] Hilda Tweedy, of the Irish Housewife's Association, noted that some letters to the newspapers argued that a twelve-year-old pregnant girl should be permitted to marry in order to legitimise her child.[52] Nevertheless, the Catholic Hierarchy gave their approval in principle to the proposed legislation, though Dr Fergus, secretary to the Hierarchy, asked for sight of the clause relating to the minimum age of marriage before it was made public. Minister for Health MacEntee obviously felt sufficiently

---

[48] They included the Catholic women's federation of secondary school unions; the National University of Ireland Women Graduates Association; the TCD Women Graduates Association; the ICA; Institute of Almoners, Save the Children's Fund; Girl's Friendly Society and the Women's National Health Association.

[49] NAI DT S17693/A/63 Marriages Bill, 25 June 1962.

[50] Hilda Tweedy, *A link in the chain, The story of the Irish housewives association, 1941–1992* (Dublin: Attic Press, 1992), p. 32.

[51] NAI S17206A/63.   [52] Tweedy, *A link in the chain*, p. 32.

confident that this would not present any major difficulties, because he arranged to bring a first reading of the bill before the Dáil before the summer recess of 1963, which only gave the short title of the bill.[53] However, the Hierarchy was evidently insisting on exemptions and negotiations continued with all churches. The matter was not resolved until 1972 when 'an interim measure' set a minimum age of sixteen with provision for exemptions.[54]

One intriguing feature of the debate over the Succession Act is the open acknowledgement of marriage breakdown. Desertion, separation and marriage breakdown were not new; for generations Irishmen had emigrated and ceased to send money home; some had established second families. This was highlighted in the early 1950s by an English Catholic social worker Maurice Foley.[55] Desertion and other marriage difficulties featured in the caseload of the Emigrants' Section of the Dublin Archdiocese's Catholic Social Welfare Bureau;[56] yet the topic attracted little public attention. Although there is no evidence that the incidence of desertion or broken marriages was rising, references to marriage breakdown and its consequences became more frequent in the 1960s. The 1964 Guardianship of Infants Act, which was ostensibly introduced to deal with custody in the event of widowhood, was increasingly used to determine child custody in cases of marriage breakdown. The legislation was guided by two principles: that the welfare of the child should be the paramount consideration, and subject to this, to give the mother and father equal rights in regard to the custody and upbringing of an infant and the administration of any property belonging to the infant. If one parent died, the surviving parent would be the sole guardian, with power to determine who would be appointed as a second guardian; a dead parent could not bind a surviving spouse in that regard. Introducing the bill in the Dáil, Minister for Justice Charles Haughey cited the judgement of the Supreme Court (1952) in the notorious Tilson case[57] that 'the Irish Constitution and especially Article 42 established the principle that the parents "have a joint power and duty in respect of the religious education of their children" and the parent . . . cannot be construed "in some generic

---

[53] NAI DT S17296A/63.
[54] DD vol. 263, col. 1912, 7 November 1972. The Act also made provision for church marriages contracted by Irish couples in Lourdes to be declared legally valid (French law required a civil ceremony), and went some way towards removing distinctions between different religions in marriage law.
[55] Daly, *Slow failure*, pp. 175–6.
[56] A. E. C. W. Spencer, *Arrangements for the integration of Irish immigrants in England and Wales*, edited by Mary E. Daly (Dublin: Irish Manuscripts Commission, 2012), pp. 56–9.
[57] For details, see J. H. Whyte, *Church and state in modern Ireland* (Dublin: G&M, 1971), pp. 169–71.

sense that included only the father when he was living". This judgement marks the establishment of the mother's equality with the father.'[58]

This Act also dealt with the guardianship of illegitimate children. Under common law the mother had custody, and while the mother was confirmed as the full (and sole) guardian of her child, with power to appoint a testamentary guardian and to apply to the court on matters regarding the child's welfare, it gave the natural father the right to apply to the court if he believed that the mother was neglecting the child.[59] In cases where a couple had secured a divorce *a mensa et thoro*,[60] the court had power to decree that the person whose misconduct gave rise to the decree could be declared unfit to have custody, and they would not be given guardianship rights in the event of the death of the other parent. However, as these cases were heard in the High Court, the absence of legal aid meant that this option was only available to prosperous families.[61] In December 1970, a woman sued her husband for divorce *a mensa a thoro* on the grounds of incompatibility: they had no interests in common, no conversation, no sex life and he didn't wash himself. The case was extensively covered in the newspapers, which gave names and graphic details.[62] Guardianship of children cases were much cheaper and were held in private. Michael Viney noted that while the cases were solely concerned with custody of children, 'this does not prevent most parents acting as if they were separation proceedings concerned with "grounds" of adultery, cruelty, desertion and so on. There are lurid descriptions of the number of occasions on which the husband has had too much to drink and equally lurid descriptions of the neurotic behaviour of the wife. The children seem often to be mere pawns in the confrontation between the spouses.'[63] But these life stories remained hidden from public scrutiny.

Deserted wives in Ireland, as elsewhere, resorted to the courts to secure maintenance. The maximum weekly maintenance that a District Court could award was £4, a sum set in 1940. Despite regular expressions of sympathy by politicians, this threshold was not raised until 1971 when it was set at £15, plus £5 for each dependent child. Many husbands evaded maintenance payments by moving to Britain. In 1973, no reciprocal arrangements existed for enforcing maintenance orders made by Irish courts in Britain: the Commission on the Status of Women expressed

---

[58] DD, vol. 207, col. 143, 29 January 1964.   [59] DD vol. 207 col. 142, 29 January 1964.
[60] Divorce without provision for remarriage.
[61] Casey, 'Law and the legal system', p. 276. Cases could only be taken in the High Court. Don Buckley, 'Women first', *IT*, 19 December 1972.
[62] *IT*, 3 December–19 December 1970.
[63] 'The broken marriage 5. Putting apart', *IT*, 30 October 1970.

the hope that this would be resolved under an EEC convention.[64] Wives who failed to secure maintenance had to apply for home assistance (discretionary means-tested payments). In 1967, 151 deserted wives were receiving home assistance in Dublin city, that is, 5 per cent of all recipients. Assistance officers referred these cases to the ISPCC or the Salvation Army, who contacted their UK counterparts in an effort to persuade husbands to return, or set up a mechanism of support.[65] In 1969, the ISPCC handled 397 new cases of desertion by the father and 65 cases of deserted mothers.[66]

In 1970, Deserted Wife's Allowance was introduced, providing a level of payments similar to widows, though the allowance was only payable to women with dependent children or women without dependent children who were over 50, whereas no age limit applied to widows. The government regarded this allowance as a last resort: Social Welfare Minister Joseph Brennan expressed the view that 'the wife should have available in so far as is possible for her, all processes, legal or otherwise (are) open to her, to effect a reconciliation or to oblige the husband to meet his responsibilities'.[67] In June 1972, the qualifying age for women without dependents was reduced to forty. By then, 1,790 women had successfully claimed the allowance.[68] Applicants had to answer thirty-seven searching questions about their efforts to secure maintenance, efforts to trace their husband and efforts to achieve reconciliation.[69]

Single mothers

Irish society had generally been unsympathetic to single mothers, though Ireland was not unique in that respect.[70] Some ended up in mother and baby homes, controlled by religious orders, which received financial support from the Irish Hospitals Commission and local authorities; some remained in the county home – a surviving legacy of the Poor Law; some women were confined by their families in Magdalen asylums; others were persuaded/forced to marry the father of their child with scant account taken of their readiness for marriage or whether he was a suitable partner. Others opted for 'the boat to England', crowding Catholic

[64] *Commission on the status of women*, para 461.
[65] Seamus Ó Cinnéide, *A law for the poor. A study of home assistance in Ireland* (Dublin: Institute of Public Administration, 1970), pp. 83–4.
[66] Viney, 'The broken marriage 2. Getting lost', *IT*, 27 October 1970.
[67] DD vol. 248, col. 999, 14 July 1970.
[68] DD vol. 262, col. 169, 28 June 1972; vol. 262, col. 505, 4 July 1972.
[69] Paul Murray, 'Divorce Irish style', 23 February 1973.
[70] Pat Thane with Tanya Evans, *Sinners? Scroungers? Saints? Unmarried motherhood in England in the 20th century* (Oxford: Oxford University Press, 2013)

mother and baby homes and creating tensions between the Irish and English Hierarchies. Some of these children were repatriated to Ireland, to mother and baby homes and perhaps for adoption.[71] In a number of families the child of an adult daughter was raised as her sibling often only discovering his/her true parentage later in life, if ever. Legal adoption was not introduced until 1952, but private adoptions/long-term fostering took place before that date, though little is known about them, and a steady stream of Irish babies were adopted by American parents from the late 1940s.[72] Private adoptions did not cease with the introduction of the 1952 Act; in 1967, the social worker in the Rotunda Hospital expressed her concern at 'some third party adoption arrangements, which took no cognisance of possible repercussions'.[73] This elliptical wording is difficult to interpret; it may refer to adoptions within a family. In 1969, 1,400 of the estimated 1,600 children born to single mothers were adopted, the highest percentage in Europe.[74] The furtive attitude towards illegitimacy was receding, but it had not disappeared. Single mothers were attending ante-natal clinics and giving birth in Dublin maternity hospitals, as opposed to being delivered and receiving ante-natal care in a mother and baby home.[75] In the National Maternity Hospital, a special ward was set aside, primarily to shield them from the hostile comments of other patients and their visitors; single mothers were referred to as 'Mrs Innupta' (unwed). In 1968, the Rotunda reported 'a sharp and sudden rise in illegitimacy'; 63 extern and 73 intern unmarried women attended the hospital in 1959; by 1968 this had risen to 131 and 126 respectively. By 1974 the National Maternity Hospital delivered one-quarter of Ireland's births outside marriage.[76] Some women would have remained at home throughout pregnancy; in other instances they availed of a family place-ment scheme operated by Rev Fergal O'Connor, a Dominican priest who lectured at UCD; he noted that these mothers were unwilling to enter

---

[71] Lindsey Earner-Byrne, 'The boat to England: an analysis of the official reactions to the emigration of single expectant Irishwomen to Britain, 1922–72', *IESH*, vol. xxx, 2003, pp 52–70; M. C. Ramblado-Minero and A. Perez-Vides (eds), *Single motherhood in 20th-centiury Ireland; cultural historical and social essays* (Lewistown: Edwin Mellen, 2006); Elaine Farrell (ed.), *'She said she was in the family way'. Pregnancy and infancy in modern Ireland'* (London: Institute of Historical Research, 2012), J. M. Smith, *Ireland's Magdalen laundries and the nations' architecture of containment* (Manchester: Manchester University Press, 2007).

[72] Mike Milotte, *Banished babies. The secret history of Ireland's baby export business* (Dublin: New Island, 1997).

[73] *Rotunda Hospital Clinical Report*, 1967, p. 65.

[74] *Hibernia*, 5–18 February 1971, Monsignor Barrett report of conference on unmarried mothers in Kilkenny November 1970.

[75] Information provided by Dr Dermot McDonald, former master of Holles St.

[76] Farmar, *Holles street*, p. 155.

mother and baby homes because of pressure from social workers to place their children for adoption. One-third of single mothers who gave birth in the Rotunda in 1968 opted to keep their babies; by 1972, the proportion was just under half. The 1969 Report of the Social Work Department noted that almost all the mothers wanted to keep their babies, but they faced major problems, the most insuperable being lack of housing. The 1972 Report adopted a more censorious tone: 'Generally speaking it is the more inadequate, immature and unstable of these patients, with rather poor insight and dull perception, who opted to keep their child and then had to struggle'[77] – this statement indicates that hostility for single parenthood persisted. Of the 120 single mothers, fifty-eight, just under half, went home to their parents after the birth; sixteen went to other relatives; twelve to live with the putative father of their child; thirteen went to their own home; and eighteen went to a mother and baby home. An increasing number of mothers subsequently married the father of her child.

Mothers who opted to keep their babies had either to provide for them by working, which was extremely difficult, if not impossible; rely on social welfare benefit, which would only provide short-term support; or apply for means-tested home assistance, or an affiliation order against the putative father – the number of affiliation orders was rising. By the early 1970s, a number of groups were campaigning for special state provision for single mothers. The Irish Women's Liberation Movement (IWLM), which published a manifesto *Chains or Change* in 1971, noted that 'The unmarried mother who keeps her child does not officially exist . . . as far as this State is concerned'; they demanded the introduction of a less punitive system of support, which was more conscious of the needs of the mother and her child. The following year saw the founding of Cherish, a non-denominational voluntary body to assist unmarried mothers.[78] The Commission on the Status of Women recommended that an unmarried mother who elected to keep her child should be eligible for social welfare payments on similar terms to a deserted wife.[79] By 1972, the government was considering introducing a specific benefit for unmarried mothers as part of an overall reform of social assistance;[80] however, following the change of government, it was a Fine Gael/Labour Coalition which introduced Unmarried Mothers' Allowance in 1973, payable until a child reached eighteen years, or twenty-one if in full-time education. The more caring attitude towards single mothers is not wholly attributable to a more humane Ireland. In 1967, Britain introduced a new abortion

---

[77] *Rotunda Hospital Clinical Reports* 1969, pp. 73–75; 1972, p. 73.
[78] Connolly, The Irish women's movement, p. 114; Gráinne Farren, *From condemnation to celebration. The story of Cherish, 1972–1997* (Dublin: Cherish, 1997).
[79] *Commission on the status of women*, para 388, p. 153.   [80] *IT*, 28 February 1973.

law, which made abortion readily available, and by 1971 at least 577 women with addresses in the Republic of Ireland had abortions in Britain.[81] More generous provision for mothers wishing to keep their babies was seen as one possible means of reducing that number.

The growing number of single mothers and greater public acknowledgement of their existence are indicative of changing sexual practice and changing social attitudes; however, the more tolerant attitudes emerged gradually and they were not necessarily universal. Throughout the late 1960s, for example, mothers giving birth in the Rotunda were still being discharged to mother and baby homes, which must indicate that they had no other option. Yet in a 1972 survey of attitudes carried out by Micheál MacGréil, 98.6 per cent of those surveyed agreed that children born out of wedlock should be treated the same as those born in marriage, and 95.3 per cent disagreed with the assertion that 'the unmarried mother should pay for her sin'.[82] Did some respondents reply in one manner and act otherwise, because these figures are not easily reconciled with continuing admissions to mother and baby homes throughout the 1970s and later. The last home closed in 1991.

Travellers

'Itinerants' or 'tinkers' had long formed part of Ireland's social landscape; travelling people were documented in detail in the Poor Inquiry of the 1830s, and they remained an integral part of rural and small-town life over the next century or more. But the appointment of a Commission on Itinerancy in 1961 represented the first official recognition of the existence of this distinct community with specific problems. Until that time the Travelling community had largely lived outside the state – coming into intermittent contact with local authorities or gardaí, but apparently having little if any contact with health, education or welfare services. The life expectancy of Travellers was much lower than the national average, and many were illiterate. While many working-class parents were brought to court for failing to ensure that their children attended school,[83] there is no evidence of efforts to enforce school attendance laws on the travelling community. Travellers were often unable to claim unemployment assistance because they were moving about.

[81] DD vol. 263, col. 515, 2 November 1972.
[82] Micheál MacGréil, *Prejudice and tolerance in Ireland* (Dublin: College of Industrial Relations, 1980), pp. 410–12.
[83] Sarah-Anne Buckley, *The cruelty man. Child welfare, the NSPCC and the state in Ireland, 1889–1956* (Manchester: Manchester University Press, 2014), p. 80.

By the 1960s, traditional markets and fairs were disappearing and increasing use of tractors killed their trade in horses; the introduction of cheap plastic utensils meant that there was no longer a demand for tinkering skills and road-site campsites were becoming dangerous because of heavier traffic. With fewer opportunities for earning money in rural areas, travellers were moving into the cities and larger towns.[84] There were growing complaints at travellers camping on open ground and other public order issues. Suburban expansion and the construction of new factories closed off many traditional camp sites.[85]

The Commission was asked to report on the economic, educational, health and social problems facing that community and to recommend measures to improve their lives and 'promote their absorption into the general community'. A growing number of Traveller families were applying for local authority housing, though the most prosperous families were least interested in being settled. Some local authorities had provided housing for travellers since the 1930s; however, plans to house Traveller families frequently gave rise to local protests, and opportunistic local councillors found that opposing traveller settlements attracted votes.[86] The Commission on Itinerancy hoped that these prejudices could be overcome if people became more aware of Travellers and their requirements. They also argued that settling traveller families would ultimately benefit the entire community.[87] Publication of the report in 1963 was followed by a systematic programme by local authorities to provide housing or halting sites, which was mandated and financially supported by the Department of Local Government. Between 1962 and 1969, local authorities provided housing for 229 families, and by 1969 they had also provided sixty-six halting sites – though Breathnach describes the provision of halting sites as 'poor'. Tigins – small shed-like units with running water, electricity and sanitary facilities with adjoining space for a caravan to be parked, similar to developments for housing nomads in the Netherlands – were built in Ballyfermot. A school for Traveller children was opened.[88] In 1967, changes to social welfare regulations enabled many Travellers to claim unemployment assistance for the first time.[89] The most significant change was probably a growing awareness of

---

[84] Michael Flynn, *Medical doctor of many parts: memoir of a public health practitioner and health manager* (Ireland: Kelmed, 2007), p. 195.

[85] Jane Helleiner, *Irish Travellers. Racism and the politics of culture* (Toronto: University of Toronto Press, 2000), p. 82.

[86] Flynn, *Medical doctor*, pp. 196–207.

[87] *Report of the Commission on Itinerancy*, chairman Hon Mr Brian Walsh, (Dublin, 1963).

[88] Flynn, *Medical doctor*, p. 196.

[89] Aoife Breathnach, *Becoming conspicuous. Irish Travellers, society and the State 1922–70* (Dublin: UCD Press, 2006), pp. 122–3; 135–6.

Travellers and their needs. This was promoted initially by the Itinerant Settlement Committee, consisting of clergy, charitable groups and committed individuals from both the Catholic and Protestant communities (an indication that denominational boundaries were easing), which spawned a network of local committees with similar profiles. The designation of Traveller Settlements Week was used as an opportunity to highlight awareness and sympathy. But the momentum was not one way; proposals to house Traveller families in local authority estates gave rise to protests, most notoriously in the Galway city community of Rahoon – which gave rise to the term 'rahoonery'.[90] There were also signs that Travellers were beginning to articulate their own needs, as opposed to passively accepting the advocacy of others on their behalf. The 1960s model was one of settlement and assimilation; halting sites were regarded as a transitional measure; the long-term history indicates a rejection of this model in favour of greater recognition of travellers' distinctive identity.

Children in institutional care

Economic growth, improved welfare supports, adoption, falling adult mortality and greater support for single mothers wishing to raise their children combined to reduce very significantly the numbers of children in institutional care. The number of children in industrial schools fell from a 1946 peak of 6,800 to 4,300 in 1960 and 1,740 by 1970.[91] Industrial schools were established in Victorian times to provide education and training for children, whose parents were deemed unable or unwilling to provide for them. They survived in Ireland, largely unchanged into the 1960s, though a number of schools closed as fewer children were committed by the courts, and religious orders increasingly preferred to turn the buildings into secondary schools. Yet in the year 1968–1969, 162 children were committed to industrial schools: fifteen for failure to attend school; seventy-nine because of lack of proper guardianship; three deemed uncontrollable; and sixty-five for committing indictable offences.[92] Children were also sent to industrial schools under the Health Acts, following the death or long-term illness of a parent or marriage breakdown. Many children committed to industrial schools had low levels of education; some were of below-average intelligence. A survey carried out in the 1960s, as part of the Kennedy Inquiry, revealed

---

[90] Helleiner, *Irish Travellers*, pp. 83–8.
[91] *Commission of inquiry into child abuse*, vol. 1, 3.02.
[92] *Annual report department of local government 1968–1969.*

that only 18 per cent 'were known to have parents who were married, alive and living together'; 18 per cent were known to be illegitimate; and 30 per cent had only one living parent. In 51 per cent of cases the school did not know whether the parent(s) were alive – a finding that raises serious questions about their concern for the child's emotional welfare and the constitutional rights of parents.[93] Some children had been transferred to industrial schools from mother and baby homes. Although most children were placed there by government agencies, and the state provided a capitation grant for each child, the schools were owned and managed by religious orders, and the state's oversight was limited; it had no role in the appointment of managers or staff. While the schools were under the control of the Department of Education, children were committed through the courts (Department of Justice) and the local health authorities. Children were often placed in schools far away from their families; brothers and sisters were separated, as were older siblings of the same sex. A number of recent enquiries have revealed that siblings often lost contact or were unaware that they had a brother or sister. In some instances one or more children might remain with a parent(s) or relative, while others were committed to an industrial school.

Children in industrial schools lived highly regimented lives; food and clothing were inadequate; educational and training opportunities limited; 'industrial' training prepared them only for work in agriculture, general labouring, messenger boys or domestic service; and a harsh regime of physical punishment prevailed. The 2009 Report of the Ryan Commission also revealed many instances of sexual and emotional abuse. The forbidding and often brutal nature of industrial schools was never a secret. Instances of brutal corporal punishment, resulting in children being injured, would have been known – at least to government officials. At intermittent intervals over the decades, questions or statements in the Dáil or Seanad, an occasional newspaper article or an inquest into the death of a child in an industrial school would highlight neglect, ill-treatment or lack of contact with a child's family. But these headline stories, or occasional parliamentary questions, never translated into a sustained campaign for reform.

This changed in the 1960s, when a diverse range of interest groups began to scrutinise conditions in the industrial schools, asking awkward questions and publicising their concerns. In 1961, the Archbishop of Dublin John Charles McQuaid asked Fr Moore, the chaplain to Artane (the largest school for boys), to report on the institution. He described the

---

[93] *Reformatory and industrial schools system report* 1970 (Kennedy Inquiry), E58, paras 3.3. 3.4; 3.11.

boys as 'badly clothed'. They had no overcoats (unless they could pay for them), only rain capes, no vests and no change of either footwear or socks. There was no such thing a boy 'having his own shirt or pyjamas – after washing, articles of clothing [were] distributed at random'. Bed clothes were inadequate. Poor-quality clothing, lack of overcoats, underwear and nightwear would not have been uncommon in poorer Irish families in earlier times, but rising living standards brought general improvements in clothing and a greater consciousness of the deprivations of industrial school children.

Fr Moore reported that the boys were 'undernourished'; medical facilities were 'appalling'. More than half of the boys were 'psychologically disturbed and in need of psychiatric treatment' that was not available in Artane.[94] In Upton, near Cork city, a 1965 inspection commented on lack of privacy in the dormitories, hard pillows, no evidence of sheets, no pyjamas and that the boys slept in their shirts.[95] When Dr Lysaght, Chief Medical Officer of the Department of Health, carried out an inspection of Artane in 1966, he reported poor standards of cleanliness and tidiness; the dormitories were 'far too big', with 100 boys sleeping in one room. 'Any such large concentration gives an impression of institutional care and regimentation which is of course objectionable and not in accordance with modern trends.' The 'institutional atmosphere' was inescapable at mealtimes. All 395 boys dined together in one very large room. Lysaght observed that such 'institutional mass feeding', together with the over concentration of boys in dormitories, tended 'to hinder or delay development of individuality'. A medical doctor wrote to the Department of Education in 1962 about twenty-eight boys from Artane that he had met at Carne Camp in Mayo where they were on holidays the previous summer. He had been 'struck by the fact that only two [in his opinion], were of average physique for their age'. He described their standard of physical development as 'very low' and suggested that this was caused by 'nutritional deficiency probably over a long period'. The boys appeared 'very susceptible to skin infections' which were slow to respond to treatment.[96] His observations were confirmed by Dr Laurence Masterson, the MOH at Artane, who reported that sixty-three of the 371 pupils in the school were 'noticeably below average physique'.[97] Corporal punishment was widely used, often in a very brutal manner: in 1963, one boy in Glin industrial school spent eight days in hospital with a

[94] Dept. Ed. MIF13 Artane 1/7./63.
[95] Dept. Ed. 06/G DOE Internal Report, St. Patrick's Upton, 11 March 1965.
[96] Dept. Ed. MIF/13 Letter to DOE, 15 December 1962.
[97] Dept. Ed. QMR/4 Medical Report of Dr. Laurence Masterson, M.O. to Artane Ind. School, 2 July 1962.

broken jaw. When the Department of Education asked for an explanation, the resident manager explained that the injury had been caused 'accidentally . . . in the administration of punishment'.[98]

Fr Moore repeated his findings in evidence given to the Inter-Departmental Committee on Prevention of Crime and Treatment of Offenders in November 1962.[99] The Department of Education responded by sending a team of senior officials to inspect Artane. Their report refuted almost all of Fr Moore's allegations. One inspector described the boys as 'well fed, warmly clothed, comfortably bedded and treated with kindness by the Christian Brothers in an atmosphere conducive to their spiritual and physical development'. He remarked on the 'very friendly relationship between the boys and the Brothers' and concluded that Artane emerged 'very creditably from the inspection. No serious fault could be found . . . and the impression of the "big happy family" atmosphere which pervaded the entire institution was inescapable.'[100] This report should be read as a whitewashing exercise, reflecting the reluctance of the Department of Education to intervene in this difficult area and to question the authority and control of the Irish Christian Brothers. When parents or foster parents complained about excessive physical punishment the Department tended to question the credibility of the complainant, describing them as 'having a record of trouble-making' or 'an irresponsible person'.[101]

But adverse publicity and complaints continued to mount. A growing number of families came to know these children through 'god-parent' schemes, and as the numbers in industrial schools fell, the remaining children were often transferred to a neighbouring national school, where again they came to the attention of the parents of their classmates.[102] In 1971, a woman wrote to the Department on behalf of the Galway God Parents' Association, a group who took children from Lenaboy – an industrial school for girls – out for day and weekend visits. The Association complained about 'a complete lack of basic hygiene and care for the children's health': children with lice-infested heads, filthy underwear and kidney infections. Although they had brought these matters to the attention

---

[98] Dept. Ed. Letter from DOE to Resident Manager, St. Joseph's Glin, 1 May 1963.
[99] Dept. Ed. G021/A Internal Memo: Note of Interview given to Fr. Moore, Chaplain to Artane Industrial School by Chairman of the Inter-Departmental Committee on Prevention of Crime & Treatment of Offenders, 26 November 1962.
[100] Dept. Ed. MIF/13, 4 January 1963.
[101] Dept. Ed. G041/A Letter from DOE to E. Kennedy, Chairman, Committee on Reformatory and Industrial Schools, 22 May 1969.
[102] Mary Raftery and Eoin O'Sullivan, *Suffer the little children. The inside story of Ireland's industrial schools* (Dublin: New Island, 1999), pp. 356–68.

of the school, they were 'apparently ignored'. Other allegations about conditions in Lenaboy were reported in a local newspaper.[103]

These low-key reports attracted little publicity. In April 1963 however, the British Sunday newspaper *The People* reported on the experiences of three sisters from St. Martha's Industrial School in Bundoran, Donegal, who were punished by having their heads shaven. One girl, thirteen-year-old Philomena Daly, wrote to her mother, who had emigrated to England in 1956 after having separated from her husband, asking for help. Her mother travelled to Donegal, removed her daughters from the school and then told the story of her 'heroic dash' to *The People*. They published the story with a photograph of the shaven daughters under the headline 'Orphanage Horror'. The school manager defended her action to the newspaper, claiming that 'Cutting off a girl's hair is a common punishment here ... but it is administered only in extreme cases'. The girls had played truant on two occasions.[104] This story attracted widespread attention: there were letters to the Department of Education criticising the nuns who managed the school; representations by the Irish Housewife's Association to the Minister for Education; and questions in Dáil Éireann. The Department of Education was aware of this incident before it was reported in *The People*, but although they determined that the punishment and other aspects of the regime followed in Bundoran were in breach of regulations, they decided not to penalise the congregation.[105] The school closed within two years; the remaining children were transferred to another school and the vacated building re-opened as a secondary school.

In 1964, *Hibernia* published 'Early Days in Letterfrack', part of a memoir by Peter Tyrrell, who had been an inmate in the industrial school, located in a remote part of Connemara from 1925 to 1933. 'A few of the boys had visits from their parents from time to time, but they would dread these visits and hide in the lavatories when the parents arrived ... parents would be ragged and badly dressed and the children were ashamed to be reminded that they were paupers. We are always being told that our parents were not good because they didn't look after us and that we were not good either ... My experiences there have haunted me all my life and even now I find it difficult to talk about them.'[106] But Tyrell's harrowing account, published with the assistance

---

[103] Dept. Ed. 23/G Letter from Sec., Galway God Parents Assoc., to Sec., DO Health (forwarded on to DOE), re condition of children maintained in St. Anne's Lenaboy, 3 February 1971.

[104] *The People*, 21 April 1963.

[105] Dept. Ed. 39/G DOE Internal Memo: 20 May 1967.   [106] *Hibernia*, June 1964.

of independent senator Owen Sheehy Skeffington and Joy Rudd, who helped Tyrell to write his story, attracted relatively little attention, in contrast to the memoirs of former inmates published in more recent times, and a recent reprint of his story. In 1967, he set fire to himself on Hampstead Heath and died from his injuries. His full memoir was not published until 2006.[107]

Tyrell contributed to the 1966 Tuairim Report, *Some of our children. A report on the residential care of the deprived child in Ireland,* written by London members of the group, under the direction of Joy Rudd. Tuairim criticised the inadequate capitation grants for children in institutional care and lack of trained childcare professionals. They noted that proportionately fewer children were in residential care in England and Wales – perhaps because the welfare services intervened at an early stage in order to pre-empt the need for institutional care, and they worked to secure early discharges. Yet, although Tuairim criticised the low ratio of staff to children in girls' industrial schools, the shabby clothing worn in the Daingean reformatory and the use of corporal punishment to punish cases of sex offences or alleged sex offences, the overall tone was not condemnatory. The section on industrial schools for senior boys, which included Artane and Letterfrack, concluded:

In the circumstances, financial and physical, the managers of these schools in keeping them going at all perform a task which no one else would contemplate. They do all and more than can be reasonably expected of them for the boys, with too little public help or support. We do not think, however, that boys' boarding schools provide a satisfactory substitute home for deprived children, and think that they should be used as special schools within the ordinary education system, not as a dumping ground for children with a variety of problems: institutionalism, destitution, deprivation, delinquency.[108]

Tuairim's criticism focused on lack of aftercare and the difficulties that 'mentally retarded and socially maladjusted' young adults faced adjusting to life outside the institution. Many former inmates emigrated to Britain; in 1965, fifty-two of the 124 inmates in borstals (young offenders institutions) born in Ireland were former inmates of industrial schools or other institutions. They recommended that all childcare services should be co-ordinated by a children's department within the Department of Health, with services supervised by child welfare officers employed by local health

---

[107] Andrée Sheehy Skeffington, *Skeff, A life of Owen Sheehy Skeffington 1909–1970* (Dublin: Lilliput, 1991), pp. 190–1. Peter Tyrell, *Founded on fear. Letterfrack industrial school, war and exile,* edited by Diarmuid Whelan (Dublin: Irish Academic Press, 2006).

[108] Tuairim, *Some of our children. A report on the residential care of the deprived child in Ireland* (Dublin, 1966), p. 31.

authorities.[109] The findings and recommendations were reported in the national media and cited in journal articles on the care for children in need.[110]

This cumulative publicity prompted the government to set up a committee of enquiry. The tipping point, ironically, appears to have been an interview on Teilifís Éireann with Brother Normoyle, the provincial of the Irish Christian Brothers, who complained about the difficulty in getting the government to articulate a policy with respect to industrial schools. He was demanding additional public funding. Taoiseach Jack Lynch contacted Minister for Education Donogh O'Malley and suggested that he respond. O'Malley's reply epitomises the confused thinking that pervades government files, acknowledging the shortcomings of the existing system combined with a failure to confront them. He admitted the lack of psychiatric services for children in residential institutions and he conceded to Brother Normoyle's assertion that the capitation grants were inadequate; however, he went on to assert that overall the schools were 'very well run'. When Paddy Lalor, a parliamentary secretary (junior minister), visited Daingean reformatory – probably the most inhumane institution – in December 1966 (it is unclear why he went) he was appalled. He claimed that 50 per cent of the buildings should be demolished; yet, he then commented that 'Great work could be done' by the Oblate Fathers, who ran the reformatory, if they had adequate facilities.[111] When the Secretary of the Department of Education T. F. Ó Raifeartaigh visited Daingean two months later, in his letter of thanks to the resident manager, he said that he was 'greatly edified' by both 'the wonderful spirit of apostolate which was evident' and by the 'wonderful work' in which the school was engaged.[112] In similar spirit, O'Malley suggested that an ad hoc committee be established to report on industrial and reform schools. 'If it were to do nothing else, it might at least have the effect of allaying public unease.'[113] He reassured the resident managers (the religious who oversaw the schools) that the committee would 'go far to dissipate the effect of ill-informed and detrimental assertions which occasionally receive publicity and which, if not thus counterbalanced, might eventually create unease in the mind of the public'.[114]

[109] Tuairim, *Some of our children*, pp. 41–6.
[110] Tomás Finn, *Tuairim, intellectual debate and policy formation: rethinking Ireland 1954–1975* (Manchester: Manchester University Press, 2012), pp. 194–5.
[111] Dept. Ed. Letter from Paddy Lalor T.D., Parl. Sec. to the Minister for Posts & Telegraphs, to Donogh O'Malley, 22 December 1966.
[112] Dept. Ed. G041/i Letter from T O'Raifeartaigh, DOE to Rev. W. McGonagle, Manager, St. Conleth's School, Daingean, 24 February 1967.
[113] NAI 98/6/156; Lynch to O'Malley 6 January 1967; O'Malley to Lynch 19 January 1967.
[114] Dept. Ed. Go41/i O'Malley to Rev William MacGonagle, chairman resident managers association 2 March 1967.

The Committee, chaired by Miss Justice Eileen Kennedy, the first and at that time the only female judge, was asked to survey industrial and reform schools and report and make recommendations to the Minister. Their remit was subsequently extended to include all children in care. The Kennedy Report, published in 1970, recommended fundamental changes in provisions for children in need. The childcare system should be designed to prevent family breakdown with residential care as a last alternative. Industrial schools should be abolished and replaced with group homes that would approximate to a family atmosphere. Daingean reformatory and the young offenders remand home – Marlborough House – should be closed. All childcare staff should have a professional qualification. The report was a serious indictment of the existing institutions, yet once again the criticism was qualified: 'were it not for the dedicated work of many of our religious bodies, the position would be a great deal worse than it is now'.[115] Failings were attributed to a lack of awareness on the part of the staff about children's needs, which in turn was due to a lack of professional training and low staff numbers.

Although the Kennedy Report recommended closing industrial schools and placing children in either foster homes or in smaller family-style group homes, the pace of change was extremely slow. Buckley is correct in concluding that 'the Kennedy Report also ignored many issues and did not effect change to the extent that history has recorded'.[116] Childcare became the responsibility of the regional health boards. The number of children in residential homes fell from 2,147 in 1968 to 1,364 in 1973; the numbers in residential special schools fell from 418 to 244.[117] But institutional care remained under the control of religious orders. It was cheaper and the attitudes reported above suggest that civil servants and politicians believed that religious orders provided a better quality of care than a system under professional lay management, despite abundant evidence of maltreatment.[118] Some of the new family-style homes opened beside former industrial schools, often on sites provided by the same religious orders. Raftery and O'Sullivan claim that 'the legacy of the old system was ever present'. 'The stark reality is that while the rhetoric associated with child care had changed, the closed and secretive practices which had allowed so much past abuse were still very much in evidence.' There were many further instances of sexual and physical abuse of children in care in the years after 1970.[119]

---

[115] *Kennedy Report*, 4.1.   [116] Buckley, *The cruelty man*, p. 146.
[117] SD – 76, col. 142, 15 November 1973.   [118] Dept. Ed. G041/B.
[119] Raftery and O'Sullivan, *Suffer the little children*, pp. 381–90.

A 1964 report by Fr Ken McCabe based on a stay of several weeks as an observer in Daingean reformatory documented severe physical punishment – well beyond what was permitted by Department regulations – shaving of boys' heads and 'serious incidents of homosexual practices'.[120] Although his evidence was available to the Minister, the Department of Education and presumably the Kennedy Committee, it was not seriously addressed by the Kennedy Report or the authorities, nor was serious consideration given to the psychological consequences for the inmates. Tyrell was not the only former inmate to speak out about his experiences at this time. One man, who was probably in his 'twenties – he had left Ireland eight years earlier 'a free individual', wrote to Jack Lynch demanding the repeal of Ireland's laws on contraception. An illegitimate child, he was sent to an orphanage at the age of two (presumably transferred from a mother and baby home) and from there at the age of ten to 'a borstal school' (probably an industrial school) until his sixteenth birthday. He claimed that successive governments 'have also made miserable the lives of thousands of unwanted babies'; he referred to 'the treatment of which helpless children are subject to, while in the care of the Irish Catholic authorities'. Another correspondent wrote of the 'sad upbringing through lack of government concern' suffered by 'unwanted children'. He asked for the opportunity to tell his story to members of the government, because he believed that 'a great deal of good could be done'. 'I myself am still suffering from the crucifying effect of my upbringing in Irish government care.... Every child should have the right to a happy childhood so far the people of Ireland have done grave psychological damage to literally thousands of young people both male and female who had even brought up as I was'.[121] But opportunities to tell these stories did not come for more than thirty years, and the lack of interest in Peter Tyrell's account suggests an unwillingness to confront these personal tragedies and what they revealed about Irish society. There was a widespread reluctance to confront the religious orders who ran these institutions, or to consider what such revelations might say about the much-admired members of religious communities. There was also a wider culture of tolerance towards physical punishment of children, and a silence with respect to the sexual abuse of children – whether it happened in institutions, within the family or was perpetrated by outsiders.

In 1968, the *Irish Times* published an article by journalist Renagh Holohan titled 'High Park: Laundry with a Difference', which opened

---

[120] Raftery and O'Sullivan, *Suffer the little children*, pp. 366–7.

[121] S2003/16/453, Contraceptives resolutions and miscellaneous correspondence.

by stating that 'High Park is a laundry that gives off emotional rather than any other kind of steam'. This 'highly efficient service' was a Magdalen Laundry run by the Sisters of Our Lady of Charity. She described how High Park took in girls who arrived from the country with no money; girls referred by the Guards or the Legion of Mary. Some only stayed for one night; others had been there for years. 'The girls in St Mary's don't pay anything for their keep but the nuns, apart from giving them pocket money and cigarettes don't pay for [sic] the girls the work they do in the laundry.' The article ended by promoting a fashion show in the Gresham Hotel, which was a fundraiser for the institution.[122] A check on the letters column in the following weeks revealed none questioning the existence of this institution, or the use of unpaid labour to run a laundry 'on a wholly commercial basis', which suggests a tacit acquiescence on the part of Irish society in such institutions. The fact that this article appeared in *Women First* page, which carried the name of women's editor Mary Maher, a section of the paper commonly cited as a torchbearer for second-wave feminism, also suggests that this acquiescence stretched far beyond the Catholic Hierarchy.

Underlying the attitude of both the state and the wider society towards industrial schools and institutions like the Magdalen Homes is a somewhat schizophrenic attitude towards the family. On the one hand, the 1937 Constitution and Catholic social teaching privileged the family and parents over the state. Where a family failed to meet acceptable standards of childcare because they were too poor, suffered from mental or physical illness or a parent had died or abandoned a spouse and children, church and state appear to have had little compunction about placing children in an industrial school, and often breaking the connections to their family – placing siblings in different institutions, ignoring requests from parents for the return of their children.[123] Some of this contempt extended to parents who might complain about excessive corporal punishment in national schools. Department of Education regulations on corporal punishment in national schools were regularly broken, with little if any sanction being imposed on teachers or school managers.[124] Changes to the regulations in 1965 made by George Colley removed the prohibition on teachers pulling children's hair, boxing their ears or caning them on parts

---

[122] *IT*, 1 October 1968.

[123] Buckley, *The cruelty man*, pp. 91–2, notes the 'distrust of [widower] fathers being left with daughters' who were often removed to an industrial school, whereas the sons remained at home. On requests for children to be returned, Buckley, p. 141.

[124] Mary E. Daly, ' "The primary and natural educator"? The role of parents in the education of their children in independent Ireland', *Éire-Ireland*, vol. 44, 2009, pp. 201–8.

of the body other than their hands.[125] *Reform*, an organisation established to campaign for the abolition of corporal punishment in schools, was not very successful. Christopher Morris, one of the founders, noted in 1968, roughly a year after its foundation, that it had approximately 100 members; he conceded that many parents were in favour of corporal punishment. The topic was aired on the *Late Late Show*, where according to one account, the chairman of *Reform* 'waving a strap seemed about to lay into Senator Brosnahan, the secretary-general of the INTO' (which favoured corporal punishment). A test case taken by the parents of ten-year-old David Moore for excessive beating at school resulted in a jury awarding him one shilling in damages – less than the cost of a newspaper; the family decided to emigrate to Canada.[126] In November 1969, the US network NBC broadcast a documentary on corporal punishment in Irish schools, which included a panel discussion. But the resulting publicity within Ireland was limited. Corporal punishment in schools was not outlawed until 1982.[127] Lack of interest in such stories, and a failure to generate public outrage, was undoubtedly a key factor in the delay.

[125] Daly, ' "The primary and natural educator"?' p. 207; Moira Maguire and Seamus Ó Cinnéide, ' "A good beating never hurts anyone'. The punishment and abuse of children I twentieth century Irealnd, *Journal of Social History*, vol. 38, no. 3, 2005, pp. 635–52.

[126] *Hibernia*, 18 October–1 November 1968.

[127] The database of Irish newspaper articles revealed only five stories relating to this programme, though it prompted acrimonious exchanges in the Seanad between Sheehy Skeffington and Sean Brosnahan, secretary of the INTO; SD, 67, 4 December 1968, cols. 330–43.

Changing attitudes towards women and children in need – however half-hearted – were partly driven by investigative journalists, including Michael Viney, a new generation of women journalists such as Mary Maher and Mary Kenny and women's pages in the daily newspapers. Catriona Clear noted that Irish women's media had not propagandised 'anything like Betty Friedan's "feminine mystique" in the 1940s and 1950s. In Irish-produced media at least, Irish women were not subjected to psychological and pseudo-scientific reinforcement of the idealisation of motherhood.'[1] Such idealisation would not have accorded well with families of five or more children. Life as a housewife, in a modern home equipped with labour-saving devices, whose husband was away throughout the working day, was a relatively new experience for Irish women, and it had scarcely begun when second-wave feminism arrived in the early 1970s. In 1971, the short-lived IWLM published a manifesto *Chains or Change* which identified 'justice for deserted wives, widows and unmarried mothers' as one of five key demands, along with equal pay, equality before the law, equal educational opportunity and contraception.[2] Within a very short time, the movement fractured over which should be the key issues in any campaign, on the modus operandi, and what stance they should take on other political causes, such as the housing action campaign and Northern Ireland.[3] The more mainstream section of women activists concentrated their efforts on issues relating to women and children. The early 1970s saw the emergence of a more radicalised National Association of Widows of Ireland, and the founding of Cherish (1972), a self-help group of single mothers,[4] ADAPT – the Association for Deserted and Alone Parents (1973) and Women's Aid – an organisation that supported battered wives. A greater awareness of the need to protect women and children in violent marriages emerged in Britain and in Ireland at

---

[1] Clear, *Women of the home*, p. 214.   [2] IWLM, *Change or chains* (Dublin 1971).
[3] Connolly, *The Irish women's movement*, pp. 111–54.
[4] Farren, *From condemnation to celebration*.

around the same time. The annual reports of the National Society for Prevention of Cruelty to Children (NSPCC) had commonly highlighted instances of 'domestic violence or 'wife beating', but 'it was acknowledged to be a private matter – not one that affected the public finances'.[5] Second-wave feminism transformed it into a public concern. The focus on the family was core to AIM – Action, Information, Motivation – which lobbied for legislation to enforce maintenance orders; joint ownership of the family home and improvements in welfare payments and legal treatment of women.[6]

The focus on campaigns for women and children could be seen as belated Irish activism in maternal feminism. Such issues did not present a direct challenge to the Catholic Church or the constitutional ban on divorce; indeed, many clergy and religious sisters supported these efforts on behalf of deserted or battered wives and single mothers. The absence of divorce from the list of five key demands in *Chains or Change* is significant. Divorce had been largely absent from Irish political debate since the 1920s, when the Irish government introduced a law to prohibit divorce, a prohibition subsequently enshrined in the 1937 Constitution. The incidence of divorce remained low in most Western countries until the 1960s, partly because social convention was strongly supportive of marriage, and also because divorce laws were restrictive. In 1951, there were 615 divorced men and 233 divorced women in Northern Ireland.[7] But the introduction of 'no fault divorce' in various US States during the 1950s, Canada (1968), England and Wales (1969), Scotland (1974) brought a significant rise in the number of divorces.[8]

In 1965, Lemass asked Justice Minister Brian Lenihan to investigate whether the Vatican Council Decree on Religious Liberty 'oblige or permit us to change the law so as to allow divorce and remarriage for those of our citizens whose religion tolerates it?'[9] There is an irony in the Taoiseach invoking a Vatican Council decree as justification for amending Ireland's constitutional prohibition on divorce. This enquiry should probably be seen as part of Lemass' overall strategy of improving relations with Northern Ireland. (see Chapter 14). An informal approach by Lenihan to Rev Maurice Sheehy, a canon lawyer (who may well have been the canon lawyer who was consulted about the age of marriage),

---

[5] Buckley, *The cruelty man*, pp. 171–2.
[6] Connolly, *The Irish women's movement*, p. 108.   [7] 1951 Census.
[8] Callum Brown, *Religion and the demographic revolution. Women and secularisation in Canada, Ireland, UK and USA since the 1960s* (Woodbridge: The Boydell Press, 2012), p. 175.
[9] Lemass to Lenihan, 25 September 1965, NAI 96/6/364 Marriage in Ireland. Constitutional and Ecclesiastical position.

reported that having consulted others – Lenihan interpreted this to mean Dr McQuaid – there would be 'violent opposition' from the Hierarchy to any proposal to allow divorce; furthermore, the matter was not related to the question of religious liberty.[10] Divorce was on the agenda, albeit in a rather low-key manner; there is no evidence of any grass-roots campaign at this time. In December 1967, an all-party committee on the constitution, established on Lemass' initiative (he became a member when he retired as Taoiseach), recommended that civil divorce should be available to Protestants, but the committee had no formal standing; it would appear that the intention was to use their report as a basis for further discussion.[11] In the event this didn't happen. In 1968, Frank Aiken (on behalf of Taoiseach Jack Lynch) indicated that it was anticipated that the committee's proposals would be discussed by the political parties, no government action was anticipated until they had responded.[12] While the proposal to remove the constitutional prohibition on divorce was welcomed by Fianna Fáil Cumainn in TCD and UCD and by the National Democratic Group at Queen's University Belfast, even the merest suggestion of reform was sufficient to bring out the opposition, which was not confined to Catholics. In 1968, Gwendolene Hart, President of the Mothers Union – an all-Ireland women's organisation with 17,500 members affiliated with the Church of Ireland – wrote to Jack Lynch from Omagh, County Tyrone, expressing 'grave concern' at the possibility of a bill permitting divorce: 'We deplore that the Government of Eire who have always stood for the permanencies of the marriage bond should now propose to lower its standard.' A woman with an address in Greystones expressed her opposition in more basic terms: 'As long as divorce is unobtainable in Ireland unthinking, greedy, selfish people will be deterred from stealing other people's marriage partners.' She urged Lynch to 'Think well before you allow your name to go down in posterity as the one who helped to topple Ireland from a high moral standard'. A more heartfelt letter came from a Finglas woman, begging that 'if you (presumably Lynch) can't pass divorce law for all grant me one and tell me which courts. Please'. She described a 'wife and family having to stand by watching the man [presumably her husband] living with a widow in the same parish and what fear and dread for them as long as he can't marry again'. She and her family were 'in great danger' because they were living in 'his house', and the widow had a grown up son who had often threatened her and her family. The hapless woman was informed that there

[10] NAI 96/6/364, Lenihan to Lemass 17 February 1966.
[11] Oireachtas. *Committee on the Constitution*, December 1969.
[12] DD 232, 8 February 1968, 797. Aiken to Cosgrave.

were no proposals to introduce legislation permitting divorce; 'your personal problem is one which you might wish to discuss with a Solicitor or with your Parish Priest'.[13]

By the early 1970s, the argument in favour of introducing divorce to diffuse the image of the Republic as a Catholic state was outweighed by a growing awareness of marital desertion, which was described as 'Divorce Irish style'. The legal and financial difficulties of deserted wives were consciously used to promote the case for divorce. In December 1972, a group of deserted wives appeared on the *Late Late Show* to tell their stories. Changes in British divorce law brought the issue to the fore. Prior to then an Irish husband who deserted his wife and moved to Britain could not obtain a divorce unless he could prove that his wife had committed a marital offence, such as adultery or cruelty. However, following the introduction of 'no fault divorce', any Irishman who could demonstrate that he was domiciled in Britain and intended to stay there could apply for a divorce, provided that he and his wife had lived apart for at least five years. Although divorce was not permitted in Ireland, the Department of Social Welfare regarded a woman whose husband had divorced her in Britain as no longer married, and therefore ineligible for deserted wife's allowance.[14] Women, whose husbands had divorced them in Britain and subsequently died, were denied a widow's pension.[15] Additional complications emerged with regard to ownership or tenancy of the family home which was commonly in the husband's name. However, a memorandum drafted in response to questions presented to Jack Lynch by the women's editor of the *Irish Times* in February 1973[16] stated that 'The Government do not accept that divorce legislation is either an appropriate or a useful means of improving the lot of deserted wives. Neither do they accept that a radical change in the law governing legal desertion would necessarily be beneficial to deserted wives.' It was government policy to secure 'consistent and considered advances even in the face of sustained criticism ... social attitudes do not change overnight but they find it regrettable that they do not always get support from the quarters from which support might be expected'. The memorandum noted that it was 'but a few years since' they were under 'concerted attack' over the Succession Act, and that attacks continued long after the legislation had been passed.[17] Divorce did not become legal until 1995. By then, the incidence of marital breakdown and cohabitation was of a scale unimagined in the 1970s, and Ireland was fully part of what has been described as the third demographic revolution.

---

[13] NAI 96/6/364/.   [14] *Commission on the Status of Women*, para 464.
[15] DD 269, col. 716 3 November 1972, Barry Desmond T.D.
[16] *IT*, 23 February 1973.   [17] NAI 2004/21/32, Illegitimate children affiliation orders.

Divorce failed to emerge as a major issue in politics or the media at this time, perhaps because the incidence of marriage breakdown, though rising, remained low. By contrast, the ban on the sale, importation and distribution of contraceptives became a battleground. Private members bills to repeal the 1935 Act were tabled in both Dáil and Seanad and the 1935 Act faced a legal challenge in the High Court and the Supreme Court. The challenges and the ensuing media attention prompted a serious debate within Cabinet about the future direction of Irish society, strong statements from the Catholic Hierarchy and the emergence of a grass-roots movement committed to upholding the status quo. By the early 1970s, an open but increasingly polarised debate on contraception had become part of a wider discourse over Northern Ireland, and the reforms necessary to make a united Ireland acceptable to Ulster Protestants and the Protestant community in the Republic. Senators Mary Robinson, John Horgan and Trevor West, sponsors of private members bills to repeal the 1935 Act, made their case, not from a feminist perspective, or the medical and family-planning needs of Irish couples; but they focused on 'the many statements made by the Taoiseach and by Deputy Dr Hillery [Minister for External Affairs] about the necessity to create a pluralist society in southern Ireland and the necessity not to discriminate on the basis of religion'.[18] Noel Browne, then a Labour TD, referred to the rights of 'the minority in a pluralist society' – the 'religious minority' and 'those Catholics who feel that they conscientiously have a right to use contraceptive methods'.[19] His co-sponsor Dr John O'Connell argued that by publishing their private members' bill, the government could prove their commitment to a '32-county non-sectarian State'.[20] Garret FitzGerald noted that 'The Republic's laws on censorship and contraception are highly contentious issues with Northern Protestant opinion ... It seems sensible, therefore, to initiate changes in the Republic ... as part of a programme designed to show Northern Protestant opinion that the will to reunification on an acceptable basis is genuine.'[21] While no bill secured a second reading, they did provoke both a public debate and a government review of options for amending or repealing the 1935 Act.

The Irish Hierarchy set out the counter-argument in a 1971 Lenten statement, which was one of the first occasions when abortion was invoked as an inevitable consequence of more liberal contraception. Abortion had come to feature in the Irish media, following the liberalisation of British laws in 1967. In 1971, 577 women giving Irish addresses

---

[18] SD, 7 July 1971 col. 966.   [19] DD 258, cols. 1436–7 9 February 1972.
[20] DD 9 February 1972 col. 1440.   [21] FitzGerald, *Towards a New Ireland*, p. 152.

had UK abortions.[22] The debate over sexual permissiveness was not unique to Ireland. In Britain, Hera Cook claims that 'From 1965 to 1969, there was a transformation of sexual mores. This happened as a result of supplying contraception to women publicly and solely for the purpose of sexual pleasure, indeed explicitly to prevent reproduction.'[23] The Irish Hierarchy was determined to prevent a similar transformation by preventing any relaxation in the laws. Their statement, issued on 11 March 1971, indicated that contraception was not simply a matter for private conscience; it had implications for the wider society. The needs of married couple were superseded by a greater imperative to prevent the spread of the permissive society.

The bishops fully share the disquiet which is widespread among the people at the present time regarding the pressure being exerted on public opinion on the question concerning civil law on divorce, contraception and abortion. These questions involve issues of great import for society as a whole, which go far beyond purely private morality or private religious belief. Civil law on these matters should respect the wishes of the people who elected the legislators and the bishops confidently hope that the legislators themselves will respect this important principle.

Dr McQuaid expanded on these themes in a subsequent statement:

The use of a contraceptive by an individual person is an act that primarily concerns that person, and as such is a matter of private morality ... Publicly to make contraceptives available is a matter of public morality. Given the proneness of our human nature to evil ... it must be evident that an access, hitherto unlawful, to contraceptive devices will prove a most certain occasion of sin, especially to immature persons. The public consequences of immorality that must follow for our whole society are only too clearly seen in other countries.

He dismissed the argument that the law should be changed to promote re-unification: 'One must know little of the Northern people, if one can fail to realise the indignant ridicule with which good Northern people would treat such an argument. It would indeed be a foul basis on which to attempt to construct the unity of our people.'[24] This statement, which was read at all masses, prompted a public demonstration and walkout by members of the IWLM.[25]

A Department of Justice memo to Cabinet in April 1971 – that is, shortly after these statements – concurred with the Hierarchy. It

---

[22] Daly, *Slow failure*, pp. 312–3.
[23] Hera Cook, *The long sexual revolution. Englishwomen, sex and contraception 1800–1975* (Oxford: Oxford University Press, 2004), p. 295.
[24] Archbishop's House 22 March 1971, Reprinted by the Association for the Protection of Irish family life. Copy on NAI DT S2003/16/453.
[25] Nuala Fennell, *Political woman. A memoir* (Dublin: Currach Press, 2009), p. 61.

acknowledged the 'difficulties in accepting unreservedly the proposition that, because an action is in the field of private morality, the State may never prohibit such action'; this would mean that the state should tolerate homosexual acts carried out in private between consenting adults and the importation of pornography and addictive drugs for private use. They saw little prospect of establishing some middle-ground between making contraceptives available to all and the status quo. Acknowledging that 'most people, including the Catholic Hierarchy' would accept that civil law should facilitate married couples, whose religion and conscience permit them to use contraceptives, 'if this can be done without serious damage to public morality or the "moral tone" of society', they noted that it would be impossible to ' keep contraceptives out of reach of young adolescents'. They agreed with the Hierarchy that the campaign to reform the laws regarding contraception was part of a wider campaign for divorce, a secular Constitution and perhaps even abortion. The arguments used to justify contraception, 'if accepted, would made (sic) divorce inevitable'. This was followed by a diatribe about 'the growth of what is usually called the permissive society'; a programme on RTÉ on Holy Thursday about 'pornography in Ireland' which opened according to the *Irish Times* with 'a film clip of any anonymous film starlet showing off her breasts and most of the rest of her anatomy to photographers in Cannes ... incredibly tasteless shots of some model girls prancing around St. Stephen's Green in hot pants with the cameras zooming in around their thighs'. What bearing this has on contraception is unclear, except that it was screened shortly after another programme where a chemist in Enniskillen described the range of contraceptives available in his shop; the RTÉ journalist bought a packet of condoms which were duly confiscated by a customs officer at the border. The Department of Justice argued that, 'never to have had a ban on contraceptives would be one thing: a change in the law to make them available to single people might seem to some, if not as an endorsement of immorality, at least an acceptance of its inevitability on a very wide scale. Young people were 'bombarded by sex ... a typical television studio audience in this country is now apt to shout down anyone who defends Christian ("establishment") thinking'; 'the positive act of publicly by law, accepting the availability of contraceptives for young, single people may appear as an official signal for a further lowering of barriers that are already under siege'.

A subsequent memorandum concluded that 'If the sale of contraceptives were to be permitted, the best that could be done by way of control would be to confine sales to certain outlets, such as registered chemists and to create an offence of knowingly selling contraceptives to a person under a given age'. However, regardless of restrictions, 'contraceptives would become available to all, irrespective of age or status'.[26] This was written a day before a group of IWLM members travelled to Belfast, purchased contraceptives; marched off the train waving them at customs' officers, challenging to arrest them, before going on to appear on *The Late Late Show*. While the incident attracted widespread publicity, many feminists regarded its provocation as counter-productive,[27] and it must have confirmed the worst fears of the nervous Cabinet ministers who were contemplating the consequences of changing the law. The Cabinet appears to have recoiled from all options presented: the agenda item was postponed on several occasions – generally a sign that ministers are divided – and was eventually withdrawn until further notice on 6 July 1971,[28] no doubt much to ministers' relief. The seizure by Customs officers of a package of spermicidal jelly addressed to Mrs Mary McGee, which she challenged in the High Court with the support of the IFPA, gave the government a breathing space. The case was heard in the High Court in June 1972 and dismissed; she then appealed to the Supreme Court, their verdict was issued in December 1973. The Supreme Court ruling made it legal to import contraceptives for private use, but did not strike down the restrictions on sale, distribution and wholesale importation of contraceptives. The court determined that if Mrs MaGee observed the prohibition on importing contraceptives, 'she will endanger the security and happiness of her marriage, she will imperil her health to the point of hazarding her life, and she will subject her family to the risk of distress and disruption. These are intrusions which she is entitled to say are incompatible with the safety of her life, the preservation of her health, her responsibility to her conscience, and the security and well-being of her marriage and family.'

The Court placed considerable emphasis on the right of a married couple to privacy. Mr Justice Brian Walsh determined that

The sexual life of a husband and wife is of necessity and by its nature an area of particular privacy. If the husband and wife decide to limit their family or to avoid having children by use of contraceptives it is a matter peculiarly within the joint decision of the husband and wife and one into which the State cannot intrude unless its intrusion can be justified by the exigencies of the common good. The question of whether the use of contraceptives by married couples within their marriage is or is not contrary to the moral code or codes to which they profess to subscribe, or is or is not regarded by them as being against their conscience, could not justify State intervention. Similarly the fact that the use of contraceptives may

---

[26] NAI 2003/16/34 Criminal Law Amendment Act. Office of the Minister for Justice. Memorandum for the Government contraceptives 21 and 30 May 1972.

[27] Connolly, *The Irish women's movement*, pp. 120–2; Fennell, *Political woman*, pp. 60–3.

[28] NAI 2003/16/34 Criminal Law Amendment Act, 30 May 1972.

offend against the moral code of the majority of the citizens of the State would not per se justify an intervention by the State to prohibit their use within marriage. The private morality of its citizens does not justify intervention by the State into the activities of those citizens unless and until the common good requires it.[29]

The Supreme Court decision meant that customs officers could no longer seize contraceptives imported for personal use either by post or in person. On the day following the Supreme Court ruling, the Attorney General issued summonses against the IFPA and Family Planning Services, a company that supplied contraceptives in return for a 'voluntary' donation.[30]

The debate on contraception provides some insights into the fears that were aroused by the prospect of a relaxation in Ireland's traditional code of sexual morality. In the mid-1960s, words like 'family planning', 'contraception' were not part of regular discourse; if/when they were mentioned, it was in the context of large families, the medical risks to mothers, or a wish by married couples to space or limit the number of children. By the early 1970s, contraception was increasingly linked with divorce, abortion, even euthanasia – as the first step on the road towards 'the permissive society'.[31]

In January 1973, Fr Paul Marx, OSA, a leading anti-abortionist in the United States, who was touring Britain paid a short visit to Ireland, where he addressed several hundred adults in a Dublin hotel and spoke to 500 teenage girls, at a Mercy Convent in Cork, showing them a 12-week old foetus which he carried around in a jar, plus 40 graphic slides of aborted foetuses. When he addressed a group of nurses in Cork, he told them 'You have in Ireland, a group which promotes contraception. I say right now that that leads to abortion.' When he paid a repeat visit in November, shortly before the Supreme Court judgment, a visit possibly timed to coincide with a further attempt to bring a Family Planning Bill before the Seanad, he claimed that 'you've the abortion ... I mean family planning clinics right here in your city. I won't go into the details.'[32] This Bill, introduced by Senators Robinson, West and Horgan, prompted a statement from the Hierarchy, 'The real question facing the legislators is: what effect would be increased availability of contraceptives have on the quality

---

[29] McGee versus Attorney General 1973.

[30] Barry Desmond, *Finally and in conclusion*, p. 230.

[31] The 1969 report by the social worker in the Rotunda referred to an 'increasingly permissive society', going on to write of marital breakdown, debt, alcoholism, and compulsive gambling.

[32] Mary Robinson attempted to introduce a private members' Family Planning Bill on 14 November 1973, SD, vol 76, cols. 3–4, 14 November 1973. *II*, 19 November 1973. Janet Martin, 'An evening with Fr. Paul Marx'.

of life in the Republic of Ireland'. They described abortion as the ultimate contraceptive.[33]

While the Supreme Court based its judgement on the rights of a married couple, there is evidence of a rising incidence of sexual activity among young people. In 1974, Emer Philbin-Bowman discovered that 47 per cent of new clients at the IFPA Clinic in Merrion Square were single, and 19 per cent were not planning to marry.[34] Irish society was changing. A survey that year by Micheál MacGréil showed that over 98 per cent of respondents believed that children born to single mothers should be treated exactly like children of married couples, and only 3 per cent of respondents believed that an unmarried mother 'should pay for her sin'. But only 45 per cent were in favour of decriminalising homosexual behaviour between consenting adults, and 57.6 per cent believed that premarital sex was always wrong.[35] A 1973 survey of married women showed that 54 per cent had tried to regulate fertility; of these 55 per cent had used natural methods, followed by 15 per cent who used the pill and 10 per cent who relied on coitus interruptus. Use of contraception and attitudes towards legislative reform were strongly correlated with age, social class, occupation and geography. Younger women, living in Dublin, members of the professional classes were the most liberal; older women in rural areas, and especially farming families, held the most conservative views. Only one-third of women in the sample were opposed to some changes in the law, though many wanted access limited to married couples. Wilson-Davis noted the conservative position of farming couples – where over one-third wished to see contraception available only on medical grounds. The majority of married couples, including those not using any form of family planning, regarded the number of children as a private matter.[36]

---

[33] *II*, 26 November 1973.

[34] Emer Philbin Bowman, 'Sexual and contraceptive attitudes and behaviour of single attenders at a Dublin family planning clinic', *Journal of Biosocial Science*, vol. 9, 1977, pp. 429–45.

[35] MacGréil, *Prejudice and tolerance*, table 149.

[36] Keith Wilson-Davis, 'Some results of an Irish family planning survey', *Journal of Biosocial Science*, vol. 7, 1975, pp. 435–44.

10   The churches

The emerging debate on contraception represented a direct challenge to the authority of the Catholic Church, though we should not overstate its extent – memoranda originating in the Department of Justice faithfully reflected Church statements on the dangers to society of liberalising access to contraception. But for a time during the 1960s, it appeared that the Church and the wider society would march arm in arm towards a modern and consensual future, marked by greater tolerance, less censoriousness and a shared commitment to social and economic progress. The Protestant churches were also changing, and there is evidence that the communities in the Republic and Northern Ireland were drifting apart, with the former identifying more strongly than before with the Irish state. Whatever divisions existed in the mid-1960s between Protestants in Ireland, north and south were seriously exacerbated after 1969 with the crisis in Northern Ireland. The 1960s also brought some erosion of deeply entrenched denominational divisions, with the emergence of more neutral social spaces such as commercial dance halls, the beginnings of more open recruitment in business and the professions, and measures to promote closer inter-church relations, which were encouraged by Pope John XXIII. But there were limits to this process. Some Protestants feared that their identity would be submerged; liberal voices within the Catholic Church faded. Yet, given the emotions aroused by violence in Northern Ireland, the lack of denominational tensions, and continuing commitment to inter-church meetings, however limited, should be applauded. And while the 1960s was a decade when greater affluence and individualism, the sexual revolution, second-wave feminism, political radicalisation and more liberal and even radical theologies combined to undermine the position of religion in Western society,[1] the impact on Ireland was limited. Callum Brown, author of a comparative study of Ireland,

[1] Hugh McLeod, *The religious crisis of the 1960s* (Oxford: Oxford University Press, 2010), p. 15.

191

Canada, Britain and the United States, concluded that 'the sixties did not have the same resonance in Ireland', as elsewhere.[2] Although the numbers entering religion peaked in the mid-1960s and declined from that point, the Irish Catholic Church continued to have more than sufficient religious to meet its pastoral requirements. In 1971, 91 per cent of the population attended church every week. The Catholic Church continued to exercise a significant influence on politics and society. Nevertheless, in contrast to the past, the relationship/concordat between the church, the state and society was now contested and unstable, at continuing risk of challenge or revision.

In the 1950s, those poor benighted Catholics on the Continent seemed to be in dire straits, mired in all kinds of theological disputes (unknown to ever-loyal Ireland), struggling with falling numbers, alienated from the working classes, and so on. This was the time when the Irish Church basked in the self-satisfied glow of almost total attendance at Sunday Mass, sufficient vocations to supply most of the English-speaking world – and no theological doubts.[3]

Rev Vincent Twomey's comment captures the complacency of Irish Catholicism in the early 1960s – the years that saw the final flourishing of Ireland's 'devotional revolution'.[4] In 1940, when John Charles McQuaid became archbishop of Dublin, there were 370 priests in the archdiocese and 99 students in the diocesan seminary; by 1965, the year of his golden jubilee, there were 550 priests and 140 seminarians.[5] In 1960, 94 priests ordained for Irish dioceses were sent abroad on loan to foreign dioceses, because they were not needed at home. A further 141 men were ordained for foreign dioceses – 75 for the United States and Canada and 50 for Britain; an additional 53 were ordained for missionary societies and 139 for religious orders and congregations – the latter would serve both in Ireland and overseas.[6] Half of all priests ordained in the early 1960s left Ireland for service overseas.[7] Although control of dioceses in Africa was passing to native-born bishops, as part of the decolonisation process, Irishmen were still being appointed as bishops in far-flung countries, and many native-African bishops had been educated in Ireland. The US Catholic Hierarchy retained a strong Irish ethnic profile, and

---

[2] Brown, *Religion and the demographic revolution*, p. 37.
[3] D. Vincent Twomey, *The end of Irish Catholicism?* (Dublin: Veritas, 2003), p. 31.
[4] Emmet Larkin, 'The devotional revolution in Ireland, 1850–75', *American Historical Review*, vol. 75, no. 3, 1972, pp. 81–98.
[5] Roland Burke Savage, 'The Church in Dublin 1940–1965: a study of the achievements and of the personality of Most Reverend John Charles Mc Quaid on the occasion of his silver jubilee', *Studies*, vol. 54, winter 1965, p. 301.
[6] *Hibernia*, April 1961.
[7] 'The modern missionary movement' in Desmond Fennell (ed.), *The changing face of Catholic Ireland* (London: G. Chapman, 1968), pp. 138–9.

with the increasing frequency of long-distance flights, contacts with Ireland's 'spiritual empire' probably strengthened. Many US or African bishops with Irish connections travelled to Ireland before or after a visit to Rome. In the early 1960s, the number of schools, hospitals and charitable institutions run by the Catholic Church was greater than at any previous time, and the role of the Catholic Church in Irish society was not facing any serious challenge. New secondary schools were opening. Ireland's first child psychology services had recently opened, with the support of the Dublin Archdiocese – compensating yet again for a major gap in state provision.[8]

Rev Twomey overstates the distinction between Ireland and elsewhere. The decades after the Second World War saw a religious revival throughout Western Europe and substantial missionary activity by religious communities from the Netherlands, Belgium and Italy. Ireland's ratio of priests to Catholic laity was not exceptionally high: 558 Catholics per priest, compared with 494 in the Netherlands and 507 in Britain. The Church of Ireland ratio was 1: 180.[9] Ireland was distinct mainly because the proportion who attended religious services regularly was much higher than that elsewhere, as was the number entering religious life. Irish clergy of all religions constituted an educated elite. In the early 1970s, 80 per cent of Catholic diocesan clergy were graduates; over 10 per cent had a postgraduate qualification; just under half of priests in religious orders were graduates; 40 per cent of brothers held university degrees, 86 per cent had a professional qualifications – mainly teacher training; 72 per cent of religious sisters held a university degree or a professional qualification, in nursing or teaching. Some of the authority exercised by Catholic religious communities reflected their superior education.

D. H. Akenson's book *Small Differences* examined the similarities and contrasts between Irish Catholic and Protestant emigrants: the phrase is equally applicable to Catholics and Protestants in mid-twentieth-century Ireland. Emigration and rural decline, the major social problems, had a disproportionate impact on Ireland's Protestant community, and although the Irish population rose between 1961 and 1971, Protestant numbers continued to decline, though at a slower pace. The Protestant community was more affluent and more middle class, nevertheless Catholics and Protestants had much in common, though they generally lived separate lives. They attended church regularly. Both communities shared a conservative attitude towards sex; both were equally fearful of

---

[8] Tom Feeney, 'Church, state and family: the advent of child guidance clinics in independent Ireland', *Social History of Medicine*, vol. 25, no. 4, 2012, pp. 848–62.
[9] Fennell (ed.), *The changing face of Catholic Ireland*, 'Time of Decision', pp. 26–7.

the threat of conversion to the other's religion. 'Mixed marriages' were not welcome in most Catholic or Protestant homes – though the *ne temere* decree where the Catholic Church required that children in inter-religious marriages should be raised as Catholics meant that Protestant hostility was greater. For many Catholics and Protestants, social life and the calendar revolved around religion: weekly church services, some additional devotions; hobbies, sports or charitable activities based around the parish. One Church of Ireland bishop found it hard to think of his 1950s childhood in the north Dublin suburb of Drumcondra, as other than a form of denominational apartheid, though 'an extremely benign and civilised apartheid . . . apartheid by mutual consent'.[10] There were separate schools, separate universities for the privileged minority of both communities, and often different employers.

For Catholics, there was little gender difference in terms of religious practice, which often extended well beyond Sunday mass to include the nine First Fridays, May devotions, membership of confraternities, pilgrimages and other devotional practices. The numbers attending the annual blessing of the throats on St Blaise's Day, in the Franciscan church at Merchant's Quay, continued to rise well into the 1960s; the recently introduced evening term-time mass for UCD students at University Church attracted 'three or four hundred holy communions or more each evening, and a confessor or two kept busy'.[11] One woman who became a nun recalled that in her childhood 'our entertainment was sort of going to the Holy Hour ... I could say "I'm going to the Holy Hours", it got you into town. [Religion] was socially *right*'.[12] Parish sales of work, parish excursions; socials organised by the Pioneer Total Abstinence Association or a sodality; trips to the seaside or the cinema for altar boys were highlights in many social calendars. Until 1966, UCD students stood in the library at noon and 6pm to recite the angelus. Radio-trains broadcasting the rosary, and occasionally Mass, carried pilgrimages to Knock; pilgrimages to Lourdes were a lucrative market for Aer Lingus and often the first or only foreign holiday for many Irish people. Religious statues, holy water fonts and holy pictures or church art calendars were common in most homes – though increasingly absent or less prominent in modern suburban living rooms. My father, an agricultural advisor who worked in counties Cavan and Monaghan, told me that

[10] Bishop Richard Clarke, in Colin Murphy and Lynne Adair (eds), *Untold stories. Protestants in the Republic of Ireland 1922–2002* (Dublin: Liffey Press, 2002), pp. 52–3.
[11] Roland Burke Savage, 'The Church in Dublin 1940–1965', p. 327.
[12] Quoted in Yvonne McKenna, *Made holy: Irish women religious at home and abroad* (Dublin: IAP, 2006), p. 52.

in farm houses, holy pictures or photographs of Queen Elizabeth II were reliable visual clues as to their religious affiliation.

The life of a young woman growing up in a Church of Ireland family in the midlands was not dramatically different to that of her Catholic neighbours: her church hosted 'a choral festival when singers would come from neighbouring parishes to sing together ... the harvest festival ... in late September or early October'. The service was followed by supper and a dance in the parish hall.[13] An elderly Protestant from Mayo described travelling in the 1950s and 1960s to Church of Ireland socials in neighbouring counties. He met his wife at one of these occasions.[14] Young people carried a card signed by their local rector, which they had to show to gain admittance.[15] Mac Gréil's survey showed that over 40 per cent of adult males were members of a voluntary group – most commonly church- or parish-based.[16] Sport was both a unifying and divisive force: GAA sports were not played in Protestant schools, and as most matches were played on Sundays, conflicting with Protestant sabbatarianism, it was difficult for Protestants to participate. Rugby – segregated more by class than religion – crossed the denominational divide. Carol Coulter, who grew up in the west of Ireland, described

the world of the south Dublin Protestant middle class in the 1960s, [as]a smug and complacent intimate world where networking assured children employment in the arenas of finance, insurance and manufacturing where the old Protestant middle class held sway. Its social life was almost hermetically sealed, with its Scout and Girl Guide troops, its tennis clubs, its youth clubs, all linked to the Church. Unlike the people I grew up with, the girls in my school – and, indeed, their parents – passed their entire lives with practically no social interaction with their Catholic neighbours.[17]

There was no anti-clerical party in Irish politics; indeed, Ó Corráin noted 'a respect for men of the cloth, irrespective of denomination, by representatives of both national and local government'.[18] Leading politicians mingled on a regular basis with religious leaders. A military guard of honour, from the nearby army base, greeted the Minister General of the Franciscan Order when he visited Gormanston College.[19] Formal arrangements for St Patrick's Day in 1959 set out that Members of the

---

[13] Gillian Lyster, in *Untold stories*, pp. 121–2.
[14] Heather Crawford, *Outside the glow. Protestants and Irishness in independent Ireland* (Dublin: UCD Press, 2010), pp. 78–9.
[15] Bishop Paul Colton, in *Untold stories*, p. 57.
[16] MacGréil, *Prejudice and tolerance in Ireland*, p. 106.
[17] Carol Coulter, in *Untold stories*, p. 65.
[18] Ó Corráin, *Rendering to God and Caesar*, pp. 75–6.
[19] Franciscan Chronicle April 1957.

Government, Parliamentary Secretaries, Chairmen of the Houses of the Oireachtas and the Attorney General would 'as usual' attend 12 o'clock High Mass at the Pro-Cathedral. Ministers would gather in the nearby presbytery and would be 'conducted to the church'. After Mass they would return to the presbytery to be received by the archbishop of Dublin.[20] Lemass travelled to Rome for ceremonies marking the eightieth birthday of Pope John XXIII.[21] When Dr Conway, Archbishop of Armagh, was elevated to the College of Cardinals, the government marked the event by releasing sixteen republican prisoners.[22]

The early 1960s brought a wave of church-building to cater for Dublin's expanding suburbs. Rev Anthony Gaughan, then a curate in Cabra West, recalls that 'Such were the crowds at Mass on each Sunday, that Masses were celebrated every half-hour from seven till noon', lasting an average of 20–25 minutes – formulaic services, where 'almost simultaneously' one priest would say Mass, one distributed communion and a third preached a sermon lasting five to seven minutes. Sodalities for men, women and teenagers, and the Legion of Mary were integral parts of parish religious life. A boys' club with gymnastics, boxing and woodwork was designed to attract the more 'intractable' boys who did not join the boy scouts. The parish hall hosted classes in Irish dancing and 'show-girl dancing' – run by former members of the Royalettes – a high stepping dance troupe attached to Dublin's Theatre Royal; there were band sessions, socials, teenage dances and concerts.[23] Weekly Bingo sessions in parish halls proved an effective method of fundraising, while giving a night out to many women, whose social outlets were otherwise limited. Dublin dockers protested because their wives were attending parish Bingo evenings twice a week.[24]

Priests were commonly regarded as some combination of political fixer, fundraiser, social worker and entrepreneur. They often led deputations seeking new factories, water schemes, new schools, or chaired committees running community shows, sports and drama activities. Some priests appear to have devoted more time to these activities than to theology or catechising. Gaughan described his parish priest in county Wicklow in 1962, spending most of his time 'putting on shows for one charity or another', many of the performers were past pupils of a school in Glasnevin where he had had served as chaplain.[25] By the 1960s, many parishes were heavily in debt; rising inflation reduced the real value of legacies and investments at a time when running costs were rising; more commercially

[20] NAI DT S10561B St Patrick's Day.   [21] Franciscan Chronicle, 7 November 1961.
[22] Matt Treacy, The IRA, 1956–69 (Manchester, 2011), p. 23.
[23] Gaughan, At the coal face, pp. 50–4.   [24] Gaughan, At the coal face, p. 80.
[25] Gaughan, At the coal face, pp. 62–3.

minded banks may well have proved less accommodating to parish over-drafts than in the past. Professional US-style fundraisers were hired to tackle the growing deficits; they toured the parish, visiting households and persuading them to commit to a fixed weekly contribution.[26] These new funding methods were not universally popular: in January 1969, Grille, a left-wing Christian group, picketed Clonliffe College in protest,[27] and although professional fundraisers succeeded in collecting more money, their intrusion into what had hitherto been a voluntary community activity did not strengthen the bond between parishioners and their church.

When Ireland celebrated the Patrician Year in 1961, marking the 1500th anniversary of the death of St Patrick, the world of Irish Catholicism appeared secure. Under almost every metric – numbers of religious; ordinations; numbers entering religious institutions – the peak years were 1965–1967, then a decline. The decline was most acute among nuns, who constituted 70 per cent of Catholic religious: 592 women joined congregations in 1966; by 1970, this had fallen to 207.[28] Between 1965 and 1970, 37 of the 102 female congregations recruited no new postulants, and the authors of a survey of Irish female religious orders expressed fears that if these trends continued, some orders would no longer be capable of staffing the schools, hospitals, and other institutions under their control.[29] Some congregations no longer accepted school-leavers. When an English translation of Heinrich Böll's *Irish Diary* was published in 1967, Böll noted in the introduction that 'to my regret, but not to that of most Irishmen, nuns have practically disappeared from the newspapers'.[30] This was probably because they were less conspicuous. Traditional religious habits, such as the elaborate 'butterfly' headdress of the French Sisters of Charity or the 'shoe-boxes' of the St Louis sisters, were replaced by short skirts and shorter veils. By the 1970s, religious sisters often wore civilian dress. Yet, in 1971 the number of priests and nuns in Ireland was almost identical to 1961. Falling vocations first impacted on the numbers serving overseas. In 1966, 206 diocesan priests were ordained, 85 for Irish dioceses; in 1974, the total had fallen to 130, but 86 were ordained for Irish dioceses. Ordinations for foreign dioceses collapsed from 121 to 44.[31] Between 1965 and 1970, 104 professed brothers and 72 priests left religious life; 297 sisters and 169

[26] *B&F*, Helen Lucy Burke, 'How parish fundraisers work', 3 December1965.
[27] *IT*, 23 January 1969.   [28] Fuller, *Irish catholicism*, p. 168.
[29] 'Survey of Catholic clergy and religious personnel 1971', by Rev James Lennon (director), Rev Liam Ryan, Rev Michael MacGréil, Nuala Drake and Carmely Perera, *Social Studies*,: Report no 3 Statistical Survey of Irish Sisters, pp. 195–7.
[30] Heinrich Böll, *Irish Journal* (London: Secker & Warburg, 1967), p. 122.
[31] *ICD*, 1974.

brothers left after taking final vows. Fuller suggests that while the number leaving religious life was low, it was 'nonetheless significant' and considerably higher than in the past.[32] There was a proportionately greater decline in the number of Church of Ireland ministers, from 552 to 428; ministers in other religions fell from 221 to 164, which might indicate that the determining factor was wider societal change, and not, as commonly assumed, a response to Vatican II. We shouldn't underestimate the impact of wider career opportunities, or the introduction of grants for higher education. Many poor and academically talented students in the past only received secondary or university education by joining a seminary.

Vatican II and Irish Catholicism

In the early 1960s, the papacy of Pope John XXIII and the Second Vatican Council seemed to promise a Catholicism more in tune with modern society; an escape from the stultifying background of censorship and old-fashioned charity, and the emergence of a Catholicism that encouraged greater lay involvement in church affairs and a more liberal approach to social reform. Lemass regularly cited John XXIII's 1961 social encyclical, *Mater et Magistra*, and he urged Cabinet ministers to keep a copy on their desks,[33] which suggests that he saw no overt conflict between economic development and an active role for the Catholic Church. The Second Vatican Council could be described as the religious and theological equivalent of free trade, EEC membership and the AIFTAA. During the sessions of Vatican II, members of the Irish Hierarchy spent long periods in Rome, where they were exposed to the ideas and issues that concerned their fellow bishops throughout the world. While Irish cardinal Paul Cullen had played a leading role at the First Vatican Council almost a century earlier, on this occasion, the Irish clergy appear to have been out of line with their fellow prelates, who were more aware of the need to address the challenges presented by modern society. The Dominican theologian Rev Austin Flannery described the response of the Irish clergy as 'we have a winning team, why change it'.[34] He noted that 'There was very little theological discussion in Ireland, very little. And the result was when the bishops went to Rome they were ill-prepared ... and some of the things that were said came as a hell of a shock.'[35] Maynooth theologian Liam Twomey claims that 'Before the Council, there was little public discussion of reform of the

---

[32] Fuller, *Irish Catholicism*, p. 167.   [33] Horgan, *Lemass*, p. 322.
[34] Francis Xavier Carty, *Hold firm. John Charles McQuaid and the second Vatican Council* (Dublin: Columba Press, 2007), pp. 42–3.
[35] Flannery, as quoted by Carty *Hold Firm*, p. 49.

liturgy, little exposure to new ideas about the nature of the Church or ecumenism, not to mention the challenge posed by atheism or the question of the relationship of the non-Christian religions to Christianity'.[36] Dr McQuaid wrote to priests in the Dublin Archdiocese before he travelled to Rome, where he suggested that 'the Faithful' should be advised against 'undue expectations of new definitions of doctrine, new laws of discipline, new or startling movements towards the unity of Christendom'. T. Commins, Irish ambassador to the Holy See, reported that 'their [the Irish hierarchy] attitude to the Council itself has been the reverse of exuberant'; he surmised that their reaction to any proposed changes 'will be supremely conservative'.[37] A year later, he noted little evidence that the Hierarchy, either as a body or as individuals, 'has moved from the largely supine and reserved approach to the Council and Council problems which has characterised their participation in the last two sessions'.[38]

Irish Catholicism before Vatican II has been described as 'institutional, authoritative and ritualistic'.[39] Desmond Fennell claims that it was 'the most thorough-going, full-blooded and successful embodiment' of 'late Tridentine Catholicism'.[40] Clergy and laity shared a common, largely unquestioning acceptance of church teaching, and parish clergy appear to have concentrated more on ritual and community service than promoting a greater understanding of theology, though there were exceptions. The Irish Hierarchy expected and generally enjoyed the unquestioning obedience of the laity. Bruce Biever, an American psychologist and Jesuit priest, who carried out a survey of Catholics in Dublin during the early 1960s, comparing their attitudes with those of Irish-American Catholics, claimed that

Despite the articulate intellectual minority, there is still in the Irish laity the deeply-held conviction that his prime function in the church is to obey and do what he is told, no matter whether this makes much sense to him or not. He has become used to the idea that he really does not have to think out many of his problems for himself, but rather the church will provide him with an answer for them, and all he has to do is follow the directions he is given.

Little value was placed on freedom of expression. Some of those who were contacted to take part in the survey, were fearful that the parish priest might hear that they had been 'talking to a foreigner' Biever was highly critical of the 'religious complacency, produced by 'this obedience syndrome', contrasting it with the more questioning attitudes of Irish-American Catholics.[41]

---

[36] Twomey, *The end of Irish Catholicism*, p. 35.
[37] Quoted in Carty *Hold Firm*, pp. 56, 59.   [38] Ó Corráin, *Rendering to Caesar*, p. 204.
[39] McKenna, *Made Holy*, p. 52.
[40] Fennell (ed.) *The changing face of Catholic Ireland*, p. 25.
[41] Bruce Biever, *Religion, culture and values. A cross-cultural analysis of motivational factors in native Irish and American Irish Catholicism* (New York: Arno Pres, 1976), pp. 495–7.

Vatican II transformed or ended many popular rituals.[42] The Council tried to bring religion back to fundamentals – a twentieth-century 'stripping of the altars' – replacing elaborate high altars with a more modest one facing the people; Mass was celebrated in English and there was less emphasis on popular devotions. While these changes prompted protests in many countries, Twomey claimed that they were introduced in Ireland without public controversy, in contrast to what happened elsewhere. 'There was simply, uncomprehending obedience ... of the new laws mostly without demur.'[43] Such acquiescence reflected the culture of conformity which epitomised Irish Catholicism. Vatican II promoted a more active role for the laity, another potential minefield for a church with a poor record of tolerating active independent lay Catholic organisations. Frank Duff, founder of the lay evangelising organisation Legion of Mary, faced major difficulties in establishing a working relationship with the clergy, 'because the priests often did not see a role for the laity in what they regarded as their own exclusive sphere of activity'.[44] In 1966, Tim Pat Coogan commented that 'In many ways the Irish Church of the past, and to some degree still today, is the Church Juridical. This may suffice even in an age when the priest is the only educated man in a backward, rural community. It will not serve in the age of the education explosion.'[45] Many committed Catholics, who were involved in charitable organisations, sodalities and regularly attended religious retreats saw Vatican II as an opportunity to take a more active role in church life. 'Paperback theology' flourished in 1960s Ireland; the publisher Michael Gill sold 'quite extraordinary' numbers of theology books in the company's Logos series; in 1966, one of the bestselling books in Dublin was by the French theologian Teilhard de Chardin.[46]

In 1964, the journalist Peter Lennon described two contrasting images, one of 'a Catholic population looking eagerly to the very reassuring developments taking place in the Ecumenical Council but having little confidence that they would soon benefit from these changes ... The other – an image of so many people harassed confused and unnecessarily guilt-ridden by official instance on the supposedly shameful aspects of almost anything connected with sexual activity.' He identified two fundamental problems: the obsession with indecency and obscenity and 'the unwillingness of people to publicly challenge an official opinion no matter

[42] G. Cholvy, Y. M. Hilaire, D. Delmaire, *Le fait religieux aujourd'hi en France* (Paris: Cerf, 2004).

[43] Twomey, *The end of Irish Catholicism*, p. 36.

[44] Finola Kennedy, *Frank Duff. A life story* (London, 2011), pp. 211–2.

[45] Tim Pat Coogan, *Ireland since the Rising* (London: Pall Mall, 1966), p. 247.

[46] Carty, *Hold firm*, p. 82; Coogan, *Ireland since the Rising*, p. 168.

how much they may deride it in private'. This was part of a series of
exchanges in *Hibernia* between Lennon and Rev Peter Connolly,
Professor of English in Maynooth College. Another article in the same
issue by Rev Thomas Halton suggested that Lennon had 'violated the
rules of the Test-Ban treaty between Irish church and State'. He was not
unsympathetic to Lennon; 'The Irish church in the eyes of many outsiders
has become over the years old-fashioned, autocratic, ritualistic, and narrowly conservative. At home there has been a fair amount of self-satisfied
backslapping, reassuring ourselves that we are unique.' Halton asked
whether some of this criticism 'is not correct?'[47]

Opinions were divided over a range of issues – social reform, censorship and sexual behaviour, and the divisions were not between clergy
and laity, but within both groups. There was a cohort of younger clergy,
who were conscious that Irish Catholicism was somewhat adrift from
developments elsewhere, and unprepared to face modern challenges.
From the late 1950s, Catholic periodicals such as *The Furrow* (edited in
the national seminary in Maynooth) and *Doctrine and Life* (edited by the
Dominican Austin Flannery) were discussing these topics and highlighting liturgical and pastoral developments elsewhere.[48] Peter
Connolly and John Kelly SJ were to the fore in challenging Ireland's
censorship laws, publishing critical reviews of books and films that were
banned in Ireland. Connolly wanted to encourage an intellectual
Catholic community; he claimed that one consequence of Ireland's
widespread and uncritical censorship was to engender 'a cynicism . . .
and contempt for Censorship in general'. He suggested that 'in face of
modern novels or films of whatever kind it was not necessary to bury
one's head in the sand, or, on the other hand, to sacrifice one jot of moral
principle'.[49] He favoured a more liberal censorship regime that would
make it possible for adults to make a critical judgement about modern
films and literature. In 1966, Peter Connolly shared a platform at a
Tuairim debate in Limerick with Edna O'Brien, where he 'praised the
"high spirits . . . and . . . cheerful natural ribaldry" of her writing, and
defended her from critics in the large audience'.[50] O'Brien, whose books
The Country Girls (1960) and *The Lonely Girl* (1962) described 'the
covert and not-so covert, rather foolish sexuality of two young girls',
convent educated, now living and working in Dublin, was probably the
most controversial Irish novelist of the decade. Her books were banned
and publicly burned in her local village (though they appear to have been

---

[47] *Hibernia*, March 1963. same edition as Lennon.
[48] Fennell, *The changing face of Catholic Ireland*, pp. 32–3; Fuller, *Irish Catholicism*,
pp. 82–96.
[49] *Hibernia*, February 1964.   [50] Finn, *Tuairim*, pp. 214–6.

widely read in Ireland).[51] O'Brien's descriptions of overt sexuality among young Irish women, whose everyday lives were typical of their generation, added to the shock. This was probably also true of John McGahern's banned novel, *The Dark*: the story of an Irish teenager who rebelled against his family. McGahern lost his job as a national teacher, apparently on the direct orders of Dr McQuaid. Both writers have described the shame and 'social disgrace' that their families experienced as a consequence.[52] Lennon complained that although McGahern's threatened dismissal was well known to Dublin journalists, they did not go public with the story until he had lost his job.[53] But as an indication of shifting or perhaps contradictory attitudes, Donald Connery noted in 1969 that when Edna O'Brien 'returns from London she is greeted as a celebrity, pictured on the front pages, and asked to air her views on television before a panel of teenagers'.[54]

In 1967, Minister for Justice Brian Lenihan introduced legislation providing that a ban imposed on a book would automatically lapse after twenty years. Before this became law, the duration was reduced to twelve years, releasing over 5,000 banned books to readers, though this was little comfort for McGahern or O'Brien, and significantly the relaxation did not apply to publications banned for advocating birth control. In 1968, Michael Adams, a committed Catholic and author of the first scholarly study of Irish censorship laws, reflected that 'The possible danger to public morality which a "marginal" book might offer is outweighed by the constant danger of heavy-handed censorship turning Ireland into a cultural ghetto–indeed, into something worse than a ghetto for, in addition to warding off foreign influences it also has expelled its own nonconformists and rejected invaluable criticism of its own social norms and customs'.[55] A review of Adams' book in the Jesuit periodical *Studies* noted that 'No one growing up in the nineteen-thirties and forties in Ireland could fail to be struck by the absence of communication between the Church and the educated Catholic ... A premium was put on the man who "never thought of thinking for himself at all". As a result, many young men became estranged from the Church; and a further result was the bitterness and the frightening lack of charity displayed towards those who held unorthodox views'.[56] McGahern commented on the anti-

---

[51] Edna O'Brien in Julia Carlson (ed.), *Banned in Ireland. Censorship and the Irish Writer* (London: Routledge, 1990), p. 71.
[52] McGahern, O'Brien, in Carlson, *Banned in Ireland*, pp. 55–79.
[53] *Hibernia*, March 1966.   [54] Connery, *The Irish*, pp.172–3.
[55] Michael Adams, *Censorship. The Irish experience* (Dublin: Scepter Books, 1968), p. 194.
[56] Andrew F. Comyn, 'Censorship in Ireland', *Studies*, vol. 58, spring 1969, p. 2.

intellectual nature of Irish Catholicism and the fact that most writers were 'lapsed Catholics'.[57]

Film censorship did not impact as directly on Irish creative artists, but Irish cinemas – which were losing audiences to television – found it increasingly difficult to get films that would pass the stringent censorship regulations, at a time when British and American films were becoming 'increasingly transgressive, youth-oriented, more sexually explicit and realist'. Between 1954 and 1964, the Appeal Board issued only eleven limited certificate – that is, licensing a film for over-eighteens; the majority of films approved had to be deemed suitable for children. Many explicit horror films given limited certificates in Britain were so approved.[58] Film critics Des Hickey (*Sunday Independent*) and Fergus Linehan (*Irish Times*) maintained a steady campaign for limited certificates and against insensitive cuts. In 1965, a new Appeal Board adopted a more liberal policy, making extensive use of limited certificates, though Rockett concludes that 'it was more than another two decades before this "liberal" policy [of limited certificates] was consolidated'. From 1965, adult cinemagoers could see sexual scenes between consenting unmarried adults, but nothing relating to homosexuality or abortion. But censorship remained quite heavy-handed, and a growing number of films were subject to cuts; Rockett concludes that by 1973, 'the limits of Irish liberalism had been defined and reached, at least for that decade'.[59] While film censorship had eased during the 1960s, it was outstripped by filmmakers, who were exploring topics and presenting images and language that went far beyond the norms of a decade earlier.

Television – a new medium in Ireland – attracted more attention from the Catholic Church than film. A reflection of Church concern is their advanced plans in preparation for its arrival. The Dublin Archdiocese established a Public Affairs Committee before a decree of Vatican II requested all dioceses to do so, and a number of priests were sent to the United States for training as television producers.[60] While this was part of the Hierarchy's efforts to gain control over religious programmes,[61] it can be argued that one of the images emerging from Teilifís Éireann in the 1960s is of a more radical, socially engaged Catholicism. Documentaries by Radharc, a production unit run by Catholic priests, such as the 'The

[57] McGahern in Carlson, *Banned in Ireland*, p. 63.
[58] Rockett, *Irish film censorship. A cultural journey from silent cinema to internet pornography* (Dublin: Four Courts, 2004), pp. 153–71.
[59] Rockett, *Irish film censorship*, p. 202.
[60] Kerry O'Hanlon, 'Irish television and the popularisation of the Catholic church in 1960s Ireland', UCD undergraduate history thesis 2014.
[61] John Bowman, *Window and mirror. RTÉ television, 1961–2011* (Cork: The Collins Press, 2011), p. 66.

Young Offender', filmed in St Patrick's Institution, 'Down and out in Dublin' and 'The boat to Euston' (on emigration), exposed some of the grimmest aspects of Irish life and asked searching questions. In 1968, Austin Flannery OP used the religious TV programme *Outlook* as a medium for publicising the Dublin housing crisis: Fuller suggests that his panel of speakers – two members of Sinn Féin, plus Michael Sweetman SJ and Michael O'Riordan, general secretary of the communist Irish Workers Party – 'underlines how much Irish society had changed in a decade'.[62] UCD Politics lecturer and Dominican priest, Fergal O'Connor became well-known from his appearances on *The Late Late Show* and other television programmes, where his views on social change, and his advocacy of socialism and industrial democracy – one writer described him as 'somewhat to the left of the Irish Labour Party'[63] – caused some parents to question the wisdom of their children studying politics in UCD. A number of younger priests became involved in political and social causes, such as the anti-apartheid movement, opposing the Vietnam War and the Dublin housing crisis. Clerical activism was not unique to Ireland or to Catholicism – clergy were prominent in Britain's 'Ban the Bomb' campaign and US protests against Vietnam. The Irish variant was less militant but nonetheless important in a society where the Catholic Church was synonymous with the status quo. The Students Christian Movement (SCM) – an ecumenical group, founded by students at UCD and TCD – participated in Dublin Housing Action Committee protests.[64] This combination of students from both Dublin universities was significant – given the continuing ban by the Dublin Archdiocese on Catholic students attending TCD.

The SCM was one manifestation of a new interest in inter-church relations, which was one of the major developments in religious affairs during these years. In June 1960, Pope John XXIII established a Secretariat for the Promotion of Christian Unity. Later that year, the Archbishop of Canterbury, Geoffrey Fisher paid a historic visit to Rome – the first meeting between a Pope and Archbishop of Canterbury since the Reformation. Catholic observers attended the 1961 assembly of the World Council of Churches (a gathering of Protestant churches).[65] However, the Irish response was neither prompt nor overly enthusiastic. Although the Society of Jesus held public lectures in Milltown Park, which provided a forum for inter-denominational contact, inter-church relationships in Ireland remained preoccupied with mixed marriages, and the *ne temere* decree. Despite the unchallenged position of the Catholic Church, McQuaid

---

[62] Fuller, *Irish Catholicism*, pp. 133–4.   [63] *Hibernia*, July 1968.
[64] *Hibernia*, October 1968.   [65] Ó Corráin, *Rendering to God and to Caesar*, pp. 196–7.

continued to fight a long-won battle for Catholic supremacy – retaining an obsession with the denominational breakdown of consultants in Dublin hospitals, boards of governors of charities and other indicators of status and influence. The Vatican Council's 1964 decree on Ecumenism – with its emphasis on what united Christians, rather than what divided them – set the scene for inter-church dialogue. A meeting in the Mansion House in January 1966 marking Christian Unity week attracted 700 people, including both Archbishops of Dublin, President de Valera; Fine Gael leader James Dillon, the Lord Mayor of Dublin, the Chief Justice and the Editor of *The Irish Times*. But the symbolism was less welcoming: Dr McQuaid sat on the podium with the papal nuncio and the speaker – a Belfast Catholic theologian, whereas the Church of Ireland Archbishop, Dr G.O. Simms, sat in the front row, though there was an empty seat on the podium. The gardaí were present to control the crowds; hundreds had to be turned away because there was no space.[66] In January 1967, McQuaid and Simms sat together at a Christian Unity event in the National Stadium (better known for staging boxing matches) – a venue chosen to cater for the large audience.[67] There would appear to have been general goodwill towards ecumenism; in 1972, 75 per cent of Protestants and 84 per cent of Catholics surveyed in the greater Dublin area expressed the opinion that 'Church unity' was desirable in principle,[68] though precisely what they understood by 'church unity' is not clear. In 1966, Catholics were permitted to attend weddings, baptisms and funerals of non-Catholics, including serving as bridesmaid or bestman, and there was a gradual relaxation of Catholic hostility towards mixed marriages, which had traditionally taken place in sacristies, with no flowers and no music,[69] often early in the morning. By 1970, the onus for raising children in a religiously mixed marriage as Catholics was placed on the Catholic partner. But the attitude of the hierarchy remained less tolerant than in other countries, where a child's religion was regarded as a matter of conscience for the parents.[70] In 1974, the funeral in St Patrick's Cathedral of Erskine Childers, President of Ireland, was attended by senior politicians of all parties – in marked contrast to the 1949 funeral in the same cathedral of Ireland's first president, Douglas Hyde, when government ministers wishing to pay their respects stood outside.[71]

But change was gradual: in 1970, the Irish Council of Churches – a council of Protestant churches – and the Catholic Church created a 'Joint Group on Social Problems', and Protestant churches took part in the

---

[66] Alice Curtayne, *The Furrow*, cited in Fuller, *Irish Catholicism*, p. 185.
[67] Carty, *Hold firm*, pp. 112–18.   [68] MacGréil, *Prejudice and tolerance*, p. 168.
[69] Viney, *The five percent*, pp. 23–5.
[70] Ó Corráin, *Rendering to God and to Caesar*, pp. 188–91.
[71] *DIB* online, Douglas Hyde.

Kilkenny conference (see below). The first formal Irish Inter-Church Meeting at Ballymascanlon (symbolically on the border with Northern Ireland) was not held until 1973.[72] Practical advances in identifying common social problems, less onerous requirements for mixed marriages or sharing experiences with regard to marriage counselling were counter-acted by the 1968 encyclical *Humanae Vitae*, which highlighted the differing attitudes of Rome and Canterbury towards contraception, by continuing Protestant resentment at *ne temere*, and the refusal to authorise adoptions by couples in religiously mixed marriages.[73] With social life moving away from the parish, and more open recruitment in traditionally Catholic or Protestant companies, the prospects of inter-faith marriages were rising, threatening to erode the number of Protestants and their separate identity. A further danger came from the influx of Catholic pupils to Protestant schools, most significantly in the Dublin suburb of Dalkey, which was strongly resisted by the local Protestant rector.[74]

However, the greatest threat to inter-church relations came from the conflict in Northern Ireland – which created even-deeper divisions in a community that was strongly segregated on the basis of religion. In 1972, the British Ambassador to Ireland Sir John Peck commented that 'the Church of Ireland has at times seems undecided whether it is the Church of Ireland, or a surviving branch of the Church of England'.[75] However, inverting a chapter title used by Roy Foster, 'How the Catholics became Protestants',[76] we could argue that in the 1960s, Protestants living in the Republic became Irish and made efforts to show that they identified fully with the state and its origins. This was expressed most clearly during the Golden Jubilee of the 1916 Rising when churches of all denominations held special services to mark the occasion, while indicating privately, to the government, that their co-religionists in Northern Ireland should not be associated with these events.[77] The outbreak of violence in 1969 brought these divisions and tensions within the Irish Protestant churches to a head, prompting a debate about Irishness and Protestantism. Northern Ireland challenged the Catholic Church to find a balance

[72] Geraldine Smyth, ' Ecumenism and interchurch relations', in James Donnelly et al. (eds), *Encyclopaedia of Irish history and culture* (Farmington Hills, Michigan: Macmillan), vol. I, pp. 182–4.

[73] *Church of Ireland Gazette*, 9 August 1968; 19 September 1969; 1 January 1971.

[74] Áine Hyland, 'The multi-denominational experience in the national school system in Ireland', *Irish educational studies*, vol. 8, 1989, pp. 96–103.

[75] TNA, FCO Annual Review, 1972 para 12.

[76] Roy Foster, *Luck and the Irish. A brief history of change 1970–2000* (London: Allen Lane, 2007), pp. 37–66.

[77] Daly, 'Less a commemoration', in Mary E. Daly and Margaret O'Callaghan (eds), *1916 in 1966. Commemorating the Easter Rising* (Dublin: Royal Irish Academy, 2007), pp. 44–50.

between condemning violence and providing pastoral care and support for families and communities who supported the IRA. It also prompted a debate about the close identification between Catholicism and independent Ireland, culminating in a referendum in December 1972, when almost 85 per cent of those who voted approved the deletion of Article 44 of the 1937 Constitution – which referred to the special position of the Roman Catholic Church. This amendment was uncontroversial. The emerging debates over divorce and contraception were more problematic, and not just for the Catholic Church. Suggestions that divorce and contraception should be available to, and were demanded by Protestants, would have made some sections of those socially conservative communities rather uncomfortable. Given the bloodshed, personal traumas and bitterness, the continuing friendships and contacts – sometimes perfunctory, often genuine, between churchmen and laity – might be described as success.

The final aspect of 1960s Catholicism that I want to examine is a changing role in relation to social policy. Radharc tackled some of the major social issues of the time, but the long-term impact is more evident away from the television screen. In 1963, the newly appointed Bishop of Ossory, Dr Peter Birch established an umbrella group in Kilkenny (his diocesan see), to co-ordinate the work of disparate voluntary organisations, local statutory bodies and religious orders. He was following models for partnership between church and state that had evolved in Flanders. Within a year, they had recruited over a hundred volunteers from all religious denominations. Kilkenny Social Service Council supplemented and co-ordinated existing services and identified local needs, such as meals and other practical supports for the elderly, housing and support for Travellers and a school for mentally handicapped children.[78] A profile in *Hibernia* described Dr Birch as 'conservative on theological issues, very active in promoting new social services and a more modern liturgy: experimenting with guitar music in church, using laymen to read the epistle at mass and trying to ensure that lay readers were drawn from diverse social backgrounds'. Kilkenny Social Service Council began to attract media attention; in 1966, Taoiseach Jack Lynch described it as a model for other communities.[79] By 1971, there were twenty-seven Social Service Councils offering a range of assistance plus thirty-two councils that focused exclusively on services for the elderly.

---

[78] Stanislaus Kennedy, *The development of Kilkenny social services 1963–1980. Who should care?* (Dublin: Turoe, 1981), pp. 16–18; Michael Ryan (ed.), *The church and the nation. The vision of Peter Birch. Bishop of Ossory 1964–1981* (Dublin: Columba Press, 1993), pp. 13, 58–9.

[79] Kennedy, *The development of Kilkenny social services*, pp. 33–4.

The template for this evolving partnership between church and state in social services was largely determined at a 1971 conference on poverty in Kilkenny, organised by the Catholic Hierarchy's Council for Social Welfare, which was attended by a cross-section of social scientists, trade unionists, public servants and representatives of the Protestant churches.[80] Dr Birch told the conference that while Ireland could not afford to copy the forms of social assistance provided in Britain, a much wealthier country, 'our people deserve equivalent supports'. He suggested that this could be achieved by using religious communities to provide services and advice.[81] The 1972 Statement on Social Policy issued by the Catholic Hierarchy's Council for Social Welfare set out a vision for 'comprehensive social services administered by caring local communities'. The over-riding aim was to strengthen family units and develop them into truly self-sustaining entities. Government department(s) would set minimum standards; services would be delivered by community centres linking statutory and voluntary bodies. The Statement also set out the principal that each household was entitled to a guaranteed minimum, adjusted for inflation and household needs.[82] While initially the Social Service Councils relied on voluntary funding, they soon became heavily dependent on the Exchequer: in 1969/70, they received only £7,000 from the Department of Health; by 1972/73, this had risen to £450,000 and voluntary agencies were employing a significant number of professional social workers. This model of state funding, channelled through voluntary organisations, often church-based, was widely found in Italy and other Catholic countries; however, in Kilkenny at least the relationship between the Council and the local health board appears to have been a difficult one at times.[83] In 1971, Seamus Ó Cinnéide noted that 'As the state assumed a greater role with respect to social services it was gradually assuming some of the responsibilities traditionally taken by the churches – though the transition from church to state was not always clear-cut and the respective lines of responsibility not properly delineated'.

Social Service Councils created a new role for the Catholic Church and religious orders at a time when Vatican II had encouraged many religious to move into the community, and the Church was developing a new strategy for public service.[84] In 1973, the FIRE Report addressed the

---

[80] The papers presented at the conference and summaries of discussion were published in *Social Studies*, vol. 1, no. 4, August, 1972.

[81] 'Points made in discussion after the papers', *Social Studies*, vol. I, pp. 467–8.

[82] *The Council on Social Welfare. A Committee of the Catholic Bishops Conference. A Statement of social policy* (1972), pp. 4, 9, 18.

[83] Kennedy, *The development of Kilkenny social services*, pp. 145–59.

[84] *Hibernia*, 14–27 March 1969.

prospect that declining numbers of religious would mean that priests, brothers and nuns would have to withdraw from some schools. It recommended that the reduced numbers should concentrate on caring for 'orphans and delinquent children, the handicapped, the educationally deprived, remedial education, counselling, adult education and catechesis'.[85] The church would withdraw its personnel from the classroom, while retaining control over the management and governance of most schools.

Irish Catholicism post Vatican II and post *Humanae Vitae*

'When the winds of change after Vatican II had blown down the thin barriers erected around it by "traditional" Irish Catholicism, the Catholic Church was exposed to the raw winds of modernity and post-modernity.'[86] The conventional wisdom suggests that Vatican II and the changes underway in Irish society combined to undermine the position of the Catholic Church and that it suffered a further body blow with the promulgation of the 1968 Papal encyclical *Humanae Vitae*. The story is more complex. One Dublin priest described the encyclical as 'a crushing blow', he reported 'a tremendous sense of depression'.[87] Twomey, then a divinity student, has described the press conference held by the Hierarchy following the promulgation of *Humanae Vitae* as 'a public relations disaster'.[88] But while many Irish clergy were dismayed at the pope's decision, few disagreed openly with the Vatican, in contrast with Britain, the United States and the Netherlands.[89] *Hibernia* claimed that liberal voices were silenced; the only priests heard on radio and television were those who approved of papal teaching; there had been 'no real change in the style of exercise of church authority in Ireland since the Vatican Council'. Council decrees on the renewal of worship had been 'largely ignored'; changes in the liturgy to promote the use of the vernacular had been minimal; most bishops remained silent on the continuing ban on Catholic attending Trinity College.[90] An editorial in *The Furrow* claimed that 'In Ireland ... the public debate, **happily** [my emphasis] never polarised around positions *for* or *against* the encyclical'.[91] Cork theology lecturer, Dr James Good, who was suspended from preaching and pastoral duties by his bishop, was the exception.[92] According to Rev Twomey, 'The others literally took to the hills, kept their mouths shut- and held on to their chairs in the various

[85] Fuller, *Irish Catholicism*, pp. 160, 171.
[86] Twomey, *The end of Irish Catholicism?*, p. 40.   [87] Carty, *Hold firm*, p. 130.
[88] Twomey, *The end of Irish Catholicism*, p. 137.
[89] McLeod, *Religious crisis*, pp. 168–96.   [90] *Hibernia*, September 1968 'silenced priests'.
[91] *The Furrow*, November 1968.   [92] Fuller, *Irish Catholicism*, p. 199.

faculties'.[93] In 2008, John A. Murphy, UCC Emeritus Professor of History, who was part of a delegation to intercede with the Bishop of Cork, Dr Cornelius Lucey on behalf of Rev James Good, stated that 'it was obvious to me that he [Dr. Lucey] was less concerned with the rights and wrongs of *Humanae Vitae* than with the disciplinary insistence that Fr Good should toe the line. Rome had spoken and that was that.'[94] Rev Good was not quite alone: over the next decade or so, a number of priests were quietly laicised; however, there was less sense of a revolt or potential schism in Ireland than elsewhere.

There was also evidence of a public lay reaction. A hastily arranged meeting to discuss *Humanae Vitae*, held at Bargy Castle Wexford in September 1968, attracted fifty 'specialists in medicine, gynaecology, biology, psychiatry, pathology, sociology, history, communications, law, philosophy, and dogmatic, moral and pastoral theology, and including a considerable number of married couples', among them Garret FitzGerald and his wife Joan. A short report of the meeting published in *The Furrow* recorded that 'the encyclical had created great problems for a significant number of people in relation to contraception itself; in relation to authority, and in relation to developing ideas about the nature of the Church'. It remarked on 'the genuine and widespread crisis of conscience aroused in Ireland among people in all walks of life, and of varying degrees of sophistication' and expressed concern 'lest undue stress be placed on absolute and unquestioning obedience' and fears that such emphasis might further disturb Catholics 'already seriously affected by the publication of the encyclical'. The Hierarchy appears to have ignored a request by the Bargy Castle group to establish study groups where priests, doctors and laity might meet 'to seek solutions to practical problems'; the group expressed the hope that 'this crisis offered a real opportunity for deeper understanding of the nature of the Church. In particular ... that it would lead to a better appreciation of the laity's special responsibility'.[95] A statement issued following the October 1968 meeting of the Hierarchy emphasised the duty of conscience to obey the authority of the Pope, while acknowledging that some Catholics had intellectual difficulties with the encyclical.[96] The majority view of the Irish clergy is represented by a letter in *The Furrow* from a Dublin parish priest, refuting all the concerns expressed in the Bargy Castle statement, which concludes with a ringing endorsement of the encyclical and papal

---

[93] Twomey, *The end of Irish Catholicism*, p. 39.   [94] *IT*, letter, 5 August 2008.

[95] Bargy Castle Meeting: 'Humanae Vitae', *The Furrow*, vol. 19, no. 11, November 1968, pp. 656–8.

[96] John Horgan, 'An emergence from religious isolationism, *IT*, 1 January 1969.

authority. 'The Pope has set out for us the vision and shown us how to acquire the strength. *Deo Gratias.*[97] The Hierarchy's 1969 Lenten pastoral reiterated the conservative church stance. One dissenting clerical voice, Rev Donal Flanagan – who was subsequently laicised – described it as 'the product of a leading body in dialogue with the past'.[98] The prospect of an educated Catholic laity, in active debate with the clergy, had vanished. A brief liberal window in Irish Catholicism had closed. Cardinal Conway had feared that any change in Church teaching on contraception would lead people to question 'the very foundations of the Church's ordinary teaching authority and indeed, the very principle of the immutability of the Church's doctrine' with respect to other matters.[99] However, whereas in other Western countries most Catholic couples were abandoning 'natural' methods of family planning by the 1960s, and continued to do so despite *Humanae Vitae*, in Ireland 'natural' family planning had not yet been widely disseminated. This contrast between Ireland and elsewhere probably bought some time for the Irish Catholic Church – as couples tried 'natural methods'. Although most couples who were using the pill in 1968 continued to do so, and others began to resort to barrier methods, the majority of Irish couples using family planning throughout the 1970s were using methods that were in accordance with church teaching, and continued to do so into the 1980s.

Likewise, the impact of Vatican II is mixed, probably because of the uncritical attitude of the Irish laity towards religious authority and the low level of education: thus the potential for a strong critical Catholic laity was limited. Admittedly, the Council exposed the theological weaknesses and conservatism of the Irish Hierarchy, but back in Ireland, the church weathered some brief flirtations with radicalism, a rapid expansion in education, changing social policies, the relaxation of censorship and pressures to reform legislation on divorce and contraception. Censorship of publications did not cease in 1967, but an increasing proportion of prohibited works were providing information about family planning. British publications continued to have advertisements for contraceptives redacted from copies sold in Ireland. Church attendance remained high well into the 1970s and indeed beyond. A survey of values carried out in the early 1980s revealed that 95 per cent of those surveyed in the Republic of Ireland believed in God; 81 per cent claimed to pray or meditate; 82 per cent

---

[97] Rev. John Kelly, *The Furrow*, vol. 20, no. 1, January 1969, pp. 28–9.
[98] 'Teachers must learn from the taught', *IT*, 19 March 1969.
[99] Ó Corráin, *Rendering to Caesar*, p. 205 quoted a confidential letter from Conway to Irish bishops January 1965.

went to church weekly or more frequently, though only 52 per cent claimed to have 'a great deal' of confidence in the church (26 per cent had quite a lot).[100] Despite suggesting that Vatican II 'was a major influence in fashioning the values and attitudes of Irish Catholics', it acknowledged that 'This new type of Catholic' one who showed 'an informed appreciation of the value of the supernatural and sacramental life of the Church but retain[ing] an independence of mind mainly on moral matters' was still in a minority.[101] This suggests that in the 1980s, a significant majority of Irish Catholics remained attached, formally at least, to a traditional Catholicism, which did not seriously question church authority.

By 1973, the Catholic Church had re-arranged its resources and priorities. They conceded the removal of Article 44 without challenge or debate; likewise, the ban on Catholics attending Trinity College – perhaps because by doing so, they protected their continuing influence in University College Dublin, where a number of priests held important positions in philosophy, ethics, sociology and social policy. While relinquishing some front-line posts in secondary schools, they retained a strong role in governance, and they successfully negotiated a new partnership between state and church in delivering social services – a partnership that proved highly significant for the remainder of the century and beyond. The 1971 Kilkenny Conference, convened by Dr Birch, set the template for social policy for decades to come. This is evident in the strong continuing presence of voluntary agencies, often church-controlled, and the involvement of the Conference of Religious of Ireland in social partnership negotiations in the past decade. Far from a story of failure and decline, I would suggest that the Catholic Church proved quite adroit at adjusting to change, and engaging in strategic planning in defence of its vital interests. The long-term interests centred primarily on sexual morality, and any relaxation of the laws or the Constitution relating to contraception, divorce and abortion, the Catholic Church justified their position, not on the basis of religious teaching but on the basis of the damage to Irish society. They also anticipated the growing emphasis on social policy, and succeeded in creating a new role for church-controlled agencies in determining policy and implementing programmes. This was not the work of a church in decline, rather a church that may well have had a clearer strategic vision for Ireland's

---

[100] Michael Fogarty, Liam Ryan, Joseph Lee, *Irish values and attitudes: the Irish report of the European value systems study* (Dublin: Dominican Publications, 1984), pp. 125–6.
[101] Fogarty et al., *Irish values*, p. 104.

future than most politicians. The long-term consequences of the adjustments made or not made in the 1960s may well have proved severe – judging by the state of the Catholic Church in the early twenty-first century, but decisions taken then ensured that the authority of the Catholic Church survived for another generation. If the 1960s spelled an end to Catholic Ireland, this proved a very long drawn-out process.

11   Education, health and welfare

Ask older people about the major changes in the 1960s and they will probably mention the introduction of free secondary schooling by Minister for Education Donogh O'Malley; free travel for old age pensioners; and perhaps the introduction of a choice of doctor for those who were entitled to medical cards. One feature common to all these initiatives is that they happened towards the end of that decade; indeed, the choice of doctor scheme was not introduced until 1972. In the late 1950s and early 1960s, advances in social provision were not on the agenda; the priority was economic growth. One of the dominant principles behind the 1958 economic programme was to concentrate public capital spending on 'productive' investment; social spending and social objectives would have to wait. The decade after the Second World War brought a significant expansion in social insurance and publicly funded access to healthcare, plus major investment in hospitals, including sanitoria for the treatment of tuberculosis. Although this fell far short of the British National Health Service and Beveridge-style welfare state, it constituted the largest single extension of health and welfare services since the foundation of the state. By contrast, the last major expansion in government support for education came in the 1931 Vocational Education Act. In the late 1930s, the share of government spending devoted to education in Ireland was among the highest in Europe, but Ireland was one of the few countries where this failed to rise in the 1950s, and in the early 1960s there was no expectation that this would change. In 1961, the government informed the OECD that they expected spending on education to increase by 28 per cent between 1958 and 1970 – one of the lowest projected increases among member countries – and significantly lower than the hoped-for rise in GNP. On these projections, Ireland would be spending half the OECD average educating five- to fourteen-year-olds in 1970, and one-third of the OECD average educating fifteen- to nineteen-year-olds. Ireland was one of only three countries not anticipating a significant increase in enrolment in higher education over the decade.[1] Yet by 1970, all children were entitled to free second-level schooling, and free transport was provided for those living some distance from schools. Means-tested grants were available for those who qualified for a university place, and the first in a network of regional technical colleges providing advanced courses in technical and applied subjects had opened. In 1972, the school-leaving age was increased from fourteen – the age set in the 1920s – to fifteen.

The expansion in state support for education happened partly because new literature on economic growth had identified investment in education as a major driver of growth,[2] and the OECD report *Investment in Education* provided strong evidence to support the case. There was also a strong popular demand for increasing access to secondary schooling and higher education. The numbers attending secondary schools and universities rose steadily in the 1950s, although there was no state capital funding and very few scholarships for those unable to pay. Many families made considerable efforts to send their children to secondary school or university, in the hope that education would give them a job in Ireland, or better prospects if they emigrated. The proportion of fifteen- and sixteen-year-olds in full-time education in the early 1960s was higher than England and Wales, Scotland and Northern Ireland, where free second-level schooling was available and the school-leaving age was fifteen, compared with fourteen in Ireland. The number of full-time university students increased by 55 per cent between 1951 and 1961.[3] A 1959 cartoon in the periodical *Dublin Opinion* showed the government presenting UCD President Michael Tierney with a shoe-horn, so that he could cram more students into grossly overcrowded city-centre buildings. UCD student numbers rose by 30 per cent from 1957/1958 to 1961/1962; the proportion of leaving certificate students progressing to university increased from 26 per cent to 31 per cent.[4] But any significant expansion in education was fraught with hazards, because it threatened to disrupt the existing relationship between church and state. This was a contentious issue in the nineteenth century, and once again in the years immediately before the foundation of the state; indeed, one reason why the Catholic Church threw its support behind Sinn Féin and the first Dáil was because they had secured commitments with respect to continuing

[1] John Vaizey, 'A note on comparative statistics', in A. H. Halsey (ed), *Ability and education opportunity* (Paris: OECD, 1961), pp. 114–28.
[2] NAI TD S12891 D/1/62 Education post-war planning T.Ó Raifeartaigh to T. K. Whitaker, 8 November 1961.
[3] Vaizey, 'A note on comparative statistics', p. 182.
[4] *Investment in education*. Report of the survey team appointed by the Minister for Education in October 1962 (Dublin, 1966: E 56), pp. 73–4, and p. 46.

church control over education. This was also ensured in the 1931 Vocational Education Act, though not without negotiations.[5]

After independence, successive governments – irrespective of political party, adopted a semi-detached attitude towards education, a strategy that minimised the dangers of a church–state clash, and one that left the church and local communities with responsibility for a significant share of the overall costs. UCD Professor John O'Meara referred to the 'State's shirking of responsibility'.[6] Most schools were owned and maintained by the churches. Elementary schooling was delivered in national schools, which were inspected by the Department of Education, who also paid teachers' salaries. However, the schools were owned and maintained (or neglected) by a manager, who was commonly a local clergyman – a system unchanged since the mid-nineteenth century. Schools generally catered for one religious denomination, and for children of one gender, though some Protestant children in remote areas attended Catholic schools, and smaller rural schools were co-educational. The national schools were often the only schools accessible to rural children, who continued to attend until their fourteenth birthday made it legally possible to leave. In 1964, more than one-quarter of thirteen-year-olds were no longer at school one year later.[7] Two-thirds of national schools, which were attended by one-third of pupils, were one- or two-teacher schools. Academic standards were low in these small schools; pupils were less likely to secure scholarships to secondary school – a critical matter at a time when secondary schools charged fees, so it was not uncommon for pupils to transfer to larger schools in nearby towns. Two-thirds of one-teacher schools were constructed before 1900. In the early 1960s, only one-third had running water and sanitation; most were heated by an open fire, and only half had electricity. The Department of Education provided grants towards the cost of a new school or for installing heating and water, but the onus was on the manager to raise part of the cost and to apply and lobby for funding; an elderly or passive parish priest could condemn pupils and teachers to decades in sub-standard classrooms.

At the other extreme, some of the largest schools in Dublin, Cork and Limerick had pupil–teacher ratios of forty-five or more. In 1964, the Minister for Education set a cap of fifty in infant classes.[8] These schools

[5] David Miller, *Church, state and nation in Ireland, 1898–1921* (Dublin, London: Macmillan, 1973), pp. 436–42. On Vocational Education Act, see Whyte, *Church and state in modern Ireland*, pp. 37–8.

[6] John O'Meara, *Reform in education* (Dublin: Mount Salus, 1958), p. 3.

[7] *Investment in education*, table 1.2.

[8] John Walsh, *The politics of expansion. The transformation of educational policy in the Republic of Ireland, 1957–72* (Manchester: Manchester University Press, 2009), p. 73.

were generally only attended by working-class children; middle-class city children attended fee-paying schools often run by religious orders, which were attached to a secondary school. Over 20 per cent of classes in national schools in the late 1950s were taught by unqualified teachers, because the marriage bar imposed on women teachers in 1933 had resulted in a shortage of qualified teachers. Some married women were rehired on temporary contracts, but many classes were taught by Junior Assistant Mistresses, who had no formal qualifications. The marriage bar was removed in 1958, despite the opposition of the Catholic Hierarchy, who suggested that the government open an additional teacher-training college to deal with the shortage; recruitment of Junior Assistant Mistresses ended the following year.[9] One-third of class time in the national school syllabus was allocated to teaching Irish.[10]

Whether a teenager attended post-primary school, and what type of school, was determined by social class, geography and gender. In 1961, 46 per cent of fifteen- to nineteen-year-olds from professional families were in school but less than 10 per cent of the children of unskilled workers. Working-class children who continued in school were more likely to attend a vocational school; middle-class children, regardless of ability, attended more academic secondary schools. Low participation rates were found in some of the poorest and some of the richest counties. Children in Donegal, Cavan, Monaghan, Laois, Meath and Kildare had a significantly lower chance of continuing in school than children from Munster or Connacht. The proportion of children from Sligo and Roscommon in secondary schools was double than that of Donegal. One-quarter of day pupils in secondary schools outside Dublin travelled more than five miles each way; distances were greatest in Ulster where 40 per cent of secondary school pupils and 60 per cent of vocational school students travelled more than five miles. Cycling was the common mode of transport, although a small number of students received 'transport scholarships'.

The wide disparity in participation rates reflects the passive attitude of the state: – there was no concept that children had the right to attend a post-primary school within easy reach. Although vocational schools were owned and controlled by local authorities, they were under no obligation to provide sufficient places for all eligible children. Longford, Leitrim and Sligo were well-supplied with vocational schools, other counties much more poorly.[11] In Virginia, county Cavan, the local agricultural show

---

[9] Walsh, *The politics of expansion*, p. 16. Séamus Ó Buachalla, *Educational policy in twentieth century Ireland* (Dublin: Wolfhound, 1988).

[10] 'The challenge', By a Tuairim Study Group, in *Educating towards a United Europe*, Tuairim pamphlet 8 (1962), p. 10.

[11] *Investment in education*, pp. 156–8.

committee raised funding and erected a school, which they handed over to the local VEC – while this reflects admirable community initiative, it should not have been necessary. In 1961, the *Western People* reported that the people of Foxford '*continued* [my emphasis] to campaign for a vocational school'.[12] *Investment in Education* suggested that the location of vocational schools was determined by 'the availability of alternative forms of post-primary education at a modest fee, the regional development of industry, interest in adult education, especially for farmers in specific areas and finally the growth of popular demand associated with the development of voluntary community organisations'.[13] Most vocational schools outside the cities were incapable of delivering a proper technical education. Half had fewer than hundred pupils. The syllabus concentrated on woodwork, rural science (boys), domestic science (girls), Irish and general subjects. Standards in science and mathematics were low because classes were often taught by woodwork, metalwork or rural science teachers.[14] The clergy who commonly chaired the VECs were often keen to ensure that vocational schools did not compete with church-controlled secondary schools. Rivalry between the Departments of Education and Agriculture hindered the development of an adequate programme of agricultural education, yet for many years vocational schools in rural areas were prevented from teaching commercial subjects lest this would encourage young people to leave the land.[15] It was almost impossible to progress to higher education from a vocational school.

Most secondary schools were owned and run by religious orders or charitable trusts. Their location reflected historical forces and random events. Prosperous Catholic farming and business communities in nineteenth-century Munster supported the foundation of Catholic schools. Catholic communities in Ulster were relatively poor and so there were few schools. A chance bequest, as in the case of a woman who left money to the Irish Christian Brothers to establish a school in Roscommon town, could also be a factor. A recalcitrant bishop, who was unwilling to permit religious communities not directly under his control, such as the Christian Brothers, to locate in his diocese, might deprive thousands of teenagers of schooling. As schools were generally single-sex, a town might offer secondary schooling for girls but not for boys. Geography was even more important for Protestants: outside a limited number of large towns and cities, secondary school meant boarding school, and while some schools offered scholarships for needy pupils, these were limited. Nevertheless, just under half of Protestant teenagers received a secondary

[12] *The Western People*, 18 February 1961.   [13] *Investment in education*, p. 283.
[14] *Investment in education*, pp. 14, 292, 301.   [15] Rouse, *Ireland's own soil*, pp. 157–61.

education, compared with one-third of Catholics. Fees varied: the Christian Brothers and the Sisters of Mercy charged modest sums and provided some free places. Some families sent children to board with relatives close to a secondary school. Sandymount High School, a lay Catholic co-educational school, and other private ventures that did not fit into the norm were regarded with suspicion by the Department of Education.[16]

Two-thirds of secondary schools had fewer than 150 places. Over 40 per cent had less than hundred pupils and almost half the places in these small schools went unfilled. Larger schools filled a much higher proportion of places, indicating that parents were making informed decisions about quality and the range of subjects. The standard secondary school curriculum was geared to the needs of seminaries that trained young men for the priesthood and university matriculation, though some schools focused on commercial subjects. Lack of grants towards the cost of constructing and equipping science laboratories and the emphasis on training seminarians militated against scientific subjects: in the early 1960s, only 8.6 per cent of graduate secondary teachers had qualifications in science – on average one teacher per school. Over 40 per cent of teachers were unregistered, and therefore unqualified, yet many graduates emigrated because they could not find jobs. The high proportion of untrained teachers reflected the precarious finances of secondary schools.[17] Many had incurred crippling debts, which they struggled to pay, and they couldn't afford to hire sufficient qualified teachers.[18] Schools were subsidised from the salaries of qualified teachers who were members of religious orders. In 1960, almost 1,100 priests were employed in educational institutions, 'including that of self-replacement' (educating future priests), and one boy in eight who sat the leaving certificate went on to study for the priesthood.[19]

In Ireland, as elsewhere, gender differences were marked. Nevertheless, US economist Dale Tussing suggested that because Irish secondary education developed with a strong religious intent, 'education of girls has always been considered to be as important as education of boys, thus accounting for higher female participation rates than in most other countries'.[20] Farmers' daughters were more likely to attend secondary school than their brothers, but girls tended to leave at an earlier

[16] Hyland, 'The investment in education report', *IES*, 2014, p. 8. S12891 D/1/62 Education: post-war planning March 1962.

[17] O'Meara, *Reform in education*, p. 9.   [18] Tuairim, *The Challenge*, p. 7.

[19] Newman, 'Priests of Ireland: a socio-religious survey', *IER*, vol. cxvii, pp. 18–19.

[20] A. Dale Tussing, *Irish educational expenditures – past, present and future*, ESRI Dublin 1978, p. 12.

age than boys with comparable educational achievements: 95 per cent of boys with an honours intermediate certificate continued in school, compared with 87 per cent of girls. Girls from modest social backgrounds were more likely to leave early. While over one-quarter of boys who sat the leaving certificate in 1963, and 42 per cent of those with an honours certificate went on to university, only 10 per cent of girls and less than 17 per cent with honours certificates did so. One-quarter attended a commercial school[21] preparatory to finding a job. The gender gap in university enrolment was wider than in Britain, where 28 per cent of girls and 44 per cent of boys with A-levels went to university. Irish parents were more willing to bear the costs of university education for a son than for a daughter, and girls were less likely to study matriculation subjects. Only one-quarter took intermediate certificate science, compared with three-quarters of boys; less than 5 per cent studied chemistry at leaving certificate, compared with almost one-third of boys.

Prior to the 1960s, Irish education was driven by a variety of agendas: government determination to use the schools as the key mechanism for reviving the Irish language; the educational and professional priorities of the Catholic Church; and the social and occupational preferences of professional, large farmers and middle-class parents. While the Irish language remained a core element of the school syllabus, and a compulsory requirement to pass all school certificate examinations, the 1964 report of the Commission on the Restoration of the Irish Language stated bluntly that 'the schools alone cannot restore Irish as the language of the people'.[22] The Commission, whose membership consisted exclusively of Irish language enthusiasts, was asked to advise on the steps necessary to hasten progress in reviving the language. Their proposals included an extensive propaganda campaign to promote Irish; lavish resources to boost its use in the Dáil and all aspects of the public service, including the requirement that state companies use a reasonable amount of Irish in publicity films and advertisements; and a significant increase in Irish language programmes on radio and television.[23]

These proposals shifted the focus from the schools as the key instrument of language revival, opening the way for a new emphasis on economic growth. Just as the OECD growth target for member states became the Irish growth target up to 1970, the OECD emphasis on the importance of education and science in promoting economic growth permeated Irish official thinking. In 1962, Minister for Education Patrick Hillery

---

[21] *Investment in education*, pp. 112, 120.
[22] *Commission on the Restoration of the Irish Language Final Report*, English language summary, July 1963, R102, p. 58.
[23] *Restoration of the Irish language*, pp. 16–30.

applied to participate in a pilot OECD study, which resulted in the land-mark 1965 report *Investment in Education*. While the research was carried out and overseen by an Irish team, the endorsement of the OECD conveyed an authority to their findings that helped to sell the message. *Investment in Education* was primarily a statistical analysis; its sole recommendation was the establishment of a Development Unit in the Department of Education. If current trends continued, it noted that over half of school-leavers between 1961 and 1971 would have either no qualification or only a primary school certificate and there would be a shortfall of 76,000 – or 40 per cent – in the numbers with a junior secondary school certificate and significant shortages of technicians.[24] *Investment in Education* and *Economic Development* are among the tiny minority of government publications that gained widespread public recognition. According to Seán O'Connor, 'The public were now aware of the deficiencies and inequalities of the system and remedial action could no longer be postponed.' He conceded that 'while we [officials in the Department of Education] were aware of the faults of the system, and some of us feared that the ills ran deep, yet even the most pessimistic among us were shocked by the magnitude of the report's disclosures'. However, Áine Hyland, a young executive officer in the Department of Education at that time, was struck by the lack of outcry in the Department at evidence showing the lack of electricity and running water in national schools and the 'haphazard availability of second-level schooling'.[25] She suggests that officials were not concerned about these shortcomings. The President of the Association of Secondary Teachers of Ireland welcomed *Investment in Education* with 'faint praise' and argued that the economist should be kept in his rightful place in education – 'a minor place'.[26]

Comprehensive Schools

Investment in Education highlighted the need to increase the number of places in second-level schools. But how should they be provided, who should control the schools, and what type of curriculum should they offer? A *Tuairim* pamphlet suggested that Ireland could no longer rely on the Catholic Church to take responsibility for providing additional school places.[27] In the mid-1950s a sub-committee of the Fianna Fáil National Executive had recommended a ten-year programme to expand

---

[24] *Investment in education*, pp. 201, 208–21.
[25] Hyland, 'The Investment in Education report', *IES*, 2014, p. 12.
[26] Seán O'Connor, *A troubled sky: reflections on the Irish educational scene* (Dublin: St. Patrick's College, 1986), pp. 120–1.
[27] Tuairim, *The challenge*, p. 7.

the number of vocational schools and raise the school-leaving age to fifteen. They envisaged a reformed curriculum in vocational schools, concentrating on agriculture and science, and changes to university matriculation requirements to enable vocational school students to progress to degrees in science, agriculture and engineering. Local authorities would provide additional university scholarships, with more generous funding for degree students in pure and applied sciences. However, the Fianna Fáil National Executive amended these proposals to provide for an expansion in both academic and vocational school places: the goal 'so far as practicable should be to give a freedom of choice to all children ... of either going to a secondary school, or a vocational school or remaining at national school'. This amendment, affirming parental choice was consistent with Catholic social teaching; it may also reflect a potential backlash against a significant expansion of vocational schooling. Nevertheless, the National Executive assumed that most additional school places would concentrate on science/agricultural science.[28]

The late 1950s and early 1960s saw a steady expansion in vocational school places; thirty nine new schools opened between 1960 and 1965.[29] In 1962, the Department of Education extended the vocational school programme to three years, so that pupils could sit the intermediate certificate. The long-term goal was to introduce a technical leaving certificate. These plans were derailed because the Department of Local Government and local authorities objected to the additional costs that this would impose on local taxation. Comprehensive schools (which were much in vogue in Britain) emerged as an alternative solution. Irish officials described them as 'an end to watertight compartments' – the formal distinction between academic and vocational schooling.[30] First proposed in 1962 by the Inter-Departmental Committee on the Problems of Small Western Farms, they would offer a combined academic and practical syllabus with a strong emphasis on agriculture and rural science. The capital cost would be met by the Exchequer as would the cost of subsidised school transport. Minister for Education Paddy Hillery urged Lemass to make comprehensive schools 'the archetype of a system of post-primary education applying to the whole country'. He warned that 'Certain vested interests' – presumably the Catholic Hierarchy – would oppose this, but if pilot schools were established in remote rural areas, as part of a comprehensive plan to save small farms (a cause championed by

[28] UCDA Fianna Fáil National Executive P175/347, 18 June 1956; 24 August 1956.
[29] Walsh, *Politics of expansion*, p. 74.
[30] The phrase appears in NAI S 17405/63 Department of Education Proposal for comprehensive post-primary education. Pilot scheme related to small farm areas, 9 January 1963.

the Catholic Church), they would find it difficult to object.[31] In May 1963, Hillery announced plans to create a network of comprehensive schools in areas lacking second-level schools and the introduction of a technical leaving certificate, to be delivered in regional technical colleges. This idea originated in an OECD report on technicians and technical education.[32] The *Irish Times* described the proposals as a 'revolutionary change'. For the first time, the state would take the initiative in providing post-primary schools; teachers would be paid directly by the state, and pupils would have free transport. Comprehensive schools were expected to cater for the estimated one-third of children who did not receive any post-primary schooling,[33] a cohort described by Hillery as 'today's Third Estate'.[34]

The Catholic Hierarchy expressed concern at the prospect of co-educational, non-denominational state comprehensive schools; however, they were given assurances that the boards of the three pilot schools – in Shannon, Carraroe and Cootehill – would be chaired by a bishop's nominee, who could veto any nominee on religious or moral grounds. They were further placated by the announcement that the government would, for the first time, provide grants towards the capital cost of privately owned secondary schools. The Hierarchy was not the only vested interest. Hillery told Lemass that 'those concerned with Vocational Education see themselves as the total answer to the educational needs of the country ... Their easy access to publicity and relatively plentiful supply of money has had a pneumatic effect on a number of them.' He believed that vocational schools offered poor value for money.[35] In 1965, George Colley, Hillery's successor as Minister for Education, announced plans for a common curriculum and common examination for twelve- to fifteen-year-olds, to be delivered in both secondary and vocational schools. He indicated that the state would take responsibility for future developments in post-primary schooling – ending the long-established position where the church, individuals or a VEC determined whether to provide or not provide a school or expand the number of places.[36] Such *dirigisme* would have marked a radical break with the past; however, it did not happen. Colley suffered 'the belt of a crozier' when the bishop of Galway, Dr Michael Browne, denounced his proposals to close small national schools, as signalling the death of rural Ireland.[37]

---

[31] NAI DT S17405/63 Hillery to Lemass 9 January 1963.
[32] Tony White, *Investing in people. Higher education in Ireland from 1960 to 2000* (Dublin: IPA, 2001), pp. 32–36.
[33] *IT*, 21 May 1963.   [34] Walsh, *Politics of expansion*, p. 87.
[35] NAI DT S17405/63 Hillery to Lemass 19 January 1963.
[36] Walsh, *Politics of expansion*, pp. 137–9.   [37] Walsh, *Politics of expansion*, pp. 123–6.

Lemass moved Colley from Education in the summer of 1966. One wonders whether this was done to placate the Hierarchy.

In September 1966, within three months of his appointment as Minister for Education, Donogh O'Malley, addressing a dinner of the National Union of Journalists, announced that free second-level schooling for all would be provided within twelve months. The story broke on that evening's television news. The proposal had not been approved by Cabinet; the Department of Finance was not consulted (despite the fact that the budgetary position was extremely difficult), and Keogh surmises that 'he may not have discussed the matter even with his own department'.[38] According to Horgan, O'Malley had given Lemass a memorandum, setting out a number of options for extending secondary schooling, and had indicated that his speech would include 'a general reference – *without going into details* – to some of the matters referred to in this Memorandum should you so approve'. Horgan determined that 'Lemass did not connive at the specific nature of O'Malley's proposals'.[39] In the eyes of the public, and in most hindsight accounts, O'Malley's initiative is seen as a triumph. By September 1967, a national system of free secondary school tuition and school transport was in place, and O'Malley, who died suddenly in 1968, had secured his place as 'the folk-hero of Irish education'.[40]

His announcement can be viewed as daring – challenging a potential veto by the Department of Finance. Alternatively, it could be seen as pre-empting a significant transformation in the syllabus and the control over second-level schooling, ensuring a significant expansion of religiously controlled schools focusing on academic subjects. The commitment to provide additional school places within twelve months left the Department of Education with no time to determine which schools should be expanded, or whether schools should be amalgamated, in order to provide a more extensive syllabus. Whitaker protested that O'Malley's announcement was 'the negation of planning',[41] and while this is a typical Department of Finance response, in this case it has some justification. Schools that abolished fees received an additional grant of £25 per pupil enrolled – equivalent to the average secondary school fee. One of the most significant aspects of O'Malley's announcement was the absence of a means-test. Given the disparities in participation rates, one could argue that middle-class families were the major beneficiaries.

Enrolment in secondary schools rose by 15,000 in 1967 and by a further 15,000 in 1968. By 1970 it was 46 per cent higher than in 1965.

---

[38] Keogh, *Jack Lynch*, p. 114.   [39] Horgan, *Lemass*, pp. 298–9;italics in Horgan.
[40] O'Connor, *A troubled sky*, p. 192.   [41] Horgan, *Lemass*, p. 298.

The percentage increase in full-time students attending vocational schools was marginally higher. In 1966, 27.2 per cent of full-time students attended vocational schools, by 1969/1970 this had increased to almost 30 per cent. If the expansion of school places had been planned and more gradual, a majority of the additional pupils would probably have been enrolled in comprehensive or vocational schools, and the expansion would have been accompanied by the merger of smaller schools. In the event, most of the additional places were provided in existing privately owned secondary schools, which proved remarkably responsive to this sudden surge in numbers. By 1968, 92 per cent of secondary school pupils attended non-fee-paying schools. A minority of schools, mainly in Dublin, continued to charge fees, but O'Connor claims that the Archbishop of Dublin put considerable pressure on at least one order of nuns to participate – probably the Dominican sisters.[42] The additional students were squashed into pre-fabricated buildings, school halls and other improvised spaces; young graduates who might otherwise have emigrated found it easy to get jobs.

By 1967, officials in the Department of Education acknowledged the widespread hostility to attempted mergers between secondary and vocational schools, so they effectively abandoned the idea. Rising enrolments weakened the case for amalgamating smaller schools. Where new schools were urgently required, they proposed to establish community schools: a partnership between the VEC and other educational authorities, with a comprehensive syllabus, generally co-educational; the capital costs would be met by a loan from the World Bank. The Catholic Hierarchy were determined that community schools would be denominational schools under their control. The battle over governance proved a lengthy affair; the VECs, teachers and parents pressed for representation on school boards. The Deed of Trust for community schools was not finally agreed until 1979, nine years after the proposals were first tabled, and the story is too tortuous to relate.[43] Suffice it to say that they were denominational schools; church authorities continued to exercise significant control, although they no longer had financial responsibility.

The Protestant churches were no less eager to retain their schools, and their requirements were respected by successive Ministers for Education. Half of Ireland's one-teacher schools were managed by the Church of Ireland; however, they anticipated the Department's proposals for amalgamation by drawing up their own scheme, which provided for pupils to be bussed to larger central schools. Minister Colley approved these

---

[42] O'Connor, *A troubled sky*, pp. 191, 152.
[43] Fuller, *Irish Catholicism since 1950*, pp. 155–60.

proposals and committed to funding school transport. O'Malley's proposals for free secondary education presented difficulties, because average fees in Protestant schools were considerably higher than the proposed £25 additional government grant, so an alternative mechanism was introduced. Protestant schools were given a block grant to provide pupils from less affluent homes with free or subsidised places – eligibility was determined by the Protestant community; grants were provided for boarding-school places for pupils from remote areas, and a more liberal school transport policy permitted Protestant pupils to bypass a nearby non-denominational vocational school to attend a more distant Protestant secondary school. Catholic pupils who opted to travel to a secondary school in similar circumstances were denied free transport.[44]

In 1968, Seán O'Connor, Assistant Secretary in the Department of Education, described the Irish school system as a 'hodge-podge of very small units'. There were fewer very small units ten years later, but the term 'hodge-podge' remains valid – with several different types of school and a variety of governance arrangements. The untidy outcome reflected the compromises reached with powerful interests such as the churches, and the resilience of the existing system. Although the syllabus was broadened to include more commercial subjects, it continued to be dominated by academic subjects. Hillery had wished to expand technical education[45]; Colley favoured a comprehensive curriculum for twelve- to fifteen-year-olds; both failed. Proposals for a technical leaving certificate that would enable students to specialise in technical or scientific subjects in their senior years were never implemented because of opposition from teachers and school managers. As a result, Irish secondary education in the mid-1970s was remarkably similar to that fifteen to twenty years earlier, with more pupils, more co-education, more modern buildings, more school buses, and fewer schools offering Latin or Greek, which had given way to modern European languages.

The most obvious change was the decline in the numbers of priests, nuns and brothers in classrooms, though they continued to serve as school principals and managers. Tussing concluded that the contribution of the new policies to participation rates was 'only marginal': only 6.4 per cent of students in secondary schools in 1974 could be attributed to changes in educational policy. Girls were major beneficiaries of the new educational order. In the early 1960s they were more likely to terminate secondary schooling at an early age than boys; by 1972 they constituted a majority of leaving certificate students.[46] While Tussing is correct that the

---

[44] Ó Corráin, *Rendering to God and Caesar*, pp. 82–88.   [45] *Hibernia*, February 1964
[46] Tussing, *Irish educational expenditures*, pp. 60, 71.

numbers attending secondary schools were rising sharply in the early 1960s and would have continued to rise in the absence of the O'Malley initiative, one thing had changed. By 1974 free secondary schooling was viewed as a right, not a privilege – and that was a significant change.

Higher education

In 1960 there were two universities: the University of Dublin, a sixteenth-century foundation, with one college, Trinity College, and the National University of Ireland (NUI), founded in 1908 with colleges in Dublin, Cork and Galway, which had prior existences as Newman's Catholic University and the Queen's Colleges. This structure was unchanged since 1908, and although the universities received some current funding from the Exchequer, the state was largely indifferent to higher education. The only major initiative since independence was the introduction of degree programmes through Irish in University College Galway (UCG). The numbers attending universities and colleges of technology (controlled by VECs) were rising sharply by the early 1960s, and this continued throughout the decade. By 1968/1969 – before there was any material change in student funding, 56 per cent more students were enrolled than in 1963/1964. University education was determined more by ability to pay than intellectual capacity. Ireland had a higher participation rate than Britain, but the matriculation standard was low, failure rates were much higher and the staff:student ratio was poor. Many students left without a degree.[47] In the early 1960s, the government discussed and rejected proposals for a comprehensive system of grants for higher education, opting to double the number of university scholarships awarded by local authorities. In 1962/1963, local authorities awarded 214 scholarships; an additional 25 scholarships were awarded by the Department of Education to students who sat their examinations through Irish and would take a degree through Irish. Scholarship holders constituted roughly one in eight of those who matriculated.

Higher education was segregated by religion; the overwhelming majority of Catholics attended NUI colleges; Protestants attended Trinity College Dublin. Only 27 of the 2,644 students in University College Cork (UCC) in 1966–1967 were not Catholics, including one Buddhist; only 3 of the 2,235 students in UCG were not Catholics.[48] Almost half of the students studied arts – the proportion was highest in TCD; the NUI had a stronger tradition of vocational programmes.

[47] Vaizey, 'A note on comparative statistics', p. 182.
[48] Ó Corráin, *Rendering to God and Caesar*, p. 92.

Foreign students accounted for one-quarter of the total; members of Catholic missionary orders, or English students, who found TCD a comforting second-best to Oxbridge. One-third of TCD students were from outside Ireland, mainly from Britain; a further third came from Northern Ireland. The ban on Catholic students imposed by Archbishop of Dublin John Charles McQuaid meant that the number of Catholics remained small.

The first glimmer of a potential strategy for higher education came in 1957 with the establishment of a commission to examine the accommodation needs of the three constituent colleges of the NUI, taking account of the national need. They reported that the system was close to breaking down, and they recommended additional capital spending at all three colleges. In 1960, the government approved capital funding for a UCD Science building, the first capital funding for universities awarded by the state. A revised Commission on Higher Education was appointed in 1960 to advise on the organisation and provision of Irish higher education, including professional and technical education, having regard to educational needs and financial and other resources. Despite being established a year before Britain's Robbins Commission on Higher Education, Robbins reported four years earlier than its Irish counterpart; they eventually produced a *summary* report in 1967.

A long gestation and multiple minority reports may explain why most of the Commission's thirty-seven recommendations were never implemented, but the conservative tone may also have been a factor. It recommended that the existing universities concentrate on liberal education as opposed to vocational programmes; any expansion in enrolment should be deferred until staff:student ratios were improved. The growing demand for higher education should be met by establishing new colleges, offering more basic and applied degrees with a vocational emphasis; and by specialist technology institutions.

The Commission's relevance was called into question within weeks of the report being published, when Donogh O'Malley announced a merger between the two largest institutions in the state – TCD and UCD. This was *not* among the thirty-seven recommendations. The idea had been floated in the late 1950s by UCD academics unhappy about the proposed move to Belfield in the Dublin suburbs. The merger was supported by the notoriously parsimonious Seán MacEntee, a former Minister for Finance, who regarded it as cheaper than funding a new university campus. At the time, Cardinal D'Alton dismissed the proposed merger as a 'union of incompatibles'. The Department of Education claimed that it would deny Catholics their legitimate right to denominational education. O'Malley tabled proposals for a merger at Cabinet in December 1966, *before* he had seen the Report of the Commission on Higher Education. Government finances were under severe pressure, and there were demands for substantial capital spending for phase two of the UCD Belfield campus (arts, library and administration buildings), and requests from Trinity College. O'Malley saw a merger as offering a solution to the 'The Problem of Trinity College Dublin'[49] (where only one-third of students came from the state), preventing 'avoidable duplication' and bringing 'a most insidious form of partition on our own doorstep' to an end. There would be one university with two complementary colleges: a multi-denominational university with two theology faculties, one in each college.[50] This announcement on 18 April 1967 came two months after Dr McQuaid had reiterated the ban on Catholics attending Trinity College in his Lenten pastoral.[51] The proposal was greeted with public acclaim and was welcomed by many academics in both universities. But relationships became fraught when it came to allocating degree programmes – most especially proposals to transfer the elite professional programmes of law and medicine to Trinity College. In 1971, the newly established Higher Education Authority recommended that there should be two universities in Dublin with a conjoint board, which was never established. The merger was finally buried in 1973 by the incoming Fine Gael/Labour government. The only outcome was an agreement to consolidate dentistry at TCD and veterinary science at UCD. By then the rationale for a merger was dwindling. By 1970, 1,400 of TCD's 4,000 students were Catholics – most of whom had been granted a dispensation to study there by Dr McQuaid, and the number of British students was declining.[52] In June 1970, the Catholic Hierarchy announced that it planned to seek approval for removing the ban – citing the proposed merger as justification for the decision. Donal McCartney has described this as 'one of the most dramatic and most significant consequences of the whole merger affair'.[53]

As happened with secondary education, most of the additional higher education places were created in existing universities, though new institutions emerged. One of the hot political issues of the 1960s was the insistent lobby for a university in Limerick.[54] The government was happy to offload responsibility for any decision to the Commission on

[49] The title of a paper that he presented to Cabinet on 9 March 1967.
[50] Theology had been part of the Trinity College programme since its foundation, but was expressly forbidden under the 1908 Act establishing the NUI.
[51] John Cooney, *John Charles Mc Quaid. Ruler of Catholic Ireland* (Dublin: G&M, 1999), pp. 386–7.
[52] Cooney, *McQuaid*, p. 410.
[53] Donal McCartney, *UCD. A national idea. The history of University College Dublin* (Dublin: UCD Press, 1999), p. 537. On the merger see pp. 307–44.
[54] Details in White, *Investing in people*, pp. 65–75.

Higher Education, who recommended establishing a New College – an offer that Limerick promptly rejected. During the by-election following the death of Donogh O'Malley (TD for Limerick), the government gave a commitment to establish some form of higher education institution; discussions over its precise remit became embroiled with the future shape of technological education. In January 1970, Ed Walsh, a twenty-nine-year-old electrical engineer, returned to Ireland from the United States to become director and chairman of the planning board of the proposed new institute. The blueprint was ill-defined, but it assumed that most students would take shorter certificate and diploma courses rather than degrees. Walsh claims that when he met Seán MacGearailt, secretary of the Department of Education, to discuss the proposed institute, 'he [MacGearailt] was unaware or uninterested in international initiatives, and what he had in mind would add little to the attraction of Ireland as a location for foreign direct investment'.[55] Walsh met industrialists in the Shannon area to discuss their requirements. They convinced him of the need for 'expertise in industrial design, advanced materials, quality manufacturing and mechanical engineering ... modern expertise in management and industrial relations ... programmes in international trade, marketing and sales' and graduates in science, engineering and business who could speak a continental language. The institute's planning board visited the recently founded Sussex University, the technological university at Eindhoven (then 14 years old) and other potential role models.[56] The Institute – which Walsh succeeded in renaming the *National* Institute for Higher Education – opened in 1972 with 115 students. The five degree programmes in applied sciences, electronic technologies, business, secretarial science and European studies, which included work placements, were markedly different to those offered in established universities, who initially viewed the Institute with suspicion, even hostility. Those who had campaigned for a university in Limerick continued to hanker after degree programmes in medicine and law and the title of university – all later achieved.

Regional technical colleges (RTCs) were the other major innovation. By 1966, the government was committed to establishing eight regional technical colleges, though it is questionable whether any Cabinet minister or senior official could have given a coherent description of their purpose or proposed programmes. They were originally devised as a technological high school, catering to students aged fifteen plus and apprentices,

[55] Ed Walsh with Kieran Fagan, *Upstart. Friends, foes and founding a university* (Cork: The Collins Press, 2011), pp. 23–5.
[56] Walsh, *Upstart*, pp. 51, 57–9.

offering courses to meet skills shortages in the labour market. The proposed programmes were clearly vocational: technical and engineering; art and design; hotel and catering; and commercial training, including modern languages (a major concern in the light of EEC membership), with students taking either a technical leaving certificate or a higher diploma. The failure to develop a technical leaving certificate, and opposition from existing second-level schools, left the colleges without a clear role. In 1970/1971, 60 per cent of the 478 students were taking second-level courses; by 1973/1974, only one-quarter of the 2,126 students were on these programmes. RTC programmes became much more popular when scholarships for certificate and diploma courses were opened up to students with a traditional leaving certificate, and when courses leading to professional qualifications in accountancy were introduced.[57] By the mid-1970s they were playing a critical role in extending opportunities for higher education throughout provincial Ireland.

In 1966, the year of the Golden Jubilee of the Easter Rising, Lemass told the IMI annual conference that '[f]or the next fifty years the symbol of patriotism is not the Army, Irish volunteers but the student in the Technical College'.[58] This statement plus the concept of 'Investment in Education' encapsulate a commitment to expand technical education as part of the drive for economic growth. Public expenditure on education as a share of GNP doubled between 1961/1972 and 1973/1974 – at a time when GNP was rising steadily.[59] Universities and traditional secondary schools opened their doors to many students from families whose education had previously terminated at national school. Students received an education not dramatically different what had been offered in the past, though pupils now had a much better prospect of studying mathematics, a modern language (overwhelmingly French) and science, and government capital spending on universities gave 1970s students more modern labs and less inadequate library spaces. By 1974, two-thirds of sixteen-year-olds were in full-time education, compared with only two in five in 1966.[60]

Ed Walsh's account suggests that civil servants made little effort to develop new programmes or institutions catering to the needs of Irish or foreign businesses. The profile of the expanded educational sector reflects the power of traditional institutions and interests, and their capacity to accommodate change and shape it to their own ends. If Ireland invested in education, the education provided remained primarily academic and

---

[57] White, *Investing in education*, p. 85; pp. 50–60 and 79–86.   [58] *Kerryman*, 23 April 1966.
[59] Tussing, *Irish educational expenditures*, p. 67.
[60] Tony McCashin, 'Social policy: 1957–82', in Litton (ed.) *Unequal achievement*, p. 210.

focused on traditional professions, because these careers were valued and understood by Irish people. By the early 1970s, the involvement of the Catholic Church in higher education was much less than before, but they remained a powerful force at primary and second levels. New entities such as comprehensive and community schools, RTCs and the NIHE in Limerick added to the diversity of the system, but they did not challenge established hierarchies, and NIHE and the RTCs were under pressure to introduce programmes that met parental aspirations for their children to enter traditional professional careers.

Health

While spending on education languished in the decade after the Second World War, public spending on health rose sharply. In 1960, it accounted for 2.9 per cent of GNP – higher than France (2.6), Belgium (2.0), the Netherlands (1.8) and only fractionally lower than Germany and Denmark.[61] The establishment of the Department of Health in 1947 was followed by a planned roll-out of new services, including the Mother and Child Scheme, a scheme providing free care for mothers and infants. These proposals aroused strong opposition from the Catholic Church and the medical profession, resulting in the most serious church–state dispute since the foundation of the state. Catholic social teaching determined that the state should not assume responsibility for matters that are properly the remit of the family; the role of the state should be subsidiary – stepping in when the family failed to meet its obligations.[62] Providing free health-care for the poor in dispensaries was acceptable if they could not provide for themselves. Free universal care was unacceptable. The 1953 Health Act was an adroit compromise between Catholic social teaching and an expanded state health service; it was enacted following negotiations between government ministers and the Catholic Hierarchy, which were brokered by the President of Ireland.[63] Comprehensive ante-natal, maternity and child healthcare was provided for the first six weeks, free to 'lower and middle income groups and to certain hardship cases'. Others could avail of these services by paying £1 a year. In keeping with Catholic social teaching, patients could choose their doctor.[64]

[61] Tom Feeney, *Seán MacEntee. A political life* (Dublin, 2009), footnote 62, p. 224.
[62] Paul Ginsborg, 'The politics of the family in twentieth century Europe', *Contemporary European history*, vol. 9, no. 3, 2000, p. 433.
[63] Ronan Fanning, *IT*, 13 and 14 February 1985.
[64] Lindsey Earner Byrne, *Mother and child. Maternity and child welfare in Dublin 1922–60* (Manchester: Manchester University Press, 2007), p. 163.

The 1953 Act also extended free or heavily subsidised hospital treatment to approximately 85 per cent of the population; entitlement was determined by income and farm size. Prior to this, free hospital treatment was provided only to 'poor law' cases – the 30 per cent of the population treated by dispensary doctors. The cost of hospital treatment was beyond the means of most families, so under Catholic social teaching it was acceptable that the state meet all or part of the cost, for all but the wealthiest families. Voluntary Health Insurance, introduced in 1955 by the Second Inter-Party Government, was designed to cover hospital treatment for those who did not qualify under the 1953 Act. There were 25,000 subscribers in 1957; 250,000 in 1966; and 500,000 by 1972.[65] VHI also limited its cover to hospital in-patient treatments.

By 1960, the population was much healthier than a decade earlier. Mortality from tuberculosis had fallen sharply, though it remained significantly higher than other developed countries. Infant mortality had halved compared with the 1940s and was now approaching the average for northern Europe. Infant mortality in Dublin, which remained significantly higher than in rural areas until the 1950s, was approaching the national average. Fewer children were dying from pneumonia or gastroenteritis, perhaps because of the availability of penicillin and antibiotics, or because of better housing and sanitary services.[66] Infectious diseases such as scarlet fever and diphtheria had been largely conquered, as had polio, which was now prevented by universal vaccination. Children aged six years and under could attend a child welfare clinic free of charge; health authorities were obliged to provide clinics in towns with a population in excess of 3,000 and some smaller towns also had clinics, but attendance was optional. Clinics concentrated on preventative medicine. Every child attending national school received three free medical checks during their school years

The expansion in publicly funded health services did not extend to general practice. By the early 1960s, the dispensary system provided free general practitioner care for approximately 800,000 people, roughly 30 per cent of the population, at a cost of £1.3 million – c. £1.50 per head (less than 3 euro). This figure included doctors' salaries, the upkeep of dispensaries and the cost of medicines. The service was largely unchanged from Victorian times, though the 1953 Health Act had

---

[65] Department of Health, *The Health Services and their future redevelopment* (Dublin, 1966, K 1966), p. 40; David Mitchell, *A 'peculiar' place. The Adelaide Hospital, Dublin. Its times, places and personalities 1839–1989* (Dublin: Blackwater, 1989), p. 207.

[66] Brona Ní Chobhtaigh, 'Preventive or curative: policy impacts on Irish infant mortality 1920–1960', UCD M Litt., 2008, concluded that improvements in housing and water supplies were probably more significant. Daly, 'Death and disease in independent Ireland, c.1920–1970', pp. 235–6. Jacques Verriere, *La population de l'Irlande* (Paris, New York, 1979), p. 337.

abolished the requirement that anybody wishing to attend had to secure a 'red ticket' from the public assistance authority, replacing it with an annual medical card, entitling the holder to unlimited visits. Entitlement to a medical card was not based on income or farm size. Some local authorities were more generous than others. In 1965, 29.2 per cent of the population had a medical card; the highest percentages were in counties Carlow (47 per cent), Longford (46 per cent), Roscommon (45 per cent), Kilkenny (44 per cent) and Monaghan (42 per cent), a list that shows no correlation with relative incomes or poverty. In Dublin city and county, only 16 and 13 per cent respectively had medical cards.[67] Dublin's poor relied on out-patient clinics in the city's voluntary hospitals to treat major and minor ailments, as they had for over a century.

In 1961, Dr T. F. O'Higgins, Fine Gael spokesman on health, claimed that spending on medicines and dressings for medical card patients amounted to only four to six shillings (30–40 cent) per capita. In the cities, public dispensaries supplied drugs to medical card patients, but elsewhere they had to rely on whatever drugs the dispensary doctor carried. Many dispensary doctors were chronically overworked; some allegedly cared for up to 2,000 patients. The 674 dispensary doctors were assisted by 171 public health nurses, whose duties also included school health examinations, immunisation and home-births. No surprise that dispensary doctors tended to 'call for the ambulance' and transfer patients who needed nursing care to hospitals.[68] Some large employers provided free medical care for workers and their families, but the majority of households paid for general practitioner services. By the early 1960s this cost approximately 15/- (1 euro) per visit, plus the cost of prescriptions.

Dispensary doctors also treated paying patients, and in many rural areas 'the dispensary' was the doctor's home. James Deeny, a former chief medical officer in the Department of Health, who worked occasionally as a locum dispensary doctor in the late 1960s, noted that 'In an ordinary rural area, the medical expectation of the dispensary population . . . was not high.' In Fanad, Co. Donegal, the dispensary opened for an hour or two in the morning twice a week. Patients visited to obtain national health insurance certificates confirming that they were medically incapable of work, new cases were seen and chronic patients were given medicine. Patients also visited the doctor in his home whenever they wanted or sent for him at any hour they liked, twenty-four hours a day, seven days a week.[69] Deeny's account is confirmed by Dr Geoffrey

[67] *The health services and their future redevelopment*, pp. 27–8.
[68] DD vol. 192, cols. 724–6 23 November 1961.
[69] Deeny, *To care and to cure*, pp. 281–2.

Dean, Director of the Medico-Social Research Board, who carried out some short-term locum appointments in the mid-1960s in order to learn about Irish medical practice. In Ballyhaunis, Co. Mayo, patients would walk into the doctor's house at any time of the day, even late at night. Half of the patients had medical cards; the remainder were private patients. When he made a house call to a medical card patient 'the man of the house would always insist on pushing two or three pounds into my hand, saying "something for your petrol doctor" '.[70] Most illnesses that he treated were 'minor', though he was 'surprised at the large number of women taking tranquilisers, usually librium or valium'. In January 1971, Drs Deeny and MacMenamin (the dispensary doctor) treated 182 cases of respiratory disease; 96 cardio-vascular diseases; 83 digestive diseases; and 80 nervous diseases in Fanad. Thirty-six per cent of those treated were over 60; 21 per cent were under ten years. One-third of children examined during a school medical inspection needed some follow-up treatment, most commonly glasses.[71] Lack of telephones and doctors' receptionists meant that appointments were uncommon. Medical card and private patients often spent long hours in waiting rooms. In one practice in Dublin's north inner city, mothers would send children to keep their place in the queue, 'which led to rows and fights'; others visited the warm waiting room to gossip with friends.[72]

It is impossible to determine the quality of general practice medicine. Deeny noted that 'Dr. MacMenamin . . . after fifty years' experience could spot a sick man or woman from 100 yards away and have a diagnosis made before they could come face-to-face with him'. Deeny decided it was advisable to examine every patient 'very carefully . . . much to the amusement of the two district nurses. Word soon went around that "the new man finds things and tries to cure them", so trade increased, until the dispensary session became a day-long affair'. The older doctor claimed that the same thing had happened when he first came to the area fifty years earlier.[73] It is even more difficult to capture patients' experiences. County council meetings occasionally report complaints from patients on the long waiting times at hospital out-patient clinics.[74] When the dispensary service was about to disappear, one doctor – presumably a district medical

---

[70] Geoffrey Dean, *The Turnstone. A doctor's story* (Liverpool: Liverpool University Press, 2002), pp. 160–2. His account of being offered payment by patients who were entitled to free medical treatment is reminiscent of stories that I heard from my hometown in the same period.

[71] Deeny, 'Fanad', p. 163.

[72] Dr Colum Killeen with Dr Ita Killeen, *Half-Century memoirs of two Dublin inner city general practitioners* (Dublin: Linden Press, 2007), pp. 90, 114.

[73] Deeny, 'Fanad', p. 282.   [74] *The Kerryman*, 4 April 1970.

officer – described it as 'the finest, most economical and most efficient medical service in Europe',[75] but this was not a universal view. Another welcomed the end of 'the poor law system and all its degrading aspects'. He believed that giving patients a choice of doctor 'will immediately establish a much better patient–doctor relationship'.[76]

For private patients, it was often cheaper to be treated in hospitals where the maximum charge for those entitled to subsidised care was ten shillings per day, two-thirds of the cost of a GP visit, and 10 per cent of the actual cost. By the early 1960s, Ireland had over 20,000 acute-care hospital beds – 7.2 beds per 1,000 of population, a figure exceeded only by Sweden and Luxembourg and substantially higher than England and Wales (4.3), Northern Ireland (5.5), or the United States (4.9).[77] In 1964, the rate of hospital admissions was 100 per 1,000 of the population, significantly higher than the 1951 figure of 60 per 1,000. The increased admissions were concentrated in acute hospitals: the proportion of patients treated in district and cottage hospitals, where care was usually provided by a general practitioner, fell from 18 per cent in 1951 to 11 per cent by 1964. The increase was greatest in voluntary and regional hospitals offering more specialist treatments.[78] Minister for Health Erskine Childers reminded the inaugural meeting of the National Health Council in February 1971 that 'we have the highest proportion of hospital beds to population in Western Europe'.[79] Irish patients spent more days in hospital – an average of 20 days in 1960 (figures exclude long-stay institutions) – and fewer patients were treated annually per hospital bed: 16 per bed compared with 19 in Sweden, 22 in England and Wales, and 30 in the United States.[80]

Yet hospital services were seriously inadequate, consisting of 'a large number of small institutions scattered throughout the country'. There were 169 hospitals providing acute medical surgical and maternity services, but only three had more than 300 beds. The dysfunctional shape of hospital services reflected the legacy of the Irish Hospitals Commission, which underwrote the deficits of voluntary hospitals, and provided easy capital funding for voluntary and public hospitals from the 1930s, without matching funding for clinical appointments. New buildings were politically popular; closing down hospitals was not. Although the

---

[75] P. B. McCarthy, 'The new Health Act: a forty-hour week for Box and Cox', *IMT*, 2 April, 1969.

[76] *IMT*, 19 November 1971.

[77] *Outline of the future hospital system*. Report of the consultative council on the general hospital services (Dublin, 1968), Prl. 154 (hereafter referenced as the *FitzGerald report*), pp. 20, 29, 49.

[78] *FitzGerald report*, p. 49.   [79] *First report national health council*, 31 March 1971, p. 8.

[80] *FitzGerald report*, p. 50 Figures exclude those in long-term institutions.

Hospitals Commission, who were responsible for allocating the proceeds of the Irish Hospitals Sweepstake, drew up a comprehensive plan for national and regional hospitals, which would have rationalised services, it was never implemented.[81] In the 1960s, county hospitals, the cornerstone of the service outside the major cities, employed one consultant surgeon and one consultant physician – who carried the titles County Surgeon and County Physician; one or two had a resident obstetrician/gynaecologist, otherwise the surgeon or physician handled obstetrics and gynaecology. One reason for long hospital stays was that patients had to await the weekly or bi-weekly visit of the radiologist or anaesthetist, or for laboratory results to come back from a regional hospital.[82] Specialist medical and surgical posts were concentrated in hospitals in Dublin, Cork and Galway, which provided clinical teaching for medical students. Voluntary hospitals could make consultant appointments without having to secure prior approval or funding from the local authority. Consultants in voluntary hospital drew most of their income from private patients who were treated in private hospitals and nursing homes, so the cost of a consultant appointment was significantly less than in a public hospital. But this system was under threat. The income of the Hospitals Sweepstake – which subsidised the deficits of voluntary hospitals – was falling and costs were rising.[83] As a further complication the voluntary hospitals were divided into two groups – those controlled by Catholic religious orders and those whose traditional links were with the Protestant community. It is not surprising that the FitzGerald Report spoke of 'a tendency to reduplicate services excessively'.[84]

While a succession of young, ambitious Ministers for Education devised new programmes in the early 1960s, pressure for changes in health services came from the opposition benches and from local authorities protesting at the impact of the rising cost of health services on local authority rates. Following the 1961 general election, which returned a minority Fianna Fáil government, the main opposition party Fine Gael identified health as an issue on which to challenge the government. Tom O'Higgins – a former Minister for Health – proposed a motion demanding the introduction of an insurance-based health service to cover the 85 per cent of the population who were entitled to subsidised hospital

[81] Mary E. Daly, ' "An atmosphere of sturdy independence": the state and the Dublin hospitals in the 1930s', in Greta Jones and Elizabeth Malcolm (eds), *Medicine, disease and the state in Ireland 1650–1940* (Cork: Cork University Press, 1999), pp. 234–52; Marie Coleman, *The Irish sweep. A history of the Irish hospitals sweepstake, 1930–87* (Dublin: UCD Press, 2009), pp. 197–223.

[82] *FitzGerald report*, pp. 16–71.

[83] Coleman, *The Irish sweep*, pp. 172–6 and Appendix.   [84] *FitzGerald report*, p. 41.

treatment. His proposals provided for free hospital, specialist and GP treatment, 'adequate' dental and ophthalmic services, a choice of doctor and an end to medical cards. The Exchequer would pay the cost of health insurance for those receiving social benefits and for small farmers and casual workers – the numbers qualifying for state-funded insurance would be greater than the existing 800,000 medical cardholders. Health insurance for employees would be financed by contributions from employers and employees. The self-employed and middling/larger farmers would pay their own insurance. Those entitled to state-funded insurance would get free prescription medicines; others would pay half the cost. The wealthiest 15 per cent would continue to pay for GP visits and prescribed medicines, with VHI covering the cost of hospital treatments. O'Higgins claimed that while a comprehensive health scheme was necessary, 'we reject the idea of it being provided free by the State'.[85] His proposal would have given Ireland an insurance-based health service, which was similar to many European countries and compatible with Catholic social teaching, but significantly different to the NHS, which was funded through general taxation and free to all users.

Lemass' minority government obviously felt under pressure from O'Higgins' motion, because Minister for Health Seán MacEntee countered by proposing to establish a select committee of the Dáil to examine 'to what extent the existing system of health services did not reasonably meet the essential medical needs of the population', 'having regard to the general structure of our society'. The committee of twenty TDs included two former Ministers for Health, Noel Browne and O'Higgins, a future Minister for Health, Donogh O'Malley, and the current minister.[86] MacEntee and the Department of Health began this exercise with a predetermined view that radical change was neither necessary nor desirable. A memorandum drafted in November 1962, before the committee met, rejected the assumption that the State had a duty to provide free healthcare to all irrespective of income, but went on to note that 'the services are not designed so that a person must show dire need before he can avail of them'. Barrington reads this statement as an indication that 'The Minister and the Department were reassuring those with a stake in the health services that they no longer contemplated any radical change in eligibility or in the role of the state. Their formulation . . . was immediately acceptable to the mores of Irish society and, over the next decade, provided a rationale for public activity in medical services.'[87]

---

[85] DD vol. 192, cols. 732–6, 23 November.
[86] DD vol. 192, col. 750, 23 November 1961.
[87] Ruth Barrington, *Health, medicine and politics in Ireland, 1900–1970* (Dublin: IPA, 1987), pp. 257–8.

Unfortunately, the only indications currently available of the findings of the select committee come from MacEntee's papers, and he is not an unbiased source. MacEntee claimed that the 'records ... show ... that the weight of evidence elicited at the hearings would not support a suggestion that the existing system of general medical services [the dispensary system] was in any radical or significant way defective'. They confirmed 'that the services in question meet "in a reasonable way and at reasonable cost the essential needs" of those sections of our people for whose benefit they have been organised'. 'In no case, however, did a witness, who was disinterested, informed and authoritative, allege that the system was unsound in its conception or defective in its general structure ... the weight of evidence tended to confirm ... the Institutional and Specialist services are also in general, satisfactory.'[88] The Select Committee collapsed because of irreconcilable disagreements between government and opposition; MacEntee wanted to concentrate on modifying existing services; O'Higgins pushed for the adoption of an insurance-based system which would, he claimed, bring Ireland into line with health services in EEC countries. MacEntee countered that services 'should be adapted to our social and economic background. In these respects we have little similarity with most of the countries of Western Europe.' Irish medical practice was different.[89]

Fine Gael's proposals for health featured prominently in the party's 1965 general election campaign. Barrington comments, 'As if to prove that elections are won and lost on issues other than the health services, Fianna Fáil was again returned to power.' She speculates that MacEntee's 'reluctance to contemplate change in the health service' might account for Lemass' announcement that he would not be reappointed as a Minister if the government was re-elected.[90] Both statements are open to question. It is unlikely that an insurance-based service would have attracted the votes of the self-employed or middling/larger farmers, who would be required to pay an insurance contribution. Farmers were actively campaigning against their rates bills (which included a significant health component); they were unlikely to agree to pay compulsory health insurance. If MacEntee is to be believed, evidence given to the Select Committee by the ICA (who surveyed their members) and the City and County Managers Association indicated no great pressure for a major extension of free GP services. A survey carried out by VHI of its members showed that GP visits and prescription medicines cost subscribers approximately £8 a year (indicating that subscribers and their families

---

[88] UCDA MacEntee Papers, P67/336 Select Committee on the Health Services.
[89] P 67/336 and 337.   [90] Barrington, *Health, medicine and politics*, p. 260.

visited a GP approximately five times a year). A recent article on the founding of the British NHS concluded that 'There was indeed no great popular demand from the average man or woman in the street for radical or overarching change. This was, at best, wishful thinking on the part of reformers.'[91] Whether Irish public opinion supported a major reform of health services at that time remains unknown.

The 1966 White Paper on the Health Services, introduced by Donogh O'Malley, could well have been drafted by MacEntee. It stated that 'the Government did not accept the proposition that the State had a duty to provide unconditionally all medical, dental and other health services free of cost for everyone, without regard to individual need or circumstances. On the other hand, no service is designed so that a person must show dire want before he can avail of it.' Free GP treatment was limited to 30 per cent of the population, 'because it is considered that the expenses arising from attending a general practitioner are not normally an undue strain on families in the middle income group'. Providing free or cheap hospital treatment was the most effective use of public money; 'the *continuing* [my emphasis] policy of the Government and the health authorities [was]to improve facilities by building new hospitals, clinics and dispensaries' extending specialist services, increasing the number of doctors, dentists and nurses and raising the standard of qualified medical personnel.[92] Middle-income families would be given financial support towards the cost of medication, but only 'when they had encountered hardship'. Public ophthalmic service would be extended to middle-income families 'as soon as is practical'. District nursing services would be provided free of charge for chronically ill and elderly members of middle-income families; state funding for home help for the elderly and infirm was under consideration.[93]

However, the White Paper announced that the dispensary service would close; while it had real merits, the fact that medical card patients were 'set apart from a person who arranges for private medical care' and were not free to choose their doctor was a major drawback. In future, those entitled to free GP care would attend a private doctor of their choice, getting a similar service to a paying patient, using the same waiting room, obtaining drugs and other medical needs (free of charge) from a retail chemist.

Future health services would be organised on a regional, not a county, basis. This change was driven by the need to restructure hospital services.

---

[91] Nick Hayes, 'Did we really want a National Health Service? Hospitals, patients and public opinions before 1948, *English historical review*, vol. cxxvii, no. 526, 2012, p. 661.
[92] *The health services and their future redevelopment*, pp. 15–16.
[93] *The health services and their future redevelopment*, p. 35.

Over half of all in-patients in acute hospitals were treated in larger regional or teaching hospitals, and many specialist services were already organised on a regional basis. The campaign against the cost of health services on local authority rates was also a factor. Between 1954 and 1965, the rate in the pound in Dublin rose by over 40 per cent and in Galway by 72 per cent; health spending accounted for most of this increase.[94] Although the Exchequer agreed to meet the full cost of additional health spending from 1966, this failed to stop the protests. In 1969, the government dissolved Dublin Corporation and appointed a commissioner to run the city, when the Corporation failed to strike a rate in protest at the health charges. In 1973, the Fine Gael/Labour coalition government threw in the towel and announced that the contribution to health expenditure from local taxes would be phased out.[95]

A consultative council established to advise on future hospital services – part of the implementation of the White Paper – proposed that hospitals should be organised into three regions, based on teaching hospitals in Dublin, Cork and Galway. The report, commonly known as the FitzGerald Report, was drawn up by eighteen hospital consultants; ten held positions in voluntary hospitals, the remainder were attached to county or regional hospitals. Their report was strongly influenced by the 1962 Hospital Plan for England and Wales.[96] Community and district hospitals, working closely with local GPs, would provide non-acute care. General hospitals with at least 300 beds would serve a population of approximately 120,000. Each hospital would have sufficient consultant physicians, surgeons, anaesthetists, gynaecologists, radiologists and pathologists to provide twenty-four-hour service and adequate training for student nurses. Regional hospitals, each linked to a medical school (there would be two in Dublin), with a minimum of 600 beds would provide services similar to a general hospital and specialist services for the region. The number of acute beds would be reduced from 7.2 to 4.15 per 1,000. County hospitals would treat non-acute cases and provide diagnostic facilities and out-patient clinics staffed by visiting consultants. The most radical aspect of the FitzGerald Report was the integration of voluntary hospitals into a national hospital service, overseen by regional hospital boards. Voluntary hospitals would agree to a service contract with the regional hospital board; ownership of public hospitals would transfer to this board. The proposals were guaranteed to arouse

[94] Barrington, *Health, medicine and politics*, p. 259.
[95] Brendan Hensey, 'The health services and their administration', in Litton (ed.), *Unequal society*, p. 157.
[96] John Mohan, *Planning markets and hospitals* (London and New York: Routledge, 2002), pp. 111–32.

considerable opposition. FitzGerald acknowledged that 'The existing County Hospitals have in nearly all cases, attracted to themselves a very real local loyalty and pride'; changing their status 'is bound to arouse some sentimental regrets, perhaps even bitter opposition'; similar considerations would apply to plans to close or amalgamate voluntary hospitals.[97] The FitzGerald plan for three hospital regions was inconsistent with the government's plan to create eight regional health authorities with responsibility for all aspects of the health service, including acute hospitals. This ultimately prevailed.

The government plan sacrificed the possibility of a national hospital service. Voluntary hospitals continued to receive funding directly from the Department of Health, whereas regional health boards were responsible for public hospitals. For the first time however, voluntary hospitals had to seek external approval from a public body Comhairle na nOispidéal (hospital council) before appointing consultants, and Comhairle was represented on selection boards. This change was welcomed by the medical unions, because it ruled out nepotism, denominational partiality and other factors that had figured prominently in voluntary hospital appointments in the past.[98] The reforms resulted in significant changes to administrative structures in voluntary hospitals. Dublin's leading Catholic hospitals, the Mater and St Vincent's appointed management boards, reducing the authority of the religious sisters who owned the hospitals to a minority presence.[99] The annual report of the Adelaide Hospital in 1971 lamented the fact that the 1970 Health Act 'marked a further stage in the process- now well established – of the gradual diminution of the powers and responsibilities of the lay personnel ... Increased State control and the trend towards the replacement of voluntary workers by civil servants was continuing and was likely to make the recruitment of competent persons to serve on the boards of voluntary hospitals an increasingly difficult task.'[100] Yet once an annual budget was agreed, and appointment procedures complied with Comhairle na nOispidéal, the voluntary hospitals retained considerable autonomy.[101] The Board of the Adelaide Hospital countered proposals to reduce the number of voluntary hospitals with a statement that 'the Adelaide Hospital would remain in its present form on its present site for many years'.[102]

---

[97] *FitzGerald report*, para 3.60, p 38; summary of conclusions pp. 55–9.
[98] *IMT*, 3 March 1972.
[99] F. O. C. Meenan, *St Vincent's Hospital, 1934–1994: an historical and social portrait* (Dublin: Gill & Macmillan, 1995), pp. 209–11.
[100] Mitchell, *A 'Peculiar Place'*, pp. 222–4.   [101] *IMT*, 1 January 1971.
[102] Mitchell, *A 'Peculiar' Place*, pp. 220–2; they were correct!

Consolidating Dublin hospitals, while not without difficulties, proved to be one of the simpler tasks. The voluntary hospitals associated with Trinity College medical school had been operating as a federation since the late 1950s. By 1970, plans were underway to construct a new hospital, St James, on the site of the former South Dublin Union as the nucleus of clinical teaching for Trinity medical school.[103] Efforts to create a federated group of voluntary hospitals in Cork proved less successful – despite the fact that the scale of the hospitals and the city made consolidation even more essential than in Dublin.[104]

The rationalisation of county hospitals proved much more controversial. In August 1970 the *Irish Medical Times* claimed that 'the FitzGerald Report is dead, certainly as far as rural hospitals are concerned, and it now looks as if there is no possibility of its implementation, outside of perhaps Dublin and Cork, for at least fifteen years'. As evidence they cited a letter from the Minister for Health to Roscommon County Council stating that changes in hospital services must be introduced on a planned basis because of the limited resources available. Priority would be given to reorganising services in Dublin and Cork. No decisions would be taken in the near future with respect to specific county hospitals. He suggested that existing hospitals should enter into 'close associations'; additional consultants might be appointed to serve a group of county hospitals. Many of the benefits of specialisation could be achieved through this mechanism. The *Irish Medical Times* suggested that this compromise was motivated by the estimated £100 million cost of implementing the FitzGerald Report,[105] but local opposition was probably the determining factor. Local authorities convened special meetings to denounce the proposals. Members of the Old IRA held a fast and vigil outside Roscommon County Hospital – one of the affected hospitals. In 1972, local hospital action committees came together to form a National Hospitalisation Organisation.[106] Critics alleged that the proposals would destroy the fabric of rural Ireland.[107] County surgeons and county physicians fought to preserve their fiefdoms. County hospitals continued to press for additional resources, complaining at the decision to prioritise construction in Cork and Dublin: 'what hospital in Dublin ever has up to five per cent of its patients accommodated on stretchers on the floor? Accommodation, staffing and facilities in general in country hospitals lag very far behind those in Dublin and the State has a duty to remedy these

---

[103] J. B. Lyons, *The quality of Mercer's: the history of Mercer's hospital, 1734–1991* (Dublin: Glendale, 1991), pp. 164–5.
[104] *IMT*, 21 May 1969.   [105] *IMT*, 28 August 1970.
[106] *IT*, 7 August 1972, 1 August 1972.
[107] *IT*, interview of Minister for Health Erskine Childers, 2 April 1970.

defects urgently. We are all Jock Tamsan's bairns.' It is extremely difficult to reconcile this statement by the Wexford county surgeon with statistics in the FitzGerald Report showing that bed occupancy in Wexford was well below and the average stay of patients well above the national average.[108]

Replacing dispensary doctors with a choice of doctor scheme was more successful, though not without difficulties. Old-fashioned dispensary doctors had tolerated patients calling to their homes at any hour; younger doctors wanted more defined working hours. One said that 'we don't want any better working hours than those granted to the ordinary labourer, but we want them at least as good'. There was no mention of 'ordinary labourer' wages! The medical press alleged that there was a crisis in general practice, with a high average age of GPs, a shortage of newly qualified doctors entering general practice and difficulties sustaining a GP service in rural areas.[109] Some former dispensary doctors claimed that their incomes would fall as patients transferred to other doctors. Fears were expressed that many remote areas would be without a resident doctor. Doctors rejected a government proposal to pay an annual capitation fee for each medical-card patient plus additional fees for special services. A study group drawn from the medical profession recommended that doctors in the new scheme should work a forty-hour week; receive a fee per consultation; higher fees for working outside normal working hours or special services, that is, road accidents; and a special fee for working in remote areas.[110] These proposals formed the basis of the new scheme. As a further sop to GPs, the Minister established a commission to examine Irish general practice – following on the Todd Report in the United Kingdom.

When the choice of doctor (GMS) scheme was introduced, 1,150 doctors were participating,[111] 50 per cent higher than the number of dispensary doctors. Dublin city doctors had an average of 330 medical-card patients on their panel; in Cork city the figure was 600, but some doctors in the west and north-west had 1,000 to 1,175 patients.[112] A 1974 report on general practice produced by a committee with a majority of medical practitioners described the new service 'as a major landmark in the history of social development in Ireland'.[113] Patients were making greater demands on family doctors than in the past, but the majority of GPs continued to operate as sole practitioners with no nurse, limited secretarial support – often provided by a doctor's wife, no access to social

[108] *IMT*, 6 April 1973.   [109] *IMT*, 9 October 1970.   [110] *IMT*, 1 October 1969.
[111] *The General Practitioner in Ireland. Report of the consultative council on general medical practice* (Dept. of Health, 1974, Z19), para 2.9.
[112] *IT*, 26 May 1972.   [113] *The General Practitioner in Ireland*, para 6.2.

workers, home helps, and so on, and no access to basic diagnostic tools. GPs protested about the heavy workload, and being overrun with trivial complaints more appropriate to a district nurse. One doctor claimed that 'These patients were coming back because it was free and they had always come back.' There was a need to educate patients that they did not necessarily need a prescription.[114] Patients complained of difficulties getting a doctor to attend in an emergency: the reluctance of some doctors to answer night calls and being seen on a night call by a locum who was not familiar with their medical history. The report concluded that 'The image and standing of the general practitioner in the community during recent years has suffered with the curtailment of his hours. It appeared to many that some doctors were now more concerned with conditions and remuneration rather than with patients. It was also felt by the public that the doctor's attitude towards the patient tended to vary with the patient's social status.'[115]

Pharmacists were major beneficiaries of the new scheme. By 1975, drugs accounted for 63 per cent of total costs, and the drugs bill was 93 per cent higher than in 1973 (the first full year of operation). The sharp increase in the cost of medicines was predictable. In the first years of the British NHS the cost of GP services was double that of pharmacy items; by 1963 the pharmacy bill exceeded the cost of GP services; in the early 1970s it amounted to 1.25 the cost of GP services.[116] Irish GPs prescribed more items than their counterparts in Northern Ireland. Antibiotics and drugs to treat infection accounted for less than one-quarter of prescriptions; 13 per cent related to tranquilisers and sedatives; 5 per cent to vitamins; and there was significant prescribing of common pain killers. GMS patients received on average 2.5 times more prescribed items than those who paid for treatment. A committee that examined GMS prescribing practices suggested that 'a level of expectation that all visits to the doctor will result in a prescription of some kind' was a factor. But their recommendation that GMS patients pay a nominal charge per prescription was not implemented.[117]

Spending on health soared from 3.5 per cent of GNP in 1968 to 4.8 in 1973 and 5.8 by 1975. Between 1968 and 1973, despite a major expansion in access, education's share of GNP was unchanged at 2.6 per cent of

[114] *IMT* 5 January 1973.   [115] *The General Practitioner in Ireland*, para 2.29.
[116] Stuart Anderson, 'Drug regulation and the welfare state. Government, the pharmaceutical industry and the health professions in Great Britain, 1940–1980', in Virginia Berridge and Kelly Loughlin (eds), *Medicine, the market and the mass media, Producing health in the twentieth century* (London and New York: Routledge, 2005), pp. 198–9.
[117] *Report of the working party on prescribing and dispensing in the general medical service*, 1976, Prl 5531, paras 6–20, pp. 11–18.

GNP, rising to 3.1 per cent by 1975.[118] While part of the increase in health spending is attributable to improved service under the GMS scheme, much of it went on drugs and salaries. In 1973, the Exchequer relieved local authorities of all health costs, yet regional health boards continued to be dominated by representatives of local authorities; they now had power without financial responsibility – probably the worst possible outcome. Regional health boards also included substantial representation from health professionals, who had strong vested interests. The *Irish Medical Times* estimate that it would take fifteen years to implement the FitzGerald hospital reforms was wildly optimistic. Additional consultants were appointed to regional and some county hospitals, but there was no significant reduction in staffing or services in county hospitals. The summer of 2011 saw protests at the withdrawal of services from Roscommon county hospital, almost identical to the protests of the early 1970s, though on this occasion they proved less effective.

The health reforms of the early 1970s retained the binary distinction between heavily subsidised hospital services for most of the population and a much more limited free GP service. The 1974 report on general practice recommended that criteria for hospital and general medical services should be identical.[119] But despite the election in 1973 of a Fine Gael–Labour coalition, no effort was made to introduce either an NHS-style service as favoured by Labour or Fine Gael's insurance-based system.[120]

The 1972 annual report of the Medico-Social Research Board noted that 'In spite of the great increase in the cost of the health service there has been no improvement during the last twenty years in the expectation of life of men in Ireland.'[121] Declining deaths from TB were offset by rising incidences of coronary heart disease, cancer – especially lung cancer, and fatal road accidents. In 1958, James Deeny, one of Ireland's leading health experts, highlighted the dramatic rise in deaths from cancers of the respiratory organs – mainly lung cancer, and warned that if current trends continued within a few years 'it will probably be our major public health problem in the middle-aged'.[122] As women had a lower incidence of these 'new epidemics', they fared marginally better – additional life expectancy for a twenty-five-year-old woman rose by one year between

---

[118] John W. O'Hagan, 'An analysis of the growth of the public sector in Ireland, 1953–77', *JSSISI*, vol. xxiv, no. 2, 1979–1980, p. 77.

[119] *The general practitioner in Ireland*, para 6.14.

[120] Universal health insurance was part of the 2011 Fine Gael election programme.

[121] *Report Medico-Social Research Board 1972*, p. 56.

[122] James Deeny, 'Cancer mortality in the Republic of Ireland; A changing pattern', *Irish Journal of medical science, sixth series*, no. 389, May 1958, pp. 199–205.

1961 and 1970/1972 – from 49.5 to 50.5 (additional life expectancy for a twenty-five-year-old man remained static at 46.3 years). Recorded maternal deaths fell from 27 in 1961 to 4 by 1975. Infant mortality fell by 40 per cent between 1961 and 1971, as did mortality for babies in the first month of life and premature infants.[123]

The government did little to advance health education and preventative programmes. A public health system designed to conquer major infectious diseases, such as tuberculosis, diphtheria or polio, failed to adapt to tackle modern epidemics, such as cancer and coronary heart disease. Ireland was not unique in this failure, which left the initiative on preventative campaigns on cancer or coronary heart disease to voluntary organisations. In 1963, a research paper by Dr Risteard Mulcahy concluded that 'heavy cigarette smoking is a most important factor in the causation of CHD (coronary-heart disease) in the Irish male population under 60 years'.[124] The sudden death following a heart attack, of the forty-six-year-old Minister for Education and former Minister for Health Donogh O'Malley put heart disease on the front page. By 1970 the Irish Heart Foundation reported that heart disease accounted for one-third of adult male deaths.[125] In 1964 and in 1965, Noel Browne introduced a private members bill to ban tobacco advertising, without success, though this probably forced tobacco manufacturers to agree on a voluntary advertising code, two years later than Britain; this was mainly designed to control advertisements targeting young people. In 1968, the Minister for Health Seán Flanagan pressed for additional voluntary controls on tobacco advertising, and higher tobacco taxes to discourage consumption, but his proposals were strongly opposed by the Minister for Finance, who feared a loss of revenue if sales fell. Cigarette packets carried health warnings from January 1973, but an advertising ban was not introduced until the late 1970s. The agricultural lobby campaigned effectively against efforts to inform consumers of the link between animal fats, high cholesterol and coronary heart disease,[126] and there were no obvious sanctions against the widespread sale of cigarettes to children.

A campaign to reform out-dated mental health treatment had some success. Mental illness was something of a taboo subject in Ireland until the 1960s. When Ivor Browne was appointed in 1965 as chief psychiatrist at St Brendan's hospital Grangegorman, the hospital was 'antiquated, appallingly overcrowded, chaotic'. Its sister hospital St Ita's at Portrane had 'old dilapidated wooden huts where the most disabled of the mentally

---

[123] Department of Health, *Statistical information relevant to the Health Services* 1977.
[124] *Journal IMA*, November 1963, p. 145.
[125] *IT*, 18 February 1970; Medico-social research board, report, 1972, p. 59.
[126] *SP*, 2 March 1969; *II*, 2 May 1974.

retarded were housed. These were known as the wet and dirty wards, full of small, gnome-like creatures in long black coats sitting and standing around on floor impregnated with years of urine'.[127] In 1969 there were more than 20,000 patients in psychiatric hospitals – double the proportion in England and Wales. Fourteen per cent of in-patients were mentally subnormal, not mentally ill, and the majority were men – whereas women constituted the majority of in-patients in England and Wales. There were six times as many men and four times as many women aged twenty- five to thirty- four in Irish mental hospitals as in England. These findings and the fact that the west of Ireland had the highest rates of admissions – strongly correlated with the proportion of the population who were unmarried, and areas of high emigration – prompted questions that went far beyond conventional clinical therapies. There was speculation that those who emigrated were less likely to suffer mental illness (recent research would question this hypothesis); loneliness and failure/inability to marry were also seen as factors. Many admissions were for alcoholism and schizophrenia.[128] Such findings challenged the romantic images of the west of Ireland, and its superior quality of life. These hypotheses also tied in with ongoing research by anthropologists and sociologists.[129] Ivor Browne and his colleague Noel Browne campaigned relentlessly to reduce the number of patients in psychiatric hospitals, which became possible, thanks to new drug therapies. Yet although the numbers fell to 16,661 by 1971, the proportion remained high, compared with international trends, and this remained the position for some decades.[130]

Alcoholism, another taboo topic, also came into the open. Formal recognition of alcoholism as a medical, perhaps a medico-social, problem came in November 1966 when the Minister for Health established an Irish National Council on Alcoholism; the director announced that his primary concern was the lack of available treatment for an estimated 60,000 alcoholics.[131] First-time admissions to mental hospitals for alcoholism were more than double those for Scotland, and more than ten times the figure for England and Wales.[132] The 1966 Commission of

---

[127] Ivor Browne, *Music and madness* (Dublin, 2008), pp. 102–3, 131.

[128] *First Report of the Medico-Social Research Council 1969*, pp. 6–7. Dean, *The Turnstone*, p. 167. Catherine Cox and Hilary Marland, 'Itineraries and experiences of insanity: Irish migration and the management of mental illness in nineteenth-century Lancashire', in Catherine Cox and Hilary Marland (eds), *Migration, health and ethnicity in the modern world* (Basingstoke: Palgrave Macmillan, 2013) pp. 36–60.

[129] Brody, *Inishkillane*; Nancy Scheper-Hughes, *Saints, scholars and schizophrenics: mental illness in rural Ireland* (Berkeley: University of California Press, 1979).

[130] Hensey, 'Health services', p. 162.   [131] Ferriter, *A nation of extremes*, pp. 219, 233.

[132] Dean, *Turnstone*, p. 168. Ireland 1969, 42.5 per 100,000; Scotland 20.6; England and Wales 3.6.

Inquiry on Mental Illness recommended that regional alcoholic units should be established, and by 1973 this was underway.[133] There was also a growing awareness of the links between mental health and social disadvantage. When Ivor Browne set up a psychiatric clinic in the working-class suburb of Ballyfermot in the early 1960s, it attracted 'a long queue of people, mostly women' – with 'horrendous social problems of all kinds' – poverty, an alcoholic husband, too many children, moneylenders. He realised that he had two options; 'Either I would have to put my head down and simply dish out tranquillisers to all and sundry for the rest of my life and give up any attempt to relate to these people as human beings, or I would have to be quite ruthless in organising my time.' He decided to see only nine or ten patients in an afternoon – all with prior appointments.[134] Data from psychiatric hospitals and the gardaí give no indication of a drugs problem before the mid-1960s, other than the occasional admission for amphetamines abuse. However, in 1969, a working party on drug abuse, established by the Minister for Health, revealed a serious drugs problem in Dublin; a Drug Advisory and Treatment Centre at Jervis St hospital was established in the same year. The principal drugs presenting to the unit in the early years were amphetamines, LSD, morphine cannabis and alcohol[135] – Ireland's drug of choice. Intravenous drugs abuse began to emerge in the early 1970s.

While the case for additional spending on education and training could be made on the basis of their contribution to economic growth, no such argument was made with respect to health – yet while we regard education as the favoured sector in the 1960s, increased spending on health far outstripped spending on education by the early 1970s. This suggests that economics was not a key factor underpinning social expenditure. There was already a strong demand for education in the 1950s: the introduction of free secondary schooling and grants for third-level students helped many students and their parents to fulfil their wishes. There were some visionary and original plans: for comprehensive schools, a technical leaving certificate, but the only one that was realised was the innovative degree programme launched in NIHE Limerick. In healthcare the attempted changes followed closely on what had been done in Britain. The outcome reflected the power of vested interests: smaller inefficient county hospitals pretending to deliver a comprehensive range of

---

[133] *Commission of Inquiry on Mental Illness* (Dublin, 1966), *IMT*, 4 March 1972.
[134] Browne, *Music and madness*, pp. 122–123.
[135] Michael G. Kelly, 'The national drug advisory and treatment centre', in Eoin O'Brien (ed.), *The Charitable Infirmary: Jervis St 1718–1987* (Dublin: Anniversary Press, 1987), p. 193.

treatments survived for decades to come, and GP service and preventative medicine continued to be under-resourced.

Public spending absorbed an increasing share of national income, rising from 29–31 per cent of GNP in the early 1960s to 40–43.5 per cent by 1971.[136] By the mid-1970s it accounted for over 50 per cent of GNP.[137] While Ireland lagged significantly behind other Western countries in the share of GNP devoted to public expenditure in the early 1960s, it had caught up by the early to mid-1970s.[138] Social spending increased in real terms throughout the period: between 1958 and 1968/1969 it rose at an annual average of 10.2 per cent – comfortably outstripping annual price increases of 7.4 per cent. Per capita spending on social welfare in real terms rose by 55 per cent between 1966 and 1973.[139] Under the *Third Programme* increased spending on social services (health, education, housing and income maintenance) was projected to account for 70 per cent of additional public spending. The 1969 *Third Programme* highlighted the 'obligation to ensure that all members of society share in economic progress', identifying 'care of the underprivileged' as a key objective.[140] The numbers receiving social assistance – that is, non-contributory payments – rose from 491,000 in 1958 to 563,000 by 1972; benefits were increased every year from 1959.[141] Increases in state pensions and welfare payments more than compensated for rising prices. New payments were introduced for widows and deserted wives. Old age pensioners received free travel on public transport, an allowance of free electricity and free television licences.[142] The old age pension doubled between 1958 and 1968; unemployment assistance rates trebled, whereas prices rose by one-third. Means-tests for various benefits were relaxed; likewise the qualifying conditions for unemployment assistance.[143] In 1968 unemployment benefit was extended from six to twelve months. The more generous treatment of the unemployed and under-employed, including those receiving 'farmers' dole', can be regarded as a response to rising levels of unemployment/underemployment. By the early 1970s the

---

[136] O'Hagan, 'An analysis of the growth of the public sector in Ireland, 1953–77', *JSSISI*, vol. xxiv, no. 2, 1979–1980, pp. 71–2.

[137] Frank Gould, 'The growth of public expenditure in Ireland, 1947–77', *Administration*, 1981, vol. 29, no. 2, p. 119.

[138] Public spending accounted for 37.1 per cent of British GDP in 1960 and 42.9 per cent by 1973. Daunton, *Just taxes*, table 1.1.

[139] *Third Programme*, p. 190. McCashin, 'Social policy', p. 209.

[140] *Third Programme*, p. 16

[141] Finola Kennedy, *Public social expenditure in Ireland* (Dublin, ESRI Broadsheet 11, 1975), p. 34; *Third Programme*, pp. 205–6.

[142] Maria Maguire, 'Ireland', in Peter Flora (ed.), *Growth to limits. The Western European Welfare States since World War II*, vol. 2 (Florence EUI, 1986), pp. 244–384.

[143] *Third Programme*, p. 207.

near full employment of the post-war years (though not in Ireland) was disappearing internationally. The numbers at work in Ireland were actually falling, so too, paradoxically, was emigration. The increase in benefits, coupled with a more difficult labour market in Britain, may have persuaded some would-be emigrants to remain in Ireland. In hindsight, it is also possible to detect the emergence in the early 1970s of a long-term unemployment problem that persisted, even during the boom years of the early twenty-first century.

Improved benefits reflected a growing awareness that Ireland lagged behind Britain, Northern Ireland and other EEC states; such comparisons were documented by a growing number of social scientists based in universities and the ESRI. In 1964 Kaim-Caudle concluded that 'It is extremely difficult to understand how thousands of people can manage to exist on unemployment assistance at all. They have to rely on help from some quarters – neighbours, emigrants' remittances, family, religious orders, food centres or charities.'[144] He highlighted the low level of benefits relative to the United Kingdom, and the shortcomings compared with EEC member states; Finola Kennedy noted that many of his recommendations for improving welfare services were implemented in the following years.[145] The *Third Programme* specifically noted that 'a re-examination of our general standards [of benefits] will be required if we join the European Economic Community'.[146] When the outbreak of violence in Northern Ireland prompted government departments to examine possible future constitutional arrangements on the island, one of the factors highlighted was the major disparity in social services between north and south; this undoubtedly encouraged government plans for expanded services.[147] Changes in electoral politics and growing competition for votes were also a factor. If Irish benefits lagged behind the United Kingdom in 1970, this was primarily because Ireland was a poorer country. Although social spending as a percentage of GNP and monetary value remained significantly lower than the EEC average, it was on a par, and occasionally higher than countries with a similar per capita income.[148]

---

[144] P. Kaim-Caudle, *Social security in Ireland and western Europe* (ESRI Dublin), paper 20, 1964, p. 24.
[145] P. Kaim-Caudle, 'The levels and trends of social expenditure in some smaller Western European Countries', ESRI memo 1968, cited in Kennedy, *Public social expenditure*, p. 31.
[146] *Third Programme*, p. 207. John W. O'Hagan, 'Demonstration, income effects and determinants of public sector expenditure shares in the Republic of Ireland', *Public Finance*, vol.3, 1980, pp. 425–35.
[147] UCDA T.K Whitaker Papers, P 175/2 p. 147; FitzGerald, *Towards a new Ireland*, App. II, pp. 181–7 compares benefits.
[148] Kennedy, *Public social expenditure*, pp. 24–27.

The rise in the proportion of GNP devoted to social expenditure is one of the major developments of the 1960s. The expansion in welfare and health provisions were mainly funded through general taxation – not through an insurance-based system as was the norm in many Western European countries, and there was limited consistency between the growing array of means-tested payments, which were often added in an ad hoc manner in response to political representations. In that respect Ireland was closer to Britain than to other EU states. Fine Gael proposals for an insurance-based health service were not seriously explored by government. While the last remnants of the nineteenth-century poor law vanished with the disappearance of dispensaries, a two-tier health service survived. By 1973, local taxation no longer contributed to the cost of health and welfare services, yet much of the control over these services remained at local level – under the regional health boards. While at first sight the role of the Catholic Church with respect to education, welfare and health had declined, this should not be exaggerated: voluntary hospitals and voluntary secondary schools remained key components of the national systems, and the new model community services developed in Kilkenny assumed a central role in Ireland's expanding welfare and health system.

Part III

Politics and international relations

12   Party politics
The revolution that never happened

In a 1964 article titled 'Ireland: the end of an era?', David Thornley, who combined an academic post in TCD with a broadcasting career in Teilifís Éireann, suggested that recent years had brought 'a series of novel political factors'. The men who came to prominence when the state was founded were retiring from active politics; it was now acknowledged that maintaining economic growth 'is the first charge upon political administration'; there was a greater awareness that the state would have to assume a more active role in improving access to education, health and welfare, and the pontificate of John XXIII, meant that the Catholic Church could no longer be seen as a conservative force. Thornley was concerned that Irish politics was incapable of dealing with these changes. There were dangers to democracy if the holders of power lagged behind 'the instincts of the community'; likewise, 'if the decision-makers respond more quickly to the challenge of change than the masses ... if the mass of the people largely deprived of secondary, technical and university education and congenitally sceptical of their political masters, turns a jaundiced ear to the new rhetoric, democracy in that society does not shatter in revolution. It wanes in political apathy'; 'as politics becomes less and less concerned with emotional stereotypes and more and more concerned with complex economic issues, it is ever more difficult to communicate its relevance to democracy.' He was highly critical of the importance attached to ' "constituency service" [as] the touchstone of electoral success', and the difficulty faced by 'a devoted handful of twentieth-century men [in] the painful, uphill struggle of educating their followers to the realisation that growth-rates and schools are more important than getting a boreen macadammed or fixing a road mender's job'.[1]

One underlying theme in this book is the relative weight of continuity and change, and the capacity of traditional values or vested interests (they can be the same and different) to continue to shape a changing Ireland.

[1] David Thornley, 'Ireland: the end of an era', *Studies*, vol. liii (spring 1964). This was later published as Tuairim pamphlet no 12, 1965.

255

These concepts are central to Thornley's argument. He suggested that Irish politicians had to steer a precarious path between Scylla – lagging behind 'the instincts of the community' and Charybdis – where the public dismissed 'the new rhetoric' of economic growth and modernity. Previous chapters suggest that the rhetoric of change was not always matched by reality. Government policy did not prioritise economic growth at the expense of local interests, or traditional aspirations to preserve rural society and the family farm. The capacity to build sufficient housing and develop new communities was seriously circumscribed because of a failure to curb the rights of landowners to cream off windfall profits. Compromises in implementing regional policy, reforms to health or education reflected 'the instincts of the community', the pressures of electoral politics, plus a strong injection of Catholic social teaching. Thornley's belief that emotional stereotypes had given way to complex economic issues is also worthy of examination, particularly in relation to Northern Ireland – where his own emotional instincts came to the fore.

So questions to examine: how does the agenda of economic change impact on politics and political parties? What messages are being communicated to voters, about the economy and about social programmes? Do Irish parties change their message and support base as a result of a changing economy, and how does socio-economic change impact on the behaviour of politicians and their constituents? How far did key decisions – such as free secondary education, health reforms, a new policy towards Northern Ireland – feature in election campaigns? My assumption – hence the decision to discuss politics in the final section and not before – is that electoral politics was essentially responding/reacting to the changes in the economy and in personal lives described above.

By the late 1950s, the dominant political parties were 'catch-all' parties, with some nuanced differences that outsiders might find it difficult to detect. The divisions over the Anglo-Irish Treaty and Ireland's constitutional relationship with Britain, which were at the root of the political distinctions between Fianna Fáil and Fine Gael, were no longer relevant; the state had achieved maximum autonomy from Britain. Ending partition was a vague aspiration which was apparently shared by all – but like St Augustine, not yet. The economy had established an equilibrium between agriculture and a protected industrial sector, albeit an equilibrium that ensured stagnation and continuing emigration. Both parties struggled to find solutions to these problems – *Economic Development* was conceived during a coalition government and completed under Fianna Fáil. Tax concessions to encourage exporting industries were introduced by Fine Gael Minister for Finance Gerard Sweetman and extended by Fianna Fáil. The dominant political party in the state, Fianna Fáil, could justifiably claim to be a 'catch-all' party, drawing substantial support from all social classes and from rural and urban Ireland. They attracted the largest share of the urban working-class vote; their farming vote tended to come from smaller farmers. During the 1950s, the party's support remained relatively constant in the most rural constituencies, but fluctuated in more urban areas, where they lost support when in government and regained it in opposition. Fine Gael traditionally drew greater support than Fianna Fáil from professionals and larger farmers. They fared poorly in western counties where farms were small and emigration was high. Fine Gael support in urban areas fluctuated much like Fianna Fáil, with voters punishing the party after a period in office, and renewing their support when Fine Gael was in opposition. By the 1950s, Protestant voters appear to have supported Fianna Fáil, rather than Fine Gael, perhaps because that party had shown somewhat less deference to the Catholic Church, particularly in relation to the Mother and Child Scheme. However, Fianna Fáil, Fine Gael and Labour were equally supportive of Catholic teachings on social and moral questions. Labour, the smallest of the three parties, drew most of its electoral support from rural labourers, which meant that its TDs represented the more prosperous farming constituencies. Labour support in Dublin was below its national share of the vote; it won only one seat in Dublin in 1957 and again in 1961.[2]

All four elections between 1948 and 1957 brought a change of government, reflecting voters' dissatisfaction, an outcome that challenges the belief that party allegiance was fossilised on the basis of civil war divisions. When political scientist Michael Gallagher assessed the geographical stability of party support from one election to the next, he identified a 'lack of stability in the Irish electorate'. Geographical support for Fine Gael and Fianna Fáil was much less stable than for the British Conservative party or the Canadian Liberals. Labour had the most stable electorate (until 1965), because the party had 'an identifiable ideological outlook'. Gallagher noted the irony of this instability given 'an image of stagnation' that was associated with Irish electoral politics.[3] In contrast to the years 1948–1957, all elections from 1957 until 1973 returned Fianna Fáil to office. This continuity suggests that voters were less disgruntled than in the past. However, it may equally reflect the fact that there was no realistic alternative to Fianna Fáil until 1973, because Labour was determined not to enter into another coalition, and neither Fine Gael nor

---

[2] Michael Gallagher, *Electoral support for Irish political parties, 1927–1973* (London: Sage, Contemporary Political Sociology, 1976), pp. 18–45.

[3] Gallagher, *Electoral support*, pp. 66–70.

Labour had a realistic prospect of forming a single-party government. In 1957, Fianna Fáil won 48.3 per cent of the total vote, giving them a very secure majority; their 43.8 per cent vote in 1961 was only fractionally above their share in 1954 when they ended up in opposition. In 1965, they bucked the trend in post-war Irish elections – the first time that a government increased its share of the vote to 47.7 per cent. In 1969, their vote slipped back to 45.7 per cent, and in 1973, despite securing 46.2 per cent of votes, they lost the election – because the two main opposition parties had agreed to transfer lower preference votes. Fine Gael's vote share fell by over 5 per cent in 1957, but by 1961, it had regained its 1954 figure of 32 per cent, rising to 34.1 per cent in 1965 and 1969 and by a further 1 per cent in 1973. The Labour vote of 9.1 per cent in 1957 had risen to 17 per cent by 1969 – a figure that it would not achieve again until the 1990s.

Economic and social issues dominated election campaigns between 1957 and 1973, as they had over the previous decade. Peter Mair's analysis of party programmes between 1961 and 1982 concluded that 30 per cent consisted of economic content, followed by 21 per cent devoted to welfare. Government authority – political stability – was an important theme up to and including 1957 and it continued to feature prominently in Fianna Fáil election campaigns.[4] The party never tired of warning that unstable coalition governments could wreck the prospects for economic growth.

The 1957 election campaign took place against a background of economic crisis and an IRA campaign of cross-border incursions. It also coincided with critical talks in Paris about the formation of a European free trade area (Ireland was represented by officials from the Department of External Affairs). Fianna Fáil linked economic recovery with a stable one-party government. Lemass (generally seen as the leader-in-waiting) claimed that Fianna Fáil had been most effective in government when it had an overall majority[5]; he urged the electorate to return them to office with an overall majority, instead of 'another weak government, dependent for support on an instable combination of minority parties'.[6] Lemass gave the party's traditional nationalist rhetoric an economic focus. 'So long as there is room for families to move to Britain, which will continue so long as there are full employment conditions in that country, our standards must approximate to British standards, or our population will go. It is the survival of the nation which is involved, and not merely our living standards, unless we can achieve by our own efforts a rapid and substantial

---

[4] Mair, *The changing Irish party system*, pp. 147–64.
[5] MacEntee, Rathmines, *IT*, 18 February 1957; Lemass, *IT*, 14 February 1957.
[6] *IT*, 11 February 1957.

increase of our resources.'[7] However, all the parties adopted a cautious attitude to the proposed European free trade area. The outgoing Fine Gael-Labour government noted that the creation of an integrated Western European market of 250 million people 'would have significant implications for Ireland's economy requiring fundamental reappraisal of economic plans and policies',[8] but opted not to spell out these implications. Labour leader William Norton gave a commitment that the present government would not agree to the 'dismantling of our Irish industry' if this was the price of joining the proposed free trade area. Lemass expressed caution about the proposal.[9]

The 1957 election was the last under de Valera's leadership. Indeed, all three main political parties changed leader in 1959/1960. Lemass, long seen as the anointed successor, became Taoiseach in 1959 when de Valera was elected President. James Dillon, son of a leading figure in the Irish Parliamentary Party at Westminster, succeeded Richard Mulcahy – another veteran of the war of independence. Brendan Corish became leader of the Labour party in succession to William Norton. Yet, it would be wrong to invest this change of leaders with the mantle of 1960s youth culture. Lemass was sixty when he became Taoiseach; James Dillon was three years younger; only Corish, born in 1918, survived as party leader and an active politician in 1970; perhaps the shorter lifespan of political leaders was a more significant development.

All-party neutrality about free trade and EEC membership fractured slightly in 1961. Lemass called a general election shortly after he had announced that Ireland would apply to join the EEC. His election message headed 'Well begun' argued that 'The new conditions affecting our trade with the countries of Western Europe are of great and immediate importance. They give Ireland many opportunities of development if we can organise ourselves properly to avail of them.'[10] Other leading figures in the party, including Frank Aiken and Seán MacEntee, spoke about the challenge of preparing for EEC membership.[11] The Fianna Fáil campaign emphasised the success of the outgoing government in rescuing the economy, before warning of 'the Great Challenge' that lay ahead – how to organise to seize the opportunities of 'one of the great events of our era', the establishment of the EEC.[12] But they gave few specifics as to what was necessary, other than greater effort. Fine Gael's message was more

[7] *IT*, 18 January 1957.   [8] *IT*, 24 January 1957.   [9] *IT*, 15 February 1957.
[10] UCDA Fianna Fáil 1961 election P176/839.
[11] Aiken: 'FF. made country ready for EEC'; MacEntee, 'Membership of the EEC vital to our survival', *IT*, 15 September 1961; report of election broadcast on Radio Éireann. *IT*, 12 September 1961.
[12] *IP*, 30 September 1961.

ambivalent – while giving a commitment to lead Ireland into the Common Market,[13] it simultaneously argued that Ireland should concentrate on expanding trading links with the United Kingdom; they saw EEC membership as a means to this end. While Lemass spoke about industrial expansion, Fine Gael reiterated the primacy of agriculture; election speeches are littered with statements such as 'prosperity must come from the land'; agriculture would be 'Ireland's mainstay' when it joined the EEC.[14] Dillon's biographer, Maurice Manning has commented that 'Dillon's thinking continued to be dominated by the centrality of agriculture in economic development, by his general scepticism about the viability of industrial growth, and by his old distrust of excessive state involvement in economic activities'.[15] Fine Gael attacked the outgoing government for neglecting rural Ireland. Party advertisements in the provincial press emphasised three issues: a united Ireland; the need to improve arable land and farming, and restoring the Irish language – including a commitment to abolish compulsory Irish in school examinations.[16] Labour ducked the question of EEC membership by promising to issue a special policy statement at a later date.[17]

Horgan claimed that approval for Ireland's application for EEC membership 'formed in effect part of the mandate' that Lemass received in the 1961 general election.[18] If so, it was a qualified mandate. Fianna Fáil lost eight seats and their overall majority. The outcome is consistent with evidence showing that most economic indices did not recover to 1956/1957 levels until 1962/1963. *Hibernia* concluded that 'the absence of de Valera cost the party considerable support . . . [Lemass'] appearances in the country during the campaign were dull and unimaginative from the vote getting point of view. He was too academic he spoke over the heads of the ordinary person. In short he was unable to sell himself to the rural voter. It is clear that the farmer is not very impressed with the modern organisation man.' They described Dillon and Corish as 'far more impressive in the country'; Dillon was 'more au fait with agricultural problems . . . Corish did a magnificent job in putting the party forward as the friend of the farmers'.[19] During the short 1961 campaign, Dillon travelled over 2,000 miles and addressed 31 meetings, and Lemass spoke at 15.[20]

[13] *II*, 22 September 1961.
[14] Sweetman, *II*, 18 September 1961; Dillon |*IP* 2 October 1961.
[15] Manning, *James Dillon. A biography* (Dublin: Wolfhound, 1999), pp. 316–7.
[16] *The Kerryman*, 23 September 1961.
[17] *II*, 1 September 1961; *IT*, 13 September 1961.   [18] Horgan, *Lemass*, p. 200.
[19] *Hibernia*, November 1961.
[20] UCDA P39 GE/125 Fine Gael papers; Analysis of 1961 general election campaign. Cornelius O'Leary, *Irish elections, 1918–1977. Parties, voters and proportional representation* (Dublin: Gill & Macmillan, 1979), p. 62.

While Lemass' leadership may have damaged Fianna Fáil support in rural Ireland, the party made significant efforts to counteract this. Fianna Fáil never produced an election manifesto during the 1960s. However, briefing manuals supplied to candidates and canvassers indicate the policies that they wished to highlight. In 1961, the manual went into considerable detail about programmes for agriculture, forestry, rural electrification, drainage, turf development and Western development. Speaking notes emphasised that 'a most attractive aspect of the Common Market from the Irish point of view is the opportunity for expansion which it may offer to our agriculture'; although the Common Market's agricultural policy had not yet been finalised, the principle had been accepted 'that **energetic, hardworking farmers should be entitled to be able to earn standards of living comparable to those of urban populations**' (bold in original). The manual was more equivocal about the impact of EEC membership on industry, noting that 'the position with regard to industry in the initial stages, will require careful planning'.[21] A summary of 'Points to note' highlighted ten issues: a rise in agricultural output and state aid in 1960, the near completion of rural electrification, piped water, forestry, land division, roads, housing, new school buildings, health and social welfare. When the party national executive discussed policies, they focused on agriculture and rural Ireland – small farms, rural housing, heifer subsidies and the succession bill – rather than the grand scheme for economic growth or preparing for EEC membership.[22] Resolutions tabled at the 1962 Ard Fheis reflect a similar emphasis: national unity, land purchase and division, forestry, small farms, decentralising industries; promoting industry in underdeveloped areas; ensuring that jobs in new industries went to Irish workers. These resolutions were not exactly in accord with Lemass' presidential address on the theme, 'Ireland in the New Europe'.[23] In 1963, the party's honorary secretaries highlighted 'the danger that lack of public understanding of the Government's policy could jeopardise its plans for the Nation's economic and social progress. The Organisation must do everything possible to inform the people fully of the aims the Government has in view and the need for steps to achieve them.'[24] There would appear to have been a tension between Lemass' agenda, and the priorities of the national executive. Lemass spoke of economic development in patriotic terms: the 1960s

---

[21] UCDA P 176/839 Notes for speakers: industrial policy accounted for seven paragraphs and just over one page of text; less than the space given to western development; and roughly one-quarter of the space devoted to agriculture.
[22] P176/348, 22 January 1964, 24 February 1964.
[23] P176/769 FF Ard Fheis resolutions November 1962.
[24] P176/770 Ard Fheis November 1963.

equivalent to the fight for Irish freedom – it is unclear whether the party rank and file fully embraced this message. There is some sense of tension between the new economic agenda and the need to reassure a more traditional rural electorate.

1965 – Generational and electoral change

In 1961, the support base for the major parties was broadly similar to all elections since 1948. But the 1965 general election reflects the impact of a period of economic growth. Numbers at work and real wages outside agriculture were rising; emigration had fallen, but farmers believed that they were not sharing the benefits. In January 1964, Lemass' minority government faced two by-elections in Cork and Kildare; if they lost both seats (one was a former Labour seat), the government would have fallen. In advance of the election, they approved an excessively generous wage agreement, and capital grants for secondary schools. Fianna Fáil took both seats, but as Horgan remarks, 'the price was a high one'.[25] During the course of another Cork by-election in March 1965, Minister for Industry and Commerce and local TD Jack Lynch promised that £11 million in industrial development planned for the Cork region would create six thousand jobs.[26] The age of auction politics had arrived.

'Let Lemass Lead on' was the party's slogan in the 1965 general election: 'Before you vote, look around you – look at what has happened, or is happening in your own city, town or country, and then decide'.[27] Canvassers highlighted falling emigration and unemployment; new industrial jobs; annual increases in social welfare benefits during the term of the current government; a trebling in grants to farmers compared with the 1954–1957 Coalition, with the Exchequer meeting 57 per cent of farmers' rates bills.[28] The 1965 general election was the first occasion since the war that an outgoing government increased its share of the vote – to 47.7 per cent, almost 4 per cent higher than in 1961, and sufficient to secure an overall majority. With an almost identical share of the vote in all types of constituency, the party could justifiably claim to be a national, catch-all party. As in 1961, notes provided to canvassers paid what might appear to be disproportionate attention to rural and farming voters: Under the heading MORE JOBS IN RURAL IRELAND, voters were told that Ireland was not the only country where people 'tend to leave the land'; indeed the fall in numbers in agriculture was the third lowest

[25] Horgan, *Lemass*, p. 204.   [26] Keogh, *Jack Lynch*, p. 90.
[27] UCDA P176.840 (25) 'Let Lemass Lead On'.
[28] UCDA P 176/840 (1) You and the General Election.

among nine leading agricultural countries; the flight from the land was slowing. They highlighted measures to provide alternative employment in forestry, turf, drainage and tourism, but made no mention of industry. Voters were continually reminded of the track record of the 1954–1957 coalition. The emphasis on forestry, drainage and new schools, as opposed to industrial development or expanding educational opportunities, again suggests that the party was under pressure to shore up traditional rural support. Although the argument that rural decline was a European-wide phenomenon was correct, how many deputies or canvassers would have said this at the church gate?

Towards a just society

Fine Gael tried to outflank Fianna Fáil, by committing to a fully planned economy that would drive higher growth and a significant expansion in social spending. Their manifesto *Towards a Just Society* [29] began by invoking papal encyclicals, almost like a protective 'scapular or holy medal' to ward off allegations of socialism, before setting out a blueprint for a planned economy with detailed targets for public and private sectors. It made the Fianna Fáil commitment to economic planning look halfhearted, dismissing both the *First* and *Second Programmes* as 'statements of policy', suggesting that the growth targets were merely aspirations. *Towards a Just Society* would implement comprehensive economic planning, overseen by a committee of the Dáil and Seanad; a Planning Board to oversee agriculture, industry, services and education; regional planning boards, and extensive layers of committees, plus a new Department for Economic Affairs (Britain's Labour government had recently introduced such a ministry). Many of the suggestions were desirable and even necessary, not least that this new department would engage in proper demographic forecasting and regional planning, and the Oireachtas would finally engage with economic plans/programmes, but whether regional plans drawn up à la *Just Society* would have had a better prospect of implementation than the Buchanan Report is doubtful. If sectors of the economy were not performing as expected, 'the government must be prepared itself to undertake the necessary economic activity, if required in the national interest'. They proposed a prices and incomes policy (very much in vogue during the 1960s); greater control by the Central Bank over the commercial banking sector and credit policy and taxes on speculative profits. However, it was quite vague on some details. If Ireland

[29] Ciara Meehan, *A Just Society for Ireland?, 1964–1987* (Basingstoke: Palgrave Macmillan, 2013).

joined the EEC, it gave a commitment 'to safeguard the interests of industrial workers and those who have invested their money in Irish industry' and an unspecific commitment to support home industry. It rejected the Fianna Fáil view that an additional 66,000 people would have left agriculture by 1970, claiming that with better advisory services and better marketing every farmer 'large and small' will be enabled to sell increasing quantities of produce 'in competition with the rest of the world' – a fantasy that took no account of global agricultural markets. Social investment would not be sacrificed in the interests of economic growth. While this was laudable, by 1965, the economy was seriously overheated, and there was not sufficient capital to finance a larger investment programme – so priorities would be needed. Other commitments included creating an insurance-based health service (see Chapter 11); comprehensive services for youth and the mentally handicapped, and a commitment to put in place a system – no details given – to enable all children who would benefit from doing so to proceed to university.[30]

While *Towards a Just Society* evaded many of the trickier issues in economic and social policy – falling numbers in agriculture, the fate of Irish industry in the EEC and how to allocate limited investment funds between social and economic projects – it presented an alternative to the Lemass argument that the economy must come first, and social development must wait. In 1965, he told voters that improvements in health, education, housing and welfare were dependent (and would follow) on increases in national output.[31] Lemass' 'rising tide' argument assumed social harmony – that all would benefit from economic development, whereas *Just Society* gave a more specific commitment to increase spending on a range of social programmes, such as housing and hospitals; pensions and tax treatment of the elderly. Quite how this would be funded, given the commitment to remove sales taxes from food and clothing, derate smaller farms and raise personal tax allowances – measures that would create a massive revenue gap – is unclear. The underlying assumption appears to have been that a more interventionist and active planning system would generate higher economic growth and enable a more generous allocation of public funding to social improvements than Fianna Fáil was committed to delivering. In that respect, there is more in common between the two parties than commonly suggested – economic growth was fundamental to both aspirations. Peter Mair however suggests that there is a distinction: Fianna Fáil's emphasis on social harmony, their 'fundamental recasting of nationalist discourse'

---

[30] Fine Gael Policy 1965. *Towards a Just Society.*
[31] UCDA P176.840 (25) 'Let Lemass Lead On'.

can be described as deploying corporatist ideology, whereas with the *Just Society*, Fine Gael was moving towards social democracy.[32]

Yet, what appeared to be a fundamental shift in the Fine Gael position was not universally accepted by party members, and many candidates in the 1965 general election would not have subscribed to the policies outlined in the *Just Society*. The document was primarily the work of Declan Costello, son of a former Taoiseach. Manning claims that the party was 'riven down the centre between the modernizers, led by and personified in Declan Costello, and the conservatives, though not necessarily traditional wing, led by Sweetman [a former Minister for Finance] and Senator E.A. McGuire', with party leader James Dillon in the middle, trying to maintain unity, though undoubtedly favouring the traditional wing. His address to the Party Ard Fheis in May 1963 (two months after Costello tabled his first version of the *Just Society*) concentrated on his proposal to end compulsory Irish, and 'well-worn Dillon themes [that] had little to suggest any real awareness of the rapid changes happening socially and economically, much less offer a plan to deal with or lead these developments'.[33] Although the parliamentary party gave support in principle in May 1964 to a revised version of Costello's proposals, which had been modified by the inclusion of policies on agriculture and rural development, momentum stalled and the final version was not yet ready when Lemass called a snap election in March 1965. Fine Gael claimed that Lemass called the election to pre-empt their efforts to draft a comprehensive policy document, but they had little cause for complaint because they had been working on it for two years! The final version was only cleared after the election had been called. Manning describes the party's acceptance of the *Just Society* as 'a coup', noting that Dillon, the party leader, had only accepted it in order to maintain party unity.[34] But its belated appearance reflected deep internal divisions,[35] as did the decision not to distribute free copies to members; they had to buy it! *Irish Times* journalist John Healy derided Fine Gael for proposing to introduce full-scale economic planning, while not being capable of getting copies of its plan to voters!.

Towards a Just Society was a radical document, committed to transforming the roles of government and the legislature with respect to the economy; its impact on the outcome of the election was paradoxical. Fine Gael failed to attract urban working-class voters. The party made its greatest gains in the poorer farming areas of the west – not areas that one would naturally associate with radical economic planning.[36] I suspect

---

[32] Mair, *Changing Irish party system*, pp. 182–6.   [33] Manning, *Dillon*, pp. 350–1.
[34] Manning, *Dillon*, p. 372.   [35] *IT*, 15 March 1965.
[36] Gallagher, *Electoral support for Irish political parties*, p. 39.

that many Fine Gael candidates cherry-picked the document, highlighting proposals to derate smaller farms, increase pensions and restore the Land Project, while ignoring proposals for a much more directive system of economic planning. An internal review of the 1965 election noted bluntly that the party had performed best in the west, where there was 'much less prosperity'.[37] (These were also the areas where the 'Save the West' campaign was strong.) Although Fine Gael increased its share of the vote by 2 per cent, the outcome was seen as disappointing. They attracted voters who had previously supported the small farming party, Clann na Talmhan, and capitalised on the appeal of party leader James Dillon, a native of Ballaghdderreen on the Roscommon/Mayo border, who was warmly remembered as a former Minister for Agriculture who had poured a lot of money into land reclamation. One disgruntled supporter, from suburban Dublin, claimed that there was a real danger that the party would lose votes because the Government was 'getting all the credit for the increase in prosperity ... those whose circumstances have greatly improved in the last few years, give credit to the government and are afraid of a change. Many who have never voted Fianna Fáil will do so.' He claimed that Fianna Fáil was benefiting from the 'the image of the young set', and the 'popular image of Lemass as the realistic businessman quietly and efficiently leading the country to prosperity'.[38] His concerns were justified.

The main story in Dublin was the strong Labour performance; their vote more than doubled from under 8 per cent and one seat to 19.5 per cent and six seats. This marked a significant realignment for Labour, from its traditional rural base to becoming an urban party. Their 1965 manifesto, *The Labour Party: the Next Five Years*, also emphasised the need to develop state-owned industry, state planning and a comprehensive, British-style national health service. Puirséil described it as 'a perfectly decent, if not particularly stellar document. Unfortunately its lack of originality led to its being completely eclipsed by Fine Gael's *Just Society* paper, published one week earlier. Declan Costello had managed to steal a march on Labour'.[39] Yet if he had, why did Labour gain votes and seats in Dublin, whereas Fine Gael didn't? This suggests that historians are in danger in attributing too much political weight to detailed, ambitious election manifestos. Labour picked up the votes of the growing number of younger city workers – often white-collar workers in state employment who were joining trade unions and may also have attracted some traditional Fianna Fáil working-class voters, who feared that their

[37] UCDA P39GE/125 1965 election.   [38] UCDA P39/GE/133. Correspondence.
[39] Niamh Puirséil, *The Irish Labour Party, 1922–73* (Dublin: UCD Press, 2007), p 233.

jobs would disappear under free trade and technological changes such as one-man buses and container ships.

Politicians – youth, change and tradition

The Irish Revolution, 1916–1922, was a young person's revolution, whose survivors remained prominent in public life for decades. In 1961, 27 TDs (19 per cent) were veterans of the revolutionary period, as were 10 per cent of those elected in 1965. But 1965 marked a transition to a younger generation. Lemass' 1965 Cabinet was described as the youngest Cabinet in Europe, though it still contained two veterans of the war of independence – Lemass and Minister for External Affairs Frank Aiken. The 1969 Cabinet was the first not to include a veteran of the war of independence. The generational change in Cabinet was mirrored in Fine Gael; after the 1965 election, no member of the civil war generation sat on the party's front bench. The outcome of the 1966 Presidential election was read as evidence that the revolutionary generation's day was over; that youth and change were synonymous with electoral appeal. The election, held in the year of the Golden Jubilee of the Easter Rising, saw 1916 veteran and Ireland's dominant political figure Eamon de Valera returned by a margin of only 10,000 votes over the Fine Gael candidate Tom O'Higgins, who was identified with the modernising wing. The O'Higgins campaign focused on youth and the future. Briefing notes distributed to party activists by the campaign press secretary Emer O'Kelly highlighted the fact that O'Higgins was not even born in 1916. Voters were reminded that the leaders of the 1916 Rising were 'young, progressive forward-looking and idealistic', who would wish to see the country represented by somebody who belonged to the generation born 'in the freedom they won for us; a man with his eyes on the future'.[40]

Yet, while momentum appeared to lie with youth and change, it would be unwise to underestimate the strength of tradition. By the mid-1960s, all three political parties were grappling with internal tensions; the divisions were most overt within Fine Gael. Within hours of 1965 Dáil assembling, Dillon resigned as party leader, and called for the immediate election of his successor. Liam Cosgrave, son of a former leader, was elected unopposed. Cosgrave was proposed by Sweetman in an effort to indicate a united party, although one Fine Gael deputy claimed that the two men did not speak during the years 1957–1965 because Cosgrave blamed Sweetman's harsh 1956 budgets for the party's poor electoral fortunes. Manning dismisses suggestions that this precipitous election

[40] UCDA P39/PR/87 (1) Guiding notes for speakers in the Presidential election campaign.

was designed to prevent Costello from becoming leader; nevertheless Cosgrave's unopposed election served to paper over fundamental divisions. While Cosgrave appeared to side with Costello at the 1964 Fine Gael Ard Fheis, he represented the middle-ground. Stephen Collins suggests that the 1966 presidential campaign aggravated divisions between Cosgrave and the progressive wing,[41] A key issue was whether Fine Gael should aim to form a single-party government, or enter coalition with Labour. Sweetman – the bête noire of the liberal wing – favoured the former position, despite the fact that it had no prospect of success; the more radical wing favoured a coalition with Labour. In 1966, Cosgrave installed Sweetman as party organiser. According to Garret FitzGerald, who joined the party in 1965 and was elected senator in the same year, 'from autumn 1966 onwards a certain tension began to develop'. Sweetman had little sympathy with younger party members, many of them UCD students, who were personally close to FitzGerald, a UCD economics lecturer. Internal tensions were aggravated when FitzGerald and a number of other Fine Gael politicians met Labour representatives to explore the possibilities of coalition or even a merger between the two parties. Strong opposition within both parties ended this initiative.[42] At the 1968 Ard Fheis, Sweetman as chairman, managed to head off an attempt by liberals to change the name of the party to Fine Gael – the Social Democratic Party. Although most delegates appeared to be in favour, he succeeded in referring the motion to a postal ballot of party members, where it was defeated by 653 votes to 81.[43]

The liberal wing of Fine Gael was seriously weakened by Labour's continuing opposition to entering coalition, and the announcement in 1967 that Declan Costello was retiring from active politics. Although Costello cited personal reasons, Michael Gallagher suggests that Labour's anti-coalition stance may have been a factor.[44] Cosgrave's support for ending PR in 1968, contrary to the position taken by the majority of the party, further weakened party solidarity; *Hibernia* wondered whether Cosgrave could maintain this stance and remain as leader.[45] Fine Gael 'young tigers', the student activists flexed their muscles, but *Hibernia* claimed that they 'did not have teeth sharp enough or claws long enough to overcome Gerard Sweetman'.[46] The divisions were evident to

[41] Stephen Collins, *The Cosgrave Legacy* (Dublin: Blackwater, 1996), pp. 84–5; 90–2. Manning, *Dillon*, p. 375.

[42] Garret FitzGerald, *All in a life. An autobiography* (Dublin: Gill & MacMillan, 1992), pp. 76–9.

[43] Collins, *The Cosgrave Legacy*, p. 94.

[44] Michael Gallagher, *The Irish Labour Party in transition, 1957–82* (Manchester: Manchester University Press, 1982), p. 169.

[45] *Hibernia*, March, 1968.   [46] *Hibernia*, June 1968.

all; *Business and Finance* claimed that Fine Gael was 'now two parties; one liberal capitalist with regrettable overtones of McCarthyism and a tendency towards scare-mongering bombastic. The other slightly to the left of Harold Wilson, preoccupied with the undoubted social injustices of modern Ireland and impatient with a leadership seemingly more concerned with words than actions. This element would welcome coalition with Labour.'[47] These divisions became even more exposed in the run-up to the 1969 general election. The redrawn constituency boundaries meant that there were fewer incumbents: 'thrusting young Fine Gael candidates are knocking against and being knocked by the Old Guard of the Coterie Party'. One 'thrusting young candidate' was Maurice O'Connell, who was selected for Dublin Central, despite the fact that he had criticised Cosgrave's leadership on television: he claimed that Cosgrave would 'eventually be replaced by somebody "more dynamic and more convincing" '.[48] When Fine Gael headquarters rejected his candidacy, several local activists resigned from the party. O'Connell stood as an independent; by splitting the Fine Gael vote, he probably helped Labour to secure a seat.[49]

The divisions within Fine Gael between traditionalists and modernisers were mirrored in the Labour party. Under Brendan Corish, who became leader in 1960, some sections of the party assumed that Irish politics was about to undergo dramatic change, reflecting the changes that were underway in the economy. Labour began to select a different type of candidate and they adopted a left-wing agenda. With bitter memories of the 1954–1957 coalition, they determined not to enter into another coalition with Fine Gael. Labour victories in the 1964 and 1966 British general elections and an upsurge of left-wing politics throughout Europe added to their belief that they could become a major force in Irish politics. The formation of ICTU in 1959, ending a split in the trade union movement which began during in the 1940s, strengthened the party, although a majority of trade unionists voted for non-Labour candidates, mainly Fianna Fáil. More importantly, the growth in waged and salaried workers, especially in the public service, appeared favourable for Labour. Ironically, these changes also represented a major challenge. Only one of the sixteen deputies elected in 1961 held a Dublin seat; the remainder were elected by a combination of farm labourers, and pockets of working-class voters, including manual workers in state enterprises such as the ESB and Bord na Móna. The traditional Labour TD relied on a personal

---

[47] *B&F*, 14 June 1969.   [48] *Hibernia*, 9–22 May 1969.
[49] Tom Garvin, 'Political parties in a Dublin Constituency', Ph.D. University of Georgia, 1972, pp. 76–7.

vote and strong constituency service. Dan Spring (Kerry) and Seán Treacy (Tipperary) owed their success as much to their involvement in the war of independence as to labour activism. A US State Department memo in August 1961 explained that party finances were weak, which meant that in selecting candidates, Labour often had to rely on 'people who as individuals are willing to stand under the Labour banner and obtain their own financial support, especially from local trade union organisations'.[50] The 1960s saw a sharp fall in the numbers of agricultural labourers. Rural protests were increasingly associated with non-party movements. Meanwhile, Labour's trade union supporters were threatened by plans to dismantle tariff protection and the arrival of new foreign-owned industries, which wanted either no trade unions or a system radically different to the existing multiple trade unions.

Labour underwent more dramatic changes than the other main parties. It began to present itself as a more disciplined opposition party within Dáil Éireann, as opposed to a loose federation of independents wearing the Labour label. For the first time, Labour TDs shadowed specific ministers. They developed more formal relationships with trade unions. The Workers Union of Ireland affiliated to the party in 1965; the ITGWU in 1967. ICTU established a joint council with Labour in the same year, though Gallagher suggests that these arrangements had a limited impact on party fortunes.[51] However, they did signify a greater distance between the trade unions and Fianna Fáil. In 1963, Noel Browne and Jack McQuillan, members of the small and short-lived National Progressive Democrats, joined Labour, strengthening the party's left-wing credentials. Yet, when Seán MacEntee, an inveterate critic of Browne, alleged that Labour was being infiltrated by Marxists, Corish, who had initially opposed admitting them to the party, responded that Labour policy continued to be based 'on good, sound, Christian principles'[52] – an indication of the potential dangers presented by a leftwards move.

The 1960s was marked by a shift in the balance of power between urban TDs with professional qualifications and traditional rural TDs who often had only primary schooling.[53] In 1965, Labour gained seats in Dublin and held its traditional provincial base to win twenty-two seats. Although Labour overtook Fine Gael to become the second party in Dublin in 1969 (after Fianna Fáil), with 30 per cent of votes and ten seats, they failed to hold this position in 1973, when they won 22 per cent of votes and seven seats. By 1969 however, gains in Dublin were exceeded

---

[50] Cited in Purséil, *The Irish Labour Party*, pp. 219–20.
[51] Gallagher, *Labour Party in transition*, pp. 55–6, 62–5.
[52] Purséil, *Irish Labour Party*, p. 227. Quoted Gallagher, *Labour party in transition*, p. 53.
[53] Brian Farrell, 'Dáil deputies: the 1969 generation', *ESR*, vol. 2, 1970/1971, p. 315.

by losses elsewhere; Labour won nineteen seats.[54] By the end of the decade, Labour could be described as an uneasy coalition of university-educated deputies and party members, who were happy to proclaim themselves as socialists, and more traditional members and deputies, who identified with issues such as rural works programmes, food subsidies, welfare benefits, and Catholic teaching on the dangers of communism and personal morality, plus a strong injection of traditional republicanism. Barry Desmond, who was first elected in 1969, claimed that there was 'acute tension between the rural and urban wings of the Labour Party' . . . There was a patronising assuming by some of the media that the men from rural Ireland were somehow uncultured, unread and uninspiring. Those with academic or professional experience were deemed politically superior.'[55] The divisions were not simply between Dublin and the provinces. Garvin described the Labour party in Dublin South-Central as having a 'bi-polar' membership – with many activists from middle-class backgrounds, educated in the elite Catholic secondary schools, and others from working-class families who were educated in vocational schools.[56]

Labour's conversion to socialism was partly due to the influx of new, younger members, many of them university students. With a membership of approximately 5,000, it was relatively easy to gain control of party conferences; whereas, the Fine Gael 'young tigers' were outmanoeuvred by the party establishment. The crowded political landscape, with Fine Gael's *Just Society* adopting social democratic programmes, and Fianna Fáil – while avoiding any such terminology – awarding regular pay increases and extending welfare benefits, not to mention its willingness to concede overly generous pay increases to militant trade unions, put Labour under pressure to adopt a more left-wing stance. This begs the question whether Labour's conversion to socialism was pragmatic, or ideological? Corish had a track record of conforming to Catholic Church teaching, as is evident in the stances that he had taken on issues such as the Mother and Child Scheme, and the notorious Fethard on Sea boycott; he often justified his socialism by referring to the encyclicals of Pope John XXIII.[57] Gallagher suggests that Fine Gael's adoption of the *Just Society* programme prompted Corish to declare that Labour was a socialist party, though the term 'socialist' was not used in their 1965 election manifesto.[58] Purséil makes a similar argument. 'With the

[54] Gallagher, *Labour Party in transition*, p. 45.
[55] Barry Desmond, *Finally and in conclusion*, pp. 31–3.
[56] Garvin, 'Political parties in a Dublin constituency' p. 121.
[57] Purséil, *Irish Labour Party*, pp. 230–1, 241.
[58] Gallagher, *Labour Party in transition*, pp. 54–7.

Taoiseach and the main opposition party encroaching more and more on Labour's would-be policy and language, Labour was faced with the need to assert its identity in more radical terms; if Lemass was "left" and Costello was "just", Labour might have to be "socialist" '.[59] Whyte claimed that in the 1965 election, Labour 'had some difficulty' maintaining its position as the most radical party. Although they were 'slightly to the left' of Fine Gael, 'by a short head', the 'most striking feature' was 'how much Fine Gael and Labour have in common'.[60] The most revealing quote comes from Michael O'Leary, a UCC graduate and trade union official, first elected in 1965, who told Labour's 1966 conference that Fianna Fáil and Fine Gael had appropriated Labour's policies: 'everything we ever looked for, they now seek. On planning, health education, they speak with the tongue of socialists.' Labour had to find a way to differentiate itself from the other parties.[61] They did this by rebranding the party as socialist. In 1966, Corish told the party conference that he stood for a socialist republic.[62] Labour's embrace of socialism was encouraged by the celebrations marking the Golden Jubilee of the 1916 Rising, an occasion that saw 1916 leader James Connolly emerge as an iconic figure.

Labour launched their new look at the 1967 conference with the slogans 'Let's build the New Republic' and 'the Seventies will be Socialist'. Corish told delegates that the party had a real prospect of gaining fifty seats and forming a government after the next election. The official party line was that Labour would force a merger between Fianna Fáil and Fine Gael, leaving Labour as either the first or second party in Irish politics. In 1967, Labour joined the Socialist International. But the 1967 local elections, when Labour gained votes in Dublin, but lost them elsewhere, were the first indication of the risks of adopting a socialist agenda. Gallagher described the period between the 1967 Party conference and the 1969 general election as 'Labour's brief golden age'. While Labour activists made liberal use of the word socialism, initially 'it remained an ill defined term, not backed up by anything tangible, and used almost as a ritual word, as proof of comradeship and as a mark of a distinctive Labour identity.'[63] By 1968, however, this ill-defined term had been translated into a series of policies, which included state control of banking; nationalising the construction industry, building societies, development land and large landed estates; workers participation in all company decisions; state control of farms if the farmer was idle or

---

[59] Purséil, *Irish Labour Party*, p. 230.   [60] *Hibernia*, April 1965.
[61] Quoted in Purséil, *Irish Labour Party*, p. 239.
[62] Gallagher, *Labour Party in transition*, p. 60.
[63] Gallagher, *Labour Party in transition*, pp. 68–9.

incompetent and taking schools and voluntary hospitals into community control. Gallagher described the proposals as betraying 'a starry-eyed naivety': 'It appeared to rest on the assumption that Labour was on the verge of a fifteen-year spell in government, and that it would find unlimited funds at its disposal upon entering office. There was no attempt to cost the various proposals.'[64]

And so to Fianna Fáil – the party in office: Whereas most discussion of the divisions within Fine Gael and Labour emphasise policy differences, in the case of Fianna Fáil, the emphasis is generally on style and personality. In some respects, this is surprising, given that Fianna Fáil had abandoned its traditional policy of self-sufficiency and appeared to be reneging on a long-standing commitment to supporting small farmers and rural Ireland, not to mention its closer links with the Northern Ireland government; yet, there is no real indication that party members were involved in those key decisions. In 1970, the British ambassador to Ireland Sir John Peck noted that 'it is vital that there is no public discussion of policy between branches [of Fianna Fáil] in various parts of the country. The normal system is that any suggestions go to the leadership, which decides the line and subsequently tells the branches what that line is.'[65] Nevertheless, the abandonment of long-held positions presented difficulties for party members, and this is most evident in the resignation of Minister for Agriculture Paddy Smith in protest at concessions to building workers, and in the opposition expressed to measures such as the Succession Act, the original drafts of what became the 1965 Land Act, and the Buchanan Plan. There were undoubted tensions between urban/rural interests and small farming and non-agricultural interests.

The party had faced divisions over policy in the past; de Valera's strategy was consensus by exhaustion – marathon meetings of Cabinet. Lemass appears to have adopted a different approach – avoiding lengthy Cabinet meetings where divisions might be thrashed out, and expanding the office of the Taoiseach by taking a much more active role in key government decisions. In a letter to Jack Lynch, Minister for Industry and Commerce, who had brokered the concessions to striking building workers, written shortly after he resigned from Cabinet, Paddy Smith protested that compromise 'is the only language understood now in Government circles and especially in your Department. They all say that the Taoiseach has taken over that place [presumably the Department of Industry and Commerce] and that it was on his

---

[64] Purséil, *Irish Labour Party*, pp. 261–2; Gallagher, *Labour party in transition*, pp. 81–2.
[65] TNA FCO33/1200 23 June 1970 Blatherwick to McGlashen.

instructions this press conference is now taking place in your Department.'[66] Farrell notes Lemass' frustration that parliamentary secretaries (junior ministers) reported to a senior Cabinet Minister, not to the Taoiseach; this limited Lemass' scope for using them to by-pass ministers whose views were not akin to his.[67] Todd Andrews, a party veteran, claimed that Lemass' leadership brought a change in 'the style of government' from de Valera's: less sense of a shared responsibility and the emergence of cabals. 'Snide remarks about one another were common enough. Accounts of cabinet proceedings were leaked and often discussed with others.' Andrews believed that there were 'personal tensions in his [Lemass'] cabinet which finally crystallised in the contest for the succession'.[68] Horgan quotes Dan Breen – a veteran backbencher – that Lemass could not keep control unlike de Valera.[69] Lemass' control over his Cabinet appears to have weakened after the 1965 general election, perhaps because of a changing political culture, and because ministers sensed that he would not remain long in office. Horgan suggests that by 1966 the 'temper of the party was becoming frayed by the increasing tempo and severity of Government cut-backs', especially cuts in the allocation for housing.[70] Haughey refused to announce cuts in capital services to Agriculture, though this would have been a normal ministerial responsibility.[71] Donogh O'Malley's announcement of free secondary education is yet another instance of a minister ignoring collective Cabinet responsibility.

The departure of the revolutionary generation brought a change in political culture, a more lavish, ostentatious lifestyle that at least super-ficially seemed to reflect the dynamic economy, plus a greater willingness to collaborate, even conspire with the media. Tim Pat Coogan described the 1965 Cabinet as 'the coming of the men in the mohair suits' – Charles Haughey, Donogh O'Malley and Brian Lenihan. Coogan described Haughey – Smith's successor – as Minister for Agriculture as 'the epi-tome of the men in the mohair suits . . . a strange blend of confidence and uncertainty, concerned for his image and sensitive to newspaper com-ment. He hunts, is a bon viveur and a generous host. (His favourite brand of port which he buys by the case, costs thirty-four shillings a bottle.)'[72] It would be naive to assume that the earlier generation of politicians did not

---

[66] UCDA MacEntee Papers P 67/335 Smith to Lynch 12 November 1964 typed letter, copy in MacEntee papers.
[67] Brian Farrell, *Seán Lemass* (Dublin: Gill & Macmillan, 1983), pp. 103–4.
[68] C. S. Andrews, *Man of no property* (Dublin: Lilliput, 2001), p. 250.
[69] Horgan, *Lemass*, p. 234.   [70] Horgan, *Lemass*, p. 238.
[71] Dermot Keogh, *Jack Lynch. A biography* (Dublin: Gill & Macmillan, 2008), p. 96.
[72] Coogan, *Ireland since the rising*, pp. 108–10.

use the press to advance their interests: the *Irish Press* was founded to promote Fianna Fáil; as Minister for Agriculture, James Dillon used his friendship with *Sunday Independent* editor Hector Legge to place stories.[73] But the 1960s brought a less deferential tone to political journalism, and some journalists and politicians developed mutually beneficial relationships. The *Irish Times* was to the fore, because as a newspaper with a small circulation, traditionally dependent on Anglo-Irish Protestant readers, it had to expand its readership in order to survive. By the mid-1960s, Irish newspapers were not simply reporting politics; they had become part of the process. Coogan claimed that John Healy 'revolutionised Irish political journalism ... developing first a political column under the pseudonym "Backbencher", which had much to do with bringing the *Irish Times* to its present position of influence in Irish society'.[74] Healy used his column to advance the careers and agendas of his ministerial friends. In the run-up to the 1965 general election, the *Irish Times* launched a sustained attack on Seán MacEntee, suggesting that it was time that he retired from politics – an attack that given MacEntee's pugilistic temperament was guaranteed to fail. MacEntee was re-elected, though he was no longer a member of the Cabinet.[75] Michael Mills, then political correspondent of the *Irish Press*, described Healy as 'a formidable supporter of the Haughey camp, and he and O'Malley became extremely close'. Mills described O'Malley as 'witty and urbane and a wonderful companion ... loved the company of journalists'.[76] The minutes of the Fianna Fáil national executive include several reminders that proceedings were confidential and deploring leaks to the media,[77] to little effect. Kevin Boland reported meeting John Healy with O'Malley in Fianna Fáil headquarters during the 1964 Roscommon by-election and ordering Healy to leave.[78]

As rumours of Lemass' retirement began to circulate in August 1966, one journalist suggested that 'Lemass' successor has got to be able to inject new incentives and new heart into the party and manage the economy with strength ... The language, the border, Dev's gospel are almost irrelevant besides the straightening out of industrial and agricultural development and entry into the Common Market.'[79] During the contest to succeed Lemass, several leading members of the party contacted Michael Mills, whose story in the *Evening Press* that Kevin Boland

---

[73] Manning, *James Dillon*, p. 254.
[74] Tim Pat Coogan, *A memoir* (London: Weidenfield & Nicholson, 2008), p. 88.
[75] UCDA P67/403 clipping of *IT* leading article 23 March 1965; report of election meeting 23 March 1965; the *II*, 22 March 1965 also suggested that he should retire.
[76] Michael Mills, *Hurler on the ditch. Memoir of a journalist who became Ireland's first Ombudsman* (Dublin: Currach, 2005), p. 40.
[77] UCDA P 176/348, 8 June 1964; P 176/349, 30 November 1964; 22 November 1965.
[78] Boland interview Horgan/Lemass files.   [79] *Hibernia*, August 1966.

was nominating Neil Blaney as a candidate against George Colley prompted Lemass to persuade Jack Lynch to stand.[80] Lemass' successor, Jack Lynch was seen as a compromise candidate – a man who was identified with neither the traditional wing of the party, which supported George Colley, nor with the 'men in the mohair suits', who did not field a candidate. Although Lynch appeared to have a strong mandate winning fifty-two votes against nineteen for Colley, his authority was always in question. The manoeuvres prior to the leadership contest had revealed the existence of several aspiring leaders – particularly Haughey and Blaney, whose hopes were kept alive in part because Lynch was initially reluctant to become Taoiseach. Although Lynch transcended the various factions, he lacked a network of close allies in Cabinet; more importantly, he lacked vision and purpose. Lee describes Lynch as 'instinctively a temporiser. Having no strong views himself, he preferred to lead from behind, and to let policy "emerge".'[81] According to Frank Dunlop, who worked closely with Lynch in the 1970s as Fianna Fáil press secretary, 'He was unwilling to confront unless forced to do so'; he 'rarely initiated anything and he was great at delegating. Most new ideas . . . came from other people.'[82] Keogh notes that as Minister for Finance, Lynch 'had been seen as a soft touch'.[83] He presided over Ireland's EEC entry otherwise his record on the economy was mixed; the growth rate fell consistently below target; industrial relations difficulties escalated; the government effectively abandoned its commitment to economic planning, but failed to substitute any alternative goals. Government control over prices and public spending, which was already slipping in Lemass' later years, deteriorated further. Lynch also vacillated on policy towards Northern Ireland. His failure to secure Cabinet support to either accept or reject the Buchanan Report is further evidence of indecisiveness, likewise the repeated postponement of any decisions on contraception. Fianna Fáil governments, unlike coalition governments, did not have a track-record of postponing items on Cabinet agendas – generally an indication of fundamental divisions among ministers; that changed under Lynch.

Yet, Lynch was more popular with the public than Lemass, and although born and raised in Cork city, he was much more at ease in provincial Ireland – probably because of his status as a GAA hurling

---

[80] Mills, *Hurler on the ditch*, p. 42. The story is confirmed by Boland's interview in the Horgan/Lemass files.
[81] Lee, *Ireland 1912–1985*, p. 409.
[82] Dunlop, *Yes, Taoiseach. Irish politics from behind closed doors* (Dublin: Penguin Ireland, 2004), p. 16.
[83] Keogh, *Jack Lynch*, p. 123. Dunlop, *Yes, Taoiseach*, pp. 21–2.

and football star, and his political philosophy appears to have been much closer to traditional values (he was a strong supporter of the Irish language, for example) than Lemass. In 1965, Fianna Fáil had fared well in Dublin; in 1969 and 1973, they fared best in the most agricultural constituencies.[84] In the 1969 general election, thanks to Boland's adroit redrawing of constituency boundaries and the failure of Labour and Fine Gael to agree on Coalition, Lynch defied most political pundits by winning an overall majority. The election was held at an opportune moment: in 1968, the economy finally rebounded after the recession of 1965/1966, and the record growth was still evident in the summer of 1969, though now coupled with rampant price and wage inflation. In substance, if not in style, the campaign remained true to the winning formulas of 1961 and 1965: the need for a stable government – which only Fianna Fáil could offer – to meet future challenges Their campaign literature was dominated by lists of the programmes introduced and increases in benefits since the previous general election. Election literature for the Kilkenny constituency listed the jobs created in the various towns and villages; the 160 new local authority houses 'ready for occupation', a new swimming pool and other amenities.[85] Party literature in Dublin South Central presented a series of 'Do you remember' points, all designed to remind voters of the failures of the 1954–1957 Coalition: empty Corporation houses, no increases in pensions and record unemployment.[86] Lemass' message about the need for a national effort to ensure continuing economic growth and the links between growth and improved services was no longer prominent; it now seemed as if all that was necessary for continuing prosperity was to re-elect the government. Fianna Fáil had taken account of Fine Gael's *Just Society* document. They ignored the sections that proposed greater state intervention in the economy, especially in banking and other elements, but adopted the message that social improvement mattered, and that what voters wanted was higher pensions, and other benefits.

1969: No turning point

Expectations of change were rife in the run-up to the 1969 general election, with local newspapers highlighting a 'Strong desire for change', predictions that the contest would be 'one of the great watersheds in Irish political history'.[87] It wasn't. When Fianna Fáil was returned with an

[84] Michael Gallagher, *Electoral support for Irish political parties*, pp. 27–8.
[85] UCDA P 176/841 (3).   [86] UCDA P 176/841.
[87] Editorials in *Sligo Champion*, 30 May 1969, and *Kilkenny People*, 13 June 1969, cited in Brian Farrell, 'Dáil Deputies: "The 1969 generation" ', p. 309.

overall majority, *Hibernia* described the result as 'a surprise', going on to note that Dublin-based political commentators 'ignored or discounted too heavily what is the most important single fact of Irish political life; the Irish electorate in both its voting habits and mould of thought is one of the most conservative in the world. The exception of Dublin City doesn't disprove this generality.'[88] The 1969 general election took place in the aftermath of 1968 – the year of protest and thwarted revolution across Europe. Dublin exhibited the same heady mixture of left-wing organisations – with a strong youth presence – as many other western cities. The most common ingredients were left-wing republicanism affiliated to Sinn Féin, and Marxist, or Maoist tendencies. In Dublin, as elsewhere, such movements attracted student support across a wide political spectrum: Republican Clubs, Connolly Youth, the Internationalists, left-wing Christian groups and university branches of Labour and Fine Gael. Protests were directed at apartheid when South African cricket or rugby teams played in Ireland; the Vietnam War – there were protests when US Senator Edward Kennedy visited Trinity College, and regular demonstrations outside the US Embassy. Housing attracted the most sustained agitation. The Dublin Housing Action Committee – which drew members from Sinn Féin and the IRA, the Irish Workers Party and Irish Communist Organisation – demonstrated outside Dublin City Hall throughout 1968.[89] Marches and squatting attracted a wide spectrum of support. According to Ruairí Quinn, the Labour party 'came to the conclusion that we should radicalise students first and presume that they would subsequently vote for Labour', so student Labour party members joined the left-wing Students for Democratic Action.[90] Professor John Kelly, a Fine Gael politician and a leading authority on constitutional law, noted signs 'that the traditional modes of keeping order are breaking down. Some groups now appear unafraid of any degree of force which the government may bring to bear, and indeed, seem anxious for long-term ends, to make martyrs ... The Irish pattern is this: arrest for breach of the peace or of a statute prohibiting certain kinds of assembly or demonstration is followed by conviction; the conviction is followed by a fine; the offenders refuse to pay the fine and are kept in prison, whereupon a hunger strike starts and some formula has to be found for saving the Government's face while releasing the offenders.'

Kelly was commenting on the Criminal Justice Bill, which was designed to strengthen the government's hand with provisions that unpaid fines or

---

[88] *Hibernia*, 27 June–17 July 1969.
[89] *Hibernia*, 1–14 November 1968; Brian Hanley and Scott Millar, *The lost revolution* (Dublin: Penguin Ireland, 2009), pp. 84–90.
[90] Quinn, *Straight left*, pp. 61–2.

unpaid rates could be recouped by withholding government grants; giving gardaí power to arrest people without a warrant if they believed that the person was likely to engage in conduct leading to a breach of the peace and powers to prevent public meetings or demonstrations, which were much wider than applied in Northern Ireland.[91] The highly controversial Bill was introduced in the Oireachtas in the spring of 1969, but had not passed into law when the general election took place. No effort was made subsequently to reintroduce it.

Television enhanced, indeed exaggerated, the impact of radical youth. The contrast between tongue-tied ministers, grimacing at the camera as the presenter questioned them, and the young articulate panellists on *Teen Talk* or the *The Late Late Show* was striking. Live programmes afforded young people the opportunity 'pour épater la bourgeoisie'; a chance for Fine Gael 'young tigers' to criticise the party leader, for panellists such as TCD student Brian Trevaskis to describe the Bishop of Galway as a 'moron'. Whether such contributions served any purpose other than to shock is questionable; Harvey O'Brien suggests that 'the casual nature of this technologically refigured fireside chat ... disabled more sustained and challenging documentary analysis of the same issues'.[92] The frequent and often noisy protests drew on a limited cohort of activists, and, as happened with international protest movements of 1968, they had little immediate electoral impact, except perhaps to weaken moderate reform and strengthen conservatism. Purséil notes that UCD's Kevin Barry Cumann – the Fianna Fáil student branch – was 'at least 50 per cent bigger than either of the Labour or Fine Gael societies'.[93] Frank Dunlop who became a member in 1969 described it as 'a desert of political thought and activity compared to the maelstrom of political activity waging through the left-wing organisations'. The Fianna Fáil national executive was extremely reluctant to sanction the creation of a youth wing, and Dunlop claims that ministers were reluctant to set foot on campus.[94] Liam Cosgrave had similar suspicions about his party's 'young tigers'. However, in an eve of election rally at the GPO – he claimed that the large number of young men and women, who were involved in the campaign, was evidence of growth and renewal, describing Fine Gael as 'a forward-looking party' though much of his speech consisted of a litany of the party's achievements when in government more than a decade earlier.[95] In 1969, younger radical members of

[91] John M. Kelly, The Criminal Justice Bill I: The Price of Public Order, *IT*, 30 July 1968.
[92] Harvey O'Brien, *The real Ireland. The evolution of Ireland in documentary film* (Manchester: Manchester University Press, 2004), p. 157.
[93] Purséil, *Irish Labour Party*, p. 241.   [94] Dunlop, *Yes, Taoiseach*, p. 1.
[95] UCDA P39GE/159 – election speeches 1969; GPO 17 June 1969.

Fine Gael held their fire and worked closely with the party organisation during the election campaign.

Many pundits assumed that the election would return a significant Labour/socialist representation. But a substantial number of the most vocal left-wingers were under twenty-one years and ineligible to vote. The election took place weeks before Northern Ireland erupted into violence. In hindsight, this gives it an air of unreality. The critical issues were Fianna Fáil's recurring theme that political stability was essential to sustain economic growth and negotiate Irish entry to the EEC; secondly, the future shape of Ireland's economy and society – would the state become more directly involved in the economy to the extent of nationalising or controlling key sectors including the banks and development land? Fine Gael fought the election with a slate of twenty-two policies – too many for the electorate to absorb, though mercifully fewer than the sixty-three items highlighted during a 1964 by-election campaign![96] Land speculation became a hot topic, with news that Charles Haughey had sold his home and surrounding lands in north Dublin for housing development. Fine Gael secured legal advice that Haughey would have been liable for a substantial tax bill on the sale, if the 1965 Finance Act had not been amended, and he had failed to inform the Dáil of this, but they do not appear to have used this information to any great effect during the campaign.[97] In the early 1970s, a briefing note by the British Embassy in Dublin on Irish political parties (written for the Foreign Secretary Sir Alec Douglas-Home) claimed that Haughey 'has acquired an estimated £1.5 million in the course of property deals which steered just clear of illegality'.[98] Although Conor Cruise O'Brien – Labour's candidate in the same constituency – was highly critical of Haughey's land sale, his criticism was somewhat blunted when it emerged that Labour candidate Justin Keating had sold his home and land for housing development to Dublin Corporation for a significant sum.[99] Housing featured prominently in the Fine Gael campaign. They promised a 'crash housing programme' and cheap serviced land to thwart land speculation. Cosgrave, in typical blunt language, promised to 'literally cut the ground from under those speculators who are now making fortunes overnight through artificial scarcity of serviced land'.[100] The party gave a commitment to end the power of the Minister for Local Government with respect to planning appeals; promised measures to reduce the cost to

[96] *Hibernia*, June 1964.   [97] UCDA P39 GE/158(1).
[98] TNA FCO33/1603. Despatches on state of political parties in the Republic of Ireland 14 December 1971.
[99] Conor Cruise O'Brien, *Memoir. My life and themes* (Dublin: Poolbeg, 1998), pp. 318–9.
[100] UCDA P39GE/159 – election speeches 1969; GPO 17 June 1969.

householders of local authority rates; a comprehensive health service based on insurance. They criticised 'spurious' promises of jobs in new factories – the failed Potez aircraft factory was repeatedly cited. The emphasis on housing and rates reflects increasing pressure on the housing market, especially in Dublin, and the rising costs of local authority services, which culminated in the dissolution of Dublin Corporation shortly before the general election for refusing to strike a rate that would cover its costs. Fine Gael appealed to rural voters with proposals to create a rural development authority under farmers' control. John Bruton, a candidate in Meath with a personal base on Dublin's door-step, lamented the 'decline of rural Ireland and the disintegration of rural communities'; he claimed that many people living in cities did not even know their next door neighbour.[101]

An editorial in *The Kerryman* commented that 'With this election Labour faces the public for the first time in doctrinaire dress.'[102] Labour had recruited several new high-profile candidates, including Justin Keating, David Thornley, Conor Cruise O'Brien – all with strong media profiles and equally strong academic credentials, who were returned for Dublin constituencies. Given that Labour's manifesto proposed to nationalise large landed estates and take neglected land into community control, it is not surprising that former NFA President Rickard Deasy failed to win a seat in Tipperary. Labour's new candidates gave Fianna Fáil ample scope for invective against Trinity College intellectuals and socialists, who were described as out of touch with the real Ireland. Seán MacEntee, though retired from active politics, assumed his traditional role as the party's Rottweiler, denouncing the Red Poster of Labour, which 'stands for the philosophy and teaching of Karl Marx'; he was one of many to play on the red scare.[103] A proposal by Conor Cruise O'Brien that Ireland should close its embassy in Portugal (still ruled by long-term dictator Salazar) and open an embassy in Cuba proved particularly inviting; the Fianna Fáil team in Dublin South Central warned voters to 'Leave Cuba to the Cubans. We can look after ourselves.'[104] Labour tried to counter the red label, by quoting the encyclicals of Pope John XXIII, but with little apparent effect. Purséil suggests that the party lost support outside Dublin in the closing weeks of the campaign because the outcome was much worse than the party's internal polls had indicated. It would be naive however to blame Labour's performance wholly on Fianna Fáil scare tactics – indeed, they provided a convenient scapegoat. Many policies would have been anathema to long-standing Labour

---

[101] UCDA, P39/GE/159 Election speeches.
[102] Farrell, 'The 1969 generation', pp. 309–11; quotation from *The Kerryman*, 31 May 1969 on p. 309.
[103] P67/411 1969 general election.   [104] P176/841 (7).

TDs. Veteran Kerry TD Dan Spring ran a personal campaign that did not mention Labour; he was re-elected. Others lost their seats, because some traditional Labour voters were uncomfortable with the new policies, and because of the naïve hubris that saw Labour running two or more candidates in constituencies in an effort to prove that they could provide an alternative government. This split the Labour vote and probably cost the party seats.[105] The 1969 general election was a shattering experience for the party. One columnist speculated that Labour secretary Brendan Halligan 'must be the most disappointed man in Ireland'.[106] Yet, predictions of a significant swing to a socialist Labour Party took little account of the social and geographic profile of the electorate – which, despite the changes over the previous decade, included significant numbers of farmers, family business owners, regular church-goers and others who were unlikely to be enamoured of plans to take control of underperforming farms or church-owned schools.

The losing parties blamed the outcome on gerrymandered constituency boundaries. There was a requirement to review, and if necessary redraw, constituency boundaries to take account of changes in the population census. In 1969 however, for the first time, constituency boundaries were redrawn, without any such need, and they were undoubtedly redrawn to maximise Fianna Fáil's electoral chances. The Minister Kevin Boland personally redrew constituency boundaries on a large map placed on the floor of his office. With the assistance of a young civil servant, who was deputed to carry out this task by senior officials who declined to become involved, District Electoral Divisions were added and subtracted from constituencies to achieve the desired population and political configuration.[107] Boland opted for three-seat constituencies in the west, where Fianna Fáil was strong, in the expectation that the party would win two seats, and four-seaters in the east where the party was weaker.[108] Boland is on record as saying some years later that 'The only political reputation I have is as an expert constituency reviser.'[109] The redrawn constituencies gave Fianna Fáil a considerable bonus. They won 51.7 per cent of the seats (74) with 45.7 per cent of the votes, two more seats than 1965, when they secured 47.7 of first preferences – a much greater deviation between seats and votes than previous elections.[110] Political

---

[105] Purséil, *Irish Labour Party*, p. 270. Gallagher, *Labour in transition*, pp. 91–102.
[106] *Hibernia*, 27 June–17 July 1969
[107] The civil servant involved has described this to me.
[108] Michael Gallagher, 'Proportionality in a proportional representation system: the Irish experience', *Political Studies*, December 1975, pp. 510–11.
[109] *Hibernia*, 22 July 1977, p. 9 as quoted in O'Leary, *Irish elections*, p. 66.
[110] O Leary, *Irish elections*, p. 104.

scientist Michael Gallagher concluded that 'Despite allegations that Fianna Fáil had done this [gerrymandering] at several revisions, only the 1969 revision seems to have been designed in this spirit.'[111] The other major criticism of the 1969 revision concerned the 'butchering' of county boundaries, at a time when regional planning appeared to be overriding historic boundaries. But the revised constituencies provide only a partial explanation for Fianna Fáil's success. Labour's refusal to enter coalition resulted in poor vote transfer between Fine Gael and Labour. It is estimated that Labour or Fine Gael could have taken seven seats won by Fianna Fáil in 1969 if there had been an effective transfer of votes between the parties.[112]

If the election failed to bring about a dramatic change in political representation, it did represent an important change in style. By 1969, Irish politics was operating in the age of television, but the medium had a complex impact on the political process. Seán Lemass had described Teilifís Éireann as 'an instrument of public policy and as such [is] responsible to the Government'.[113] He believed that the station should preach the need for pay restraint, higher productivity and support for government objectives. Ministers protested at even the merest break with the deference traditionally shown to them by Radio Éireann, as when press statements were edited or summarised in television news bulletins. Perhaps for this reason, Teilifís Éireann was slow to engage directly with politics and current affairs. Although they covered the 1965 general election count extensively, it was only in the autumn of 1966, with the launch of two new programmes – *Division* and *Seven Days* – that the station began to provide systematic coverage of politics and current affairs.[114] Current affairs soon fell foul of the government, when they determined to proceed with an interview with NFA President Rickard Deasy, despite the refusal of Minister for Agriculture Charles Haughey to appear on the programme; Haughey presumably assumed that his refusal would kill the item. Documentaries focusing on topics such as homelessness, young offenders and emigration had the potential to influence political debate, and it is probable that their impact was by definition critical of the status quo and of government. Purséil comments that within the Labour party, 'personality clashes which would have taken place behind closed doors were now becoming increasingly public, as a

[111] Michael Gallagher, 'Proportionality in a proportional representation system', p. 512.
[112] James Knight and Nicolas Baxter-Moore, *Republic of Ireland. The general elections of 1969 and 1973* (London: Arthur McDougall Fund, 1973), p. 14.
[113] DD vol. 224, cols. 1045-8, 12 October 1966.
[114] Bowman, *Window and mirror*, pp. 70, 74.

fracas on *The Late Late Show* between MacAonghusa, Michael O'Leary and Noel Browne illustrated'.[115]

But after a brief loss of nerve, politicians showed a growing ability to control the medium in their own interests. In the 1966 presidential election campaign, Fianna Fáil Director of elections Charles Haughey decided that President Eamon de Valera would not formally campaign for re-election, forcing Teilifís Éireann effectively to ignore the highly telegenic campaign staged by Tom O'Higgins. In 1969, by selecting candidates who were household names thanks to TV, Labour saved time and money, and significantly increased their election prospects. Lynch's 1969 general election campaign was also designed for media – even down to photographs of him canvassing convents, which may have been influenced by an earlier photograph of Northern Ireland Prime Minister Terence O'Neill visiting a convent (the first such visit by a Prime Minister of Northern Ireland). Irish politicians had been visiting convents for generations; the easing of enclosure rules on nuns during Vatican II meant that some nuns voted for the first time, and press photographers could capture the occasion. Since 1969, every Irish election or referendum has included mandatory shots of a nun at a polling station. Between 27 May and 15 June, Lynch visited all the main towns in three whistle-stop tours. Most stops allowed little more than an opportunity to shake hands with local activists, and nuns, but they provided good copy for local newspapers and the television news. On Friday, 6 June, for example, Lynch visited Strokestown; Ballaghdderreen; Charlestown; Tubbercurry, Boyle, Collooney and Sligo, where the day ended with a public meeting at 9 pm. This was the standard format: several short stops in smaller towns concluding with a public meeting in a major town. On Saturday, 14 June, the final weekend before the election, he addressed a public meeting at 8 pm in Ennis, and one in Limerick at 10 pm. Lynch's campaign was obviously modelled on Tom O'Higgins' 1966 presidential campaign, which included 85 to 100 meetings over a six-week campaign, culminating in a rally at the GPO. Fine Gael drew comparisons between O'Higgins' campaign and John F. Kennedy 'who also insisted on meeting individually as many of his supporters as possible'. [I suspect that the model was Kennedy's Irish visit rather than his Presidential campaign]. O'Higgins was invariably accompanied by his wife – a first in Irish campaigns, and as Fine Gael noted, 'The Candidate has stressed the importance of rousing the interest of women voters as well as of men in his campaign and many essentially feminine functions have been taking place during the past weeks, to which Mr O'Higgins has accompanied his wife

---

[115] Purséil, *Irish Labour Party*, p. 245.

whenever possible.'[116] Maureen Lynch, like Terry O'Higgins, was at her husband's side throughout the 1969 campaign. These campaigns mark the first apparent efforts to appeal to women voters – though whether women were swayed by seeing the candidate's wife on the campaign trail is unknown.[117] Only three women were returned in the 1969 election. 1969 was the last occasion that the main parties ended their campaigns with traditional rallies outside the GPO. These came to an end because of security concerns following the outbreak of violence in Northern Ireland,[118] though the changing nature of political campaigns might well have brought them to an end regardless of this. The final Fine Gael rally was a test of stamina; the programme provided for ten speakers – beginning with a twenty-minute address by Liam Cosgrave, ten minutes from Tom O'Higgins, followed by eight candidates representing Dublin constituencies who were scheduled to speak for six minutes apiece.[119]

The outcome of the 1969 election indicated that Ireland was not about to transform itself into a radical socialist republic. By 1969/1970, left-wing revolution was a spent force throughout Western Europe. This dose of reality administered by the electorate in 1969 probably determined the outcome of the 1973 election – because it forced Labour and Fine Gael to acknowledge that coalition offered both parties the only realistic prospect of government and emboldened party members who favoured coalition.[120] While Labour and Fine Gael might rightly protest that the redrawn constituency boundaries had ensured Fianna Fáil's victory, a more realistic verdict might be that radical politics had a limited appeal for Irish voters. Labour was forced to row back on its socialist ideology; within Fine Gael, the result strengthened the hand of Cosgrave and his supporters against the more radical wing. In the autumn of 1969, Fine Gael expelled six younger members – they included journalist Vincent Browne and Henry Kelly, who became a TV personality in Britain. But this failed to stem dissent – on the contrary, some months later Dublin TD Richie Ryan alleged that 'a junta' existed, who were determined to destroy the party. [121]

The winners, Fianna Fáil, were arguably least affected by the election. Lynch had defied all expectations by winning an overall majority, yet there is no evidence that this strengthened his position. When he tried to shift Kevin Boland, from Local Government to Social Welfare – the

---

[116] UCDA P 67/408 Material provided at 1966 Fine Gael Press Conference.
[117] UCDA P39GE/159 – election speeches 1969; GPO 17 June 1969; P 39GE/.160 Garret FitzGerald speech.
[118] FitzGerald, *All in a Life*, p. 86.   [119] P39/GE/167.
[120] Paddy Harte, *Young Tigers and Mongrel Foxes: [a life in politics]* (Dublin: O'Brien, 2005), pp. 221–2.
[121] *Hibernia*, 12–25 September 1969; 19 December 1969–8 January 1970.

portfolio he held from 1961 to 1966 – Boland threatened not to serve in Cabinet. Lynch then agreed that Boland should combine the two posts – a concession that made no sense, given the heavy workloads associated with both departments. Lynch proposed to split the Local Government portfolio by creating a new department with responsibility for housing, construction and physical planning, under Neil Blaney, who would also continue as Minister for Agriculture – another key department.[122] This messy compromise, which appeared unworkable – there was a case for a separate housing minister, but not as a joint ministry with agriculture – undermined Lynch's authority. Hillery's biographer described some Cabinet ministers as operating 'like feudal barons from an earlier age, acknowledging only the most grudging fealty to a distant and barely tolerated overlord'.[123] Boland and Blaney were powerful figures within Fianna Fáil. They held key roles in election campaigns – especially by-elections– and were officer-holders within the party – activities which gave them independent power bases and influence and had earned them the loyalty and support of many TDs. In 1968, *Hibernia* – no fan of Blaney's – claimed that 'If any other politicians has as much influence as Neil Blaney it is a well-kept secret'; he ensured that party members were appointed as 'judges … rate collectors, sub-postmasters, state solicitors, road gangers, contractors of all description, police of high rank; army officers; directors of state bodies, county managers etc.'. Blaney had 'resolutely undermined the NFA and its sources of power and support' even cancelling Department of Agriculture advertisements in the *Irish Farmers' Journal*.[124]

The fault-lines within Lynch's government opened in the months following the outbreak of violence in Northern Ireland in August 1969, culminating in the Arms Crisis in May 1970, when four Cabinet ministers and one parliamentary secretary were either dismissed or resigned. While events in Northern Ireland precipitated open divisions, the government was deeply factionalised even before that crisis; indeed, the roots can be traced back to Lemass' government. By 1969, it was evident that the mould of Irish party politics would not break. The existing parties would survive, though all were deeply divided on various issues. When faced with a choice between change and continuity, modernisation and tradition, all three parties compromised, veering more towards continuity than change. All three parties could be described as internal coalitions, with factions representing both continuity and change.

[122] Keogh, *Jack Lynch*, pp. 158–61; DD, 241, 2 July cols. 23–4.
[123] Walsh, *Patrick Hillery*, pp. 167–70.   [124] *Hibernia*, April 1968.

From the national to the local: the continuing strength of the parish pump

One explanation for continuity in Irish electoral politics can be found in the micro details: the candidates and what voters sought from their TDs. Although the 1960s were marked by significant generational change – evident in the number of by-elections caused by the death of sitting TDs – this was combined with strong familial continuity. By 1965, forty-one TDs, more than one-quarter of the total, were related to former or current elected representatives, including four widows, twenty-seven sons, one daughter, six nephews, one brother and one brother-in law.[125] *Hibernia* titled an article on the 1964 Galway by-election, when John Donnellan, son of the deceased TD, was returned, 'Another family seat in the Dáil'. John Whyte suggested that the practice of nominating close relatives of deceased deputies in by-elections had grown from a former 'trickle' to a 'flood'. 'At every single by-election in the present Dáil, a near relative of the TD whose death has caused the vacancy has stood as a candidate'.[126] Most female deputies were widows of former TDs. Dynastic succession was not limited to the rank and file. Lemass' 1965 Cabinet included his son-in-law, Charles Haughey, and George Colley, Kevin Boland and Neil Blaney – all sons of former deputies. One of Jack Lynch's liabilities as leader of Fianna Fáil was a lack of family connections with the party or the struggle for independence. In 1965, Fine Gael leader James Dillon, son of a former leader of the Irish Party, was succeeded by Liam Cosgrave, son of a former head of government; the leading ranks of Fine Gael included Declan Costello, son of a former Taoiseach and Garret FitzGerald, son of a former Cabinet minister. Labour leader Brendan Corish succeeded his father as a TD for Wexford on the latter's death.

Brian Farrell described the members of the 1969 Dáil as 'a small tightly-knit political elite'; 'so many of these "heirs" are related to former ministers of state'.[127] The other common routes to electoral success (now that service in the war of independence no longer applied) were sport, especially Gaelic games, and local government. Fifteen per cent of those elected in 1965, including Jack Lynch, were well-known GAA stars. On the eve of the 1969 general election, one sports columnist suggested that 'All going well the GAA could have in the region of thirty members in the new Dáil.' This was a conservative prediction. Farrell identified four current GAA officials, fifteen star players and a further twenty-five who were currently or formerly active in the GAA, among the elected

---

[125] John Whyte, *Dáil Deputies. Their work; its difficulties; possible remedies* (Dublin: Tuairim, 1966), p. 31.
[126] *Hibernia*, January 1965.   [127] Farrell, 'the 1969 generation', p. 320.

TDs.[128] Local connections were more critical than in the past. By the 1960s, three-quarters of TDs lived in their constituencies, and over 60 per cent were born there – whereas some members of the revolutionary generation, notably de Valera, never lived in their constituency or held clinics. Seventy per cent of the 1965 Dáil had experience in local government; 55 per cent were members of local authorities before their first election to Dáil Éireann.[129] By 1971, at least two-thirds of deputies were current or former members of local authorities.[130] Bax noted that the men who succeeded 'the revolutionary elite ... lack a national record with which to attract supporters. Therefore, they, more than their predecessors, are compelled to build up a following by rendering as many services as possible'.[131] This linkage between local authority membership and success in Dáil elections developed after the Second World War, when political parties became important in local politics – paradoxically, as the power of local authorities was reduced.[132]

'The parish pump has long been the true symbol of the "hidden Ireland" '.[133] Theo Hoppen made this statement, when writing about mid-nineteenth century Ireland, but his observation is equally applicable to the 1960s. In 1961, when the Dáil was in session, Michael Carty, Fianna Fáil TD for Galway East and chairman of Galway County Council met 10–20 constituents every Sunday from after Mass until 2 pm; on Mondays, he met approximately 200 constituents from 10 am until 8 pm.[134] Chubb determined that approximately half of the questions tabled in the Dáil or Seanad 'are clearly and explicitly personal or local and many more have some bearing on a local interest of the questioner'.[135] A 1964 questionnaire asking TDs about the most satisfactory and the most burdensome aspects of their role confirmed the dominance of local, clientelist matters: 55 of the 109 who replied listed 'Achieving something for constituents; helping those in need and other comment relating to service to constituents' as the most satisfactory aspect of their work, while forty-five of eighty-seven respondents identified 'doing errands for constituents, having them call at inconvenient times, being unable to help them when he is in need, trying to persuade them that they have no grievance, writing

---

[128] *SP*, 8 June 1969 quoted by Farrell, 'the 1969 generation', p. 321.
[129] Whyte, *Dáil Deputies*, Appendix, pp. 30–1.
[130] Farrell, 'the 1969 generation', p. 320.   [131] Bax, *Harpstrings and confessions*, p 188.
[132] Paul Sacks, *The Donegal Mafia. An Irish political machine* (New Haven and London: Yale University Press, 1976), p. 62.
[133] Hoppen, *Elections, politics, and society in Ireland*, p. 436.
[134] Evidence given to High Court case regarding the ratio of TDs to voters in rural Ireland, reported in *IT*, 12 January 1961, as cited by Basil Chubb, 'Going about persecuting civil servants', *Political Studies*, vol. 11, 1963, p. 281.
[135] Chubb, 'Going about persecuting civil servants', p. 280.

letter, etc.' as the most burdensome aspect. Party differences were not significant. One deputy complained about 'those who make unreasonable demands, or are suffering from imaginary grievances, or who think things can be got by "pull" '.[136]

Chubb titled an article about the working lives of TD, 'Going about persecuting civil servants'. Yet, civil servants were equally complicit: their letters to TDs in response to constituency queries came with a carbon copy attached (this was in the days before photocopying), which could be forwarded to the constituent. Most public sector jobs were filled by open recruitment based on examinations or interviews, and not by patronage; the exceptions were rate collectors, postmen, road workers and messengers. Medical cards and some other welfare benefits were discretionary and therefore open to influence. Chubb quotes a senator who expressed alarm that applications for old age pensions, children's allowances and other statutory entitlements were channelled through TDs.[137] Could this possibly reflect low literacy standards, or complex application forms? Paul Sacks, who studied constituency politics in north-east Donegal, concluded that there was a high element of 'symbolic patronage'.[138] TDs acted as brokers between voters and public bodies; Chubb described their role as 'local spokesman, ombudsman and influence peddler'.[139]

A TD ignored constituency business at his peril. Former diplomat and intellectual, Conor Cruise O'Brien, who was elected as Labour TD for Dublin-North-East in 1969, was the antithesis of the traditional constituency politician; yet, his papers contain correspondence relating to dental treatment for a child, requests to find a job in Dublin in catering or a hotel, for somebody from provincial Ireland, and a letter from a constituent who wished to join the garda síochána.[140] Donncha Ó Briain, first elected as Fianna Fáil TD for Limerick West in 1933, was a more traditional politician, interested only in the Irish language, and his constituency. In 1961, one constituent asked his assistance in securing a job with the state-owned Irish Sugar Company, and whereas there is no evidence that Cruise O'Brien took any steps with regard to job requests, Ó Briain wrote to the CEO, M. J. Costello, who reported that the candidate did not meet the required standard, but recommended that he apply for another vacant position, though he would have to be interviewed. Ó Briain contacted the matron of a Dublin hospital on behalf a young woman, who was seeking a trainee place; the matron indicated that

---

[136] Whyte, *Dáil Deputies*, pp. 8–10.
[137] Chubb, 'Going about persecuting civil servants', pp. 278–9.
[138] Sacks, *Donegal Mafia*, p. 100; Farrell, 'Dáil deputies', p. 124.
[139] Bax, *Harpstrings and confessions*, pp. 50–2.
[140] UCDA Conor Cruise O'Brien Papers, P82/186 – constituency matters 1969–1973.

she did not meet the required educational standard. Although his constituency business was dominated by pensions, and land distribution – as
it had been for decades – there were signs of change, such as his involvement in a meeting between the Drumcollogher and District Development
Association and the Department of Education. The Development
Association wanted to recruit a part-time ceramics teacher, in the hope
of developing a local industry. Ó Briain also responded to protests by the
Newcastle West Chamber of Commerce against the introduction of turnover tax. A letter from a nun on behalf of her niece, who had applied for a
place on the domestic science teacher training course in Sion Hill, reflects
a widespread belief in the importance of patronage: 'Could you use your
influence . . . I'm sure all the other candidates too will need influence to
get called to training'. 'In this particular examination the examiners like to
know the circumstances and background of the candidate, and a word in
her favour from you would mean a great deal.'[141]

Most representations to Cruise O'Brien related to housing and local
services; there was an acute housing shortage in Dublin and his constituency included several new estates. There were letters from men who had
returned from England but were unable to find housing for their families;
requests for transfers from a Corporation flat or house, to another area.
Residents associations contacted him about unfinished estates, lack of a
bus service, traffic bollards, inadequate fire and ambulance services, lack
of open space, or protesting that open spaces were being developed for
housing or commercial purposes. The majority of representations related
to matters controlled by the local authority, not Dáil Éireann.[142] This
appears to have been the norm: one Fianna Fáil TD claimed to spend 50
per cent of his time on local authority matters.[143] Competition within
multi-seat constituencies forced TDs to keep up to the mark, regardless of
whether a constituent's representation was a matter for the local authorities or a government department. Chubb claimed that 'a candidate
cannot fight his fellow party candidates on policy; he tries to rival them
in service'.[144] The 1969 general election in Clare 'was as much a contest'
between Minister for Labour Patrick Hillery and fellow Fianna Fáil
candidate, local auctioneer Sylvester Barrett 'as it was between Fianna
Fáil and the fragmented forces of the Opposition'.[145] One man who
lobbied Cruise O'Brien about some unspecified matter relating to the
Department of Industry and Commerce responded to his letter: 'I note
you are not very sanguine as to the reply you may get to your

[141] UCDA Donncha Ó Briain Papers, P 83/120.   [142] UCDA P82/186.
[143] Donegal NE TD Liam Cunningham, quoted in Sacks, *Donegal Mafia*, p. 70.
[144] Chubb, 'Going about persecuting civil servants', p. 284.
[145] Walsh, *Patrick Hillery*, p. 163.

representations on my behalf. However in addition to you a number of Fianna Fáil deputies have taken this matter up for me and something may yet result.'[146] A friend of Donncha Ó Briain warned him that 'Mick has some kind of craze for writing letters to TDs and Ministers and Union officials. Don't take any notice of anymore of his letters, burn them.'[147] But few deputies would take this risk.

Fianna Fáil had the most proficient and extensive support for constituency representations; Garvin concluded that in Dublin South-Central – a constituency with a mixed social background – the party had 'twice as many caseworkers as Labour and nearly four times as many as Fine Gael'. Fine Gael's lack of engagement reflected the fact that its core middle-class vote needed less assistance in dealing with government agencies.[148] Liam Cosgrave never held a clinic, relying on councillors and party members to do this work.[149] But candidates ignored constituency service at their peril. The Fine Gael inquest after the 1961 general election concluded that 'Dublin was disappointing. We ought to have done much better there ... candidates were little known and time too short to make themselves better known. The moral seems to be that potential candidates will have to work in the constituency long before an election. Another cause of relatively poor showing in Dublin is that Deputies have shown little interest in the affairs of their constituencies – the whole future in Dublin depends on a greater show of activity by Dublin deputies.' Candidates should be 'in the field in good time ... Deputies and senators must be more active, travel through their constituencies frequently, ventilate the grievances of their constituents in Dáil Éireann or local councils and the local press'.[150] But a review of the party's performance after the 1965 general election suggests that little had changed. 'Only 14 [of a total of 38] constituencies had selected candidates before the election was announced ... Directives and advice to have the candidates selected and in the field were ignored.' There was a long delay in getting the campaign underway in some constituencies 'because of poor organisation, and slothful, negligent officials'.[151] As TDs had no secretarial support, most of O'Brien's correspondence was handled by his wife, likewise his fellow Labour TD Barry Desmond. A Labour Party 'clinic' in Liberty Hall run by the ITGWU assisted TDs who were sponsored by the union. The O'Brien and Ó Briain archives reveal some of the hidden costs of being a TD. Conor Cruise O'Brien made numerous donations to local groups, such as the Clontarf Lawn Tennis Club, GAA clubs, an Old Folks Society, a school

---

[146] UCDA P82/186.   [147] UCDA P83/120.
[148] Garvin, 'Political parties in a Dublin constituency', pp. 153–4.
[149] Desmond, *Finally and in conclusion*, pp. 44–5.
[150] UCDA, P 39/GE 94 (1) 8 November 1961.   [151] P 39/GE 125 1965 campaign.

for children with special needs, and other voluntary organisations. Donncha Ó Briain acted as guarantor for a number of small bank loans to constituents: one woman, who made recurring demands of this nature, repeatedly assured him that this would be the last. A wife tried to engage his support in persuading her husband that he must sign over the family farm before he could qualify for an old age pension: 'If you could convince him while he has the farm that he hasn't a chance.'[152] At one of his first constituency clinics, a week after he was elected, a woman presented Des O'Malley with her television licence, which had expired, and explained that his late uncle Donogh had 'always paid it for me'.[153] Fianna Fáil TD Padraig Faulkner, first elected in 1957, was occasionally offered payment 'in cash or in kind' by constituents he had assisted, which he declined; some callers to his clinic asked for loans.[154] Barry Desmond was one of many deputies who sent numerous Christmas cards – 'All my Labour colleagues at national level, the secretary and chairperson of every resi-dents' association, all old folks groups, sports, clubs, county council and corporation staffs, local party members of whom there were 150 and a wide circle of friends received a card . . . personally signed.'[155] Fine Gael constituency files for Roscommon contain copies of numerous letters of sympathy to constituents on the death of a close relative, despatched by party Secretary Commandant Sanfey at the request of Joan Burke TD.[156]

Local and constituency issues did not become less relevant; indeed, they may well have become more important during these years. In a stagnant economy, with limited social welfare provisions, the scope for political representation was obviously limited – though perhaps for that reason, a temporary job as a local authority labourer, or entitlement to discretionary home assistance was important. But by early 1970s, the scope for political representations was expanding – both in relation to individual voters and the constituency – with prospects now emerging for planning permission, industrial estates, new factories or grants for local small industries, plus a greater range of benefits, many of them means-tested or requiring some degree of verification – all grist to the politician's mill. These new possibilities for patronage coincided with the rising cost of election campaigns – more sophisticated postering and media cam-paigns – all demanding greater funding. The traditional source of party funding, the annual church-gate collection was no longer adequate to

---

[152] P83/120; Desmond, *Finally and in conclusion*, p. 38.
[153] O'Malley, *Conduct unbecoming*, p. 32.
[154] Padraig Faulkner, *As I saw it. Reviewing over 30 years of Fianna Fáil and Irish politics* (Dublin: Wolfhound, 2005), p. 37.
[155] Desmond, *Finally and in conclusion*, p. 42.
[156] UCDA Fine Gael Papers, P39/C/RL 9 and 10.

support a major political campaign. In 1964, the Fianna Fáil national collection raised a record £23,606, a figure not achieved against until 1967,[157] but insufficient to support a professional media and organisation team. Lemass oversaw the establishment of a new fund-raising committee chaired by Dublin businessman John Reihill, which contacted companies who might contribute to party funds.[158] In 1966, the party put this operation on a more systematic basis, with the creation of Taca – a fundraising organisation with an annual membership fee of £100. The 500 subscribers were promised opportunities to meet leading members of the party at dinners and other social gatherings. In 1969, an election year, journalist Michael Mc Inerney estimated that Taca raised £40,000, which was equivalent to the proceeds of the annual collection.[159] Taca, which was operated from an office in Dublin's Burlington Hotel, reflected a more overt relationship between the party in government and business, especially property developers. Des O'Malley claimed that it was 'dominated by builders and property developers as well as ambitious ancillaries of that industry, such as architects, solicitors, quantity surveyors, and engineers'.[160] Although many members of Fianna Fáil were uncomfortable about the image that it presented, the 1968 Ard Fheis (annual conference) rejected a resolution calling for its abolition. A decision was taken to bring it under the control of a committee appointed by the national executive, and membership was broadened by reducing the minimum annual donation to a modest £5 with a maximum of £100.[161] While these changes may have diffused internal party tensions, Fianna Fáil continued to receive significant financial support from businessmen; 'the party just found more discreet ways of doing it'.[162]

Funding was more precarious in the Labour party. In 1970, the party appealed to members to contribute to central funds: 'A modern political organisation depends almost as much on activity generated at a central level as it does on constituency organisation.' They were urged to make a voluntary contribution of one shilling a month (twice the price of a daily newspaper) in aid of head office; the other fund-raising activity proposed was a raffle.[163] A cursory comparison between fundraising by political parties and the Catholic Church shows that the latter was much more effective at raising money, though by the 1960s both were under pressure. The Labour party accounts in Dublin-North-East, probably for 1970, show total income of just over £300, half coming from the local TD; a

---

[157] Figures taken from P 176 – successive Ard Fheiseanna files.
[158] Horgan, *Lemass*, p. 330.   [159] Byrne, *Political corruption in Ireland*, p. 89.
[160] O'Malley, *Conduct unbecoming*, p. 39.
[161] P176/348 11 November 1968; 10 December 1968.
[162] Dunlop, *Yes, Taoiseach*, p. 18.   [163] UCDA P82/122.

raffle raised £29, branches contributed £4–£5 each but several made no contribution.[164] The lack of reliable funding left Labour heavily dependent on the trade unions, and their sponsorship of candidates. It made it more difficult to discipline recalcitrant candidates, who might be in a financial position to run an election campaign. One such example was Limerick TD Steve Coughlan, who, despite making outrageously racist comments about Jews and apartheid in South Africa, was permitted to stand as a Labour candidate.[165]

Continuities

In 1958, John A. Costello, who was Taoiseach from 1948 to 1951 and 1954 to 1957 mused about the future shape of Irish politics.

Who can tell what will happen here when Deputy de Valera, the present Taoiseach, either retires or dies? What conditions shall we have?

We are coming to the end of an era. We do not know how Parties may split up. We do not know how the electorate may transfer their allegiance. There may very well be what I might describe, not with any over-emphasis, as a Radical Party. Certainly, in a few years there will be a break-up of the present political Parties. God alone knows what will be the result . . .

We have had experience over the last few years of the political apathy, cynicism and disillusion which exist throughout the country . . . We are now on the threshold of a radical change. Members on both sides of the House who took part in the Treaty controversies and subsequently in the Civil War are not far off, however many years they may still have before them, from their end certainly as active politicians.

The young people are coming on, desirous of forgetting these conflicts and controversies, forming new ideas, looking to the future and not to the past, indeed not even interested in the past for inspiration. What will happen?[166]

What happened was that the parties that were prominent in 1958 survived, though the personnel had changed, as had the style of electioneering and some elements of their electoral support base (This was particularly so with respect to Labour which finally became an urban party.) But the choice for voters – if they were given a choice, which they weren't in 1961, 1965 or 1969 – was between a Fine Gael/Labour Coalition and Fianna Fáil, who had defied predictions by surviving the departure of de Valera, and securing overall majorities in both 1965 and 1969. This had not been expected. In 1959 and again in 1968, Fianna

---

[164] UCDA P82/90 Constituency Finances.
[165] Purséil, *The Irish Labour Party*, pp. 278–9, 294.
[166] DD, vol. 171, cols. 1025–6, 26 November 1958: Third Amendment of the Constitution Bill, 1958, second stage, John A. Costello.

Fáil held referendums to change the electoral system from multi-seat proportional representation to a British-style 'first past the post', in the belief that only this change could ensure the continuation of single-party governments. The electorate defeated this proposal twice; on the first occasion by a relatively narrow margin. A referendum in 1959 was defeated by 33,000 votes: the rural majority in favour of change was more than offset by a strong no vote in Dublin and Cork cities, where a trade union campaign in favour of PR may have determined the outcome.[167] Given that de Valera was elected President by a margin of 120,000 over Fine Gael candidate, Seán MacEoin, the outcome suggests that voters made a conscious decision to stick with the existing system. In the 1968 referendum, Jack Lynch tried to play the economy card, arguing that strong single party government was necessary to support economic expansion. PR was unlikely to deliver this; indeed might make it impossible to form a government. But that referendum was doomed when political scientists Basil Chubb and David Thornley presented their calculations on the current affairs programme *Seven Days*, showing that a re-run of the 1965 general election with single- member constituencies and a single vote, would result in a Fianna Fáil landslide – ninety-three seats (compared with seventy-two in 1965).[168] Lynch told John Bowman some years later that these forecasts 'with certainty killed our aspirations about the change in the system'.[169] There is an irony in this outcome, given that Chubb and Thornley were highly critical of the clientelist politics fostered by Ireland's multi-seat constituencies. There is a real possibility that the electoral system might have been changed, if de Valera or Lynch had opted for the compromise of single-seat constituencies and transferable votes. In 1959, Fine Gael Deputy James Dillon – soon to become leader – supported this option; Labour TD Patrick Norton attempted to have it added to the ballot in 1968. A number of political scientists favoured the single transferable vote.[170] Such an outcome might have reduced the impact of clientelist politics and strengthened the hand of national parties.

But in 1973, the political parties carried the same names as in the 1950s, and many of the family names remained the same. Personalities, family connections, local constituents' interests remained the dominant forces in electoral politics, partly because of the survival of multi-party constituencies. The primacy of the personal helps to explain why no

---

[167] O'Leary, *Irish elections*, pp. 57–8.
[168] Muiris MacConghail, '"He boxed light in the interview but intended to land a punch"': David Thornley at RTE, 1966–69', in Yseult Thornley (ed.), *Unquiet spirit. Essays in memory of David Thornley* (Dublin: Liberties Press, 2008), pp. 122–3.
[169] Bowman, *Window and mirror*, p. 74.
[170] O'Leary, *Irish elections*, pp. 68–9; Garret FitzGerald, *IT*, 15 April 1965.

major realignment of the main political parties occurred, and why the parties survived often despite significant internal policy differences. By 1973 Irish politicians were expected to deliver strong personal service to voters – assisting them in securing pensions, medical cards, and housing grants, as they had done for many years. But politicians were now saddled with wider expectations on the part of voters – additional benefits, lower taxes, rising incomes, even the abolition of an unpopular tax such as rates. Minister for Finance George Colley's announcement of a planned budget deficit in 1972, the first in the history of the state, can be seen as an opening gambit in the anticipated general election. Lynch's government no longer had a majority in Dáil Éireann, and he wanted to go to the country before the new electoral register, came into effect, giving votes to eighteen- to twenty-one-year-olds, because this was expected to favour Labour. For the first time in more than a decade, voters had a real choice of government. Within days of the election being called, the Fine Gael and Labour leaders had signed a 'statement of intent', which emphasised that there was a national crisis and a change of government was needed. They set out a manifesto for a 'modern and progressive society'. While Fianna Fáil initially tried to campaign on a slogan of 'Progress and Stability', their claim to offer the only prospect of stable government lacked credibility. In the end, the election was fought on domestic issues, as both potential governments competed with promises to cut (Fine Gael/Labour) or abolish (Fianna Fáil) rates; remove VAT on food (Fine Gael/Labour) and improve social benefits – all parties included. Only 12 per cent of those sampled identified Northern Ireland as the most important issue, compared with 28 per cent who identified inflation and 25 per cent who saw education and welfare as the most important issues.[171] The major impact of a growing economy on electoral politics was the expectation on the part of voters and political parties that elections would involve competing offers of material benefits.

---

[171] Richard Sinnott, *Irish voters decide. Voting behaviour in elections and referendums since 1918* (Manchester, 1995), pp. 177–8.

13   International relations

The overriding sense of Ireland in the years after the Second World War is of semi-detachment from the Western world. Neutrality in the Second World War – a decision taken to ensure the stability of the new state – had significant long-term costs, including delayed entry to the UN, and lingering resentment, even hostility on the part of British and US politicians and officials. By comparison, the government of Northern Ireland undoubtedly gained sympathy and influence from its wartime service. The immediate post-war years were marked by an anti-partition campaign that engaged all the main political parties, and for a time partition appeared to constitute Ireland's overriding foreign policy issue. The campaign was predicated on the belief that partition could be ended by putting pressure on Britain, using all international channels available. The most unrealistic instance of this was when the First Inter-Party Government of 1948–1951 rejected an invitation to join NATO, in the mistaken belief that it was possible to bargain NATO membership in return for a US commitment to bring pressure on Britain to end partition, a gross misreading of Anglo-American relations, and one that reinforced Ireland's post-war isolation.[1] Reading key documents relating to Irish foreign policy in the early 1950s today leaves an overriding impression of unreality. Ireland's self-absorbed preoccupation with partition, the Vatican and Catholic Church concerns shows no serious appreciation of the threats to world peace, the devastating aftermath of the Second World War, or the long-term damage to Ireland's international reputation resulting from war-time neutrality.[2] John Horgan notes that 'In the minds of the populace at large, neutrality rapidly became elevated to a principle', whereas government files reveal 'that behind much of the official posturing on neutrality the concept was regarded by those in power as a

---

[1] Ronan Fanning, 'Irish neutrality: an historical review', *ISIA*, vol. I, no. 3, 1982, pp. 34–6
[2] Catriona Crowe, Ronan Fanning, Michael Kennedy, Dermot Keogh, Eunan O'Halpin and Kate O' Malley (eds), *Documents in Irish Foreign Policy, VII* (Dublin, 2014).

highly tradeable commodity'.[3] Ireland's neutrality was highly ambiguous – not a NATO member, yet firmly anti-communist, and, as Salmon emphasises, unlike Switzerland or Sweden, it was not enforced by a strong army.[4] Wylie describes Ireland's efforts to claim an independent position in foreign policy as 'more erratic than reasoned, almost schizophrenic'.[5]

Semi-detachment characterised Ireland's relationship with Western Europe. There was a decided lack of engagement with Marshall Aid and a failure to make full use of these funds and related programmes to transform the economy. Ireland was slow in grasping the significance of OEEC moves towards a European free trade area, or the political significance of organisations such as the European Coal and Steel Community and the EEC. The failure to engage with these international organisations reflected a continuing attachment to economic self-sufficiency plus the fact that international economic relations remained almost exclusively focused on Britain, and Irish semi-detachment mirrored Britain's. Neutrality and geography – an island off the west coast of Europe, remote from any imminent threat of Soviet invasion – left the country at a physical and mental distance from the tensions of the Cold War. This safe location appears to have attracted some German settlers to Ireland; it also fostered a relaxed attitude towards the nuclear threat. While British youth marched to 'ban the bomb', this was of little immediate concern to Ireland.[6] The 1957 fire at Windscale, a nuclear reprocessing plant on the west coast of England, was reported in the newspapers, but primarily as a British story, with no attention given to the potential threat that it might pose to Ireland, though this became a significant issue many decades later.[7] While newspapers and radio/television reported on the shooting down of Gary Powers' U2 mission, the Berlin Wall and other incidents that increased the threat of a thermo-nuclear war, they all seemed rather remote. The most immediate local impact came in the form of photos of Nikita Khruschev, secretary-general of the USSR Communist Party, banging his shoe in temper during the 1960 UN General Assembly and being called to order by the chairman,

---

[3] John Horgan, 'Irish foreign policy, Northern Ireland, neutrality and the commonwealth: the historical roots of a current controversy', *ISIA*, vol. 10, 1999, pp. 136–7.

[4] Trevor Salmon, *Unneutral Ireland: an ambivalent and unique security policy* (Oxford: Oxford University Press, 1989).

[5] Paula Wylie, *Ireland and the Cold War: diplomacy and recognition, 1949–63* (Dublin: Irish Academic Press, 2006), p. 29.

[6] An anti-nuclear movement does not emerge until the late 1970s when there were plans to construct a nuclear power station at Carnsore Point in county Wexford.

[7] The story was covered in the *Irish Press*, *Irish Independent*, *Irish Times* and the *Irish Farmer's Journal*, which was the only newspaper to mention any possible consequence for Ireland from the release of radiation. Most stories concerned the ban on milk from neighbouring farms. *IP*, 16, 28 October 1957; *IFJ*, 16 November 1957.

Irish diplomat Freddie Boland, who broke his gavel.[8] Irish school children, unlike their US counterparts, did not practice what to do in the event of a nuclear attack. In 1960, Radio Éireann planned to broadcast a programme highlighting the lack of preparation in the event of a nuclear explosion. It would open with the sounds of a hydrogen bomb, exploding on central Dublin, before going on to discuss the implications with civil defence personnel. The script, by Proinsias MacAonghusa, included the statement: 'You people in Galway – you people in Cork, you people in Antrim – you people in Dublin – and your children will die a horrible death. This is the belief of many thousands of experts.' The programme was withdrawn following complaints from the Department of Defence; one official noted that 'while he appreciated the need for the producer to adopt a neutral attitude, the general effect of the programme must be to impress people favourably with Civil Defence'.[9] While the controversy is almost amusing, and an indication of the extent of government control of the state broad-casting station, it also reflects Irish isolation from the major global/ European issues of the period. Television began to spread throughout Ireland from 1962, but it was only in 1966 that a majority of households had a television set; television undoubtedly made people more aware of international events. Newspaper coverage of foreign stories was generally taken from international news agencies. In the days before television, popular knowledge of the world beyond Western Europe and North America often came through religious magazines, slide shows and talks by visiting Irish missionaries trying to raise funds or recruit candidates to religious life. Religious magazines and sermons highlighted their version of the Cold War; stories of missionaries suffering Communist persecution featured prominently in popular Catholic and Irish discourse during the post-war years, though they faded during the more liberal 1960s.

Once Ireland determined to abandon protectionism and apply for EEC membership, Ireland's international relations necessarily had to change: the impact was not limited to the economy; indeed, any close analysis of post-war international relations reveals the vital importance of econom-ics, trade and finance, and their interaction with more narrowly political issues. The obsession with partition of the early 1950s receded, and economic development and EEC membership became the paramount foreign policy concerns. Salmon suggests that 'In the period 1956–72, therefore, the Irish had to wrestle with their equivocation between what might be termed two foreign policies, the one reflecting their aspiration

---

[8] Michael Kennedy, 'Persuade an alternative European candidate to stand', in Michael Kennedy and Deirdre McMahon (eds), *Obligations and responsibilities: Ireland and the United Nations, 1955–2005* (Dublin: Institute of Public Administration, 2005), pp. 172–3.

[9] NAI DT S33532C/63.

for "neutrality" and "non-alignment" and the other pragmatic and aimed at promoting material prosperity'.[10] But 'neutrality' and 'non-alignment' was always a rather quixotic goal – though one that continued to feature in many speeches by Irish politicians. Ireland was finally admitted to the UN in 1955 on a list of Western nations, which was carefully balanced by an equal number of countries in the Soviet sphere of influence, as part of a sixteen nation deal negotiated between East and West.[11] During the first year of membership when the Second Inter-Party Government (a Fine Gael/Labour Coalition) was in office, Ireland voted in line with the Western powers. This changed in 1957 when Fianna Fáil returned to office. In 1957, Aiken voted to discuss admitting China to the UN. This change in Ireland's position was not signalled in advance to the US authorities; it brought the wrath of New York's Cardinal Francis Spellman down on the Irish delegation and gave rise to protests from strongly anti-Communist Irish-Americans.[12] Aiken was not wholly in sympathy with the United States and its policies – this had been the case also during the Second World War. He adopted the United Nations as his pet project, remaining in New York for the entire autumn session – the only foreign minister to do so. This was highly unusual at a time when Irish ministers made few overseas trips, and it smacks of self-indulgence, though perhaps Lemass was more comfortable with Aiken – a maverick politician – several thousand miles from home. Working closely with Conor Cruise O'Brien – Counsellor to the UN mission – Aiken adopted a much more independent line on key issues, but there is a degree of fantasy about this independent stance. While NATO members did not regard Ireland as wholly supportive of the Western Alliance, the USSR placed the country firmly in the western camp. Ireland was not invited to attend the first non-aligned summit in Belgrade in 1961, and never attended any meetings of this group, which Ireland regarded as sympathetic to Communism.[13] Nevertheless, for a brief period in the late 1950s, Ireland could claim to occupy an independent position, between two hostile blocks – Western countries/NATO members, and Soviet allies, part of a tiny minority belonging to neither group. In 1957, there were few UN members from sub-Saharan Africa, few former colonies. The balance of power changed significantly in 1960 when sixteen African countries – all former colonies – were admitted, heralding the emergence of a more conscious non-aligned group of Asian and African countries. Regardless

---

[10] Salmon, *Unneutral Ireland*, p. 4
[11] Joseph Skelly, 'Ireland, the department of external affairs and the United Nations, 1946–55: a new look', *ISIA*, vol. 7, 1996, pp. 63–80.
[12] NAI DT S16057 Foreign policy general file.
[13] Salmon, *Unneutral Ireland*, pp. 202–3

of Irish statements about neutrality, and speeches recalling that Ireland
had for centuries been occupied by a foreign power, and therefore shared
'a sense of brotherhood with the newly emerging peoples of today',[14]
these former colonies viewed Ireland as a Western power. However, even
if the balance of power at the UN had not shifted, it is highly probable that
Ireland's independent foreign policy would have been reined in, as part of
the efforts to promote Ireland's case for EEC membership.

In June 1961, the Gallup organisation conducted the first public opinion poll carried out in Ireland. The primary purpose of the poll, which
was commissioned by the *Irish Press* – a newspaper controlled by the de
Valera family – was to collect information about knowledge and attitudes
towards the EEC in advance of Ireland's application for membership.
The poll also asked about Ireland's international relationships; 95 per
cent of respondents regarded a close relationship with Britain as important; 89 per cent said likewise about relations with the United States and
62 per cent about relations with Europe. Asked about Ireland's most
important relationship, 62 per cent identified Britain, 29 per cent the
United States, 1 per cent said others and 5 per cent saw relations with no
country as important. The importance attached to Anglo-Irish relations
was highlighted by the fact that 38 per cent would oppose Ireland joining
the EEC without Britain, and only 36 per cent would be in favour.[15]
Voters regarded a close relationship with the United States and the
United Kingdom as critical to Ireland's future; such views were somewhat
at variance with efforts to craft an independent foreign policy.

Ireland–US relations – from partition to investment

The shift in relative priorities between anti-partition and economic development is clearly evident in Ireland's relationship with the United States,
where attracting US industrial investment, export orders and tourists
emerged as key priorities, which might involve some distancing from
traditional Irish-American groups, who remained preoccupied with
bringing an end to partition, and supportive of the IRA's border campaign. In 1958, Irish consulates in the United States were asked to submit
reports on the economic influence of the Irish community, an exercise
that appears to have been carried out as part of the pre-planning for
Economic Development. John Conway, consul-general in New York

---

[14] Aiken, October 1960, as cited by Joseph Skelly, *Irish diplomacy at the United Nations,
1945–1965: national interests and the international order* (Dublin: Irish Academic Press,
1997), pp. 21–2.
[15] The poll was given extensive coverage in *IP*, 11–13 July 1961; the detailed results
appeared on 12 July 1961.

claimed that the Irish carried little political or economic influence. The number of residents of Irish birth was falling rapidly; 'influence solely through them is a diminishing possibility'. Although recent emigrants had a somewhat higher economic status than earlier generations, it was probably below the general average, 'although by no means poor by Irish or, for that matter, British standards'. The County Clubs, the main organizations for Irish immigrants, had only 'a few thousand' members, and attendance at social events, such as annual dances, was falling. Membership was overwhelmingly drawn from blue-collar workers; the clubs made no real effort to attract professional and white-collar immigrants. Conway believed that the leadership and membership of County Clubs carried 'little economic or social weight'. Relations between the County Clubs and the consulate were poor, because the Irish Institute, which acted as an effective headquarters for the clubs, disagreed with the government's tough stance towards the IRA's border campaign (Operation Harvest) and its director – Mayo-born lawyer Paul O'Dwyer, brother of former New York Mayor, William O'Dwyer – had adopted an attitude towards the Dublin government that was 'unfriendly and at times even offensive'. Conway claimed that most members of the county clubs shared O'Dwyer's attitude. He lamented the absence of a non-political organisation 'of a middle-class social or cultural nature' that would attract professional and white-collar emigrants. Because no such organization existed, the influence of middle-class Irish immigrants was 'scattered and virtually valueless'.[16]

The election of John F. Kennedy as President of the United States reinforced the wish to focus attention on successful Irish-Americans, often second- or third-generation emigrants. Kennedy was of 100 per cent Irish ancestry; his family had achieved major successes in business and politics. Irish newspapers welcomed his election, though the emphasis was as much on his youth and his Catholicism, as on his Irishness.[17] T. J. Kiernan, the Irish ambassador to the United States, described Kennedy as 'the first Irish President of the US'[18] – a comment that ignores the many US Presidents of Ulster Scots ancestry. Yet, the Irish authorities were cautious about inviting Kennedy to visit his ancestral country. It appears that the invitation was first issued by Dublin Lord Mayor Robert Briscoe. Kennedy's visit to Ireland in the summer of 1963 was Ireland's first modern media event. TV sales and rentals soared, business life came to a halt to watch coverage of the event, which seriously strained the fledgling TV service and Ireland's primitive telephone network. Kennedy's public appearances – in an open car,

---

[16] NAI DFA P 115/1.   [17] US Presidential inauguration, *II*, 5 January 1961.
[18] NAI DT S17401, A Kennedy Visit to Ireland.

surrounded by thousands of cheering people – recall a more innocent trusting age; they are also poignant, given his assassination in a Dallas motorcade some months later.[19] But Kennedy successfully compartmentalised his family ties to Ireland and US interests. He had a close personal relationship with British Prime Minister Harold Macmillan – a valuable European ally in the Cold War. As a young senator, Kennedy had co-sponsored a Senate resolution on partition, but when Ambassador Kiernan broached the possibility that the President might urge the British to make a public statement indicating that 'a solution of partition question is desirable from the point of view of both Britain and Ireland', Kennedy expressed the opinion that 'no British Minister would feel able to make a public statement of the kind suggested'. Kiernan added that 'He [Kennedy] is by his education, British-inclined. And in the present international conjuncture, he makes no secret of his firm attachment to Britain. So that, to raise a new issue (or renew an old issue) now when Britain has so many pressing problems to solve, is something he would avoid and would seek an alternative. He would, therefore regard our suggestion as embarrassing to the British at this troubled stage in their history.'[20] Aiken persisted in trying to use the Kennedy visit to exert pressure on Britain over partition – an indication that the post-war anti-partition mindset was not entirely dead. Kiernan was armed with forty-four pages of statements by US and other political leaders, including Gladstone, supporting the case for Irish unity, and he was urged to present these to the President, in the hope of persuading him 'to avail himself of any suitable opportunity with the British to encourage them to play their part in bringing Partition to an end'. When Kiernan raised the matter with Kennedy, and summarised some of the extracts, Kiernan reported that 'The President looked as if another headache had struck him and asked me was he expected to say anything in public. I repeated we were not asking for this but only that we hoped for his continued goodwill towards a solution of the reunification of the country.'[21] Partition did not figure at any point in Kennedy's visit.

Kennedy's visit to Ireland formed the backdrop for Lemass' US visit in September 1963, which was designed to promote US investment in Ireland and strengthen economic ties. A cover story in *Time* magazine in July provided excellent advance publicity. Lemass' agenda included lunch with Chicago business leaders and a private dinner hosted by J. Peter Grace, of W.R. Grace and company – a firm with industrial interests in Ireland – a speech at the UN General Assembly and several

---

[19] Ryan Tubridy, *JFK in Ireland* (London: Collins, 2010).
[20] NAI S17401B, Kennedy visit to Ireland Cable 19 March 1963 Kiernan to McCann.
[21] S17401B, 17 June 1963.

events with Irish-American groups, including a speech at Boston College. Journalist Dermot Mullane, who covered the trip, noted that 'Lemass's real purpose throughout has been an economic one', presenting Ireland as a destination for US investment.[22] The year 1963 also saw the formation of the Irish-American Council for Industry and Commerce which was designed to attract the prosperous influential middle-class network, whose absence was lamented in Conway's report.[23] In the process, Irish-America was redefined as a business/cultural network of men and women, whose biological links with Ireland were often distant, even non-existent.[24]

But partition could not be avoided. Lemass addressed the topic in his address to the Washington Press Club and again in Chicago, where the consul-general advised that he should do so. His Washington speech referred to the 'winds of change' – Britain's changing policies on decolonisation in Africa; he called on Britain to issue a clear statement agreeing to abandon partition of Ireland 'when Irishmen want to get rid of it'.[25] This was precisely what Kiernan had asked Kennedy to raise with Macmillan. But Lemass' statement was too moderate to placate Irish-American activists; yet, it damaged his efforts to develop a working relationship with Northern Ireland Prime Minister Terence O'Neill. In 1966, during the ceremonies marking the Golden Jubilee of the 1916 Rising, it was evident that the relationship between some Irish-American organisations and consular officials was an unhappy one. While the Irish consul-general in Chicago was speaking about economic development and 'the restoration of national unity through peace and friendship', a local Congressman celebrated the blowing-up of Dublin's Nelson's Pillar, and a possible violent campaign to end partition.[26] Nevertheless, Clan na nGael, the IRA's main support network in the United States, appeared to be a spent force. Only five Clan supporters picketed Lemass in Philadelphia, and the FBI had reduced its surveillance.[27] In 1968, new US immigration laws ended ethnic quotas, and effectively closed the door to Irish emigrants. The changes gave rise to protests in some Irish American communities, notably Boston; the Irish authorities in Washington had taken no steps to lobby against the new immigration

---

[22] *IT*, 23 October 1963.
[23] NAI DT S15245 A, B/62, B/63 Irish Chamber of Commerce in USA.
[24] Mary E. Daly, 'Nationalism, sentiment and economics: relations between Ireland and Irish-America in the postwar years', *Éire/Ireland*, vol. xxxvii, no. 1&2, 2002, pp. 86–91.
[25] *IT*, 17 October 1963.
[26] Mary E. Daly, 'Less a commemoration of the actual achievements and more a commemoration of the hopes of the men of 1916', in Mary E. Daly and Margaret O'Callaghan (eds), *1916 in 1966. Commemorating the Easter rising*, pp. 64–6.
[27] Hanley and Millar, *The lost revolution*, pp. 47–8.

laws, believing that with Ireland's prospering economy, emigration was no longer a matter of concern.[28]

Joining the EEC

When the Gallup organisation surveyed Irish opinion about EEC membership in June 1961, the returns indicated that most people had a positive attitude towards membership, though 36 per cent of those polled had never heard of the Common Market, and only 9 per cent claimed to have a good knowledge. Nevertheless, 76 per cent were in favour of membership and only 7 per cent were opposed; support was greatest among those who were better informed. Farmers were noticeably more enthusiastic than the rest of the population; 60 per cent were in favour of full membership, compared with 45 per cent of the overall poll, perhaps because farmers were better informed. Two-thirds of farmers believed that membership would bring a higher standard of living, compared with just under half of other respondents; and there were significantly fewer 'don't knows' among farmers: 6 per cent against 25 per cent. The poll asked about potential loss of sovereignty resulting from EEC membership: 39 per cent believed that the common agricultural policy and common social policies would present serious difficulties, but 52 per cent believed that gains from membership would outweigh any losses, only 10 per cent held a contrary opinion. 41 per cent of respondents regarded a united states of Europe as a good idea, only 6 per cent were opposed. Once again support was greatest among those who claimed to be better informed. But, as noted earlier, 38 per cent would oppose Ireland joining the EEC without Britain, and only 36 per cent would be in favour.[29] One of the key difficulties that Ireland faced in its application for membership was how to reconcile its close association with Britain – and the fact that many European countries viewed it as effectively a British satellite – with efforts to develop an independent identity. The second key issue, especially in the early years, was persuading EEC member states that membership was not incompatible with Ireland's non-membership of NATO.[30]

When a German radio station invited Lemass to make a statement about Irish foreign policy in January 1961 (part of Lemass' strategy of winning international support for Irish membership), he began by stating

---

[28] Daly, 'Nationalism', pp. 90–1. A number of retired Irish diplomats have informed me that a memo was issued instructing them not to lobby for a continuing Irish immigration quota, but to date I have failed to find a copy.

[29] *IP*, 11–13 July 1961.

[30] For a detailed analysis of the attitudes of EEC member states towards Ireland's application, see O'Driscoll, Keogh and aan de Wiel (eds), *Ireland through European eyes*.

that the 'Principles which shape Ireland's policy in international affairs are part of Ireland's heritage: freedom, dignity of the human person, the inherent evil of all forms of persecution and oppression, the right of nations to self-determination without outside interference and a world order based on justice and rule of law'. When he moved on to the details, he began with a familiar trope: 'First and foremost we wish to see the re-unification of Ireland restored . . . by every test' Ireland was one nation; he expressed the hope that in time unification would be achieved 'in har-mony and agreement'. Ireland was not party to any military alliance. The decision to remain outside NATO was 'to some extent due to partition'. Ireland could not join any organisation that involved members having an obligation to safeguard the integrity of each other's territory; this would amount to de facto recognition of partition. It would be a matter for the parliament of a united Ireland to decide whether to join NATO. But while not a NATO member, Ireland should 'not be regarded as neutral in the ideological conflict which divided the world'; she was 'unequivocally on the side of nations that supported the democratic principles enshrined in the Irish Constitution'.[31] In this statement, Lemass reiterated the official position of successive Irish governments: explaining Ireland's refusal to join NATO with reference to partition. However, he also emphasised that non-membership of NATO did not mean that Ireland was not wholly supportive of the political and diplomatic goals of NATO members.

The EEC was established to create a strong alliance of Western European countries at a time when Europe was divided between east and west. Economic integration was seen as a means of promoting pros-perity and political co-operation – removing the prospect of future wars between France and Germany and creating a strong bulwark against the Soviet bloc. There were hopes that in time economic integration might lead to a united Europe. All the founding members of the EEC were NATO members. US President Eisenhower was in favour of the EEC because he believed that the political benefits out-weighed any damage to US economic interests. By contrast, the United States was unenthusiastic about EFTA, which was simply a free trade area. President Kennedy encouraged Britain to join the EEC – again with the perspective of the Cold War in mind; the United States regarded Britain as a reliable Western ally, specifically in the light of US fears of a neutral Germany, as the possible prelude to a united Germany.[32] During Kennedy's pre-sidency, the United States favoured an enlarged EEC which would

---

[31] NAI DT S16057G/61.
[32] Richard Griffiths and Stuart Ward, *Courting the Common Market. The first attempt to enlarge the European Community 1961–63* (London: Lothian Foundation 1996), pp. 3–4.

include Britain, and possibly Denmark and Norway (both NATO members),[33] but Ireland was not mentioned in talks between the United States and EEC over enlargement.[34]

The UN was the international forum where Ireland's attitude towards major foreign policy issues was most clearly expressed, and this assumed greater importance in the light of Ireland's application for EEC membership. Skelly claims that the shift in Ireland's voting pattern happened after Lemass became Taoiseach, and before Ireland formally applied for EEC membership. Ireland increasingly voted in line with NATO/EEC members. Lemass informed the Fianna Fáil Ard Fheis in 1959 that Ireland would not support China's admission to the UN unless 'very specific safeguards were forthcoming in relation to the rights of the Chinese people, particularly in regard to religious freedom'.[35] Aiken's UN speech in December 1961 was consistent with this point of view.[36] It was also in line with Western thinking. Ireland supported a two-China strategy – admitting Peking and retaining Taiwan as a member – something that Peking would never accept. Ireland reversed its position on Algeria and South Tyrol, and now voted with EEC countries, supporting Italy (EEC member) against neutral Austria on the question of the German-speaking minority in Süd-Tirol and upholding France's position as the colonial power in Algeria.[37] Ireland's attitude towards Britain's policy in Southern Rhodesia (now Zimbabwe) was not unsympathetic to Britain.[38] Lemass also determined that Ireland should become a candidate for membership of the UN Security Council in 1961. Kennedy claims that he took this decision 'without seeking Aiken's advice'. Ireland's candidacy was successful because Western powers needed a European candidate, known to be pro-Western as a compromise candidate in a crisis.[39]

While Ireland's non-aligned status at the UN diminished significantly in the early 1960s, Aiken continued his personal crusade to prevent the proliferation of nuclear weapons. He first raised the issue in 1958; during the next session, Boland claimed that non-proliferation absorbed Aiken's 'energies to the virtual exclusion of everything else'.[40] In 1961, the UN

---

[33] Corso P. Boccia, 'The Kennedy administration and the first attempt to enlarge the EEC, 1961–1963', in Griffiths and Ward (eds), *Courting the Common Market*, p. 173.

[34] Michael Geary, *An inconvenient wait. Ireland's quest for membership of the EEC 1957–73* (Dublin: Institute of Public Administration, 2009), p. 39. US Secretary of State George Ball was opposed to neutrals becoming members of the EEC.

[35] Skelly, *Irish diplomacy*, p. 226 quoting *IT*, 11 November 1959.

[36] Skelly, *Irish diplomacy*, p. 233.   [37] Skelly, *Irish diplomacy*, pp. 219–26.

[38] Aoife Bhreathnach, 'A friend of the colonial powers? Frank Aiken, Ireland's United Nations alignment and decolonizations', in Kennedy and McMahon (eds), *Obligations and responsibilities*, pp. 182–99.

[39] Kennedy, 'Persuade an alternative European candidate to stand', p. 176.

[40] As quoted in Skelly, *Irish diplomacy*, p. 255.

General Assembly unanimously adopted a resolution sponsored by Ireland on 'Prevention of the wider dissemination of nuclear weapons', which would commit nuclear powers to preventing either nuclear weapons or weapons technology being transmitted to other states. Aiken's role was formally acknowledged in 1968 when all the nuclear powers signed the Nuclear Non-Proliferation Treaty in Moscow, and he was invited to be the first signatory to the treaty. Skelly highlights 'the realistic streak', shown by Aiken in this campaign. The initiative was a success because 'it jettisoned a comprehensive approach to general disarmament and concentrated instead on just one of its dimensions: non-proliferation', and Ireland's careful liaison with the United States at critical points.[41]

While Non-Proliferation was a pet project for Aiken, at critical moments Lemass determined Ireland's vote at the UN. During the 1962 Cuban Missile crisis, President Kennedy wrote a personal letter to Lemass, seeking Ireland's support. Lemass, who was in Bonn, as part of the EEC membership campaign, made a public statement that Ireland's UN delegation would support any proposal coming before the Security Council (of which Ireland was then a member) 'calling for the abolition of weapons of aggression in Cuba'.[42] Ireland generally supported the Western powers on issues such as the Middle East, the 1968 Soviet invasion of Czechoslovakia, and China – moving in 1970 from supporting the two-China Strategy to advocating the replacement of Taiwan and the People's Republic, the position increasingly adopted by EEC member states, though not by the United States. Ireland was least likely to be wholly in line with Western powers on questions of decolonisation, though the Irish position was not that of newly independent African states.[43] Pragmatism dictated Ireland's refusal to recognise the government of Biafra, a breakaway province of Nigeria, despite strong pressure from the Irish Holy Ghost fathers and some church groups who had missions in the province, and support for Biafra from a number of TDs and the *Irish Independent*. This stance was in line with the position adopted by other Western countries; it also protected the interests of Irish missionaries in other parts of Nigeria.[44] Ireland's growing interest in international development can also be seen as reflecting a national interest which was wholly in line with the thinking of the Western powers. The OECD increasingly saw aid to developing countries both as a means of counteracting the attraction of Communism and as an opportunity to

[41] Skelly, *Irish diplomacy*, pp. 247–65.   [42] Skelly, *Irish diplomacy*, pp. 240–1.
[43] Greg Spelman, 'Ireland at the United Nations. 1965–69: evolving policy and changing presence', in Kennedy and Mc Mahon (eds), *Obligations and responsibilities*, pp. 224–52.
[44] Enda Staunton, 'The Case of Biafra: Ireland and the Nigerian civil war', *IHS*, vol. xxxi, no. 124, November 1999, pp. 513–34.

develop new markets that would fuel economic growth. Ireland hoped that food aid would provide a new market for agricultural produce and technical expertise.[45]

But while Ireland was using the UN to demonstrate its support for EEC member countries and the Western alliance, it had to confront the strong opinion of EEC member states that a neutral Ireland should not be admitted to full membership. The Cold War raged strongly in 1961 – the year when the Berlin Wall was constructed. On 18 July 1961 – shortly before Ireland announced its determination to apply for membership – EEC heads of state or government[46] issued the Bonn declaration. This stated that only a united Europe, allied to the United States and other free peoples, 'is in a position to face the dangers that menace the existence of Europe and of the whole free world ... [they] resolved to develop their political co-operation with a view to the union of Europe'. The Declaration referred to 'the will for political union already implicit in the Treaties establishing the European Communities'; steps taken to 'progressively create the conditions for a common policy'; regular meetings 'to concert their policies and to reach common positions in order to further the political union of Europe, thereby strengthening the Atlantic alliance'. [NATO] Member states affirmed their commitment to extend co-operation beyond politics to include education, culture and research.[47] The Bonn statement posed a major threat to Irish membership, which was driven almost exclusively by economic objectives.

In September 1961, Lemass sent Whitaker and Con Cremin, secretaries of the Departments of Finance and External Affairs respectively, on a mission to EEC member capitals. They reported that the EEC tended to divide countries into two groups: Britain and Denmark – who were also candidates for membership, were NATO members and grouped accordingly; Ireland was grouped with neutral countries such as Austria and Switzerland. They reported that 'Acceptance by a potential member of the over-riding political objectives of the Community is of course essential. This is not, however, enough. Danger threatens Western Europe now and only if the Community is united can it hope to have the opportunity to move forward to its ideals. The countries joined in NATO have a defensive alliance ... the Community would expect a new member to make an

[45] HAEU, OECD 1029 AGR 62 (61).
[46] France was represented by the President (head of state); the other countries by their prime ministers.
[47] European Parliament: Political Committee, *Towards Political Union A selection of documents*, with a foreword by M Emilio Battista (January, 1964), pp. 9–10. A separate declaration issued on the same day announced the establishment of a European University. The declaration was reproduced in full in DD, vol 193, col. 15, 14 February 1962.

effective, positive, contribution, whether through NATO or otherwise, to the preservation of the existing foundations for advance towards the ideal of European unity.'[48] A report from Brussels in December 1961 noted that there was 'considerable reluctance on the part of the EEC Commission to allow Sweden, Switzerland and Austria to have associate status under Treaty of Rome if their present neutrality is retained'. There was a feeling that 'loose association would dilute considerably the political solidarity of the EEC'; associate membership would only be offered to less-developed countries such as Greece.[49] EEC memoranda referred to Ireland's 'special circumstances' or 'special problems'.[50] Whitaker, who was probably the strongest advocate of membership, was quite explicit that Ireland should reconsider the policy of neutrality. He told Finance Minister James Ryan that 'Nobody has yet told us that this [neutrality] is a condition of membership of the EEC. On the other hand, nobody so loves us as to want us in the EEC on our own terms.' Whitaker was concerned that Ireland might be seen as a ' "contrary" new member' ... it was our own propaganda which has given such an artificial significance to NATO in relation to partition'. There was 'not necessarily incompatibility' between NATO membership and Ireland's position on partition. He warned that 'To others it may seem that we are treating a narrow national interest as being more important than unity and co-operation in the defence of Western civilisation.'[51] He also suggested that EEC membership (with Britain) offered the best prospects for achieving a united Ireland.[52]

Whitaker appears to have had a major influence on the speech that Lemass gave in Brussels in January 1962, when he formally tabled Ireland's application for membership. An earlier draft contained a lengthy justification for not joining NATO, including a statement that if NATO membership was an essential precondition 'it would confuse Irish public opinion as to the aims of EEC and might operate to lessen enthusiasm for the whole concept of Western European unity. This is a political consideration to which the Irish Government must have regard in the light of their desire to secure near unanimous acceptance by the Irish people of the political aims of the European Community.'[53] Wisely, these sentences

[48] NAI DT S16877, 20 September 1961, as quoted in Dermot Keogh, 'Irish neutrality and the first application for EEC membership', in Michael Kennedy and Joseph Skelly (eds), *Irish foreign policy, 1919–66. From independence to internationalism* (Dublin: Four Courts, 1999), p. 269.

[49] NAI DT S14291B, 4 December 1961.

[50] Denis Maher, *The tortuous path, The course of Ireland's entry into the EEC 1948–73* (Dublin: Institute of Public Administration, 1986), p. 142.

[51] Whitaker to Ryan, 5 January 1962, as quoted in Horgan, *Lemass*, pp. 137–8.

[52] Keogh, 'Irish neutrality', in Kennedy and Skelly (eds), *Irish foreign policy*, pp. 273–6.

[53] NAI DT S14291B/61.

did not feature in Lemass' speech. He opened with a clear statement that 'Ireland belongs to Europe by history, tradition and sentiment no less than by geography'. Although Ireland was not a member of NATO, 'we have always agreed with the general aim of that Treaty'. He reiterated Ireland's 'will and desire to play a positive part ... in the achievement of European unity but also of our capacity, granted an appropriate rhythm to accept and discharge the economic obligations of membership'. Ireland was fully aware of the Bonn Declaration and the importance attached to political objectives and shared these ideals.[54] Responding shortly after this speech to a Dáil Question, as to whether NATO membership would be a condition of membership, Lemass reiterated that 'it would be highly undesirable that remarks made here should give the impression in Europe that there is a public opinion in this country which regards membership of NATO as something discreditable. The view of the Government in that regard has been made clear. We think the existence of NATO is necessary for the preservation of peace and for the defence of the countries of Western Europe, including this country. Although we are not members of NATO, we are in full agreement with its aims.'[55] Ireland's application attracted considerable attention from foreign media – both press and television, and Lemass used interviews with foreign media to emphasise the fact that Ireland was not neutral between east and west.[56] In July 1962, he gave an interview to the *New York Times*, in an attempt to counter the hostility of the US State Department towards Ireland's application; he noted that Ireland 'recognised[d] that a military commitment will be an inevitable consequence of our joining the Common Market and ultimately we would be prepared to yield even the technical label of neutrality'.[57] On a number of occasions, he indicated that Ireland was committed to Western European integration, acknowledging that this would involve member states co-ordinating their foreign and defence policies; he questioned whether NATO membership would involve recognising the partition of Ireland, but tended to skirt around the question of Ireland joining NATO.[58] In reality, Irish membership or non-membership was largely symbolical. Having read a memo on the topic by an official in the British embassy in Dublin, an official in the Commonwealth Office minuted that 'The Irish will not be joining NATO. This does not matter much.'[59]

---

[54] Full text of speech in Appendix II of Maher, *The tortuous path*, pp. 375–85.
[55] DD, vol. 193, cols. 6 and 7, 14 February 1962.
[56] NAI DT S16699D/61 Questions and answers to Desmond Wilcox for ITV programme, *This Week*, 30 October 1961.
[57] Quoted in Maher, *The tortuous path*, p. 152.
[58] Keogh, 'Irish neutrality', in Kennedy and Skelly (eds), *Irish foreign policy*, pp. 273–6.
[59] TNA FO0371/153790.

Despite these protestations, Ireland's application was put on hold while formal talks opened with Britain and Denmark. Jean Rey, the EEC Commissioner responsible for external relations, was favourably disposed towards Britain and Denmark; France and Germany appeared well-disposed towards Denmark.[60] Ireland's application suffered from two serious drawbacks – the perception that Ireland was an underdeveloped economy – a perception for which Ireland was largely responsible because of demands to be treated as such during earlier talks on a European free trade area. Neutrality was also a critical factor, especially for Hallstein and Mansholt.[61] The government tried to persuade the EEC to open formal negotiations on membership; the Irish Council of the European Movement visited Brussels; journalists from member countries were invited to Dublin for briefing sessions with Lemass. In the autumn of 1962, Lemass visited EEC capital cities to press Ireland's case and while in Bonn, he was informed that formal negotiations would be opened, though at a date to be determined.[62] Keatinge suggests that the failure of the Department of External Affairs to promote Ireland's case for membership may have contributed to the delay.[63] The DEA did not appoint a separate mission to the EEC until 1966, and only did so following criticism of its laid-back approach to membership. In July 1966, Garret FitzGerald noted that in the annual debates on financial estimate for the DEA over the three previous years, Frank Aiken had devoted only 58 words out of 20,000 words to the EEC.[64] While individual diplomats were undoubtedly working to promote Irish membership, Aiken's semi-detached attitude cannot have been an asset.

Negotiations on Irish membership had not commenced when Charles d e Gaulle vetoed Britain's membership application in January 1963. The French veto was tied up with European foreign policy and the development of an independent European nuclear deterrent.[65] De Gaulle questioned Britain's willingness to integrate into the EEC. He expressed fears that a larger EEC would lose cohesion; member states might be less capable of resisting pressure from the USA. The veto was a blessing for

[60] Johnny N Laursen, 'Next in line: Denmark and the EEC challenge', in Griffiths and Ward (eds), *Courting the Common Market*, p. 223.

[61] Brian Girvin 'Economic development and the politics of EC entry: Ireland 1956–63', in Griffiths and Ward (eds), *Courting the Common Market*, pp. 251–7. On Hallstein see Geary, *An inconvenient wait*, p. 48.

[62] Maher, *The tortuous path*, p. 160.

[63] Patrick Keatinge, *The formulation of Irish foreign policy* (Dublin: Institute of Public Administration, 1973), p. 131.

[64] SD, vol. 61, 14 July 1966, col. 1852.

[65] Anne Deighton, The United Kingdom application for EEC membership', in Griffiths and Ward (eds), *Courting the Common Market*, pp. 40–53.

Ireland; it gave the country 'a breathing space'.[66] If negotiations had not halted, there is a real possibility that Britain and perhaps Denmark would have become full members, with Ireland either relegated to associate membership or excluded. The veto gave Ireland time to develop the economy and to take significant steps to liberalise its trade; negotiating the AIFTAA, and applying for membership of GATT – the General Agreement on Tariffs and Trade. Ireland became a member in December 1967.[67] As time passed, NATO and neutrality assumed less importance in the evolution of the EEC. Aspirations of EEC founders for a united Europe were scaled back. Maher claims that de Gaulle's veto in January 1963 'had the effect of blunting further the drive for closer political integration'.[68] This drive became even more attenuated, during the 'empty chair' crisis – when France absented itself from heads of government meetings in the autumn of 1965, bringing the evolution of EEC policy to a standstill and halting plans to give the Commission extensive budgetary powers, and introduce majority voting – that is, an end to national vetoes. The 1966 Luxembourg compromise, which ended the dispute, meant that the EEC evolved less as a proto-united Europe, more as a consensual group of member nations. National vetoes survived, aspirations for a common foreign policy remained but the momentum towards a united Europe slowed.

Irish economic growth stalled in 1965/1966, bringing a realisation that growth was not inevitable. Mass protests by the farming lobby about low prices and lack of government assistance made EEC membership even more necessary and desirable. Geary suggests that a visit to Brussels by Aiken and Lynch (then Minister for Finance) in September 1966 and a subsequent up-beat press statement were designed to counteract media criticism of the lack of momentum regarding membership.[69] Yet, while farming interests suggested that Ireland could join the EEC independently of Britain, the two applications were inextricably linked and those links were strengthened significantly following the signing of the AITFAA. It became a matter of waiting for Britain's application to be reactivated. Ireland's second membership application does not merit lengthy discussion. It was submitted in May 1967, almost simultaneously with Britain's; Denmark and Norway also reapplied. But there was mutual suspicion about the other's intent. During the summer of 1967, George Brown, British Foreign Secretary, had suggested that negotiations on Britain's membership should precede other applications.[70] In the event all candidate countries held a common line, perhaps because there

[66] Griffiths and Ward, *Courting the Common Market*, p. 4.
[67] Maher, *Tortuous path*, pp. 191–5.   [68] Maher, *Tortuous path*, p. 169.
[69] Geary, *An inconvenient wait*, p. 92.   [70] Geary, *An inconvenient wait*, p. 116

were few benefits from doing otherwise. On 29 September, the Council of Ministers agreed to open negotiations with applicants to see 'whether arrangements could be made under which the indispensible cohesion and dynamism will be maintained in an enlarged Community'.[71] But when sterling was devalued on 18 November, de Gaulle used this as an argument against British membership; 'What France cannot do is to enter into a negotiation with the British and their associates which would lead to the destruction of the Europe structure of which she is a part.' Although it appeared other members were prepared to open negotiations, France exercised its veto in December 1968.[72]

De Gaulle's retirement from politics in 1969 re-opened the possibility of Britain and Ireland joining the EEC. After the general election in June 1969, Lynch appointed Patrick Hillery as Minister for External Affairs. Hillery, in contrast to Aiken, was strongly pro-Europe, and within weeks of his appointment, he made a tour of all EEC capitals to press Ireland's case for membership and to counter apparent moves for Britain to be admitted before other applicants.[73] Securing simultaneous negotiations and simultaneous membership with Britain became a key consideration. Hillery's appointment meant that primary responsibility for EEC membership shifted to the Department of External Affairs, whereas the earlier momentum came from Finance. His personal commitment also ensured that the EEC became a priority for all diplomatic missions.

The green light came in the autumn/winter of 1969. The Commission presented the Council of Ministers with an *avis*, recommending that negotiations should open shortly with all applicants for membership; it advised a common accession date. The process of economic integration within the Community should continue, while talks on enlargement were proceeding. In December 1969, the Council of Ministers agreed to open talks with applicants for membership.[74] Following a meeting with George Thomson, the British minister responsible for overseeing Britain's application, Britain and Ireland agreed that officials in both countries would keep in touch during accession talks. British and Irish officials met on four occasions (in Dublin and London) between December 1969 and October 1970.[75] Ireland made similar arrangements with Denmark, and both countries agreed to trade information about British actions.[76]

[71] Maher, *Tortuous path*, p. 228.
[72] Con O'Neill, *Britain's entry into the European Community. Report on the negotiations of 1970–72* (London: Frank Cass, 2000), p. 11.
[73] Geary, *An inconvenient wait*, pp. 160–5.
[74] Keogh, *Jack Lynch*, pp. 290–1; Walsh, *Patrick Hillery*, pp. 292–4.
[75] O' Neill, *Britain's entry*, p. 285.
[76] Keogh, *Jack Lynch*, pp. 291–2; Geary, *An inconvenient wait*, p. 163.

Formal membership negotiations opened on 30 July 1970, though this was purely a ceremonial occasion; the first working meeting took place on 21 September. According to British diplomat Sir David Hannay, membership negotiations 'was not, however, a negotiation like just any other. It was a new species with a new style, which had emerged in the period after the Second World War, as part of the rapid expansion of multilateral diplomacy; and within that new species, it was one of the earliest in a series of sub-species relating to negotiating with, or about the development of, the European Community ... Many of the issues involved were not those formerly considered as a suitable subject of international negotiations at all ... Seldom had technical issues assumed such an importance at a multilateral level.' Negotiations involved a combination of formal meetings in Brussels and Luxembourg, plus diplomatic contacts in the various capitals, a complex process that, according to Hannay, 'developed into a kind of three-dimensional game of chess'.[77] Although Lynch determined that Ireland's negotiating team would be led by the Minister for External Affairs, the White Paper setting out the implications of membership was drafted by the Department of Finance. Hillery's biographer Walsh speculates that the decision to put Hillery in charge of negotiations might have been influenced by 'the imminent breakdown of his [Lynch's] relations with Haughey', though he also notes that negotiating sessions (involving ministers) were chaired by the foreign ministers of member states.[78]

For Ireland, the key issues were transition arrangements for agriculture and industry; protecting Ireland's industrial development incentives[79]; protecting the provisions of the AIFTAA during the transitional period, regional policy and Ireland's contribution to the EEC budget. The negotiations involved a lot of technical detail. The Hague communiqué of 2 December 1969, announcing the opening of enlargement talks, specified that all applicants had to accept 'the treaties and their political finality, the decisions taken since the entering into force of the treaties'.[80] This meant that the Common Agriculture Policy (CAP) and the community budgetary process were not open to negotiation, neither was the Common Fisheries Policy (CFP), despite the fact that it was only adopted as negotiations opened with new members, and the CFP would give all member states access to coastal waters throughout the community on

---

[77] Sir David Hannay, foreword to O'Neill, *Britain's entry into the European Community*, pp. x–xi.
[78] Walsh, *Patrick Hillery*, pp. 299–300.
[79] Export profits tax relief (see Chapter 3) was in conflict with article 98 of the Treaty of Rome.
[80] Quoted in O'Neill, *Britain's entry*, p. 18.

identical terms, after a short transition period. This was arguably a rather underhand act given that the four applicants for membership – Britain, Ireland, Norway and Denmark – had extensive coastal waters and a combined fish catch double that of existing member states.[81] The CFP was one issue where the accession countries (with the possible exception of Denmark) had a common interest, but although Britain and Ireland liaised closely, Norway went solo demanding permanent protection of its national waters, which might in hindsight be seen as an augury of their eventual decision not to become a member. Britain and Ireland were able to protect their national waters for a ten-year period, and they secured some commitments about renegotiating the CFP before that period ended, but no long-term safeguards.[82]

Britain's chief negotiator Sir Con O'Neill claimed that 'on the whole we kept each other fully informed' on all aspects of the negotiations, though he noted 'a slight disposition on the part of the Irish, for which I hardly blame them, to keep some of their objectives and their ideas about timing to themselves. Where these special interests were concerned, the Irish were inclined to bide their time and then dart in suddenly to strike the Community iron when they judged it hot.'[83] With the exception of the CFP, Ireland was broadly satisfied with the accession arrangements. They secured a prolonged transition for car assembly, which required some renegotiation of the AIFTAA with Britain, an agreement that tax concessions already granted to industrialists would continue to be honoured. After accession, Ireland would be permitted to introduce a revised tax relief scheme to attract industrial investment that would comply with the Treaty of Rome. The most significant achievement was securing a separate Protocol 30 'on Ireland', setting out the Community's undertakings to protect Irish interests on issues such as economic development, under-employment and regional incentives – a protocol that Con O'Neill described as 'Ireland seemingly singled out for special treatment'.[84]

Ministers were careful to emphasise that Ireland accepted all the political obligations of membership.[85] This commitment presented no great difficulties, because the future political shape of the EEC, its foreign and defence policies had not been determined or articulated. Indeed, a senior EEC official Dr Nass claimed that the great issues of European integration were never discussed during the negotiations – matters such as the future policies of the enlarged Community or the relationship of the EEC with the rest of the world.[86] Neutrality assumed much less importance

[81] Hannay, *Britain's entry*, p. xiv.   [82] Walsh, *Patrick Hillery*, pp. 316–23.
[83] O Neill, *Britain's entry*, p. 285.
[84] Walsh, *Patrick Hillery*, pp. 307–16; O'Neill, *Britain's entry*, pp. 386–7.
[85] Walsh, *Patrick Hillery*, p. 297.   [86] O Neill, *Britain's entry*, p. 38.

than in the early 1960s. A memorandum by Sir Con O'Neill noted that 'the Irish did not [feel] and fortunately for them the Community did not feel either, any difficulties or scruples arising from their neutral status'. He claimed that the Irish Ambassador to the United Kingdom told him that 'the present Irish Government saw no difficulty about accepting defence commitments in Europe, even if it were to mean – and he hardly thought it would – membership of NATO ... The general attitude of the Community seems to have been that though the Irish Republic was neutral, it was less neutral than others.'[87] Lynch played down the political aspects of membership. He informed the Dáil that the 'provisions of the treaties themselves and the implementing legislation are solely concerned with economic and commercial activities and related social matters'. The Community was committed to evolving towards political union at some future date, and Ireland would play a full part in any negotiations on this matter.[88]

The main farming and employer organisations were strongly in favour of membership, as was Fine Gael, the main opposition party. The opposition included most, though not all members of the Labour Party, Sinn Féin, trade unions, representatives of small farmers, and the Common Market Defence Campaign – a network of intellectuals, artists and left-wing activists. The 'yes' campaign emphasised the benefits for farm incomes, social welfare (the additional revenue available from no longer having to pay farm subsidies) and the prospects of higher living standards and increased foreign industrial investment. The government deployed the IDA regional jobs targets as evidence that membership would benefit all communities. Opposition focussed on the threat to jobs in industry as a result of free trade; claims that the CAP would mean the extinction of small farmers – a credible argument in light of the Mansholt Plan, which proposed the elimination of many smaller holdings – and the fact that the CFP would make it difficult, if not impossible to develop a strong indigenous fisheries industry. The referendum on membership in May 1972 was a landslide, with 83 per cent of those who voted in favour – a margin substantially higher than anticipated.[89] Opponents focused on the loss of sovereignty, especially the threat to Ireland's neutral status, given that all other member-states were members of NATO, and prospects of a common defence policy or a common foreign policy. Tony Coughlan, a leading figure in Common Market Defence Campaign, claimed that 'the Irish Parliament would hand over to the Council of Ministers and

---

[87] Quoted in Keogh, *Jack Lynch*, p. 294.   [88] DD, vol. 247, col. 1648, 23 June 1970.
[89] Gary Murphy and Niamh Purséil, ' "Is it a new allowance?" Irish entry to the EEC and popular opinion', *IPS*, vol. 23, no. 4, December 2008, p. 550.

the Commission in Brussels the power of legislating for Ireland'. The British Embassy summarised the arguments of the 'No' campaign as 'Brussels rule, the re-emergence of big-scale and probably foreign landlords, the gradual domination of multi-national companies over Irish industry, the submersion of the Irish way of life and language and the final abandonment of "real" Irish independence'.[90] Opponents highlighted the democratic deficit within the Community – including the limited powers of the European Parliament and that fact that its members were not directly elected.[91] While EEC membership had long-term implications for many dimensions of Ireland's domestic and international relations, it is symptomatic of the era that the discussion was dominated by economic and social issues.

Anglo-Irish relations

By the 1950s, the high-level negotiations between Dublin and London over Ireland's constitutional status were in the past. Ireland became a republic in 1949, which removed the last residues of the 1921 Anglo-Irish Treaty. In the same year, Britain passed the Ireland Act, which stated that any change in the status of Northern Ireland was a matter for the Northern Ireland parliament, effectively closing the door on Anglo-Irish negotiations on Northern Ireland. Anglo-Irish relations in the 1950s and most of the 1960s were concerned with economic matters. Ireland remained a member of the sterling area; international financial transactions were carried out through London; Irish interest rates were determined by London rates. Irish people retained the freedom to live and work in Britain without restriction, despite leaving the Commonwealth in 1949, and the number of Irish in Britain rose significantly in the 1950s. Indeed one of the major concerns for the Irish embassy in Britain was that Britain might restrict Irish immigration under the 1962 Commonwealth Immigration Act.[92] Economic relations and a common interest in EEC membership dominated the relationship throughout the 1960s. Britain regarded Lemass as a more modern man, whose pragmatism and focus on economics contrasted with de Valera's opaque references to Ireland's history; he generally received positive coverage both in print and on British television. Although 'Operation Harvest', the IRA border campaign, dragged on until February 1962, it appears to have caused little strain in the relationship. A private visit by Princess Margaret and her

---

[90] TNA FCO 87/ 38 Economic situation, EEC Campaign memo Sir John Peck 18 May 1972.
[91] Direct elections were introduced in 1979.   [92] Daly, *Slow failure*, p. 210.

husband to visit relatives in Ireland provoked minor protests by the IRA and splinter republican groups, as did visits by British naval vessels to Irish ports.[93] Ireland viewed the election of a Labour government in 1964 as an opportunity to improve Anglo-Irish relations. Under the Wilson government, some long-term irritants were solved or ameliorated. An agreement was reached to permit the loan of pictures from the disputed Lane Bequest to the Dublin Municipal Art Gallery. Britain returned the remains of Roger Casement, on condition that burial would be in Glasnevin, not in County Antrim, and the British Ambassador Geoffrey Tory marched in Casement's funeral cortege and attended the funeral mass in the Pro-Cathedral.[94] Minister for External Affairs Frank Aiken represented Ireland at the state funeral of Sir Winston Churchill in 1965 and Lemass deliberately digressed from his speech on a Finance motion in Dáil Éireann, to make a statement describing Churchill as 'a great English leader, who during his life, served the interests of his country to the best of his very high abilities'. He went on to reject criticism of Ireland's representation at Churchill's funeral, irrespective of whether it came from 'the leader writers and letter writers of the *Irish Times* or the tree fellers at Abbeyleix [a reference to the protests against a visit by Princess Margaret and her husband]. The world will respect us in the degree to which we respect ourselves. There may be a need for a public education campaign to promote understanding of what national self-respect requires in individual and group behaviour.'[95] A small group protested outside Teilifís Éireann at the decision to broadcast a one-hour programme about Churchill, but most critics were of the opinion that de Valera or Lemass should have attended his funeral.[96]

When the British Ambassador to Ireland Sir Geoffrey Tory had a private meeting with Hugh McCann in October 1965, he remarked on the 'improving trend in Anglo-Irish relations', though he was conscious 'that there are still some people in the country who did not relish the change that had taken place'. At this time, the final terms of AIFTAA had not yet been determined, and McCann minuted that 'if, on purely economic grounds, the Agreement should appear ... to be tipped slightly against Britain, then the political factor should tip the scale in their

---

[93] *IP*, 20 January 1965, 'Ten injured in Laois riots', *SP*, 3 October 1965, 'Cork asked to boycott warship.

[94] Chris Reeves, 'The penultimate Irish problem: Britain, Ireland and the exhumation of Roger Casement', *ISIA*, vol. 12, 2001, pp. 151–78.

[95] DD, vol. 214, cols. 585–6, 17 February 1965. Lemass's description used almost identical words to de Valera's tribute. For events at Abbeyleix, *IP*, 20 January 1965.

[96] *II*, 25 January 1965; *IP*, 4 February 1965; *Southern Star*, 30 January1965.

favour'.[97] Craig noted that one of the functions of the British embassy in Ireland was 'the delicate maintenance of British army recruitment in Ireland, run from the Dublin embassy'.[98] For this reason the ambassador was keen to promote courtesy visits to Ireland by British naval vessels, despite the danger of protests. He described such visits as 'part of the normal intercourse between friendly countries ... they were welcomed by many people here, and if, by yielding to threats by the IRA, they were stopped they would be missed and their absence would be commented on'. McCann reminded him that 'There were historical reasons why visits of British naval vessels to Ireland were not on the same footing as courtesy calls to, say, the Scandinavian countries. In our joint effort to promote good relations between the two countries, one must move carefully and avoid action which would arouse hostility.' The ambassador asked whether the diplomatic corps would be expected to attend official ceremonies associated with the Golden Jubilee of the Easter Rising, and whether the commemoration 'would be oriented towards the future or a re-enactment of the past'. McCann reassured him that 'the Commemoration would be a forward-looking occasion without any attempt to re-open old wounds'.[99] Britain returned the flag that flew over the GPO during Easter Week (which had been held in the Imperial War Museum), shortly before the Jubilee, but the ambassador insisted on the handover taking place in a private ceremony to avoid a repeat of the criticism in Britain resulting from his presence at the Casement funeral. Most British coverage of 1916 was quite sympathetic to Ireland. The concluding sentence in a series of articles in the *Daily Express* said: 'We are friends again now. Principally because of that preposterous, foolish, bungled, costly, brave Easter Rebellion of 1916'.[100] Irish officials were angered at the *Sunday Times* colour supplement, featuring a cover picture of Pearse's revolver, and an inside article about the current strength of the IRA, though their anger was primarily directed at the author, Irish journalist Tim Pat Coogan. But the British authorities remained relaxed, despite the fact that a petrol bomb was thrown at the home of the British military attaché,[101] by an IRA splinter group. The Irish government shared its intelligence regarding the IRA with the British authorities, and it appears that the latter accepted the Irish assessment that the threat was limited, rather than the more inflated warnings which they received from the Northern Ireland authorities.[102]

---

[97] Report of interview with British Ambassador 1/6/495 2 October 1965 Copy on NAI 98/6/495.
[98] Craig, *Crisis of confidence*, p. 11.
[99] *Report of interview*, 2 October 1965 Copy on 98/6/495.
[100] Donald Seaman, 'Six days that changed history', *Daily Express*, 26 March 1966.
[101] TNA DO 182/139.   [102] Craig, *Crisis of confidence*, pp. 14–17.

Britain loomed much larger for the Irish government than Ireland did for Britain. Sir Geoffrey Tory told Hugh McCann that 'because of the pre-occupation of British Ministers with such a multitude of problems, both international and domestic, it was difficult to bring a point [relating to Ireland] to the notice of Ministers personally'.[103] It is highly unlikely that the 1965 Agreement would have been negotiated without Lemass' determination. But despite Harold Wilson's jocular manner, and his claim to represent more Irish voters in his Liverpool constituency of Huyton, than any Irish TD, British interests remained paramount in trade as in other respects, and the Anglo-Irish economic relationship, though close, were not always a happy one. The vulnerable state of sterling and the wider British economy disrupted the Irish economy, and despite the AIFTAA, Ireland remained very much at the mercy of British economic policies. British industrial investment in Ireland was restricted by a 'voluntary' code imposed by the UK government; the AIFTAA failed to deliver the expected security for Irish farmers, and by the end of the decade, it was seriously eroding the domestic market for Irish manufacturers. Ireland's economic strategy was to reduce its dependence on Britain, so that while the AIFTAA appeared to bring a return to the free trade relationship that prevailed before 1932, Ireland regarded it as an interim step towards EEC membership and less dependency on Britain. By January 1972, sterling accounted for 57 per cent of official external reserves, compared with 90 per cent only five years earlier. By 1974, Ireland's first year as a member of the EEC, Britain and Northern Ireland was the destination for just over half of Irish exports (51.6 per cent), compared with over 76 per cent in 1956.[104] But if economic dependency was waning, the Northern Ireland crisis meant that constitutional issues had re-emerged as the primary concern.

A steep learning curve

Foreign relations was a challenging area for Ireland, and there are many indications of naïveté, such as the belief that newly independent African colonies would regard Ireland as soul-brothers, the debacles and near-misses of the Irish mission to the Congo;[105] suggestions that displaying the

---

[103] NAI 98/6/495.   [104] *Central Bank Quarterly Report* spring 1972.
[105] Lemass told the Dáil that UN Secretary-General Dag Hammarskjöld had requested Irish troops because Ireland 'occupied a "special position in world affairs because of its impartial stance at the UN and its" national traditions and outlook', Michael Kennedy and Art Magennis, *Ireland, the United Nations and the Congo* (Dublin, 2014), p. 24 and more generally on the Congo.

treasures of Ireland's Golden Age – the early medieval period, when Irish monks evangelised Europe – might enhance Irish candidacy for membership, or a belief that the friendlier relationship with Britain might translate into Ireland being given a role in Northern Ireland in 1969. Yet, officials and ministers successfully managed the complex negotiations on EEC membership.

14   Northern Ireland

Northern Ireland is yet another instance where economic development appeared to offer a new approach to an old problem. Lemass' meeting with Northern Ireland Prime Minister Terence O'Neill in January 1965, the first meeting between the two heads of government since the early 1920s, is commonly seen as one of the highlights of the decade. Ken Whitaker – a key intermediary in the prior negotiations for the meeting – has described the 'minor thrill – of a James Bond kind – of making sure that the secrecy desired by the Northern Premier was observed. He wanted the news to break only at 1 o'clock, when Mr Lemass and I would already have arrived at Stormont'. O'Neill described the meeting as a historic one – meriting champagne; the wine served was Chateauneuf du Pape, [1] presumably selected either as a bridge-building gesture or somebody's private joke. Garvin claims that Lemass' 'dramatic and unheralded visit . . . ended a sterile cold war between the two Irish states'.[2]

Lemass and O'Neill were pragmatists who were primarily concerned with economic development. In 1961, a joint report by the British and Stormont governments on the economy of Northern Ireland painted a bleak picture and suggested that unemployed workers should be encouraged to emigrate in search of work.[3] The economic challenge confronting O'Neill was equal to that facing Lemass; economic development was the primary objective for both prime ministers. Nevertheless, O'Neill remained 'very fundamentally a unionist',[4] who believed that Northern Ireland nationalists would come to see 'the economic sense of the

---

[1] Terence O'Neill, *The autobiography of Terence O'Neill* (London: Hart-Davis, 1972), pp. 68–76; Kenneth Bloomfield, *Stormont in Crisis* (Belfast: Blackstaff, 1994), pp. 80–2; UCDA P 175/1, Whitaker Northern Ireland papers gives two accounts – a formal minute of the event and a more informal account that Whitaker gave to the BBC in 1975 See also Chambers, *Whitaker*, pp. 257–63.
[2] Tom Garvin, *Judging Lemass: the measure of the man* (Dublin: Royal Irish Academy, 2009), p. xiv.
[3] Marc Mulholland, *Terence O'Neill* (Dublin: UCD Press, 2013), p. 24.
[4] Bloomfield, *Stormont in crisis*, p. 76.

Union'.[5] Lemass likewise was convinced that hard-headed Ulster unionists could be persuaded to develop closer links with the Republic, even perhaps supporting a united Ireland, if this offered economic benefits. In a speech to the Fianna Fáil party in May 1961, he stressed that 'this economic effort is of special and immediate significance and importance in relation to our aim of reuniting the Irish people and ending partition'. He invited the people of Northern Ireland to contrast the economic success of independent Ireland with the 'despondency' regarding the Northern economy.[6] According to Patterson, 'the idea that northerners could only be attracted by a higher standard of living in the Republic – had already been articulated by de Valera'. However, he concedes that Lemass' 'premiership was notable for a serious attempt to implement ideas that de Valera had articulated but had done little about for fear of more republican sections of the party'.[7]

Lemass folded Northern Ireland into a wider programme of economic liberalisation. He believed that joint membership of the EEC and the AIFTAA would foster closer links with Northern Ireland. Initial discussions on north-south trade took place between Dublin and Whitehall, with follow-up talks between Northern Ireland business interests and Irish officials. In 1962, the Irish government introduced licences providing for duty-free imports of electrical motors and paint from Northern Ireland; a unilateral reduction on import duties on linens and furniture followed some months later. [8] The Northern Ireland government refused to take part in these talks until Dublin had formally recognised the Northern state. O'Neill's election as Prime Minister in March 1963, following the retirement of Lord Brookeborough, brought no immediate change in attitude. In July 1963, Lemass accorded a rather grudging de facto recognition to Northern Ireland and expressed a willingness to accept some form of federal settlement for a united Ireland, when he stated that 'the Government and Parliament there exist with the support of the majority in the Six Counties area, artificial although that area is. We see it functioning within its powers ... within an all-Ireland constitution, for as long as it is desired to have them.' He called for both governments to co-operate on matters of mutual benefit: this had of course been happening for many years. O' Neill responded to this speech after 'a considerable

[5] Marc Mulholland, *Northern Ireland at the Crossroads: Ulster unionism in the O'Neill years* (London: Macmillan, 2000), p. 63.
[6] Daly, *Slow Failure*, pp. 217–8.
[7] Henry Patterson, *Ireland since 1939* (Oxford: Blackwell 2002), pp. 155–6; Horgan, *Lemass*, pp. 169–71.
[8] Michael Kennedy and Joseph Skelly (eds), *Division and consensus. The politics of cross-border relations in Ireland 1926–1968* (Dublin: Institute of Public Administration, 2000), pp. 183–9.

lapse of time' with what Mulholland describes as a 'supercilious rebuke' and 'an invitation to treat'. But the Northern government then took umbrage at references to partition in Lemass' speech to the National Press Club in Washington (see p. 304). Mulholland suggests that 'it is clear that Northern Ireland feared an all-Ireland détente more than the Republic'. O'Neill was in a much weaker political position than Lemass; however, the threat that Brian Faulkner, the ambitious Minister for Commerce and his potential rival, would engage in ministerial talks with Dublin 'virtually coerced' O'Neill into inviting Lemass to Stormont.[9] Kennedy suggests that the invitation was prompted by pressure from British Prime Minister Harold Wilson.[10] Both interpretations suggest that O'Neill was a reluctant participant, and the choreography of the event reflects his weak political position. While Lemass informed his Cabinet of the meeting in advance, O'Neill confided in a much smaller group, though once news of the visit became public, ministers were invited to join Lemass for tea.[11]

By the 1960s, the gap between Ireland North and South was probably greater than ever before. One important factor to bear in mind is that Dublin's policy towards Northern Ireland was being constructed on the basis of minimal knowledge and little if any research. Few Irish ministers and civil servants had first-hand knowledge of Northern Ireland. Regular visits by members of the Department of External Affairs, which were a feature of the early and mid-1950s, ended for reasons that are unclear.[12] Fanning notes that when Northern Ireland crashed to the top of the agenda in 1968/69 'There was then no Anglo-Irish division in the Department of External Affairs, and not a single official in Iveagh House was assigned to the issue of Northern Ireland. Nor was there anyone in the Taoiseach's Department working on Northern Ireland.'[13] It is no coincidence that the first meeting between Lemass and O'Neill was arranged by the then-Secretary of the Department of Finance T. K. Whitaker, who became acquainted with O'Neill when they both attended a World Bank conference some years earlier and were introduced by a mutual contact.[14]

---

[9] Mulholland, *Northern Ireland at the Crossroads*, pp. 80–2.

[10] Kennedy, *Division and consensus*, p. 229.

[11] Kennedy, *Division and consensus*, p. 233.

[12] D. H. Akenson, *Conor. A biography of Conor Cruise O'Brien* (Montreal: McGill University Press, 1994), pp. 145–7.

[13] Ronan Fanning, 'Playing it cool: the response of the British and Irish government to the crisis in Northern Ireland, 1968–9', *ISIA*, vol. 12, 2001, p. 59.

[14] Information supplied by T.K. Whitaker. Whitaker told David McCann that they first met on a trans-Atlantic liner. David McCann, 'Mr Whitaker and Northern Ireland policy from 1959 to 1973', *ISIA*, vol. 23, no. 201, 2012, p. 174. Chambers claims that they first met in Paris at the opening of the World Bank's European office. They were introduced by Tyrone-born Sir William Iliff, vice-president of the World Bank, Chambers, *Whitaker*, p. 254. Whitaker told me that Iliff introduced him to O'Neill.

Recourse to this informal channel reflects the absence of more formal contacts between the two governments.

The post-war anti-partition campaign had done little to cement a close relationship between the two Irelands. By the early 1950s, Northern nationalists were decrying a lack of support from Dublin for the campaign.[15] Fianna Fáil and Fine Gael united in opposing their demands to have a presence in Dáil Éireann; both parties concurred in urging them to take their seats in Stormont.[16] Yet according to Horgan, the Irish Government 'and Fianna Fáil especially, were held in Messiah like reverence for decades by nationalists in the North', though few ministers appear to have been conscious of this.[17] Northern nationalists continued to make highly unrealistic demands on the Dublin government: financial support for Catholic schools and Belfast's Mater hospital (which remained outside the NHS); industries to be established along the border, to provide jobs for Northern nationalists; funding for religious houses in Northern Ireland; and extending Irish Arts Council grants to Northern Ireland.[18] In 1964, in response to the report of a Commission on the Irish Language hundreds of Northern nationalists dispatched petitions to Dublin demanding government support for Irish language teaching for Northern Irish students, arguing that 'when the six north-eastern counties will be integrated in [a united Ireland] .... the Irish language as the common inheritance of all our people will be not only a symbol and seal of our nationhood but will be, as well a great and unbreakable bond of unity'.[19] Northern nationalists were also eager to watch Teilifís Éireann, most especially GAA games, but the Irish government argued that they were bound by a 1952 Stockholm Agreement limiting the power of Irish transmitters to a level that would minimise overspill into Northern Ireland, despite the fact that substantial areas of the Republic received two British television stations. A judicious locating of transmitters would have enabled Teilifís Éireann to reach most of west Ulster and even Belfast, yet this was never contemplated.[20] When the British authorities had to renegotiate on transmitters in 1959, Savage notes that they pressed the Irish government 'to accept the principle of not intentionally broadcasting into Northern Ireland, and

---

[15] Brendan Lynn, *Holding the ground: the Nationalist party in Northern Ireland, 1945–72* (Aldershot: Ashgate, 1997), p. 98.
[16] Lynn, *Holding the ground*, p. 101.   [17] Horgan, *Lemass*, p. 267.
[18] Enda Staunton, *The Nationalists of Northern Ireland 1918–1973* (Dublin: Columba, 2001), pp. 181–92.
[19] NAI DT S17627a/95. Commisiún um Athbheocháin na Gaeilge.
[20] Robert Savage, *Irish television. The political and social origins* (Cork: Cork University Press, 1996), pp. 134–5.

Dublin acquiesced'.[21] Northern ministers were extremely concerned that Irish television programmes might be received in Northern Ireland and explicitly forbade any cable companies from transmitting Irish television (they were also extremely active in ensuring that British channels did not broadcast programmes that were critical of Northern Ireland). Savage suggests that any concerted effort to transmit into Northern Ireland would have been strongly opposed – not just by Belfast, but by London. In 1970, only 14 per cent of the population of Northern Ireland could receive Teilifís Éireann, whereas 35 per cent of homes in the Republic could receive British stations and the number was rising.[22] Dublin's acquiescence with Britain's and Stormont's wishes may have been determined by Lemass' wish to work more closely with the Northern government.

Lemass' focus on closer practical links with the government and business communities left little room for a working relationship with Northern nationalists, and it might explain the unwillingness to beam Teilifís Éireann into Northern Ireland. Horgan describes Northern nationalists as 'fairly far down the queue' in Lemass' priorities, 'partly because they had no political power, did not figure very largely in the immediate calculations of a leader for whom executive power was the primary language of political communication'.[23] Constitutional nationalism in Northern Ireland was little more a collection of individual fiefdoms with nothing approaching proper party structures or policies. The nationalist party was almost a sub-branch of the Catholic Church. Such an archaic and powerless entity was unlikely to attract Lemass' attention– it offered no opportunities for advancing his policy. Lemass' speeches contain many overtures towards the Northern government and the Unionist community, but significantly fewer references to Northern nationalists. A Department of External Affairs memo on the proposed guest list for the Kennedy visit suggests that Northern nationalists were regarded somewhat akin to irritating relatives who had outworn their welcome. Having noted that, in line with 'our long-standing practice', the draft invitation list for the state reception at Iveagh House included all the 'six-county [sic] anti-partitionist MPs and Senators', plus the editor and manager of the Belfast nationalist newspaper the *Irish News*, it queried whether this practice should continue; Northern political representatives were being treated more generously than TDs and senators, not all of whom would receive invitations.[24] Dublin's efforts to engage with the Northern Ireland

---

[21] Robert Savage, *A loss of innocence? Television and Irish society 1960–72* (Manchester: Manchester University Press, 2010), pp. 328.

[22] Savage, *Loss of innocence*, pp. 340–1; 343–5; *Hibernia*, 14 July 1972.

[23] Horgan, *Lemass*, pp. 265–6.   [24] NAI, DT S17401A, 17 May 1963.

government and business community prompted fears and even resentment on the part of Northern nationalists. When Northern nationalist leader Eddie McAteer met Lemass shortly after the first O'Neill/Lemass meeting, McAteer recorded that he was 'more worried than ever. I get neither the encouragement nor understanding of our position that I expected.' He claimed that Lemass viewed northern Catholics as 'just as intractable as the Protestants'. McAteer left the meeting 'with the conviction that as far as Seán Lemass was concerned, the Northern Irish were very much on their own'.[25] In 1968, Gerry Fitt, Westminster MP for West Belfast, claimed that for the nationalist minority, the O'Neill/Lemass meeting seemed 'to consolidate the existence of the unnatural divisions of this country. Those people living in the North who have yearned for reunification, received a resounding kick in the teeth from Mr. Lemass who, on his resignation as Taoiseach, stated at Queen's University that "one side is as bad as the other".'[26] Kennedy presents a more positive version of the 1965 McAteer/Lemass meeting (drawn from Irish government archives); he claims that Lemass encouraged McAteer to take up the position of official opposition at Stormont.[27] But on the eve of the Westminster elections of March 1966, McAteer noted that this decision 'had got little response from the O'Neill government'.[28] He was not paid the leader of the opposition's allowance, and O'Neill rebuffed his offer to meet to discuss matters of mutual agreement.[29]

By the early 1960s there was evidence that some Northern Catholics were prepared to work within the framework of the United Kingdom and/ or the Northern Ireland state, a decision prompted by an awareness that the United Kingdom offered significantly better health, education and welfare services than the Republic. A 1964 article in the *Irish Times* on 'The Northern Catholic' by a young Derry school-teacher John Hume explained:

The crux of the matter for the younger generations is the continued existence, particularly among the Catholics of great social problems of housing, unemployment and emigration. It is the struggle for priority in their minds between such problems and the ideal of a United Ireland with which they have been bred that has produced the frustration and the large number of political wanderers that Michael Viney met on his tour. It may be that the present generation of younger Catholics in the North are more materialistic than their fathers but there is little

[25] Frank Curran, *Derry. Countdown to disaster* (Dublin: Gill & Macmillan, 1980), pp. 38–9.
[26] *IT*, 9 November 1968.   [27] Kennedy, *Division and consensus*, p.237.
[28] *Derry Journal* 22 February 1966, and 25 March 1966, quoted in O'Callaghan, 'Commemorating the Rising in Northern Ireland', p. 92.
[29] Mulholland, *Northern Ireland at the Crossroads*, pp. 134–5.

doubt that their thinking is principally geared towards the solution of social and economic problems. This has led to a deep questioning of traditional Nationalist attitudes.[30]

One of Lemass' most significant gestures was to use the term 'Northern Ireland' in place of 'Six Counties'– the designation commonly used in Irish official documents and speeches. But this change of name was not officially decreed, and 'Six Counties' remained in use, even in documents originating in the Department of the Taoiseach. [31] Yet there is no evidence that Lemass abandoned the goal of a united Ireland, though Conor Cruise O'Brien claimed that he made it 'a remote platonic ideal'.[32] Evidence that a united Ireland remained part of official thinking can be seen in a memo for Cabinet on the economic social and political impact of a peaceful 're-integration of the national territory', written in 1966/1967, which concluded that 'We are no nearer to success than in 1923.' It noted the difficulties presented by superior social services in Northern Ireland and acknowledged that any settlement must address the long-standing fears of Northern Protestants – that they would be dominated by Roman Catholics and that their economy would be ruined. Membership of NATO and Ireland's possible return to the Commonwealth were mooted as possible steps in bringing an end to partition. The memo distinguished between the 'bitter men of the west' [west of the Bann], who tended to lobby Dublin, and 'the more level headed nationalists of Belfast'.[33] This is indicative of a more realistic approach to reunification, not its abandonment.

Although the Irish government was well informed about discrimination against the Catholic population, they tended to use this evidence as justification for a united Ireland, rather than lobby for reform, and they offered scant support to the groups who were campaigning against discrimination. When Cahir Healy, Northern Nationalist MP, urged that Ireland raise discrimination against Northern Catholics at the United Nations, Lemass placated him by asking for up-to-date information, but there is no indication that any use was made of the fat file supplied.[34] Dublin avoided any official connection with the Campaign for Social Justice (CSJ) – an organisation founded by middle-class Catholics to

---

[30] 'The Northern Catholic', by John Hume, *IT*, 18 May, 1964. This piece emerged as a consequence of a series of articles about Northern Ireland by Michael Viney.
[31] Horgan, *Lemass*, pp. 260–2. The official *Statistical Abstract* continued to use 'Six Counties', in the early 1970s.
[32] Conor Cruise O' Brien, *States of Ireland* (London: Panther, 1974 edition), p. 140.
[33] Staunton, *Nationalists of Northern Ireland*, pp. 214–6, S9361G. Kennedy, *Division and consensus*, p. 168.
[34] Horgan, *Lemass*, pp. 267–8.

publicise discrimination in housing and social services. Irish diplomats were advised to adopt a similar line because of fears that any contact might jeopardise a closer relationship with the Northern government.[35] Dr Conn McCluskey, who with his wife founded the CSJ in 1963, contacted the *Irish Press* and *Irish Independent* asking for publicity; they informed him that discrimination in Northern Ireland was not newsworthy.[36] The CSJ emphasised that Northern Ireland was part of the United Kingdom, and its citizens sought the rights common to British citizens.[37] In 1964, when National Unity sought financial support for its journal *New Nation*, the Minister for External Affairs Frank Aiken advised that the request be refused. Sarah Campbell concludes that 'Dublin thus missed the opportunity to direct Northern politics away from the constitutional issue and towards participation within the state.'[38] Reviewing Irish government policy towards Northern Ireland in the early 1960s, Staunton commented that 'It seems a paradoxical position to on the one hand abandon traditional anti-partitionism yet on the other to refrain from following through on the logic of this by supporting the increasingly reformist initiatives emanating from within the minority community.' According to Staunton, the Irish government was keen to get Britain to state that they had no interest in maintaining partition, and in order to achieve this were prepared to soft pedal on issues such as discrimination.[39] Kennedy claimed that 'By ignoring the position of nationalists through the 1960s and making their peace with unionism, the authorities in Dublin had lost touch with the minority community in Northern Ireland.'[40] Furthermore, by following Dublin's advice to integrate into the Northern Ireland parliamentary system, Northern nationalists lost credibility with their constituents. Yet an opinion poll by the *Belfast Telegraph* in December 1967 suggests that northern Catholics subscribed to Lemass' rhetoric on Northern Ireland: '67 per cent of Catholics and 70 per cent of nationalist voters believed that joining the EEC would hasten reunification; they also believed that economic co-operation between north and south would make the border superfluous; 67 per cent believed that the border would disappear – the majority of these expected it to vanish within 10–20 years'.[41]

[35] Mulholland, *Northern Ireland at the Crossroads*, p. 137; Staunton, *Nationalists of Northern Ireland*, p. 248.

[36] Conn McCluskey, *Up off their knees: a commentary on the civil rights movement in Northern Ireland* (Dungannon: Conn McCluskey and Associates, 1989), p. 22.

[37] Lynn, *Holding the ground*, p. 171.

[38] Sarah Campbell, 'New nationalism? The origins of the SDLP, 1969–1974', (Ph.D., UCD, 2010), p. 20.

[39] Staunton, *Nationalists of Northern Ireland*, pp. 233–4.

[40] Kennedy, *Division and consensus*, p. 308.

[41] Mulholland, *Northern Ireland at the Crossroads*, p. 5.

The official celebrations marking the Golden Jubilee of the Easter Rising reflected the distance between the two nationalist traditions. In Dublin, the government used the Jubilee to celebrate the achievements of an independent Ireland and committed the state to providing improved socio-economic and educational opportunities for its citizens. Margaret O'Callaghan noted that 'If any cabinet or commemoration committee discussions of the implications or consequences of the state-planned commemorations for nationalists in a northern context took place no record of these has been found.' Nevertheless, 'The fact of the commemoration reminded people that they were a part of the Irish nation, even if the Irish state did not have much to say to them.' The Irish government blocked requests for a special train to carry republican supporters to the Belfast commemoration one week after the main Dublin event. Northern Ireland authorities alerted Dublin (via Whitaker) of their plans to seal the border over that weekend. Partition featured only marginally in the Dublin celebrations. De Valera referred twice in general terms to his hopes that a united Ireland would be achieved by uniting all the people and forgetting past differences and dissensions. In a special Irish supplement of *The Statist*, Lemass spoke of his desire to strengthen contacts and co-operation between the two parts of Ireland, before going on to express a wish 'to see a clear statement by British political leaders that there is no British interest in maintaining partition'. Northern nationalists were invited to two of the less important official events: a showing of the documentary *An Tine Bheo* and a reception hosted by the Taoiseach on the closing Sunday of the week of celebrations.[42] They were not invited however to the GPO on Easter Sunday or to the state reception that evening. The Jubilee united all nationalist factions in Northern Ireland. One underlying trend was the call to mark the Jubilee through local events, and not by travelling to Dublin. O'Callaghan concludes that the commemorations in Northern Ireland 'underlined the fact that however deep the divisions within Northern nationalists went, they were as nothing to the divide between Northern nationalists and an Irish state that seemed capable of conceiving of itself as a nation without them'.[43]

The summer of 1966 was a turning point in north–south relations.[44] O'Neill's failure to prevent the 1916 commemoration in Northern Ireland fuelled unionist extremism, and the commemoration undoubtedly damaged whatever progress was being made in official contacts between the two governments. Visits to Belfast by Dublin civil servants

[42] Margaret O'Callaghan, 'Commemorating the Rising in Northern Ireland in 1966', pp. 95 and 140; Daly, 'Less a commemoration', pp. 56–7.
[43] O Callaghan, 'Commemorating the Rising in Northern Ireland in 1966', p. 138.
[44] Kennedy, *Division and Consensus*, p. 271.

were suspended when sectarian tensions increased. Although meetings on north-south co-operation continued until 1969, the pace slackened. Agreement was reached on a number of non-contentious issues; for example, Dublin agreed to recognise the qualifications of teachers trained in Northern Ireland. Mulholland describes the practical benefits as 'relatively limited',[45] and I would agree. Ken Bloomfield, a senior Northern Ireland civil servant, claimed that 'Although substantive issues were, of course, discussed, I always felt that these meetings were more about symbolism than substance ... Northern Ireland could not play on two different teams at the same time.'[46] Attitudes were not dramatically different in the Republic. While the symbolism of Lemass' visit to Stormont and the return trip to Dublin by O'Neill and his wife was welcomed, it remains unclear how far Irish ministers were prepared to go in promoting meaningful cross-border co-operation. A review of actual and potential areas for co-operation in the autumn of 1963, that is, before the landmark meeting, indicated several areas where civil servants believed that Northern Ireland was blocking co-operation; however, there was little enthusiasm in Dublin for extending existing co-operative arrangements.[47] The O'Neill/Lemass meeting did not alter this position significantly; the secretaries of the Departments of Agriculture and Industry and Commerce were unwilling to extend further trade concessions to Northern Ireland.[48] Lemass' commitment to closer relations with Northern Ireland cannot be questioned, but in many respects the policy was flawed. Northern businessmen were happy to take advantage of tariff reductions and other unilateral concessions by Dublin, but that did not translate into a closer political relationship, and Northern Ireland ministers were apprehensive about the implications of AIFTAA for their farmers. O'Neill was under almost continuous pressure from his own party – leadership heaves were afoot from 1964 onwards. When Ulster Unionists criticised O'Neill, his meetings with Lemass and toleration of the Golden Jubilee celebrations were high on the list of shortcomings. The Young Unionists refused to express support for the O'Neill/Lemass meetings, despite having been Lemass' guest some years earlier.[49] Groups associated with Rev Ian Paisley campaigned against any gestures of friendship towards the Catholic Church or the Dublin government. Garvin, whose opinion of Lemass borders on hagiography, suggests, I believe correctly,

---

[45] Mulholland, *Northern Ireland at the Crossroads*, pp. 86–8.
[46] Bloomfield, *Stormont in Crisis*, p. 83.
[47] Kennedy, *Division and Consensus*, pp. 202–7.
[48] David McCann, 'Whitaker and Northern Ireland policy from 1959 to 1972', *ISIA*, vol. 23, 2012, pp. 176–8.
[49] Mulholland, *Northern Ireland at the Crossroads*, pp. 110, 144.

that Lemass 'did to some extent, and like most southerners, retain a certain innocence about northern realities, in particular the implacable collective resistance of the Unionist population to anything that looked even vaguely like a Dublin takeover bid or anything that seemed to threaten the union with Britain'. 'Eventually, the North was to defeat him, and he ended up engaged with the problem but openly baffled by it.'[50]

Officially Jack Lynch's policy was a continuation of Lemass': promoting north-south co-operation without making concessions on political and constitutional matters. Yet although Lynch described O'Neill as 'a most enlightened man', the *Irish Times* suggested that Lynch was more doctrinaire than Lemass; he described the border as unnatural. Ryle Dwyer remarked that in his first speech to Dáil Éireann as Taoiseach, Lynch expressed support for de Valera's goals of reviving the Irish language and ending partition – but Lynch didn't mention de Valera, and what he said about partition was not noticeably different to Lemass.[51] Briefing notes for Lynch's first meeting as Taoiseach with British Prime Minister Harold Wilson in December 1966 reiterated the message that north-south co-operation would promote peaceful reunification. They also suggested that he ask Wilson about prospects of electoral reform in Northern Ireland and British intervention on the question of discrimination against Catholics.[52] But Ireland's priorities were trade and EEC membership. Northern Ireland only ranked fourth in a list of priorities given to the Irish ambassador in London in 1966.[53] Brian Harrison summarised Britain's position towards Northern Ireland as follows: 'as long as no major abuses were exposed or discontent erupted, British governments of either party let well or ill alone'.[54] Britain was determined not to become involved in north-south discussions, and equally determined not to discuss political and social reform in Northern Ireland with the Irish government.[55]

Although Lynch met Wilson within weeks of becoming Taoiseach, it was a further year before he met O'Neill. Their meeting covered a standard repertoire of safe topics: cooperation on tourism, electricity

---

[50] Garvin, *Judging Lemass*, pp. 219–20.
[51] T. Ryle Dwyer, *Nice Fellow. A biography of Jack Lynch* (Cork: Mercier, 2001), p. 141; DD 225, 16 November 1966, cols. 1183–4.
[52] Dwyer, *Nice Fellow*, p. 143.
[53] First was British foreign and defence policies; second EEC and EFTA developments; third British policy on major international issues such as Britain east of Suez, Vietnam, NATO, Cyprus. Craig, *Crisis of confidence*, p. 8.
[54] Brian Harrison, *Seeking a role. The United Kingdom 1951–1970* (Oxford: Oxford University Press, 2009), p. 426.
[55] Kennedy, *Division and consensus*, pp. 282–3.

and cultural exchanges, and the possibility of opening Irish government contracts to Northern Ireland businesses.[56] But whereas the first O'Neill/ Lemass meeting got a very positive reception in Northern Ireland, Lynch's visit took place against a background of growing unionist opposition, which extended far beyond the snowballs that Ian Paisley threw at Lynch's car. When O'Neill paid a second visit to Iveagh House, he returned to Belfast by a circuitous route to avoid protesters.[57] An editorial in the next day's *Irish Press* referred to a 'sickness in Northern society' and warned of the dangers of accommodating such a society; the only merits of a closer relationship was to help achieve a united Ireland. In subsequent months the *Irish Press* published a growing number of letters criticising Irish ministers for meeting Northern Ireland ministers, while remaining silent about discrimination against Catholics.[58]

Lynch is widely seen as letting policy on Northern Ireland drift until the Arms Crisis of May 1970, though Kennedy suggests that this judgement fails to take account of the growing resistance to change in Northern Ireland. He notes that Lynch was relying on the same advisors as Lemass, and when tensions increased during 1966, they had urged caution.[59] Yet there is little evidence that Lynch's Cabinet was committed to fostering practical co-operation with the Northern government. Neil Blaney refused to attend meetings with his British counterpart if a civil servant from the Northern Ireland Ministry of Agriculture was present. In 1968, the British ambassador in Dublin, Sir Andrew Gilchrist reported that Hugh McCann, Secretary of the DEA, 'like others in his Department [he] was puzzled by Blaney's attitude to Northern Ireland officials; there was perhaps a political point about Republican Cabinet Ministers not sitting down tripartitely with Ulster Ministers but on officials he (personally) saw no real difficulty and would try to sort the thing out'. McCann brokered a compromise where Northern Ireland officials could be present as observers, but not form part of the team.[60] By 1968, Lemass' policy towards Northern Ireland, which had relied heavily on O'Neill and on pragmatic unionist goodwill, was unravelling.

In the spring of 1968, Whitaker broached the topic of partition with Sir Arthur Snelling, Deputy Under-secretary of State in the FCO, during a meeting to discuss Ireland's sterling reserves. Whitaker claimed to be speaking 'not as an Irish official but merely as an Irish citizen'. Snelling minuted that 'His question proved to have a financial twist. He asked the

---

[56] Keogh, *Jack Lynch*, pp. 135–6.   [57] Dwyer, *Nice Fellow*, p. 154.
[58] Frank Foley, 'North-South relations and the outbreak of the Troubles in Northern Ireland, 1968–9: the response of the "Irish Press"', *ISIA*, vol. 14, 2003, pp. 11–12.
[59] Kennedy, *Division and consensus*, p. 296.
[60] TNA FCO 62/91. Craig, *Crisis of confidence*, pp. 22–4.

familiar question whether the British attitude was that ending partition was a matter which could be left to Northern and Southern Ireland. I said it was primarily the job of the man in the South to woo the girl in the North. If successful I thought we would be prepared to give the bride away and lead her to the altar but not prepared to put pressure on her.' Whitaker admitted that 'if partition ended tomorrow and Britain ceased to subsidise the North, the standard of living of the North would fall'. He estimated the British subsidy at approximately £30 million, the majority for agriculture and social security. He asked if there was any hope that Britain would be willing to continue to subsidise Northern Ireland 'on this scale' after partition ended. Snelling replied that 'it was a new thought to me and I could not imagine an enthusiastic reception in any quarter of London. However we had to remember that we were now seeing the beginning of a trend towards greater regionalism in Britain and that we might be faced with more Northern Irelands.'[61] Given Lynch's reliance on Whitaker as a key advisor on Northern Ireland, this conversation may indicate that Lynch's mind was already focusing on partition rather than north–south co-operation. Whitaker's question could be seen either as prompted by Lynch or as an attempt to collect evidence to dissuade Lynch from fantasising about reunification. He seriously under-estimated Britain's financial contribution; a later study put the 1967/8 figure at £126 million[62] – further evidence of Dublin's lack of knowledge about Northern Ireland.

The informal all-party Committee on the Constitution, which reported in 1967, recommended changes to several key articles in order to make it more acceptable to unionists, including rewriting Article 3 and dividing it into two clauses: 3.1 'The Irish nation hereby proclaims its firm will that its territory be re-united in harmony and brotherly affection between all Irishmen. 3.2. The laws enacted by the Parliament established by this Constitution shall, until the achievement of the nation's unity shall other-wise require, have the like area and extent of application as the laws of Saorstát Éireann and the like extra-territorial effect.' The Committee recommended amending the constitution to permit divorce for those whose church permitted it and deleting Article 44 – which referred to 'the special position of the Catholic Church'. But the Committee on the Constitution was Lemass' initiative. Lynch gave the impression that he was determined to bury it. His decision to embark on a referendum to abolish PR ended all prospects of cross-party support for constitutional

[61] FCO 48/26 Sterling Irish republic diversification of.
[62] John Simpson, 'Regional analysis: the Northern Ireland experience', *ESR*, vol. 2, no. 4, July 1971, pp. 5–29.

change, and it showed scant regard for Northern nationalists who were demanding the reintroduction of PR. The timing could scarcely have been worse; the vote took place less than two weeks after a civil rights march in Derry, which resulted in serious violence. One Monaghan councillor suggested that events in Derry 'should be a warning to them at the polls on Wednesday not to allow the same electoral system that was the cause of the troubles in Derry to be foisted on them'.[63] Frank Curran, then editor of the *Derry Journal*, claimed that 'The Fianna Fáil push against PR altered many of the perceptions of that party's dedication to the interests of the northern minority. Fianna Fáil ceased to be the respected guardians of the nationalist and national rights'.[64]

The year 1968 was a year of protest throughout the Western world, and this militancy infected civil rights groups in Northern Ireland, which had previously concentrated on lobbying and petitioning for change. In August, the Northern Ireland Civil Rights Association (NICRA) orga-nised the first civil rights march from Coalisland to Dungannon. The march, which attracted 2,000 people, was modelled on US civil rights marches; members of the IRA acted as stewards, the AOH and nationalist bands also took part.[65] Fanning claims that 'the silence of the Irish archives suggests that the civil rights march in August 1968, which many historians have identified as the first spark in the coming conflagra-tion, made no impact upon Jack Lynch's government'; this was also the case with the civil rights march in Derry on 5 October, when a baton charge by the RUC led to 50 people being admitted to hospital.[66] The Derry marchers included three British Labour MPs plus Gerry Fitt, which ensured that the event was noticed in Britain; the MPs briefed Wilson on their experience. Thanks to Teilifís Éireann cameraman Gay O'Brien, the baton charge in Derry was seen and heard around the world.[67] Irish viewers were conscious of international parallels; one Monaghan councillor compared events in Derry with 'what happened in Chicago' – a reference to the brutal riots during the 1968 Democratic Party Convention.[68] Speaking in Kilkenny the day after the Derry march, Lynch blamed the violence on 'the methods necessary to maintain Partition against the wishes of the vast majority of the Irish people'. The

[63] 'Monaghan views on Derry scenes', *Anglo-Celt*, 18 October 1968.
[64] Curran, *Derry*, pp. 86–7.
[65] Mulholland, *Northern Ireland at the Crossroads*, pp. 7–8, 15; Simon Prince, *Northern Ireland '68: civil rights, global revolt and the origins of The Troubles* (Dublin; Irish Academic Press, 2007); Hanley and Millar, *The lost revolution*, pp. 101–3.
[66] Fanning, 'Playing it cool', p. 59.
[67] John Horgan, *Broadcasting and public life RTÉ news and current affairs 1926–1997* (Dublin: Four Courts, 2004), p. 74.
[68] *Anglo-Celt*, 18 October 1968.

emphasis on partition jarred with the remainder of the speech which called for efforts to improve community relations, eliminate discrimination and introduced full democratic rights (in Northern Ireland). Although copies were distributed to Irish embassies, Aiken instructed diplomats not to become involved in debates or public controversy about Northern Ireland.[69] The Kilkenny speech is representative of many later Lynch speeches in veering from more traditional anti-partition rhetoric to demands for internal reform – symptomatic of Lynch's twin-track approach – or more realistically his efforts to placate the diverse views within Fianna Fáil.

When Lynch met Wilson on 30 October, three weeks after the Derry march, his briefing notes recommended that he should press for political reform in Northern Ireland and not be deflected into the details of housing and job discrimination; he was also advised to press for an end to the convention where Northern Ireland was not discussed at Westminster. Fanning describes the notes as 'remarkably devoid of old-style anti-partitionist cant'. But Lynch deviated from his script, identifying partition as the basic cause of events in Northern Ireland.[70] He spoke in similar terms when he addressed the Westminster Anglo-Irish Parliamentary Group at a lunch before his meeting with Wilson, and at a post-meeting press conference in the Irish embassy, when he said that 'partition was the greatest bugbear to harmony in Northern Ireland'. He suggested that the British government 'is not particularly interested in the continuation of Partition'.[71] While such rhetoric may have protected him against Fianna Fáil militants, this maladroit intervention was unwise. Fanning suggested that 'Lynch's exploitation of his October meeting with Wilson for domestic policy purposes damaged the fragile relationship between Dublin and London; it also explains why both Wilson and his successor, Ted Heath, were so reluctant to meet Lynch in 1969–70.'[72] Lynch's government was also in danger of alienating the new generation of Northern nationalists. When Blaney made a strong speech against partition on 8 November, it drew criticism from Gerry Fitt, who suggested that the speech was not calculated to help the civil rights movement or to further the cause of Irish unity.[73]

Whitaker tried to persuade Lynch to continue Lemass' policy of unity by agreement: 'a long-term policy requiring patience, understanding forbearance and resolute resistance to emotionalism and opportunism. It is none the less patriotic for that'. He cautioned that 'any other policy

---

[69] Keogh, *Jack Lynch*, pp138–9.   [70] Fanning, 'Playing it cool', p. 60.
[71] *II*, 31 October 1968.   [72] Fanning, 'Playing it cool', p. 62.
[73] *IT*, 9 November 1968.

risks creating a deeper and more real partition than has ever existed in the past . . . Relying on Britain to solve Partition is also futile.' All that could be expected was 'a benevolent neutrality – that no British interest will be interposed to prevent the re-unification of Ireland when Irishmen, North and South, have reached agreement'. Whitaker warned of the economic cost of unification and expressed fears that some Labour MPs would like to expel Northern Ireland from the United Kingdom; any suspicion that Dublin was trying to force Britain to disengage from Northern Ireland or reduce financial support would be damaging. The government should not be concerned that O'Neill's reforms would 'seduce' Northern nationalists into becoming 'happy citizens of a Northern Ireland within the U.K. . . . O'Neill's policy, besides being best for our Nationalist brethren in the short-run, is most likely to loosen the roots of Partition and prepare the way for agreement between North and South on some from [sic] of re-unification.' 'The patient good-neighbour policy aimed at "ultimate agreement in Ireland between Irishmen" ' offered the only hope of success. The government could 'leave it mostly to public opinion and to pressure from the British Parliament and Government to prod the Northern Ireland Government into more vigorous and effective reforms regarding social conditions and the local franchise'. If progress remained slow 'we might consider what we could do vis-à-vis the Belfast, in preference to the London Government'. In a further effort to counter any naive fantasies about imminent reunification, he set out the extent of British financial subsidies to Northern Ireland.

Whitaker's realism about the cost of a united Ireland contrasts with his naïve optimism about prospects for internal reform in Northern Ireland. He believed that increased prosperity throughout Ireland, full employment and satisfying housing needs would remove Northern Unionist fears and bring to an end 'the root cause of discrimination'.[74] His advice was that the government should express a wish for reunification by consent, work to foster co-operation with Northern Ireland, but rely on O'Neill to implement reforms, while not doing anything in public or in private to press for reform. This amounted to a very passive role, which left it to Stormont and Whitehall to address Northern minority demands. Like Lemass, Whitaker underestimated the strength of Ulster unionism as an ideology. His advice ruled out any engagement with the nationalist community, the civil rights movement and probably also with the UK authorities. *Hibernia* suggested, 'If the Taoiseach with the Cabinet is convinced that the Lemass initiative has proven futile then he has a responsibility to produce something else.'[75] 'Something else' was not

[74] UCDA P 175/1.   [75] *Hibernia*, 15–28 November 1968.

forthcoming. Whitaker's advice of silence and continuing to trust O'Neill was not a workable policy.

On 22 November 1968, under pressure from Wilson, and following a lengthy Cabinet session, O' Neill announced a five-point programme of reforms, which significantly did not include one-man one-vote in local elections. Civil rights activists regarded the concessions as too little and too late, but they proved too radical for many Ulster unionists. O'Neill tried to overcome the growing challenge to his leadership within the parliamentary party by appealing to the public. In his famous 'Ulster at the Crossroads' speech on 9 December, he appealed to the middle-ground, asking: 'What kind of Ulster do you want?'[76] His speech attracted extensive support, especially in Belfast. *Sunday Independent* readers voted him 'Man of the Year', though he only received 2,000 plus votes. The *Irish Press* published the full text and praised O'Neill's 'resolution and statesmanship', while denouncing the Unionist establishment.[77] The speech brought a temporary truce in demonstrations by moderate civil rights campaigners, but the radical student group, People's Democracy, refused to call off a planned march from Belfast to Derry. They were attacked en route at Burntollet bridge; once again the photographs were seen around the world. Brian Faulkner, Minister for Commerce, O'Neill's most powerful challenger, resigned from Cabinet shortly after this. O'Neill's final throw of the dice was to call a general election.

Despite the obvious weakening of O'Neill's position, most Dublin-based media continued to cling to the possibility of a benevolent outcome. Wesley Boyd claimed that Douglas Gageby, editor of the *Irish Times*, 'viewed the evolving events there, certainly up to the start of the Troubles in 1969, with benign optimism'.[78] When O'Neill called a general election in February 1969, 'Gageby and Healy [the *Irish Times* political correspondent] convinced themselves that O'Neill would wipe out his opponents, and credited him with wholly imaginary political skills. Most weirdly, Healy wrote about old-time republicans overcoming their prejudices and coming down from the hills to campaign for him in his Antrim constituency. In all my life I have never heard anything resembling confirmation of this. I regard it as fantasy.'[79] The belief that O'Neill was a reforming prime minister was not confined to the *Irish Times*. In October 1968, following the Derry civil rights march, the chairman of

---

[76] Mulholland *Northern Ireland at the Crossroads*, pp. 165–70.

[77] Foley, 'North-South Relations', p. 19.

[78] Wesley Boyd, 'The mantle of Wolfe Tone', in Andrew Whitaker (ed.), *Bright, brilliant days. Douglas Gageby and* The Irish Times (Dublin: A&A Farmar, 2006), p. 78.

[79] James Downey, 'Irish Catholics' favourite Protestant editor', in Whitaker (ed.), *Bright, brilliant days*, p. 26.

Monaghan County Council noted that O' Neill and nationalist MP Eddie McAteer were going to London to meet Harold Wilson. 'He hoped some good would come.' [80] Dublin newspapers predicted an O'Neill landslide on several occasions in the run-up to the election. The *Irish Independent* carried an article by Barry White, political correspondent of the *Belfast Telegraph*, predicting a split in the Unionist party. All who wished to see the Unionist stranglehold broken would be 'eternally grateful' to O'Neill; he predicted that O'Neill would attract a substantial Catholic vote. [81] When the results showed that O'Neill had failed to secure a strong mandate, the *Irish Independent* suggested that O'Neill 'may congratulate himself on achieving objectives which may well prove of inestimable value to the North eventually'; he had exposed the divisions in unionism and showed that there was a substantial number who accepted the need for a 'levelling-up in the rights denied to thousands'. [82] Such wishful thinking – the belief that reform would ultimately triumph – may account for Lynch's inactivity. Fanning notes that 'many of the more seductively titled files' on Northern Ireland 'are largely composed of newspaper clippings and transcripts of radio and television broadcasts', [83] produced by journalists with no real knowledge of Northern Ireland. RTÉ had no resident correspondent, neither did any of the four daily newspapers. [84] The *Irish Press* described February 1969 as 'one of the most baffling elections of all time'; while they had urged Catholics not to endorse O'Neill, they failed to anticipate the collapse of the Nationalist Party and the triumph of new nationalist politicians, such as John Hume. [85] There is no indication that the Dublin government made any effort to get to know these men.

In a note titled 'The IRA and the Republic', dated July 1968, Sir Andrew Gilchrist, the British ambassador, asserted: 'Scratch them on partition and you will rouse Irish emotions, that is certain.' [86] By the winter of 1968/9 emotions were rising. TV news bulletins carried pictures of protests and police violence in Northern Ireland, which were often followed or preceded by pictures of war in Vietnam or international anti-war protests. The *Irish Press* began to publish pages of photographs of marches and demonstrations. [87] Civil rights agitation in Northern Ireland attracted support from left-wing groups, such as the Dublin Housing Action Committee, which was controlled by the IRA. Left-wing protest movements in north and south appeared to be coalescing, which was the goal of the republican movement. Sinn Féin President Tomás Mac Giolla

[80] *Anglo-Celt*, 18 October 1968.   [81] *II*, 22 February. 1969.   [82] *II*, 26 February 1969.
[83] Fanning, 'Playing it cool', pp. 59–60.   [84] Keogh, *Lynch*, p. 152.
[85] Foley, 'North-South Relations', pp. 16–18.
[86] Quoted by Craig, *Crisis of confidence*, p. 12.   [87] Foley, 'North-South Relations', p. 23.

predicted the disintegration of Fianna Fáil and the Ulster Unionist Party.[88] Several thousands attended a People's Democracy meeting outside the GPO. Foley claims that the *Irish Press* was 'relishing what it believed to be the results of violence and instability in Northern Ireland – an increasing potential for constitutional change'.[89] They were probably not alone.

With events in Northern Ireland attracting growing international attention, the Department of External Affairs issued a circular to all embassies in March 1969 instructing them that 'the less said the better' and urging diplomats to avoid giving public speeches or interviews relating to Northern Ireland.[90] Riots in Derry and the bombing of Belfast's main reservoir led to British troops being deployed to guard strategic sites. O'Neill's position became increasingly precarious. He resigned on 28 April. On 21 April, Whitaker, now Governor of the Central Bank, sent a letter to Charles Haughey, apparently at Lynch's behest, urging caution. Whitaker's growing foreboding is evident. He suggested that extremists were manipulating the civil rights movement in the hope of fomenting disorder; he warned that civil war 'or anything near it would make real unity impossible'. The Irish authorities should 'convey to the UK Government our anxiety that they should act with the greatest care so as not to add to an inflammatory situation which might easily spread to the whole of this partitioned island and use their influence to secure an effective remedying of the immediate (and at least long-term remedying of the ultimate) causes of the present crisis'. The Taoiseach should take the first opportunity to make 'a full and authoritative statement' of the government's policy on partition: 'i.e. a peaceful solution based on agreement between North and South and British support and goodwill'.[91] This reads like an attempt by an increasingly beleaguered Lynch to invoke Whitaker's assistance in keeping Haughey in line – an interesting intervention given that Haughey had made no recent public statement on Northern Ireland.[92]

Given the increasing tension, it is quite remarkable that Northern Ireland barely featured in the Irish general election campaign of May/June,[93] though Fianna Fáil was more than happy to highlight the threat

---

[88] Hanley and Millar, *Lost revolution*, pp. 107–10.
[89] Foley, 'North–South Relations', p. 24.   [90] Fanning, 'Playing it cool', p. 67.
[91] UCDA P175/56.
[92] Stephen Kelly, 'Fresh evidence from the archives: the genesis of Charles J. Haughey's attitude to Northern Ireland', *ISIA*, vol. 23, 2012, pp. 155–70. In an exchange of memos between Haughey and Whitaker in 1968, in relation to the Committee on the Constitution, Haughey wrote that 'we would never abandon the moral right to use force. We have the right to use force to defend the national territory'. Chambers, *Whitaker*, p. 272.
[93] A search of the *Irish Times* uncovered no significant statements from any candidate regarding Northern Ireland, other than comparisons by Labour candidates between the Criminal Justice Bill and legislation in Northern Ireland, but these comparisons were made to highlight domestic issues.

presented by left-wing 'Communist' groups.[94] ' "Support for the objectives of the Civil Rights movement" was common to all parties.'[95] According to Sinnott, only 1 per cent identified Northern Ireland as the most important issue, compared with over 20 per cent who identified inflation, education and welfare, labour relations or unemployment.[96] When Lynch returned to office, Hillery became Minister for External Affairs, succeeding Aiken – who, as a native of South Armagh, had first-hand knowledge of Northern Ireland. During his final months as minister, Aiken had been extremely careful not to do or say anything that would damage relations with Britain.[97] Hillery by contrast had no direct experience of Northern Ireland or foreign affairs. On 1 August he travelled to London to meet British Foreign Secretary Michael Stewart, with a request that Britain should prevent the Apprentice Boys from marching in Derry on 12 August. Stewart reiterated that Northern Ireland was a matter for Stormont and Whitehall – Dublin had no role to play. Hillery indicated that if violence increased he would be under pressure to raise the question of Northern Ireland at the United Nations.[98]

As is well known and widely documented, 12 August saw the first significant violence of the Northern Ireland conflict, beginning in Derry and spreading to Belfast. There are lengthy and occasionally conflicting accounts about what happened around the Cabinet table during the emergency meetings that began on 13 August. Hillery has described the meetings as like 'a ballad session ... They were all talking patriotic.'[99] There is widespread agreement that militants – probably Haughey, Boland and Blaney – raised the possibility that the Irish army might intervene, though how seriously this was entertained is unclear. According to Padraig Faulkner (a moderate), 'the possibility of incursions into the North was raised but quickly dismissed. As far as I can remember the matter was raised in a rather haphazard way and was given little or no consideration.' Stephen Collins suggests that the talk was about contingency plans, not an immediate incursion.[100] Des O'Malley, who was present as Chief Whip, has stated that 'The possibility of some form of humanitarian incursion into the North was contemplated if needed; but it was a discussion in the context of a possible serious attack on nationalists

---

[94] Hanley and Millar, *Lost revolution*, pp. 119–21.

[95] Cruise O'Brien, *States of Ireland*, p. 178.

[96] Sinnott, *Irish voters decide*, p. 178, table 7.4; voters could identify more than one issue.

[97] Craig, *Crisis of confidence*, p. 47; Fanning, 'Playing it cool', pp. 67–70.

[98] Fanning, 'Playing it cool', p. 71.

[99] In an interview with Ronan Fanning, 20 June 2001 as cited by Fanning, 'Playing it cool', p. 74.

[100] Keogh, *Lynch*, pp. 168–9; Faulkner, *As I saw it*, pp. 89–91; Stephen Collins, *The power game: Ireland under Fianna Fáil* (Dublin: O'Brien Press, 2001).

close to the border and consequent loss of life.'[101] On 13 August Boland
indicated that he was resigning from the government because he had
failed to secure support for military intervention, but was persuaded to
withdraw his resignation. On 11 August (before the march) the *Irish Press*
had published a call by Eddie McAteer, the former Nationalist MP, for
the Irish army to intervene if Derry Catholics were attacked.[102] Rumours
of Irish army intervention were rife in Derry. As John Hume walked to his
home on the evening of 13 August, 'people spontaneously spilled out on
the streets shouting "The Irish army's coming!" ' His wife, who had
watched Lynch's television broadcast told him that this was not the
case.[103]

The initial draft of Lynch's television speech, written in Iveagh House,
was amended by the Cabinet. Faulkner said that Blaney later claimed that
'the speech was no longer the Taoiseach's but really expressed his and
like-minded minister's views', though Faulkner disagreed. Lynch's biographer Dermot Keogh rejected accusations that Lynch lost control of the
government and 'capitulate[d] to the hawks',[104] but this begs the question – what were Lynch's views? We know that Lynch amended the
speech after the Cabinet meeting ended; the final version had to be
typed in the television centre. He was in an extremely nervous state; he
made the broadcast fortified by a 'stiffener of Paddy'.[105] Lynch adopted a
militant tone, but stopped short of committing to immediate intervention
in Northern Ireland. He emphasised that the government had made their
concerns known to the British government. Up to this point they had
'acted with great restraint' and were careful 'to do nothing that would
exacerbate the situation'. This would no longer be the case: 'the Irish
Government can no longer stand by and see innocent people injured and
perhaps worse'. The Stormont Government was no longer in control; the
RUC was no longer accepted as an impartial police force, and the British
army (who were not yet on the streets of Northern Ireland) would not be
acceptable. He called on Britain to request the United Nations to send an
immediate peace-keeping force to Northern Ireland and to ensure that
attacks by the police on the people of Derry cease immediately. [Both
messages had already been communicated to Whitehall.] The Irish army
was sending field hospitals to border areas to treat 'many of the people
who do not wish to be treated in Six County Hospitals'. The closing
section dealt with partition: he requested the British government to enter
into negotiations 'to review the present constitutional position of the Six

[101] O'Malley, *Conduct unbecoming*, p. 54.   [102] Foley, 'North-south relations', pp. 26–7.
[103] Barry White, *John Hume. Statesman of the troubles* (Belfast: Blackstaff, 1984), p. 84.
[104] Faulkner, *As I saw it*, p. 91. Keogh, *Lynch*, p. 170.
[105] Fisher, 'Irishman's Diary', *IT*, 25 October 1999.

Counties of Northern Ireland'.[106] Britain responded to this speech, predictably, by reiterating that Northern Ireland would remain part of the United Kingdom unless the people of Northern Ireland decided otherwise. As Northern Ireland was part of the United Kingdom, there was no question of UN intervention.

On the night of 13/14 August, the Northern Ireland government deployed the B-Specials on the streets and violence spread to Belfast, where seven people were killed and over 150, mainly Catholic homes, destroyed. Patterson suggests that 'the Lynch broadcast and the mobilization of the B Specials contributed powerfully to the worst outbreak of communal violence since the 1920s'.[107] Blaney contacted Iveagh House demanding action – a blatant example of a minister bypassing Cabinet protocol and his Taoiseach. The Cabinet meeting on 14 August appears to have been equally heated, despite Boland's absence. Hillery, who had been absent the previous day, was instructed to travel to Britain to meet either the Prime Minister or Foreign Secretary to reiterate demands for UN intervention and an end to police violence in Derry – demands which Britain had already rejected. Troops would be sent to protect the field hospitals – a further escalation of military activity. The Minister for Justice was instructed to expand the Garda's intelligence service in 'the Six Counties' and a committee of the secretaries of the Departments of Justice, External Affairs, Defence and Local Government was established 'to keep the situation under continuous review'. British troops arrived on the streets of Derry that evening – a move broadly welcomed by Northern nationalists and by many in the Republic. When the Cabinet met on August 15 it decided to call up the first line army reserves 'in readiness for participation in peace-keeping operations'. The presence of Irish troops on the border fuelled rumours that an incursion into Northern Ireland was contemplated; Kennedy suggests that the Cabinet agreed 'off the record the contingency of a doomsday scenario in which Southern troops would invade Northern Ireland to create an international incident and thereby bring in the United Nations',[108] though what was decided, and the proposed extent of any such invasion, continues to be contested.

Although Britain was extremely reluctant to intervene in Northern Ireland, during the winter of 1968/69, Wilson's government devised contingency plans for dealing with various levels of crisis, and these were implemented in August 1969. Britain was determined to take any action short of direct rule. By contrast, the Irish government was scrabbling around, uncertain how to respond. The pressure from Northern

---

[106] Keogh, *Lynch*, pp. 170–2.   [107] Patterson, *Ireland since 1939*, p. 215.
[108] Kennedy, *Division and Consensus*, p. 342.

nationalist groups should not be under-estimated. Austin Currie met Lynch to discuss the situation in Dungannon and urged him to refer to the 'protection' of the Catholic population in any future statements. Lynch also met Armagh nationalist Senator James Lennon.[109] Bernadette Devlin of People's Democracy contacted the Department of Defence demanding gas masks, tear gas and troops to repel 'a united force of police and Paisleyites'. On the evening of August 16, Northern MPs Paddy Devlin, Paddy O'Hanlon and Paddy Kennedy arrived at Iveagh House demanding arms to protect Belfast Catholics; when their demand was rejected, they insisted on meeting Lynch (also refused).[110] They indicated that they would hold the Dublin government responsible for Catholic deaths if their demands were not met.[111] Michael Mills claims that 'requests for guns were made to almost every journalist from Dublin visiting Belfast at the time'.[112] On the other hand, John Hume tried to ring Lynch on 13 August to advise caution.[113] Hillery's meeting with two British junior ministers produced nothing, other than a request that the Irish government 'do nothing to make the situation worse'.[114] Hume suggested that Lynch's speech on TV provided 'an outlet for popular feeling'.[115] Justin O'Brien described it as 'a holding operation'.[116] While the ambiguous language may have been effective in conveying different messages to a spectrum of nationalist opinion, it provided hostages for the future.

Sir Andrew Gilchrist reported that the events of August 1969 prompted 'a wave of incoherent popular enthusiasm' to which the government had to respond with 'some dramatic eye-catching gesture'.[117] According to Conor Cruise O'Brien, 'For most viewers in the Republic a feeling of identification with the Bogsiders was immediate, as if instinctive, and yet somehow unreal, like sympathy with a family ghost; or, more precisely, with a member of the family writing from emigration, with alarming news imperfectly understood.'[118] There were mass meetings outside the GPO; 4,000 people marched to the British embassy, and some demonstrators were involved in scuffles with the gardaí.[119] TDs and councillors called public meetings to express outrage and sympathy. A civil rights meeting in Monaghan addressed by Austin Currie attracted a large crowd, despite the fact that it was only publicised at the last minute via a loudspeaker

---

[109] Kennedy, *Division and Consensus*, pp. 343–4.   [110] NAI 2000/5/42.
[111] NAI 2000/6/538 Visit of northern MPs 18 August 1969.
[112] Mills, *Hurler on the ditch*, p. 62.   [113] White, *John Hume*, p. 84.
[114] Fanning, 'Playing it cool', p. 74.   [115] White, *John Hume*, p. 85.
[116] Justin O'Brien, *The Arms Trial* (Dublin: Gill & Macmillan, 2000), p. 43.
[117] TNA FCO33/1200.   [118] Cruise O'Brien, *States of Ireland*, pp. 184–5.
[119] Hanley and Millar, *Lost revolution*, p. 131.

travelling through the town. There was widespread sympathy for Northern refugees; one Monaghan councillor emphasised that they were 'just as much refugees as those who fled from Czechoslovakia' [when Russian troops invaded the previous summer], 'but these are your own people'. Over 3,000 refugees were accommodated in army camps.[120] Relief efforts provided an outlet for constructive sympathy; local Red Cross units and voluntary agencies collected food and clothing. But as the 1970 Arms Crisis revealed, refugees provided useful cover for financing armed republicans. There was widespread support for a UN peacekeeping force in Northern Ireland, which might include Irish troops – evidence of Ireland's positive attitude towards such missions, probably because of Irish troops' involvement in the Congo. The violence of August 1969 acted as an effective recruitment opportunity for the IRA. My sister has described a meeting in Carrickmacross, in August 1969, where she and my brother met a teenager who seemed determined to invade Northern Ireland single-handedly that night; he later served a long sentence for IRA offences. Hanley and Millar describe busloads of young people setting off in a surge of emotion to fight in Northern Ireland; the majority hitched back home.[121] According to Bosi, many who became IRA prisoners joined the movement in response to violence or police raids on their community; those who were active before 1969 belonged to families with a republican tradition.[122] Nevertheless, while republican sentiment was gaining ground, in 1969 majority opinion in the Republic was probably prepared to trust the British government and its army.

August 1969 left the Irish government with an urgent need to rebuild relations with the British government, Northern nationalists and Irish-American sympathisers, while keeping a close eye on the popular mood. This was a tall order given the divisions within Cabinet. Efforts to bring international pressure to bear on Britain failed miserably. The press officers (drawn from state agencies such as Bord Fáilte), who were dispatched to Irish embassies to publicise the government's point of view, were called home in the early autumn; there is no evidence that they had any impact.[123] The US State Department declined to become involved, and Ireland failed to have a resolution on Northern Ireland put to the vote at either the UN Security Council or the

[120] Keogh, *Twentieth-century Ireland. Nation and state* (Dublin: Gill & Macmillan, 1984), p. 301.

[121] Hanley and Millar, *Lost revolution*, p. 132.

[122] Lorenzo Bosi, 'Explaining pathways to armed activism in the Provisional Irish Republican Army, 1969–72', *Social Science History*, vol. 36, no. 3, Fall 2012, pp. 347–90.

[123] Keogh, *Lynch*, p. 189.

General Assembly[124] – an indication that Ireland's international influence remained marginal, despite more than a decade of active involvement in the United Nations. Hillery made what he has described as 'a low-key presentation' to the General Assembly. Fanning claims that this initiative 'at least enabled the Lynch government to appear to be doing something when, in fact, there was very little they could do. In that sense it served as a safety-valve to ease the domestic pressures for action.'[125] Even this low-key intervention touched a raw nerve in Britain.[126]

Anger was the dominant tone in Lynch's speech of 28 August; he objected to the presence of British troops in Northern Ireland and reiterated that partition was the root cause of the present troubles; he dismissed even an accelerated programme of reform as only an interim solution.[127] He adopted a more moderate line in Tralee on 20 September. On this occasion Whitaker was the main author; his draft emphasised that the long-term goal was unity by agreement; there was no wish 'to extend the domination of Dublin'. Whitaker later wrote to Lynch, welcoming the positive reception for the speech '(though it was somewhat less conciliatory than I would have liked)'.[128] Lynch had substituted 'Six Counties' and 'Government of the North of Ireland' for 'Northern Ireland', and he ignored Whitaker's advice that he should announce that the army reserve was being stood down, 'unless there are strong reasons to the contrary from your Intelligence Services'.[129] Nevertheless, the speech signalled a calmer, more reflective response.

By this time, devising a policy for Northern Ireland and gaining control of that policy had turned into a competitive exercise within the Irish civil service. The DEA's Eamonn Gallagher, a native of Donegal, took a personal initiative in establishing contact with Northern nationalists, most significantly with John Hume. Hugh McCann the Secretary of DEA encouraged him to continue doing so. Lynch increasingly relied on Gallagher as a source of information and speech-writer. Gallagher recommended that policy should concentrate on supporting Northern nationalists and moderate Unionists, while maintaining pressure on London to continue the programme of reform; according to Fanning, 'he [Gallagher] sought to pin responsibility on London and not on Belfast – an approach that marked a deliberate change of direction

---

[124] Daniel Williamson, 'Taking the Troubles across the Atlantic: Ireland's UN Initiatives and Irish-US diplomatic relations in the early years of the conflict in Northern Ireland', *ISIA*, vol. 18, 2007, pp. 175–89.

[125] Fanning, 'Playing it cool', p. 77.

[126] TNA FCO33/1200 Annual Review for the Republic of Ireland 1969.

[127] UCDA 175/1, p. 108.   [128] P175/1, p. 188 Whitaker to Lynch 22 September.

[129] UCDA P 175/1, pp. 111–2. Whitaker, 13 September draft speech for Taoiseach; McCann, 'Whitaker and Northern Ireland', pp. 182–3; Craig, *Crisis of confidence*, p. 62.

from the days of Lemass – O'Neill rapprochement'.[130] The British ambassador described Gallagher as 'a powerful and thrusting backseat driver'.[131] A brief for Cabinet drafted by the DEA stated that the goal should be to secure reunification 'by peaceful means through cooperation, agreement and consent between Irishmen'. It ruled out international action through the United Nations and noted that 'Care should be taken to avoid action leading to direct rule from Westminster which would make the North a closer integral part of the United Kingdom – unless of course Stormont should ultimately reject genuine reform.' The focus should be on 'discreet contact with London', reiterating Dublin's right to be heard; meetings 'in the full glare of publicity' should be avoided; north–south contacts should be maximised. At a domestic level it suggested that barriers to unity be removed – that is birth control and the Irish language. A section within the Department of External Affairs with responsibility for Northern Ireland should be established, which would act as a clearing house for the activities of other departments in this area.

Although this was the model that ultimately prevailed, it faced competition.[132] Whitaker was keen to remain involved, despite no longer being a civil servant. He enlisted the assistance of Denis Maher, Assistant Secretary in the Department of Finance and other former colleagues. In September 1969, Maher sent Whitaker the draft of a letter, which he proposed to send to all relevant government departments. It opened with the statement that 'Events in Northern Ireland in recent months have led to a state of affairs which casts doubts on the permanence of the existing constitutional arrangements in that area. This brings to the forefront the attitude which we, as a Government, should adopt to the various possibilities that may be opened up, and, indeed, the question of the kind of initiative we might undertake, if the opportunity should present itself, in support of our objective of the erosion of the Border.' He proposed a series of papers to examine 'the practical problems that must be overcome' in relation to constitutional issues, finance and comparative services in both parts of Ireland, 'with a view to identifying the main problems of assimilation'.[133] A long document on the constitutional position of Northern Ireland, produced by this Finance/Whitaker initiative, acknowledged that it was unlikely that majority opinion in Northern Ireland would opt for an end to partition and equally improbable that Britain would coerce Northern Ireland into a united Ireland. Having

---

[130] Fanning, 'Playing it cool', p. 80.
[131] TNA FCO/033/1200 Annual review for the Republic of Ireland 1969.
[132] Fanning, 'Playing it cool', p. 82.   [133] UCDA P 175/1, p. 123.

reviewed possible means of bringing partition to an end, it determined that the only option was a 'policy of friendship with Northern Ireland' and 'being prepared to accept a future structural set-up between the two parts of Ireland which would allay Northern Ireland fears and safeguard her interests'. The main preconditions for a successful outcome were a satisfactory rate of economic growth in the Republic, maintaining agricultural subsidies and welfare services in Northern Ireland at their current level, EEC membership, or failing that some form of economic union with Britain. It recognised the need to respect Northern unionist wishes on matters such as the Irish language, divorce and contraception, but did not anticipate extending divorce and contraception to the entire population.[134] It expressed the hope that Britain would continue to pick up the cost of supporting services in Northern Ireland, at least on an interim base, while ceding constitutional control to some form of condominium or federation – two states with a federal authority, linking the two.[135] Whitaker urged Lynch to permit Maher and his colleagues to continue this work, but Lynch apparently wanted it to be handled by a group reporting to the Attorney-General. Whitaker argued that 'One of the crucial elements in any plausible solution is how to keep the British £100 million a year for the North, and to work this requirement into a constitutional arrangement demands some knowledge of Common Markets, Customs Unions etc. – economic information not normally possessed by lawyers.'[136] (In 1969, Ireland collected £81 million from income tax.)

The Protestant minority in the Republic was almost uniformly horrified by events in Northern Ireland; on 21 August, the *Irish Times* carried an advertisement by Mr and Mrs O'Callaghan-Westropp, members of a Clare landed family, indicating that they no longer wished to be called Protestant. This and other articles prompted an extensive series of letters – drawing distinctions between the treatment of Protestants in the Republic and Catholics in Northern Ireland and raising questions about the Irish Constitution. [137] But there is no evidence that the government deployed influential members of the Republic's protestant community – especially churchmen and others with close cross-border contacts – to promote a 'policy of friendship'. In 1972, the British reported that 'Mr Lynch has

---

[134] This is consistent with the stance of the Committee on the Constitution which proposed to remove the constitutional prohibition on divorce where it was permitted by the church who had carried out the ceremony. Brian Girvin, ' "Lemass's brainchild": the 1966 informal committee on the constitution and change in Ireland, 1966–73', *IHS*, vol. xxxviii, no. 151, May, 2013, pp. 415–7.

[135] UCDA P 175/2, pp. 145–8.

[136] P175/1 188, 22 September 1969 Whitaker to Taoiseach.

[137] *IT*, 21 August – c 20 September 1969.

failed to establish substantive links with Northern Protestants, largely owing to pressures within Fianna Fáil.[138] *Hibernia* criticised the government for failing to grasp the nettle and draw up a constitution for a united Ireland.[139] But the political appetite for constitutional reform appears to have been limited, not just in Fianna Fáil. More to the point, time was not on the side of this 'policy of friendship', even if there had been a significant momentum for constitutional reform and other measures designed to win over the majority Northern population. News bulletins were dominated by bombings, shootings and bank robberies, and the deteriorating relationship between Northern nationalists and the British army. Violence no longer stopped at the border and armed robberies became common; in April 1970, Richard Fallon became the first garda killed in the course of duty since the 1940s during a bank rate organised by Saor Éire, a left-wing republican group.

December/January 1969/70 saw a split in the IRA and Sinn Féin. While Sinn Féin ostensibly split over the issue of abstention – one wing wished to take their seats in Dáil Éireann – the IRA split reflected a division between those who were determined to achieve social revolution throughout the island (Official IRA) and others, soon known as the Provisional IRA, who preferred to wage a traditional military campaign against British troops and the Northern government. Official IRA continued to protest against the Vietnam War; they held fish-ins protesting against exclusive fishing rights on rivers and lakes; joined forces with those agitating for civil rights of small farmers and regeneration in Connemara; and developed links with the emerging Irish feminist movement.[140] The number of IRA recruits was rising and some traditionalists who had been disenchanted with the IRA's socialist activism rejoined the Provisionals. Blaney gave a speech in Letterkenny, where he stated that Fianna Fáil had never taken a decision to rule out the use of force 'if the circumstances in the Six Counties so demand', going on to quote Lynch's television address of 13 August.[141] The Fianna Fáil Ard Fheis in January 1970 heard militant speeches from Boland and Blaney, followed by Lynch's address emphasising that partition would only end by peaceful means: Unionists could not be coerced into a united Ireland. Perhaps ominously Lynch's question, 'Is this the kind of Ireland we want?' echoed O'Neill's *Crossroads* speech. The Ard Fheis made no attempt to reconcile the obvious differences between both camps.

The Arms Crisis of May 1970, which saw the dismissal of two Cabinet ministers – Blaney and Haughey, and the resignation of a third, Kevin

---

[138] FCO Diplomatic Report 433/72 Irish Republic 18 September 1972.
[139] *Hibernia*, 18 February 1972.   [140] Hanley and Millar, *Lost revolution*, pp. 234–42.
[141] Keogh, *Lynch*, p. 221.

Boland (Minister for Justice Michael Moran resigned the previous day, ostensibly on health grounds), was the gravest threat to the survival of the state since the 1920s.[142] The origins lie in the Cabinet decision of August 1969 to create a mechanism for permanent liaison with 'opinion in the Six Counties' and to set aside a sum of money (£100,000 was the amount later agreed), controlled by the Minister for Finance, for the relief of distress in Northern Ireland. A Cabinet sub-committee on Northern Ireland was established, consisting of Haughey (Finance) and three ministers representing border constituencies – Blaney, Faulkner and Brennan, which only met once. Some of the £100,000 was used to finance the *Northern Voice*, a newspaper directed at nationalist opinion in Northern Ireland; intelligence officers in the Irish army were in contact with northern republicans, and there were various attempts to import guns for distribution in Northern Ireland. While the story is murky, it is highly probable that Lynch had some knowledge of the conspiracy for some time before he acted, and that the Minister for Defence James Gibbons was also aware of at least some of these activities.[143] The decision to sack key Cabinet ministers was precipitated by Liam Cosgrave, leader of the opposition, who had been made aware of a pending importation of arms, and would have gone public if Lynch had not acted. [144] The entire episode reflects Lynch's lack of control over his Cabinet, and at least a tacit willingness to turn a blind eye to defiant ministers, plus a lazy approach to procedures. *Hibernia* commented that it would be 'impossible to imagine a Minister in a De Valera, Costello or Lemass Cabinet becoming involved in even a suspicion of such conduct'.[145]

While Lynch secured the support of the parliamentary party and the Dáil, he did so on a procedural matter – the right of the Taoiseach to fire and appoint ministers, not a vote of confidence.[146] The party remained deeply divided, and unusually for Fianna Fáil, the divisions were aired in public. Lynch faced a further test in October 1970 when the courts acquitted Haughey, Blaney and fellow-defendants. Blaney, Boland and back-bencher Des Foley voted with the opposition on the subsequent vote of confidence; Haughey supported the government. The divisions were rehashed very passionately and publicly at the party's Ard Fheis in

---

[142] For detailed accounts see O'Brien, *The arms trial*; Diarmaid Ferriter, *Ambiguous Republic. Ireland in the 1970s* (London: Profile, 2012), pp. 141–50.

[143] Vincent Browne, 'The Arms Crisis', *Magill*, May 1980, pp. 35–56. This reproduced the diaries of Peter Berry, Secretary of the Department of Justice. O'Malley claims that the Berry diaries were written retrospectively and argues that Lynch and Gibbons did not have prior knowledge. *Conduct Unbecoming*, pp. 59–73.

[144] O'Brien, *The Arms Trial*; Ferriter, *Ambiguous Republic*, pp. 141–50.

[145] *Hibernia*, 15–28 May 1970.   [146] Keogh, *Lynch*, p. 263.

February 1971. Sir John Peck who described 1970 as 'a very odd year' attributed Fianna Fáil's survival to 'their ability to close ranks when threatened' and 'the disarray of the opposition'.[147] Describing the 1971 Ard Fheis, he noted that 'When Fianna Fáil determines to pursue a certain course, follow a certain leader, and crush internal opposition, it is efficient, ruthless and none too scrupulous. The uproar created at the opening of the Conference, and at intervals during it, by the minority who still followed Mr Boland, was a wild gesture of frustrated helplessness as the great party machine ground relentlessly on.' TV viewers witnessed scenes of near-riot with Hillery screaming that 'You can have Boland, but you can't have Fianna Fáil.' Peck concluded that 'Mr Lynch has won because he has correctly interpreted and broadly expressed what the Irish people want, and his opponents within the party have not. For most of them that is enough. They are not demanding reunification tomorrow. It is enough to know that their Taoiseach is standing up to the English on behalf of those whom they regard as "their people" in the North, and that one day Ireland will be one country.'[148]

Relations with Britain improved somewhat after a low point in August 1969. The failure to secure the intervention of the US State Department or the United Nations meant that where Northern Ireland was concerned, Britain was Ireland's only foreign relation. Britain, however reluctantly, also had to take account of the Irish government's position. A review of 1969 by the FCO, which carried the heading Ireland – carried a note that the title was chosen deliberately. 'Although officially the FCO's subject is the RoI (Republic of Ireland) leaving the HO (Home Office) to deal with N I (Northern Ireland) in practice the two subjects are almost indivisible. The Irish have no greater problem than Northern Ireland (or "the Border" "Partition" 'a United Ireland' the terms are almost synonymous); and their lesser problems (EEC, AIFTA etc.) cause us little trouble.' It noted that for the FCO the Republic was 'a non-subject until 1969 ... We began at a time when British and Irish Ministers did not know each other, the Irish Ambassador hardly figured and the HO were deeply suspicious of all things Southern Irish ... The Irish were virtually demanding to share the problem and its solving.' By 1970, Hillery and British ministers were meeting regularly, as were senior officials in the Foreign Office and DFA,[149] often discussing Anglo-Irish relations on the side of EEC negotiations. But this closer relationship did not bring any immediate dividends for Lynch's government.

[147] TNA FCO33/1595, Annual Review 1970.
[148] TNA FCO33/1596 Sir John Peck report to Sir Alex Douglas-Home 9 March 1971.
[149] FCO33/1200.

Irish policy on Northern Ireland was buffeted by conflicting interests and agendas: the Fianna Fáil party and Irish public opinion; a growing security crisis; moderate nationalists in Northern Ireland, as represented by the SDLP; and efforts to secure a voice in Britain's Northern policy. When news of the Arms Crisis broke, the British embassy in Dublin noted 'surprise tinged with admiration that Mr Lynch should have demanded the resignations' of Haughey and Blaney; they cited an *Irish Times* editorial which pointed out that moderates were under threat in both parts of Ireland, adding that 'the crisis has shown that southern self-righteousness about the north is unfounded'. Britain continued its efforts to persuade the Irish government 'to treat Northern Ireland as our business though a point of mutual concern', but the Dublin embassy feared that this would be more difficult 'with hawks breathing down Lynch's neck'.[150] The Conservative victory in the British general election of June 1970 brought a change of ministers and the need to build new relationships. The Falls Road Belfast Curfew, imposed shortly after the Conservatives took office, suggested a tougher regime in Northern Ireland, and that together with Hillery's unannounced visit to the Falls Road in July meant that relations started badly and did not improve. On 1 June 1971, Sir John Peck reported on a recent conversation with Hillery, who warned that Lynch's position was 'beginning to show signs of crumbling'; party stalwarts were beginning to ask 'does anything come of trusting the British'; Peck urged that reforms in Northern Ireland should be speeded up to protect Lynch's position.[151] In July, the SDLP formally withdrew from Stormont in protest against the deaths of two men in Derry and announced plans to establish an alternative assembly – on similar lines to the First Dáil in 1919. August brought the introduction of internment, a one-sided measure directed only at republicans. Several thousand refugees came south of the border, as did many leading IRA men. Internment sparked a wave of protests in the Republic, reminiscent of August 1969. On this occasion, however, many protests were openly organised by Sinn Féin, and public sentiment was more militantly anti-British. Internment brought a new low in Anglo-Irish relations. A government press statement expressed 'the sympathies of the Government and of the vast majority of the Irish people North and South', with 'the Nationalist minority ... again victimised by an attempt to maintain a regime which has long since shown itself incapable of just Government'.[152] The Irish government agreed to fund the SDLP's proposed alternative assembly.[153] Heath rejected

---

[150] TNA FCO33/1206 Changes in Government of ROI Telegrams, 6 and 7 May; Cabinet 7 May speaking notes.
[151] FCO33/1596, 1 June 1971 to Sir Stewart Crawford.   [152] *IP*, 10 August 1971.
[153] Campbell, 'New nationalism?', pp. 73–4.

Lynch's advice as 'unacceptable in its attempt to interfere in the affairs of the United Kingdom'.[154] Popular revulsion at internment ramped up, following reports that internees were mis-treated. Internment had been successfully deployed in Northern Ireland and the Republic to deal with the 1957 IRA border campaign, and in December 1970, Minister for Justice Des O'Malley had announced that the government was considering reintroducing internment to deal with a secret armed conspiracy involving kidnappings, murder and armed robberies. Those charged with crimes relating to Republican activities were often acquitted, because witnesses were reluctant to give evidence, and juries unwilling to convict. But widespread opposition in the Republic to internment in Northern Ireland removed this option. In December 1971, 'The Men behind the Wire', a ballad about the internees, became Ireland's best-selling record. Internment failed to reduce violence in Northern Ireland; indeed the numbers killed and injured rose significantly; nationalists were utterly alienated. A paper by the Central Policy Review Staff in Whitehall asked whether Northern Ireland 'could be the United Kingdom's Vietnam'.[155] In November, one FCO official minuted that 'I cannot help wondering, on the basis, admittedly of only a few weeks at the desk, whether we are succeeding adequately in getting across to the HO and the MOD (Ministry of Defence) a full appraisal of the Irish Republic Government's statements on the North, in particularly the extent to which current policies in the North are inevitably making it that much harder for reason and goodwill to prevail among the Fianna Fáil rank and file.' He also remarked on the 'notable feeling at least at junior level in HO and MOD that Peck is too close to the Irish to view the situation in the North sufficiently dispassionately'.[156] Britain's policy remained as in 1968: keep the Northern Ireland government in office and avoid direct rule. However, a meeting between Lynch and Heath, planned for December, was brought forward to 27/28 September. For the first time the British and Irish prime ministers talked over two days about Northern Ireland; the talks were followed by a meeting between Lynch, Heath and Brian Faulkner, Prime Minister of Northern Ireland: the first meeting of the three prime ministers for more than seventy years.[157] While Craig describes these meetings as 'a somewhat cynical attempt to create a new political initiative', Garret FitzGerald and other Irish commentators are more positive, seeing it as evidence that Britain recognised that the Irish government had a 'legitimate interest in a situation threatening the security of both parts of the island'.[158]

[154] Campbell, 'New nationalism?', p. 83.   [155] Campbell, 'New nationalism?', p. 84.
[156] TNA FCO33/1596 25 November R. Bone.   [157] Keogh, *Lynch*, p. 318.
[158] Craig, *Crisis of confidence*, p. 100; FitzGerald, *All in a life*, p. 99.

Whatever advances had been made in Anglo-Irish relations evaporated in February 1972 with the killing of twelve civilians (a thirteenth died later from his injuries) when British troops opened fire on a banned civil rights march in Derry and the subsequent burning of the British embassy in Dublin. It seems inappropriate to pass over these events speedily, but they have been extensively described and analysed, and the story stretches well into the twenty-first century. Ireland withdrew its ambassador in London. Lynch and his Cabinet ministers attended the funerals in Derry, as did leading politicians from other parties. But the real impact of what became known as 'another Bloody Sunday' – a reference to November 1920 when British troops opened fire on a crowd attending a GAA match in Croke Park in retaliation at the assassination of British special agents earlier that day – was on the streets. Hanley sees this as 'a key event in radicalising opinion'.[159] Businesses and schools closed on the day of the funeral. People crowded into churches to attend requiem masses; the Church of Ireland held memorial services for all who had died in the northern violence, especially the Derry dead. The IRA and associated groups organised rituals designed to link those killed in Derry with earlier republican martyrs. Empty coffins draped with a tricolour or a black flag paraded through Kerry towns – similar mock funerals were common in 1867 following the deaths of the Manchester Martyrs. In Killorglin, after requiem mass, thirteen young men marched to the Republican plot in a nearby cemetery where they fired a volley of shots. The ESB offices in Tralee flew a black flag and a tricolour (half-mast). A speaker in Castleisland described events in Northern Ireland as 'the third reign of the Tans'.[160]

In Dublin, the day of the funerals ended with a mass meeting outside the British embassy, which culminated in a petrol bomb attack and the burning of the embassy building, 'the first occasion when a British Embassy in Europe has been burnt by a rioting mob'.[161] Many commentators suggest that this was a cathartic moment; the IRA carried out the arson attack taking advantage of the mass protest. Minister for Justice Des O'Malley later said that 'the emotions of the times spent themselves in the flames of that building'.[162] When the Dáil met the following day, Garret FitzGerald claims that inflammatory speeches by Blaney and other Fianna Fáil dissidents 'evoked an immediate, instinctive, response from both the Government and opposition benches: a response that

---

[159] Brian Hanley, ' "But then they started all this killing": attitudes to the I.R.A. in the Irish Republic since 1969', *IHS*, vol. xxxviii, no. 15, May 2013, p. 443.
[160] *Connacht Tribune*, 4 February 1972; *Kerryman*, 5 February 1972.
[161] TNA FCO Review of 1972, Sir John Peck, 4 January 1973.
[162] Cited by Ferriter, *Ambiguous Republic*, p. 122.

demonstrated the strength of our democratic system and the ability of our politicians in a crisis to transcend their differences in the interest of the country. Every contribution was directed towards taking the heat out of the situation and reducing the tension. Instinctively, and without concert, all concerned resisted the temptation to hit out blindly at the authors of this tragedy; too much was at stake for that: peace, itself, in fact.'[163] FitzGerald may reflect opinion in Dáil Éireann, but he fails to capture the wider public mood. Page 1 of the *Kerryman* carried an opinion piece headed 'War on the Irish People':

People who were apathetic up to last Sunday are now displaying a remarkable solidarity with the Irishmen and women who are being shot, wounded, harassed, interned, discriminated against, unemployed in the part of Ireland that the British claim as their own against the facts of history and geography.

. . .

The Irish people are in a mood to be led to the achievement of freedom for all Ireland. Unless the leadership that is so needed when people are aroused is forthcoming, the mood may not last.

A leader is wanted . . . 'Standing idly by' is no excuse for a policy. The people have now taken the bit between their teeth if Wednesday's Day of Mourning has any meaning other than a gesture of sympathy for sorely tried Irishmen and women in Derry.[164]

The *Connacht Tribune* suggested that public opinion was being transformed, as happened after the 1916 Rising. 'Is Britain going to resist that new-found Irish strength just as it resisted the aspirations of the Irish people when Sinn Féin swept the country in 1917?' Internment and Bloody Sunday provided the IRA with ample material for winning hearts and minds. Echoing the strategy followed in the aftermath of the 1916 Rising, local committees raised funds for the Derry families or the dependents of internees. Families built personal links with the families of internees, taking their children for holidays. The GAA and Macra na Feirme were among the community organisations that held fund-raising dances for internees' families. There were large attendances at social events organised by Provisional Sinn Féin, which often featured speeches by IRA leader Dáithí Ó Conaill or an escaped internee. British-owned holiday homes were damaged in the aftermath of Bloody Sunday (three in Oughterard county Galway), and there were demands for a boycott of British goods. The Scottish and Welsh rugby teams refused to travel to Dublin for international fixtures, and the British equestrian team did not attend the Dublin Horse Show. Tourist companies cancelled bookings; the cost of insuring British tour buses travelling to Ireland soared. IDA

---

[163] FitzGerald, *All in a Life*, pp. 103–4.   [164] *Kerryman*, 5 February 1972.

managing director Michael Killeen said that 'The burning of the British embassy had particular significance. The Americans regard embassies as symbols of stability. They could not believe it when an embassy was burned in a peaceful country like Ireland.'[165]

The government abandoned the traditional military parade on Easter Sunday to commemorate the 1916 Rising because of fears that it would be disrupted. President de Valera and government leaders attended a flag-raising ceremony at the GPO, before laying a wreath at the Garden of Remembrance in Parnell Square. But the *Irish Press* reported that 1916 ceremonies outside Dublin had attracted the largest attendance for some years; the number of ceremonies was proliferating as both wings of Sinn Fein/IRA ran separate events. Public opinion vacillated, often determined by 'the politics of the last atrocity'[166] – growing anger and sympathy for republican causes if the perpetrator was the British army or Protestant paramilitaries, and a sombre, reflective response when the IRA was the killer.

The spillover of the Northern Ireland crisis into domestic politics increased significantly from the autumn of 1971. Kevin Boland, former Fianna Fáil minister, founded Aontacht Éireann – a Republican Unity Party in September 1971, resulting in some defections from Fianna Fáil – though fewer than might have been anticipated. Neil Blaney was expelled from the parliamentary party in November 1971 having abstained in a vote of confidence relating to James Gibbons; he was expelled as an ordinary party member some months later for 'conduct unbecoming a member of the organisation' – his followers had organised a Fianna Fáil collection independent of the national organisation[167] – yet another instance where Fianna Fáil maintained party discipline while failing to confront critical ideological and political issues. Haughey, who remained within the party, became one of the five vice-presidents at the 1972 Ard Fheis.[168]

Irish media made up for its previous neglect of Northern Ireland, appointing correspondents in Belfast and dedicating extensive space and time to the topic. When RTÉ interviewed the leaders of both the Provisional and Official IRA in October 1971, Minister for Posts and Telegraphs Gerard Collins invoked Article 31 of the 1960 Broadcasting Authority Act, ordering RTÉ 'to refrain from broadcasting any matter

---

[165] *IT*, 8 March 1972, quoted in Paul Bew, Peter Gibbon and Henry Patterson, *Northern Ireland 1921–1996. Political forces and social classes* (London: Serif, revised 1996 edition), p. 169.
[166] Cruise O'Brien, *States of Ireland*, p. 265. The phrase was used by Ernest Holmes chairman of the Northern Ireland Labour Party.
[167] Neil Blaney, *DIB* online.   [168] *IP*, 18 February 1972.

that could be calculated to promote the aims or activities of any organisation which engages in, promotes encourages, or advocates the attaining of
any political objective by violent means'.[169] In May 1972, shortly after
voters had approved the referendum on EEC membership, the government invoked a section of the Offences Against the State Act to establish
the Special Criminal Court in cases where the normal operation of justice
had broken down. The three-man juryless courts would try those arrested
for scheduled offences, including offences committed by paramilitaries.
Following a mass riot in Mountjoy Prison, also in May, they passed
legislation, making it possible to hold prisoners in military custody. An
IRA Truce in June provided only a brief respite; it ended on 'Bloody
Friday' when a series of bombs planted by the IRA in Belfast on 21 July
killed 11 people and injured over 130. High-profile republicans arrested
in 1972 included Provisional Sinn Féin President Ruairí Ó Bradaigh and
Belfast Republican Joe Cahill. When Seán MacStiofáin, leader of the
Provisional IRA, was arrested in November, and went on hunger strike,
he was visited by the retired archbishop of Dublin Dr McQuaid and his
successor Dr Dermot Ryan. RTÉ journalist Kevin O'Kelly interviewed
Mac Stiofáin; although the interview was not broadcast, O'Kelly related
its contents in detail. The government regarded this as a direct challenge
to Section 31 and they dismissed the RTÉ authority.[170] Encroachments
on civil liberties gave rise to strong opposition from groups such as the
Irish Council for Civil Liberties, journalists and Labour politicians.

Northern Ireland divided opinion in all the main political parties. A
British embassy observer noted that at the Fine Gael Ard Fheis in May
1971 there were calls to substitute Six Counties for Northern Ireland in
motions and demands for a vote of sympathy with the 'beleagured
minority'.[171] Garret FitzGerald claimed that 'differences between what
seemed to have become two wings of the party, deriving primarily from
disagreements on domestic issues, were intensified by different
approaches on Northern Ireland'.[172] There was a strong element of
competition and personal resentment between Richie Ryan – the party's
spokesman on Northern Ireland – and the ever-active FitzGerald.
Liberals sought to make a united Ireland more amenable to unionists by
pressing for internal reform, and they opposed the government's tougher
security laws. But party leader Liam Cosgrave showed little sympathy
with even non-violent protests. Tensions came to a head when Fine Gael
met to determine their response to the Offences Against the State

[169] Bowman, *Window and Mirror*, p. 123.
[170] Bowman, *Window and mirror*, pp. 123–4.
[171] TNA FCO33/1601 Fine Gael, Blatherwick.   [172] FitzGerald, *All in a Life*, p. 105.

Amendment Bill – which provided that a statement by a garda chief superintendant that he believed a person to be a member of the IRA could be accepted as evidence by the court. Cosgrave expressed support for the measure, whereas a majority of the parliamentary party were highly critical of the threat that it represented to civil liberties. During the debate on the second reading, Cosgrave criticised 'Communists and their fellow-travellers . . . soft-headed liberals . . . anti-apartheid protest marches'. All members of the parliamentary party except Cosgrave and Paddy Donegan were determined to oppose the bill. But shortly before the vote took place, two bombs exploded in Dublin, killing two men and injuring 127 people – prompting a last-minute decision by Fine Gael to abstain. If Lynch had lost the vote he would have called a general election, appealing to voters on a question of national security. If Cosgrave had voted with the government, he would have been forced to resign as leader of Fine Gael.

Divisions within the Labour Party were on a par with those in Fianna Fáil, perhaps even greater, though they were less significant because Labour was not in government. Many grass-roots Labour supporters were sympathetic towards the IRA campaign in Northern Ireland. According to an opinion poll carried out in 1970, almost 25 per cent of Labour supporters favoured armed intervention in a crisis in Northern Ireland compared with 18 per cent of Fianna Fáil and 12 per cent of Fine Gael supporters.[173] In July 1971, Conor Cruise O'Brien made a strong statement opposing violence and expressing fears that the Provisional IRA campaign would result in civil war in the North, and perhaps throughout the island. O'Brien argued that there were two nations on the island – unionists and nationalists – and therefore no case for a united Ireland. Thornley, who like O'Brien formed part of the 'new' intake of Labour MPs, presented the contrary argument with equal passion. Thornley, 'guardian of the Labour Party's republican conscience',[174] invoked the 1916 leader James Connolly in support of a united Ireland. But while Thornley represented the most militantly nationalist wing of the party, O'Brien's analysis was equally unappetising to moderate nationalists, and to the SDLP, especially the more nationalist John Hume wing. In August 1971, Labour issued a joint six-point communiqué with the SDLP expressing support for unity by consent. Thornley's speeches became increasingly controversial. In December 1971, he told the Dáil that the death of Northern Ireland senator John Barnhill – who was murdered by the Official IRA – had been 'excessively

[173] Hanley, 'But then they started all the killing', p. 440.
[174] *Hibernia*, 24 September–7 October 1971.

deplored'. The British embassy described this speech as 'a "provisional" speech' – a speech that supported the views of Provisional Sinn Fein.[175] Although Labour threatened to expel Thornley and two other TDs who held similar views, they prevaricated. Northern Ireland was the most divisive issue at the party's annual conference in February 1972. However, the leadership succeeded in getting the conference to approve a statement expressing support for a socialist, non-sectarian, united Ireland, while rejecting any attempt to achieve this 'by force of arms'. The support of party chairman Roddy Connolly, son of the 1916 leader, was a major asset. The conference rejected a vote of no confidence in Conor Cruise O'Brien.[176] But divisions remained: in November 1972, Thornley visited MacStiofáin on hunger strike and was prominent in a demonstration protesting at his arrest. Meanwhile, O'Brien continued to articulate his argument against a united Ireland, most significantly in his 1972 book *States of Ireland*. Labour voted against the Offences Against the State Amendment Bill.

After August 1969, the government's policy on Northern Ireland had refocused on Britain and away from the Northern government. The suspension of Stormont and the introduction of Direct Rule from Westminster in March 1972 confirmed the primacy of Anglo-Irish relations as key. This strategy was reinforced by Lynch's emphasis on reunification by agreement as the overriding goal. But Direct Rule increased the danger of disputes between Britain and Ireland, because Britain now had full control over security – so complaints about bombings launched from south of the border, cratering of border roads or British troop incursions into the Republic were now matters between Dublin and London, and Dublin had to confront Britain's wish to make security the paramount issue in Anglo-Irish relations.[177] Britain kept the Irish government informed about its talks with the IRA, during the ceasefire, and Dublin had advance knowledge of 'operation Motorman', which removed the barricades in Derry's Bogside and Catholic areas of Belfast. But information did not amount to consultation; indeed, Dublin was angered by Britain's negotiations with the Provisional IRA. By the summer of 1972, Craig notes, with negotiations on EEC entry now complete, 'there were now *fewer* forums in which the Irish and British governments could meet bilaterally'.[178] On 30 October, William Whitelaw, British Secretary of State for Northern Ireland, finally

---

[175] TNA FCO 33/1603, Labour Party activities.
[176] *IT*, 28 February 1972, Purséil, *Irish Labour Party*, pp. 288–99.
[177] Catherine O'Donnell, *Fianna Fáil. Irish Republicanism and the Northern Ireland Troubles 1968–2005* (Dublin: Irish Academic Press, 2007), pp. 34–8.
[178] Craig, *Crisis of Confidence*, pp. 125–6.

published *The Future of Northern Ireland: A Paper for Discussion.* The green paper included a section headed 'The Irish Dimension' which declared that no British government wished to impede the unity of Irish by consent. This can be seen as a triumph for Lynch's government; it marked the first occasion that Britain formally acknowledged 'an Irish dimension' in a Northern Ireland settlement, paving the way for the Irish government's participation in the Sunningdale talks of December 1973 and talks and other agreements in decades to come.

The Northern Ireland crisis brought to an end the mood of optimism that characterised Irish politics in the 1960s. While the economy and related social programmes remained the dominant concerns for voters, Northern Ireland forced political parties to think about nationalism, unionism, civil rights, freedom of speech and national security. The spillover effects of the Northern crisis were significant in many Irish communities, stirring up latent sympathies for military activism, threatening critical tourist earnings, prompting the government to curtail civil liberties and bringing violent crime – such as armed robberies – into communities that had been almost crime-free for decades. It refocused Irish foreign policy, most especially Anglo-Irish relations, away from the economy to more complex issues of security and constitutional status. Yet while Northern Ireland challenged the political parties, exposing deep internal divisions, the Irish party system was not changed by either the Northern conflict or by economic growth. While the years after 1969 made the people of the Republic much more aware of Northern Ireland than in the past, and resulted in much greater contact between the two Irelands, this greater awareness reinforced the sense that the North remained 'a place apart'.[179]

---

[179] *A Place apart* is the title of travel writer Dervla Murphy's 1978 book describing her journey around Northern Ireland.

Conclusion
Abandoning the past?

The conception of the Irish as a people mainly preoccupied with historic grievances and indifferent to the opportunities for development was probably never true, but certainly it has no relation to the situation of today. The Irish are aware of their history ... the consequences of struggles and sacrifices ... fully alive to the need for maintaining maximum efficiency ... industrial growth.[1]

Ireland has passed through her period of revolution and the turbulent aftermath, and her long hard climb to economic prosperity is nearing success. She has reached a watershed in her development wherein the emphasis is no longer on political or constitutional transformation but on economic and social change. Her wounds have healed, or nearly so. She is now able to see herself for what she is: a small nation with much to be proud of, particularly in the field of international affairs; a nation not afraid to face up to its problems.[2]

One of the recurrent themes in the 1960s was that Ireland had abandoned its preoccupation with the past to focus on the present, redirecting its energies towards economic and social development instead of the previous fixation on national sovereignty. National pride and national commitment were increasingly linked with economic success and Ireland's greater involvement in world affairs. Economic development was welcome because it would bring an end to emigration, while offering a mechanism for building a new relationship with both Britain and Northern Ireland. But the outbreak of violence in Northern Ireland in 1969 forced both the government and the wider society to reconsider the origins of the state, and its political and ideological identity – issues that could not be resolved by economic development. Yet even before 1969, when an economic agenda was paramount, the drive for economic growth was moderated by a wish to preserve existing social structures.

The year 1966 marked the Golden Jubilee of the Easter Rising, the event most commonly seen as sparking the revolution that resulted in an

---

[1] NAI S16699F/95 Seán Lemass UPI interview, 24 November 1964.
[2] Coogan, *Ireland since the rising*, p. xi.

independent Ireland. The celebrations were subsequently condemned for reigniting physical force republicanism and armed conflict in Northern Ireland, though I question that simplistic analysis. One striking feature of the official commemoration was the rather self-congratulatory celebration of the success of the Irish state, and the emphasis that was placed on future challenges and aspirations. There was an element of farewell to the founding generation of national leaders, and implicitly a farewell to their preoccupations with the civil war, partition and language revival. The Jubilee prompted a welter of conferences, speeches and essays, which ostensibly drew on the spirit of 1916 and its leaders to provide lessons for contemporary Ireland. A minority focused on the failure to secure a united Ireland and revive the Irish language, but these were swamped by contributions that concentrated on socio-economic themes. Irish-American historian Joseph Curran welcomed the passing of the 'Old Guard of 1916–22'; he believed that their long 'oligarchical rule' had hindered national progress. 'At last there is real hope that the highest aims of 1916 will be achieved – real economic opportunity and a decent standard of living for all, cultural creativity, friendly co-operation with Britain and Ulster, and a full share in world affairs.'[3] Pearse was widely recalled as a pioneering educator – cue for speeches about the need to expand educational opportunities or the announcement of a new scholarship programme. Lemass urged all parties involved in wage negotiations and industrial relations disputes to emulate the spirit of 1916 by subordinating their self-interest to the national good. National unity was another underlying theme – an end to the divisions between pro- and anti-Treaty sides, and some modest recognition of Irishmen who fought in the Great War – but national unity within a sovereign twenty-six county state. To say that a united Ireland featured even marginally in this combination of celebration and reflection would be an overstatement. The government regarded the Jubilee as an opportunity to showcase the achievements of an independent Ireland. They insisted on inserting images of factories, power stations and other trappings of modern life in a documentary about the Easter Rising, which was distributed to foreign television stations, though most stations that showed the film omitted the contemporary scenes. Given the determination to project an image of a modern, prospering nation, Irish officials were more irritated by the articles written by the widely syndicated US journalist Jimmy Breslin, who described the tenements in central Dublin as largely unchanged since the 1916 Rising, than at the exaggerated accounts of the security threat from republican groups that appeared in the *New York Times*.[4]

---

[3] Joseph M. Curran, 'Ireland since 1916', *Éire-Ireland*, vol. I, no. 3, 1966, p. 28.
[4] Daly, 'Less a commemoration', pp. 18–86.

This determination to present Ireland as a modern nation, which had moved beyond past insularity and local preoccupations, is central to contemporary images of the 1960s. The focus was overwhelmingly on material and social improvement and the capacity of the state to achieve this. Connery noted that independence had been followed by 'slowly drawn-out political changes which scarcely affected the resigned and often desperate way of life of ordinary Irishmen. The dreamed-of social and economic upheaval never happened.' He was not alone in seeing this belated upheaval, and 'the trappings of the affluent society and the welfare state' – occurring in the 1960s.[5]

Terence Brown, quoting Thornley's article 'Ireland: the end of an era' (see pp. 255–6), referred to 'Thornley's near incredulity at Ireland's rapid transition from a society ostensibly dedicated to economic nationalism and its social and cultural concomitants, to a society prepared to abandon much of its past in the interests of swift growth in the context of modern British and Western European economies [which] has been shared by other historians and commentators'.[6] Any trawl through the social history of Ireland in the early years of the century throws up a remarkable quantity of censorious commentary about modern life and its dangers: criticism of mixed bathing, 'pin-money girls' – young women ostensibly working to fund their frivolous spending – jazz, city life, the cinema and other pernicious features of twentieth-century life. Such comments become much less common in the 1960s. Heinrich Böll lamented the disappearance of the lifestyle of the peasantry of the west of Ireland – but he was a German artist, whose regrets might be seen as akin to a modern tourist lamenting the disappearance of an exotic primitive society.

I must say something about poverty ... I believe that even the poorest inhabitant of a village in the west of Ireland is richer than he knows – his house, his turf, potatoes, milk butter and eggs, he owes allegiance to no master; enjoys magnificent air and scenery and he is free. I personally consider him to be richer than the occupant of a two-roomed flat in any industrial city in England, America or Germany.

It is the job of statisticians and economists to show economic progress of a country – it would bore any author to distraction for progress is much the same everywhere; bulldozers, building materials, concrete, plastics, factories, blocks of flats – it is no different in Stalingrad, than it is in Gelsenkirchen, Limerick or Appeldoorn. Almost every day I read advertisements in the German papers inviting industrialists to build factories in your country. The family and I read the advertisements not without sadness. We know that industries must exist in order that emigration shall cease, that this painful problem shall be solved. But we

---

[5] Connery, *The Irish*, pp. 20–1.   [6] Brown, *Ireland. A social and cultural history*, p. 232.

know too that industry changes both a land and its people and we do not believe that the spirit of industrial progress has much regard for people.[7]

Böll was by no means alone in his ambivalence about economic development. *Irish Times* journalist John Healy lamented the changes taking place in his hometown of Charlestown since the 1930s: 'In our town in those years life seemed snug and warm and self-contained. Above all it seemed permanent' ... 'farmers with hundreds of bags of potatoes. Outside them were carts of turnips, farmers with cabbage plants in season and big bundles of sally rods to be sold to the thatcher and the ciseán maker. Fat women waddled in with wicker baskets of eggs and rolls of butter.' He contrasts these images with the 'false vitality' of the present: 'the fresh paint merely throws into relief the shuttered houses; the new shop fronts bring the eye to the mortally wounded old businesses'.[8] But such comments reflect nostalgia for a life-style that is being romanticised – and they fail to capture the poverty, ill-health, premature deaths and lack of choice open to these rural families, or to the less-noticed and less romantic urban labourers. Böll may have believed that the Western peasant owed 'allegiance to no master', but his teenage sons and daughters, who were shipped off to England to work as labourers or servants, with instructions to send money home, would not have agreed. Healy's claim that Charlestown was dying is overstated – the fall in population was marginal, and it rose in subsequent decades. For Ireland, it can be argued that the 1960s was much less disruptive of family life than the previous decade, which saw over 500,000 people emigrate, and the level of disruption does not compare with other parts of Western Europe. Over 9 million Italians migrated within Italy, mainly from north to south between 1955 and 1971 (equivalent to approximately 600,000 migrating within Ireland), and the geographical and social gap between Milan and the Italian Mezzogiorno was far greater than the gap between Dublin and the west of Ireland. By the late 1960s, 500,000–700,000 'guest workers' were arriving each year in West Germany.[9] In Ireland, falling emigration meant that more young adults settled close to home than in the past. The rise in the population of Dublin and other urban areas appeared significant only by comparison with past stagnation – though local authorities were ill-prepared to cope with a growing population, hence the housing shortages, lack of infrastructure and soaring house and land prices. Most

---

[7] Henrich Böll, 'A reply to critics of *Children of Eire*', *Hibernia*, March 1965.
[8] Healy, *Death of an Irish town*, pp. 8, 17.
[9] Paul Ginsborg, *A history of contemporary Italy, 1943–1980* (London: Penguin, 1990), pp. 218–20; John Salt, 'International labour migration: the geographical pattern of demand', in John Salt and Hugh Clout (eds), *Migration in postwar Europe. Geographical essays* (Oxford: Oxford University Press, 1976), pp. 80–91.

new factories were small and widely dispersed. Shannon, Ireland's only new town, was on a very small scale by international standards, with a population of 3,657 in 1971.

A sense of insecurity about Irish modernity is evident in the hypersensitivity to foreign representations – as when an editorial in the *Irish Independent* in May 1963 headed 'Begorrah Now' reproduced some of the advance coverage of US President John F. Kennedy's impending visit:

> If all the leprechauns were tossed off the shamrocks this morning and the mountains trembled from Slieve Naght to McGillacuddy Reeks, it was because of the arrival in Dublin of two advance agents of the White House ... Not only is he coming for sure, but the dates have been arranged. And many's the unearned smile and proffer of a Guinness or a Jameson that has been the reward of the American pilgrim who saw no harm in encouraging as a probability the view expressed that, in all those foreign travels, 'he' was after making, Eire would certainly be included 'if twas God's will'.

The *Irish Independent* commented that 'If the *New York Times* can print this sort of stuff under the heading, "The greatest Event since Independence" meaning Irish independence, we shudder to think of what is going to appear in its less inhibited contemporaries.'[10] Government planning for the visit and concerns whether there would be sufficient telephone lines to meet the needs of the travelling press corps are further indications of this insecurity. A letter writer to the *Irish Press* was 'horrified' by a Canadian Broadcasting Company film titled 'Horseman Pass By', which included images of Puck Fair, 'where the cameras lingered long and lovingly for the next fifteen minutes in the atmosphere of a public house ... ample view of stout poured, counters wiped; customers – man flat against the wall in advanced state of drunkenness; voice of another drunk interrupting and fiddle played by tinker man; more beer poured, more mopping counters ... more tinkers – two women about to start a fight'.[11] Department of External Affairs officials were worried about 'pigs in kitchens etc' in US media coverage of the Kennedy visit.[12] The most heated reaction came in 1961 when the Irish embassy in Bonn contacted the German foreign ministry with a request that the German TV film 'Ireland and Her Children', a documentary based on German writer Heinrich Böll's book *Irisches Tagebuch* (*Irish Diary*), be withdrawn from the Prix Italia – the prestigious international competition for television documentaries. The film had already been shown on German television, and the embassy feared that a screening or award at the Prix Italia would result in it being shown by other networks. The ambassador was 'disappointed' by 'its emphasis on poverty

---

[10] *II*, 15 May 1963, cutting on NAI S 17401A Kennedy visit.
[11] S16699/f/95 *IP*, 6 May 1964.   [12] S17401A, 17 May 1963.

and emigration'; he had hoped for a 'more discerning' programme, given that Böll had a home in Achill, though the ambassador conceded that 'his [Böll's] principal concern is to portray Ireland in a romantic light and to dwell on those aspects of the Irish scene which might be expected to interest a German audience because of their strangeness and quaintness'.[13] The reaction reflected fears that the portrayal might damage efforts to attract German investment; the finessing of Ireland's international image was designed to attract investment and strengthen the case for full membership of the EEC. But Böll's depiction also challenged the desire of a poor nation to boast about its new-found affluence. Yet this affluence was fragile and partial; images of a prosperous modern Ireland clashed with photographs of collapsing Dublin tenements. Despite the introduction of free secondary education, local and national newspapers at the close of the decade still carried advertisements by Hynes Catholic Agency, recruiting teenage girls to work as servants and child-minders in Britain and the United States.

Some of the most vocal critics of a changing Ireland were members of the Irish language lobby, which moved from being a pillar of the establishment to join the ranks of protesters. Coogan, writing in 1966, stated that 'The Irish language movement is, after Partition, the most controversial subject in Ireland'; its protagonists included 'some of the most dedicated intelligent and likeable people in the state', and others who gave the language movement 'the appearance of having not only a lunatic fringe but also a lunatic core'.[14] The most prominent protest during the Golden Jubilee of the Easter Rising was staged by Misneach, whose members staged a hunger strike to protest at the failure to revive the Irish language as the language of the people. The hunger strike formed part of a wider series of protests during these years by groups such as Gael Linn or Cearta Sibhialta na Gaeltachta (Gaeltacht Civil Rights Movement). Gael Linn was aggrieved at their failure to secure control over Teilifís Éireann; at the absence of Irish language programmes in prime-time slots; and at the apparent lack of government commitment to implementing the proposals outlined in the Report of the Commission on the Irish Language. The emphasis on economic development was regarded as a direct threat to the language. The priority formerly given to the Irish language in education was being superseded by a new emphasis on economic growth and modern continental languages which were seen as essential to support EEC membership; the campaign for the abolition of compulsory Irish in state examinations was a further cause for concern. Yet claims that the

---

[13] S14463B Ireland: Foreign articles and comments.
[14] Coogan, *Ireland since the Rising*, p. 183.

Irish language was in crisis were misplaced. Irish remained a compulsory subject in school examinations; indeed, rising enrolment in secondary schools could be seen as potentially strengthening the language in the younger population. But aligning the Irish language and its culture with a more modern Ireland would have required a mental and cultural change – toning down the traditional linkages between the language and a cultural and economic life centred on remote, western, agrarian and fishing communities. Yet the subsequent history of the language, the expansion of Irish language schools in urban areas, the development of modern Irish language media and the popularity of Irish traditional music suggest that economic development was not an automatic death sentence; indeed, the emergence of language lobby groups in Wales, Brittany or Catalonia offered the potential to create new international networks to support minority languages.

However, the more common response was to welcome economic growth, provided that it was not left wholly to market forces. The publication in 1961 of Pope John XXIII's encyclical *Mater et Magistra*, which acknowledged and even welcomed economic growth and technological change, made it easy for the Irish Hierarchy to adopt a position of qualified support. The core argument in *Mater et Magistra* was that 'Economic progress must be accompanied by a corresponding social progress so that all classes of citizens can participate in the increased productivity.' It called on the state to take steps to reduce fluctuation in the economic cycle, prevent mass unemployment and address the imbalance between agriculture and other sections of the economy.[15] When Dr Rodgers, the Bishop of Killaloe, dedicated two new churches in Kilkee parish on the same day, he spoke of 'a fresh resurgence of national development sweeping the land and the optimism and hope which was replacing cynicism and apathy'.[16] While the Hierarchy was concerned at the threat to faith and family resulting from the decline in the rural population and the temptations of urban life, they were conscious that emigration presented a much greater threat. When Dr Thomas Ryan, the newly consecrated bishop of Clonfert – an overwhelmingly rural diocese in the west of Ireland – gave an address in Loughrea town hall, he cited the emphasis in *Mater et Magistra* on 'the desirability of making life in the countryside more attractive and easy for the people ... so as to stop people going from the countryside to the cities, above all, from leaving Ireland for overseas ... the dangers to body and soul lying behind the outward

[15] Encyclical letter *Mater et Magistra: on recent developments of the social question in the light of Christian teaching* (Rome, 1961).
[16] *ICD*, 1964, 'Some notable events in the Catholic life of Ireland in the year 1963', 14 July, p. 745.

appearance of good wages in other countries'.[17] Factories in provincial towns were welcome if they sustained the rural population. Many priests served on local development committees that lobbied for new factories. The Hierarchy demanded policies that preserved rural society and redistributed incomes and wealth to those in material need; their demands were not significantly different to those made by rural TDs and not noticeably out of line with government policies. If the government was criticised for failing to meet these goals, this was simply because expectations far outstripped resources. By the end of the decade, the Catholic Hierarchy was increasingly articulating the language of 'social justice' – urging that the benefits of economic growth should be apportioned between higher incomes and higher social spending – including financial support for Third World development. They remained ambivalent about city life; they were concerned at the threats posed by television, advertising and the growth in consumer credit, and like the rest of the population they appear to have taken economic growth and higher productivity for granted, seeing it as a means of delivering much-needed benefits to society.[18] If economic development and urban expansion presented a serious threat, giving rise to 'the neuroses of contemporary urban industrial society', Jeremiah Newman, the church's leading sociologist, expressed the opinion in 1970 that 'these problems are as yet unfelt in Ireland'. He believed that they could be averted by 'preserving a balance between urban and rural culture'.[19] It is striking that the Catholic Church apparently believed that a more prosperous rural society would have the strength to withstand the 'neuroses' of modern life. While Brendan Walsh suggests that the changes in marriage and fertility first evident in Dublin in the early 1960s soon spread throughout Ireland,[20] there are significant distinctions in the 1970s and 1980s between rural and urban attitudes towards contraception and divorce, with farmers consistently emerging as the most conservative group. The shoring up of rural Ireland through the dispersal of factories and preservation of family farms undoubtedly served to delay reform relating to divorce and contraception.[21]

According to Paul Ginsborg, 'Italy's modernization, as so many others, was not based on collective responsibility or collective action, but on the opportunities it afforded individual families to transform their lives'.[22]

[17] *ICD*, 1964, p. 743.
[18] John Brady, SJ, 'Beyond the Third Programme', *Christus Rex*, vol. xxiv, no. 3, July 1970, pp. 163–72.
[19] Jeremiah Newman, 'Progress and Planning', *Christus Rex*, vol. xxiv, no. 3, July 1970, p. 175.
[20] Walsh, 'Ireland's demographic transition', pp. 251–72.
[21] *II*, 23 March 1973 MRBI Poll; *II*, 3 October 1975; *Magill*, October 1977.
[22] Ginsborg, *A history of contemporary Italy*, p. 342.

This was also true for Irish families. The 1960s offered an escape from the constraints of the past. Couples were free to marry at an earlier age; the numbers marrying rose steadily as more jobs outside farming meant that farmers' sons no longer had to wait to inherit the farm – indeed parents increasingly had to persuade a son to stay. Young couples started married life in a home of their own – perhaps heavily mortgaged, but with a modern kitchen, hot water on tap, a bathroom and a television set – modest comforts by today's standards, but luxurious when compared with the past. Parents could aspire to their children completing secondary school, even going on to university or a technological college, with the prospect of finding a secure job and settling in Ireland. These changes strengthened the family and Irish society. While younger couples were beginning to experiment with family planning, this was masked by the booming marriage and birth rates, which left Ireland as an outlier in terms of fertility and family size. Better marriage opportunities went in step with a relaxation of social controls. For young women whose feminist consciousness had not yet been activated, the decade offered much more fun: opportunities to dance, go to a lounge bar, a ballad session; plenty of secretarial jobs– though little prospect of promotion or career advancement; marriage; and, thanks to the pill, the capacity to regulate births in the early years of marriage. For older married women, the 1960s bought rising living standards, running water, a bathroom, a washing machine and other material comforts and more opportunities for 'getting out of the house'. Family outings became easier with rising car ownership; there were more festivals in provincial towns and more weddings to attend, and television provided entertainment at home. But there is little evidence that Irish women had become frustrated with enforced domesticity; for many it was a new luxury. The 1960s strengthened the nuclear family centred on the male breadwinner and the full-time mother/homemaker, who was more focused on domesticity and family duties than ever before. Fewer women were now involved in family farms or family businesses, and a higher proportion of women experienced marriage and motherhood than in the past. The changing legal and economic environment did not revolutionise gender roles; it merely remedied a number of glaring disadvantages for women, with respect to inheritance, work, pay and benefit. While the 'contraceptive train' and strident feminist arguments on *The Late Late Show* has tended to be seen as the dominant images of Irish feminism in the early 1970s, they distort the picture. Most women's organisations focused their attention on cohorts of women who had been neglected, ignored or mistreated: widows, deserted wives, establishing refuges for women fleeing violent partners, securing the right of women to serve on juries.

In the quotation cited at the beginning of this chapter, Coogan suggested that Irish society was beginning to 'face up to its problems'. This is correct to a point. Alcoholism, mental handicap, travellers, the problems facing emigrants and conditions in industrial schools were examined and discussed openly – in Dáil Éireann, in newspapers, on television and in many homes. Women's refuges, established in the 1970s, marked a public acknowledgement of domestic violence.[23] But there were limits to this investigative process. For example, despite the extensive exposés of conditions in industrial schools, there was no serious effort to examine why so many children were in institutional care; why young women were in Magdalen laundries; or why the proportion of Irish people in psychiatric hospitals was significantly higher than in any other Western country. While the Irish state was making better provision for its citizens, and addressing the needs of groups who had been neglected or ignored in the past, there would appear to have been a general unwillingness to excavate some of the darker aspects of society, presumably because such an interrogation might challenge public representations of core institutions such as the family or the Catholic church.

In 1962, Lemass believed that by 1970 inefficient industrialists, traditional farmers and old-style trade union leaders would 'have become anachronistic relics of a dead past'.[24] It didn't happen, though the industrialists were probably the most vulnerable of the three categories. For many people, including many politicians, economic development and reorienting the economy were seen as a means of protecting institutions and values that were central to Irish society – the family farm, ending a century of population decline, and promoting family life by making it possible for more men and women to marry and for their children to remain in Ireland. Ireland's past had involved a hard-fought land war, and by the time of independence protecting private property – provided that it was not owned by an Anglo-Irish landlord – had become a core political principle, hence the emphasis on home ownership, the failure to tax windfall gains from rezoning land or redistribute neglected farms. Other survivals of 'the past' include an industrial policy that continued to give preference to jobs for men, not for women – a policy first articulated in the 1930s, which survived until the end of the 1970s; the continuing in office of local political dynasties; the primacy of the 'parish-pump'; and a continuing, though modified, role for the Catholic Church in education and social policy. Ireland's response to second-wave feminism was to remove regulations that were causing local difficulties – such as the

[23] Nuala Fennell, *Political Woman.*
[24] Lee, *Ireland 1912–1985*, p. 400, quoting Tobin, *Best of decades*, p. 71.

marriage bar for women working in the public service and to improve conditions for 'deserving' women while holding the line on divorce and contraception. Far from the 1960s marking the end of Ireland's preoccupation with sexual morality, any cursory look at Irish media, political debates or files in the National Archives during the 1970s and 1980s suggests that more time than ever was devoted to arguments about the links between traditional standards of sexual morality and core Irish values.

Political parties were one of the most stable elements. At first sight this is surprising, given that the two main parties originated in the split over the Anglo-Irish Treaty, an event long consigned to history. Many predicted that the party system would change to reflect a changing society. Labour flirted with socialism in the belief that a more industrialised Ireland would inevitably mean a stronger working class committed to a left-wing ideology. Yet many of the new trade union members and factory workers aspired to a middle-class life style – owning a modern home, a car and other trappings of modern affluence. Fine Gael tried to transform itself from a conservative party supported by business and professional voters and larger farmers to something akin to a social democratic party – appealing to voters with a comprehensive package of welfare and health services – but they pulled back from full-scale commitment. The stability of Irish political parties reflected their weak attachment to ideology and the strength of family dynasties and parish-pump politics. A younger generation of politicians, who now sat in Leinster House, gave equal if not greater attention to constituency matters than their predecessors. All the main parties could embrace higher public spending without any apparent sacrifice of principles, provided that proposals on tax and spending respected deeply held beliefs about private property, the family farm and the role of the churches. Labour suffered a major backlash in the 1969 general election when their policies appeared to pose a threat to property rights. Economic growth, new foreign-owned factories and improved health and welfare services gave politicians additional opportunities to lobby on behalf of constituents. EEC membership offered further scope for political brokerage. Brian Farrell notes that Seán Lemass was 'willing to sacrifice economic good sense on the altar of electoral necessity',[25] and the temptation to do this grew steadily over this period. Fianna Fáil in government facilitated and indeed connived at the survival of parish pump politics (Cabinet ministers were first and foremost TDs with a local constituency), soft-pedalling on proposals to centralise hospital services and other difficult decisions. Planning regulations – and the

[25] Farrell, *Seán Lemass*, p. 121.

power given to local councillors to determine zoning – provided developers and some councillors with significant opportunities for personal enrichment. Plans for a major reform of local government – which would have reduced the number of councils and councillors – were abandoned. The 1969 general election was won by the party that had undergone the least ideological reflection and reform, but the party with the best track record of delivering benefits to constituents. While Fianna Fáil's success can be attributed to the astute redrawing – gerrymandering – of constituency boundaries, and the absence of an alternative government, because Labour refused to enter coalition, the result was a signal that Irish politics was not going to realign on a left–right axis. Labour and Fine Gael won the 1973 general election, less because of their commitments to higher spending – which Fianna Fáil by and large matched – but because of the widespread belief that Fianna Fáil had overstayed its time in office, and the fallout from the 1970 Arms Crisis. Thus the party structures and grass-roots politics of the early 1970s and indeed the early twenty-first century are recognisable as the linear descendant of the system that existed twenty or thirty years earlier – old parties offering voters new spending programmes – testimony to the pragmatic, but historical and familial basis of party politics, though this may be changing in the aftermath of the economic crisis post-2008.

While the years 1957–1973 have a unity, a break/fault-line can be detected around the end of the 1960s – internationally and in Ireland. Rising inflation and the collapse of the post-war Bretton Woods model for regulating international monetary affairs were indications that the 'Golden Age of Economic Growth' was coming to an end. The wave of protests during 1968, and their growing radicalism, resulted in a backlash and the regrouping of conservative forces. Three events marked this process in Ireland. The 1969 general election confirmed that Irish politics was not about to experience a revolution; any change of government would have to be accommodated within the existing party system. The 1969 Lenten pastoral issued by the Hierarchy, which reiterated papal teaching on divorce and contraception, was the first significant pronouncement for many years to challenge a growing liberalism in Irish society (the only other example was in 1967 when the Archbishop of Dublin reiterated the ban on Catholics attending Trinity College). August 1969 shattered the fantasy that reform in Northern Ireland could be achieved peacefully and that the two parts of Ireland could move towards some form of friendly co-existence, lubricated by shared membership of the EEC and a common interest in economic development. Religion and nationalist ideologies reasserted their position in political discourse as divisive topics; economics was no longer the dominant paradigm.

The changing national mood is evident if we contrast the euphoria surrounding the 1966 Golden Jubilee of the Easter Rising and the much more sombre and contested celebration of the Golden Jubilee of the establishment of Dáil Éireann three years later, which was marked by pickets and protests. When President de Valera addressed a specially convened joint session of the Houses of the Oireachtas in the Mansion House (the setting for the first meeting of Dáil Éireann), in January 1969 he told his audience that 'cosmopolitanism is very much in the air, some would say that the ideas of nationality which we held some fifty years ago are out of date. Small nations are again in danger of being pushed aside or completely absorbed. I hope that it will not be so with us and that this grand old nation of ours, which has maintained its identity and individuality at great cost, will be preserved.'[26] Reading this speech it is no surprise that de Valera probably voted against Ireland's membership of the EEC.[27] But the circumstances of the time testify to the real limitations on the sovereignty of a small nation, such as Ireland. By the late 1950s Ireland had no alternative other than to secure a free trade agreement with Britain, apply for EEC membership and attract foreign companies with the expertise and resources to provide jobs and export earnings, if it was to deliver the living standards demanded by its citizens. Ireland's currency was pegged to sterling; the exchange rate and interest rates were determined in Whitehall and the City of London, with the requirements of sterling and the British economy as the foremost considerations. In trade negotiations or the implementation of bilateral agreements with Britain, Ireland was invariably the weaker party: subject to unilaterally imposed import deposit schemes, reductions in dairy quotas or restrictions on UK investment in Ireland. The capacity to exercise a meaningful and independent foreign policy was also constrained. By the 1960s, the United Nations was effectively controlled by major voting blocs: NATO members, the Eastern bloc and former colonies in Africa and South-East Asia. Ireland's UN votes were increasingly aligned with those of EEC/NATO members – primarily because this generally reflected Ireland's ideological position and this voting pattern helped to smooth the path for EEC membership, overcoming the potential threat presented by Ireland's neutral status. Ireland's inability to use the United Nations to secure any international leverage over British policy in Northern Ireland

---

[26] NAI S2005/15/16. My thanks to Dr Brian Murphy for alerting me to this speech.
[27] Diarmaid Ferriter, *Judging Dev: a reassessment of the life and legacy of Eamon de Valera* (Dublin, 2007), pp. 352–3. Information given to me by the late Brian Lenihan junior, who was told this by his father Brian Lenihan.

reflected the realities of international relations: the unwillingness of Western powers to act against Britain's interests and the dominance of the UN General Assembly by Afro-Asian countries.

Yet, on 1 January 1973, Ireland became a member of the EEC, without abandoning its policy of neutrality and non-membership of NATO, something that could not have been predicted in the early 1960s. The referendum on EEC membership in May 1972 was a landslide, with a turnout of 71 per cent, and 83 per cent of those who voted in favour of membership.[28] While economic arguments were paramount, sovereignty emerged as an issue in the Dáil and during the campaign, with those opposed to membership warning of the threats posed by a future EEC foreign policy. The government argued that small nations in isolation had very limited sovereignty in the modern world, and that consequently sovereignty would be strengthened by membership. Perhaps the clearest statements to this effect came from Liam Cosgrave, the leader of the opposition: 'Although we won full political independence, in the world in which we find ourselves independence is not always meaningful. The great powers act ultimately to suit themselves. The small countries have no ultimate sanction of force to defend their rights.' It had proved difficult for Ireland to make 'a reality of independence because we have been so heavily overshadowed by our powerful neighbour, Britain'. For Cosgrave, 'the most important result of our membership, will, therefore, be the prospect of escaping from this long period of economic dominance by Britain' and 'a realistic opportunity to take our place on equal terms alongside the other sovereign nations of Europe'.[29]

If 'economic dominance by Britain' was receding somewhat (though the relationship between the two economies remained and remains close), the crisis in Northern Ireland meant that Anglo-Irish relations reverted to issues that had been dominant in the early years after independence – constitutional relationships, ideology, nationalism, history, rather than the cheese quotas, or tubercular cattle that predominated in the 1960s. There was also something of a return to the past with respect to Ireland's relationship with the United States, a need to restore links with Irish-America and to communicate Ireland's position on Northern Ireland to the White House, the State Department and Capitol Hill, as opposed to the 1960s focus on attracting investment, trade and tourism – yet another instance of economic objectives being relegated to second place. Nevertheless, while August 1969 marked a return to the politics of

---

[28] aan de Wiel, 'The Commission, the Council and the Irish application for the EEC, 1961–73', p. 380.
[29] DD, 23 June 1970, cols. 1659–1960.

the past, it was the first occasion that Northern Ireland featured prominently on the Irish Cabinet agenda over a sustained period: the first
occasion that ministers and civil servants explored the realities of
Northern Ireland, as opposed to fantasising about reunification.

The unfolding crisis in Northern Ireland prompted a series of inter-
connected debates across politics and society. What was the role of
armed insurrection, instigated by a minority, in achieving independence? Did the precedent offered by the 1916 Rising, which did not
command popular support at the time, give legitimacy to an armed
struggle in Northern Ireland? Did the population of the island of
Ireland consist of one nation or two? Did Ulster unionism represent a
distinct religious and cultural tradition, or was partition an artificial
division imposed on a united island? What obligations did the Irish
state and its people have towards the minority in Northern Ireland?
The debates stretch far beyond the time period of this book, and many
of the critical contributions to the debate on historical revisionism fall
into this later period.[30] If, as Coogan claimed, the 'wounds of the past'
had almost healed, some were re-opened after 1969. Rhetoric about a
united Ireland and the iniquity of partition had formed part of Irish
political discourse since the 1920s. All the main parties came together in
a vocal anti-partition campaign in the late 1940s and early 1950s. But
these activities were at some remove from political reality; there was
little expectation that an Irish government would have to take any
immediate steps to bring about a united Ireland. The 1970s saw the
past coming back to haunt Lynch's government, as speeches about the
evils of partition by de Valera and other party leaders in earlier years or
the ghosts of 1916 were invoked to support armed republicans in
Northern Ireland. On 8 May 1970, during the heated debate on the
Arms Crisis, Kevin Boland, who had recently resigned from the
Cabinet, told the Dáil that while it was appropriate to rule out the use
of force in 'this 26 County State ... there is no doubt that the people in
the Six Counties are, in fact, in the same position as the people in the
whole country were in before 1916, and they are entitled to make their
own decisions'.[31] Yet if the Irish state had failed to escape its past, the
debate that opened up was quite new. This was the first occasion that
serious consideration was given to the implications and possible configuration of a united Ireland; the first time that a serious effort was made to
comprehend Ulster unionism. Reviewing the memoranda, speeches and

---

[30] The literature on this topic is voluminous, a good starting point is Ciaran Brady (ed.),
Interpreting Irish history: the debate on historical revisionism, 1938–1994 (Dublin, 1994).
[31] DD, vol. 260, col. 750, 8 May 1970.

published works from that time, the most striking feature is the expectation that constitutional change on the island was imminent.

As for the implications of such a change, the issues highlighted included the cost – Britain's annual subvention to Northern Ireland of £100 million – and the legal and constitutional changes that were seen as necessary. While the economic cost was to the fore in Whitaker's memoranda, and predictably in Garret FitzGerald's 1972 *Towards a United Ireland*, finance attracted much less public attention than legal and constitutional issues. The conflict in Northern Ireland focused attention on the role of religion as a badge of identity – something that divided communities within Northern Ireland and divided North and South. Michael Heslinga, lecturer in human geography in Amsterdam, determined that Ireland's borders – whether with the rest of the United Kingdom or between the two parts of Ireland – were 'in the last resort religious frontiers'.[32] Conor Cruise O'Brien described the subject of his 1971 book *States of Ireland* as 'the relations between Catholics and Protestants and two political entities created by those relations'. FitzGerald also highlighted religions as a historic dividing line (the seventeenth-century Ulster Plantation) and a continuing barrier to a united Ireland. He was among those who regarded legislation banning contraception, the constitutional prohibition on divorce and Article 44, which referred to the special place of the Catholic Church, as barriers to a united Ireland. At the end of a chapter titled 'The Religious Issue', he concluded that 'There is room for agreement on these issues, and a strong motivation towards such agreement exists among Catholic churchmen, who would not wish to appear to stand in the way of the achievement of reunification by consent, should this become a real possibility.'[33] This statement was naïvely optimistic. In hindsight, it is highly questionable whether reunification by consent was ever a realistic possibility in the early 1970s, and it is equally questionable whether amendments to Ireland's laws and constitution to permit divorce and contraception would have seriously changed the picture. Although Irish voters agreed by a large majority to remove Article 44 from the constitution, the referendum was conducted almost in silence – the opportunity was not taken to debate the role of religion in politics and society, or how it might figure in some form of closer relationship between the two Irelands.

The debate over divorce and contraception is more informative about independent Ireland than about Ulster unionism. While the Irish Hierarchy happily agreed to the removal of Article 44 – which was purely

---

[32] Michael Heslinga, *The Irish border as a cultural divide* (Assen: Gorcum, 1971), p. 203.
[33] FitzGerald, *Towards a new Ireland*, p. 101.

of symbolic value – they made it known that they would strongly oppose any changes with respect to divorce and contraception. In 1972, Cardinal Conway, commenting on a recent report on divorce by the Irish Theological Association, emphasised that the prohibition on divorce in the Irish constitution 'sustains and strengthens the fabric of family life'.[34] The position adopted by the Catholic Church at the time was very much in line with majority opinion in the state. In 1971, an opinion poll showed only 22 per cent in favour of divorce (34 per cent of those under thirty-four years).[35] It is questionable whether many opponents of divorce would have switched sides in order to facilitate a united Ireland. While hostility to divorce reflects the influence of the Catholic Church on Irish society, it is also symptomatic of an underlying conservatism that valued continuity, the family, private property and what was seen as Ireland's traditional way of life. The groups who campaigned to 'Save the West' and prevent the transfer of land out of the family and those who demanded that factories be decentralised would not have countenanced divorce or more liberal contraception; yet paradoxically, they were also the groups most in favour of a united Ireland.[36] A majority of the adult population had left school at fourteen. The priest was still the best-educated and best-read person in most rural parishes and small towns. His authority was being challenged by other media – notably television – but we should not overstate the pace and extent of change. Quite what would have happened if the Sunningdale Agreement signed in December 1973 had survived will ever remain an unanswered question. The agreement between the British and Irish governments and a power-sharing executive designate in Northern Ireland provided for the establishment of a Council of Ireland, with 'executive and harmonising functions and a consultative role, and a consultative assembly with advisory and review functions', relating to all Ireland. But as McDaid shows, 'The Irish government's view of what the role and functions of a Council of Ireland should be moderated significantly between 1973 and 1974 … As time progressed, however, the government effectively decided that the council would have little more than symbolic importance.' The Department of Foreign Affairs was the only department to show any real enthusiasm for the concept; McDaid concluded that there is no evidence that the attitude of a Fianna Fáil government would have been different.[37] The Agreement collapsed in the spring of 1974 when the

---

[34] *ICD* 1973, diary 4 June 1972, p. 734.   [35] FitzGerald, *Towards a new Ireland*, p. 30
[36] *Magill* October 1977 opinion poll.
[37] Shaun McDaid, 'The Irish Government and the Sunningdale Council of Ireland: a vehicle for unity', *IHS*, vol. xxviii, no. 150, November 2012, pp. 283–303; quotation p. 297.

power-sharing executive collapsed following a major strike by the Ulster Workers Council. This may have enabled the Irish government and indeed the wider society to avoid confronting the limits of their commitment to an effective all-Ireland executive body. While the 1998 Good Friday Agreement resulted in major changes to Articles 2 and 3 of the 1937 Constitution, which was overwhelmingly approved by voters, the all-Ireland dimension continues to be largely a matter of ministerial meetings and some high-level agreements; it has had significantly less impact on everyday life than EEC membership.

The story of Ireland 1957–1973 is one of partial transformation. When British sociologist John Goldthorpe tried to analyse the Irish experience in the concluding chapter of a collection of essays on the development of industrial society in Ireland up to the early 1990s, he emphasised the constraints imposed by the self-maintaining properties of 'social structures and processes expressing established relationships of power and advantage within Irish society',[38] but he does not offer an explanation for this continuity. The major social revolution in Ireland – the near disappearance of the rural proletariat after the famine and the emergence of peasant proprietorship – predated the state. Although successive governments introduced measures to alleviate poverty, provide employment and access to land, none of these programmes were designed to effect a social revolution – on the contrary. Wartime neutrality meant that Ireland was spared the shocks that affected all combatant nations.[39] Mass emigration served to arrest change and cement social structures, as did the economic policies pursued since independence. Kissane concluded that Irish society was 'relatively modernised by 1921, with high levels of education and urbanisation'. By the late 1950s however, Irish levels of industrialisation, enrolment in secondary and university education, and urbanisation were relatively low compared with other European countries.[40] Lee, who examined the process of socio-economic change through the lens of 'the performer ethic', concluded that the competitive (performance ethic) education system was primarily 'directed to the goal of security', education for the professions.[41] Kelly suggests that 'Home Rulers at their most open-minded and progressive, articulated their politics in terms of pluralism and tolerance', whereas the constitutional

---

[38] Goldthorpe, 'The theory of industrialism and the Irish case', in Goldthorpe and Whelan (eds), *Development of industrial society in Ireland*, p. 431.

[39] Mancur Olsen, *The rise and decline of nations* (Newhaven: Yale University Press, 1982), contrasted the dynamism of postwar Germany which had suffered major discontinuities with the comparative stagnation of societies that had not undergone a similar experience.

[40] Bill Kissane, *Explaining Irish democracy* (Dublin: UCD Press, 2002), pp. 27–44.

[41] J.J. Lee, *Ireland 1912–1983. Politics and society*, pp. 390–5.

settlement that resulted in the Irish Free State 'created one of the most religiously homogeneous societies in modern Europe',[42] though a comparison of Ireland north and south in terms of religious and social values suggests that though divided they had much in common, and the argument that a united Ireland would have adopted more liberal attitudes towards sexual morality is unproven and unprovable.

There is broad consensus about lack of social change pre the 1960s – but Lee claimed:

> The turning of the tide during the Lemass years did not therefore simply mark one more turn of the generational wheel. Instead, it represented a reversal of the dominant ethos not just of a generation, but of a century. The essence of the Lemass approach can be defined as the attempt to substitute the performance principle for the possessor principle in Irish life. To fully grasp the magnitude of the challenge confronting him, we must delineate the nature of the inherited ethos. For the primacy of the possess or principle owed its power not to the whims of individuals, but to attitudes deeply rooted in social structure and historical experience.[43]

But if the tide turned, it was more a course correction than a major transformation. When Ireland finally made the transition from an agrarian to an industrial society in the 1960s, the change was muted – partly because Ireland left it rather late to industrialise. The early 1950s saw massive expansion in industrial employment throughout parts of Europe which had formerly been agrarian, though not in Ireland; by the late 1960s the age of mass industrialisation in countries with relatively high wages and social costs was coming to an end, and the long-drawn out process of falling employment, especially for skilled male workers, was underway. The discontinuities in terms of Ireland's industrial sector – with the loss of jobs in protected industries and the emergence of new foreign-owned firms, often employing different workers in different locations – retarded the formation of a mature industrial culture. The leadership in most foreign firms was based outside Ireland, which meant that industrialists failed to emerge as an identifiable elite interest group that might challenge the farmers, or indigenous businessmen, whose interests were more likely to be in property or distribution. The dispersed foreign industrial sector and the absence of linkage with existing industries retarded the development of emerging entrepreneurs. However, we need to know much more about Irish businesses; their access to capital and technical expertise; and their medium and long-term history.

---

[42] Matthew Kelly, 'Home Rule and its enemies', in Alvin Jackson (ed.), *The Oxford handbook of modern Irish history* (Oxford: Oxford University Press, 2014), p. 598.
[43] Lee, *Ireland, 1912–1985*, p. 390.

Farming was less subject to disruption than the industrial sector. Farming was protected by the CAP, whereas traditional Irish industrial communities and the small Irish coalmines in Arigna and Castlecomer were not. Farmers also benefited from an unwillingness to challenge property rights and a welfare regime that provided income support without the socially damaging requirement that the claimant should be unemployed; this preserved their identity as property-owners, despite relying on benefits. Existing social structures were also reinforced by the expansion in educational opportunity – which extended access to academic secondary schools and places in traditional university programmes – which meant that the aspirations of parents and students continued to focus heavily on traditional professions such as law and medicine, as they had in the past. Yet by 1980s, over 30 per cent of fifteen- to nineteen-year-old children of unskilled workers were in education, compared with less than 10 per cent in 1961/62.[44] Demography is yet another instance of partial change and continuity. Ireland remained a demographic outlier – with cyclical periods of emigration, and a significantly higher birth rate than other Western European nations, and this high dependency rate until the 1990s was one of the factors that retarded the capacity to catch up with the average income level of EEC members.

In 1964, during a debate on the Budget, Lemass said that 'Only the Government can achieve a balance between national resources and the often conflicting desires of every section, and take the decisions which determine the rate of economic or social progress and keep the country moving in line on a common front. As President Kennedy said, "A rising tide lifts all boats" '.[45] This quotation encapsulates two assumptions that were central, not just to government policy during the 1960s, but over a longer period. The first is the assumption that government has the capacity to exercise significant influence over the economy – for good or ill – a belief that predates the formation of the state; it was a core tenet of nineteenth-century Irish nationalism. The second element, 'the rising tide', suggests that a national economic policy will be socially neutral – that all will benefit; existing hierarchies or interests will not be disturbed. This quotation begs the question whether Lee's belief that Lemass wanted to overturn 'the dominant ethos ... of a century' is correct, or to 'lift all boats'? The quasi-corporatist bodies that emerged during the 1960s promoted a sense of what Mair has described as 'The Politics of the National Interest'[46] – harnessing trade unions and industrialists to a

---

[44] Brendan M. Walsh, 'Interpreting modern Ireland: time for a new view', *Studies*, vol. 80, no. 350, Winter 1991, p. 402.
[45] DD, vol. 208, col. 1791, 15 April 1964.
[46] Mair, *The changing Irish party system*, pp. 177, 183.

national purpose (farmers less effectively), which served to blur potential class divisions, at least at elite level. A steady increase in welfare payments and the articulated belief that economic growth would lift all boats created a sense of national purpose that served to create a belief that economic growth was a national enterprise, and not one that privileged one social class or interest group over another. But there is no indication that these interest groups were prepared to put the national interest ahead of self or sectional interests.

Government efforts to retain this social equilibrium were at the core of the 1960s development process; the question was who would control the process? In *Economic Development* and the associated discussions, Whitaker made a strong case for the process to be controlled by civil servants and that civil servants should be authorised to communicate with the public; he referred to the 'talent ... locked up in the civil service'.[47] The post-war years saw several instances internationally where talented civil servants played a critical role in diagnosing social problems and determining policies to address these. Heclo argues that civil servants in Britain and Sweden were more influential in determining social policy than political parties or interest groups.[48] From the 1950s onwards Irish civil servants travelled regularly to meetings of the OEEC/OECD, whereas Irish ministers were rarely present. These meetings would have given Irish civil servants access to current European thinking on key policies and the awareness that public servants elsewhere were playing a key role in determining policy. But as we have seen, despite Whitaker's reference to 'talent ... locked up in the civil service', such talent was limited, and leading civil servants were not always in agreement as to national policy – sectional/departmental interests remained foremost for many senior civil servants.

Yet the initial momentum for Ireland's EEC membership undoubtedly originated with civil servants (and with the NFA). During the 1957 general election campaign, all the main political parties sat on the fence on the question of a European free trade area. The first official document to suggest that Ireland must take that direction was the early drafts of *Economic Development*, an example of what Hugh Heclo as described as 'autonomous state action'. But when Whitaker suggested that oversight of the 1958 *Programme for Economic Expansion* should be carried out by external experts, Lemass countered by insisting that political control must remain paramount. Yet the political control was ministerial,

[47] Has Ireland a Future? Copy on NAI DT, S16660A.
[48] Hugh Heclo, *Modern social politics: from relief to income maintenance* (Newhaven and London: Yale University Press, 1974).

rather than by the legislature. This had long been characteristic of Fianna Fáil in government; in 1933, de Valera mused that the Dáil should be given six months holidays to enable the Cabinet to get their work done,[49] implying that Dáil scrutiny was hampering government efforts to implement its programme. While de Valera's Cabinets scrutinised all major policies at length, the evidence suggests that this did not happen under either Lemass or Lynch. A review of political material – election manifestos/briefing notes/agendas for annual conferences and related matter – indicates limited engagement (and perhaps not even that) by rank-and-file party members in the details of Ireland's economic development policies. Proposals in Fine Gael's *Just Society* that all aspects of economic planning should be scrutinised by a Dáil committee highlight the absence of such oversight, though it would be naïve to assume that the rank and file of Fine Gael played a key part in drafting that document.

If the 1960s development strategy had little input from TDs or political parties, it did create a new elite: the Taoiseach and some key economic ministers, senior civil servants, business and trade union leaders, plus some academics, who met on a regular basis. But while these organisations came up with programmes, targets, recommendations – some of which bore fruit in tax concessions, grants and other initiatives – we should not exaggerate their influence on policy. It is possible that their real influence was exercised in a more personal, informal manner, because many of these reports had limited impact. Many key decisions were made in a more ad hoc manner. Donogh O'Malley's proposal for free education and how it should be implemented appears to have been determined solely by himself; no prior memoranda setting out the case of this approach have come to light, and the policy was at variance with proposals that were being developed in the Department of Education. Nor is there evidence that O'Malley's proposals were the *direct* result of influence by the Catholic Church – though they did reflect the church's wishes, and also the wishes of parents that traditional secondary schooling should be available to their children. Farming organisations did not sit round the table at corporate meetings; they probably had fewer formal meetings with ministers and civil servants than leading industrialists and trade unionists, and this absence may have influenced policy in the early 1960s. But agricultural interests were foremost in the minds of those who negotiated the AIFTAA (the fact that it failed to meet farming expectations was not the fault of Irish politicians or officials), and by the latter half of the decade agriculture was commanding a steadily increasing share of Exchequer funding. The farming influence was felt in NFA protests and

[49] DD, vol. 46, col. 2657, 7 April 1933.

in local and national electoral politics. While trade union leaders attended meetings to determine policies on retraining, industrial estates and economic planning, it was arguably the pressure exercised by striking workers that determined pay increases.

Nevertheless, there is a real sense of a gulf between the elite and the masses, in terms of involvement in policy discussions, commitment to EEC membership, economic programmes and other developments. Such a gulf is also evident with regard to Northern Ireland, where Lemass and others in a relatively small circle – whose extent remains uncertain, but I suspect that it was small – were consciously working to befriend the government of Northern Ireland and the almost exclusively Unionist Northern business elite. Yet when violence broke out in 1969, traditional anti-partitionist rhetoric re-emerged among politicians of all parties, and more widely throughout the community. The fact that the rhetoric did not translate into more widespread support for the IRA is not especially surprising: this also marks a reversion to traditional attitudes – active support for a united Ireland, as opposed to spouting anti-partition rhetoric was always a minority position. Support for the argument that constitutional changes should be implemented in order to bring about a united Ireland was limited, and when FitzGerald or Whitaker recommended removing the constitutional ban on divorce, they envisaged divorce being available to those in Northern Ireland/or Protestants, not to all citizens. Murphy and Purséil suggest that there was a significant gulf between the elite and the masses with regard to EEC membership – 'despite the large "yes" vote [in the 1972 referendum] Irish people were less enthusiastic than the result implies and can more accurately be termed reluctant Europeans as the sense of inevitability of the outcome of a decade-long process left them with little choice but to sign up for membership'.[50] But if that is so, the mass vote in favour suggests a capacity by the government, the main opposition party, farming and elite interests to convince the majority to accept change, though acceptance was linked to perceived material benefits.

The 1950s saw a crisis of confidence in the capacity of a native government to meet the aspirations of its citizens. The political and economic developments of the 1960s restored that confidence by setting new national goals of economic development and EEC membership; repeated references to Ireland's economic success that masked underlying realities such as the continuing failure to catch-up with the rest of Western Europe or provide all citizens with a realistic prospect of employment; an emphasis on the government's role in delivering this success. By 1973, average

[50] Murphy and Purseil, 'Irish entry to the EEC', p. 534.

living standards were approximately half those in other EEC member states, though I doubt that many citizens were aware of this. Projections in the NIEC *Report on Full Employment* (1967) showed that emigration or higher unemployment were inevitable in the future, unless the rate of investment and economic growth rose substantially.[51] In 1959 John Cahan, with uncanny foresight, predicted that Ireland would have a hard road ahead until the end of the century: it was only in the mid-1990s that Ireland belatedly began to catch up on other Western European economies.[52]

Ultimately, this is a story of political rather than economic success – the capacity to present the case for economic growth and EEC membership in terms of national interest and to share the benefits of rising living standards sufficiently widely to placate very diverse communities and interest groups. But the government's commitment to change did not extend beyond the economy and programmes such as education and health. Political pragmatism and an understanding of the electorate meant that there was no serious momentum on constitutional reform other than the removal of Article 44, which was of purely symbolic value, a (non)-decision to leave access to contraception to the courts and to avoid legislation. One explanation for the combination of continuity and limited change may lie in the longevity of Ireland's political tradition – traditions often forgotten by those who emphasise Ireland's revolutionary past. Yet mass movements beginning with Daniel O'Connell, and continuing through Parnell and the Irish Party, to the advertising campaigns of Cumann na nGaedheal and the establishment of Fianna Fáil show a considerable sophistication in wooing the electorate, with national goals to the fore. Hayward has described the politics of adaptation in early twenty-first-century Ireland – a time of rapid economic, social and cultural change – as 'the "recycling" of what has constituted the political fabric of the Irish state since its inception'. She argues that 'the Irish state remains "unique": it is addressing issues that transcend national boundaries in a national way'.[53] The national agenda of the 1970s was increasingly focused on economic development, but another national agenda recognised the need to protect 'Our Way of Life'. A 1971 opinion poll on EEC membership showed that a substantial minority were concerned about the potential impact of membership on

---

[51] NIEC, *Report on full employment* (1967), F66/18.
[52] FitzGerald, 'The story of Ireland's failure – and belated success', in Nolan et al. (eds), *Bust to boom*, pp. 27–57.
[53] Katy Hayward, 'Introduction: The politics of adaptation in Ireland', in Katy Hayward and Muiris MacCarthaigh (eds), *Recycling the state. The politics of adaptation in Ireland* (Dublin: Irish Academic Press, 2007), pp. 1–3.

morality, though not apparently on Irish culture.[54] In July1982, in the run-up to the 1983 Pro-Life Amendment, Martin Mansergh, then an advisor to the Taoiseach, Charles Haughey, commented: 'We have a distinctive way of life here, are proud of it, and wish to protect and develop it. The State is taking a positive stand against what is perceived to be one of the evils of our time.'[55] This can be read as a post-1973 'recycling' of Irish identity – a combination of an open economy and continued protection of what was seen as Ireland's 'distinct way of life'.

As we approach the centenary of the 1916 Rising – the most significant event in the emergence of an independent Ireland – the Ireland of 1957–1973 is increasingly a foreign place. The political configuration that has dominated the state since independence may be dissolving; though given the predictions that this would happen in the 1960s, caution is advised. The certainties associated with EEC membership are being undermined by a faltering European economy and the threat of British exit. While the constitutional position of Northern Ireland was transformed after the 1998 Good Friday Agreement, the future direction of North–South relations is uncertain in the light of the potential dismantling of the United Kingdom and the increasing likelihood of a Catholic majority in Northern Ireland combined with a growing proportion of people identifying themselves as Northern Irish (not Irish or British).[56] Ireland's individuality as a country with 'certain distinctive Christian values' has largely disappeared, though the birth-rate remains significantly higher than other European countries, and the propensity to emigrate remains strong. Ethnic and racial homogeneity has given way to a much more diverse population. Political and economic debates are increasingly couched in terms of competing classes and interests, rather than in national terms. The importance of foreign multinationals is arguably one of the strongest continuities. The economic and fiscal crisis that occurred post-2008 has frequently been described as a 'loss of sovereignty'. The widespread use of this terminology to describe a socio-economic and a psychological crisis testifies to the continuing emotional power of national rhetoric in contemporary Ireland.

[54] Murphy and Purséil, 'Ireland and EEC entry', pp. 544–5.
[55] NAI, 2012/90/667 Pro-Life Amendment.
[56] In the 2011 Census 39.89 per cent identified themselves as British only, 25.26 per cent as Irish only and 20.94 as Northern Irish only.

Bibliography

Dublin Diocesan Archives

John Charles McQuaid Papers

Historical Archives of the European Union, Florence (now in Fiesole)

Hallstein papers
OECD Agriculture Committee Files
OECD Economic Policy Committee Files
OECD Education Directorate Files
OEEC and OECD Executive Committee Files

National Archives, Ireland

Cabinet Minutes
Department of Foreign Affairs Files
Department of the Taoiseach Files
Government Information Bureau Files
Tweedy Papers

National Library of Ireland

Records of Irish Countrywomen's Association

The National Archives, Kew

Foreign and Commonwealth Office Files

University College Dublin Archives

Conor Cruise O'Brien Papers
Donncha Ó Briain Papers
Fianna Fáil Archives

Fine Gael Archives
Seán MacEntee Papers
T.K. Whitaker Papers

Newspapers and periodicals

Anglo-Celt
Belfast Newsletter
Business and Finance
Catholic Standard
Church of Ireland Gazette
Christus Rex
Connacht Tribune
Hibernia
Irish Catholic Directory
Irish Farmers' Journal
Irish Independent
Irish Medical Times
Irish Press
Journal of the Irish Medical Association
Sunday Independent
Sunday Press
The Economist
The Furrow
The Irish Times
The Kerryman
The Western People
Woman's Choice

Oireachtas

Dáil Debates; Seanad Debates

Official Publications, Ireland

An Comisiún um Athbheochan na Gaelige. [*Commission on the Restoration of the Irish Language*] *Final Report,* English language summary, July 1963, R102.
An Foras Forbartha, Colin Buchanan and partners, *Regional Studies in Ireland,* Dublin, 1969.
An Foras Talúntais, *West Cork Resource Survey* 1963.
Central Bank, Quarterly Reports.
Commission on Emigration and other Population Problems, 1948–54, 1955, R63.
Commission on the Status of Women – interim report, 1970, R114.
Commission on the Status of Women, 1972, R117.

Commission on the Garda Síochána: Report on Remuneration and Conditions of Service, 1970, R119.

Department of Agriculture, *Advisory Committee on the Marketing of Agricultural Produce*. Seven reports 1958–59, A42–47.

Survey of Agricultural Credit in Ireland by Fred Gilmore, Department of Agriculture, 1959.

Inter-Departmental Committee on the problems of small western farms, Report on Pilot Area Development, 1964, A52/1.

Agriculture in the Second Programme for Economic Expansion, 1964, A55.

John J. Scully, *Agriculture in the West of Ireland: a study of the low farm income problem*, 1971, A67.

Department of Education, *Investment in Education. Report of the survey team appointed by the Minister for Education in October 1962* (Dublin: 1966), E56.

Commission on Higher Education 1960–67, 2 vols, E59.1–2.

Reformatory and Industrial Schools System report 1970. E58.

Department of Finance, *Economic Development*, 1958, F58.

Programme for Economic Expansion, 1958, F57.

Second Programme for Economic Expansion, Part 1, 1963, F57/1.

Second Programme for Economic Expansion, Part 2, 1964, F57/2.

Third Programme. Economic and Social Development, 1969–72, F57/7.

NIEC *Report on Economic Planning*, 1965, F66/7.

NIEC *Comments on the report of committee on development centres and industrial estates*, 1965, F66/8.

NIEC *Report on Full Employment* 1967, F66/19.

NIEC *Report on Physical Planning* 1969, F66.27.

Report of public service organisation review group, 1966–69, F81 [Devlin Report].

—

Department of Health, *The Health Services and their future redevelopment*, 1966, K87.

Commission of Inquiry into mental illness, 1967, K1966.

Outline of the future hospital system. Report of the consultative council on the general hospital services, 1968, Z1.

The General Practitioner in Ireland. Report of the consultative council on general medical practice, 1974, Z19.

Report of the working party on prescribing and dispensing in the general medical service, 1976, R133.

Statistical information relevant to the Health Services, 1976, Z23.

Department of Industry and Commerce. IBEC Technical Services Corporation, *An appraisal of Ireland's industrial potential*, 1952, I98.

CIO *Interim Report on State Aid,* 1962, I109.

CIO *A Synthesis of Reports by the Survey Teams on 22 Industries,* 1965, I 109.24.

CIO *Final Report,* 1965, I109.31.

Report of Committee on Development Centres and Industrial Estates, 1965, I110.

The Committee on Industrial Progress, *Report on the Irish Footwear Industry,* 1971, I131/7.

Department of Labour.

Final Report of the Committee on industrial relations in the Electricity Supply Board, 1969, V2/1.

Report of inquiry into strikes in Bord na Mona in November 1967 and February/March 1968 conducted by Charles Mulvey, 1968, V5.

Department of Local Government. Annual Reports.

The Dublin Region. Advisory Regional Plan and Final Report. Parts One and Two. Myles Wright, 1967, K85/1–2.

Nathaniel Lichfield and Associates, *Report and Outline for the Limerick Region,* 1967, K88/2.

Committee on the Price of Building Land. Report to the Minister for Local Government, 1973, K119.

Industrial Development Authority Reports (on) Reported Industrial Plans 1972, 173–7.

Arthur D. Little, *Review of the structure of the Industrial Development Authority* (May 1967).

NESC, *Regional Policy in Ireland: a review* (1974).

Industrial policy and development: a survey of literature from the early 1960s, 1980.

Report on dispute of 1970 between the Associated Banks and the Irish Bank Officials' Association and recommendations as to what action might be taken to avoid the risk of closures through industrial action in the future, by Michael P. Fogarty at the request of Joseph Brennan, 1971, R112.

Commission of Inquiry into Child Abuse, 5 vols, 2009, Z210/01–05.

The Tribunal of Inquiry into certain planning matters & payments. The final report, March 201 www.planningtribunal.ie

Annual Reports.

Other official publications

Maud Committee on the Management of Local Government, HMSO 1967, vol. 1.

The Civil Service/Chairman: Lord Fulton, vol. I (*Report of the Committee 1966–68,* HMS) 1968.

UK Department of Trade and Industry, *Multi-national investment strategies in the British Isles,* HMSO 1983, by Neil Hood and Stephen Young.

European Parliament: Political Committee, Towards Political Union A selection of documents, with a foreword by M Emilio Battista (Jan. 1964).
European Social Charter, Collected texts, 6th edition, 30 June 2008.

Books and journals

Adams, Michael, *Censorship. The Irish experience* (Dublin: Scepter Books, 1968).
Akenson, D. H., *Small differences: Irish Catholics and Irish Protestants, 1815–1922: an international perspective* (Dublin: Gill & Macmillan, 1991).
Conor. A biography of Conor Cruise O'Brien (Montreal: McGill UP, 1994).
Anderson, Stuart, 'Drug regulation and the welfare state. Government, the pharmaceutical industry and the health professions in Great Britain, 1940–1980', in Virginia Berridge and Kelly Loughlin (eds), *Medicine, the market and the mass media, producing health in the twentieth century* (London and New York: Routledge, 2005), pp. 192–218.
Andrews, C. S., *Man of no property* (Dublin: Lilliput, 2001).
Arensberg, Conrad and Solon T. Kimball, *Family and community in Ireland* (Cambridge MA: Harvard UP, second edition, 1968).
Baker, T. J. and M. Ross, 'The changing regional pattern in Ireland', *ESR*, vol. 1, no. 1, 1969, pp. 155–65.
Bailey, Martha J. and Sheldon Danziger (eds), *Legacies of the war on poverty* (New York: Russell Sage Foundation, 2013).
Barrington, Ruth, *Health, medicine and politics in Ireland, 1900–1970* (Dublin: Institute of Public Administration, 1987).
Barrington, Tom, 'The structure of the civil service 2. Elaborate contrivance', *Administration*, vol. 3, 1955, pp. 94–108.
From big government to local government. The road to decentralisation (Dublin: Institute of Public Administration, 1975).
Barry, Frank, 'Economic integration and convergence. Processes in the EU cohesion countries', *Journal of Common Market Studies*, 2003, vol. 41, no. 5, pp. 897–921.
Bax, Mart, *Harpstrings and confessions. Machine-style politics in the Irish Republic* (Assen and Amsterdam: Van Gorcum, 1976).
Bew, Paul and Henry Patterson, *Seán Lemass and the making of modern Ireland* (Dublin: Gill & Macmillan, 1982).
Bew, Paul, Peter Gibbon and Henry Patterson, *Northern Ireland 1921–1996. Political forces and social classes* (London: Serif, 1996, revised edition).
Biever, Bruce, *Religion, culture and values. A cross-cultural analysis of motivational factors in native Irish and American Irish Catholicism* (New York: Arno Press, 1976).
Blackwell, John, *Transport in the developing economy of Ireland* (Dublin: ESRI paper 47, 1969).
Bloomfield, Kenneth, *Stormont in crisis* (Belfast: Blackstaff, 1994).
Boel, Bent, *The European productivity agency and transatlantic relations 1953–1961* (Copenhagen: Museum Tusculanum Press, 2003).
Boltho, Andrea (ed.), *The European economy. Growth and crisis* (Oxford: Oxford University Press, 1982).

Böll, Heinrich, *Irish Journal* (London: Secker & Warburg, 1967).

Bowman, Emer Philbin, 'Sexual and contraceptive attitudes and behaviour of single attenders at a Dublin family planning clinic', *Journal of Biosocial Science*, vol. 9, 1977, pp. 429–45.

Bowman, John, *Window and mirror. RTÉ television, 1961–2011* (Cork: Collins, 2011).

Brady, Ciaran (ed.), *Interpreting Irish history: the debate on historical revisionism, 1938–1994* (Dublin: Irish Academic Press, 1994).

Brady, John SJ, 'Beyond the Third Programme', *Christus Rex*, vol. xxiv, no. 3, July 1970, pp. 163–72.

Breathnach, Aoife, *Becoming conspicuous. Irish travellers, society and the state 1922–70* (Dublin: UCD Press, 2006).

Breen, Richard, Damien Hannan, David Rottman, and Christopher T Whelan, eds., *Understanding contemporary Ireland: state, class, and development in the Republic of Ireland* (Dublin: Gill & Macmillan, 1990).

Bristow, J. A. and A. A. Tait (eds), *Economic policy in Ireland* (Dublin: Institute of Public Administration, 1968).

Brittain, Samuel, *Inquest on planning in Britain* (London: PEP pamphlets, no. 499, Jan., 1967).

Brody, Hugh, *Inishkillane: change and decline in the west of Ireland* (London: Jill Norman & Hobhouse, 1982).

Brown, Callum, *Religion and the demographic revolution. Women and secularisation in Canada, Ireland, UK and USA since the 1960s* (Woodbridge: Boydell Press, 2012).

Brown, Terence, *Ireland. A social and cultural history 1922–1979* (London: Fontana 1981).

Ireland. A social and cultural history 1922–2002 (London: Harper Perennial, 2004).

Browne, Ivor, *Music and madness* (Cork: Atrium, 2008).

Browne, Vincent, 'The arms crisis', *Magill*, May 1980.

Bryson, Anna, *No coward soul. A biography of Thekla Beere* (Dublin: Institute of Public Administration, 2009).

Buckley, Sarah-Anne, *The cruelty man. Child welfare, the NSPCC and the state in Ireland. 1889–1956* (Manchester: Manchester University Press, 2014).

Bugler, Jeremy, 'Ireland's economy under fire', *New Society*, 2 September, 1965.

Byrne, Elaine A., *Political corruption in Ireland 1922–2010. A crooked harp?* (Manchester: Manchester University Press, 2012).

Earner-Byrne, Lindsey, 'The boat to England: an analysis of the official reactions to the emigration of single expectant Irishwomen to Britain, 1922–72', *IESH*, no. xxx, 2003, pp. 52–70.

Mother and child. Maternity and child welfare in Dublin, 1922–60 (Manchester: Manchester University Press, 2007).

' "Aphrodite rising from the waves", Women's voluntary activism and the women's movement in twentieth-century Ireland', in Ester Breitenbach and Pat Thane (eds), *Women and citizenship in Britain and Ireland in the Twentieth Century. What difference did the vote make?* (London: Continuum 2010), pp. 95–112.

Cairncross, Alec, *The British economy since 1945. Economic policy and performance, 1945–1990* (Oxford: Oxford University Press, 1992).

Callanan, Brian, *Ireland's Shannon Story. Leaders, visions and networks. A case study of local and regional development* (Dublin: Irish Academic Press, 2000).

Campbell, Fergus, *The Irish establishment, 1879–1914* (Oxford: Oxford University Press, 2009).

Campbell, Sarah, *Gerry Fitt and the SDLP. 'In a minority of one'* (Manchester: Manchester University Press, 2015).

Carlson, Julia (ed.), *Banned in Ireland. Censorship and the Irish writer* (London: Routledge, 1990).

Carty, Francis Xavier, *Hold Firm. John Charles McQuaid and the Second Vatican Council* (Dublin: Columba Press, 2007).

Kaim-Caudle, P., *Social security in Ireland and Western Europe* (Dublin: ESRI, paper 20, 1964).

Chambers, Anne, *T.K. Whitaker. Portrait of a patriot* (London: Doubleday, 2014).

Cholvy, G., Y. M. Hilaire, D. Delmaire, *Le fait religieux contemporain en France. Les trente dernières années (1974–2004)* (Paris: Cerf, 2004).

Chubb, Basil, 'Going about persecuting civil servants', *Political Studies*, vol. 11, 1963, pp. 272–86.

Chubb, Basil and Patrick Lynch (eds), *Economic Development and Planning*, vol. 1 (Dublin: Institute of Public Administration, 1969), p. 266.

Clarke, Peter, 'The introduction of exports sales relief – a fifty year review', *Accountancy Ireland*, vol. 38, no. 1, February 2006, pp. 85–6

Clear, Caitriona, *Women of the house: women's household work in Ireland, 1926–1961: discourses, experiences, memories* (Dublin: Irish Academic Press, 2000).

Connery, Donald, *The Irish* (London: Eyre & Spottiswoode, 1969).

Cogan, D. J., *The Irish services sector. A study of productive efficiency* (Dublin: Government Stationery Office, 1978).

Coleman, Marie, *The Irish Sweep. A history of the Irish Hospitals Sweepstake, 1930–87* (Dublin: UCD Press, 2009).

Collins, Stephen, *The Cosgrave Legacy* (Dublin: Blackwater, 1996).

The power game: Ireland under Fianna Fáil (Dublin: O'Brien Press, 2001 edition).

Conniffe, Denis and Kieran A. Kennedy (eds), *Employment and unemployment policy for Ireland* (Dublin: ESRI, 1984).

Connolly, Linda, *The Irish women's movement. From revolution to devolution* (Basingstoke: Palgrave Macmillan, 2002).

Coogan, Tim Pat, *Ireland since the Rising* (London: Pall Mall, 1966).

A memoir (London: Weidenfeld & Nicholson, 2008).

Coombe Hospital Clinical Reports, 1960–73.

Cook, Hera, *The long sexual revolution. Englishwomen, sex and contraception, 1800–1975* (Oxford: Oxford University Press, 2004).

Cooney, John, *John Charles Mc Quaid. Ruler of Catholic Ireland* (Dublin: O'Brien Press, 1999).

The Council for Social Welfare. A Committee of the Catholic Bishops Conference. *A Statement of social policy* (Dublin, 1972).

Comyn, Andrew, 'Censorship in Ireland', *Studies*, vol. 58, spring 1969, pp. 42–50.

Cox, Catherine and Hilary Marland, 'Itineraries and experiences of insanity: Irish migration and the management of mental illness in nineteenth-century Lancashire', in Catherine Cox and Hilary Marland (eds), *Migration, health and ethnicity in the modern world* (Basingstoke: Palgrave Macmillan, 2013), pp.36–60.

Cox, Tom, *The making of managers. A history of the Irish Management Institute 1952–2002* (Cork: Oak Tree, 2002).

Crafts, Nicholas and Gianni Toniolo (eds), *Economic growth in Europe since 1945* (Cambridge: Cambridge University Press, 1996).

Craig, Anthony, *Crisis of confidence. Anglo-Irish relations in the Early Troubles* (Dublin: Irish Academic Press, 2010).

Crawford, Heather, *Outside the glow. Protestants and Irishness in independent Ireland* (Dublin: UCD Press, 2010).

Cresswell, Robert, *Une communauté rurale d'Irlande* (Paris: Institut d'ethnologie, 1969).

Crowe, Catriona, Ronan Fanning, Michael Kennedy, Dermot Keogh, Eunan O'Halpin and Kate O' Malley (eds), *Documents in Irish Foreign Policy, VII* (Dublin: Royal Irish Academy, 2014).

Curran, Frank, *Derry. Countdown to disaster* (Dublin: Gill & Macmillan, 1980).

Curran, Joseph M., 'Ireland since 1916', *Éire-Ireland*, vol. 1, no. 3, 1966, pp. 14–28.

Curtin, D., R. C. Geary, T. A. Grimes, B. Mention, *Population growth and other statistics of middle-sized Irish towns* (Dublin: ESRI paper 85, April 1976).

Daly, Mary E., 'Women work and trade unionism', in Margaret MacCurtain and Donncha Ó Corráin (eds), *Women in Irish society. The historical dimension* (Dublin: Arlen House, 1978), pp. 71–80.

' "An Irish-Ireland for industry"? The control of manufactures acts, 1932 and 1934', *IHS*, vol. 24, no. 94, Nov. 1984, pp. 246–72.

Industrial development and Irish national identity, 1922–39 (Syracuse: Syracuse UP, 1992).

The Buffer State. The historical roots of the Department of the Environment (Dublin: IPA, 1997).

' "An atmosphere of sturdy independence": the state and the Dublin hospitals in the 1930s', in Greta Jones and Elizabeth Malcolm (eds), *Medicine, disease and the state in Ireland, 1650–1940* (Cork: Cork UP, 1999), pp. 234–52.

'Nationalism, sentiment and economics: relations between Ireland and Irish-America in the postwar years', *Éire/Ireland*, vol. xxxvii, no. 1&2, 2002, pp. 263–80.

The First Department. A history of the Department of Agriculture (Dublin: Institute of Public Administration, 2002).

The slow failure. Population decline and independent Ireland, 1920–1973 (Madison, WI: University of Wisconsin Press, 2006).

and Margaret O'Callaghan (eds), *1916 in 1966. Commemorating the Easter Rising* (Dublin: Royal Irish Academy, 2007).

' "The primary and natural educator"? The role of parents in the education of their children in independent Ireland, *Éire-Ireland*, vol. 44, 2009, pp. 194–217.

'Death and disease in independent Ireland c.1920–c.1970: a research agenda', in Catherine Cox and Maria Luddy (eds), *Cultures of care in Irish medical history, 1750–1970* (Basingstoke: Palgrave Macmillan, 2010), pp. 229–50.

Daunton, Martin, *Just taxes. The politics of taxation in Britain, 1914–1979* (Cambridge: Cambridge University Press, 2002).

Wilson-Davis, Keith, 'Some results of an Irish family planning survey', *Journal of Biosocial Science*, vol. 7, 1975, pp. 435–44.

Dean, Geoffrey, *The Turnstone. A doctor's story* (Liverpool: Liverpool University Press, 2002).

Deeny, James, 'Cancer mortality in the Republic of Ireland; A changing pattern', *Irish Journal of Medical Science, sixth series*, vol. 127, no. 389, May 1958, pp. 199–205.

The end of an epidemic. Essays in Irish public health, 1935–65 (Dublin: A&A Farmar, 1995).

Delaney, Enda, *Demography, state and society: Irish migration to Britain, 1921–1971* (Liverpool: Liverpool University Press, 2002).

The Irish in post-war Britain (Oxford: Oxford University Press, 2007).

'Modernity, the past and politics in post-war Ireland', in Thomas E. Hachey (ed.), *Turning-points in twentieth-century Irish history* (Dublin: Irish Academic Press, 2012), pp. 103–18.

Desmond, Barry, *Finally and in conclusion* (Dublin: New Island, 2000).

Deutsch, Karl, *Nationalism and social communication. An inquiry into the foundation of nationality* (Cambridge MA: MIT Press, 1966).

Dooley, Terence, *The land for the people. The land question in independent Ireland* (Dublin: UCD Press, 2004).

Donaldson, Loraine, *Development planning in Ireland* (London: Praegar, 1966).

Dunlop, Frank, *Yes, Taoiseach. Irish politics from behind closed doors* (Dublin: Penguin Ireland, 2004).

Dwyer, T. Ryle, *Nice Fellow. A biography of Jack Lynch* (Cork: Mercier, 2001).

Eichengreen, Barry, *The European economy since 1945: coordinated capitalism and beyond* (Princeton: Princeton University Press, 2007).

Encyclical letter, *Mater et Magistra: on recent developments of the social question in the light of Christian teaching* (The Vatican: 1961).

Evans, Bryce and Stephen Kelly (eds), *Frank Aiken. Nationalist and internationalist* (Dublin: Irish Academic Press, 2014).

Evans, Peter, Dietrich Rueschemeyer, and Theda Skocpol (eds), *Bringing the state back in* (Princeton: Princeton University Press, 1988).

Fanning, Ronan, *The Irish Department of Finance, 1922–58* (Dublin: Institute of Public Administration, 1978).

'Irish neutrality: an historical review', *ISIA*, vol. I, no. 3, 1982, pp. 23–38.

'Playing it cool: the response of the British and Irish government to the crisis in Northern Ireland, 1968–9', *ISIA*, vol. 12, 2001, pp. 57–85.

Farmar, Tony, *Holles Street 1894–1994, The National Maternity Hospital – a centenary history* (Dublin: A&A Farmar, 1994).

Farrell, Brian, 'Dáil deputies: the 1969 generation', *ESR*, vol. 2, 1970/1971, pp. 309–27.

Seán Lemass (Dublin: Gill & Macmillan, 1983).

Farrell, Elaine (ed.), *'She said she was in the family way'. Pregnancy and infancy in modern Ireland'* (London: Institute of Historical Research, 2012).

Fennell, Desmond (ed.), *The Changing Face of Catholic Ireland* (London: G. Chapman, 1968).

Fennell, Nuala, *Political woman. A memoir* (Dublin: Currach, 2009).

Farren, Grainne, *From condemnation to celebration. The story of Cherish, 1972–1997* (Dublin: Cherish, 1997).

Faulkner, Padraig, *As I saw it. Reviewing over 30 years of Fianna Fáil and Irish politics* (Dublin:Wolfhound, 2005).

Feeney, Tom, *Seán MacEntee: a political life* (Dublin: Irish Academic Press, 2009).

'Church, state and family: the advent of child guidance clinics in independent Ireland, *Social History of Medicine*, vol. 25, no. 4, 2012, pp.848–62.

Ferriter, Diarmaid, *A nation of extremes. The Pioneers in twentieth-century Ireland* (Dublin: Irish Academic Press, 1998).

The transformation of Ireland 1900–2000 (London: Profile, 2004).

Judging Dev: a reassessment of the life and legacy of Eamon de Valera (Dublin: Royal Irish Academy, 2007).

Ambiguous Republic. Ireland in the 1970s (London: Profile, 2011).

Fine Gael *Towards a just society* (Dublin: Fine Gael Party, 1965).

Finn, Tomás, *Tuairim, intellectual debate and policy formation: rethinking Ireland, 1954–1975* (Manchester: Manchester University Press, 2012).

Fisher, Kate, *Birth control, sex & marriage in Britain, 1918–1960* (Oxford: OUP, 2006).

FitzGerald, Garret, *Planning in Ireland* (Dublin and London: Institute of Public Administration, Political and Economic Planning, 1968).

Towards a New Ireland (Dublin: Torc, 1973).

All in a Life. An autobiography (Dublin: Gill & Macmillan, 1992).

Fitzgerald, Maurice, *Protectionism to liberalisation. Ireland and the EEC, 1957 to 1966* (Aldershot: Ashgate, 2000).

Fitzsimons, Jack, *Bungalow Bashing* (Kells: Kells Publishing Co., 1990).

Flanagan, Robert J., David W. Soskice and Lloyd Ulman, *Unionism, economic stabilization and incomes policies. European experience* (Washington: Brookings Institution, 1983).

Flynn, Michael, *Medical doctor of many parts: memoir of a public health practitioner and health manager* (Ireland:Kelmed, 2002).

Fogarty, Michael, Joseph Lee and Liam Ryan, *Irish values and attitudes: the Irish report of the European Value Systems Study* (Dublin: Dominican publications, 1984).

Fogel, Robert W, Enid Fogel, Mark Guglielmo and Nathaniel Grotte, *Political arithmetic. Simon Kuznets and the empirical tradition in economics* (Chicago: Chicago University Press 2013).

Foley, Frank, 'North-South relations and the outbreak of the Troubles in Northern Ireland, 1968–9: the response of the 'Irish Press', *ISIA*, vol. 14, 2003, pp. 9–31.

Foster, Roy, *Luck and the Irish. A brief history of change 1970–2000* (London: Allen Lane, 2007).

Fuchs, Joseph, 'The pill', *Studies*, vol. liii, Winter 1964, pp. 352–71.

Fuller, Louise, *Irish Catholicism since 1950. The undoing of a culture* (Dublin: Gill & Macmillan, 2002).

Gallagher, Michael, 'Proportionality in a proportional representation system: the Irish experience', *Political Studies*, December 1975, pp. 501–13.

Electoral support for Irish political parties, 1927–1973 (London: Sage, Contemporary political sociology series, 1976).

The Irish Labour party in transition, 1957–82 (Manchester: Manchester UP, 1982).

Garvin, Tom, *Preventing the future. Why was Ireland so poor for so long* (Dublin: Gill & Macmillan, 2004).

Judging Lemass: the measure of the man (Dublin: Royal Irish Academy, 2009).

Gaughan, Anthony, *At the coalface. Recollections of a city and country priest, 1950–2000* (Dublin: Columba, 2000).

Geary, Michael, *An inconvenient wait. Ireland's quest for membership of the EEC, 1957–73* (Dublin: IPA, 2009).

Ginsborg, Paul, *A history of contemporary Italy, 1943–1980* (London: Penguin, 1990).

'The politics of the family in twentieth century Europe', *Contemporary European history*, vol. 9, no. 3, 2000, pp. 411–44.

Girvin, Brian, 'Trade unions and economic development', in Donal Nevin (ed.), *Trade Union Century* (Cork: Mercier, 1994).

Between Two Worlds. Politics and economy in independent Ireland (Dublin: Gill & Macmillan, 1989).

and Gary Murphy (eds), *The Lemass era. Politics and society in the era of Seán Lemass* (Dublin: UCD Press, 2005).

' "Lemass's brainchild": the 1966 informal committee on the constitution and change in Ireland, 1966–73', *IHS*, vol. xxxviii, no. 151, May 2013, pp. 406–21.

Gould, Frank, 'The growth of public expenditure in Ireland, 1947–77', *Administration*, vol. 29, no. 2, 1981, pp. 119, 115–35.

Goldthorpe, John H. and Christopher T. Whelan (eds), *The development of industrial society in Ireland* (Oxford: Oxford University Press, 1992).

Griffiths, Richard and Stuart Ward, *Courting the Common Market. The first attempt to enlarge the European Community, 1961–63* (London: Lothian Foundation, 1996).

Hanley, Brian and Scott Millar, *The lost revolution: the story of the official IRA and the Workers' Party* (Dublin: Penguin Ireland, 2009).

' "But then they started all this killing" attitudes to the I.R.A. in the Irish Republic since 1969', *IHS*, vol. xxxviii, no. 15 (May 2013), pp. 439–56.

Hanna, Erika, *Modern Dublin. Urban change and the Irish past, 1957–1973* (Oxford: Oxford University Press, 2013).

Hannan, Damien, *Rural Exodus. A study of the forces influencing large-scale migration of Irish rural youth* (London: Geoffrey Chapman, 1970).

'Kinship, neighbourhood and social change in Irish rural communities', *ESR*, vol. 3, 1972, pp. 163–88.

and Louise Katsaiouni, *Traditional Families? From culturally prescribed to negotiated roles in farm families* (Dublin: ESRI, 1977).

Displacement and development: class, kinship and social change in Irish rural communities (Dublin: ESRI, 1979).

Hardiman, Niamh, *Pay, politics, and economic performance in Ireland, 1970–1987* (Oxford: Oxford University Press, 1988).

Harrison, Brian, *Seeking a role. The United Kingdom 1951–1970* (Oxford: Oxford University Press, 2009).

Harte, Paddy, *Young Tigers and Mongrel Foxes: [a life in politics]* (Dublin: O'Brien, 2005).

Hayes, Nick, 'Did we really want a National Health Service? Hospitals, patients and public opinions before 1948', *English Historical Review*, vol. cxxvii, 2012, pp. 625–61.

Hayward, Katy and Muiris MacCarthaigh, (eds), Recycling the state. The politics of adaptation in Ireland,(Dublin: Irish Academic Press, 2007).

Healy, John, *The death of an Irish town* (Cork: Mercier, 1968).

Heath, Anthony, Richard Breen and Christopher Whelan (eds), *Ireland: north and south. Perspectives from the social sciences* (Oxford: Oxford University Press, 1999).

Heclo, Hugh, *Modern social politics: from relief to income maintenance* (Newhaven and London, Yale UP, 1974).

Helleiner, Jane, *Irish Travellers. Racism and the politics of culture* (Toronto: University of Toronto Press, 2000).

Hennessy, Peter, *Having it so good. Britain in the fifties* (London: Allen Lane, 2006).

Heslinga, Michael, *The Irish border as a cultural divide. A contribution to the study of regionalism in the British Isles* (Assen: Van Gorcum, 1971).

Hoppen, K. T., *Elections, politics and society in Ireland, 1832–1885* (Oxford: Clarendon, 1984).

Horgan, John, *Seán Lemass: the enigmatic patriot* (Dublin: Gill & Macmillan, 1997).
'Irish foreign policy, Northern Ireland, neutrality and the commonwealth: the historical roots of a current controversy', *ISIA*, vol. 10, 1999, pp. 135–47.
Broadcasting and public life RTE news and current affairs, 1926–1997 (Dublin: Four Courts, 2004).

Hutchinson, Bertram, *Social status and inter-generational social mobility in Ireland* (Dublin: ESRI, 1969).
Social status in Dublin: marriage mobility and first employment (Dublin: ESRI paper 67, 1973).

Hyland, Áine, 'The multi-denominational experience in the national school system in Ireland', *Irish Educational Studies*, vol. 8, 1989, pp. 96–103.
'The investment in education report 1965 – recollections and reminiscences', *Irish Educational Studies*, vol. 33, no. 2, 2014, pp.123–40.

Jackson, Alvin (ed.), *The Oxford handbook of modern Irish history* (Oxford: Oxford University Press, 2014).

Jacobsen, David Kurt, *Chasing progress in the Irish Republic. Ideology, democracy and dependent development* (Cambridge: Cambridge University Press, 1994).

Kaeble, Hartmut, *A social history of Europe, 1945–2000. Recovery and transformation after two world wars* (New York and Oxford: Oxford University Press, 2013).

Kealy, Alacoque, *Irish Radio Data: 1926–80* (Dublin: RTÉ, 1981).

Keatinge, Patrick, *The formulation of Irish foreign policy* (Dublin: Institute of Public Administration, 1973).

Kelly, Matthew, 'Home rule and its enemies', in Alvin Jackson (ed.), *The Oxford handbook of modern Irish History* (Oxford: Oxford University Press, 2014), pp. 582–602.

Kelly, Michael G., 'The national drug advisory and treatment centre', in Eoin O'Brien (ed.), *The Charitable Infirmary: Jervis St 1718–1987* (Dublin: Anniversary Press, 1987), pp. 193–8.

Kelly, Stephen, 'Fresh evidence from the archives: the genesis of Charles J. Haughey's attitude to Northern Ireland', *ISIA*, vol. 23, 2012, pp.155–70.

Kennedy, Finola, *Cottage to crèche. Family change in Ireland* (Dublin: IPA, 2001).

Frank Duff. A life story (London: Continuum, 2011).

Kennedy, Kieran and Brendan Dowling, *Economic growth in Ireland: the experience since 1947* (Dublin: Gill & Macmillan/ESRI, 1975).

Thomas Giblin and Deirdre McHugh, *The economic development of Ireland in the twentieth century* (London: Routledge, 1988).

Kennedy, Michael and Joseph Skelly (eds), *Irish foreign policy, 1919–66. From independence to internationalism* (Dublin: Four Courts, 1999).

Division and consensus. The politics of cross-border relations in Ireland, 1926–1968 (Dublin: Institute of Public Administration, 2000).

and Deirdre McMahon (eds), *Obligations and responsibilities: Ireland and the United Nations, 1955–2005* (Dublin: Institute of Public Administration, 2005).

and Art Magennis, *Ireland, the United Nations and the Congo* (Dublin: Four Courts, 2014).

Kennedy, Robert, *The Irish: Emigration, marriage and fertility* (Berkeley: University of California Press, 1973).

Kennedy, Stanislaus, *The development of Kilkenny Social Services, 1963–1980. Who Should Care?* (Dublin: Turoe, 1981).

Kenny, Ivor, *In good company. Conversations with Irish leaders* (Dublin: Gill & Macmillan, 1987).

Kenny, Ivor, *Out on their own. Conversations with Irish entrepreneurs*, (Dublin: Gill & Macmillan, 1991),

Keogh, Dermot, *Twentieth-century Ireland. Nation and state* (Dublin: Gill & Macmillan, 1984).

Jack Lynch. A biography (Dublin: Gill & Macmillan, 2008).

Killeen, Dr Colum, with Dr Ita Killeen, *Half-century memoirs of two Dublin inner city general practitioners* (Dublin: Linden, 2007).

'Kilkenny Conference on Poverty, Papers and Proceedings', *Social Studies*, vol. 1, no. 2, 1972.

Kissane, Bill, *Explaining Irish democracy* (Dublin: UCD Press, 2002), pp. 27–44.

Knudsen, Anna-Christina Lauring, 'Romanticising Europe? Rural images in European Union policies', *Kontur*, vol. 12, 2005, pp. 49–58.

Farmers on welfare. The making of Europe's Common Agricultural Policy (Ithaca: Cornell University Press, 2009).

Larkin, Emmet, 'The devotional revolution in Ireland, 1850–75', *American Historical Review*, vol. 75, no. 3, 1972, pp. 81–98.

Lee, J., 'Workers and society in modern Ireland', in Donal Nevin (ed.), *Trade unions and change in Irish society* (Cork: Mercier Press, 1980), pp. 11–25.

Ireland 1912–1985. Politics and society (Cambridge: Cambridge University Press, 1989).

Lemass, Seán, 'The Organisation behind the economic programme', *Administration*, vol. 9, no. 1, 1961, pp. 3–10.

Lennon, James (director), Liam Ryan, Micheál MacGréil, Nuala Drake and Carmely Perera, 'Survey of Catholic clergy and religious personnel', *Social Studies*, vol. 1, 1971, pp. 137–230.

Litton, Frank (ed.), *Unequal achievement: the Irish experience, 1957–82* (Dublin: Institute of Public Administration, 1982).

Denis, I. F. Lucey and Donald R. Kaldor, *Rural industrialization. The impact of industrialization on two rural communities in western Ireland* (London: Chapman, 1969).

Lynch, Patrick, 'The Economics of Independence: Some unsettled questions of Irish economics', *Administration*, vol. 7, no. 2, 1959, pp. 91–108.

Lynn, Brendan, *Holding the ground: the Nationalist party in Northern Ireland, 1945–72* (Aldershot: Ashgate, 1997).

Lyons, J. B., *The quality of Mercer's: the history of Mercer's hospital, 1734–1991* (Dun Laoghaire: Glendale, 1991).

MacGréil, Micheál, *Prejudice and tolerance in Ireland* (Dublin: College of Industrial Relations, 1977).

Maguire, Maria, 'Ireland', in Peter Flora (ed.), *Growth to limits. The Western European welfare states since World War II*, vol. 2 (Florence: EUI, 1986), pp. 244–384.

Maguire, Moira and Seamus Ó Cinnéide, ' "A good beating never hurts anyone". The punishment and abuse of children in twentieth century Ireland', *Journal of Social History*, vol. 38, no. 3, 2005, pp. 635–52.

Maguire, Martin, *Servants to the public. A history of the local government and public services union* (Dublin: Institute of Public Administration, 1998).

Massé, Pierre, 'French Planning', in Patrick Lynch and Basil Chubb (eds), *Economic development and planning* (Dublin: Institute of Public Administration, 1969), pp. 219–232.

Mathúna, S Ó, 'The Christian Brothers and the civil service', *Administration*, vol. 3, 1955, pp. 69–74.

McCourt, Kevin C., Broadcasting – A community service, *Administration*, vol. 15, no. 3, Autumn 1967, pp. 173–81.

Maher, D. J., *The tortuous path: the course of Ireland's entry into the EEC, 1948–1973* (Dublin: Institute of Public Administration, 1986).

Mair, Peter, *The changing Irish party system: organisation, ideology and electoral competition* (London: Pinter 1987).

Manning, Maurice, *James Dillon. A biography* (Dublin: Wolfhound, 1999).

Mansergh, Martin (ed.), *The spirit of the nation: speeches and statements of Charles J. Haughey (1957–86)* (Cork: Mercier, 1986).

Marwick, Arthur, *The Sixties* (Oxford: Oxford University Press, 1998).

McAleese, Dermot, *Effective tariffs and the structure of industrial protection in Ireland* (Dublin: ESRI paper 62, 1971).

A profile of grant-aided industry in Ireland (Dublin: IDA, 1977).

McCague, Eugene, *My dear Mr McCourt* (Dublin: Gill & Macmillan, 2009).

McCann, David, 'Whitaker and Northern Ireland policy from 1959 to 1972', *ISIA*, vol. 23, 2012, pp. 171–89.

McCarthy, Charles, *The decade of upheaval. Irish trade unions in the nineteen sixties* (Dublin: Institute of Public Administration, 1973).

McCarthy, John F. (ed.), *Planning Ireland's future. The legacy of T.K. Whitaker* (Dublin: Glendale, 1990).

McCartney, Donal, *UCD. A national idea. The history of University College Dublin* (Dublin: UCD Press, 1999).

McCluskey, Conn, *Up off their knees: a commentary on the civil rights movement in Northern Ireland* (Dungannon: Conn McCluskey and Associates, 1989).

McDaid, Shaun, 'The Irish government and the Sunningdale council of Ireland: a vehicle for unity', *IHS*, vol. xxviii, no. 150, November 2012, pp. 283–303.

McDonald, Frank, *The destruction of Dublin* (Dublin: Gill & Macmillan, 1985).

McKenna, Yvonne, *Made holy: Irish women religious at home and abroad* (Dublin: Irish Academic Press, 2006).

McLeod, Hugh, *The religious crisis of the 1960s* (Oxford: Oxford University Press, 2010).

McLoone, Martin and John MacMahon (eds), *Television and Irish society: 21 years of Irish television* (Dublin: RTÉ, 1984).

Meehan, Ciara, *A Just Society for Ireland? 1964–1987* (Basingstoke: Palgrave Macmillan, 2013).

Meenan, F. O. C., *St Vincent's hospital, 1934–1994: an historical and social portrait* (Dublin: Gill & Macmillan, 1995).

Mendras, Henri, *The vanishing peasant. Innovation and change in French agriculture* (Cambridge MA, London: MIT Press, 1970).

Messenger, John, *Inis Beag: Isle of Ireland* (London and New York: Holt, Rinehart & Winston, 1969).

Miller, David, *Church, state and nation in Ireland, 1898–1921* (Dublin: London: Macmillan, 1973).

Mills, Michael, *Hurler on the ditch. Memoir of a journalist who became Ireland's first Ombudsman* (Dublin: Currach, 2005).

Milotte, Mike, *Banished babies. The secret history of Ireland's baby export business* (Dublin: New Island, 1997)

Mitchell, David, *A 'peculiar' place. The Adelaide Hospital, Dublin. Its times, places and personalities, 1839–1989* (Dublin: Blackwater, 1989).

Mjoset, Lars, *The Irish economy in a comparative institutional perspective* (Dublin: NESC, 1992).

Mohan, John, *Planning markets and hospitals* (London and New York: Routledge, 2002).

Mulholland, Marc, *Northern Ireland at the Crossroads: Ulster unionism in the O'Neill years* (London: Macmillan, 2000).

Terence O'Neill (Dublin: UCD Press, 2013).

Murphy, Colin and Lynne Adair (eds), *Untold stories. Protestants in the Republic of Ireland, 1922–2002* (Dublin: Liffey Press, 2002).

Murphy, Dervla, *A place apart* (London: Murray, 1976).

Murphy, Gary and Niamh Purséil, ' "Is it a new allowance?" Irish entry to the EEC and popular opinion', *IPS*, vol. 23, no. 4, December 2008, pp. 533–53.

Murray, Peter, *Facilitating the future. US Aid. European integration and Irish industrial viability, 1948–73* (Dublin: UCD Press, 2009).

National Maternity Hospital, Clinical Reports, 1960–73.

Newman, Jeremiah, 'Priests of Ireland: a socio-religious survey', *IER*, vol. cxvii, xcviii, 1962, pp. 1–28, 65–91.

(ed.), *Limerick rural survey, 1958–64* (Tipperary: Muintir na Tíre, 1964).

'Progress and planning', *Christus Rex*, vol. xxiv, no. 3, July 1970, pp. 173–86.

Nevin, Donal, *Trade unions and change in Irish society* (Cork: Mercier 1980).

Trade union century (Cork: Mercier, 1994).

Nolan, Brian, Philip J. O'Connell and Christopher T. Whelan (eds), *Bust to Boom? The Irish experience of growth and inequality* (Dublin: ESRI, 2000).

O'Brien, Conor Cruise, *States of Ireland* (London: Panther, 1974 edition).

Memoir. My life and themes (Dublin: Poolbeg, 1998).

O'Brien, Harvey, *The real Ireland. The evolution of Ireland in documentary film* (Manchester: Manchester University Press, 2004).

O'Brien, James F., *A study of national wage agreements in Ireland* (Dublin: ESRI, 1981), ESRI paper no. 104.

O'Brien, Justin, *The Arms Trial* (Dublin: Gill & Macmillan, 2000).

Ó Buachalla, Séamus, *Educational policy in twentieth century Ireland* (Dublin: Wolfhound, 1988).

Ó Cinnéide, Seamus, *A law for the poor. A study of home assistance in Ireland* (Dublin: Institute of Public Administration, 1970).

O'Connor, Seán, *A troubled sky: reflections on the Irish educational scene* (Dublin: St Patrick's College, 1986).

Ó Corráin, Daithí, *Rendering to God and to Caesar: the Irish churches and the two states in Ireland, 1949–73* (Manchester: Manchester University Press, 2008).

O'Donnell, Catherine, *Fianna Fáil. Irish Republicanism and the Northern Ireland Troubles 1968–2005* (Dublin: Irish Academic Press, 2007).

O'Driscoll, Mervyn, Dermot Keogh and Jérôme aan de Wiel (eds), *Ireland through European eyes. Western Europe, the EEC and Ireland, 1945–1973* (Cork: Cork UP, 2013).

O'Farrell, P. N., *Regional industrial development trends in Ireland, 1960–1973* (Dublin: Institute of Public Administration, 1975).

Ó Gráda, Cormac and Kevin O'Rourke, 'Irish economic growth 1945–88', in Nicholas Crafts and Gianni Toniolo (eds), *Economic growth in Europe since 1945* (Cambridge: Cambridge University Press, 1996), pp. 388–427.

A rocky road: the Irish economy since the 1920s (Manchester: Manchester University Press, 1997).

O'Hagan, John, 'An analysis of the growth of the public sector in Ireland, 1953–77', *JSSISI*, vol. xxiv, no. 2, 1979–80, pp. 69–98.

'Demonstration, income effects and determinants of public sector expenditure shares in the Republic of Ireland', *Public Finance*, vol. 3, 1980, pp. 425–35.

O'Hara, Patricia, *Partners in production? Women, farm and family in Ireland* (New York/Oxford: Berghahn, 1998).

O'Leary, Cornelius, *Irish elections, 1918–1977: parties, voters and proportional representation* (Dublin: Gill & Macmillan, 1979).

Olsen, Mancur, *The rise and decline of nations* (Newhaven: Yale UP, 1982).

O'Malley, Desmond, *Conduct unbecoming. A memoir* (Dublin: Gill & Macmillan, 2014).

O'Meara, John, *Reform in education* (Dublin: Mount Salus, 1958).

O'Neill, Con, Britain's entry into the European community. Report on the negotiations of 1970–72 (London: Frank Cass, 2000).

O'Neill, Terence, *The autobiography of Terence O'Neill* (London: Hart-Davis, 1972).

Patterson, Henry, *Ireland since 1939* (Oxford: Blackwell, 2002).

Prince, Simon, *Northern Ireland '68: civil rights, global revolt and the origins of the troubles* (Dublin: Irish Academic Press, 2007).

Press, Jon, *The footwear industry and Ireland, 1922–1973* (Dublin: Irish Academic Press, 1989).

Radio Éireann: *Annual Reports*, Dublin.

Puirséil, Niamh, *The Irish Labour Party, 1922–73* (Dublin: UCD Press, 2007).

Quinn, Ruairi, *Straight left. A journey in politics* (Dublin: Hodder Headline Ireland, 2005).

Raftery, Mary and Eoin O'Sullivan, *Suffer the little children. The inside story of Ireland's industrial schools* (Dublin: New Island, 1999).

Ramblado-MInero, M. C. and A. Perez-Vides (eds), *Single motherhood in 20th-centiury Ireland; cultural historical and social essays* (Lewistown: Edwin Mellen, 2006).

First Report of the Medico-Social Research Council 1969.

Reeves, Chris, 'The penultimate Irish problem: Britain, Ireland and the exhumation of Roger Casement', *ISIA*, vol. 12, 2001, pp. 151–78.

Reynolds, Albert, *My autobiography* (London: Transworld Ireland, 2009).

Rockett, Kevin, *Irish film censorship. A cultural journey from silent cinema to internet pornography* (Dublin: Four Courts, 2004).

Roche, William K., 'State strategies and the politics of industrial relations inIreland since 1945', in T. Murphy (ed.), *Industrial relations in Ireland. Contemporary trends and developments* (Dublin: UCD, 1987), pp. 115–32.

Rohan, Dorine, *Marriage Irish style* (Cork: Mercier, 1969).

Ross, M., *Further data on county incomes in the sixties* (Dublin: ESRI paper 64, May 1972).

Rotunda Hospital Clinical Reports, 1960–74.

Rouse, Paul, *Ireland's own soil. Government and agriculture in Ireland, 1945–1965* (Dublin: Irish Farmers' Journal, 2000).

and Mark Duncan, *Handling change. A history of the Irish Bank Officials Association* (Cork: The Collins Press, 2012).

Ryan, Liam, *Social dynamite. A study of early school-leavers* (UCC, Sociology Dept. c 1970).

Ryan, Michael (ed.), *The church and the nation. The vision of Peter Birch. Bishop of Ossory, 1964–1981* (Dublin: Columba, 1993).

Ryan, Paul, *Asking Angela Macnamara, an intimate history of Irish lives* (Dublin: Irish Academic Press, 2012).

Ryan, W. J. L., 'The need for structural change in Irish industry', *Irish Banking Review*, March 1961, pp. 9–15.

'The methodology of the Second Programme of Economic Expansion', *JSSISI*, vol. xxi, no. ii, 1963–1964, pp. 120–43.

Sacks, Paul, *The Donegal Mafia. An Irish political machine* (New Haven and London: Yale UP, 1976), p. 62.

Salmon, Trevor, *Unneutral Ireland: an ambivalent and unique security policy* (Oxford: Oxford University Press, 1989).

Savage, Robert J., *Irish television. The political and social origins* (Cork: Cork University Press, 1996).

A loss of innocence? Television and Irish society 1960–72 (Manchester: Manchester University Press, 2010).

Savage, Roland Burke, 'The Church in Dublin 1940–1965: a study of the achievements and of the personality of Most Reverend John Charles Mc Quaid on the occasion of his silver jubilee', *Studies*, vol. 54, winter, 1965, pp. 297–346.

Salt, John, 'International labour migration: the geographical pattern of demand', in John Salt and Hugh Clout (eds), *Migration in postwar Europe. Geographical essays* (London: Oxford University Press, 1976), pp.80–91.

Sandbrook, Dominic, *White Heat, A history of Britain in the swinging sixties* (London: Little Brown, 2006).

Scheper-Hughes, Nancy, *Saints scholars and schizophrenics. Mental illness in rural Ireland* (Berkeley: University of California Press, 1981).

Schonfield, Andrew, *Modern Capitalism. The changing balance of public and private power* (Oxford: Oxford University Press, 1970 edition).

Share, Bernard, *Shannon departures, a study in regional initiatives* (Dublin: Gill & Macmillan, 1992).

Shields, Hugh, 'Printed aids to folk singing 1700–1900', in Mary E. Daly and David Dickson (eds), *The origins of popular literacy in Ireland: Language change and educational development, 1700–1920* (Dublin: TCD&UCD history departments, 1990), pp. 139–52.

Skeffington, Andrée Sheehy, *Skeff, A life of Owen Sheehy Skeffington, 1909–1970* (Dublin: Lilliput, 1991).

Sheingate, Adam, *The rise of the agricultural welfare state. Institutions and interest group power in the United States, France and Japan* (Princeton: Princeton University Press, 2001).

Shiel, Michael, *The Quiet Revolution. The electrification of rural Ireland* (Dublin: O'Brien, 1984).

Simpson, John, 'Regional analysis: the Northern Ireland experience', *ESR*, vol. 2, no. 4, 1971, pp. 5–29.

Sinnott, Richard, *Irish voters decide. Voting behaviour in elections and referendums since 1918* (Manchester: Manchester University Press, 1995).

Skelly, Joseph, 'Ireland, the Department of External Affairs and the United Nations, 1946–55: a new look', *ISIA*, vol. 7, 1996, pp. 63–80.

Irish diplomacy at the United Nations, 1945–1965: national interests and the international order (Dublin: Irish Academic Press, 1997).

Smith, J. M., *Ireland's Magdalen laundries and the nations' architecture of containment* (Manchester: Manchester University Press, 2007).

Smith, Louis and Sean Healy, *Farm organisations in Ireland. A century of progress* (Dublin: Four Courts, 1996).

Smurfit, Michael, *A life worth living* (Cork: Oak Tree, 2014).

Smyth, Geraldine, 'Ecumenism and interchurch relations', in James Donnelly et al. (eds), *Encyclopaedia of Irish history and culture*, 2 vols (Farmington Hills, MI: Macmillan Reference USA), pp. 182–4.

Solomons, Michael, *Pro Life? The Irish question* (Dublin: Lilliput, 1992).

Somerville-Woodward, Robert, *Ballymun. A history, c 1600–1997.* 2 volumes (Dublin: Ballymun Regeneration, 2002).

Spencer, A. E. C. W., *Arrangements for the integration of Irish immigrants in England and Wales*, edited by Mary E. Daly (Dublin: Irish Manuscripts Commission, 2012).

Staunton, Enda, *The Nationalists of Northern Ireland, 1918–1973* (Dublin: Columba, 2001).

'The case of Biafra: Ireland and the Nigerian civil war', *IHS*, vol. xxxi, no. 124, November 1999, pp.513–34.

Thane, Pat with Tanya Evans, *Sinners? Scroungers? Saints? Unmarried motherhood in England in the 20th century* (Oxford: Oxford University Press, 2013).

Thornley, David, *Ireland: the end of an era* (Dublin: Tuairim pamphlet no. 12, 1965).

Thornley, Yseult (ed.), *Unquiet spirit. Essays in memory of David Thornley* (Dublin: Liberties Press, 2008).

Toibín, Fergal, *The best of decades: Ireland in the 1960s* (Dublin: Gill & Macmillan, 1996).

Tomlin, Breffni, *The management of Irish Industry. A research report by the Irish Management Institute* (Dublin: IMI, 1966).

Treacy, Matt, *The IRA, 1956–69* (Manchester: Manchester University Press, 2011).

Tucker, Vincent, 'Images of development and underdevelopment in Glencolumbkille, County Donegal, 1830–1970', in John Davis (ed.), *Rural change in Ireland* (Belfast: Queen's University Institute of Irish Studies, 1999), pp. 84–115.

Tuairim Group, *Educating towards a United Europe*, Tuairim pamphlet no. 8 (Dublin: Tuairim, 1962).

Some of our children. A report on the residential care of the deprived child in Ireland (Dublin: Tuairim, 1966).

Tubridy, Ryan, *JFK in Ireland* (London: Collins, 2010).

Tussing, A. Dale, *Irish educational expenditures – past, present and future* (Dublin: ESRI 1978).

Tweedy, Hilda, *A link in the chain, The story of the Irish Housewives Association, 1941–1992* (Dublin: Attic, 1992).

Twomey, D. Vincent, *The end of Irish Catholicism?* (Dublin: Veritas, 2003).

Tyrell, Peter, *Founded on fear. Letterfrack industrial school, war and exile*, edited by Diarmuid Whelan (Dublin: Irish Academic Press, 2006).

Vaizey, John, 'A note on comparative statistics', in A. H. Halsey (ed.), *Ability and education opportunity* (Paris: OECD, 1961), pp. 114–28.

Verrire, Jacques, *La population de l: Irlande* (Paris, New York: Mouton, 1979).

Viney, Michael, *The five per cent. A survey of Protestants in the Republic* (Dublin: Irish Times, 1965).

von Bothmer, Bernard, *Framing the sixties. The use and abuse of a decade from Ronald Reagan to Greorge W. Bush* (Amherst & Boston: Univeristy of Massachusetts Press, 2010).

Walsh, Brendan, 'Ireland's demographic transition, 1958–70', *ESR*, vol. III, no. 2, 1972, pp.251–72.

'Aspects of labour supply and demand with special reference to the employment of women in Ireland', *JSSISI*, vol. xxxii, part iii, 1971, pp. 88–12.

'Interpreting modern Ireland: time for a new view', *Studies*, vol. 80, no. 350, winter 1991, pp. 400–7.

'Labour force participation and the growth of women's employment, Ireland 1971–1991', *ESR*, vol. 24, no. 4, 1993, pp. 369–400.

Walsh, Ed, with Kieran Fagan, *Upstart; friends, foes and founding a university* (Cork: Collins, 2011).

Walsh, John, *The politics of expansion. The transformation of educational policy in the Republic of Ireland, 1957–72* (Manchester: Manchester UP, 2009).

Patrick Hillery. The official biography (Dublin: New Island, 2008).

Whelan, Bernadette, *Ireland and the Marshall Plan, 1947–1957* (Dublin: Four Courts, 2000).

Whitaker, Andrew (ed.), *Bright, brilliant days. Douglas Gageby and the Irish Times* (Dublin: A&A Farmar, 2006), p. 78.

White, Barry, *John Hume. Statesman of the troubles* (Belfast: Blackstaff, 1984), p. 84.

White, Tony, *Investing in people. Higher education in Ireland from 1960 to 2000* (Dublin: Institute of Public Administration, 2001).

Whyte, John, *Dáil deputies. Their work; its difficulties; possible remedies* (Dublin: Tuairim, 1966).

Church and state in modern Ireland (Dublin: Gill & Macmillan, 1971).

Williamson, Daniel C., 'Taking the troubles across the Atlantic: Ireland's UN initiatives and Irish-US diplomatic relations in the early years of the conflict in Northern Ireland', *ISIA*, vol. 18, 2007, pp. 175–89.

Wylie, Paula, *Ireland and the Cold War: diplomacy and recognition, 1949–63* (Dublin: Irish Academic Press, 2006).

Unpublished theses and unpublished research papers

Barry, Frank, Linda Barry, Aisling Menton, 'Foreign ownership and external licensing of Irish business under protection', Research paper, August 2012.

Campbell, Sarah, 'New nationalism? The origins of the SDLP, 1969–1974' (Ph. D., UCD, 2010).

Garvin, Tom, 'Political parties in a Dublin Constituency' (Ph.D., University of Georgia, 1972).

Holohan, Carole, 'Every generation has its task: attitudes to Irish youth in the "sixties" ' (Ph.D., UCD, 2009).

Knight, James and Nicolas Baxter-Moore, *Republic of Ireland. The general elections of 1969 and 1973* (Thesis: Arthur McDougall Fund London, 1973).

Ní Chobhtaigh, Brona, 'Preventive or curative: policy impacts on Irish infant mortality 1920–1960' (M. Litt. Thesis, UCD, 2008).

O'Hanlon, Kerry, 'Irish television and the popularisation of the Catholic Church in 1960s Ireland' (UCD undergraduate history thesis, 2014).

Reference works

Flora, Peter, *State, economy and society in Western Europe, 1815–1974: a data handbook*, vols I and II (London: Macmillan, 1987).

Royal Irish Academy (RIA), Dictionary of Irish Biography, DIB Online.

CSO Statistical Abstracts.

Census of Population Ireland, 1951, 1956, 1961, 1966 and 1971.

Index